# THE
# OXFORD HISTORY
# OF THE
# FRENCH
# REVOLUTION

# THE
# OXFORD HISTORY
# OF THE
# FRENCH
# REVOLUTION

BY

WILLIAM DOYLE

CLARENDON PRESS · OXFORD

Oxford University Press, Walton Street, Oxford OX2 6DP
Oxford New York Toronto
Delhi Bombay Calcutta Madras Karachi
Petaling Jaya Singapore Hong Kong Tokyo
Nairobi Dar es Salaam Cape Town
Melbourne Auckland
and associated companies in
Berlin Ibadan

Oxford is a trade mark of Oxford University Press

Published in the United States
by Oxford University Press, New York

First published 1989
Reprinted 1989 (twice)

British Library Cataloguing in Publication Data
Doyle, William, 1942–
The Oxford history of the French Revolution
1. French Revolution, 1789–1799
1. Title
944.04
ISBN 0–19–822781–7

Library of Congress Cataloging in Publication Data
Doyle, William, 1942–
The Oxford history of the French Revolution
William Doyle.
Bibliography: p.       Includes index
1. France—History—Revolution, 1789–1799.   2. Europe—
History—1789–1815.   I. Title.
DC148.D69   1989   944.04'03'21—dc19   88–37235
ISBN 0–19–822781–7

Printed in Great Britain by
Butler & Tanner Ltd, Frome and London

From Number Six

# Contents

LIST OF ILLUSTRATIONS    ix

LIST OF MAPS    xi

1. France under Louis XVI    1
2. Enlightened Opinion    44
3. Crisis and Collapse, 1776–1788    66
4. The Estates-General, September 1788–July 1789    86
5. The Principles of 1789 and the Reform of France    112
6. The Breakdown of the Revolutionary Consensus, 1790–1791    136
7. Europe and the Revolution, 1788–1791    159
8. The Republican Revolution, October 1791–January 1793    174
9. War against Europe, 1792–1797    197
10. The Revolt of the Provinces    220
11. Government by Terror, 1793–1794    247
12. Thermidor, 1794–1795    272
13. Counter-Revolution, 1789–1795    297
14. The Directory, 1795–1799    318
15. Occupied Europe, 1794–1799    341
16. An End to Revolution, 1799–1802    369
17. The Revolution in Perspective    391

Notes    426

Appendices:
1. Chronology of the French Revolution    434
2. The Revolutionary Calendar    442

BIBLIOGRAPHY    444

INDEX    449

# List of Illustrations

(*Between pages 114 and 115*)

1. Louis XVI in full state robes
2. Vergennes, architect of the fateful American War
3. Necker, the Swiss wonder-worker
4. Calonne, as Comptroller-General of the Finances
5. The last chief minister of the Ancien Régime: Loménie de Brienne
6. The Royal Session in the Parlement of Paris, 19 November 1787
7. Troops fire on the Reveillon rioters, April 1789
8. The Tennis Court Oath, 20 June 1789. David's commemorative picture
9. The attack on the Bastille, 14 July 1789
10. Sieyès in 1789, while still a priest
11. Lafayette at the height of his power: the festival of the Federation, 14 July 1790
12. Mirabeau, demagogue and royalist plotter
13. Barnave: Protestant, Patriot, Feuillant
14. The women of Paris march back from Versailles, October 1789

(*Between pages 242 and 243*)

15. The Festival of the Federation, 14 July 1790
16. Brissot: a journalist in power
17. Robespierre in 1789
18. Dumouriez, patriotic general and traitor
19. Danton at the height of his revolutionary prestige
20. The overthrow of the monarchy, 10 August 1792
21. Louis XVI in the Temple, shortly before his execution
22. Sketch by David of Marie-Antoinette on the way to the scaffold
23. Marat, the 'People's Friend'
24. Carnot, 'Organizer of Victory' and Director
25. Vendéan generals: Stofflet
26. Vendéan generals: Charette
27. The contrast between the old and new France, as seen by Gillray, whose anti-French cartoons aroused deep resentment among revolutionaries

28. A little-known David. Outraged by Gillray, the artist responded with a number of anti-coalition cartoons of his own

29. The first public audience of the Directory, November 1795

30. Barras in directorial robes

31. La Révellière-Lépeaux, depicted as a republican intransigent

32. Bonaparte in 1799

# ACKNOWLEDGEMENTS

Illustration no. 4 is reproduced by gracious permission of Her Majesty the Queen.

Photographs and illustrations were supplied by, or reproduced by kind permission of, the following: Bibliothèque Nationale: 3, 7, 9, 10, 13, 23, 25, 30, 31; Musée Carnavalet, Paris: 11 (Photo Bridgeman Art Library); 15, 16, 19 (Musées de la Ville de Paris © by SPADEM 1989/DACS); Musée du Louvre (cliché des Musées Nationaux, Paris): 22, 32; Mansell Collection: 5, 6, 8, 14, 17, 18, 21, 24, 26, 27, 29; Musée de la Révolution Française: 28; Musée du Château de Versailles (cliché des Musées Nationaux, Paris): 1, 2, 12, 20.

# List of Maps

1. Pre-revolutionary France: principal administrative, judicial, and fiscal subdivisions      3
2. The departments of revolutionary France      126
3. Revolutionary Paris: the sections and main places and streets mentioned in the text      128
4. Resistance to the Revolution, 1793–1799      225
5. The expansion of revolutionary France      344

Le mal de changer est-il toujours moins grand que le mal de souffrir?

Montesquieu, *De l'esprit des lois,* bk. XXIX, ch. XVIII

# France under Louis XVI

THE king of France needed no coronation. He reigned by the grace of God from the moment his predecessor breathed his last, and a coronation was purely customary. So the argument was heard, even in the highest circles, that the elaborate consecration of Louis XVI, arranged for 11 June 1775 in the traditional setting of Rheims cathedral, was a waste of public money. A month beforehand, the countryside around Paris, and many districts of the city, had been shaken by rioting against high flour and bread prices. The disturbances led to talk of postponing the ceremony, and the approaches to Rheims were ringed with precautionary troops. And far fewer people than expected made the journey to the capital of Champagne to witness the historic spectacle. Innkeepers complained of unlet rooms, and caterers of wasted supplies. But when, that brilliant morning, the cathedral doors were flung open to reveal the young monarch crowned and enthroned in glory, invested with the sceptre of Charlemagne and anointed with the holy oil of Clovis, men broke down and wept despite themselves.

The son of St Louis, the Most Christian King of France and Navarre, had sworn that day to uphold the peace of the Church, prevent disorder, impose justice, exterminate heretics, maintain forever the prerogatives of the Order of the Holy Spirit, and pardon no duellist. Three days later, in the summer heat, he ritually touched 2,400 stinking sufferers from scrofula, the disfiguring disease believed by countless generations to be curable through the miraculous touch of an anointed king. And all this still left him time to write letters to his 74-year-old chief minister, who had remained at Versailles; and to resist the attempts of an empty-headed queen to have her favourites given office. Court intrigues could not be expected to stop merely because the king was being crowned. And so the ceremonies that Louis XVI observed that week, the motions he went through, were a strange blend of momentous and trivial, significant and purely formal, meaningful and empty. The powers he exercised, the promises he made, the regalia he wore, all resulted from a long, tortuous, and often haphazard evolution.

Few knew or remembered why things had to be the way they were. And this was typical of the kingdom over which he had ruled since 10 May 1774.

The domains of the king of France in the 1770s, excluding overseas territories in the Americas and east of the Cape, covered some 277,200 square miles and had over 27 million inhabitants. By 1789 there would be a million more. These realms had been built up since the early Middle Ages by a process of conquest and dynastic accident or design, and during the last century of the monarchy they were still being added to. In 1678 Louis XIV acquired Franche Comté, in 1766 Louis XV inherited Lorraine, and in 1768 he took over Corsica. But deep inside French territory Avignon and its surrounding district still belonged to the Pope, and in Alsace there were islands of territory nominally under the sovereignty of German princes and an independent city-state at Mulhouse. Nobody thought such enclaves anomalous, for they were well established by law, prescription, and international consensus. In any case, they were only extreme examples of the variety which prevailed within the kingdom itself.

Its most ancient division was into provinces. Originating as independent feudal domains that had been progressively swallowed up by the kings of France, they varied enormously in size. Vast regions like Languedoc, Dauphiné, or Brittany counted as provinces alongside tiny Pyrenean counties like Foix or narrow frontier strips like Flanders or Roussillon. Even the precise number of provinces was uncertain, for historical traditions were often far from explicit, but in 1776 39 provincial governorships were recognized. The functions of governors were largely honorific, however, since for most administrative purposes the kingdom was divided into 36 generalities, each presided over by an intendant. The origin of the generalities was much less ancient, and it was still only a century since intendants had become established everywhere. But these administrative units were far more uniform in size than the old provinces, and consequently their boundaries seldom coincided. Closer to provinces in this respect were the *ressorts* or jurisdictional areas of the parlements, the 13 sovereign courts of appeal. That of Paris, for example, covered a third of the kingdom, whereas those of Pau or Douai were scarcely larger than the smallest provinces. The parlements had their origins in the supreme courts of the great feudal rulers of medieval times. When their lands fell to the king of France, he tended to accept or adapt the institutions he found there rather than impose his own. Normans still called the parlement of Rouen the Exchequer 500 years after the English king had ceased to be their duke and hold court there; and the last parlement was established at Nancy in succession to the old ducal court of Lorraine only in 1775. But inevitably

MAP 1. Pre-revolutionary France: principal administrative, judicial, and fiscal subdivisions

*Source*: W. Doyle, *Old European Order* (Oxford, 1978).

most *ressorts* took in all or part of several provinces and generalities, a rich source of conflicts of jurisdiction. And the Church, meanwhile, divided up the kingdom in its own way, into 18 archiepiscopal provinces and 136 dioceses. The majority were in the south, where dioceses were much smaller and older. But many bishops enjoyed enclaves of jurisdiction in dioceses other than their own: the bishop of Dol in Brittany had no less than 33. Such uneven, illogical patterns of organization were repeated in a thousand different ways at the more local levels of town and village.

Nor did complexity end there. Apart from royal edicts on certain general issues, the king's domains were subject to no law and no administrative practice common to them all without exception. Southern provinces regulated their affairs by written, Roman law; but even there, in isolated regions like the Pyrenees, local customs were more important. In northern France they were all-important. Here nearly all law was customary, and at least 65 general customs and 300 local ones were observed. This meant that the law relating to marriage, inheritance, and tenure of property could differ in important respects from one district to another; and those who had property in several might hold it on widely differing terms. Every district, too, had its own range of weights and measures, and the same term often meant different values in different places. In these circumstances fraud, or fear of it, bedevilled all exchanges and provided endless business for the hundreds of petty courts and jurisdictions on the lower slopes of the judicial pyramid. So did taxation, where again there was no uniformity. Northern and central France notoriously bore a heavier tax-burden than the south, or the periphery of the kingdom in general. The main direct tax, the *taille*, was levied on persons in central provinces, but on land in peripheral ones like Languedoc. The salt tax, the notorious *gabelle*, was levied at six different rates according to area, while six other specially privileged districts, including Brittany, were exempt. And the whole country was criss-crossed with innumerable internal customs barriers, whether at the gates of towns, along rivers, or between provinces, where excises, tolls, and tariffs could be collected—again at a bewildering series of rates, on a limitless range of items. Goods shipped down the Saône and Rhône from Franche Comté to the Mediterranean, for example, paid duty at 36 separate customs barriers, some public and some private, on the way. To rational observers such complexities appear, and appeared, an arbitrary shambles; the product of routine and meaningless historical traditions. But these traditions were often as not rooted in geography, climate, culture, and economic necessity, as any traveller could readily testify.

The kingdom of France had originated, and first expanded, in the rolling, open country of the Paris basin where communications were easy. The river systems of the Seine and the Loire were navigable, or easily made so, and gave ready access to the sea. Paris stood at the centre of overland routes that were little diverted by natural obstacles for miles on end; and by the late eighteenth century the main roads were constructed to a standard unparalleled elsewhere in Europe, and the wonder of foreigners. With a temperate climate, fertile soils, and ready access to markets, the agriculture of the Paris basin, especially north of the capital and towards the Flemish lowlands, was the most advanced and commercialized in the kingdom. It sustained not only the 650,000 inhabitants of Paris itself, but also the most densely concentrated population in France, along the Channel coast. Rouen, the capital of Normandy, drew on these abundant reserves of manpower to work the expanding cotton industry, which made it, as all English travellers agreed, the Manchester of France. Rich in resources and tightly organized, the Paris basin was a metropolitan area, easily dominated by central authority. More people could read and write there than in any other part of the kingdom, and all spoke recognizable French. But none of this could be taken for granted more than 150 miles from the capital.

In western Normandy and on the borders of the rocky Breton peninsula, the open spaces gave way to a landscape of small fields divided by high mounds and tree-strewn hedges, scattered farmsteads and deep sunken roads—the *bocage*. Further west still, the peasantry spoke Breton, not French, and dressed in a distinctive local costume. Arthur Young, the English traveller famous for his minute observations of the French scene in the late 1780s, was appalled by the poverty-stricken air of this region: 'Brittany, Maine and Anjou have the appearance of deserts.'[1] Yet Brittany at least was heavily populated, lightly taxed, and from the 1760s well served by good main roads. Bretons were proud of their distinctive character. Through their truculent parlement and tumultuous estates meeting in Rennes every year they enjoyed more self-government than most provinces. And they were linked to a world beyond France by the sea. In Brest, they boasted France's principal Atlantic naval port; Lorient was the main gateway to French interests in the Indian Ocean; while booming Nantes was the capital of the French slave-trade and second only to Bordeaux in commerce with the West Indies. South of the Loire there was more *bocage* country in the low hills of the Vendée, with characteristic isolated farmsteads or hamlets but few larger settlements. But the lack of ports along its low, marshy coastline meant the Vendée was bypassed by all major lines of communication, and so intensely inward-looking; an area of subsistence agriculture supplemented here and there by low-grade textile production exported through Nantes.

The contrast with the basin of the Garonne, which with its provinces of Aunis, Saintonge, Guyenne, and Gascony stretched to the foothills of the Pyrenees, could scarcely have been greater. This was another zone of navigable rivers and good communications. Apart from the sandy heaths of the *Landes*, to the south of the Gironde, it was a fertile region whose warm, damp climate favoured great agricultural diversity. Even the stony gravels around Bordeaux were perfect for growing what were already acknowledged to be the best wines in the world; and on the upper Garonne and the Pyrenean foothills the introduction of maize in the late seventeenth century had transformed the face of the country and the rural economy. But south-western agriculture was not as commercialized as that of the northern plains. Southwards from the Loire stretched a region of petty cultivation (*petite culture*) carried on by a mixture of small peasant proprietors and share-croppers leasing from landlords who plainly did not expect high profits. Centuries of English rule during the Middle Ages had bequeathed no profound sense of separate identity comparable to that of Brittany. Basque and Béarnais were spoken in the extreme south, but the nasal Gascon accent of much of the south-west was recognizably the *langue d'oil* of northern France. Only Bordeaux, the undisputed regional capital, which had revolted twice against the Crown in the previous century, remained suspicious of authorities still five or six days distant. They were thought all too likely to interfere damagingly with the surging commercial prosperity which had created Europe's second busiest port and boosted the city's population from 45,000 to 111,000 since the beginning of the century.

Apart from the monotonous plains of the Beauce, to the south of Paris, the landscape of northern and western France was very varied, with many hilly regions. But hardly anywhere did the land rise much above 600 feet. South and east of a line running roughly from Bayonne in the south to Sedan in the north, however, all the land was higher except for the valley floors of the Rhône and the upper Garonne, and the Mediterranean littoral around the Gulf of Lions. Mediterranean France, the Midi, was largely cut off from the northern lowlands by the impenetrable plateau of the Massif Central, a remote, mountainous region whose poverty-stricken economy only survived thanks to large-scale seasonal migrations of manpower to more favoured lowland regions, often as far away as Catalonia. There certainly were fertile valleys in the Massif, and on the higher lands many of the peasants owned their plots; but they were subsistence farmers, and were relying increasingly on chestnuts rather than grain to feed the burgeoning population. The southern Massif fell within the vast province of Languedoc, which derived its name from the distinctive strain of French spoken in the south. In Provence, the accent of the Midi almost became a separate language; it certainly marked all southerners out as closer cousins of the Italians or Spaniards than their fellow subjects north of the Massif. So did the climate, with its dry, searing summers and short winters, so suitable for vines, olives, and mulberries on almost any soil, with hillsides often terraced to the top in order to take them. Languedoc was the home of a quarter of a million Protestants, largely concentrated in and around Nîmes, Montauban, and the Cévennes mountains which formed the southern wall of the Massif. Since 1685 they had enjoyed no toleration, and the bitter and savage uprising of fanatical Bible-bred peasants in the Cévennes, the Camisards, during the first decade of the century had inflamed sectarian antagonisms and suspicions that, though abating, were far from dead by the day Louis XVI swore to extirpate heresy. However reluctant central authority might be, as time went by, to invoke the full rigour of the law against dissent, its power was limited in a province with strong autonomous traditions. The estates of Languedoc, meeting annually in Montpellier, were run by bishops, and since 1762 the bigotry of the parlement of Toulouse had been notorious thanks to Voltaire's vilification of them as judicial murderers of the Protestant Jean Calas.*

Provence shared Languedoc's autonomous traditions, although uniquely, at Aix, its parlement was presided over by the intendant. Taxation was raised by the Assembly of the Communities, a stopgap for estates that had not met since 1639. Most of the province was wild and rocky country, of no great prosperity; but isolated on its southern tip was Toulon, a bustling naval base and penal colony. Further west lay Marseilles, a major port commanding the mouth of the Rhône, whose valley was the main corridor between northern and southern France. Marseilles virtually monopolized France's Mediterranean and Levant trade, but had important outlets to the Atlantic, too. Devastated by the last great outbreak of plague in France in 1720, two generations later the population had recovered buoyantly. 'The common people', wrote an English visitor,[2] 'have a brutality and rudeness of manners more characteristic of a republican than a monarchical state.' Many northerners would have found this true of most inhabitants of the Midi.

Doubtless they were not well prepared for meeting this alien world by their journey down the narrow Rhône valley, swept at alarming speed along the fast-flowing stream and shooting through the perilous arches of the bridge at Pont Saint-Esprit, or plodding along the narrow trunk road at

* See below, p. 55

24 miles a day, from Lyons, 200 to the north. The Alpine fastnesses of
Dauphiné, to the east, certainly did not tempt them to stray off, with their
high, cold valleys and largely pastoral economy. Dauphiné had once
governed itself through estates, and memories of this lost autonomy
lingered on in a region of isolated valleys where the authority of central
government was seldom felt. Everybody in the lowlands was familiar,
however, with the mountain men of Dauphiné, who descended every
winter to the valleys in search of work, leaving their womenfolk no
competitors for strictly limited stocks of food. One of the most obvious
magnets for such migrants was Lyons, France's second city, with 146,000
inhabitants. Standing at the crossroads of routes where Rhône and Saône
meet, Lyons was a city of commerce and industry, proud to be
unencumbered by the swarming lawyers who plagued the seats of
parlements. Economic life was dominated by the fortunes of the silk trade,
in which over 60,000 earned their living, and which in the mid-1770s was
on the crest of a wave of prosperity that was about to break.

Though as far from the capital as Bordeaux, Lyons was within the
jurisdiction of the parlement of Paris, whereas the province of Burgundy, to
the north, had its own parlement at Dijon, and indeed its own estates.
Much damaged in the wars of the early seventeenth century, Burgundy
ceased to be a frontier province when Franche Comté was annexed, and
this brought a peace which facilitated the redevelopment of its famous
vineyards straddling the main routes from Paris to the south. The good
communications of Burgundy also favoured the establishment of industry,
and around the coal and iron deposits of Le Creusot the 1780s were to
witness the foundation of the most advanced industrial complex in Europe,
producing munitions, hardware, and glass with coke-smelting techniques
borrowed from England. The real centres of French metallurgy, however,
lay north-west of Burgundy, in the wooded hills of Lorraine, where
smelting still relied for heat on traditional charcoal, and enterprises were
still small-scale. Lorraine had only just become French, but in reality it had
been under French control since 1738, and surrounded by French
territory for much longer. For beyond it lay Franche Comté and Alsace,
frontier provinces bounded by the Jura mountains and the Rhine. After its
annexation from the Spaniards, Franche Comté slumbered throughout the
eighteenth century undisturbed by international conflict, largely preoccupied with its own affairs. The chief focus of interest in the province was the
bitter infighting between factions within the parlement of Besançon; and
the most noteworthy feature of its social structure was the presence of most
of France's 140,000 remaining serfs, whose land was technically forfeit to
their lords when they died. Spanish rule had left the Comtois with a

reputation for extreme piety and orthodoxy, in marked contrast to the Alsatians to the north of them. There, 200,000 Protestants, Lutherans distinct from the Calvinists of Languedoc, and almost a third of the population, enjoyed religious toleration under the Peace of Westphalia of 1648 that had made the province French. There were also some 30,000 Jews, spilling over into neighbouring Lorraine. Cut off from the Paris basin by the steep, wooded ridges of the Vosges, Alsace looked towards Germany, most of its inhabitants were German-speaking, and its economic life was dominated by its position along the great commercial artery of the Rhine. From the Germans its peasants had learned to cultivate, and like, potatoes, and the agriculture of the fertile Rhine valley was, as Arthur Young put it, 'one of the richest scenes of soil and cultivation to be met with in France'.[3]

Young was not often moved to such praise on his journeyings round France. In general he found French agriculture backward and unenterprising and few historians since have disagreed. Productivity was low, technology conservative, and methods wasteful. Throughout the middle years of the century a small group of writers energetically advocated the adoption of new methods, largely copied from England. The government lent them its support, and tried to foster greater public discussion of agricultural questions. But none of this activity had the slightest effect on everyday agriculture or the peasants who carried it on. The root of the problem, in Young's view, lay in the morcellation of rural property. All the legal systems of France stipulated one form or another of partible inheritance. Property was divided up between heirs each generation. Entails, which kept vast estates together down the generations in most other European countries, were either unknown or weak and limited, and in any case peasants could not afford them. So even the largest French estates were not enormous by international standards, only property owned by the Church escaped regular redistribution, and there were no fewer than four million small owner-occupiers. Between them, the tiny plots of these peasants made up perhaps a quarter of the kingdom's surface area. Much of the rest was not owned in compact units either, and leasing it out piecemeal to small tenants was the only practicable way of managing it. Perhaps three-quarters of the rented land in France was leased to peasants on share-cropping contracts (*métayage*) under which the lessee undertook to work the land and provide implements, and the lessor provided seed and received in return half or some other agreed proportion of the crop. Such leases recognized that the yield of small plots was too unpredictable to produce a regular fixed rent. In fact the yield of most peasant plots, whether owned or leased, was seldom enough by itself to keep a peasant family, let alone produce a marketable surplus. It was notorious, and the lament of agrarian improvers, that all French peasants seemed to care about was producing enough grain to feed their own families. Their ambitions seldom went beyond having just enough land to supply these needs.

Obsession with grain growing sprang, of course, from an age-old but well-justified fear of famine. But it also prevented the diversification which might have made harvest failure less catastrophic. It is true that in some areas a breakthrough had been made into high-yield crops. In the south-west peasants lived on maize and sold their wheat. In Alsace and Lorraine potatoes were widely cultivated. In both cases the new crops only took hold after catastrophic harvest failures—in the 1690s in the south-west, and between 1737 and 1741 in the east. But maize would not grow in northern France, and potatoes were still thought of by most peasants as fit only for animals. In any case, both crops required far more fertilizer than grain, and manure was already in short supply. This was because pasture was normally sacrificed to arable, and livestock was left to graze on commons or fallow land. In competition with human beings for what the land produced, flocks and herds were neither numerous enough nor well enough nourished to provide adequate manure. The very fallow they grazed on was a colossal waste of resources, as Arthur Young never ceased to proclaim. In northern provinces, land was customarily rested every third year, while in the south every second year was more usual; so a huge proportion of the country's cultivable land lay unproductive at any one time. Only in Flanders and a few contiguous districts was grain rotated with soil-restoring fodder crops, such as clover, lucerne, and sainfoin, and fallow thus eliminated. It was no coincidence that crop yields in these extreme northern districts was the highest in the kingdom, and had been for centuries.

These advances had come about in Flanders in response to demand for food from the most highly urbanized region of early modern Europe. A substantial and accessible market had prompted productive innovation. Similar demands, this time from Paris and the densely populated northern coasts, had produced the only large-scale farming to be found in France, in the open country of the Paris basin. Here the profits to be made from supplying insatiable urban markets made it worthwhile for landlords to lease out their estates in big units, and for enterprising tenants (*gros fermiers*) to take on the spiralling rents they demanded. Farming more than a handful of acres was expensive. Ploughs, teams to draw them, and semi-skilled labour to work them were all costly. This was why, in a rural world where most cultivators relied on spades and hoes, the term *laboureur* (ploughman) denoted a person of some means. But *gros fermiers* were seldom popular figures in the rural community, where they tended to accumulate the best land, turned arable into pasture, enclosed fields hitherto open, and spurned ancient communal rights such as gleaning and free grazing. They were a disturbing element in a rural society where neither landlord nor peasant showed much interest in profit-seeking by improving the land. Outside their ranks hardly any surpluses apart from seed were ever reinvested, and Young was repeatedly struck by the dilapidated appearance of most French farm buildings and the poor condition of the implements in use. Most cultivators, and many owners, too, were simply not involved in growing for the market. Or if they were, the market was a strictly limited local or regional one.

Transport costs alone made this inevitable, and contemporaries could not imagine how these could be much diminished. Roads and rivers could be improved, canals built, and some hoped the system of tolls and customs could be rationalized. But until the coming of the railways, which nobody could foresee, resulting benefits would still be marginal. Much more hope was placed in diminishing the burdens on production which ate into profits. Taxation, for example, might be reorganized so as to take less than the usual 10–15 per cent of a peasant's gross product. Tithes, destined for the upkeep of the parish clergy but often impropriated by monasteries or laymen, took around another 8 per cent on average. The *corvée*, forced labour for road construction and maintenance, took hands away from the fields for substantial periods every year; and when, under Louis XVI, it began to be commuted, the cost was added to the tax-bill. Above all there was the burden of what contemporaries called 'feudalism'. It was infinitely variable, from a few per cent around Paris or in Maine, 10 per cent in the Massif, 15 per cent around Toulouse, up to 25 per cent in parts of Brittany or Burgundy. Here and there a few islands of allodial tenure, free of all burdens, survived from distant times. But in the vast majority of the medieval territories that later became France there had been no land without a lord. This was still the case under Louis XVI, although by now lordship and ownership had become largely divorced. The 'feudal' rights that lords could exercise over land they might no longer truly own were infinite. They always included a token money rent (*cens*), but often extended to heavier payments in cash or kind too. Almost invariably they included hunting and shooting rights. Sometimes they included manorial monopolies (*banalités*) which compelled producers to use a lord's mill or wine-press; and all such rights were normally enforceable through the lord's own court. Even this is to simplify. Many leases blended feudal and ordinary cash rents indiscriminately. Over much of Brittany, under a system known as *domaine congéable*, tenants on nine-year leases payable in a mixture of cash and kind were deemed proprietors of the buildings and fruit-trees on their plots, could not be evicted unless their landlord bought them out, and so effectively enjoyed permanent tenure. Whether this amounted to ownership, and whether it was strictly feudal in character, were questions of little practical interest—until 1789, when they suddenly assumed crucial, and fateful, importance.

Despite low productivity, antiquated methods, and little sign of improvement, French agriculture had prospered in the middle decades of the century. Increasing demand from an expanding population coincided with a long series of good harvests to bring excellent prices and a sustained rise in rents and land values. From the late 1760s onwards, however, harvests became more uncertain and yields began to fluctuate sharply. Only three harvests between 1770 and 1789 were abundant everywhere, and provinces with shortfalls found it hard to import adequate extra supplies. The wine crop, upon which many peasants relied to supplement inadequate resources, also proved abnormally volatile during these years, failing completely in 1778 and over-producing subsequently. There were shortages in the mid-1780s too of flax and forage crops. Cattle owners unable to feed their stock adequately had to slaughter and sell at rock-bottom prices since everybody was doing the same. None of this dented the rise in rents and land values. Landlords and big farmers continued to do well. But for the small proprietors, leaseholders, and share-croppers who dominated French agriculture the reign of Louis XVI was to prove a time of difficulty and disruption. And because agriculture was far and away the most important economic activity in the kingdom, the shock waves were felt throughout economic life.

There was, in fact, no clear distinction between agricultural and industrial workers. Most industry was rurally based. Even ostensibly urban trades like construction, a major growth industry that was transforming the appearance of Paris and greater provincial cities, were largely dependent on migrant workers who took their earnings home to the country each winter. Metallurgy, scarcely yet affected by coal and coke technology, was a business of small-scale concerns located in remote forests where charcoal was plentiful. It is true that the biggest industry of all, textiles, was centred on cities—woollens on Amiens, Abbeville, Sedan, or Clermont-de-Lodève; cottons on Rouen and Elbeuf; silk on Nîmes and Lyons. But only in Lyons was much actual production concentrated in the town. The other textile towns were primarily markets, centres of distribution and finance, with most of their spinning and weaving carried on in peasant households anything up to 50 miles distant. Around Rouen that meant that perhaps 300,000 peasants were involved in cotton production. But if most of the industrial work-force were peasants, so were most of the consumers; and when harvests failed they had less money to spend on clothing themselves, or indeed on other manufactures. So demand fluctuated according to the harvests, and this made Louis XVI's reign an uncertain time in industrial as well as agricultural terms. The silk industry of Lyons lurched from crisis to crisis. Markets for woollens and linens became extremely erratic, too. Only cottons continued the sustained expansion that all textiles had experienced in mid-century, and this was because their main markets were not in France but abroad, in southern Europe and the tropical colonies.

France did not have many such colonies by the 1770s. The British had practically expelled her from India in mid-century, and elsewhere east of the Cape only the Île de France (Mauritius) and the Île Bourbon (Réunion) were still in her hands. In the Caribbean she had managed to hang on to Martinique, Guadeloupe, and above all Saint-Domingue (present-day Haiti). But the value of these tropical islands was out of all proportion to their size. At the peace of Paris in 1763 Louis XV had been glad to give up the whole of Canada in order to get back Guadeloupe, and on the eve of the Revolution Saint-Domingue was the richest piece of territory in the world. Colonial wealth derived from the production of sugar, coffee, and other tropical luxuries by the labour of black slaves. There were half a million of them in Saint-Domingue alone, and transporting replacements from Africa was yet another aspect of a complex Atlantic trading network whose nerve-centres were the great seaports. Thanks largely to the output of these colonies, France's overseas trade grew fivefold over the century, and the booming population, lavish rebuilding, and crowded harbours of Bordeaux, Nantes, Le Havre, and even Mediterranean Marseilles testified to their prosperity. Nor, unlike the rest of the economy, did it show much sign of flagging, except during the war with Great Britain between 1778 and 1783. Even then British action did far less damage than in previous wars, and when peace was restored the boom reached new heights. But not much of this commercial opulence reached far inland. The real profits of the colonial trade came from re-exporting the precious luxuries to the ports of northern Europe. Even when trading profits were reinvested in land, as they often were, it was to secure assets rather than put them to further productive use.

There were, therefore, two French economies, only tenuously linked. Coastal regions, and the navigable lower reaches of the four great river systems, were integrated with international and intercontinental trading networks and shared in their benefits, which seemed destined to go on improving. But most of Louis XVI's subjects lived in the interior, where communications were poor, economic life sluggish, and such improvements as good harvests had brought in mid-century were being eroded by climatic deterioration and an inexorably rising population. The famines of the seventeenth century, when hundreds of thousands died, were fading from memory; but thinking men became increasingly worried, as each harvest shortfall plunged whole populations into beggary, about the ability of existing institutions to take the strains they were coming under.

Poverty was France's most visible social problem. Nobody could overlook it. All travellers noticed the misery of rural housing, and the poor appearance of the peasantry. 'All the country girls and women', noted Arthur Young in Quercy, 'are without shoes or stockings; and the ploughmen at their work have neither sabots nor stockings to their feet. This is a poverty that strikes at the root of national prosperity. . . . It reminded me of the misery of Ireland.'[4] Bands of roving vagabonds struck terror into the hearts of isolated farmers; and the streets of most towns swarmed with beggars. The poor, meaning those without adequate employment or other assured means of support, numbered at the best of times almost a third of the population; eight million people. In bad times two or three millions more might join them, as crops failed and jobs disappeared. Most of the poor were people too old, or too young, or too ill to earn their living, people whose families could not afford to feed them either. But as the population grew, increasing numbers of the able-bodied also had difficulty in finding work, or enough of it to make ends meet. Over the century prices rose three times faster than wages. 'Workmen today', wrote Jean-Marie Roland, inspector of manufactures in Picardy in 1777,[5] 'need twice as much money for their subsistence, yet they earn no more than fifty years ago when living was half as cheap.' The result was described by a Norman parish priest.[6]

Day labourers, workmen, journeymen [he wrote in 1774] and all those whose occupation does not provide for much more than food and clothing are the ones who make beggars. As young men they work, and when by their work they have got themselves decent clothing and something to pay their wedding costs, they marry, raise a first child, have much trouble in raising two, and if a third comes along their work is no longer enough for food, and the expense. At such a time they do not hesitate to take up the beggar's staff and take to the road.

Often that road would lead to the town, which offered (or so it was hoped) more opportunities of work.

Most town-dwellers were country people by birth who had left their over-populated villages early in life in search of a livelihood. The death rate in the insanitary towns was so high, especially among children, that they could not have flourished without this steady inflow of man and woman power. And even if no work materialized, in towns immigrants could find monasteries and convents distributing alms, hospitals and poor houses endowed to take in and relieve those no longer able to fend for themselves, and more chance of private charity than in native villages where everyone was as poor as themselves. Yet when they arrived, all too many immigrants found that none of these resources was remotely adequate. Under Louis XVI they were in fact becoming steadily less adequate, and not merely because of mounting claims on their services. Monasteries were cutting back on bread doles under criticism that indiscriminate charity fostered idleness. Hospitals and poor houses found the charitable bequests on which they had always relied dwindling, and as ecclesiastical institutions they were cut off from further endowments by legislation of 1749 restricting mortmain. Revenues from investment in government securities suffered as a result of state bankruptcies and debt consolidations over the century, while inflation eroded the amount of supplies hospitals could afford from their shrinking resources. Here and there concerned laymen began later in the century to experiment with new approaches to poor relief. Masonic lodges set up charitable funds, and in several cities philanthropic societies were established in the 1780s to tap the wealth of the rich for the poor. The government began, gingerly, to toy with schemes of relief on a national scale, such as the establishment of workhouses (*dépôts de mendicité*) in each generality from the 1760s, and charitable workshops (*ateliers de charité*) from the 1770s. The background to these departures was mounting public concern about the problem of the poor. Vigorous debates, in the press, in the world of letters, and in learned societies and academies, testified to the worries of educated men that they faced a crisis that would soon be beyond control.

These fears were fuelled by the way the poor behaved. Naturally they took what work they could find; but when they failed, they turned to begging without shame. The sheer professionalism of many beggars made those they assailed suspect their good faith; and indeed faked ailments and hard-luck stories were common enough. Anything that made the better-off pay up was worth trying. When appeals to pity failed, intimidation might work better, and from there it was a very short step to crime. Petty theft was every pauper's standby. Another was smuggling, in a land criss-crossed by countless tolls and internal customs barriers. In the country, there was poaching; in town, women in desperate straits became prostitutes, despite the fact that this almost invariably led to disease and further degradation. In the 1760s there were 25,000 prostitutes in Paris.

The classic pattern was for a girl newly arrived from the country to be taken on as a maid, become pregnant, lose her job, and take to the streets to feed the child. Alternatively she might abandon it, and not only unmarried mothers adopted this way out of feeding an extra mouth. One of the most graphic indicators of the growth in poverty was the rise in the number of foundlings and abandoned children. They tripled over the century. By the 1780s perhaps 40,000 a year was the national figure. In Paris alone it was about 8,000 and even a small provincial town like Bayeux, with 10,000 inhabitants, produced about 50 annually. The hospitals who took such babies in could not possibly cope with their numbers. They tended to farm them out to wet-nurses, themselves usually poverty-stricken; and in these hands the majority were dead before their fifth birthday. Better-off observers thought all this was evidence of increasing moral depravity among the lower orders, and they agonized over how far it was safe to try to educate them out of it. Yet the heart of the matter was that the French economy could not provide a decent living for all the people being born in the countryside.

Peasants accounted for 80 per cent of the French population. Only a fifth of Louis XVI's subjects lived in communities of more than 2,000 people. A good quarter of a million probably lived in no community at all, a floating population of vagrants, feared and despised by more settled folk, an awful warning of what might happen at any time to millions who lived on or just beyond the poverty line. The livelihood of most peasant families was an amalgam of makeshifts. Even those with land seldom had enough, so like the landless they were dependent on income from day or seasonal labour, cottage industry, or exporting surplus members of the family to places where work was known, or thought, to be available. 'The only industry the inhabitants have', noted a report on an Auvergne parish in 1769, 'is to leave home for nine months of the year.'[7] Yet paradoxically families in circumstances like these were the mainstay of rural communities. Not only did they constitute a majority of the inhabitants; they found valuable extra resources in the communal rights which most villages enjoyed. On common lands they could pasture a cow and gather firewood. In the open-field areas of northern France they could glean after harvest and their cattle could graze on the stubble. In some areas, too, especially in the south, there were powerful traditions of communal defence against threats to local customs. Communities could sue lords who tried to levy excessive seigneurial dues or exercise dubious rights. From the 1760s onwards the enclosure and division of common lands and the termination of collective rights was authorized in many eastern and certain south-western districts; but little was done to take advantage of this legislation. Those lords or large landowners tempted to do so were deterred by the obvious readiness of village communities to fight the issue through the courts, not to mention by riot or other more passive ways of resisting. Similar tactics could be employed against tithe-gatherers, especially when the proceeds went to lay or monastic impropriators rather than the parish priest for whom God had ordained them. The *curé*, after all, was an important figure in every village. In most he was probably the only resident of education and authority, a natural leader quite apart from his spiritual power and guardianship of the only common building in most parishes, the church. As such, he was a powerful cement to village solidarity. Traditionally his most persistent opponents were those who shared least in that solidarity—the small minority of fortunate peasants who owned or leased enough land to be economically independent.

So much marked this prosperous handful off from the bulk of their fellow inhabitants. They alone had no fear of ruin if famine or disease struck. They alone in the village had jobs to distribute, since they farmed too much land to work entirely by themselves. Only they owned equipment, carts, and draught animals in any quantity. Others had to hire from them, just as they came to them to borrow seed or ready cash in difficult times. When, as often happened, the hapless debtors could not repay them, they would foreclose and thereby accumulate yet more property. It is true that these were the men whom communities normally nominated as syndics, local tax-collectors, or churchwardens. But only they had the leisure and resources to shoulder such duties. It was not necessarily any tribute to their popularity. The only solidarity they normally showed with their fellow villagers was in resistance to outsiders, such as *gros fermiers* who threatened to outbid them for leases, tax-exempt nobles or townsmen whose privilege pushed up everyone else's tax-bill if they bought land in the parish, or lords whose hunting and shooting rights, manorial monopolies, or feudal dues and levies in cash or kind damaged the assets and ate into the profits of rich and poor peasants alike. But *coqs de village* regarded rich outsiders and lords of the manor primarily in the same light as the parish priest: as rivals for power and authority within the village community. When the opportunity came to strike such rivals down, it was eagerly seized.

There was a sense in which this tight-fisted minority of independent yeomen were the truest countrymen: they alone could shun the towns. The rest of rural society was far more bound up with urban life than first appearance might suggest. The majority who could not grow all the food they needed had to buy in local market towns. The networks of cottage industry were organized from towns too, and its products were marketed in them. Few peasant families did not have some member who had worked for a spell in some distant city, or who had migrated there permanently. In all these ways urban and rural life interlocked. Nor was the distinction between towns and villages always obvious. Animals were raised and pastured and crops grown even in the heart of the most densely populated conurbations. Ninety per cent of French towns had less than 10,000 inhabitants, and only nine cities had more than 50,000. Nevertheless, the eighteenth century was a period of rapid urban growth. Paris grew by perhaps 100,000 people, Bordeaux and Nantes more than doubled in size, and Lyons and Marseilles expanded by more than half. It is true that towns bypassed in the commercial expansion of the century—places like Toulouse, Besançon, or innumerable small cities vegetating behind crumbling ramparts unmanned for over a century—had tended to stagnate. But a third more of the French population lived in towns under Louis XVI than at the beginning of the century, and they included nearly all the richest, best educated, and most dynamic of the king's subjects.

Even so, most town-dwellers were poor, and completely unskilled. Urban poverty was concentrated and eye-catching, a pool of labour there was never enough work to drain. 'Misery . . .', complained a Rennes magistrate in 1772, 'has thrown into the towns people who overburden them with their uselessness, and who find nothing to do, because there is not enough for the people who live there.'[8] From these ranks were recruited the innumerable casual labourers, porters, chairmen, dockers, waiters, shoeshine boys, general dealers, old-clothes merchants, and hucksters who could be met in any city street. They lived crowded together in cellars or the upper storeys (four or five floors up in Paris) of lodging houses. When times were hard and they could not pay the rent they swamped the hospitals and the criminal courts. The lucky ones among unskilled immigrants became domestic servants, perhaps the largest single occupational group in most towns of any size. In Paris there were 40,000 or 50,000 of them; in most provincial cities they made up anything between 5 and 7 per cent of the population. Sheltered, fed, often clothed as well as paid by their employers, servants had a privileged existence that other unskilled workers might well envy them. As often as not, in fact, they appear to have despised them. For servants were dependent, completely at their masters' mercy, with little real life of their own. Condemned to celibacy because married servants were expensive and inconvenient, their proverbial cupidity arose as often as not from saving to buy themselves out of service and into family life. The turnover of servants in most households was notoriously high, suggesting that for all its apparent security a life of subjection to the whims of the better-off brought more than its share of tensions and dissatisfactions. Among the floating population of casual labourers, beggars, petty criminals, and prostitutes of every town there must have been many who had at some time glimpsed a more fortunate world during a spell in service. They knew what they were missing; and no doubt they felt it all the more acutely from the certain knowledge that they could never hope themselves to break into that world—unless perhaps as burglars.

They had little chance, either, of penetrating the world of skilled craftsmen. Most of these trades were tightly organized, exclusive, and tended to recruit among townsmen born and bred, natives even of the district in which each trade was concentrated. Even trades where immigrants predominated, such as building and stone-cutting, recruited largely from well-defined provinces like Limousin. Skills required training, and the organization of most arts and crafts enshrined a hierarchy of attainment. At the bottom were apprentices, learning the trade. After four or five years they would qualify as journeymen (*compagnons*), the backbone of all the trades, and in many they would go on to acquire experience by taking to the road. Jacques-Louis Ménétra, a Parisian glazier who left a remarkable set of memoirs,[9] spent most of his twenties, between 1757 and 1764, tramping over 1,500 miles from town to town throughout southern France. To facilitate the search for work, at the outset he joined one of the three great craftsmen's unions (*compagnonnages*) which helped their members on this *tour de France* to find work and accommodation at each stop. But the *compagnonnages* had no legal standing, and were frowned upon by the authorities everywhere: they were effective organizers of strikes and boycotts, not to mention fierce fights against one another. The officially recognized form of organization for most skilled trades was the guild (*jurande*), and technically nobody could exercise his skill without belonging to the appropriate one. Every town had a clear hierarchy of guilds, each governed by its body of masters. The masters set the standards of their craft, they alone could become independent employers in it, and they were recruited from journeymen who could pay an entry fee and present a 'masterpiece' as proof of their acquired skills. But sons of masters, like Ménétra, were at a distinct advantage here, and when he became one after eight years as a journeyman he got in without a masterpiece. Much was made of such inequities when guilds had become a thing of the past; but mastership was not an automatic passport to commercial success, and in most guilds access to it does not appear to have been seriously restricted. Quite the reverse. In the great silk workers' guild of Lyons, the 60,000 strong *Fabrique*, there were more masters than journeymen, while in Paris between 1785 and 1789 alone nearly 7,000 new masters were admitted to the various guilds of the city. And proliferation of masters meant that most workplaces were small. The average number of workers in Parisian workshops was 16 or 17 in 1789. Although working hours were long, sixteen hours a day for six days a week being common, most artisans set their own pace of work and by modern standards it appears to have been an extremely slow and leisurely one. Here and there more disciplined working environments were emerging, notably textile printing works like that of Christoff Oberkampf, employing almost 1,000 operatives at Jouy, or that of Garnier, Danse, and Thevard with their 800 employees at Beauvais. In Paris the most noteworthy early factories of this sort were the royal glassworks, employing 500, or Reveillon's wallpaper works, with 300 employees, both in the eastern Saint-Antoine district. But their scale, organization, and guild-free atmosphere made such work places quite exceptional, and indeed objects of some suspicion. Not only did guilds safeguard traditional standards of quality and workmanship, they offered a well-tried means of keeping workers under control. Even the ever-growing number of free trades (*métiers libres*), which were not organized into guilds, were subjected to close supervision through an elaborate network of regulations. But doubts about such controls were spreading.

In 1776 an attempt was made to abolish the whole structure of guilds, and Parisian artisans celebrated in the streets at the news. A few months later, however, the old structure was largely restored; and in 1781 new controls were introduced in the form of what came to be known as the *livret*, a work-record which all employees had to carry and which needed the employer's endorsement whenever they left. Such developments, and the slow erosion of real wages caused by two generations of inflation, made Louis XVI's reign a time of increasing industrial unrest. Insubordination, noted Louis-Sébastien Mercier, the author of vivid scenes of Parisian life in the 1780s, 'has been visible among the people for some years now and above all among craftsmen. Apprentices and young workers want to show themselves independent; they lack respect for their masters, they form combinations.'[10] Their eye caught by increasingly frequent strikes and boycotts, such observers perhaps underestimated the deeper sense of solidarity between masters and their men fostered by a common craft and cultural background, familiar guild procedures, and the personal atmosphere of small workshops. The most vivid example was in Lyons, where masters and journeymen of the *Fabrique* united to clash repeatedly with the handful of great merchants who monopolized the buying and marketing of what they produced. And masters and journeymen everywhere were at one in their response to sudden jumps in the cost of living when harvests were deficient. It seldom occurred to artisans at such times to press for higher wages, and it never occurred to masters to pay them. Both—and their wives, who often led public protests on these occasions—expected the authorities to hold down food prices without regard to the state of the market.

Sudden rises in the price of bread or grain were universally recognized as the most dangerous moments for public order, and towns were the places it was most likely to break down. Even unrest involving peasants tended to occur when they came together in towns on market days. Everybody believed that the price of bread should be controlled and held at a level which ordinary people could afford. When it rose above that level, they felt morally entitled to take action to hold it down. This might involve threatening bakers or corn chandlers, and even lynching those who proved slow to respond. Or mobs might break into shops or warehouses and organize sales of their contents at what they considered a fair or just price. 'Hoarding' in times of scarcity was regarded as the worst of crimes. Alternatively riotous crowds would try to intimidate local magistrates into fixing acceptable prices, which was seen anyway as nothing less than their duty. Most magistrates readily agreed, and kept bread and grain prices within their jurisdiction under weekly review. In the case of Paris this was considered a matter of national importance; if the capital went hungry the stability of the state itself might be endangered, and the needs of Paris took priority in all markets within a radius of about 100 miles, and were a powerful influence at up to twice that distance. Even the most careful monitoring, however, could not anticipate every shortage, and although the years of good harvests between the 1740s and 1760s were relatively trouble-free (with the exception of 1752) the decade between 1768 and 1778 brought disturbances in many parts of the country. Harvests were uncertain during these years, and their effects were aggravated by the first attempts of the government to disengage from controlling the grain trade. Partially lifted in the 1760s, controls were reimposed in the early 1770s and then lifted again in 1775. The effect was to throw prices and expectations into chaos when stocks were short. In 1768 there were riots and popular price-fixing in Le Havre and Nantes, in 1770 at Rheims. Attempts in 1770 to regularize supplies in the hands of a few chosen merchants led to rumours of a 'famine pact' devised by rascally ministers to starve the king's subjects. In any case the return to controls did not prevent further shortages in 1773, during which Bordeaux narrowly escaped being sacked by hungry mobs. Worst of all, however, was the 'Flour War' of 1775, just before the coronation. Despite the poor harvest of 1774, the minister Turgot insisted on removing all controls in the belief that a free market would best avert shortages. By the spring, bread prices in

Paris had risen by more than 50 per cent, and riots which began on 27 April at Beaumont-sur-Oise, 25 miles to the north, spread within a week throughout the Île de France, to the gates of the royal palace at Versailles, and to the bread markets of the capital itself. It took troops, hundreds of arrests, and two public executions to restore order, and by then much of north-eastern France had been disturbed for over two weeks. In 1778 it was the turn of several southern cities—Grenoble, Toulouse, Bordeaux again—to witness riots or tensions after harvest shortfalls, and in 1784 and 1785, Normandy. But for a dozen years after the Flour War Paris was calm, and successive ministries anxious not to repeat Turgot's mistake intervened in the grain market to maintain that calm. Only after a bumper harvest in 1787 was the grip relaxed. And then once again it was at just the wrong moment.

Educated onlookers invariably blamed bread riots on the poor—the beggars, vagrants, and petty criminals who made everyday life in city streets so hazardous and disagreeable. People with nothing to lose, they thought, had everything to gain from chaos. But in fact most of these disturbances were the work of people with everything to lose. It was that which made them so frenzied. Bread made up three-quarters of most ordinary people's diet, and in normal times the poorest wage-earner might spend a third or even a half of his income on it. When it rose in price his whole livelihood was threatened, since it left him with less for other food, clothing, heating, and rent, and opened the prospect of destitution. Those who wrote and spoke with such confidence about the 'rabble' or 'dregs of the people' fomenting disorders like those of 1775 had mostly never known what it was to calculate domestic budgets so finely. The vast majority of French people who were not destitute lived under constant threat of becoming so, and were prepared to use violence to avoid such a fate. When they did, they terrified the narrow, secure social élites who in normal times dominated urban life and who never had to worry about the price of a four-pound loaf.

These groups never made up more than a small proportion of the population of most towns—seldom beyond one-fifth, and usually a good deal less. Among them were always a handful of successful master craftsmen; but the true hallmark of those in easy circumstances was that they did not work with their hands. Soft hands, formal clothing, servants, effortless literacy, and incomes and possessions far beyond the dreams of the average Frenchman or woman marked out the members of the dominant classes. They numbered about $2\frac{3}{4}$ million, and all of them except a few hundred thousand nobles and clerics were members of the middle class—the bourgeoisie. There were three times more bourgeois under

Louis XVI than in the last years of Louis XIV. Over the same period the population as a whole had only grown by about a quarter, so that the relative weight of the bourgeoisie in society was increasing even more rapidly than their numbers. Their share of national wealth was enormous. Most industrial and almost all commercial capital, amounting to almost a fifth of all French private wealth, was bourgeois owned. Perhaps a quarter of the land belonged to them, and a significant (though uncertain) proportion of government stock. So probably did the greater part of the capital invested in a field tht had proved peculiarly successful in France since the sixteenth century—venal public offices. Bourgeois competition for such offices was pushing the price of many of them to unprecedented heights by the 1780s. Bourgeois spending was also reflected in the handsome new architecture that was transforming the appearance of so many towns, and in the expansion of the luxury trades. Most of the demand for Lyons silk, sugar and coffee from the West Indies, and decorative materials such as prints and wallpaper came from bourgeois taste. Bourgeois capital helped to build lavish new theatres in Paris and provincial cities like Bordeaux and Nantes; bourgeois ticket-buyers kept them solvent. Bourgeois keenness to invest in education and culture funded a remarkable expansion in schools and colleges, booming growth in the book market, and important new developments such as the establishment of newspapers, public libraries, reading rooms, and innumerable clubs and cultural societies. All this was spectacular evidence that, as the poor grew poorer and more numerous, the rich too were growing in numbers and getting richer. 'The distance', wrote Mercier in 1783, 'which separates the rich from other citizens is growing daily and poverty becomes more insupportable at the sight of the astonishing progress of luxury which tires the view of the indigent. Hatred grows more bitter and the state is divided into two classes: the greedy and insensitive, and murmuring malcontents.'[11]

The ultimate source of this enrichment was the extraordinary commercial and industrial expansion of the eighteenth century. All bourgeois fortunes began in business, and more were being made as the century progressed. The greatest success stories caught every eye. 'The mode of living that takes place here among merchants', wrote Young in Bordeaux, 'is highly luxurious. Their houses and establishments are on expensive scales. Great entertainments, and many served on plate. High play is a much worse thing; and the scandalous chronicle speaks of merchants keeping the dancing and singing girls of the theatre at salaries which ought to import no good to their credit.'[12] All this was a world away from the traditional picture of the sober, frugal, calculating *Parfait*

*Négociant* celebrated by Jacques Savary in a famous and much reprinted manual of 1675. But it was doubtless a world away, too, from the lives of most of those engaged in trade or business. Among the bourgeoisie, as among all social groups, the opulent handful stood out much more than the modest majority. Yet fundamentally the differences were largely a matter of scale. In many ways the behaviour of the commercial bourgeoisie was much the same at whatever level it occurred. Hardly any of them, above all, were content to leave money where it had been made. Trade and manufacture, however profitable, were not secure; and so as soon as there was money to spare the first instinct was to buy land with it. While wholesale colonial shippers or metropolitan bankers used their millions to accumulate manors, country houses, or far-flung lordships in choice locations, successful small-town tradesmen picked up houses down the street or patches of garden outside the walls. Land was safe. Its profits might be low, but they were steady. Above all, land had prestige. All the best people, and the people who had governed the country since time immemorial, were landowners. Nobody, therefore, with any aspirations to social consequence could afford to be landless; and those whose ambitions were really serious knew that sooner or later they would have to get out of trade altogether.

Very few bourgeois families remained in the business that had enriched them for more than a single generation—unless they were Protestants or Jews debarred by law from everything except making money. Profits not spent on buying property went into buying the next generation a superior education. With that, the way was open to the professions, where mercantile origins could be forgotten. This pattern was very long established, and although it was becoming fashionable to extol the usefulness of merchants and lament the way they abandoned their calling as soon as it had enriched them, there was little sign that much was changing in practice.

I ought not to pass over in silence [wrote a Lyons litigant about his adversary in 1780] . . . I who am the offspring of a generally loved and respected merchant, the outrage done by Mr. Gesse to commerce in describing those who exercise this profession as 'persons from the dregs of the people'; it is thus that he speaks of a profession as honorable as it is honoured in its country; yet remember that Mr. Gesse is, as I am, a merchant's son; he disowns his stock, whereas I honour mine.[13]

The writer, however, was a judge in a local court. Evidently the paternal calling was chiefly to be honoured for producing enough money to buy the son an office. And nothing testifies more eloquently to the continuing desire of the bourgeoisie to escape from the stigma of commerce than the booming market for offices. Originating in the sixteenth century as a way of enabling the king to borrow money, in the seventeenth the sale of public offices became a basic institution of French social life when office-holders were permitted, on payment of an annual tax, to pass them on to their children or re-sell them to third parties. This made offices as sound a social investment as land, and in response to continued demand the Crown made most public functions venal. The whole judicial hierarchy, from the highest presidents in the parlements to the humble tipstaff in the obscurest rural jurisdiction, bought their positions. So did thousands of other public officials at all levels. Under Louis XVI there were well over 50,000 venal offices, representing a capital value of perhaps a billion *livres*, increasing rapidly as the market value of most of them went up. Only offices traditionally closed to bourgeois, like those in the parlements, or ones which seemed threatened by perpetual fiscal tinkering, were failing to rise in value. All the rest were shooting up under the impulsion of the bourgeoisie's seemingly insatiable desire for a life of respectable, professional dignity as far removed as possible from the hurly-burly of business.

It seemed to matter little that few fortunes were made in the professions. It was true that people like notaries could do very well in Paris or the more prosperous provincial centres. A talented—or, as many thought, plain lucky—handful might shine and prosper at the bar. For the first time in history, too, there were writers who found it possible to live by their pens. But all these success stories were exceptional. The lot—and often indeed the aim—of most professional bourgeois was to vegetate in modest, undemanding, but comfortable circumstances, finding wives of similar background and being succeeded in their office or calling by their children and grandchildren. Maximilien Robespierre, destined to become the most famous provincial bourgeois of his time, came from a family that had practised law in Artois for five generations, and before 1788 it does not seem to have occurred to him to do anything else either. In sleepy, provincial Arras he made a modest living at the bar from such cases as came his way, supplemented his income with a petty judgeship in one of the myriad special jurisdictions to be found anywhere, read widely in his ample spare time, wrote poems and entered literary competitions, and became a member of the local academy. In other towns innumerable counterparts lived similar, humdrum, unexciting lives. Many sought to spice them by joining masonic lodges, with their high ideals and mystic, supposedly secret, rituals. Others found diversion in the countless occasions offered by the narrow, under-occupied world of middle-class self-esteem for feeling slighted, nursing petty triumphs or resentments, or pursuing vicious little quarrels and vendettas. Excluded from a discussion group formed by other local lawyers, Robespierre denounced them in a bitter pamphlet. In Grenoble another small-town lawyer, Antoine-Pierre Barnave, enjoyed being recognized as the man who, at the age of 10, had been thrown with his mother out of an empty theatre box reserved for a noble friend of the provincial governor. It made the bourgeois (and Protestant) Barnaves into social and religious martyrs, a distinction they clearly treasured. Barnave later claimed the incident gave his life a mission—'to raise the caste to which he belonged from the state of humiliation to which it seemed condemned'. But the determination of his pretentious mother to use the famous box (while his father sat in the pit) is a vivid example of the most burning of bourgeois obsessions: their love-hate relationship with the nobility.

The most highly regarded of all bourgeois were those who 'lived nobly'. That meant they lived without exercising any profession, on the proceeds of investments or landed revenues. Bourgeois living nobly were a rare breed, however, since anybody who could afford to live like a noble could equally well afford to become one; and ennoblement was the ultimate recognition of social success that all bourgeois dreamed of. Nor did men of means find it hard to achieve. Upwards of 3,700 of the most sought-after venal offices conferred nobility on their holders, and by this and a number of less important avenues anything between 5,500 and 7,500 individuals (which if their families are included means perhaps 33,000–45,000 people) left the bourgeoisie for the nobility in the course of the eighteenth century. Most ennobling offices, it is true, required two successive generations to hold them if the nobility thereby acquired was to be fully hereditary; but the 819 offices of King's Secretary, with no duties to speak of, ennobled completely and at once. 'Soap for scum' (*savonnettes à vilain*) they were called, but they were much in demand among financiers, merchants, and industrialists, who pushed their price to unparalleled heights in the 1780s. Nothing outraged the professional bourgeoisie more than to see self-made businessmen leapfrogging them into the highest levels of society. It made nonsense of their assumption that tradesmen, of whatever sort, were their inferiors. But the prices parvenus were prepared to pay put most ennobling offices far beyond the reach of professional men, however worthy. All they could do was petition (as the members of local civil and criminal courts constantly did) to have their own offices made ennobling ones; or try to get away with usurping noble status. Forging false genealogies was a minor industry, and the number of later revolutionary leaders who tried to make their names sound noble is striking. Before 1789 we meet D'Anton, de Robespierre, and de Marat, while Brissot qualified himself de Warville, and Roland, de la Platière. Nor was it any consolation to know that nobles thought little of brash intruders into their order either. When parlements voted (as several did between the 1760s and 1780s) not to admit members without several generations of noble ancestry, or when in 1781 the notorious 'Ségur Ordinance' decreed that army officers would henceforth need at least four degrees of nobility, bourgeois opinion was shocked. These measures were largely directed against that same moneyed interest whose ability to buy their way into the nobility so disturbed professional people's sense of propriety. But from outside they looked like attempts to exclude all bourgeois from the most desirable public employments. In practice few bourgeois had ever got that far without becoming noble first, but to formalize the situation publicly was provocative in an age when the education, values, and outlook of nobles and bourgeois were increasingly indistinguishable.

What then made nobility so desirable? Obviously there was the glamour, distinction, and recognition that noble status had always brought. Then there was a range of privileges which all nobles enjoyed. The bourgeoisie were themselves no strangers to privilege in a society where most people benefited from some special rights or exemptions by virtue of the corporations, groups, towns, or even provinces to which they belonged. Privilege was the hallmark of a country without uniform laws or institutions. But nobles were entitled to more privileges than most. They formed a separate order or estate in society, and all the rest of the king's subjects, from the most wretched beggar to Young's great colonial shipper dining off plate, were *roturiers*, commoners. Nobles took precedence on public occasions, carried swords, and made display of special coats of arms. They were entitled to trial in special courts, and even to a distinctive mode of execution—decapitation—if convicted of a capital offence. They were not subject to the *corvée*, billeting of troops, or conscription into the militia. Above all they enjoyed substantial fiscal advantages. They escaped much of the weight of the *gabelle*, the hated, extortionate, salt monopoly; they paid no mutation duties on transferring feudal property (*franc-fief*); and nobility conferred exemption from the basic direct tax, the *taille*. It was true that many bourgeois escaped it too, as citizens of towns which had been granted exemption; and that many nobles in the *pays d'états*, where it fell on lands not persons, found themselves subject to it while non-noble neighbours owning fiefs were not. And there were certainly no exemptions for nobles from more recent direct taxes such as the capitation (1698) and the *vingtième* (1749). But *taille* exemption remained, in most people's eyes, the quintessential badge of nobility; a tangible link with chivalric times when those whose duty was to risk their lives to defend the country were not expected to contribute money as well. The same warrior associations made it dishonourable for nobles to engage in retail trade. Those who did so risked loss of status (*dérogeance*), and reduction to the ranks of the *taillables*. Few chose to imperil the advantages of nobility by flouting this law, or the deep prejudices which lay behind it. In any case they had their children to think of; nobility was a family affair, a distinction only truly worth having if it could be passed on down the generations. Besides, nobles were presumed to have more important things to do than make their fortunes. They were society's traditional rulers—yet another reason why aspiring bourgeois were so keen to join them.

Nobody knew, or knows, for certain how many nobles there were. Credible estimates vary between 120,000 and 350,000. But members of this tiny fragment of the nation owned between a quarter and a third of the land, and most of the feudal rights over the rest. They owned all the most valuable venal offices, huge amounts of government stock, and up to a quarter of the Church's revenues went into the pockets of noble priests and monks. Most heavy industry was noble-controlled, either through investments or outright ownership in fields like mining and metallurgy which, being land-based, were not deemed commercial. Even the prohibition on trading had its loopholes. Wholesale trade had been open to nobles for generations, and King's Secretaries, most of whom were great merchants or financiers, were not required to give up business on purchase of this ennobling office. And because it was so easy for successful bourgeois to join the nobility in this way, the wealth of the order was constantly being supplemented by the riches they brought in with them, not to mention the dowries of bourgeois heiresses with which impecunious gentlemen were always eager to 'regild their arms'. Thus the growing wealth of the bourgeoisie also enriched the nobility, and helped it maintain its leading position. Nobility was a club which every wealthy man felt entitled, indeed obliged, to join. Not all nobles, by any means, were rich, but sooner or later all the rich ended up noble.

And along with noble wealth went influence and power. The king, the 'first gentleman of the realm', passed his whole life among noble courtiers. Technically only those with long pedigrees might even meet him. All his ministers were nobles: it caused a sensation in 1776 when Louis XVI gave office to Jacques Necker, a Swiss, Protestant commoner. All the senior members of the administration—ambassadors, governors, councillors of state, intendants—were nobles, as were all senior military and naval officers and most junior ones, too. Most of the great financiers and tax-farmers who kept central government solvent had invested in nobility, and since every office in every sovereign court was an ennobling one, the whole upper judiciary were members of the order. In the Church, nobles occupied all bishoprics and all the choicest abbacies and canonries, and under Louis XVI it became a matter of policy that they should. The motive was one that lay behind the Ségur Ordinance of 1781—to reserve some part of the public service for a group without other resources: the poor nobility.

For in reality France under Louis XVI was governed not by the nobility, but by a plutocracy in which the majority of nobles had no share. Half or more of the nobility were no better off than the average bourgeois, and many were a good deal poorer. The nobility of Boulogne, noted Tobias Smollett in 1763,

are vain, proud, poor, and slothful . . . They allow their country houses to go to decay, and their gardens and fields to waste; and reside in dark holes in the Upper Town . . . without light, air, or convenience. There they starve within doors, that they may have the wherewithall to purchase fine cloaths, and appear dressed once a day . . . They have no education, no taste for reading, no housewifery, nor indeed any earthly occupation, but that of dressing their hair, and adorning their bodies. They hate walking, and would never go abroad, if they were not stimulated by the vanity of being seen . . . They pretend to be jealous of their rank, and will entertain no correspondence with merchants, whom they term plebeians.[14]

At Court, and in Paris, wealth opened every door, and dukes and peers happily married the well-endowed daughters of great financiers. Necker's passport to power was his opulence as a banker. There was similar mingling of rank and riches in some provincial capitals, especially if they were ports. But away from such centres of conspicuous consumption, the nobility often consisted of threadbare gentry with impeccable lineages but no resources. These were the only nobles most peasants, and therefore most Frenchmen, ever came across. They found them haughty, keen to exact their feudal dues and exercise their seigneurial prerogatives, and ferociously attached to their ancestry and privileges as noblemen. 'It generally happened', recalled Count de Ségur in 1825, looking back on the years before the Revolution, 'that there was less cause of complaint against the higher nobility or persons attached to the court than against the country nobility, who were poor and unenlightened. This ought to occasion no surprise, for the latter had nothing but their titles, which they were continually opposing to the real superiority of some of the middle classes whose knowledge and wealth embarrassed and humbled them.'[15] Among nobles of this sort prejudice against trade was at its most virulent. In Brittany, gentlemen fallen on hard times were allowed to 'put their nobility to sleep' while they restored their fortunes in commerce. But even those who did so, like Chateaubriand's father, who eventually managed to buy back the ancestral castle, spent all they had made in the process, and were then content to resume lives of straitened but genteel idleness. Lack of money closed the judicial bench to such people: the price of offices was beyond them, nor could they have afforded the education indispensable for sovereign court magistrates. They took solace in sneering at what they chose (erroneously, often enough) to think of as the recent origins of the nobility of the robe. They saw themselves, on the contrary, as the only true nobility, a nobility of the sword. Their vocation, inherited with the blood of their ancestors, was to fight. They had a duty to serve the king—as officers, of course—in his armies. And he in turn had a duty to give them that opportunity. The problem was that all military commissions were subject to purchase, and here again plutocrats priced them out of the market. In mid-century there had been a lively public debate about the problem of the poor nobility. In *La Noblesse commerçante* of 1756 the Abbé Coyer had argued that the solution was to encourage them to trade. But in *La Noblesse militaire ou Le Patriote français*, the Chevalier d'Arc, illegitimate grandson of Louis XIV, responded by denouncing the power of money and advocating a noble monopoly of military commissions with promotion on merit alone. This would both give poor nobles a guaranteed livelihood and make for more dedicated, professional officers. Such debates culminated in 1776 in the establishment of a system of twelve military schools like that of Brienne, where young Napoleon Bonaparte, from a poor noble family in newly acquired Corsica, learned the rudiments of the military arts. The Ségur Ordinance had the same aim—to purge the body of army officers of rich playboys just up from the bourgeoisie, more interested in the glamour and social recognition of a uniform than in military efficiency. The flaw was that it did nothing about courtier playboys, whose pedigrees were excellent, who were just as rich, but whose commitment to the military life was just as token. Either way those with talent or abilities seemed doomed to take second place to people endowed by chance of birth with riches or noble ancestors: and not only in the army. The whole of society, many thought, worked too obviously in this way. 'What being is most alien to those around him?' mused Chamfort, a self-made man of letters, whose aristocratic contacts propelled him into the Académie française in 1781. '. . . Might it not perchance be a man of merit without gold or title-deeds, in the midst of those who possess one of these two advantages, or both together?'[16]

It was scarcely a coincidence that public dissatisfaction should become focused on the army. The record of the French armed forces in the wars of mid-century had been lamentable. Swept from the seas by the British, and mauled on the battlefield by the Prussians, no other institutions had had their inadequacies so spectacularly demonstrated. Reforms like the introduction of military academies and the Ségur Ordinance were part of a sustained attempt to restore the tarnished prestige of an army that had been the admiration of Europe in the days of Louis XIV. That role had now been inherited by the army of Frederick the Great, and it provided the model of many of the French reforms. Successive war ministers sought not only to build a Prussian-style officer-corps, but also introduced Prussian tactics and manoeuvres, Prussian uniforms, and even Prussian discipline. Controversy raged over every aspect of this policy, and polemics flew over such questions as whether French soldiers could honourably be punished for military offences in the German way by beating with the flat of a sword. And certainly Louis XVI's army was very differently constituted from that of Frederick. Most of his soldiers were his own subjects, and volunteers too. There were indeed twenty-three foreign regiments, including the redoubtable Swiss Guards permanently attached to the royal household, but they barely accounted for one-seventh of the entire strength. And conscription was only used to recruit the militia, a reserve army never now mobilized except in wartime. Lots were drawn to select the conscripts required from each district, but exemption was so widespread that only the poorest peasants failed to avoid the draw. Even though the risk of the militia being embodied was now small, it was deeply unpopular in the countryside. The military life had little appeal for even the most miserable of peasants. The ranks of the regular army were drawn overwhelmingly from the highly urbanized, heavily garrisoned northern and eastern frontier districts. Most recruits stayed with the colours for the full eight years of their engagement, and losses of 3,000 a year through desertion were low by international standards. So was the relative weight of the military in society. The 180,000 strong army represented one soldier for every 156 of the king's subjects (as compared with 1 in 29 in Prussia), and its regional concentration meant it impinged little on the lives of whole provinces in the centre, south, and west of the country. French troops had not fought on their own soil for three generations, and in the eighteenth century they were seldom called upon to deal with civil unrest. Despite, therefore, the increasing sums being spent on it, the army was becoming more and more a world apart, making little impact on areas or populations not already militarized for generations. But even within the army there were separate worlds. Most officers, endowed with generous leave, saw little of their subordinates and cared less. The Prussian models so fashionable among military theorists, which called for mindless automatons in the ranks, did nothing to bring them closer together. Nor did attempts to restrict access to commissions. In their anxiety to exclude rich commoners, they also kept out or kept down talented 'officers of fortune' with long and valuable experience in other, lower, ranks.

Such distance was impossible in the navy, where a ship's complement all lived on top of one another for months on end, and each officer needed a thorough understanding of navigation and the duties of a crew. It was true that throughout the French navy's history repeated attempts had been made to restrict the recruitment of officers to nobles. Naval schools (*compagnies de gardes de la marine*) at Brest, Rochefort, and Toulon were intended to supply all the service's needs and were theoretically open only to nobles. But the latter found far less attraction in the rigours of seagoing than in the army; and although the 'red' officers produced by the schools dominated the service, in wartime they were outnumbered by 'blues' recruited from a wide spectrum of maritime society. There was no purchase in the navy, and few courtiers were interested in even the highest ranks, so social rivalries were far less pronounced at every level. What counted at sea was competence and experience, and ever since the time of Colbert a system of naval conscription had operated in order to ensure that even the lower decks had these qualities. In coastal districts and navigable river valleys every man under 60 with experience afloat was required to register for assignment to a 'class', or naval reserve category, liable for mobilization if the need arose. The system was as unpopular among sailors, fishermen, and bargemen as the draw for the militia was among peasants; but it produced better crews for warships than the British press-gang, and ones which had their revenge on the British during the American War of Independence. This war seemed to vindicate the massive programme of naval expansion and re-equipment that had been pursued since the end of the previous one in 1763. By 1780 there were 86 frigates and 79 ships of the line in French service, and the annual cost of the navy almost quadrupled between 1776 and 1783. These efforts were crucial in securing American independence, and even after the war ended Louis XVI remained determined to keep France a major naval power. The only time he saw the sea, or visited any of his kingdom outside the Île de France before 1791, was in 1786, when he travelled to Cherbourg to inspect progress on a vast new naval harbour. 3,000 men were employed on the works, which deeply impressed Arthur Young when he viewed them late in August 1788. Young wondered, however, whether such a stupendous project could be completed without bankrupting the kingdom. In fact it took another 65 years to complete. And defence spending on this scale had already brought bankruptcy just eleven days before Young arrived in Cherbourg.

Nobles tended to justify their grip on the armed forces by arguing that their order existed to fight; and this argument served to defend their tax-exemptions as well. It went back to the classic medieval division of society into those who worked, those who fought, and those who prayed. Naturally those who prayed, the clergy, invoked similar arguments, for the same functional principle underlay the extensive privileges which they enjoyed, too. In law the clergy ranked ahead of the nobility as the first order of the realm, for they were the custodians of the community's spiritual welfare and its moral standards. They numbered about 130,000, but over half were in regular orders (two-thirds of them women) and many of the seculars were canons without cure of souls as members of 496 cathedral or collegiate chapters. Parish priests, therefore, were in a minority, and their distribution across the country averaged one for every 400 or 500 inhabitants. But the clerical presence, like everything else in the kingdom, was unevenly distributed. In the countryside the *curé* was often the only ecclesiastic his parishioners ever came across; whereas townscapes were dominated by convents, seminaries, schools, and hospitals, all run by clerics, not to mention cathedrals, collegiate churches, and innumerable parish churches within sight of one another and within sound of each other's bells. In many a small town the church was the chief source of employment. In Chartres, the cathedral chapter alone gave direct employment to 500 or 600 of the 12,000 inhabitants, and was the main source of business for many more. The money thus spent came from over 17,000 acres and 124 feudal lordships in the surrounding district. In Bayeux, a town of 10,000, it was estimated that the total annual contribution of all ecclesiastical institutions to the town's economy was worth 400,000 L. Over France as a whole about a tenth of the land was in the hands of the Church, although much more in the north than the south; and in the form of the tithe, the parish clergy were theoretically entitled to a tenth of every person's livelihood for their upkeep. In practice the tithe was far more patchily levied, and seldom took as much as a tenth even from those who failed to avoid it. But, with the exception of provinces added to the kingdom since 1561, and thereby 'reputed foreign', all these ecclesiastical revenues were exempt from ordinary taxation. Unlike the nobility, the clergy had consistently fought off every attempt by the government to breach this principle. The most recent battle had occurred between 1749 and 1751, when the *vingtième* had been introduced. The clergy won it because they were well organized. Unlike the second or third estates, they had a representative General Assembly which convened every five years. When it was not in session the collective affairs of the order were managed by a permanent General Agency headed by two carefully chosen Agents-General, ambitious young priests with names to make. Most of their business was financial, since exemption from taxation did not mean that the clergy contributed nothing to the royal revenues. Every ten years a 'free gift' was negotiated, made up by an internal levy on clerical income. Further sums were raised to pay interest on extensive loans which the clergy used its superior credit to float on the State's behalf. Altogether the clergy paid out about 16 millions annually to or for the State, but since they had revenues of perhaps a quarter of a billion the proportion of their income was nowhere near that demanded of the laity.

Nor was the weight of clerical taxation equitably distributed within the order. The parish clergy, dependent on tithes, fees, and if they were lucky a little glebe land, paid almost half the total raised, yet had little say in its allocation within each diocese. Positions of power or influence in the hierarchy were monopolized by canons and other representatives of the great chapters and monasteries who owned most of the Church's landed wealth. And the richest of these corporations, in turn, were invariably dominated by the nobility, who saw in them an important, comfortable, and well-paid refuge for over-numerous sons and daughters otherwise burdensome to family fortunes. Ever since the Concordat of 1516 between Francis I and Pope Leo X the king had appointed all bishops and the abbots of greater monasteries. In the eighteenth century he distributed this huge fund of patronage on the advice of a bishop entrusted with what was known as the benefice portfolio (*feuille des bénéfices*). None of its holders, however, proved able to resist the enormous pressure they were subjected to by courtier families anxious to place their members, friends, and dependants in lucrative clerical comfort. The rise in landed revenues over the century only increased the demand. The greater archbishops all enjoyed six-figure incomes, and very few prelates brought in less than 20,000 L. A commendatory abbot of one of the greater monasteries might draw more than many a bishop. Accordingly most of these much sought-after benefices went to younger sons of the greater nobility. In 1789 the entire episcopate (bar one) was of noble birth, and a quarter of all sees were in the hands of just thirteen families. Many of the beneficiaries of this system were appointed very young after truncated studies, lightning ordination, and rapid progress through a hierarchy of lesser dignitaries. Talleyrand, condemned to a clerical rather than a military career by an accident in infancy which stunted one of his legs, was ordained a subdeacon at 21, canon of Rheims within weeks, an abbot within months, yet did not become a priest until four years later. Another year saw him one of the two Agents-General of the Clergy, and at 34, in 1788, he was bishop of Autun. Few of Louis XVI's bishops were as cynical and cold-blooded as Talleyrand was to prove, and most were to stand by their vocation with more or less zeal when it was put to the test. But they had all climbed the ladder of preferment in the same way, for there was no other. And if such a system produced tepid pastors, it made the bishops of the Gallican Church formidable politicians and powerbrokers. When Loménie de Brienne, archbishop of Toulouse, became chief minister in May 1787, it was the fulfilment of an ambition openly pursued for years. The examples earlier in the century of Fleury, Bernis, and Terray showed that Louis XIV's principle of never giving high secular office to clerics had died with him.

Brienne had made his name as a church reformer. In 1766 he had been made chairman of the Commission of Regulars established by the Assembly of the Clergy to investigate and if necessary close or amalgamate under-occupied monasteries or convents. This reforming gesture was undertaken in the aftermath of the greatest religious upheaval of the century, the expulsion of the Jesuits from the kingdom in 1764. Resulting in many ways from a string of improbable accidents, this removal by the secular power of one of the most vigorous and influential orders in French religious and educational life nevertheless vividly demonstrated how vulnerable a Church that refused to reform itself might be. Reading these warning signs, the Church looked around for soft targets. Contemplative orders, faltering in their recruitment and condemned by an increasingly utilitarian public opinion as useless hoarders of wealth and bolt-holes for idlers, were obviously in an exposed position. Between 1768 and 1780, accordingly, 458 smaller monasteries were dissolved. Their capital assets, estimated at 642,029 L., were redistributed to hospitals, poor houses, and seminaries. But larger, richer houses continued unscathed, and nothing was done about the problems of the parish clergy, the Church's undervalued, underprivileged workhorses. Few parish priests came from really poor backgrounds. The costs of acquiring the education necessary for the priesthood alone ensured that. Nor could the majority of beneficed parish priests be considered poverty-stricken by the standards of most of the population. But many resented the inequitable distribution of the Church's wealth, their exclusion from any say in how the Church was governed, and the complete absence of promotion prospects. Improving agricultural prices brought growing prosperity to those who enjoyed tithes, but in many towns tithes were a thing of the past, and even in the country about a third of the beneficed clergy had no right to their parish's tithes. They had been impropriated, sometimes by laymen but more often by monasteries or other ecclesiastical corporations, who only paid the incumbent a fixed share of the yield, known as the *portion congrue*. The inflation of the century constantly eroded the value of what was in effect a salary; and in 1768 and again in 1786 royal edicts imposed rises. On both occasions they were denounced as inadequate, yet rather than pay them many tithe-owners abandoned their rights to incumbents. Now it was their turn to incur the odium of tithe collection, and to find that the yield was often less than that of the *congrue*. In the 1770s the discontents of the parish clergy erupted in many dioceses in the form of mutinous assemblies which denounced the inadequacies of the *congrue*, the unfairness of clerical taxation, domination of diocesan administration by canons and regulars, and the 'despotism' of bishops, whose authority stood behind so many of these practices. The bishops' response, in the Assembly of the Clergy of 1780, was to reiterate long-standing prohibitions on unauthorized clerical gatherings. Their stance was reinforced by a royal edict of 1782 which apparently brought an end to the so-called 'revolt of the *curés*'. It did nothing to tackle its causes, however, at a time when the Church was under unprecedented attack from critical laymen.

Nothing infuriated the Church's critics more than its political power. It held a monopoly of public worship, and all the king's subjects were legally Catholics. Protestants enjoyed no legal toleration, except in Alsace, and no civil rights. As recently as 1762 a pastor had been executed, and the last Protestant galley-slaves were released only in 1775. The Church controlled almost the entire educational system, and the bulk of poor relief and hospital provision. It had extensive powers of censorship, and the pulpit was used constantly by the secular authorities for important public announcements and warnings. All this reinforced the unique God-given moral authority to which the Church laid claim. Its importance in keeping the king's subjects docile and obedient was incalculable in a country where the everyday forces of law and order were very thinly stretched.

Apart from the army, law-enforcement throughout most of the kingdom was in the hands of the *Maréchaussée*, a mounted police force barely 3,000 strong. Additionally all towns of any size employed watchmen, but even in the largest their complement seldom ran to three figures. Only Paris was considered well policed, with almost 2,000 officers serving a variety of agencies in addition to the French and Swiss guards. France, in fact, had far more magistrates than policemen, their numbers swelled by the sale of offices in earlier centuries. At the lowest level were thousands of petty jurisdictions, many private, but all fully staffed by a complement of judges, clerks, procurators, ushers, and tipstaffs. Angers alone, a city of 26,000 inhabitants, had 53 different courts or tribunals, none of them near the top of the judicial hierarchy. Besançon, somewhat larger but with a parlement, had a legal population of around 500, which meant almost one-twelfth of the population probably depended directly on the law for their existence, and many more indirectly. The delays and costs of this judicial labyrinth were notorious. 'Do we not see every day', noted the procurator-general of the parlement of Paris (who ought to have known) in 1763,[17] 'people obliged to go to law over two or three years and at great cost to find out which judges they will have the misfortune to appear before?' Yet so long as France lacked a uniform set of laws and the government felt unable to buy out venal office-holders the problem seemed insoluble. Such reforms and rationalizations as did occur, between 1771 and 1774 or again in 1788, were fragmentary, came as by-products of political conflict between the government and the parlements, and proved as transient as the circumstances that had facilitated them.

The parlements sat at the summit of the judicial hierarchy, the supreme and final courts of appeal for their own regions. They also enjoyed extensive administrative powers which brought them into regular conflict with governors and intendants. Above all they had a crucial role in the legislative process. All laws, to be valid, needed to be registered in their records, and they had the right to point out any defects in new legislation by sending the king remonstrances. By deferring registration pending the king's reply they were able to delay and obstruct government policy, and since the death of Louis XIV they had developed this technique into a major vehicle of opposition. Strictly speaking remonstrances were confidential communications between the king and his courts, but over the same period it had become normal for parlements to marshal public opinion on their side by printing and selling them. Often they would renew remonstrances after the king's reply, and later in the century they extended their means of resistance to judicial strikes and occasional mass resignations. Everyone knew, however, that ultimately the king had the last word. He could silence all opposition by coming in person (or in the provinces sending a personal representative) to the court and dictating registration of the contentious measures in a session known as a *lit de justice*. In the presence of the monarch, the fount of justice, the delegated authority of his magistrates was nullified. Parlements usually protested at such displays of sovereignty, but they seldom continued to resist after them. Honour was satisfied, and beyond lay outright rebellion, which none of them was prepared to contemplate. Nor did most contentious issues need the extreme response of a *lit de justice* to resolve them. The exceptions were matters of religion and finance. Even here the expulsion of the Jesuits in the 1760s, which they largely brought about, marked the end as well as the high-point of the parlements' interference in religious questions. Financial confrontations, however, could only get worse in an age of ever-spiralling military expenditure and constant attempts to increase taxes and borrowing to meet it. In the first half of the century the parlement of Paris, by far the most important sovereign court, with a jurisdiction covering a third of France, spoke out almost alone on such matters. But from the introduction of the *vingtième* in 1749 the provincial courts also began to assert themselves, both on financial matters and against what they saw as the attempts of agents of central government in the provinces to extend their own authority. The 1760s were particularly stormy, witnessing serious clashes with the parlements of Besançon, Toulouse, Bordeaux, Pau, and Rennes, and periodic lesser confrontations with others, too. The suspicion grew that the sovereign courts were acting in secret concert to discredit and usurp royal power, and in 1766 Louis XV felt obliged to reassert his absolute and unlimited authority in blunt terms. In what those present remembered as a 'scourging session', the king came in person to the parlement of Paris and declared that:

It is in my person alone that sovereign power resides . . . It is from me alone that my courts derive their authority; and the plenitude of this authority, which they exercise only in my name, remains always in me . . . It is to me alone that legislative power belongs, without any dependence and without any division . . . The whole public order emanates from me, and the rights and interests of the nation . . . are necessarily joined with mine and rest only in my hands.

But clashes continued, as it proved impossible in peacetime to reduce the burden of taxes first justified by the demands of mid-century wars. In 1771 they reached a further climax when a new chancellor, Maupeou, provoked the parlement of Paris into refusing all co-operation. Maupeou reacted by exiling its magistrates and replacing them with more docile collaborators. He also took the opportunity to abolish venality of offices in the parlement and set up a new structure of subordinate courts throughout the parlement's *ressort*. When the provincial parlements protested, they too were remodelled. Surprising numbers of existing magistrates co-operated in this operation, but those who suffered exile and dispossession raised a huge clamour at what they claimed was the overthrow of the kingdom's constitution. The king was deluged with remonstrances before the courts were silenced by the reform, and despite a carefully orchestrated propaganda campaign, the government was unable to convince the bulk of public opinion of the value of what it had done. The new system had still put down no deep roots when, three years after its introduction, Louis XV died. What to do about the parlements was therefore the first major political decision faced by Louis XVI on his accession. Within months he decided to restore them, Maupeou was dismissed, and all his innovations abandoned. The new monarch's most influential ministers had persuaded him that public opinion would have no faith in his good intentions if he did not bring back the tried and trusted defenders of public liberties. And so by the time of the coronation the old judiciary had been reintegrated, venality restored, and the parlement of Paris was once again remonstrating and obstructing the registration of new laws. But those who thought nothing had changed were wrong. The parlements had been shown that they were not invulnerable, and the public had been shown what feeble checks on a determined government they were. The parlement of Paris, having proved to its own satisfaction by its remonstrances of 1775 and 1776 that it was as formidable as ever, lapsed into a relative quiescence that lasted a decade. Several of its provincial counterparts were torn for years by unseemly internal recriminations between magistrates who had co-operated with Maupeou and those who had not. The chancellor (France's last, since he refused to resign on dismissal, and only died in 1792) had shattered the parlements' political credibility, and even their complete restoration was unable to rebuild it.

Nor did the damage end there. The Crown, too, was indelibly tainted by the memory of Maupeou. Louis XV's willingness to tolerate a measure of defiance from his sovereign courts, despite the extreme claims he had made for his own authority in 1766, had marked the French monarchy out as law-abiding and receptive to the legitimate expression of the subjects' discontents. The parlements enjoyed considerable popular support, and the king's occasional concessions to their opposition served to reassure his subjects that he was no tyrant. Maupeou, supported by a monarch now ageing and tired of endless obstruction, swept this subtle structure of confidence away. His attack on courts of law which traced their origins and powers almost as far back as the monarchy itself showed him up as the agent of despotism, of government by no law except the monarch's will, where no person and no property was secure against his whims. If Louis XVI had kept Maupeou in power, and preserved his reforms, he would have been called a tyrant seventeen years before he was. But even the restoration of the former parlements could not efface the memory of their suppression. Frenchmen now knew what power their king might deploy if he had a mind to, and few of them found much comfort in the knowledge. The institutions and the men of before 1771 were brought back, but the atmosphere of political confidence, innocence even, in which they had operated was irrecoverable.

The magistrates of the parlements numbered around 1,200. Together with perhaps 1,000 more officers in other sovereign courts mainly exercising special financial and fiscal jurisdiction, they made up the 'nobility of the robe'. All sovereign court offices ennobled, but few members of the parlements by now owed their nobility to their offices. Mostly they had several generations of noble forebears behind them, and by this time a number of parlements had decided to admit nobody without such credentials. In their provinces these men dominated all local affairs, which was why they so often came into conflict with intendants and governors. In Paris they dominated national affairs. Not only did the parlement and certain other metropolitan sovereign courts enjoy wider powers and jurisdiction than their provincial counterparts; the Parisian robe nobility also provided most of those who went on to become intendants, councillors of state, and ministers. After a few years on the bench, young magistrates of ambition would seek to buy one of the 80 offices of Master of Requests. By shining there they could legitimately hope to be appointed to one of the 34 intendancies, which were always filled from their ranks. And whereas most intendants never ended up as ministers, many ministers had served their time as intendants. All this meant that the worlds of government and the law in the capital were closely linked, and the intermarriage common in these circles made the relationship yet closer. Everybody involved in political conflicts had relatives on both sides, and the great confrontations were not always as serious as they appeared. Knowing each other intimately, those involved realized their opponents had appearances to maintain. Maupeou, himself recently first president of the Paris parlement, shocked this cosy world when he exiled the most vocal of his former colleagues to places seemingly chosen for their discomfort. No wonder he aroused such personal hatred. And when, to fill up the posts in his new system, he brought in outsiders, 'intruders' as they were known, he only compounded the insult. The narrow legal and administrative élite who controlled most of the levers of power in the kingdom did not welcome new blood, and even members of the provincial 'robe' only broke in occasionally. Only two other groups enjoyed as much say in the government of the kingdom; and one of these had only attained complete respectability within living memory.

This group was that of the financiers, or 'finance' as contemporaries called it. Numbering no more than two or three hundred individuals, it kept the government solvent by handling its revenues and outgoings, providing short-term credit, and raising longer-term loans from contacts in the private world of banking and trade. Most of the indirect taxes were collected by the Farmers-General, a rich syndicate who leased the monopoly under a contract renewed every six years. Revenue from direct taxes was received and paid out by venal office-holders who were also financiers. They made their living from handling public funds, and the spectacular profits of this activity placed them among the king's richest subjects. Few of them were far from humble, mercantile beginnings; but few omitted, either, to buy themselves ennoblement, and their daughters were among the most prized heiresses in the kingdom. They lived in ostentatious luxury, and the fact that this dazzling wealth came from public resources created the suspicion that it had been made at public expense. So financiers were widely hated. Old nobles regarded them as jumped-up—although they were eager enough to 'regild the arms' with their daughters' dowries. Professional men thought the same, while envying their success. And taxpayers considered them public blood-suckers, regretting the days, still just within living memory, when financiers were put on trial for embezzlement whenever a new reign began. In 1774 there was no question of that: they were now too influential. Attempts were made by successive finance ministers during the decade to eliminate some of the offices through which financiers operated, but in 1781 these efforts were abandoned. Four years later the Farmers-General began to build a new ten-foot-high wall around Paris to prevent evasion of entry tolls. The gates or barriers they commissioned were severe masterpieces of modern design. To ordinary Parisians, however, they were hated symbols of fiscal oppression and misapplication of the king's revenues.

To find a really staggering example of extravagance at the taxpayers' expense, however, it was necessary to travel twelve miles to the west, to Versailles. Here was the seat of the royal Court, and of the courtiers who constituted the third key power-group within the French body politic. Fifty thousand people lived in Versailles, making it France's tenth largest town. Ten thousand of them lived or worked in the palace, the king's household, and the whole life of the town depended on it. Thirty-five million *livres*, or about 5 per cent of the king's annual revenue, were spent on the Court, and most of this outlay ended up in the pockets of a few hundred courtiers. Anybody who was decently dressed could enter the palace of Versailles: 'It is impossible', marvelled Arthur Young,[18] 'not to like this careless indifference and freedom from suspicion.' But only those who had been presented to the king and hunted with him were true courtiers, and to be admitted to these 'Honours of the Court' one had to have authentic proofs of noble ancestry reaching back to 1400, or enjoy exemption by special favour. Less than a thousand families had this distinction, and many of those took no advantage of it after presentation, since life at Versailles was ruinously expensive. Only the richest could afford the clothes, the retinue, the entertaining, and the upkeep of quarters both there and in Paris that were essential to lead the life of high fashion. Those who could afford it were the kingdom's uncontested social élite, the cream of the nobility, dukes, peers, and other holders of exalted titles, great officers of the Crown,

ministers, generals, and archbishops, or simply favourites of the monarch
or his consort. And most of them would still have found it difficult without
further pensions, sinecures, and other lucrative orders and distinctions in
the gift of the king. This was entirely as Louis XIV, the architect of the
whole system, had intended. His aim had been to assemble the great of the
kingdom around his person, where he could see and control them. Those
who came were richly rewarded—and thereby domesticated and made
dependent. All Louis XIV denied them was real power in the form of high
political office; but by Louis XVI's time courtiers had reconquered even
that. From the late 1750s dukes and peers were found holding ministerial
portfolios alongside the professionals of the robe. And even without
formally holding office, people who mingled daily with the king, his
ministers, and favourites could hardly fail to be influential. Life at Court
was in fact an endless pursuit of advantage, status, pensions, offices, and
perquisites from those whom royal favour endowed with power to bestow
them. News of the death of Louis XV came to his successor, Marie
Antoinette's lady-in-waiting recalled,[19] when 'A terrible noise exactly like
thunder was heard in the outer room of his apartments: it was the crowd of
courtiers deserting the antechamber of the dead sovereign to come and
greet the new power of Louis XVI.' Such graphic recollections fill the pages
of countless diarists and memorialists who chronicled the intrigues of the
Court in loving detail from the time of Louis XIV onwards. Most of them
sound astonishingly trivial, but the prestige, wealth, and power they were
about were real enough. France was ruled from Versailles, and the rewards
of success at Court were limitless.

Some measured it by the public money they were able to amass. At the
height of their influence in the 1780s the family of the Duchess de
Polignac, the queen's closest friend, were together drawing an annual
438,000 L. in pensions and salaries. When she retired from Court in 1775
on the death of her royal lover, Mme Du Barry, who had started out in life
as a penniless but stunningly pretty milliner, sold her three houses in
Versailles but eventually went to live, on a generous pension, in a lavishly
furnished country house a few miles away, owning a fortune in jewels.
Under the lascivious Louis XV, indeed, royal mistresses could make or
break ministers. The Duke de Choiseul, greatest of his servants, reached the
highest office by persistent cultivation of Mme de Pompadour; Count de
Maurepas, Secretary of State for the Navy, was disgraced and exiled in
1749 for circulating smutty verses about her. He remained in exile until
1774, when a new king, who was not interested in mistresses, plucked him
out of oblivion to make him his chief minister and adviser. Until he died in
1781, Maurepas had a hand in the appointment and dismissal of every

holder of the four secretaryships of state (foreign affairs, war, the navy and the royal household), the offices of Comptroller-General of the Finances and Keeper of the Seals (head of the judiciary), and all other places of importance such as intendancies and the Paris lieutenancy of police. As the principal minister of state, with a seat on the most important of the royal councils, he had a predominant voice in all policy-making, and the young monarch gladly yielded to his knowledge and experience even though it had been gained more than a generation previously, when the problems facing the government had been far less acute.

But who else could he turn to? His parents were long dead, and his grandfather Louis XV had done little to initiate him into the duties and mysteries of kingship. He was just 20 when he inherited the throne. His wife, who had been 15 when she had married him in 1770, had been born an archduchess of Austria, but she was still a girl who thought of little but pleasure, and she resented his disinclination to perform his husbandly duties. He had been carefully educated, read several languages, and was conventionally devout. He had a strong sense of duty, and was determined to rule well. That was why he recalled Maurepas, of whom his old tutor had always spoken highly. But his podgy appearance and waddling gait were unimpressive ('the King looks', sneered an English nobleman in 1780,[20] 'much like a Castrato') and the attack of smallpox which unexpectedly carried off Louis XV left his heir feeling, as he put it, as if the universe were falling in on him. He came to the throne, he wailed, too young. There was nothing like the effortless assumption of authority and clear plan of action shown by the 22-year-old Louis XIV, 114 years beforehand, on the day Mazarin died. All Louis XVI had was good intentions.

His Majesty wishes to place Himself out of the Reach of all Intrigue [observed the British ambassador]. This, however, is a vain Expectation, and the Chimera of a Young, inexperienced Mind. The throne He fills, far from raising him above Intrigue, places Him in the Centre of it. Great and Eminent Superiority of Talents might, indeed, crush these Cabals, but as there is no Reason to believe Him possessed of that Superiority, I think, He will be a prey to them and find Himself more and more entangled every Day.[21]

# Enlightened Opinion

THE Court of Versailles, where Louis XVI passed his days according to a timetable first elaborated a century earlier, was Louis XIV's most spectacular legacy. Nor was its influence confined to France. By the early eighteenth century admiring fellow monarchs were building imitations of the sprawling palace and its lavish ornamental gardens all over Europe. From Tsarskoje Selo outside St Petersburg in the east to Aranjuez near Madrid in the west; from Drottningholm, refuge of Swedish monarchs, in the north to Caserta in the Neapolitan south, rulers built themselves out-of-town seats to display their power and flaunt their pleasures. Nor were such piles the only homage paid by foreigners to French cultural prestige in the afterglow of the Sun King. French architecture, French furniture, French fashions dominated continental taste down to the middle of the eighteenth century; and even when, after that, things English came into vogue they made their appearance in a French mirror. Above all, educated Europe adopted the French language. With the exception of England and Spain, it was the preferred tongue of courts everywhere. Recalling court life at Schönbrunn under the Empress Maria Theresia, one of her familiars noted that 'French was then the language of the upper classes and indeed of cultivated society in general . . . In those days, the greater part of high society in Vienna could say: I speak French like Diderot and German . . . like my nurse.'[1] In Frederick II's Berlin or Catherine II's St Petersburg monarchs gorged on Parisian culture created an atmosphere in which their courtiers almost completely forgot their native languages from lack of use; but even at lower levels nobody now considered themselves educated without a thorough familiarity with French. By the 1770s a certain backlash was beginning. Writers like Herder in Germany or Alfieri in Italy were raging against their compatriots' servile deference to an alien culture. But as yet their followers were few. Meanwhile, people of education found themselves unprecedentedly well equipped to follow events in France, form judgements about what was happening there, and absorb the ever-swelling outpourings of French literary life.

While monarchs willingly subscribed to the *Correspondance littéraire* issued from Paris by the expatriate German Baron Grimm, from 1754, their subjects, at less cost, found an expanding range of other journals to keep them well informed. The unadventurous could confine themselves to the long-established *Mercure de France* for news of public events, or the *Journal des savants* for learned ones; but both these periodicals were semi-official and subject to close government censorship. From mid-century a wide range of more independent journals, some specialized and some not, became available. Most had an ephemeral existence, and few of those which survived could have done so without the efforts of one or two persistent individuals. Nevertheless in the seventy years between 1715 and 1785 the number almost quadrupled (from 22 to 79), and it was quite beyond the government's resources to supervise the contents of them all. Indeed, the one it was always keenest to censor, the Jansenist *Nouvelles ecclésiastiques*, which from 1728 onwards kept up a regular critical commentary on the management and outlook of the established Church, always eluded attempts to find its presses. Journals identified openly with particular individuals, such as the popular, conservative *Année littéraire* of Fréron, (appearing from 1754) or the unpredictable *Annales politiques civiles et littéraires* produced from 1777 by Linguet, were more vulnerable. Linguet spent the years 1780–2 in the Bastille for his journalistic excesses. But even then surrogates kept his fortnightly commentary going, and the memoirs he wrote on his release, initially appearing in his *Annales* before separate publication, became a best-seller with their lurid evocation of the living death suffered by all those whom the whim of despotism chose to consign to that lowering and mysterious fortress. Henceforth, however, Linguet took the precaution of publishing outside French jurisdiction, in the Austrian Netherlands. In fact, the boldest French language periodicals had always been produced beyong the frontier. Oldest and most respectable was the *Gazette de Leyde*, founded in Holland by Huguenot refugees in 1677 and still under Protestant direction. It provided its readers with detailed and well-informed accounts of French domestic politics and the issues at stake in them, with a gentle but persistent bias against authority. Almost as popular, though less well known, was the fortnightly *Courrier d'Avignon*, published from 1733 in that enclave of papal territory in the south. The more conservative but well-informed *Courrier du Bas Rhin* was produced in Prussian Cleves; while the intellectually radical *Journal encyclopédique* came out in the tiny independent south Belgian principality of Bouillon.

The circulation of such journals was Europe-wide; and demand for them grew enormously in the news-laden 1770s, with major political upheavals to report from Scandinavia, Russia, and Poland, not to mention France itself and—greatest of all—the American struggle for independence. From a few hundred in the 1750s, the *Gazette de Leyde* was producing around 4,200 copies by 1785. Over half of these were sold outside France; but inevitably by far the biggest single market for French-language journalism was within the kingdom itself. There, local papers also made their appearance. Paris had a weekly news and advertising sheet from early in the century, Lyons had one from 1748, and by the 1780s no self-respecting provincial centre was without one. The *Journal de Paris* came out daily from 1777. These developments were paralleled by book production, in so far as fragmentary evidence allows us to reconstruct it. Expanding steadily down to the 1770s, it leaped dramatically after that and went on at an accelerated rate down to the Revolution—though with some spectacular vicissitudes as censorship policies fluctuated. Technically all books, and journals too, could only be published if passed—or awarded the 'privilege' of being printed, as it was technically known— by a board of censors headed by an official known as the Director of the Book Trade (*Librairie*). To win such a privilege they had to contain nothing contrary to religion, government, and morals. The very number of censors, rising from 41 in the 1720s to 178 in 1789, reflects the expanding volume of their work. But, in practice, very few books were banned. Most of those which the censors felt unable to invest with the positive approval signified by a privilege were nevertheless granted 'tacit permission' to publish; and even more dubious ones could appear 'on simple tolerance', with the mere assurance that the police would not act against them. Nothing short of a full privilege, however, could indemnify a book from independent persecution by either the Sorbonne or a parlement; and the government normally stood aside when a sovereign court condemned a book to be publicly torn up and burned for the subversiveness of its contents. Everybody except (seemingly) the magistrates realized that there was no better way to give a book free publicity. But like journals, an important proportion of the books sold in France came from abroad—from Holland, from Avignon, from Geneva, or from Neuchâtel, another Prussian enclave whose main export appears to have been books in French. Most of these imports were unauthorized, and came in by tortuous routes to avoid the vigilance of customs men. Even authorized imports were sometimes cut to a trickle, as in the early 1770s, by punitive increases in import duties; and in 1783 the whole book trade was plunged into chaos when it was decreed that all imports would have to be inspected by the booksellers' guild in Paris before delivery to any destination within France. The aim was to weed out pornography, sedition, and pirated editions, but the effect was to make transport costs prohibitive for all books, even in the booming market that had now established itself.

Who bought these ever-proliferating journals, newspapers, and books? Over a third of Louis XVI's subjects could read and write, and there was a steady market for cheap popular literature such as almanacks and traditional tales of wonder, sold by travelling hawkers and known from their covers as the 'blue library'. But cost alone restricted the sale of more sophisticated books and journals. A subscription to the *Gazette de Leyde* cost 36 *livres* a year, the *Année littéraire* and the *Journal encyclopédique* were 24 *livres* each, and the *Courrier d'Avignon*, 18. Even the most skilled craftsman would not earn more than 30 *livres* a week, and most earned half that or less, making even the purchase of an occasional book all but impossible. The better-off themselves might find the cost of keeping up with literature and current affairs daunting; but it was much eased in the course of the century by the appearance of subscription libraries and reading rooms, with membership fees around the cost of a single journal subscription. The first to be recorded appeared in Nantes in 1759, and thirty years later there were five more in this same city, housing more than 3,000 volumes between them. During that time similar institutions sprang up throughout the provinces, devoted, like that established in Bayeux in 1770, to 'finding decent diversion . . . in reading literary and political news'.[2] Sometimes they had rooms set aside for conversation, too; but discussion was the main function of a different type of institution which also blossomed over the eighteenth century—the literary society. They too had libraries, and subscribed to journals, but they also held regular public sessions, sometimes interspersed with concerts, at which their members read their own works or debated questions of the day. Sometimes, too, they organized public lectures and essay competitions. Open to all, but usually with a much higher subscription than the average reading room, they often adopted high-sounding names: Société de philalèthes, Société de philosophie et des belles-lettres, Logopanthée, Musée, Société patriotique. By 1787, noted a Dijon newspaper,[3] 'One sees societies of this sort in almost all the towns of the kingdom . . . such an agreeable resource for the select class of citizens in all walks of life'. The most select of all such bodies, however, were the Academies, where membership was by election only, numbers were often deliberately limited, and the society enjoyed the official recognition of royal Letters-Patent. They, too, were largely a product of the eighteenth century. In 1700, apart from the great metropolitan bodies like the Académie française, the Académie des sciences, and the Académie des inscriptions et belles-lettres, only seven provincial academies existed. By

1789 the number had risen to 35. Most had their own premises and libraries, and had in fact usually evolved from humbler literary societies; but in the end academic exclusivism was probably one reason why the latter spread so rapidly. Only 6,000 Frenchmen secured membership of an academy over the whole century, and of these a disproportionate 37 per cent or more were nobles. Yet their cultural pre-eminence was undoubted. Their rare public sessions commanded unrivalled attention, their lists of foreign associates and correspondents conferred unique prestige, and their essay competitions attracted literary hopefuls from far and wide and sometimes helped to launch a promising career: the most famous case was Jean Jacques Rousseau's triumph in the Dijon Academy's competition of 1750.

Access to literature, therefore, was not confined to individual buyers of books and journals; but there was no great social difference between those who bought for themselves and those who relied on institutional libraries. The reading classes were overwhelmingly made up of nobles, clerics, and the professional bourgeoisie. Mostly they lived in towns, and uncommercial towns at that. Merchants and manufacturers were far less interested in the world of ideas than magistrates, lawyers, administrators, and army officers. 'I do not expect you will be able to sell any here', wrote a bookseller in Bar-le-Duc to the Neuchâtel publishers promoting a new, expanded edition of the famous *Encyclopédie*, in 1780.[4] 'Having offered them to everybody here, nobody so far has come looking for a copy. They are more avid for trade than for reading, and their education is quite neglected . . . the merchants prefer to teach their children that 5 and 4 make 9 minus 2 equals 7 than in telling them to refine their minds.' To join the expanding cultivated élite, in fact, disposable income needed to be spent not only on reading, but before that on the right sort of education.

When Louis XVI came to the throne the French educational system was in turmoil, as was that of much of Catholic Europe. The cause was the dissolution of the Jesuits, who had dominated the higher education of Catholic élites since the late sixteenth century. Finally disbanded by the Pope in 1773, they had been expelled from France in 1764, and their 113 colleges (out of a total nearing 400) had been sequestrated. Some disappeared, some passed into the hands of other regular orders, some were taken over by secular priests under municipal supervision. In these varying circumstances, the fairly uniform curriculum they had taught dissolved, and although there was much public discussion of what to put in its place, no action on a kingdom-wide scale was taken. In 1789 one boy in 52 out of the 8–18 age range was attending a college, but the educational experience of them and their predecessors over a generation was much more diverse than that of their fathers and grandfathers. Many more were now boarders, too, cut off for long periods from their families. Even so, solid grounding in the Latin classics was still regarded as the essential foundation of a superior education. Four hours a day of Ancient Rome, its language, and its culture occupied six years of most college courses. Much of the time remaining was devoted to the inculcation of Catholic orthodoxy, although after 1760 there was time in some courses for a little geography, and some French history. Those who went beyond this basic cycle of the humanities, however—and most of those hoping for professional careers did—went on to take a further two years conventionally called 'philosophy', where they were introduced to the natural sciences. Here too tradition ostensibly ruled, and the authority of Aristotle went formally unchallenged. But behind this façade the lessons of the scientific revolution of the previous century, and the methods and approaches that had brought them about, had been widely propagated in the colleges from the 1690s onwards. Neither Ancient Rome nor the Christian religion had played much part in the triumph of a rational, experimental approach to natural phenomena, and it was impossible to disguise the fact. Nevertheless the new principles continued to be taught, and by the 1760s Newtonian physics in one form or another were standard fare in most colleges. Nature was to be evaluated in terms of what could be shown to work and achieve useful results. It could scarcely be expected that some at least of those who learned this lesson should not have thought about judging human affairs by the same standards, for all the precepts of obedience and orthodoxy instilled into them in earlier school years.

That, indeed, was the object of the Enlightenment, whose writers set the intellectual agenda for this generation of unprecedented literacy. It was a movement of criticism, whose advocates believed that nothing was beyond rational improvement, and that nothing was justifiable that could not be shown to be useful to humanity, or to promote human happiness. They called themselves philosophers, by which they meant independent thinkers committed to the practical improvement of the lot of their fellow men. Most of them thought the way to achieve it lay in appealing to the educated general public in works of polemic, simplification, and popularization—the very opposite, as their opponents did not fail to point out, of the traditional, detached notion of a philosopher. The supreme example, it has always been agreed, was Voltaire. Born in the last years of the seventeenth century and Jesuit-educated, by the time he was 30 he had already won a reputation for witty anti-clerical writings, and he was to remain a prolific poet and playwright all his life. But the direction of that life was changed when, in 1728, he travelled to England. Here he saw the benefits of religious pluralism and toleration, discovered the psychology of Locke, the physics of Newton, and the theoretical empiricism of Bacon. He was overwhelmed: and five years later conveyed his discoveries to compatriots largely ignorant of English in his *Lettres philosophiques*. Banned and publicly burned by the parlement, they nevertheless sold sensationally well, making Locke and Newton household names in educated French circles. Voltaire also wrote works of history—indeed, he became historiographer-royal—and in 1746 was elected to the Académie française. But his brushes with authority were as constant as his jibing against the Church, and finally, in 1759, he took up permanent residence at Ferney, close to the safety of the Swiss border. Here he almost literally held court, receiving eminent pilgrims from all over Europe, conducting a voluminous correspondence, and launching ferocious propaganda campaigns against the 'infamy' of religious intolerance and barbarous miscarriages of justice. In 1778, after an absence of 28 years, he made a triumphal return to Paris, where he was lionized for four months in a way few writers can ever have experienced. The strain killed him. The example of his success, however, was an inspiration to innumerable ambitious scribblers throughout the later decades of the century, and later revolutionaries would look back on this tireless critic and campaigner against intolerance and injustice as one of their most distinguished intellectual ancestors.

They were more ambivalent about Montesquieu—a magistrate in the parlement of Bordeaux, a feudal lord living in a moated castle, and an apologist for noble power. Yet arguably his intellectual importance was far greater. Five years older than Voltaire, he died in 1755, leaving a much less voluminous body of writings. But he, too, first made his name in the freer-breathing days of the Regency, after Louis XIV's death, with the satirical, titillating *Lettres persanes* (1721). He, too, was deeply impressed by a visit to England in 1729, a year after his election to the Académie française. But after that he fell largely silent until 1748, when he published (in Geneva) the sprawling, untidy collection of reflections entitled *De l'esprit des lois*. It proved the most fertile and challenging work of political thought of the century. Setting out to analyse rather than prescribe, Montesquieu argued that forms of government are the products of natural and historical circumstances and cannot therefore be varied at will. Such arguments offered comfort to all established authorities. Yet he also roundly condemned despotism, the government of one man according to no law but his own caprice; and implied that even true monarchs, who ruled only according to law, were always under the temptation and danger of becoming despotic. Intermediary powers were needed, buffers between them and their subjects, to restrain that tendency. Montesquieu suggested that in France the nobility and the parlements constituted such buffers, and not surprisingly these bodies were eager to invoke his authority in later struggles against the government. Despotism became a convenient battle cry against any exercise of power, arbitrary or not. And despite preaching that no form of government is appropriate in all circumstances, in attempting to provide an explanation for that of England Montesquieu was led to propound an ideal type most calculated to promote and preserve liberty. Political liberty could only flourish, he argued, under moderate governments; and what kept them moderate was the balance and separation of the three arms of the executive, the legislative, and the judiciary: 'In order that power be not abused, things should be so disposed, that power checks power.'[5] In a number of ways, Montesquieu seriously misunderstood how the English constitution actually worked; but the principles he thought he saw in it were to prove widely inspirational on both sides of the Atlantic, and not least in revolutionary France.

By the time Montesquieu died the Enlightenment as a movement was beginning to come together. Persecution and harassment at the hands of the Church, or those under priestly influence, had given a growing band of speculative writers a sense of common purpose. Nowhere was it better expressed than in the great project launched in 1751 by Diderot (perhaps the first writer to live exclusively by his pen) and the mathematician D'Alembert for a multi-authored French version of a successful English compendium of current knowledge, Chambers's *Cyclopaedia*. The *Encyclopédie* was, however, intended from the start to be more than a simple factual work of reference. Its purpose was to advance knowledge as well as summarize it, and to promote a critical attitude to everything. Its articles would, wrote D'Alembert in a foreword to the third volume (1753), 'often give occasion for philosophic reflexions, for which the public seems today to have more taste than ever; thus it is by the philosophic spirit that we shall attempt to distinguish this dictionary. It is in that way above all that it will win the approval for which we are most anxious.' By then its publication had already been suspended once by order of the royal Council, and as successive volumes continued to appear (soon dwarfing the two of its original model) it came under repeated attack as a repository of scepticism, atheism, and sedition. In 1759, after eight volumes, the whole project nearly foundered when its privilege to publish was withdrawn. It was only saved when Malesherbes, the liberal magistrate who was director of the book trade between 1750 and 1763, granted tacit permission to continue. The remaining volumes, bringing the entire text to seventeen, were published in 1765. No sooner was the *Encyclopédie* complete, however, than new and expanded editions began to appear, and in handier formats than the original heavy and expensive folios. By 1789, therefore, something like 25,000 copies of one version or another of this great compendium had been sold, perhaps half of them in France. And although it undoubtedly did constitute a work of reference of unprecedented quality, what sold it was its notoriety—its contempt for authority and its constant irreverent digs at the Church and religion in general. Yet by the time it became a best-seller such criticisms had become much more open and widespread, making the subterfuges and ambiguities behind which it veiled its early audacities seem timid. Diderot, disgusted with the whole enterprise long before the first edition was completed, turned from religious and philosophical to political and economic radicalism in his later years, although long habit had taught him to cover his tracks. When he died in 1784 he was chiefly known as a sentimental playwright and art critic. Nevertheless, few works were more important than the *Encyclopédie* which he had orchestrated and edited in promoting the values of independent thinking and indifference to authority. 'Encyclopedism' became a synonym for a refusal to accept anything uncritically.

Yet even Encyclopedism had its orthodoxies. Hostile to organized religion and intolerance as manifestations of vestigial barbarism and superstition, it held that philosophers were engaged in a winning battle for progress. The world was changing, nothing was doing more than 'philosophy' to promote that change, and it was change for the better. The material progress of the arts and sciences (of which the *Encyclopédie* proclaimed itself a 'reasoned dictionary') was inexorably improving the lot of mankind. Even if natural disasters like the Lisbon earthquake of 1755 shook their faith in the benevolence of nature, those who considered themselves enlightened continued to believe in the improvement of human institutions. The one significant exception was Rousseau. An autodidact from Geneva, in the 1740s Rousseau made a living in Paris copying music, but moving in aspiring literary circles. He knew Diderot, and collaborated in the early stages of the *Encyclopédie*. He made his name, however, by disputing Enlightenment orthodoxies, and by the late 1750s had fallen out with all the movement's leading figures. In the work which first won him public notice, an entry for the Academy of Dijon's essay-prize competition of 1750, he argued that progress in the arts and sciences had corrupted rather than improved mankind. 'Man is naturally good', he later wrote, recalling the moment when this intuition first struck him,[6] 'and has only become bad because of . . . institutions.' This conviction suffused all his writings, emphasized by a direct, emotional style which electrified the reading public throughout Europe. His novels, *Julie, ou La Nouvelle Héloïse*

(1761) and *Émile, ou l'Education* (1762), were best-sellers, moving their readers to tears at the prospect of innocence and virtue preserved and uncorrupted in the face of the snares and iniquities of established society. These triumphs were, however, the achievement of individuals. Rousseau offered no programme for changing society wholesale to restore mankind in general to its primal innocence and goodness. Even his most enduring work, the *Social Contract* (1762), was not a prescription for political change, but rather a highly theoretical sketch for how political authority might be established legitimately without men losing their natural liberty. It could only work, Rousseau emphasized, in small city-states. Yet coming from the pen of one who had denounced existing society as rotten and depraving, vaunting the sovereignty of a 'general will' which was always for the best and never wrong, and full of striking formulas such as its very first sentence which proclaimed that men were born free but were everywhere in chains, it could not fail to stir thoughts of practical change. Though he was at pains to stress that the general will was not necessarily the will of the majority, the term passed quickly into normal usage as meaning just that. And when the established form of government and society collapsed, barely a decade after Rousseau's death in 1778, he was remembered by those welcoming the new times as a prophet who had seen the future, and even bequeathed it a pattern-book for organizing a regenerated nation along juster and more virtuous lines.

   Both *Émile* and the *Social Contract* were condemned when they appeared, and Rousseau fled the country, only returning permanently after eight years of wanderings. But it was not the political content of either work that the parlement of Paris, decreeing his arrest, found offensive. It was the affront to religion in his remarks on civil religion in the *Social Contract*, and the moving 'Profession of faith of the Savoyard curate' in *Émile*. The former declared Christianity a perpetual source of civil disorders, and denounced priests; the latter proclaimed that the true gospel was belief in a benevolent god of nature rather than any particular body of Christian doctrine. Rousseau's temperament was emotional and religious, but in the eyes of the devout he appeared no less blasphemous than the mocking, irreverent Voltaire. To stem the rising tide of irreligion increasingly came to appear as the main task confronting the Church. Refutations of philosophic impieties poured from the presses, and pious laymen in positions of authority used every available means to suppress dissent. But the Church itself was not united, and its divisions opened it to yet further ridicule. Bitter quarrels over the bull *Unigenitus*, promulgated in 1713 against Jansenism, lasted half a century, and only died down in the late 1760s. Jansenists rejected many of the doctrines and emphases imposed on the Church after the sixteenth-century Council of Trent. The puritans of the Catholic Church, they opposed lax theology, excessive papal and episcopal power, and above all the influence of the Jesuits in Church and State. It was Jansenists in the parlement of Paris who engineered the Jesuits' downfall, although philosophers appalled by the prospect of a Jansenist-dominated Church hurriedly claimed it as a victory for Enlightenment. But the course of the previous quarrel, with its persecution of priestly dissidents, refusal of sacraments to dying opponents of *Unigenitus*, and occasional spectacular displays of hysteria and holy-rolling (the so-called 'convulsionaries' of Saint-Médard), brought no credit or dignity to any of those involved. So it was not only the scoffing of infidels which spread the conviction that the religious life of France needed comprehensive reform. Besides, sensibilities were changing even among the orthodox. Less ostentatious forms of piety were finding greater favour. When they made wills, testators endowed fewer memorial masses, and expressed their dying beliefs in less elaborate terms. Alive, they lit fewer votive candles, and showed less interest in religious confraternities or the austerities of the monastic life. Horace Walpole, prizing in France the romantic devotional trappings that England had lost at the Reformation, was disappointed at the change of atmosphere he found in the convents of Paris in 1771:

It is very singular that I have not half the satisfaction in going into churches and convents that I used to have. The consciousness that the vision is dispelled, the want of fervour so obvious in the religious, the solitude that one knows proceeds from contempt, not from contemplation, make these places appear like abandoned theatres destined to destruction. The monks trot about as if they had not long to stay there; and what used to be holy gloom is now but dirt and darkness.[7]

By then, smaller monasteries were being suppressed or merged wholesale. By then, too, the quarrels over *Unigenitus* had lost their urgency with the defeat of the Jesuits. And, beset by unbelievers, Catholics were even showing themselves more tolerant towards French Protestants. Since the revocation of the Edict of Nantes in 1685, Protestants had enjoyed no legal existence. Their baptisms, marriages, and burials enjoyed no status at law, and their pastors committed a capital offence in conducting services. In the course of the 1760s, however, active persecution of pastors ceased, and the open-air services traditional among the Protestants of Languedoc were no longer molested. Parish priests might still fulminate against heresy, but the barbarity of intolerance was the preferred theme of many of their bishops; and while the civil authorities still sent out troops to break up Protestant services, they always sent them deliberately in the wrong direction. The horrors of intolerance seemed vividly demonstrated when, in 1762, the Toulouse Protestant Jean Calas was put to death by the parlement of Languedoc for allegedly murdering his son to prevent him embracing Catholicism. Voltaire, appalled by recent news of what proved to be the last execution of a pastor in the same area, concluded that this was a case of judicial murder inspired by superstitious bigotry. He launched a furious journalistic campaign to rehabilitate Calas, which in 1765 achieved success before the king's Council. In 1775, after a longer struggle, he secured rehabilitation of the Sirven family, also condemned in Languedoc for murdering an apostate daughter, although they had escaped Calas's fate by fleeing to Switzerland. Such cases stirred the conscience of educated laymen; and by the 1780s few could be found, openly at least, to uphold the penal laws against Protestants. In Necker, Louis XVI even had a Protestant minister between 1777 and 1781. The final abrogation of their disabilities, already in practical abeyance, seemed only a matter of time.

It was not only the bigotry of the Toulouse judges that outraged Voltaire. It was also the cruelty and injustice of the laws which they applied. Calas was broken on the wheel, a grisly process in which the condemned person's limbs were smashed with iron bars and the mutilated corpse raised up for public display on a cartwheel. Even more atrocious punishments were possible. Damiens, a dim-witted jobbing servant who stabbed Louis XV with a penknife in 1757, was first tortured to obtain the names of accomplices, then pinched with red-hot irons, after which four horses tried (in vain) to pull him apart. Regicide was of course a particularly heinous crime, with dreadful echoes in French history, and Damiens's execution was based on carefully researched precedents. Thousands thronged the place de Grève, outside the Paris Hôtel de Ville, to watch these once-in-a-lifetime refinements on the everyday spectacle of public execution. Another case Voltaire took up was that of La Barre, who in 1766, convicted of various petty adolescent acts of blasphemy and sacrilege, was tortured and burned at the stake. A copy of Voltaire's own *Philosophical Dictionary* was thrown into the flames after him. Laws which condoned such things, the philosopher argued, were monstrous, irrational, and absurd, and he welcomed the French translation in 1765 of Beccaria's plea for a more measured, humane, and torture-free system of criminal justice, *Of Crimes and Punishments* (1764). By the early 1770s the government was announcing plans for a general reform and codification of the laws, and Voltaire led the applause for this promise. Nothing, however, emerged during his lifetime, or for a decade afterwards, apart from the abolition in 1780 of torture to obtain confessions. But in the mid-1780s there surfaced a whole series of miscarriages of justice, which, exploited by an able younger generation of publicists, renewed public concern at the law's cruelties, inconsistencies, and failure to safeguard innocence.

Their inspiration was Voltaire's campaign over Calas. In order to restore the dead martyr's name, he had successfully mobilized public opinion. The very idea of public opinion was new in France when he did so. It only appeared in the course of the 1750s. 'Among the singularities which mark out the age we live in from all others', wrote Rousseau in 1776,[8] 'is the methodical and sustained spirit which has guided public opinions over the last twenty years. Until now these opinions wandered aimless and unregulated at the whim of men's passions, and the endless interplay of these passions made the public float from one to another without any constant direction.' Philosophers sought to provide such direction, and after his success over Calas, Voltaire believed it was possible. 'Opinion governs the world,' he wrote,[9] 'and in the end philosophers govern men's opinions.' But in fact they were not the first in the field. Both sides in the religious quarrels of mid-century had sought to whip up public support, the Jansenists with their elusive, secretly published *Nouvelles ecclésiastiques*, the Jesuits with their *Journal de Trévoux*, not to mention furious pamphleteering by each. And even further back, the parlements during the Regency had begun to print and publicly distribute their remonstrances, a deliberate tactic to involve educated readers in their political disagreements with the government. These techniques became standard in the 1750s as religious and financial disputes between the Crown and the sovereign courts reached a new intensity. The years between 1758 and 1764 saw a last attempt by the traditional organs of censorship to prevent open discussion of matters of state, whether religious, administrative, or financial. Attempts to suppress the *Encyclopédie*, the works of Rousseau, and other speculative writings were part of this pattern. So was a royal declaration of 1764 prohibiting public sale of any works relating to the finances or administration of the State. But the line could not be held; and indeed government ministers themselves came increasingly to feel that it was perhaps better for the public to be well informed than uninformed. They even turned to courting opinion for themselves. Preambles to royal edicts grew longer and longer. Unwelcome remonstrances from the parlements were not only quashed, they were refuted. When Maupeou remodelled the parlements, he hired a team of writers to praise and defend what he was doing. But, mused an anxious and well-placed observer, 'each step makes matters worse. Somebody writes, another replies . . . everybody will want to analyse the constitution of the state; tempers will be lost. Issues are being raised which nobody would have dared think of . . . the knowledge the peoples are acquiring must, a little sooner or a little later, bring about revolutions.'[10]

Nothing did more to fuel this surge of public discussion than the Seven Years War. Undertaken with no clear aims, in alliance with Austria, a traditional enemy of centuries' standing, it led to humiliating defeats on land and sea at what seemed like enormous economic cost. Taxes and state borrowing had soared, but there was nothing to show for such efforts. In these circumstances an inquest began which spared no aspect of French society or institutions, and was encouraged at a certain level by the government itself. In 1763, unprecedentedly, it even asked the parlements to make proposals for economic and fiscal reform—which produced nothing very constructive, unwisely flattered their pretensions, and left them aggrieved when, ignoring their suggestions, ministers turned in preference to the untried theories of a group calling themselves by the new and unfamiliar name of 'Economists'.

Their founder was a royal doctor, Quesnay, who in a number of articles in the *Encyclopédie* in 1756, and later in his *Tableau économique* (1758), argued (in curious parallel to Rousseau) that there existed a natural, benevolent economic order which had been distorted by ill-judged and artificial human intervention. Economic wealth could only be unlocked by removing all unnatural burdens, parrticularly on agriculture, which was the only true productive activity. These ideas were developed by a number of other authors throughout the 1760s, including Mirabeau, Le Mercier de la Rivière, and Dupont de Nemours, whose book *Physiocracy* (1768) gave the Economists an alternative name. Paradoxically, the economic freedom preached by the Physiocrats implied a powerful, interventionist role for governments, for only they had the strength to sweep away artificial impediments to the natural economic order. Le Mercier even advocated a sort of despotism, which he called legal because its sole purpose would be to bring in the greatest of all laws, that of nature itself. Ministers had no wish to be thought despotic, but they were attracted to Physiocracy because it promised wealth. A natural, free market, with all artificial constraints removed, would make producers rich. They could then pay more taxes. As Quesnay had put it in the *Encyclopédie*: poor peasant, poor kingdom.

The constraints on free production were of course innumerable— customary and collective methods, feudal dues, indirect taxes, internal tolls and customs barriers, productive monopolies like guilds, local and sectional privileges. No wonder it would take a despot to remove them all. But one seemed easier to deal with than the others, since it had always been closely co-ordinated by the central government. The whole elaborate apparatus of controls on the grain trade, fixing prices and limiting export and even inter-provincial commerce, seemed ripe for rationalization. The trade had always been so carefully controlled, of course, because guaranteed supplies of bread were deemed fundamental in ensuring public order. But Physiocrats argued that freedom would create greater abundance, thereby banishing the fears immemorially associated with famine. Accordingly, in May 1763, a free internal market in grain was proclaimed, and just over a year later free export was also allowed when prices were below a certain level. A generation's good harvests underlay the optimism behind this policy, but in the late 1760s they came to an end. When crops failed no amount of administrative tinkering could guarantee abundance, and the new freedom was blamed for aggravating if not causing the shortages of these years. A furious public debate broke out, in which partisans of the old controls accused the reformers of starving the king's subjects and abandoning, at the behest of visionary theorists, the Crown's age-old commitment to keeping them alive. To arguments that in the long run the high prices resulting from lack of controls would stimulate production and so eventually bring prices down, magistrates facing bread riots replied by urging practical realism. 'The people are not wrong to complain, they are in no state to pay for their bread,' wrote the first president of the parlement of Bordeaux to the province's governor in 1773, after tumults which he thought had come within inches of putting the city to sack.[11] '. . . their normal remark is to say we prefer to die on a gibbet rather than die of hunger, it's shorter . . . Why insist on keeping up the price of bread? As for me, I confess, it seems to me that in a country where taxes are carried to excess, the king is bound to assure his subjects the only thing they have left: their lives.' Faced with such problems, ministers wavered, but attempts to reimpose controls through preferential contracting in the early 1770s scarcely restored confidence. They were now accused of deliberately plotting to starve the people by putting the trade in the hands of a profiteering private monopoly.

Around 1770, in fact, confidence in the way France was governed in general rapidly began to run out. Although some of the losses of the Seven Years War were made up with the annexation of Lorraine (1766) and Corsica (1768), the Austrian alliance, which survived the war, remained deeply unpopular. When it was renewed in 1770 with the marriage of Louis XV's grandson and heir to the Archduchess Marie Antoinette, celebrations in Paris went wrong, and 136 people were killed when a crowd stampeded. It seemed like an omen; and the feasting which continued at Versailles left bitter memories in the capital. By now the insatiable sexual appetites of Louis XV were common knowledge, and although French subjects did not begrudge their kings manly pleasures (the equally insatiable Henry IV remained the popular ideal of a good king) the latest official mistress, Mme Du Barry, was little more than a prostitute from the streets of Paris. Her position made it impossible for her not to be drawn into politics, but her role was much criticized, for she was associated with the rise of Maupeou and Terray, and the fall of the popular Duke de Choiseul. Terray, in addition to arousing popular suspicions of promoting a famine pact, declared a partial bankruptcy which outraged all holders of government stocks. His later attempts to revise tax-assessments and improve the efficiency of their collection soon won him the reputation of an extortioner. Maupeou's attacks on the parlements, meanwhile, raised a nation-wide outcry. Although Voltaire, who always believed a strong and benevolent monarch was the best means of achieving reforms, applauded the striking down of a magistracy whom he saw as the obscurantist murderers of Calas and La Barre, most other philosophers joined the general protest. 'We are on the verge of a crisis', wrote Diderot as Maupeou struck,[12] 'which will end in slavery or in freedom; if it is slavery, it will be a slavery similar to that existing in Morocco or at Constantinople. If all the parlements are dissolved . . . farewell any . . . corrective principle preventing the monarch from degenerating into despotism.' He, like everybody else, had absorbed the lessons of Montesquieu. A monarchy untempered by intermediary powers was a despotism, the worst of all governments, whose subjects enjoyed no rights, and no security. The parlements, whatever their flaws, had seemed to offer Frenchmen some protection against authority. It was now shown to be an illusion. In the protests which greeted Maupeou's action, whether in printed remonstrances from the stricken courts or individual pamphlets, a new theme was heard: the Estates-General. The ancient national representative body had not met since 1614, and nobody had more than the haziest notion of its composition or powers; but few doubted that it would have more authority than the parlements. As Maupeou's reforms established themselves, and the initial clamour against him died down, so did the calls for the Estates-General. But the idea was launched, and it kept recurring in political discussion over the ensuing decade and a half.

After these traumas the accession of Louis XVI was widely regarded as an opportunity for a new start. As the coffin of Louis XV was hustled away under cover of darkness, boundless hopes and expectations were invested in the unsullied young monarch. But his unsullied qualities rapidly became a public joke. Married since 1770, he seemed incapable of siring an heir, if not positively disinclined even to try. His first child, a daughter, only arrived in 1778, after medical attention. Meanwhile pamphleteering ribaldry ran riot, much of it directed against the presumed frustrations of his queen. Her extravagance, frivolity, and indiscreet political meddling in turn made her an easy target, as her unpredictable brother the Emperor Joseph II blundered through international affairs threatening to drag France at any moment into war on Austrian coat-tails. When in 1785 rumours arose that she wished to buy a fabulously expensive diamond necklace, nobody was surprised. A credulous courtier prelate, the Cardinal de Rohan, sought to ingratiate himself with her by securing it, but found himself merely the victim of an elaborate swindle. The queen was not involved, but Rohan had to vindicate himself before the parlement of Paris in 1786 in a show trial which inevitably cast implicit aspersions on her conduct. She took his acquittal as a personal insult, even though the perpetrators of the fraud were punished. The huge crowds which fêted the cardinal after his release were plainly delighted at her humiliation, and went on to condemn the petulance of the royal reaction which sent the acquitted Rohan immediately into provincial exile. With two sons now to his credit (born in 1781 and 1785), the king himself stood perhaps higher in public esteem than a decade earlier. But the scandal brought the whole world of the Court into a disrepute every bit as deep as that of Louis XV's final years—especially when, in 1787, its cost to the taxpayers was revealed for the first time.

Nor did the restoration of the parlements bring back the political confidence shattered by Maupeou. They returned to their various seats amid huge displays of popularity, but several soon squandered their credit in vicious quarrels between 'returner' magistrates who had been exiled under Maupeou and 'remainers' who had co-operated with him. That of Paris, after a show of resistance to the reforms of the Physiocrat minister Turgot in 1775 and 1776, took no further stands against authority. 'No doubt,' remarked a disgusted provincial judge in 1783,[13] 'there was a time when the magistrates of that august tribunal, animated by the public weal ... gave forceful opposition to the ruinous enterprises of ministers ... Today, enervated by the pleasures of a voluptuous life, led by ambition, they yield with blind deference to the monarch's wishes.' The search therefore continued for institutions that would give France more effective protection against despotism—whether ministerial, at the centre, or local, in the form of the intendants who wielded royal authority in the provinces. The intendants had never been mere passive agents of their master. Their duties were so widely defined that the scope for independent initiative had always been wide. But during the later eighteenth century they seemed to be interfering in more and more aspects of provincial life, driven by a mission to improve the lot of those whom (as they put it) they administered, whether the latter liked it or not. Some were avowed disciples of the

Physiocrats, like Turgot himself before he became a minister. All were believers in rationalizing wherever they could, and putting the latest knowledge to practical public use. But, whether in forcing the alignment of streets, promoting inoculation against smallpox, moving insanitary graveyards from town centres, refusing to control bread prices, preventing the sale of diseased cattle, or devising schemes for forcing the poor to work, they outraged popular prejudices and intensified their basic unpopularity as agents of taxation. Their activity also brought them into conflict with other authorities like parlements or provincial estates, whose members did not necessarily disagree with their enlightened ends, but challenged their authority to pursue them. An intendant, declared the parlement of Besançon in September 1787,[14] 'is subject to no inspection; . . . his arbitrary activities, arbitrarily directed and executed, are regulated by no principle other than the most blind Despotism . . . His absolute power, like that of his underlings, is completely exempt from all accountability . . . and may with impunity effect the most shocking vexations.'

The answer to such problems was increasingly seen as some form of provincial representative bodies. Some provinces had them already, of course, in the form of estates. *Pays d'états* had intendants like other regions, but at least they could bargain with them, and share some of their powers. In Brittany, the mid-1780s were marked by repeated clashes between the two. Despite the obvious challenge to their own authority, more thoughtful magistrates in the parlements had begun to advocate the establishment of estates, or restoration of long-defunct ones, in their respective provinces from the late 1750s. In the 1770s a number of sovereign courts, like the Paris Court of Aids and the parlements of Grenoble and Bordeaux, took up the call, at least intermittently. Assemblies of leading landowners were also a favourite proposal among the Physiocrats, although they had increasing doubts about estates as a model: they were too heterogeneous and tradition-bound. Turgot and his adviser while in office Dupont de Nemours dreamed of a uniform hierarchy of assemblies representing landowners from village (or 'municipality') level up to that of provinces. The only practical step to be taken before 1787, however, was the introduction of 'provincial administrations' by Necker in 1778. These bodies of landowners, nominated in the first instance and comprising (like the estates of Languedoc) a quarter nobles, a quarter clergy, and one-half members of the third estate, sat not as representatives of ancient provinces but as adjuncts to intendants in their generalities. Berry and upper Guyenne received them first, and a third one was projected for the area around Boulogne when Necker lost power in 1781. It never came to fruition; but the other two, and their intermediary commissions when they were not sitting, functioned smoothly right down to the Revolution, a working if much debated model for a more representative way of administering the kingdom.

Everything Necker did was much debated. In fact his whole career and outlook was a standing challenge to established ways of doing things. A Swiss Protestant banker, largely self-made, he became well known in Paris intellectual society in the 1760s and early 1770s thanks to his wife's much-frequented salon. Here, while he sat silent and inscrutable, she carefully cultivated his reputation for financial wizardry and general wisdom. Then in the spring of 1775, at the height of the 'Flour War', he published a book advocating a controlled grain trade, much to the fury of Turgot and his free-trading supporters. It won him enormous popularity—the beginning of a 'Neckeromania' that lasted, with ups and downs, until 1790—and carried him, though a foreigner and member of a proscribed faith, to the directorship of the treasury. Failure to find a more orthodox candidate showed how far established circles had already lost faith in their own capacities. In addition to his spectacular management of the finances,* Necker began to reorganize central accounting procedures and the structure of taxation, commissioned a nationwide survey of venality of offices in the hope of bringing about its abolition, and set up provincial assemblies in part at least to offset the influence of the parlements. Above all he made constant efforts to keep public opinion on his side, recognizing more clearly than anybody so far the political importance of this new force that had emerged since mid-century. He discovered its limits too: when in 1781 he attempted to use his popularity to win a greater say in high policy-making, he was rebuffed. Nor was Louis XVI intimidated when, in another break with precedent, he resigned in protest. But that only led him further down the path of innovation. Instead of returning to banking, he spent the next few years writing a defence of his record, *De l'Administration des Finances*, which laid bare in great detail how central government worked. Appearing in three volumes in 1785, it was an international best-seller, setting out its author's claims to be regarded as the natural alternative minister, whom the king must sooner or later recall to power if his government were to have any hope of retaining public confidence.

But that was only the Neckerite view. Ministers still in power felt that they had every right to public confidence. The most important policy the king had pursued, after all, had been gloriously successful. The humiliations of the Seven Years War were finally avenged in 1783 when Great Britain was forced to recognize the independence of her North American

* See below, pp. 66–8.

colonies. French help, on both land and sea, had played a crucial part in this achievement. Scarcely less impressive had been the way peace was maintained on the European continent while the overseas struggle went on. No wonder Vergennes, the architect of these achievements and most important of the king's ministers after Maurepas died, viewed Necker's antics with some contempt. But apart from its cost, involvement in America raised a whole range of further discontents in France.

Conservatives warned from the start that a king was unwise to give support to republican rebels against a fellow monarch; but public interest in America had been stirred long before the colonists declared their independence by the quarrels that preceded the break. Readers were prepared for it, too, by the *Histoire philosophique des deux Indes* appearing in 1772 under the name of the Abbé Raynal (though in fact a co-operative work whose contributors included Diderot). A sensational attack on European overseas expansion, it predicted the independence of colonial settlements, and, as its prophecies came true, went through over fifty editions before the end of the century. From the start of their quarrel with British authority the Americans used the language of liberty and representation, striking immediate echoes in a France obsessed with despotism. When John Adams arrived in Bordeaux in 1778, the first president of the local parlement welcomed him with the declaration that:[15] 'He could not avoid sympathising with every sincere friend of Liberty in the world . . . He had reason he said to feel for the Sufferers in the Cause of Liberty, because he had suffered many Years in that cause himself. He had been banished . . . in the time of Louis the fifteenth, for . . . Remonstrances against the arbitrary Conduct and pernicious Edicts of the Court.' Few Frenchmen knew much about America first hand, until the return of the 8,000 soldiers who served there, after the peace of 1783. Raynal, who published a further book on the revolt in 1780, had never made the voyage, and nor had the authors of many of the accounts of life in the new world which attempted to satisfy public enthusiasm. But translations soon appeared of the key documents in the struggle—pamphlets like Paine's *Common Sense*, the Declaration of Independence, and the constitutions of several of the new states. And Parisian high society was conquered between 1777 and 1783 by the brilliant propaganda of Franklin, the new republic's ambassador. Already famous as the inventor of the lightning conductor, his homespun philosophizing and simple style charmed the world of the Court and the intellectual salons alike. He seemed a living advertisement for the virtues of Rousseauistic simplicity, the product of a sylvan paradise far from the jaded artificiality of Europe. And although he flourished amid metropolitan glitter, and declared publicly that he saw no prospect of changing it, he sponsored the first open attack on the principle of nobility. The renegade Count de Mirabeau's *Considerations on the Order of Cincinnatus* (1784) condemned a hereditary order of chivalry which officers in the War of Independence had set up to commemorate their involvement. It was Franklin who brought the issue to Mirabeau's attention as returned French officers like the vainglorious Lafayette appeared in Paris flaunting the new society's insignia. Thus issues raised in America reflected critically on French society as well as French politics, and interest in the new republic and the principles it stood for continued unabated after the peace. With the return of the veterans, it even grew better informed.

But the most important thing about America did not depend on accurate information. It was the simple fact that new starts had been shown to be possible. Existing political authority could be thrown off, and institutions rebuilt from their foundations on more rational, freer lines. The improvement, the regeneration, of human laws and institutions was no longer a mere matter of Utopian dreaming. It was happening before men's eyes in America. As Jacques-Pierre Brissot, a jobbing journalist quick to cash in on every passing fashion, wrote when he read the most popular account of America, Crevecoeur's *Letters of an American Farmer*, in 1784,[16]

These letters will inspire or reawaken perhaps in blasé souls of Europeans the taste for virtue and the simple life . . . Energetic souls will find in them something more. They will see here a country, a government, where the desires of their hearts have been realised, a land which speaks to them in their own language. The happiness for which they have sighed finally does in truth exist.

America appealed, in fact, to what Jean-Joseph Mounier, one of the leading revolutionaries of 1789, would later remember as 'a general restlessness and desire for change'.[17] It manifested itself in the vogue for wonders of all sorts, whether Franklin's lightning rod, or the first manned flights in the hot-air balloons seen rising over so many cities in 1783 and 1784, or a craze for Mesmerism and miraculous cures effected by tapping the supposedly hidden natural forces of 'animal magnetism'. Established religion might be losing its mystic appeal, but science was bringing other miracles to light. Seekers after this newer, truer, wisdom believed themselves most likely to find it in the 'royal art' of freemasonry. Between 800 and 900 masonic lodges were founded in France between 1732 and 1793, two-thirds of them after 1760. Between 1773 and 1779 well over 20,000 members were recruited. Few towns of any consequence were without one or more lodges by the 1780s and, despite several papal condemnations of a deistic cult that had originated in Protestant England, the élite of society flocked to join. Voltaire was drafted in on his last visit to Paris, and it was before the assembled brethren of the Nine Sisters Lodge that he exchanged symbolic embraces with Franklin. Masonry was riddled with hierarchy. Women were excluded, men tended to join lodges where they would find their social peers, and there were innumerable grades of perfection through which adepts could pass. But within the lodges masons spoke of themselves as brothers and equals, and they elected their officers according to their talents, not their rank. Like the members of the literary societies mushrooming everywhere over the same period, most masons were well-educated commoners—often in fact the same people—and in masonry their cultural equality was fully recognized. And whereas most masonic assemblies consisted of rituals, followed by much eating and drinking, some brothers dreamed of putting the organization to more practical use. Philanthropic collections were organized; and the Nine Sisters Lodge threw itself into the vindication of wronged innocence in the judicial crusades of the mid-1780s. Mostly they steered clear of politics; but the sensational exposure in 1787 of a plot by self-styled *Illuminati* to use masonic organization to subvert the government of Bavaria threw general suspicion on to a movement much of whose appeal lay in its secrecy. Belief in plots and conspiracies was yet another sign of the credulity of the times. The same cast of mind also tended to seek simple, universal formulae to resolve any problem, no matter how complex. Its limitations would be tragically exposed in the storm that was about to break.

# 3

# Crisis and Collapse
# 1776–1788

EVER since the disasters of the Seven Years War Frenchmen had longed to see British arrogance humbled, and the power of 'the modern Carthage' broken. By the time Louis XVI ascended the throne that process seemed well under way, as the quarrel between Great Britain and her thirteen North American colonies deepened. French observers looked on with growing interest, and by the spring of 1776 Vergennes, the Foreign Secretary, was convinced that 'Providence had marked out this moment for the humiliation of England'.[1] He persuaded the king that it would be to France's advantage to intervene. In April secret supplies began to be sent to the Americans, and the first steps were taken to mobilize French naval strength. Thus began a deterioration in French relations with the British which culminated in February 1778 in a treaty of alliance between France and the United States, followed by five years of all-out warfare. When it ended, the British empire did indeed appear to have been shattered, France was revenged, and her international prestige stood gloriously restored. But the effort had brought the State to the brink of financial exhaustion.

It had not been unforeseeable. Aware of the burden of debt bequeathed by previous wars, Turgot had warned the king on assuming office as Comptroller-General in 1774 that economies were essential to the restoration of financial health. Otherwise 'the first gunshot will drive the State to bankruptcy'.[2] A month before his fall from power in May 1776 Turgot denounced Vergennes's proposal to intervene in America on the grounds that the cost would permanently destroy all hope of financial reform without necessarily helping to weaken Great Britain at all. On both counts time proved him right. In 1776, however, Turgot's fellow ministers had lost faith in both his policies and his judgement; and in any case within six months a successor had been found who seemed confident of squaring the circle. In October 1776 Necker was appointed Director of the Treasury.

Necker was not plucked from obscurity. He had carefully established himself as a man of influence and ability who offered alternatives to Turgot's austere policies, and his appointment aroused high expectations. He was determined not to increase taxes. He believed that ordinary income and expenditure could be brought into balance by economies and reorganization of budgetary structures to eliminate profiteering by financiers. Order in the finances would engender confidence; and confidence would enable the king to borrow money to meet extraordinary expenditure. The most extraordinary of all expenditure was that incurred by war.

Necker financed French involvement in the American war entirely by loans. No new taxation was imposed while he was in power. Interest incurred on the loans was charged to ordinary expenditure, and Necker claimed to have found the extra money for this from economies and 'ameliorations'. Under this system he raised 520 million *livres* in loans between 1777 and his resignation in May 1781. Most of them were fully subscribed with remarkable speed, and the parlement of Paris only raised difficulties over registering the first. Generous terms and high interest rates accounted for some of this success, but Necker believed its true foundation was public confidence in his management. In February 1781, beset by a whispering campaign organized by ministerial rivals and discontented financiers, he sought to sustain that confidence with an unprecedented gesture. With the consent of the king he published the first ever public balance sheet of the French monarchy's finances, the *Compte rendu au roi*. It showed ordinary revenues to be exceeding expenditure by over 10 million *livres*, after three years of war and no increases in taxation. The public, which bought thousands of copies, was convinced. Nobody asked about extraordinary accounts, where the real cost of the war was recorded. For the next seven years people would say, whenever ministers complained of financial difficulties, that affairs had been under control in Necker's time. This conviction would carry him back to power in 1788. But in 1781 the *Compte rendu* prepared his downfall. Buoyed up by the public adulation it brought him, he sought to force the king to admit him to the innermost council, from which he was excluded by his religion. The king, advised by Maurepas and Vergennes, refused, and Necker resigned.

The *Compte rendu* had so identified Necker's personal credit with that of the State that the blow to confidence was substantial. His successor Joly de Fleury felt obliged at last to increase taxation, with predictable objections from several of the parlements. These were overridden without much difficulty, however, and the new revenues enabled the Crown to offer interest on further loans. Between May 1781 and the end of 1782, accordingly, almost 252 millions more were raised. All told the American war cost France something over 1,066 million *livres*; and the expense did not end with the conclusion of peace in 1783. The third *vingtième* tax, introduced in July 1782, was to run until three years after the war ended; and Calonne, who became Comptroller-General in November 1783, found himself obliged to go on borrowing.

Calonne was intendant of Flanders, his native province, returning there in 1778 after a thirteen-year absence. On his rise through the administrative hierarchy he had acquired the reputation of a slippery time-server with naked ambitions. But his connections at Court were excellent, and he was trusted by Vergennes, now the dominant minister of state. Calonne's appointment was popular at Versailles, and he certainly made no efforts to impose economies on the Court, as Turgot and Necker had. Indeed, he believed that lavish spending on 'useful splendour' was good for credit. It appeared to work: between 1783 and 1787 Calonne was able to borrow over 653 millions. But by 1785 doubts were surfacing about how long this could go on. In that year Necker published his *Administration des Finances*, at once a vindication of his own record and an implicit condemnation of Calonne's. The parlement of Paris, which had not demurred at registering new loans since 1777, objected so vehemently to that of December 1785 that its members had to be called in a body to Versailles and told explicitly by the king that he had the fullest confidence in his Comptroller-General. Even so the loan, despite generous terms, was subscribed only sluggishly, and throughout the spring of 1786 there were persistent rumours in Paris that Calonne was about to be dismissed. The queen and her favourites were certainly throwing all their influence behind his ministerial rivals; but with Vergennes on his side he was safe. 'There appears at present no disposition whatever to economy in the finances of this kingdom', noted the sharp-eyed British chargé d'affaires with some disgust on 24 August 1786[3]

. . . Purchases of great value continue to be made and works of immense expense to be carried on in different Royal establishments. M. de Calonne by his unbounded liberality and complaisance to people of high rank and distinction, supports himself still in his most important situation, but the easing the burdens of the people and the interest of the Nation seem to be as perfectly disregarded as they ever were by the most corrupt of his predecessors.

He did not know that four days beforehand Calonne had proposed to Louis XVI the most radical and comprehensive plan of reform in the monarchy's history.

Calonne claimed that he had been working on his *Plan for the*

*Improvement of the Finances* for two years before he presented it to the king. It certainly took Louis XVI several months to understand it and authorize its implementation. At the outset Calonne had to convince the monarch that it was necessary at all. In 1786, the Comptroller-General explained, there would be a deficit of 112 millions, almost a quarter of expected income. Yet at the end of the year the third *vingtième* would expire, and for the next ten there would be a heavy annual burden of debt redemption on short-term loans raised since the beginning of the American war. Almost half the annual revenue was absorbed by debt-service. Well over half the next year's revenue had been spent in advance in short-term loans (*anticipations*) raised from financiers on the security of expected tax-yields—a normal enough practice, but not on this colossal scale.

It is impossible [Calonne concluded] to tax further, ruinous to be always borrowing, and not enough to confine ourselves to economical reforms . . . with matters as they are, ordinary ways being unable to lead us to our goal, the only effective remedy, the only course left to take, the only means of managing finally to put the finances truly in order, must consist in revivifying the entire state by recasting all that is vicious in its constitution.[4]

That would involve a three-part programme. First came a series of sweeping fiscal and administrative reforms designed to 'establish a more uniform order'. They centred around the proposal to abolish the existing three *vingtièmes* and their various surcharges, along with all the exemptions, compoundings, and special provisions enjoyed by privileged groups and corporations. This complex structure would be replaced by a 'territorial subvention', a permanent direct tax levied in kind on all landowners, with no exemptions, at the moment of harvest. The new tax would be assessed and administered by the taxpayers themselves in provincial representative assemblies working in co-operation with the intendants. Calonne estimated that this new tax would bring in 35 millions more than the *vingtièmes*; and it would be augmented yet further by a whole range of other innovations such as an extended stamp tax and better administration of the royal domain.

Even more impressive yields could be expected if the taxpayers could be made more prosperous; and Calonne planned to achieve this by the second part of his programme, aimed at economic stimulation. Advised by Dupont de Nemours, the former associate of Turgot, Calonne took up several of the Physiocratic policies that had lapsed when the latter fell in 1776. He proposed to abandon controls on the grain trade, abolish internal customs barriers, and commute the *corvée* into a tax where this had not already happened. Vergennes, meanwhile, in September 1786, concluded a free-trade treaty with Great Britain which was expected to benefit French agriculture. But neither these measures nor the fiscal reforms could be expected to show instant results. Time would have to be bought, and the immediate crisis averted, by further borrowing. The third part of Calonne's plan was designed to create the confidence to sustain new loans. Before sending his measures to the parlements for registration, Calonne proposed to have them endorsed by a show of national consensus, which would disarm any criticism in advance and persuade lenders that the country was behind the minister in his determination to restore financial health. The obvious forum for seeking such support, much discussed since the political crisis of 1771, was the Estates-General. Calonne considered the idea, only to reject such an unwieldy body as too unpredictable. Remonstrances from the parlements were bad enough: obstruction from people who saw themselves as the nation's elected representatives might be far worse. Besides, precedents also existed for another kind of representative body, an Assembly of Notables, whose members were all royal nominees and could therefore be handpicked. They would of course be 'People of weight, worthy of the public's confidence and such that their approbation would powerfully influence general opinion'.[5] But the honour of being chosen alone ought to make them docile. With a public show of backing from the leading men of the kingdom for his plans, Calonne did not doubt that the loans to make them possible would be forthcoming.

Louis XVI finally authorized this plan on 29 December 1786. An Assembly of Notables was ordered to convene at Versailles on 29 January 1787 to consider the king's views on 'the relief of his peoples, the ordering of his finances and the reform of various abuses'. No other details were given and speculation ran riot. In the event the Assembly did not convene until 22 February as first Calonne and then Vergennes fell ill. Vergennes, the only minister who supported Calonne whole-heartedly, died on 13 February. During all these delays the 144 chosen nominees had plenty of time to get to know each other, and the 64 provincials among them were able to sense the mood of the capital. Less than ten of the Notables were non-nobles; 18 were clerics, 7 were princes of the blood, each assigned to preside over a working party (*bureau*). Most of the 36 dukes, peers, and other great lords were generals, provincial governors, and others with experience of authority; but they included ambitious celebrities like Lafayette, the self-proclaimed hero of the American war. There were also 12 senior administrators, 38 sovereign court magistrates, 12 representatives of the *pays d'états*, and 25 civic dignitaries. And as soon as they met, and heard what the Comptroller-General proposed, it became apparent that the Notables would not be the meek and ductile collaborators Calonne had expected. Inexperienced as he was in managing political assemblies, he totally miscalculated the forces he had let loose, and how to handle them.

In a controversial political career Calonne had made many enemies, and they were well represented in the Assembly. Members of the parlements had been hostile to him ever since the 1760s, when he had been closely involved in authoritarian moves against them. The first president of the parlement of Paris, a Notable like most of his provincial counterparts, was a personal enemy. Leading prelates had been alienated by attempts since 1783 to bully the clergy into increasing its contributions to the royal finances; yet in choosing the clerical contingent Calonne was content to act on the advice of Loménie de Brienne, archbishop of Toulouse, skilled from years of manipulating clerical assemblies and the estates of Languedoc in the politics of intrigue, and known to harbour his own ministerial ambitions. Only Vergennes among Calonne's ministerial colleagues had been fully aware of his plans, and the rest felt no commitment to supporting him. Some hoped to use the Assembly to destroy him; others were known disciples of Necker. And the Swiss wonder-worker himself, though not a member of the Notables, was a central figure in their deliberations from the very start. He had many admirers in the Assembly; and when Calonne, in his opening speech, declared that the royal finances were running a substantial deficit, everyone immediately thought of the *Compte rendu*. If Necker could achieve a surplus after three years of war and no new taxation, why now was there a deficit after three years of peace and a third *vingtième?* Calonne's lavish spending and heavy borrowing were notorious. There was a perfectly reasonable suspicion that if there was a crisis—and at this stage the minister offered no figures to prove that there was—then he was responsible.

Yet if Calonne's proposals had come from anybody else there is little doubt that the Notables would have welcomed them more warmly. They were, after all, 'More or less the result of all that good minds have been thinking for several years', as Talleyrand put it.[6] And in the event the vast majority of them were accepted with very little complaint. Criticism was largely confined to the territorial subvention, the provincial assemblies, and a proposal to force the clergy to redeem its corporate debt. Even then the Notables declared themselves unequivocally in favour of the basic principles of equality of taxation and representation of the taxpayers in its assessment and apportionment. But, landowners as all the Notables were, they questioned whether a perpetual, variable tax falling entirely on people like themselves was fair, and whether the proposal to levy it in kind was practicable. And, members as they all were of the first two orders of the realm, they thought nobles and clergy should be guaranteed a proportion of the seats in the provincial assemblies, and that the work of these bodies, if they were to be truly representative, should not be subject to the veto of the intendants. The bishops, finally, saw the proposal for redemption of the clerical debt as a prolongation of the minister's earlier attacks on the Church. They knew that if their debt, incurred on the government's behalf, was liquidated, they would lose the best guarantee of the clergy's time-honoured right of self-taxation. They declared themselves incapable of assenting to any changes touching the Church without the authorization of the Assembly of the Clergy. Magistrates, likewise, announced that they could not predetermine the attitude of the sovereign courts they sat in. Most of the Notables, indeed, felt uncertain about who they spoke for. 'We were not the representatives of the Nation', Lafayette later wrote to George Washington,[7] 'but . . . we declared that altho' we had no right to impede, it was our right not to advise unless we thought the measures were proper, and that we could not think of new taxes unless we knew the returns of expenditure and the plans of economy.' This proved the real sticking-point during the first week of the Assembly. At first Calonne contended that since the king had seen the full accounts they should accept his good faith. The Notables countered that in that case there was no point in soliciting their support. Eventually, on 2 March, Calonne reluctantly revealed his estimates, and in doing so explicitly condemned the *Compte rendu* of 1781 as false and misleading. The Neckerites were outraged, while those who did not know who to believe demanded to see even more detailed accounts in order to make up their own minds. On 3 March came the first overt claim that the Notables had no power to approve new taxation. That right, declared Leblanc de Castillon, procurator-general of the parlement of Aix, belonged only to the Estates-General.

All these proceedings had formally taken place in secret. The public was agog to have news of the Assembly, rumours abounded, and a good deal of more or less accurate information leaked out. It fuelled a flurry of pamphleteering, most of it hostile to the minister. In addition to despotism, profligacy, and incompetence, it was now alleged by the most notorious pen-for-hire of the day, the dissolute Count de Mirabeau, that Calonne was also guilty of shady stock-exchange dealings. This atmosphere encouraged the Notables in their demand for full accounts, and in detailed criticism of Calonne's plan. They were all the more scandalized, therefore, when on 12 March he blandly observed at a plenary session that the king was glad to note their broad approval. Despite vehement protests, Calonne proceeded to publish this speech, which proved the first sign of a fundamental change of tactics. Having failed to browbeat the Notables in private, he now attempted to take advantage of the intense public interest to subject them to outside pressure. On 18 March he sponsored a pamphlet calling for the full proceedings of the Assembly to be made public. On 31 March, with the ground thus prepared, he published the full original texts of his proposals. They were accompanied by an introduction (*Avertissement*), which was also separately printed and circulated free to parish clergy with the request that they read it from the pulpit. It was clearly designed to arouse public suspicion about the motives of Calonne's critics. The Notables' doubts, it implied, were mere pretexts:

We will be paying more! . . . No doubt; but who? Only those who were not paying enough; they will pay what they owe according to a just proportion, and nobody will be overburdened.

Privileges will be sacrificed! . . . Yes: justice demands it, need requires it. Would it be better to put further burdens on the unprivileged, the people?

There will be a great outcry! . . . That was to be expected. Can general good be done without bruising a few individual interests? Can there be reform without some complaints?[8]

But this bold attempt to foment social antagonisms against the minister's leading critics fell flat. The Notables sent further indignant protests to the king, and the public proved completely unresponsive to Calonne's appeal. It was received as a desperate last throw by a discredited political gambler. And so it proved to be. Even the king was now dismayed by the lack of progress in the Assembly, and his minister's seeming inability to convince anyone of his honesty and good intentions. Courtiers, ministerial rivals, and men of ambition moved in for the kill. Louis XVI, committed to the reforms, resisted to the last; and on the morning of 8 April he dismissed Miromesnil, head of the judiciary and his longest-serving minister, ostensibly for failing to support Calonne. But later that day the Comptroller-General himself was dismissed. The king had clearly concluded that only new men could hope to push any reforms at all through; and the general celebration which greeted the news of Calonne's fall certainly seemed to promise an improvement in the political atmosphere.

But finding a replacement did not prove easy. Miromesnil was succeeded by Lamoignon, a member of the Notables, long known as one of the more able presidents of the parlement of Paris, and an advocate of judicial reforms. The appointment was popular, but the central problem confronting the State was financial, and capable men willing to take over the fallen minister's programme were not so readily found. Necker was still the public's favourite, but the king disliked him. On the very weekend of Calonne's dismissal he had flouted express royal instructions not to publish a vindication of the *Compte rendu* against the minister's attacks. He was exiled from Paris for his effrontery. The other obvious candidate was Brienne, who from the start had hoped to use the Notables as a stepping-stone to power. The king disliked him, too, but after entrusting the finances for three weeks to a bureaucratic nonentity who proved quite unable to handle the Notables, he yielded. Informed that royal stock was steadily falling and that without some gesture to restore confidence credit might soon run out, the king, on 1 May, appointed Brienne Chief of the Royal Council of Finances. Credit revived instantly. Nobody seemed more likely to be able to engineer a successful outcome to an experiment that had already gone seriously wrong than one of the Notables' own most capable, intelligent, and flexible members.

Brienne himself was also confident of success. He thought that if the territorial subvention could be modified to a tax in cash yielding a prearranged amount over a set and limited number of years, and if the clergy and nobility could be guaranteed seats in the provincial assemblies, the Notables would be satisfied. He presented these modifications to leading members of the Assembly on 9 May. But during the ministerial upheavals of the preceding month the Notables had done little but scrutinize the accounts, and the more they saw the more confused they had become. Before agreeing even to a modified version of the Calonne plan, they now insisted that the true condition of the finances must be established beyond dispute. The best way of achieving this, more and more of them were coming to believe, was through a permanent commission of auditors. Brienne had no objections to the idea, but the king thought it an unacceptable infringement of his prerogative. He vetoed it. His decision brought all constructive activity in the Assembly to an end. They had no authority, the Notables now declared, to consent to or authorize new taxes. 'It seems to me', declared Lafayette in the *bureau* where he sat on 21 May,[9] 'that this is the moment for us to beseech His Majesty to fix, immediately, in order to render account to him of all measures and settle their happy outcome forever, the convocation of a truly national assembly.' 'What, Sir,' burst out the Count d'Artois, the king's brother, 'are you calling for the Estates-General?' 'Yes, my lord,' replied the young glory-hunter, 'and even better than that.'

This now became the universal cry; and Brienne quickly recognized that no further progress with the Notables was likely. They had to be brought to an end before irreparable damage was done; and on 25 May they were. In an uncontested closing speech Brienne announced that he intended to press on with the modified territorial subvention, the provincial assemblies, and various other measures in the plan originally formulated by

Calonne. Having so ringingly declared that they represented nobody, the Notables had no alternative to accepting their dismissal on these terms. 'At least,' the mayor of Montauban explained,[10] 'you cannot say we have voted for any taxes.' Nevertheless the Assembly was a turning-point. It marked the beginning of a political crisis that was only to be resolved by revolution. Convoked to deal with hitherto unacknowledged financial problems, its three-month sitting revealed in rare detail to the country and to the world how serious they were. The effect was to throw public doubt on the capacity of absolute monarchy to manage the nation's affairs, and to encourage subsequent resistance to any measures the Crown might propose. Brienne saw this clearly enough.

If the Assembly of Notables [he had predicted to the king (who agreed) on 16 April] separates without having assured a balance between receipts and expenses, and it becomes necessary, after its separation, to have recourse to taxes, it is to be feared that great resistance will be encountered. This assembly was called because it was judged that its opinion would overcome all foreseeable obstacles. Lack of that opinion would produce much the same effect as outright opposition.[11]

But opposition there had been, and it had culminated in loud calls for the institution which Calonne had ruled out in his original strategy as too dangerous—the Estates-General. This stance was bequeathed to future opponents of the government's plans, and it was extremely popular. The unprecedented political spectacle of the Assembly of Notables had involved public opinion in politics to an extent not seen since 1771 and this time the interest aroused did not die away. Calonne himself had helped to sustain it by his ill-judged attempt to bring pressure on the Notables with the *Avertissement*. His fall from power discredited him entirely and vindicated the Notables in public esteem. The parlements, which were now required to register the modified remnants of his plan, knew that the public expected a resolute show of opposition.

Brienne's ministry (in August he was awarded the title of Principal Minister, unused since 1726) also felt obliged to press ahead with a programme of reforms. After all, the difficulties which had led Calonne to formulate his original plan—the lapse of the third *vingtième* and heavy debt redemptions falling due—were still there. And although the archbishop's arrival in power revived credit sufficiently to float a successful new loan in early May, it could only be a stopgap. Besides, the international situation had suddenly darkened over the spring. The Dutch Republic had been teetering on the brink of civil war for four years as self-styled 'patriots' sought to curtail the constitutional role of the Stadtholder William V of Orange. Vergennes's policy had been to support the patriots, but the British and the Prussians were now encouraging a princely counter-offensive. To lend the patriots further support might require military intervention, with all its attendant costs. Some resolution of the budgetary crisis was therefore a matter of increasing urgency.

The ministry began to send its measures for registration in the parlements at the end of June. Some of them encountered little resistance. Free trade in grain, the commutation of the *corvée* into a tax, and even the edict setting up provincial assemblies passed in Paris without trouble. Only the parlement of Bordeaux, which had been on record since 1779 as an advocate of strong provincial estates for the province of Guyenne, voiced more than formal reservations about the vagueness of the powers these assemblies were to exercise. It refused to register this or anything else until they were clarified. But the focus of public attention was the parlement of Paris where, thanks to its status as the Court of Peers, no fewer than twenty-one former Notables were entitled to sit and opine. Everybody knew that the real battle would be joined over the taxation edicts which were the kernel of the government's programme. First to arrive, on 2 July, was the extension of stamp duty, and on this the parlement clearly established its general position. It refused to register until the government justified the tax-increase by producing accounts. The king replied that there were enough former Notables in the court to know how matters stood; in any case the parlement had no right to vet the royal finances. He ordered immediate registration. Instead of that, however, the parlement decided to send further remonstrances in which it declared itself incapable of sanctioning a perpetual tax. That right belonged solely, it declared, to the Estates-General. Rather than take issue with this argument, the government now sent the territorial subvention for registration. It, too, was rejected after a long discussion, not unanimously but by a clear majority, on 30 July. Again the Estates-General were called for, and there was no doubting the popularity of the magistrates' stand. Great crowds assembled whenever the parlement met, the salons of high society were almost unanimous in urging the magistrates to keep up their opposition, and all over the capital political clubs and discussion groups were mushrooming, reading together and sometimes sponsoring an ever-swelling flow of pamphlets and broadsheets, now appearing at a rate of more than one a day. When the government decided, on 6 August, to force registration of the new taxes in a *lit de justice*, the ceremony was held at Versailles, away from the rebellious atmosphere of the capital. On this occasion a whole programme of administrative economies was announced, in the hope of softening the blow of a forced registration; and the atmosphere was so calm that Louis XVI snored audibly through much of the proceedings. But back in Paris the next day the biggest crowd anyone could remember thronged the palace of justice as the parlement debated its response. It declared the forced registration null and illegal. Three days later it voted to proceed against Calonne for criminal mismanagement of public funds; and on the thirteenth it condemned the forcibly registered laws once more to thunderous applause. Ministers were now growing alarmed. Even those who had doubted the wisdom of so rapid a recourse to a *lit de justice* recognized that the Crown must quickly recapture the initiative and calm the effervescence in the capital. So they all supported the next step, a time-honoured one in conflicts with the sovereign courts. On 15 August the parlement was exiled to Troyes.

Defiant though the leaders of the parlement felt, none of them thought of resisting the royal orders. History suggested that such exiles were never permanent, and were usually ended by some compromise or even surrender on the Crown's part. Older and more hesitant magistrates willingly complied in the hope that a calmer atmosphere would now descend. But initially there were tumultuous protests in Paris, led by law clerks thrown out of work by the transfer of legal activity to the provinces. Forced registration of the tax-edicts in other Parisian sovereign courts, carried out by the king's brothers, produced catcalls, jostling, and clashes with the princes' escort of guards. In the days following there was open defiance of the city police, and talk of a mass march to Versailles. 'The abuse bestowed on the King and Queen and the Archbishop of Toulouse', noted an English observer,[12] is incredible.' But the government continued to act with new-found vigour. All clubs were now closed. Booksellers were ordered to clamp down on unauthorized publications. Troops cleared the palace of justice and began to patrol the streets day and night. Meanwhile proceedings against Calonne were quashed (although by now he had fled to England), and to show that the new firm policy applied outside the capital too, the parlement of Bordeaux was also exiled to Libourne, a small town some distance from its normal seat. By the first week in September, the government appeared to be back in control, although the Paris parlement had ordered its subordinate courts not to register or publish the tax-edicts, and protests were now pouring in from provincial parlements about the whole drift of royal policy. What the government could not control was the situation in the Dutch Republic. There, a confrontation between the Hohenzollern princess of Orange and the patriots at the end of June had led to a Prussian ultimatum. On 13 September Prussian troops crossed the frontier, with the open connivance of Great Britain, and by the beginning of October they were masters of the entire Republic. French intervention to support the patriots was generally expected. 'The political conversation of every company I have seen', observed Arthur Young on 16 September,[13] 'is much more on the affairs of Holland than on those of France.' But on 28 September the French foreign secretary Montmorin admitted that there was no possibility of intervention. The financial crisis had meant that throughout the summer no proper preparations had been made. The contrast with the resolute days of Vergennes was glaring, another blow to the government's prestige. A lasting resolution of the country's internal problems offered the only serious prospect of restoring it.

Lamoignon, who dreamed of a comprehensive reform of the French law, was beginning to talk about action on the scale of Maupeou to break the parlements' powers of resistance once and for all. Brienne preferred negotiation with the exiles of Troyes, sensing that many of the magistrates had been pushed by the electric atmosphere of the capital beyond what they knew were the limits of wisdom. Besides, by mid-September he had elaborated a new plan. Ever since the Notables the Crown's leading critics had been calling for full accounts and drastic economies as prerequisites of new taxation. He now proposed to offer both, in the context of a five-year programme designed to restore financial health by 1792. Neither the stamp tax nor the territorial subvention, he now announced, were necessary to the success of this plan, provided the two existing *vingtièmes* could be prolonged and levied on a more equitable basis. He therefore offered to terminate the parlement's exile and withdraw the two new taxes in return for registration of the prolongation of the old. A majority of magistrates was persuaded to agree. On 20 September, accordingly, the exile was revoked, and the parlement entered at once upon its normal autumn vacation. It was understood that, on reassembling in November, it would be presented with a new loan edict intended to keep the government afloat during its five-year retrenchment.

Public reaction to this compromise was a mixture of scepticism and disgust. Although the parlement had declared once again, in agreeing to prolong the *vingtièmes*, that only the Estates-General could sanction new taxation, it appeared by the very act of registration to have abandoned that principle. The provincial parlements, who had rallied round their exiled colleagues, felt betrayed—especially that of Bordeaux, which remained in exile. The law clerks of Paris spent three days and nights celebrating the end of the exile with fireworks and bonfires where Calonne was burned in effigy. But pamphleteers were less flattering, and hostility to the government continued unabated.

The feeling of everybody [Arthur Young recorded in Paris on 13 October] seems to be that the Archbishop will not be able to do anything towards exonerating the State from the burden of its present situation; some think that he has not the inclination; others that he has not the courage; others that he has not the ability. By some he is thought to be attentive only to his own interest; and by others that the finances are too much deranged to be within the power of any system to recover, short of the States-General of the kingdom; and that it is impossible for such an assembly to meet without a revolution in the government ensuing.[14]

Brienne's own optimism, however, continued incorrigible. Even the idea of the Estates-General no longer alarmed him. Indeed, he now resolved to incorporate it in his five-year plan. By 1792, he thought, with the hand of government immeasurably strengthened by the plan's success, the Estates might be safely assembled to celebrate recovery. And to promise this now, before the plan even went into operation, would surely induce the parlement not to obstruct the loans essential to its working.

Nevertheless the archbishop left nothing to chance. Before presenting the loans for registration he took good care to ascertain that a broad spectrum of opinion in the parlement would view them favourably. And in order to invest the parlement's registration with added authority, he decided that it should take place in the king's presence, at an unprecedented Royal Session. It would not be a *lit de justice*, since all present would be allowed to opine freely. Approval given in these circumstances would carry the sort of weight once hoped for from the Assembly of Notables. The session took place on 19 November, with the peers present in force. It began with the introduction of an edict, long known to be in gestation, according civil rights to French Protestants. The aim was to foster an atmosphere of good will. Protestant refugees from Orange reprisals in Holland now pouring into northern France made its promulgation at this moment particularly appropriate. But the real business of the session was a proposal to borrow no less than 420 millions between 1788 and 1792, falling annually from 120 millions in the first year to 60 in the last. These funds would be used to pay off short-term debts due for redemption over that period, and bring down the level of *anticipations*. Stringent economies were also promised over the same period, including rationalization of the royal household, the armed forces, and the financial bureaucracy. Brienne gave notice that he was resuming the policy of Terray, Turgot, and Necker, abandoned by Calonne, of eliminating the role of private financiers in budgetary administration, and centralizing operations in a single, bureaucratically organized royal treasury. For $8\frac{1}{4}$ hours members of the parlement delivered their opinions. Even the acknowledged leader of the younger extremists among the magistrates, Duval d'Eprémesnil, supported the loans, although he called for the Estates-General to be convened in 1789. Others preferred 1788. And even though some spoke against the loans, there seemed to be a clear majority in favour. But it was never put to the test. At the end of the proceedings the king reiterated the promise of the Estates by 1792, and ordered registration of the loans as if this were a *lit de justice*. To general astonishment the Duke d'Orléans, head of the junior branch of the royal family and heir to a long tradition of obstructionism, suddenly rose and protested that this was not legal. At one of the most finely balanced moments in his country's history, the king of France was caught completely off guard. 'I don't care . . .', he stammered, 'it's up to you . . . yes . . . it's legal because I wish it.'

In a country so exercised about the threat and the evils of despotism, no reply could have been more catastrophic. Government by whim was what was presumed to have produced the malversations of Calonne; it was what the Estates-General were intended to remedy. Therefore the king's words turned what seemed destined to be a governmental triumph into a disaster. The loans were registered; but when the king had gone (watched by silent crowds) the parlement continued to sit. After $3\frac{1}{2}$ more hours of lively debate, joined in by Orléans, it formally dissociated itself from the registration. The next day Orléans and the two leaders of the protests after the king's departure, Fréteau and Sabatier, were exiled to the country by *lettres de cachet*. On the day following, the peers were forbidden to take their seats in the parlement. It was now open war between the court and the ministry. The king quashed the proceedings which had followed his departure on the nineteenth. When the magistrates called for the revocation of the exiles, they were brushed aside. They responded by prevaricating over the registration of the edict on Protestantism, which had not been considered at the Royal Session. It was only registered on 29 January 1788, after the parlement had adopted a new line of attack on despotism by denouncing all *lettres de cachet* as illegal and contrary to public and natural law (4 January 1788). The king had the declaration struck from the registers in his presence, and on 13 March this procedure was itself denounced in new remonstrances. Provincial parlements now joined in the hue and cry. Bordeaux, still in exile at Libourne, denounced *lettres de cachet* and refused to transact any business or register any new laws. Others delayed registration of the prolonged *vingtièmes*, or refused it outright. Several sent remonstrances, and all joined in the clamour for an immediate meeting of the Estates-General. And although all except Bordeaux had registered the edict establishing provincial assemblies, a number now followed the Gascon court in expressing a preference for provincial estates, with their wider constituencies and stronger powers. The conduct of such provincial assemblies as had met since the previous summer only strengthened these doubts. Nominated rather than elected, most of them agreed to compound in advance their *vingtièmes*, a practice which Brienne (following Calonne) had promised to abandon. Those refusing to compound had been subjected to punitively heavy assessments. All this seemed to vindicate the doubts expressed by the parlement of Bordeaux and, less vehemently, by others. Only the *pays d'états* proved able to bargain with a government that now seemed determined to press on with its programme in the teeth of every protest.

It was much fortified by the success of the loans registered on 19 November. The first one was fully subscribed within days, no doubt reflecting the extremely favourable terms on which it was offered. Assured thus of paying its way for the moment, the government was able to turn its full attention to dealing with the parlements. Rumours of a general remodelling even more thorough than that of 1771 were circulating as early as January. By April they had reached the most distant provinces, and nobody doubted them. Accordingly, the parlement of Paris spent that month staking out its constitutional position in unambiguous terms so that there could be no doubt of the good cause in which it was destined to suffer. On the thirteenth it sent remonstrances denouncing the irregular conduct of the Royal Session of the previous November. On the twenty-ninth it forbade tax-collectors to bring in new assessments for the *vingtièmes*. The next day it voted to remonstrate yet again against the king's reply to the protestations of the thirteenth. He had then made the time-worn accusation that the pretensions of the courts reduced the kingdom to an aristocracy of magistrates. Their consistent advocacy of the Estates-General since the previous July, they countered, gave the lie to that: 'No, Sire, there is no aristocracy in France, but no despotism; such is the Constitution.'[15] And they went on to enumerate what the constitution guaranteed:

The heir to the Crown is designated by the law; the Nation has its rights; the Peerage likewise; the Magistracy is irremovable; each province has its customs, its capitations; each subject has his natural judges, each citizen has his property; if he is poor, at least he has his liberty. Yet we dare to ask: which of these rights, which of these laws can stand up against the claims by your ministers in Your Majesty's name?

These remonstrances were presented on 4 May. The day before, on the motion of d'Eprémesnil, the parlement issued a solemn declaration of what it saw as the fundamental laws of the realm, including 'the right of the Nation freely to grant subsidies through the organ of the Estates-General regularly convoked and composed', the right of the parlements to register new laws, and the freedom of all Frenchmen from arbitrary arrest. It bound its members not to co-operate in any measures directed against it. Not even in 1771 had such extreme language been heard, and on 4 May the king ordered the arrest of its movers, Goislard de Montsabert and d'Eprémesnil. They took refuge with the parlement, which voted to remain in session until the crisis was resolved. For eleven hours during the night of 5–6 May the court refused to surrender them to the military officers sent to take them into custody. 'Arrest us all!', the magistrates cried, and only the next morning, with armed troops surrounding the palace of justice, did the two give themselves up. They were whisked away to state prisons in the south, watched by apprehensive crowds who were once more thronging the approaches to the parlement. No doubt this was why the long-awaited moves against the court were promulgated at Versailles, where the magistrates were convoked for a *lit de justice* on 8 May.

The judicial reforms there announced were the last attempt by the French monarchy to remain absolute. They sought to destroy permanently the ability of the parlements to obstruct policy by manipulating their rights of registration and remonstrance. These powers were now to be vested in a Plenary Court made up of a selection of prominent persons reminiscent of the Assembly of Notables. The parlements were to be reduced to simple appeal courts; while at the same time their jurisdiction was to be diminished from below by upgrading forty-seven subordinate courts to the status of *grand bailliage*. The diminution of business that was bound to result would make many magistrates redundant, so large numbers of offices were to be suppressed. But, as on 19 November, contentious measures were preceded by one designed to win over enlightened opinion. This time it was a series of reforms intended to eliminate from the criminal law abuses and anomalies highlighted by several spectacular miscarriages of justice that had come to light since 1785. Further reforms were promised. A few days beforehand, after much advance publicity, the government had also published a new *Compte rendu* designed to reassure the public that financial reforms were under way and working. Brienne and Lamoignon clearly recognized that their measures must carry public opinion if they were to succeed.

For a moment it looked as if they might. Paris seemed stunned by the long-awaited blow, and remained, as the British ambassador reported, 'perfectly quiet'.[16] The parlement, and the other sovereign courts of the capital where the king's brothers had conducted simultaneous *lits de justice*, were put at once into vacation, with orders not to reassemble until further notice. In the provinces, where governors on 8 May imposed the same laws, along with any still unregistered since the previous year, at military sessions, the presence of troops guaranteed order. But within days murmurs of protest began to be heard, and by the beginning of June they had grown into a deafening, nationwide roar.

In Paris the lower courts refused to register the new laws and had to be forced. The bar voted not to co-operate with any of the new judicial structure, and the members of a commission of jurists set up by Lamoignon a few months beforehand to advise him on criminal law reform all resigned. In the provinces most sovereign courts flouted the order putting them into vacation and reassembled to pass defiant resolutions. In Bordeaux, where the parlement's exile was terminated on 8 May, huge popular demonstrations, fireworks, and a general illumination of windows greeted the return of leading magistrates from Libourne. Other parlements renewed the call for the Estates-General, and at Toulouse, Besançon, Dijon, Metz, and Rouen their members had to be silenced and exiled from the town by mass distributions of *lettres de cachet*. When the military governor of Dauphiné attempted to do the same at Grenoble on 7 June, there were riots during which four people were killed and around forty injured. Troops were bombarded from the rooftops in what would be remembered as the 'Day of Tiles'. In Pau on 29 June angry crowds smashed in the locked doors of the parlement and reinstalled the magistrates. In Rennes the authorities lost control of the streets for almost two months to mobs of law clerks, students, and chairmen who drove the intendant out of the city on 9 July. He blamed the local commandant for this ignominy. 'I never complained that we had not soldiers enough;' he protested to Brienne,[17] 'decisive orders were what we were most in need of.' But the commandant in Brittany was not the only army officer reluctant to order his men to fire on rioters. All over the country rumours circulated of officers openly hostile to the government. Brienne's reforms and economies, after all, had not spared the army; many proud units had been cut or disbanded, and military careers disrupted. In the end no officer disobeyed decisive orders; but civilian nobles in many parts held unauthorized assemblies which passed resolutions backing the parlements and calling for Estates, both national and provincial. The nobility of turbulent Brittany dispatched a deputation to Versailles with orders to denounce the king's ministers as criminals; the deputies were arrested in the road and thrown into the Bastille. Louis XVI was scandalized by this 'noble revolt'; but not only nobles were involved. The clergy, Brienne's own order, joined in the protests. Finally assembling early in May to discuss plans for the Church pending since the Assembly of Notables, its representatives offered a derisory *don gratuit* and petitioned the king for an immediate meeting of the Estates-General and regular ones thereafter. And while all this clamour was going on, justice came to a standstill as most lower courts refused to recognize the new order. A few, dazzled by the prospect of promotion to the status of *grand bailliage* and anxious to revenge themselves for generations of haughty disdain on the part of the parlements, offered tentative compliance. Most, even if tempted by this line of conduct, saw the future as too uncertain to risk offending superiors who might yet return in triumph, as in 1774.

Brienne and Lamoignon thought strong nerves would be enough to face out the clamour. It had worked for Maupeou in 1771. The memory of the chancellor, still alive and watching events with a grim sense of vindication from his fourteen-year exile, haunted everybody involved in the crisis. One key to his success in 1771 had been to split the opposition, and this appears to have been the main aim of Brienne's next move. On 5 July he announced that the king would welcome views or ideas on how the promised Estates-General should be constituted. The declared intention was to establish the national body on the best possible lines; but the hope was to distract public attention from the judicial reforms, divide opinion along new lines, sow dissension among the different interest groups and estates of the realm, perhaps even produce ideas that would make any meeting more manageable, and reassure the public, finally, that the Estates-General were to meet despite the recent reassertion of authority. In provincial town halls civic officials began to comb through their records for precedents; but the outpouring of hostile pamphlets—534 between May and September, and mostly now in the provinces—was hardly affected at all. Not until Brienne and Lamoignon had fallen from power did the public at large turn its attention seriously to the question of the form of the Estates-General.

They were brought down by what every measure introduced by successive ministers over the preceding eighteen months had been intended to avoid—bankruptcy. The underlying position remained sound enough thanks to the loans of the previous November, although the despotism of the May coup, evoking as it did memories of the partial bankruptcies which had accompanied Maupeou's reforms, left the markets nervous. The weak spot of the published budget for 1788 lay in the 240 millions worth of *anticipations* required to balance it. The confident calculations of Brienne's *Compte rendu* took no account of the fiscal chaos and tax-arrears produced by months of attempted reform and hasty changes of policy. If defiance of the government on the scale of May and June continued, that position could only get worse, and then the anticipated tax-revenues might well not materialize. And on 13 July something happened which made it unlikely that they would in any case. A colossal hail storm destroyed much of the harvest in the Paris basin. This, and bad weather elsewhere in the country, meant that peasants would have difficulty meeting tax-demands in 1789. *Anticipations* were therefore unattractive, even to the financiers who normally covered them; and since Brienne's known intention was to resume the policy of Terray, Turgot, and Necker and gradually eliminate these same financiers from their traditional role, they felt even less obligation to come to his assistance. The blow fell at the beginning of August, when Brienne was told that the treasury was empty and nobody would accept any further *anticipations*. In a desperate attempt to reanimate credit with a bold political gesture, on 8 August Brienne announced a specific meeting date for the Estates-General: 1 May 1789. But this time the markets did not react. On 16 August, accordingly, the treasury suspended payments. Creditors were forced to accept interest-bearing government paper, a sort of forced loan. The long-dreaded bankruptcy had at last arrived, and panic seized the stock market as government funds plummeted and there was a run on the most important bank. Brienne, at the end of his resources, recognized that only one man now enjoyed the credit, prestige, and seemingly flawless public record to restore calm: Necker. His last act as principal minister was to persuade a reluctant king to recall the popular idol. It took a week of negotiations and importunity, but on 24 August Necker agreed to serve. The next day Brienne resigned.

His was the last attempt to save the old regime, and it had failed. His entire programme disappeared with him, as did Lamoignon and his. Necker made it clear from the start that he regarded himself as little more than a caretaker until the Estates-General met. The bankruptcy of the monarchy was therefore not only financial, but political and intellectual, too. It had collapsed in every sense, leaving an enormous vacuum of power.

# 4

# The Estates–General
# September 1788–July 1789

THE freak storm which swept across northern France on 13 July 1788, with hailstones so big that they killed men and animals and devastated hundreds of square miles of crops on the eve of harvest, came half-way through a year of catastrophic weather. Even out of the storm's path the harvest proved poor, thanks to a long spring drought which had failed to swell the grain. Unusually, these conditions affected almost every region of the kingdom. Summer disasters were followed in the first months of 1789 by the longest, coldest winter within living memory. Northern France was in the grip of snow and ice from December to April, while in Provence and Languedoc delicate vines and olive-trees were killed in their thousands by frost. The whole of Louis XVI's reign had been a time of economic difficulties, with wildly fluctuating grain, fodder, and grape harvests causing repeated disruption. Even good crops did not necessarily restore stability. A bumper harvest in 1785 had made grain cheap and abundant the year after, but any remaining surpluses were dissipated in 1787 by the removal of all controls from the grain trade in one of the few components of Calonne's reform plan to meet no educated opposition. Necker, on resuming office in August 1788, immediately reimposed controls, but by then the damage was done. Grain prices had already begun to climb, and they went on doing so throughout the winter. They peaked in Paris, at their highest level since Louis XIV's time, on 14 July 1789.

Steep rises in the price of grain, flour, and bread posed serious problems for that vast majority of Frenchmen who were wage-earners. In normal times bread absorbed anything between a third and a half of an urban worker's wage, and from landless agricultural labourers it might take even more. As prices climbed over the spring of 1789 the proportion rose to two-thirds for the best-off and perhaps even nine-tenths for the worst. In these circumstances people had less to spend on other foodstuffs, heating, and lighting. So that bitter winter was particularly miserable even for those not thrown out of work entirely by frozen rivers, blocked roads, and immobilized mills and workshops. 'The wretchedness of the poor people during this inclement season', wrote the Duke of Dorset from Paris on 8 January 1789,[1] 'surpasses all description.' There was certainly nothing to spare for consumer goods; and this produced a dramatic slump in demand for industrial products. In some areas production fell by up to 50 per cent, and there were widespread redundancies in textile towns like Rouen, Lyons, and Nîmes. Between 20,000 and 30,000 silk workers were said to be without employment in Lyons; while spinning and weaving as an extra source of income for hard-pressed country people disappeared as goods became unsaleable. People blamed new technology for undercutting the products of more expensive traditional methods. In Rouen spinning-jennies were smashed and workshops producing them sacked. Above all they blamed another of Calonne's legacies, the 1786 commercial treaty with Great Britain, which opened up the French market to British manufacturers. The agreement only came into operation in mid-1787, so that British imports, though undeniably cheaper and of higher quality, scarcely had time to do all the damage attributed to them by 1788 and 1789. But they clearly aggravated an already serious industrial depression, and provided one more reason, along with free trade in grain, for the working populace to blame the government. Over the winter of 1788 and spring of 1789 hardly anybody in France regretted the passing of the old political order. It had failed or let down too many people. Everybody assumed that change could only be for the better. But the process of working out what change there was to be took place in an atmosphere made tense by this acute and worsening economic crisis.

Necker's return to power was greeted by several weeks of popular jubilation on the streets of Paris. Bonfires were lit, and his fallen predecessors were burned in effigy. On the Pont Neuf, excited crowds stopped passing coaches and forced those inside to emerge and bow to the statue of the legendary 'good king' Henry IV. But symbols of authority, such as guard posts and the houses of prominent officials, were also attacked, and troops were called out several times to clear the streets. They fired into the crowds, killing several demonstrators and wounding many more. The climax of these commotions came during the fourth week of September, when the parlement returned in triumph from its exile. Necker knew that nothing less than the abandonment of the previous ministry's entire programme would satisfy public demand, and the recall of the parlements with all their old powers was the keystone of this policy.

Accordingly, the Paris parlement reconvened on 24 September, amid renewed demonstrations and further bloodshed. The court's first act was to ban all further tumults, while opening a judicial inquiry into the conduct of the police authorities. The magistrates realized, as they watched the price of bread inching upwards, that public effervescence could easily slip beyond anybody's control. The return of the provincial parlements in the course of October, however, proved less turbulent. The days of bonfires, fireworks, and parades that greeted the restoration of the martyred 'senators' passed off in good humour. The first edict that the restored courts were required to register was the convocation of the Estates-General, which, in a further attempt to boost confidence, Necker now brought forward to January 1789.

No parlement hesitated to register. This was, after all, what they had been clamouring for for over a year. But the Parisian magistrates remained deeply suspicious of the government's intentions. They remembered that in July Brienne had invited all and sundry to propose ideas for how the Estates should be constituted, while reserving the king's own position. The edict now before them said nothing about the form of the assembly, or how it was to be chosen. Many wondered whether the intention was to establish a body as docile and powerless as the provincial assemblies had proved to be. It was to thwart such despotic wishes in advance that the parlement declared, in its formula of registration, that the constitution of the Estates-General must follow the last recorded precedent. It should meet 'according to the forms observed in 1614'.

In 1614 the Estates-General (which had achieved very little) had met in three almost numerically equal but separately elected chambers representing the orders of clergy, nobility, and third estate. They had voted separately, by order. Throughout eighteen months of clamour for the Estates, hardly anybody appears to have been aware of this, or thought the question worth investigation. Even now it was several days before the truth became common knowledge. But once it did, the implications, if this precedent were followed, were obvious. The nobility and clergy would be enormously over-represented, both numerically and in terms of their share of the national wealth. Together they would always be able to outvote the third estate.

None of the provincial assemblies established in 1778 or 1787 had followed these principles. In them, third-estate numbers had been doubled, and voting was by head. Even the ancient but still active estates of Languedoc had double third-estate representation. And fresh in everybody's mind, above all, was the example set in Dauphiné since the summer. In several provinces the noblemen who led the protests against the

Lamoignon coup turned to the idea of resurrecting long-defunct provincial estates as a better shield against despotism than the parlements had proved to be. When, in the aftermath of the Day of Tiles, 106 noblemen of Dauphiné assembled to draft a petition to the king calling for provincial representation to be restored, they found themselves supported by the three orders of the city of Grenoble. At the prompting of the non-noble leaders of this urban movement, the judge Mounier and the young Protestant advocate Barnave, it was agreed to summon a meeting of representatives of the three orders of the entire province. They came together on 21 July in a nobleman's mansion at Vizille, calling for the Estates-General, the return of the parlements, and the restoration of the province's estates. Third-estate deputies at Vizille outnumbered the other two orders put together; and all present agreed that in the restored estates the third should be double the size of the other two, all deputies should be elected, and voting should be by head. On 2 August Brienne, now desperate for support from any quarter, agreed to revive the Dauphiné estates. Naturally enough other provinces without estates at once began to clamour for similar treatment, on similar terms; but before he fell Brienne only had time to authorize further progress in Dauphiné itself. He announced an assembly of the three orders of the province to draw up a constitution for the restored estates. It met at Romans on 5 September, and by the end of the month had produced a plan incorporating all the Vizille principles. It offered an obvious model for the Estates-General, beside which the forms of 1614 looked absurdly retrograde. By the beginning of October the pamphleteers of Paris were falling over themselves to point this out.

Nor did Necker do anything to discourage them. On taking office he released all journalists imprisoned under Brienne for writing anti-ministerial tracts, and made it clear that he no longer intended to operate traditional controls on the press and publishing. He clearly believed that the wider the public debate the freer he would be in making final decisions about the form the Estates would take. But he had not expected the parlements' intervention, and he was anxious not to let it pre-empt the issue. This was why, on 5 October, he announced that the Assembly of Notables would be reconvened in November to advise the king on all the problems involved. The effect was to fan public excitement still further and concentrate the attention of all educated men on the question of how best the nation could be represented. And since the parlement had thrown its weighty support behind the forms of 1614, the debate was initially conducted in terms of them. From the very start it was clear that most non-nobles found them unacceptable. How could what was good for Dauphiné not be good for the nation as a whole? And what were the real motives of the parlement? Was its intention merely to preserve the inequitable privileges of the first two orders, while keeping the most numerous and productive citizens in permanent political subjection? Now at last hostility to the 'privileged orders', which Calonne had tried so unsuccessfully to foment in March 1787, began to develop; and by the time the Notables convened on 6 November many of them were thoroughly alarmed. The magistrates of the parlement, so recently national heroes, now found themselves treated with hostility and suspicion, as did anybody who spoke up for the forms of 1614. By now, something like a nation-wide consensus seemed to be emerging in favour of 'doubling the third' and vote by head.

Nor did all nobles oppose it. In fact one largely noble group did a good deal to consolidate the consensus during the sittings of the Notables. Another of Brienne's prohibitions revoked by Necker was the ban on political clubs. Throughout September and October they mushroomed in Paris, and early in November a particularly distinguished group began to meet at the house of one of the parlement's leading radical magistrates, Adrien Duport. Later it would be remembered as the Society of Thirty, although its membership was nearer sixty. Drawn from the cream of the capital's legal, literary, and social life, it included five peers, two dozen magistrates, celebrities like Lafayette, the mathematician Condorcet, and Target, the leading advocate of the Paris bar. There was Talleyrand, the newly appointed bishop of Autun; and Mirabeau, who described the society as 'a conspiracy of decent folk' (*honnêtes gens*). Nine-tenths of them were noblemen, but their aim was not to defend noble interests. What they opposed was the forms of 1614, and privileges of all sorts. 'War on the privileged and privileges, that's my motto', Mirabeau had written in August,[2] 'Privileges are useful against Kings, but are contemptible against Nations and ours will never have any public spirit until it is rid of them.' The society now bent all its efforts towards whipping up this public spirit by deliberately playing on the social anxieties and resentments of the bourgeoisie. In pamphlets commissioned by the society, and distributed in both capital and provinces at the affluent members' expense, the middle classes were assured that the forms of 1614 were a plot by the privileged orders to keep them down. Typical enough was the *Essai sur les Privilèges* by the salon-haunting canon Sieyès of Chartres. Denouncing privilege as parasitic and socially divisive, creating unearned expectations, he implied (quite misleadingly) that privilege was a noble and clerical monopoly. Meanwhile the society was also circulating model petitions around the provinces on which municipalities could base appeals to Necker for doubling the third and vote by head; and in the course of November a national petitioning movement took shape. In towns all over the country the municipal authorities came under pressure from respectable bourgeois, who had often discussed the issues and concerted their actions in local literary clubs and discussion circles, to assemble town meetings to press the king for equitable third-estate representation. By the end of December over 800 petitions had been received. All this activity proved self-accelerating, and was soon far beyond the control of societies like Duport's which had done so much to focus it. 'Here one great issue absorbs all other objects', an anonymous Parisian correspondent could write to Poland by 24 November.[3] 'There is no talk of anything but the claims of the third estate; nothing is written but pamphlets about the form of the Estates-General.'

The second Assembly of Notables met on 6 November against this background. It was not expected to sit for long, but in the event it went on until 12 December, amid mounting public agitation. A handful of new members had been added to those summoned in 1787, but they did not affect the Assembly's overwhelmingly noble character. Necker confronted it with fifty-four questions about the form of the Estates, but by now the public was only interested in two. Strenuous efforts were made by certain members, led by the elder of the king's two brothers, Provence, and Orléans, hungry as ever for popular acclaim, to persuade the Assembly to reject the forms of 1614. But most members seem to have been scared by the popular passions aroused since September, and they feared that if the traditional forms of the Estates were abandoned, the nobility and clergy might be swamped. And so only 33 Notables voted in favour of doubling the third, with 111 against. Vote by head, it is true, was only openly opposed by 50, but nobody voted in favour of it. Most thought this issue should be decided by the Estates themselves, once they met. Every word uttered in the second Assembly of Notables was known outside almost at once, and it was being denounced long before it broke up as a mere mouthpiece for the privileged orders. Even when it unanimously reiterated its commitment of 1787 to fiscal equality nobody was impressed. All its long proceedings achieved was to make a meeting of the Estates on 1 January impossible. They were now postponed until April or May, amid suspicions that they might yet not be allowed to convene at all.

Opponents of the forms of 1614 had more success in the unlikely quarter of the parlement of Paris. On 5 December, after a carefully planned lobbying operation by Duport and d'Eprémesnil, now back from his summer-long exile and anxious to retain his popularity, the court was persuaded by a narrow majority to qualify its disastrous declaration of 25 September. All it had meant by the forms of 1614, it now announced, was that the electoral constituencies should be the ancient jurisdictions of *bailliages* (in the north) and *sénéchaussées* (in the south). But the narrowness of the majority for this statement was eye-catching, and it was noticed that the parlement had not endorsed the third estate's claims. And any conciliatory impact the movers of this declaration may have helped to make was eclipsed when, soon after the Notables dispersed, five of the seven princes of the blood petitioned the king not to grant either a doubling of the third or vote by head. The third should be content, they said, with fiscal equality. To give in to their other aspirations under pressure from outrageous public clamour would open the floodgates to attacks on wealth and property as well as privilege. It would lead on to complete destruction of the king's faithful nobility. The king, however, was still smarting from the 'noble revolt' of the previous summer, and regarded his nobility as anything but faithful. He ignored the princes' petition (which raised a new outcry against the intransigence of the privileged when it appeared in print) and tersely informed the parlement that he was not interested in their views on public affairs. These were now matters between him and the assembled nation—which many took as a hint that in the end the monarch's natural benevolence would put him on the third estate's side.

By mid-December Necker knew that crucial decisions could not be put off much longer. Quite apart from the clamour of public debate and pamphleteering in Paris, there was growing confusion in the provinces over the issue of provincial estates. On this the minister obviously had no coherent policy. It was generally expected that estates like those of Dauphiné would soon be established where they did not exist; and there was a widespread assumption that deputies to the Estates-General would be chosen by them. Consequently the form of provincial estates was of particular importance. But few nobles, even if they accepted doubling the third, seemed prepared to abandon vote by order; and where estates already existed they showed no desire to give up traditional forms and procedures. How could the third be effectively doubled in Brittany, where every nobleman enjoyed a right to sit in person, and they regularly turned up in their hundreds? Any practical reform was bound to deprive most noblemen of their time-honoured political rights. Non-noble Bretons had in fact been complaining for years about under-representation in the provincial estates, and they now saw that if the Vizille principles were to be adopted in other provinces their position would become even more glaringly anomalous. So when a meeting of the Breton estates was announced for January, a town meeting in Rennes demanded that it should abolish all tax privileges in the province and widen third-estate representation. Prosperous, commercial Nantes went even further. On 4 November it called for limitation of noble and clerical numbers and demanded that the first two orders agree to these changes in advance or face a strike by third-estate deputies. Meanwhile meetings of other provincial estates were being authorized; and only in Dauphiné, where the pattern elaborated at Romans in September was followed, was there no serious dissension. Elsewhere those with privileged representation showed themselves determined to maintain it, even against fellow members of their own orders. In Provence, Artois, and Franche Comté only certain types of noble had traditionally participated, but they adamantly refused to admit others even for the purpose of electing deputies to the Estates-General. At the same time they spurned third-estate claims to increased representation and open election of members. Inevitably, the disappointed groups deluged the government with petitions.

These were the circumstances in which the first great decision about the Estates-General was taken. Necker spent the whole of the week before Christmas with the king, and on 27 December, in a document entitled *Result of the King's Council of State*, he finally pronounced on the central questions in public debate since September. The third estate in the Estates-General was to be doubled. The advice of the Notables was therefore rejected, and the public pressure built up over the autumn had triumphed. The Notables had also opposed allowing deputies to be elected for and by orders other than their own. This, too, Necker ignored, to the alarm of some third-estate supporters who feared that highly placed noble or clerical candidates might be elected by over-deferential commoners. But in one thing he followed the Notables. He did not concede vote by head. He expressed the hope that, once the Estates had met, they would agree to deliberate and vote in common; but it must be by their own free choice. In this way Necker was able to avoid alienating the first two orders while retaining the good will of the third. And so the popularity he craved so much remained unimpaired. But the price of this achievement was to leave a fundamental issue unresolved. Every elector casting his vote in the subsequent spring was aware that those he was helping to choose would need to confront it before they considered anything else.

The *Result of the Council* marked the end of the first phase in the electoral campaign. It had witnessed a transformation in the political atmosphere whose speed and scale astonished everyone. Since September public opinion had completely repolarized. The political consensus against despotism, which had exulted in the downfall of Brienne and Lamoignon and brought Necker to new peaks of public idolatry, still existed; but constitutional questions had now been pushed into the background by social ones, and on them the consensus had broken down. The bourgeoisie, hitherto mere spectators in public life, had suddenly realized that they were being offered a permanent role in it, and that by their own efforts they might make it a dominant role. But in the process all their latent resentments and antagonisms towards what were now always described as the privileged orders were aroused and inflamed. Not all those involved in this campaign were members of the third estate. Most of Duport's society certainly were not. But in their own orders such people remained a minority, and the ferocity of the anti-noble and anti-clerical sentiments soon being widely expressed ensured that they made few further converts. Instead, alarmed nobles and clerics sought protection in the very precedents and privileges that educated commoners were now finding so obnoxious. Bourgeois fury at their intransigence then redoubled. It found its most eloquent expression in January 1789 in Sieyès's pamphlet *What is the Third Estate?* which argued that there was no place in a properly constituted nation for privileged groups of any sort. The third estate, which had hitherto counted for nothing in the political order, was in fact everything; for a nation, Sieyès declared, was a body of associates living under a common law, and privileges by definition were exceptions to common law. The nobility were a caste of idle, burdensome usurpers, and there should be no question of allowing them to be chosen as third-estate deputies. Sieyès refused completely to believe in the good faith of nobles who had renounced fiscal privileges, pointing to a whole range of others they had not offered up. He suggested that the third-estate deputies, once elected, should set themselves up without further ado as a national assembly, and have no dealings with the other two orders. By now, indeed, it was a commonplace for the third-estate cause to be called national; and 'patriotism', which ever since the crisis of 1771 had meant opposition to despotic government, was increasingly taken over as a label for third-estate aspirations.

   *What is the Third Estate?* was only the most eloquent among hundreds of no less vehement pamphlets denouncing the privileged orders appearing over the winter. And events in certain provinces seemed to bear out all their worst predictions. In Brittany the news of the *Result of the Council* became known as the third-estate deputies were arriving for the estates. They promptly agreed to transact no business until reform of the estates was accepted by the other two orders. The nobility, who had flocked in in unprecedented numbers for such an important meeting, refused all compromise, and on 3 January a royal order suspended proceedings for a month to allow tempers to cool. The nobility, enraged, continued to deliberate, in the teeth of bitter and increasingly violent denunciations from most of the province's major towns. When the aristocratic parlement of Rennes forbade illicit municipal assemblies it was ignored, and some of its staunchest traditional supporters, the city's law students, forsook it to join in the demands for reform of the estates. In an ill-judged attempt to exploit popular animosity towards the well-heeled bourgeois who led the reform movement, certain nobles set their chairmen, servants, and other dependants to organizing demonstrations against reform. On 26 January a vast crowd was assembled in the city centre calling for the maintenance of the Breton constitution and a lowering of the price of bread. It was attacked by bands of patriotic students, and several days of fighting culminated in the nobility being besieged in their meeting hall. In the end they fought their way out, sword in hand, and several people were killed. By the beginning of February the tumults had subsided somewhat; but the estates had achieved nothing, all hope of reconciliation between nobles and third estate in Brittany had gone; and the whole country had witnessed nobles prepared to fight rather than abandon their privileges.

These months also witnessed the emergence of third-estate leaders. Before November 1788 there had hardly been any. Only the names of the foremost Grenoble patriots, Mounier and Barnave, were widely known, and the campaign for doubling the third and vote by head had to be launched and orchestrated by the metropolitan aristocrats of Duport's society. But once launched it was soon beyond the society's control, and commoners began to speak for themselves. They wrote pamphlets: Volney's periodical *La Sentinelle du Peuple* did much to articulate and focus bourgeois grievances in Brittany, in the south the burden of generations of civil disabilities inspired the pen of the protestant pastor Rabaut de Saint-Étienne, while Robespierre's first foray into politics was his appeal *To the Artesian Nation* to abandon the archaic and privilege-ridden structure of the provincial estates of Artois. They organized town meetings and drafted petitions to local, provincial, and central authorities. In Brittany the patriots of Nantes and other cities marshalled bands of volunteers to go to Rennes to fight the 'iron swords'. And setting the pace of this activity almost everywhere were lawyers. 'Everything would have been calm in Franche Comté', a bitter Besançon nobleman confided to his diary,[4] 'if ten advocates had been hanged.' Ever since the end of the first Assembly of Notables the constitutional crisis had revolved around an attempt to browbeat the courts, raising issues to which no lawyer could remain indifferent. And once the Estates-General were won, the problem of their composition was a lawyer's paradise. Besides, petty judges and advocates were the only members of the third estate with wide experience of public life, and the confidence to speak out which it bred. Such men expected their talents to be recognized and drawn upon in the new political order, resenting any suggestion of limiting their opportunities. Noble insistence on maintaining political privileges reminded them of the pride and arrogance of aristocratic magistrates whom they had all encountered in their professional lives, qualified to sit in judgement not by ability and knowledge, but by birth and wealth. The annals of judicial life in the later eighteenth century were littered with quarrels and clashes between bench and bar, petty and sovereign courts, whose legacy of bitterness, hitherto accepted as one of the unavoidable tribulations of the calling, now surfaced. Further occasions for such antagonisms to work themselves out were provided by the elections of the spring.

The system by which the deputies of 1789 were chosen was extremely complex. Regulations issued on 24 January prescribed that the basic constituencies should be the ancient *bailliage* and *sénéchaussée* jurisdictions. In order to ensure a rough parity of size and population, however, smaller (or 'secondary') *bailliages* and *sénéchaussées* were grouped. There were other exceptions, too. Eight major towns, including Lyons, Rouen, and Paris itself, were accorded separate representation. A number of small districts not granted separate representation initially were also accorded it later after petitions of protest. The greatest exception of all was the treatment of certain *pays d'états*. The regulation of 24 January effectively ended agitation for reforming or reviving provincial estates by making clear that they would not, contrary to earlier expectations, be the means of electing the national deputies. Nevertheless it was thought prudent to allow this right to the newly constituted estates of Dauphiné, and those of the technically distinct kingdom of Navarre. Brittany might have won it too, had it not been for the bitter quarrels that had marked the last attempts to convene the estates. After that it was decided to elect the Breton third-estate deputies by *bailliages*, the nobility and clergy choosing theirs in special assemblies representing the whole province.

With these exceptions, each of the 234 constituencies was to have an electoral assembly for each order. Every noble enjoying full transmissible nobility was entitled to participate in the noble assemblies, as was every beneficed clergyman in the clerical ones. Monasteries and chapters, however, were only allowed elected representatives; and the very numbers of the third estate made indirect representation the only possibility. Accordingly, every male taxpayer over 25 had the right to attend a primary assembly, which chose two delegates for every hundred households to sit in the assembly electing the ultimate third-estate deputies. Each constituency was to be represented in the Estates-General by two clerical, two noble, and four third-estate deputies, and choosing them was the main function of the electoral assemblies. But they were also required by tradition to draw up *cahiers*, or grievance-lists, to guide the deputies in their deliberations. In the third estate every village and every urban guild and corporation was entitled to send one in, and they were conflated at the local electoral assembly into a single *cahier* for the order. Inevitably in this process many of the concerns of the king's poorer subjects were edited out. In many districts the ultimate text of *cahiers* was transparently based on models carefully put together and circulated by patriotic activists. Nevertheless the *cahiers* produced a picture of the outlook and preoccupations of a whole nation unique in Europe before the twentieth century. And the very fact of being asked to articulate their grievances and aspirations (with the implicit promise of redress) concentrated the minds of everybody involved on the seriousness of what was at stake. Throughout 1788 popular involvement in public affairs had been unprecedented, but still confined to a few major cities. The drafting of the *cahiers* drew in people throughout the country. The elections of 1789 were the most democratic spectacle ever seen in the history of Europe, and nothing comparable occurred again until far into the next century.

Nor did the government make any serious attempts to influence the outcome. It was rumoured that ministers hoped to use the diplomatic embarrassments created by Mirabeau's scurrilous *Histoire Secrète de la Cour de Berlin*, published in January, to prevent its notorious author from being elected; but if that was so they failed. Necker in any case thought that government interference in the elections would do more harm than good, creating bad blood in an assembly that ought to be inspired by goodwill. And yet the very rules he laid down affected the results in important ways. They ensured that the electoral assemblies of the first estate were dominated by parish priests rather than members of the ecclesiastical corporations who had hitherto monopolized the government of the Church. They excluded from the second-estate assemblies all new nobles whose status had not yet become fully hereditary, and swamped formerly dominant groups, such as courtiers and sovereign court magistrates, with petty nobles of long lineage, slender means, and little public experience. And the indirect system adopted for the third estate effectively eliminated peasants, artisans, and everybody without abundant leisure from the stage at which deputies were chosen, while allowing the election of members of the other two orders.

The Estates-General were summoned to meet at Versailles on 27 April, and the elections ordered to be completed by then. In the event the Estates did not convene until 5 May, and the last elections were not over until far into July. These late elections, including those of Paris which were only completed in May, were influenced by the course of events in the body to which they were electing. But most went forward in March and April, and their background was continual pamphleteering, prolonged cold weather, and a slowly rising level of popular discontent as the harvest shortfalls of the previous summer pushed bread prices inexorably upwards, and the attendant industrial crisis swelled the ranks of the unemployed. Incidents were reported from all over the country of market-day riots, popular price-fixing, and ransacking of barns, warehouses, monasteries, and country houses where hoarding of grain and flour was suspected. In Provence there was also widespread refusal to pay tithes or taxes, and at Marseilles men of property became so alarmed at the inability of the established authorities to maintain order that on 23 March electors of all three estates combined to take over the city's government and set up a 'patriotic guard' of substantial citizens. It was an idea with an important future nationally, but at this stage many found the overthrow of legitimate authorities shocking.

In any case, though stretched, the normal forces of law and order still seemed capable of preventing popular passions from boiling over completely. This was most graphically shown when, late in April, disorder reached Paris. The outbreak was precipitated by electoral excitement following the first meetings of the sixty districts in which members of the capital's third-estate electoral assembly were to be chosen, on 21 April. On the twenty-third, as the assembly of the Sainte-Marguérite district was discussing its *cahier*, one of its more prominent members, the wallpaper manufacturer Reveillon, remarked that the price of bread ought to be brought down to levels that wage-earners on 15 *sous* a day could afford. Reveillon was well known for his benevolence towards the unemployed, but in the highly charged atmosphere of the occasion his words were interpreted as a call for wage reductions. Similar remarks by Henriot, a saltpetre manufacturer, in another electoral assembly had the same effect. Over the next few days rumours of wage reductions swept the faubourg Saint-Antoine, the capital's working east end, and on the twenty-seventh Henriot's house was sacked by angry crowds. In response, troops posted in the district were reinforced, but the next day they were swamped by several thousand rioters who stormed Reveillon's house and factory and destroyed everything in them. In the evening a strong detachment of the French Guards was brought in and opened fire; after two hours of further tumult the crowd dispersed leaving twenty-five dead and almost as many more wounded. Rumour magnified the casualties to hundreds, and there was much dark talk of plots. This was the atmosphere that greeted the deputies now arriving at Versailles for the opening of the Estates. The rioters were known to have cheered the names of the king, of Necker, and the third estate. But they had also shouted 'down with the rich!' as they sacked prominent citizens' property, and the full force of authority had been deployed too late to prevent them. The capital must have appeared to the deputies even more disturbed than their native provinces.

Who then were these men, in whom the boundless hopes and expectations aroused by months of frenzied debate and discussion were invested? What sort of deputies had the elections produced? The first-estate deputation represented a clear defeat for the established Church hierarchy. Amost two-thirds of the 303 clerical deputies elected were ordinary parish priests. Only 51 were bishops; so that the nobles, canons, and regulars who had hitherto controlled all the levers of power in the Church were exposed as lacking the confidence of their subordinates. The clerical *cahiers* reinforced this impression, with demands for higher stipends, abolition of tithe impropriation, unrestricted access to diocesan administrative posts, canonries, and bishoprics, and church government by elected synods. Third-estate propagandists had campaigned hard for such results, and welcomed them as a sign that the clergy would be sympathetic in the Estates to the 'patriotic' cause. They paid less attention to issues on which the clergy were united: the need to retain and indeed increase the Church's control over education, to maintain censorship against the impieties of the Enlightenment, and to limit the toleration enjoyed by Protestants. In return for the surrender of their fiscal privileges, the clergy expected that the new order would confirm and reinforce the authority of the Catholic Church within the nation. The clerical consensus on these matters far outweighed the order's internal disagreements about the position of parish priests, but such deeper solidarities escaped the notice of most observers in the excitement of the elections. Their true importance would only emerge at a later stage, as yet scarcely foreseen by anybody.

In the case of the nobility, too, the elections brought rejection of groups hitherto taken for leaders of the order. Courtiers expected almost automatic election. ('Most of the young Nobility', reported the Duke of Dorset on 19 February,[5] 'are . . . quitting this Capital, ambitious of being deputed to the great National Assembly.') But once in the long-unvisited provinces where their estates lay, they frequently found themselves bitterly opposed by local squires resentful of their lofty ways. Often they were returned with great difficulty, although in the end they did better than the bishops in the clerical order, securing around a third of the representation. Among them were the Duke d'Orléans, and several members of the Society of Thirty such as Lafayette. On the other hand the elections were a complete disaster for the robe nobility of the sovereign courts. Only twenty-two members of this proud, articulate, and self-confident oligarchy secured seats, although they included heroes of the 1788 struggles like Duport, Fréteau, and d'Eprémesnil. The majority of the 282 deputies returned were petty provincial noblemen whose only previous experience of public life, if they had any at all, had been in the army. Like the parish clergy, they recognized that they were being presented with a unique opportunity to vent the frustrations and resentments of generations, and many of the noble electoral assemblies were extremely stormy. Some split, returned rival lists of deputies, and drew up rival *cahiers*. The nobility of Brittany, outraged that their province's delegation was not to be returned by its estates, voted to boycott the elections, and no Breton nobles ever sat in the Estates-General.

Noble *cahiers* reflected their authors' disarray. Only on agreement to give up all fiscal privileges was there near unanimity. A mere 8 per cent of *cahiers*, it is true, called for voting by head in the Estates; but the number insisting on vote by order on all occasions barely exceeded 40 per cent, the rest being prepared from one form or another of compromise. Nobility, almost 40 per cent thought, should be the reward of services and talent rather than riches; but no other question rallied opinion on a comparable scale. After the Estates met, the noble deputies would polarize into a 'liberal' minority of around ninety who were prepared to seek ways of coming to terms with third-estate aspirations, and an intransigent majority. The liberals tended to be younger, more urban, better travelled, and better read; but they were drawn, like their opponents, from right across the social spectrum of the nobility. The second order in the State, therefore, came to the political tests of 1789 in confusion. Prepared and in many ways eager for change, they were nevertheless unnerved by the hostility towards them that had sprung up since the autumn; and, torn apart by internal resentments and snobberies far more complex than those affecting the clergy, they had none of the first order's deeper unity to fall back on. For all its impressive combination of wealth, power, and place, the French nobility was far weaker, less well organized, and less self-confident than its third-estate opponents imagined. These disadvantages were fully mirrored by the deputies sent to represent it at Versailles.

The third-estate deputies, by contrast, were remarkably homogeneous and united. No peasants or artisans got beyond the first electoral stage, when the minority who voted at all (in Paris, even, only a quarter of the 50,000 or so electors chose to exercise their right) tended to be people of some education and leisure, and to prefer others like themselves. Those who went to the secondary assemblies, not to mention those finally returned for the Estates-General, were expected to pay their own expenses. More important still, the elections were inevitably dominated by people experienced in public speaking, handling meetings, and drafting documents. This meant above all the lawyers and office-holders who had been so conspicuous in all the public agitation since September 1788. Two-thirds of those elected had some form or other of legal qualifications. A quarter were advocates or notaries, among them people like Barnave and Robespierre. Forty-three per cent (278) were holders of venal offices, including many senior judges from *bailliage* and *sénéchaussée* courts who had been entrusted by electoral regulations with the organization of the third-estate assemblies. In contrast there were only 85 deputies involved in trade or industry. Only 9 members of the other two orders benefited from Necker's decision to allow electors to choose outside their orders, although they included Sieyès from the clergy and Mirabeau from the nobility. But although the third-estate contingent boasted these and other celebrities who had come to public notice during the struggles of the preceding two years—men like Mounier, the leader of the Dauphiné patriots, Target the pride of the Parisian bar, and eminent scientists like the astronomer Bailly—most of the deputies were unknown and untested outside their own localities. Apart from their similar social and educational background, what united them more than anything was their commitment to voting by head and civil and fiscal equality. Any doubts about this commitment did not survive the first days of the Estates' meeting.

The opening session of the Estates-General eventually took place on 5 May, amid great pomp and ceremonial. After a solemn service of dedication the afternoon before, the three orders processed to the largest hall in Versailles in the costume dictated by precedent—the clergy in their vestments, the nobility in silk, swords, cloth-of-gold waistcoats, and white-plumed hats, and the third in sober black. Huge and expectant crowds watched the parade, and it would probably have been impossible for any of the opening speeches to match the hopes placed in them. But nobody had expected to be bored, which was what the speeches of the Keeper of the Seals and Necker achieved. The former was completely inaudible; and the latter's voice gave out half an hour into his three-hour oration, which then had to be read out for him. Nor, despite repeated bursts of enthusiastic applause, were the issues on everybody's mind squarely addressed. While insisting that the Estates had not been convoked for reasons of financial necessity, Necker nevertheless concentrated most of his remarks on fiscal and budgetary matters. He promised royal and ministerial support for a whole range of administrative and judicial reforms, although he hinted that in the last resort the king would retain the power to reject measures he did not like. But on the question of voting he continued to sit on the fence. While recommending common voting on the most momentous or urgent issues, he declared that on others vote by order might be more appropriate; and in any case the question must be settled not by authority, but by the free agreement of the clergy and nobility to give up vote by order. They could only do this by first convening separately to verify the election returns of their respective orders. Over the preceding week the air had been full of far from groundless rumours that a party at Court led by Artois and the queen were pressing for Necker's dismissal; and shrewder members of his audience guessed that in drafting the speech the minister had not enjoyed a free hand. But most—on all sides—were disappointed by his equivocations, and extremists left the hall determined to settle the question of verification clearly before any other business was transacted.

The struggle began the next morning. Amid the confusion and hesitations of deputies still unfamiliar with each other and awed by the momentousness of what they were involved in, men who knew clearly what they wanted made the running. In the third estate representatives from Brittany and Dauphiné, whose provincial political experience over preceding months was far wider than that of others, argued that separate verification would inevitably lead to separate voting too. It must therefore be opposed. After a prolonged and chaotic debate the third (whose idea of themselves was reflected in their adoption of the tendentious title, 'the Commons') agreed not to verify any of their powers, or indeed transact any business at all, in isolation. The nobility, meanwhile, showed no hesitation. On 7 May they voted by 188 votes to 46 to proceed with separate verification. By the eleventh it was complete, and the order declared itself constituted. The clergy, too, voted to proceed with separate verification, but only after lengthy debate, and only by 133 votes to 114. Nor, when the process was complete, did they go so far as to declare themselves constituted. Earnest and sincere ministers of the gospel as most of them were, they hoped to find some harmonious compromise. And so they welcomed a deputation sent by the third on 7 May asking for tripartite discussions about common verification and called upon the nobility to do the same. A week later the nobility agreed; but when the representatives of the three orders met they found the third's mandated to accept nothing but vote by head. Responding in kind, the nobles argued that all the precedents were against common verification, and on 26 May they withdrew from the talks. The third, now reinforced by the arrival of deputies from Paris, thereupon renewed its appeals to the clergy, inviting them 'in the name of the God of peace and the national interest, to join with them in the general assembly hall, and there act in concert to bring about union and concord'. As the clergy agonized over this further assault on their conscience, on the twenty-ninth the king himself intervened to condemn the inaction of the Estates. He urged resumption of conciliatory talks, and they were resumed, but with no more positive result than before. Meanwhile, on 4 June, the heir to the throne died, plunging the king into days of gloomy inertia which paralysed all ministerial activity. By the second week of the month third-estate patience was running out. Against their previous resolutions, they had already begun to organize themselves and establish procedures, and on 3 June they elected Bailly as their president. There was now constant talk of unilateral action, of declaring the 'Commons' to be the national assembly, and of proceeding to verification of powers on that basis without further reference to the other two orders. On 10 June this talk at last culminated in a formal motion, moved by Sieyès, that a final appeal should be sent to the other two orders to join at once in common verification. Failing that, the Commons would proceed anyway. The motion was carried by 493 votes to 41. The message was transmitted the next day; and when, on the twelfth, no response was received from the other two orders, the roll-call began.

With it began the true revolutionary struggle. If the king had authorized vote by head the previous December, or if the nobility and clergy had agreed to common verification when the Estates had first met, all would have been in order, and the chain of the law remained unbroken. The time they waited before 'cutting the cable' (in Sieyès's phrase) shows how reluctant the law-soaked deputies of the third were to flout legality. For to declare themselves the only legitimate body of national representatives without reference to the other two orders was in effect to take the law into their own hands. They recognized, too, that there was no going back. The decision was taken in public, for unlike the other two orders the third had admitted spectators from the very beginning, and as the stalemate continued the numbers flocking daily from Paris to Versailles steadily increased. There was no support among these onlookers for the nobility or the clergy, whereas every intransigent speech in the 'Commons' was greeted with wild applause. Pleas for caution and restraint from the minority who still clung to dwindling hopes of agreement were drowned with jeers and catcalls.

Nor is there much doubt that the unruly crowds at Versailles represented a much wider public opinion, aroused by months of frenzied publicity and now by daily newspaper accounts of what the Estates-General were doing, or rather not doing. Leading this field were Mirabeau's *Letters to his Constituents*, in which one of the most prominent deputies produced regular and accurate (though scarcely unbiased) reports of everything that happened in the great assembly. Nobody had trusted

Mirabeau when the Estates began; but he soon demonstrated hitherto untried oratorical powers, and an unerring talent for expressing precisely what his fellow deputies were merely groping towards. Soon he was marshalling the thousands of subscribers to his journal behind the 'patriotic' cause, especially in Paris where the long-drawn-out elections also sustained the political temperature. And although the focus of political attention was obviously at Versailles, the forcing-house of political opinion was in the fashionable west end of the capital, in the arcades, cafés, and walks of the Palais Royal. Thrown open to the public as a pleasure garden in 1780 by its owner, the Duke d'Orléans, by 1789 it had become a centre for rumour, debate, and pamphleteering.

I went to the Palais-Royal [wrote Arthur Young on 9 June] to see what new things were published, and to procure a catalogue of all. Every hour produces something new. Thirteen came out today, sixteen yesterday, and ninety-two last week . . . one can scarcely squeeze from the door to the counter . . . Nineteen twentieths of these productions are in favour of liberty, and commonly violent against the clergy and nobility . . . But the coffee-houses in the Palais-Royal present yet more singular and astonishing spectacles; they are not only crowded within, but other expectant crowds are at the doors and windows, listening *à gorge déployée* to certain orators, who from chairs and tables harangue each his little audience. The eagerness with which they are heard, and the thunder of applause they receive for every sentiment of more than common hardiness or violence against the present government, cannot easily be imagined.[6]

What perhaps can be imagined is the excitement at Versailles when, on 13 June, as the deputies from Poitou were called, three parish priests presented their credentials. There was ecstatic applause. The long-strained solidarity of the clerical order had at last cracked; and over the next few days sixteen other clerics also broke ranks. But that left a problem once the roll-call was complete. Who did the deputies now speak for? Clearly they represented more than just the third. Sieyès, following the logic of his own *What is the Third Estate?*, believed they were already a fully fledged national assembly, and many of the more outspoken deputies agreed with him. But others feared that to take this title would blight still-lingering hopes of conciliation with the nobility and majority of the clergy, and on 15 June Sieyès tried to accommodate such reservations by moving that they call themselves 'Assembly of the known and verified representatives of the French Nation'. Two days of debate followed, producing formulations ever more tortuous and wordy, amid signs of growing impatience from the public galleries. It all played into Sieyès's hands, and by the seventeenth he felt able to propose the title he had always wanted. By then an overwhelming majority recognized that there was no sensible alternative, and the name National Assembly was adopted by 491 votes to 89. In the euphoria of that moment cool-headed radicals went even further. Target and Le Chapelier, the leading Breton deputy, proposed that all existing taxes be declared illegal but provisionally sanctioned until a new system could be devised. Authorization would lapse if ever the Assembly ceased to meet. The implications were clear, but carried unanimously. The Assembly was claiming sovereignty, and inviting taxpayers to defy any government which tried to dissolve it. The challenge now was not merely to the other two orders, but to royal authority itself. As the British ambassador (a duke) reported to his foreign secretary (another) the next day:[7] 'If His Majesty once gives His decided approbation of the proceedings, such as they have hitherto been, of the Tiers-Etat, it will be little short of laying His Crown at their feet.'

All the king's ministers and advisers recognized the danger; but they were divided over how to deal with it. Unknown to his master or Necker, the war minister began to reinforce the garrisons around Paris, a move welcomed by the queen and the Count d'Artois, who had been advocating strong measures for weeks. Necker, while disapproving of the third's assertion of sovereignty, believed that they must be conciliated. He proposed that the king hold a 'Royal Session' to reassert his authority while proposing a programme of popular concessions. The plan was agreed, but the draft speeches which Necker had prepared for the occasion were significantly modified in his absence by the queen and her party, and the decision to hold a Royal Session was not formally notified to any of the three orders before they arrived at their respective meeting places on the morning of Saturday 20 June, to find the doors locked and guarded by soldiers. On the previous day, the clergy had at last voted by a narrow majority to join the National Assembly, and the excited deputies arrived the next morning expecting to give them a triumphant reception. Locked doors and soldiers stunned them, and posters announcing the Royal Session for the following Monday merely aroused suspicion that a dissolution was imminent. Even those who had opposed the decisions of 17 June were outraged by this 'act of despotism',[8] and it became a point of principle to carry on meeting despite the royal prohibition. A nearby indoor tennis-court was commandeered, and there, with indignant crowds packing all approaches, the deputies took a solemn oath never to disperse until 'the constitution of the Realm and public regeneration are established and assured'. When, the following Monday, the Royal Session was postponed by a day, the Assembly made a point of sitting again. This time it was able to welcome the majority of the clergy and, to general jubilation, three noblemen from Dauphiné. The solidarity and determination of the other two orders was evidently now crumbling fast.

Nor did the Royal Session do anything to restore it. Necker, who over the weekend had taken elaborate steps to reassure the public that no dissolution was intended, felt compromised by the changes made to his plans in council, and ostentatiously stayed away. And when the king began, as in a *lit de justice* under what men were already starting to call the old order, by nullifying the decisions of 17 June, nobles were seen to smile and 'patriots' in all three orders prepared for the worst. In fact the programme put forward by the king was quite imaginative, and most observers agreed, at the time and later, that if it had been put forward in May it would have been generally acclaimed. In a thirty-five-point declaration he promised that in future no taxes and loans would be raised without the consent of the Estates-General, and that several unpopular taxes would be abolished or modified. He promised to abolish arbitrary imprisonment, forced labour on the roads, and serfdom. He announced the general establishment of provincial estates. But he also declared all feudal rights to be inviolable property, and he merely urged, and did not order, the nobility and clergy to give up their fiscal privileges. All this was preceded by a declaration that the three orders were sacrosanct. The first two were indeed exhorted to join with the third to discuss matters of common concern; and to ease the tender consciences of nobles who felt bound to separate deliberation by mandates from their electors, all binding mandates were declared invalid. But the nobility and clergy were accorded a veto on all matters concerning their particular interests and privileges; and spectators, who had done so much to encourage the third's boldness, were excluded from all future sessions. Unprecedented numbers of troops surrounded the meeting hall that day, and the king concluded the proceedings with an overt threat. Nothing the Estates did, he declared, was valid without his approval. If they refused to co-operate, he would 'see to the wellbeing of my peoples' alone, considering himself their only true representative. Then he ordered the deputies to disperse, and resume deliberations, separately, the next day.

What happened next proved a turning-point. As nobles and clerics obediently filed out of the hall, the third, and the clergy who had joined them over the previous few days, stood their ground. When the Grand Master of Ceremonies reiterated the king's orders, Mirabeau declared that nothing but bayonets could force the National Assembly to move. There was a general shout of approval, and the Assembly went on to renew the Tennis Court Oath, reiterate all it had done since the seventeenth and declare its members inviolable. The king, meanwhile, had emerged from the Royal Session to be confronted with Necker's resignation. So distracted was he that, when told that the third estate was refusing to move, he said they might stay. As in a previous Royal Session on 19 November 1787, with one word a whole strategy was thrown away. Later that night Necker was persuaded to withdraw his resignation, but by then news of his absence from the Royal Session had reached Paris, and been taken as a sign of his dismissal. The Palais Royal exploded.

The ferment in Paris [noted Young the next day] is beyond conception; 10,000 people have been all this day in the Palais Royal . . . To my surprise, the King's propositions are received with universal disgust . . . the people seem, with a sort of frenzy, to reject all idea of compromise, and to insist on the necessity of the orders uniting . . . They are also full of suspicions at M. Necker's offering to resign, to which circumstance they seem to look more than to much more essential points.[9]

Volatile crowds also roamed the streets of Versailles and burst into the palace past troops who offered no resistance. When Necker appeared he was hailed as father of the people, and grandiloquently promised he would not abandon them; but known opponents of the patriotic cause were mobbed, jostled, and had the windows of their lodgings broken. Troops saved the archbishop of Paris from being lynched, but boasted of doing so without firing an unpatriotic shot. In Paris on the twenty-fourth two companies of the French Guards, the same regiment that had shot down the Reveillon rioters two months beforehand, refused public-order duties. 'Who could prevent this disorder?', wrote a worried, though not unpatriotic, Parisian on the twenty-fifth.[10] 'The police has no strength and no credit.'

   Yet these events brought victory to the National Assembly. The king's failure to respond to their defiance and the massive popular backing they obviously enjoyed were enough for all but a handful of the remaining separate clergy. On the twenty-fourth most of them came over. Ever since the seventeenth Orléans and a minority of other nobles had been trying to persuade their own order to agree to common verification. On the twenty-fourth they made one last effort, to no avail. The next day forty-eight of them appeared in what was now being called the 'National Hall'. Forty or fifty more were plainly on the point of following them. Clearly the king could no longer rely on the first two orders to obey him, and the wavering of the French Guards suggested that even force might fail. In these circumstances he made the final surrender. On 27 June he wrote to the presidents of the clerical and noble orders ordering them to join the National Assembly. A few felt betrayed, and tried to protest, but even they soon recognized that they had no choice. And when that news broke, there were huge displays of popular jubilation and fireworks in both Paris and

Versailles. The king and queen, appearing in tears on the balcony of the palace, were cheered deafeningly. 'The whole business now seems over', Authur Young wrote,[11] 'and the revolution complete.'

Deputies on all sides certainly hoped so, and there was now much talk of getting down to business and constructing a constitution. Everybody, even third-estate deputies, had been unnerved by the scale and vigour of the popular ferment unleashed over the preceding fortnight. Responsible men now looked forward to a period of dignified calm, allowing a return to normality and social harmony. Yet as July began there was little sign of that. On 30 June a crowd of 4,000 stormed a prison on the left bank where ten mutinous French Guards were awaiting transfer to closer confinement. They released them, carried them back in triumph to the Palais Royal, and fêted them with a public collection. Such incidents suggested that the ferment was far from over. Despite the euphoric scenes of 27 June, suspicion of the Court's motives was still widespread and profound. What was more, it was justified. On 26 June four regiments were ordered from the frontiers to the Paris region, and around the same time the king asked the veteran Marshal de Broglie to assume supreme command. On 1 July more troops were ordered up, making a fivefold increase, to well over 20,000, in less than a week. Nobody could fail to notice the build-up, or the number of foreign regiments involved, presumed to be more reliable than French ones. On 8 July Mirabeau moved a motion in the Assembly that the king be petitioned to withdraw the soldiers, and nobody spoke against it. The king's bland reply was that their presence was necessary to preserve public order. It seems clear, however, that their true purpose was what everyone suspected: to intimidate Paris and reverse concessions made since mid-June. At Court, the queen and Artois remained determined to get rid of Necker. Persuading him to stay on 23 June had been a temporary necessity in their eyes, but they continued to try to exclude him from all important decisions while they cast about for more pliable replacements. By 11 July they thought they had found them. That afternoon, the minister was presented with a royal letter dismissing him and ordering him to leave the country immediately. He complied at once, shocked though he was. Three other ministers fell the next day; Broglie became minister of war and Breteuil, an old rival of Calonne and a known authoritarian, was made chief of the Council. Precisely what the new ministry intended to do is not clear. For once the news of Necker's fall broke, it scarcely had time to do anything.

The changes could hardly have been more ill timed. Everybody was frightened and unnerved by two weeks of troop movements. As 12 July was a Sunday, nobody was at work. Above all, the food shortages and high prices which had been foreseeable since the previous summer were reaching their peak, the dangerous midsummer weeks between the exhaustion of old stocks and the harvesting of new. Necker, of course, stood for control of the grain trade and subsidized bread prices. Over the spring he had fought a losing battle to keep Paris cheaply supplied, but one consequence was to drain other markets, and May was marked by bread riots all over Flanders, Artois, Picardy, and Normandy. News of them did much to persuade conscience-stricken clergy to break ranks and join the third in June, so that some action might be taken. But by the time the orders merged, disturbances were occurring much closer to the capital, and early in July news arrived that at Lyons riots against high prices had culminated in the destruction of the city's ring of toll-gates. Between 4 and 7 July the Assembly debated the grain trade, although inconclusively, since most deputies believed it ought to be free but given the popular mood were reluctant to say so. And meanwhile bread prices in Paris crept up towards their highest level in twenty years.

News of Necker's dismissal reached the Palais Royal in the afternoon of the twelfth. Everyone sensed that a decisive trial of strength had begun. At once crowds flocked to the theatres and forced them to close as a sign of mourning. Later in the day groups milling in the Tuileries gardens were set upon by German cavalry who had been ordered to clear the area. It looked like the beginning of the long-dreaded military action; and although, after some uncertain skirmishing, the troops withdrew at nightfall, the whole city was by then frantically trying to arm itself. And once armed, the populace did not hesitate to act. That night, following the example from Lyons, they attacked the toll-gates around the city and broke down sections of the customs wall. The night sky was lit up by fires which destroyed most of the gatehouses. The next morning they turned their attention to places where arms were thought to be stored, starting with the abbey of Saint-Lazare. Blackest popular suspicions were confirmed when substantial stocks of grain were also found there, and the monastery was looted amid ominous scenes of sacrilege and anti-clericalism. Men of property were now seriously alarmed. The preceding Saturday the electors of Paris, who had continued to meet unofficially after their electoral duties had been discharged late in May, had already agreed to set up a citizens' militia to maintain order when troops could not be trusted. Now they hurried to activate their decision, and by the evening of the thirteenth patrols were out. 'But', wrote a member of one of them,[12] 'we made a sorry showing; we could not contain the people's fury; if we had gone too far, they would have exterminated us. It is not the moment to reason with them.'

On the morning of the fourteenth it was the turn of the Invalides, the military veterans' hospital, where cannon were found as well as small arms. They were dragged across the city to the place de Grève, in front of the Hôtel de Ville. From there it was only a few hundred yards to the most formidable of all arsenals, the towering state prison of the Bastille. Here was the next obvious place to search, but it did not seem possible to storm such a fortress, and nobody knew until afterwards how poorly manned and defended it was. So first the electors tried to negotiate a handover. But when impatient crowds forced an entry to the inner courtyard the garrison panicked and opened fire, killing almost a hundred. Now military expertise intervened. Discipline in the French Guards regiment had never recovered after the mutinies and desertions of the last week in June. New defections, followed by bibulous celebrations in the Palais Royal, were reported daily. But experience had not gone the way of discipline, and French Guards now appeared before the Bastille with the cannon brought from the Invalides. The drawbridge and gates could not have withstood them at point-blank range, and the governor knew it. The Bastille surrendered.

During all this time the Assembly was sitting at Versailles, and as the news from the capital filtered in they issued ever more anguished appeals to the king to pull back the troops. He countered initially that in the circumstances the troops were more necessary than ever. But then, on the afternoon of the fifteenth, he came to the Assembly in person to declare that he was ordering the army encamped around Paris to disperse. The delirious deputies cheered him, threw their hats in the air, and escorted him in a body back to the palace, where the tearful scenes of 27 June were re-enacted. There was much talk of his natural goodness and concern for the well-being of his peoples. But it was not that which had produced such a spectacular change of policy. Throughout the thirteenth and fourteenth the army had indeed been poised to restore order in Paris, and there were enough troops to do it, even if the carnage would have been fearful. But the example of the French Guards was disquieting. Might other regiments follow their example? Morale was certainly under pressure from forced marches, poor quarters, and constant appeals by anxious civilians not to act against defenceless patriots. Commanders were increasingly reluctant to put their men's discipline to the test, and Broglie was too experienced an officer to take risks in such circumstances. He advised the king that he could no longer rely on his army.

Louis XVI's acceptance of that advice marked the end of royal authority. The monarch recognized that he no longer had the power to enforce his will. He was therefore compelled finally to accept all that had been done since mid-June. The Estates-General had gone. They had been replaced by a single National Assembly with no distinction of orders, claiming sovereignty in the name of the nation, and a mission to endow France with a constitution. For four tense weeks the queen, Artois, and their coterie had plotted and schemed to reverse these achievements. Ultimately they were foiled by a wave of popular support for the stand taken by the third estate and fellow-travellers in the other two orders, an atmosphere so intoxicating that the very forces the Court was calling up to contain it were infected. The storming of the Bastille marked the climax of the movement. Challenged by it, Louis XVI drew back, leaving the people of Paris convinced that they alone had saved the National Assembly from destruction. Henceforth they would see themselves as guardians of the liberty won that day. This was no ordinary revolt, as the Duke de La Rochefoucauld-Liancourt is reputed, perhaps apocryphally, to have told Louis XVI. Apocryphal or not, it was still true. This was a Revolution.

# 5

# The Principles of 1789
# and the Reform of France

Royal authority had evaporated. Nobody could misread the signs of that in the days following Louis XVI's decision to pull back his troops. Early on 17 June the Count d'Artois left Versailles for the north-east frontier, to be followed over subsequent weeks by many of the courtiers who had supported his intrigues. Their emigration clearly showed that for the moment they thought the royal cause lost. And later the same day the king made his way, escorted only by a handful of deputies, to the Hôtel de Ville of Paris to confirm that the troops were withdrawing and announce that Necker had been recalled. He also confirmed the nomination of Bailly as mayor of Paris (a new title) and Lafayette as commander of the new citizens' militia, now being called the National Guard. It was said that 150,000 armed citizens were on the streets that day, all wearing cockades in red and blue, the colours both of the city and the Duke d'Orléans. Later in the month Lafayette would splice them with Bourbon white for the uniform of his National Guardsmen, and so the patriotic tricolour was born. The king accepted a cockade and stuck it in his hat on arrival at the Hôtel de Ville; and then, for the first time, people began to cheer him. Just along the road, a contractor was already setting his workmen to demolish the Bastille.

But the excitement and tension of that week did not evaporate so easily. The price of bread remained high, supplies uncertain, and rumours of starvation plots were readily believed. Violence against those suspected of opposing the patriotic cause was all too tempting a response for a populace that on the fourteenth had hacked the governor of the Bastille to pieces and massacred the city's chief magistrate, Flesselles, who had delayed the issue of arms. Their heads were paraded through the streets on pikes. On the twenty-second Bertier de Sauvigny, intendant of Paris, was caught trying to emigrate and brought back to the city. He and his father-in-law Foulon, who had briefly accepted office in Breteuil's ill-fated ministry, were lynched and decapitated under suspicion of trying to starve the city the previous week. A few public men, carried away by the excitement, attempted to justify these killings. Barnave, in a phrase that was to dog the rest of his career, asked what was so pure about the blood shed. But most educated onlookers were appalled by such scenes of unbridled savagery. Lafayette, feeling that the newly established National Guard should have prevented them, tried to resign his command, but was pressed from all sides to stay on. Feeble though it was, the citizens' militia was the only public force patriots trusted, and it needed to be reliably led and organized in these formative days. News now pouring in from the provinces only reinforced this conviction.

Arthur Young, who had left Paris on 28 June convinced that the Revolution was over, was told in Nancy on 15 July that provincial towns would not stir until they knew what Paris had done. But in other places the established authorities had already been challenged for failing to deal with bread shortages. The militia set up in Marseilles in March was soon imitated in other southern towns, and in the last days of June, as the constitutional struggle at Versailles hung in the balance, many municipal authorities came under increasing pressure from electors or self-appointed notables for failing to take precautionary steps against the dual threat of popular violence and despotism's revenge. News of Necker's dismissal made the movement general, and in most of the kingdom's major towns the third week of July saw the establishment of revolutionary committees which either supplanted the old authorities or worked alongside them, monitoring their every move. Usually they assumed power amid scenes of riot. In Strasbourg the town hall was sacked. In Rouen grain stores were pillaged and textile workers smashed spinning-jennies. In Rennes soldiers refused to defend the citadel and joined crowds who drove their commander out of the city. Everywhere there were calls for cheaper bread, and in some places people denounced all taxes. The self-appointed committees of this municipal revolution made it their first priority to contain the effervescence, and citizens' militias were hurriedly set up everywhere. Subsequently they busied themselves with securing grain supplies, and not least with sending congratulatory addresses to the National Assembly on its providential escape from destruction. Prominent in these movements were the lawyers who had played such a central part in the spring elections; but all property owners were drawn together by the fear of anarchy, and in commercial and industrial centres businessmen threw themselves into political activity where they had earlier been mere tongue-tied onlookers. Nobles and clergy often proffered assistance too, but they were regarded as too close to the municipalities now being supplanted, and in any case the earlier intransigence of the noble and clerical deputies at Versailles threw suspicion on all those who had elected them. In Dijon nobles and clergy were put under precautionary house arrest. Nor was exclusion from local power the only blow the privileged orders were to suffer in these weeks. Even more serious was an attack on their authority in the countryside.

Rural unrest had been growing in many parts of the kingdom as the grain shortage worsened over the spring. Only the limitless hopes raised by the drafting of the *cahiers* and subsequent elections had held an anxious and hungry peasantry back from wholesale attacks on grain stores and defiance of the demands made by tax-, tithe-, and due-collectors. They clearly expected a spectacular lightening of their burdens. During the rumour-filled weeks of deadlock at Versailles the number of incidents increased, and tales of riots and tumults in Paris and other cities fanned rural impatience. News of the king's surrender to popular resistance broke all restraints. His acquiescence in the defeat of the privileged orders was taken as a signal to all his subjects to take their own measures against public enemies. The prolonged political crisis had spawned countless wild rumours of plots to thwart the patriotic cause by starving the people. Monastic and noble granaries, reputedly bulging with the proceeds of the previous season's rents, dues, and tithes, seemed obvious evidence of their owners' wicked intentions. Equally suspicious were urban merchants scouring country markets far beyond their usual circuits to provide bread for hungry townsmen. Besides, the roads were thronged with unprecedented numbers of men seeking work as a result of the slump. Farmers had good reason to dread the depredations of bands of travelling vagrants, and now took little persuading that the kingdom was alive with brigands in aristocratic pay. It was just a year since the notorious storms of July 1788, and as a promising harvest began to ripen country people were particularly nervous. All this produced the 'Great Fear', a massive panic that swept whole provinces in the last weeks of July and left only the most peripheral regions untouched. Peasants assembled, armed themselves, and prepared to fight off the ruthless hirelings of aristocracy. Seen from a distance, such armed bands were often taken for brigands themselves, and so the panic spread.

In many areas villagers did not wait for the marauders to arrive. Then it would be too late. They were determined to make sure of aristocratic defeat by striking pre-emptively. After all, they would only be anticipating what the Assembly was bound to decree. As one country priest explained, 'When the inhabitants heard that everything was going to be different they began

1. Louis XVI in full state robes

3. Necker, the Swiss wonder-worker

2. Vergennes, architect of the fateful
American War

4. Calonne, as Comptroller-General of
the Finances

5. The last chief minister of the Ancien
Régime: Loménie de Brienne

6. The Royal Session in the Parlement of Paris, 19 November 1787

7. Troops fire on the Reveillon rioters, April 1789

8. The Tennis Court Oath, 20 June 1789. David's commemorative picture

9. The attack on the Bastille, 14 July 1789

10. Sieyès in 1789, while still a priest

11. Lafayette at the height of his power: the festival of the Federation, 14 July 1790

12. Mirabeau, demagogue and royalist plotter

13. Barnave: Protestant, Patriot, Feuillant

14. The women of Paris march back from Versailles, October 1789

to refuse to pay both tithes and dues, considering themselves so permitted, they said, by the new law to come.'[1] In other places they raided barns to repossess what had already been paid, and in certain regions, such as western Normandy, Burgundy, Hainault, Alsace, Franche Comté, and Dauphiné, there were mass attacks on manor houses and castles. Even so there was little indiscriminate destruction or looting, except where lords offered resistance. The attackers made for the symbols of feudalism—dovecotes, seigneurial ovens and wine-presses, weather-vanes. Above all they made for muniment rooms, where terriers and other records of feudal obligations were held. The rooms were ransacked, their contents burned, and distantly glimpsed smoke palls from bonfires of legal papers made their own contributions to the general panic. When lords were in residence, they were often compelled to make formal renunciations of their rights. If they refused, or if their records were not found, whole buildings might be burned down. On 19 July intruders at the manor house of a particularly unpopular Franche Comté landlord at Quincey, near Vesoul, were blown up in a huge explosion which destroyed the building. Nobody blamed the intruders—it was assumed that this was the revenge any lord would take given the chance. News of the incident soon spread over all eastern France, constantly embroidered, and led to a new wave of sacking castles and rich abbeys which went on well into August.

Townsmen were appalled. Urban upheavals taking place simultaneously had done much to inflame the peasantry, but they were over fairly quickly, and citizens' militias seemed to have the situation in most towns under reasonable control. In some places they even felt safe enough to send their forces out into the surrounding countryside to restore order. But as yet they had little training or experience, nobody trusted regular troops, and remoter rural districts seemed completely out of control. From Paris and Versailles, with reports of riot, pillage, and arson pouring in from all points of the compass, the situation looked even worse. 'By letters from every province', declared the spokesman of the National Assembly's reports committee on 3 August,[2] 'it appears that properties of whatever sort are falling prey to the most disgraceful brigandage; on all sides castles are being burned, monasteries destroyed, farms given up to pillage. Taxes, payments to lords, all are destroyed; the law is powerless, magistrates without authority, and justice is a mere phantom sought from the courts in vain.' He moved a motion urging citizens to keep calm, and continue paying their taxes, tithes, and dues until the Assembly decreed a new order of things. But more radical members thought such an appeal unlikely to work without more tangible incentives. Deputies from Brittany, whose regular meetings to concert a common approach were winning them notice as the 'Breton Club', decided that a more spectacular act, 'a kind of magic' as one of them termed it, was required if public effervescence was to be calmed. The whole of feudalism, they thought, should be abolished in one grand gesture. It was going to happen anyway: *cahiers*, which another committee of the Assembly was now busily analysing, had demanded it. They persuaded the Duke d'Aiguillon, a rich young courtier of liberal views who had been active in the Committee of Thirty, to propose abolition as an amendment to the original motion. They timed his intervention for the evening of Tuesday 4 August when they expected a thin attendance in the chamber, but when the radical Breton Le Chapelier would be in the chair. It proved to be the most sweeping and radical legislative session of the whole French Revolution.

It began as chaotically as it was to continue. Before d'Aiguillon could speak another nobleman, the Viscount de Noailles, doubtless aware of what was afoot, came forward and moved his own version of abolition. D'Aiguillon could only support him, but the effect of two similar proposals coming in quick succession was to start an auction. Both had called for redemption of dues and abolition of serfdom and labour services; but others saw that feudalism did not end there. Hunting rights were soon being denounced, then private courts, then tolls. The original motion, and its purpose of calming the countryside, was soon lost sight of in a torrent of denunciations and renunciations, each carried by acclaim. The all-night session would be remembered as a display of boundless altruism and, as one nobleman carried away by emotion termed it, a 'moment of patriotic intoxication'.[3] But old scores were also settled amid the enthusiasm. Country nobles made sure that the courtiers who had deprived them of their manorial prerogatives did not escape with their pensions and sinecures. A bishop, it was noted, had been the first to denounce hunting rights, and this led an angry duke to call for an end to tithes. Vestry fees and pluralism soon went the same way, and by the time dawn broke the parish clergy had been stripped of much of their income. In the small hours the session developed into a general assault on privileges of all sorts. Representatives of corporate towns and whole provinces came forward to renounce liberties and exemptions accumulated over half a millennium. Magistrates abandoned the privileges of their offices, declared for free justice, and raised no demur when venality of office, the basis of their tenure, was thrown on to the bonfire in turn. Every public employment, the consensus was, would now be open to all according to their talents. Frenchmen would henceforth enjoy complete civil and fiscal equality. It was past two in the morning when the sitting came to a close with the deputies ordering a *Te Deum* to be sung throughout the kingdom, and the striking of a commemorative medal depicting themselves abandoning all privileges on one side, and Louis XVI, now proclaimed 'Restorer of French Liberty', on the other.

Nobody who was not there, Rabaut de Saint-Étienne later recalled, could know what this extraordinary session had been like. Even those who had been there had conflicting memories. Only scanty minutes had been kept; it took a week to draft all the decisions taken into a formal decree, and a further six months before all the technical details were settled. In cold legal language it all sounded, and was, less generous and expansive than it had seemed in the emotional candlelight of a summer night. The decree of 11 August began with a ringing declaration that 'The National Assembly entirely destroys the feudal regime'. What it actually did was lay down that most feudal dues were redeemable, and should continue to be collected until compensation was paid. They were, after all, property, just like the venal offices for which compensation was also laid down. Tithe, on the other hand, was abolished outright, despite protests from the clergy. Some deputies were heard to declare ominously that all ecclesiastical property ought to be at the disposal of the nation. Yet in the event it proved irrelevant whether compensation had been decreed or not. By 11 August peasants all over France had stopped paying both dues and tithes (not to mention taxes), and they took the decree as a vindication of their stand. They did not now intend to start paying again, on however limited a basis, and few of them did. It was they, rather than the National Assembly, who really destroyed the feudal regime by refusing to co-operate even in its orderly winding up. So the decree's most important effect, along with the need to get back into the fields to gather in the harvest, was simply to calm the countryside down; and by the end of the month the worst of the rural unrest and panic had died away.

But far more than feudalism had been cast aside on the night of 4 August. Privilege, that fundamental principle of social and institutional life since time immemorial, had been renounced. With it went the whole structure of provincial, local, and municipal government. For three centuries French social mobility had largely been channelled through the sale of offices, but that too now stood condemned. So did the system by which the pastoral clergy had always been supported, although the estates of the Church (minus feudal rights) remained for the moment intact. Nothing so sweeping had been in the minds of most French people when 1789 began. Many deputies, indeed, had had positive mandates from their electors not to support measures like the destruction of local and provincial privileges; and there had been overwhelming support for paying the parish clergy more, rather than destroying their income altogether. But by now the deputies at Versailles had gone far beyond their mandates on a wide range of issues. The merger of the orders itself could not have taken place if mandates had been strictly respected by nobles and clergy; and one of the National Assembly's first formal acts was to vote, on 8 July, for the abrogation of all binding mandates. This left the representatives of the sovereign nation free, without referring back, to decree the destruction of whatever they saw fit. It also left them at liberty to reconstruct their country on entirely new lines.

All the deputies assembled at Versailles in May 1789 believed that they had been elected to endow France with a constitution. As early as 7 July they had voted to call themselves the National Constituent Assembly. And there was remarkable agreement across all three orders, and in the *cahiers*, about what the constitution should contain. Most deputies believed (although some deplored giving such hostages to fortune) that it should be prefaced by a declaration of rights along the lines pioneered in the 1780s by certain American states. Between 9 and 28 July a score of drafts were submitted by various deputies, and on 4 August, the afternoon before the famous all-night session, the Assembly agreed to promulgate a declaration as a matter of urgency. On 26 August, after a week of discussion spun out by clerical reluctance to concede total freedom of thought and worship, the Declaration of the Rights of Man and the Citizen was finally voted. The Assembly reserved the right to add to or alter it when the constitution itself was finally promulgated, but when that moment came two years later nobody dared. The declaration had become the founding document of the Revolution and, as such, sacrosanct.

The keynote of the declaration was the rule of law. It is specifically referred to in nine of the seventeen articles. Article VI defines law as the expression of the general will, made by the direct or indirect participation of all citizens; an implicit condemnation of the legislative sovereignty claimed by kings under the old order. Sovereignty in any case, article III declares, 'rests essentially in the nation'. No body and no individual (which meant no king) might exercise any authority not expressly emanating from the nation. In the eyes of the law all citizens are equal, for, states the very first article, men are born and remain free and equal in rights. The aim of all political associations (art. II) is the preservation of the natural rights of liberty, property, security, and resistance to oppression. Hitherto, the inference was these rights had been ignored in France. That was why it was necessary for the declaration to condemn arbitrary arrest and imprisonment (art. VII), presumption of guilt before judgement (art. IX), public officials who were not accountable (art. XV), and insecurity of property (art. XVII). 'Any society', article XVI specifies, 'in which the guarantee of rights is not assured or the separation of powers not determined has no constitution.' And equality before the law meant the end of privilege. Taxation henceforth would be 'apportioned equally among all citizens according to their capacity to pay' (art. XIII), and appointment to public positions would be open to all citizens 'according to their capacity, and with no other distinction than that of their virtues and talents' (art. VI). Only on freedom of thought is the declaration somewhat equivocal. Although free communication of thought and opinion is singled out as 'one of the most precious of the rights of man (art. XI) it is noted that it can be abused, in ways the law will define. And although no one may be disturbed for his opinions, even (in a rebuff to clerical arguments for a continued Catholic monopoly of public worship) religious ones, a limit may be set if their manifestation threatens public order (art. X). This was one of the few hints in the declaration that men and citizens had duties as well as rights, although some early drafts had sought to list duties, too. To have done so would certainly have made the whole document less memorable. As it was, it long outlived the constitution to which it was a preamble; and has been looked to ever since by all who derive inspiration from the French Revolution as the movement's first great manifesto, enshrining the fundamental principles of 1789.

Its drafters could not have hoped for more; but from the start they realized that something else was required to endow the declaration with the full solemnity they intended. It needed the assent of the king. So did the decree of 11 August. If the monarch did not openly and freely associate himself in this way with the destruction of the *ancien régime*, the whole work of the Assembly would be vitiated. Yet could the king really be free without the right to refuse? The issue plunged the deputies at once into the intricacies of constitution-making.

Admirers of the checks and balances of the British constitution dominated the Assembly's constitutional committee, and they believed that the king should have the same powers of veto as the British monarch. They also believed that the democratic element of an elective National Assembly should be balanced by a second chamber or senate whose members sat for life. Led by Mounier, Malouet, and a handful of rich and eloquent metropolitan nobles like Lally-Tollendal and Clermont-Tonnerre, and energetically supported by Mirabeau, these *monarchiens* (as their opponents dubbed them) spent the first two weeks of September trying to hustle the Assembly into accepting their programme. But the alliance of patriotic heroes of July like Mounier and Mirabeau with notorious conservatives like Malouet provoked widespread surprise and suspicion;

provincial noble deputies mistrusted rich former courtiers when they advocated what looked like a House of Lords which only the great would enter; while ordinary third-estate deputies saw no point in dividing a legislature that had been unified after a tremendous struggle only a few months beforehand. On 10 September a second chamber was decisively rejected by 490 votes to 89, and the *monarchien*-dominated constitutional committee dissolved. The veto question was even more hotly contested. The king seemed in no hurry to sanction the August decrees, and that seemed evidence of the danger of allowing him an unlimited veto. But only a handful of deputies, such as Sieyès and the prolix but still uninfluential Robespierre, believed that once the National Assembly had pronounced the monarch should have no veto at all. Most, including patriotic leaders like Barnave, Duport, and the noble Lameth brothers, were attracted to the idea of a temporary or 'suspensive' veto; and when Necker let it be known that this was also the king's preference, they detected a hint that the August decrees would be sanctioned if it was carried. Consequently the suspensive veto passed overwhelmingly (673 votes to 352) on 15 September.

It was the first time the Assembly had flouted popular sentiment, for in Paris and many of the provinces it was clear than any form of veto aroused deep mistrust. As soon as the issue arose there was uproar at the Palais Royal, and on 30 August a renegade nobleman who spent his time there, the Marquis de Saint-Huruge, attempted to drum up a protest march to Versailles. The king and Assembly, the marchers declared, should be brought to Paris where they would be under constant scrutiny. There were only a few hundred of them, and they were stopped by the National Guard; but nobody was in a position to stop anti-veto agitation in pamphlets and the periodical press which had established itself as a permanent feature of political life in the capital since July. A whole new paper, in fact, was launched on 12 September with denunciations of the Assembly's equivocations over the veto. It was called *Le Publiciste Parisien*, but soon changed its name to *L'Ami du Peuple*. With it the charlatan adventurer Jean-Paul Marat at last found his vocation after years of failure and rejection. Marat throve on an atmosphere of plots and suspicion, and called for the Assembly to be purged of unreliable members. The lesson of the previous July was that the people should never shrink from direct action in the public interest. Nor was Marat alone in this view. The constant talk in Paris, noted an apprehensive bookseller, was of lynching, or 'the lamp-post; everyone called an aristocrat is threatened with it; and aristocrat is a name for anybody you don't like. Imagine the alarm in certain circles, people of wealth, title or ability, everybody in fact whom the populace and others once feared or envied. Fear of the lamp-post stops the plotting of a few mischief-makers, but it also terrifies many honest folk who pass for enemies of the new order of things but really are not.'[4] Such paranoid attitudes were compounded by persistent economic difficulties in the capital. After falling somewhat in late July and August, the price of bread began to climb again and supplies became irregular, just at the time of year when a good harvest should have banished all food worries for a twelvemonth. But the fine, still weather that had ripened the grain had also dried up rivers and immobilized mills. Grain riots began to be reported from markets in outlying districts around the capital, and by mid-September rowdy groups of women were stopping grain convoys within the city and petitioning the municipal authorities to bring prices and supplies under closer control. Guards were placed on bakers' shops, and Lafayette and his militia found themselves hard pressed to contain all the incidents that occurred.

Parallels with the situation early in July escaped no one. All that was needed to reproduce it exactly was a military threat; and that, too, soon materialized. Alarmed at persistent rumours of being taken by force to Paris, on 14 September the king summoned the notoriously well-disciplined Flanders Regiment from the north-east frontier to Versailles. It arrived a week later, and at the palace was rapturously received. Encouraged by the security it seemed to promise, the king broke silence on the August decrees. On 18 September, in a long letter drafted by Necker, he explained that he was prepared to accept some parts of the 11 August decree but not others. The deputies felt betrayed. They petitioned the king to promulgate the decree at once, without amendments. He said he would 'publish' it but not promulgate it. Then on 4 October he voiced reservations about the Declaration of Rights. By now, however, Paris was alive with rumours about a reception given by the King's bodyguard on 1 October to welcome the Flanders Regiment. After many noisy toasts had been drunk, and none to the nation, the national cockade was said to have been trampled as the air rang with unpatriotic slogans. Banquets themselves seemed unpatriotic when bread was so scarce, and by 4 October all Paris believed that counter-revolutionary orgies at Versailles were the prelude to a new attempt to starve the capital. The next morning, several districts of the city were awakened by the ringing of the tocsin from church bell-towers, recognized ever since the days of July as a call to arms. Crowds of women began to assemble at markets, from where they marched to the Hôtel de Ville. After surging through the building to impress the city authorities with their determination, late in the morning they set off for Versailles dragging cannon and brandishing whatever makeshift weapons they could lay hands on, recruiting newcomers as they went along. Perhaps 7,000 of them reached Versailles early in the evening and invaded the National Assembly, calling for bread and punishment for those who had insulted the national cockade. The unprotected deputies had no alternative but to welcome them with mollifying speeches. They were visibly relieved when a deputation went on to confront the king. Many of them recognized, however, that popular intervention had probably been the only way to make the king assent unambiguously to their decrees; and he was quick to do so once the crowds of women appeared. The problem was how to disperse the demonstration and restore calm once this object had been achieved. The forces of order, in the shape of Lafayette and 20,000 National Guardsmen, arrived in Versailles later that night after a forced march through an autumnal downpour. Lafayette had been reluctant to come at all, leaving Paris unpoliced and thereby risking accusations that he was in complicity with the demonstrators. But his men insisted, and crowds outside the Hôtel de Ville were muttering about stringing him and Bailly up if they continued to temporize. When he arrived all he could do was try to ensure that what the populace wanted was brought about without disorder, and he formally requested the king, in the name of Paris, to return to the capital with him and take up residence in the Tuileries palace. The king made no promises that night, but early the next morning a number of Parisians found their way into the palace precincts and were fired on by royal bodyguards. Thereupon an enraged mob poured into the palace, massacred two guardsmen, and almost broke into the queen's apartments. Only prompt action by unco-ordinated units of the National Guard contained them, and Lafayette bundled the royal family onto the palace balcony to stand under his personal protection. The impact on the volatile crowd milling below was favourable, but constant shouts of 'To Paris!' made clear that only one thing would really satisfy them. Late in the morning of 6 October the king announced that he would go.

A procession 60,000 strong accompanied Louis XVI and his queen on their nine-hour journey back to his capital that afternoon. As a gesture of goodwill, they brought wagonloads of flour from the palace stores, and the crowds as they marched sang the praises of 'the baker, the baker's wife, and the baker's boy'—a reference to the dauphin, who travelled in his parents' coach. In fact there was little the king could do to remedy a bread shortage caused by natural accidents and administrative upheavals. It was November before cheaper and more regular supplies were available, and market-day riots came to an end. Nevertheless in the history of the Revolution the 'October Days' were decisive. Louis XVI never returned to

Versailles. Henceforth he and his family would be confined to Paris, as a British observer put it,[5] 'more like prisoners than Princes'. A few days later the National Assembly followed him there, and by November was established in a converted riding-school a stone's throw from the Tuileries. The central authorities of the regenerate French State were now at the mercy of Paris, and time and time again over the next five years Parisians would intervene in national politics in the role of self-appointed watchdogs of the Revolution.

Few foresaw the extent of this danger in 1789. It seemed as if the August decrees could not have secured royal assent by any other means. Only some of the *monarchiens* thought all was already lost—although they included Mounier, who, though president of the National Assembly during the October Days, now slipped away home to Dauphiné to preach the dangers of metropolitan popular despotism. A new wave of emigration among great nobles and army officers certainly followed the October Days; but these were people who had been appalled at the course of the Revolution almost from the start, and took the abandonment of Versailles and the end of royal resistance to the Assembly's work as a sign that the movement was now irreversible. They were right, too. All open attempts on the king's part to resist the reform of France now came to an end. Twenty-one months later he too would try to emigrate. But between October 1789 and that moment the Assembly would have transformed the country out of all recognition.

The essence of the constitution of 1791, as the work the Constituent Assembly was now embarked on would be called, was to keep the executive weak. Despotism must have no opportunity ever to revive in France. And so the King of the French (a new title, intended to make clear that he did not own the kingdom) was to enjoy hardly any powers not subject to review by the legislature. He could propose no laws, and could only use his suspensive veto to block legislation he did not like for the length of a legislative sitting, a maximum of two years. His income, the civil list, would be determined by legislative vote; and although he alone appointed ministers, they were open to legislative impeachment. Nor was his choice of ministers entirely free: they could not be chosen from, or sit in, the legislature. This was entirely in accord with the separation of powers principle derived from Montesquieu and set out in the Declaration of the Rights of Man and the Citizen as one of the criteria of a true constitution. But it might not have been so firmly embedded in the 1791 constitution without an ill-timed intervention by Mirabeau in one of the earliest debates after the Assembly moved to Paris. On 6 November he moved that the king should choose ministers from the Assembly, on the British model. His earlier support for the *monarchiens*, however, had rekindled old suspicions, and it was widely rumoured that he was himself hoping to enter the ministry. Nobody believed his protestations to the contrary, and the debate ended with a decision that no deputy might become a minister or join the government until three years after leaving the Assembly.

Future Legislative Assemblies, as the successors to the Constituent were to be called, were to contain 745 seats and sit for two years. They were to be elected indirectly, and by far from universal suffrage. The deputies certainly did not intend to allow any say in political power under constitutional government to the sort of people who had come to their aid, but whom they had barely been able to control, in July and the first weeks of October. And so by the decree of 29 October 1789 they introduced the famous category of active citizens. Only active citizens might vote, and they were defined as men over 25 paying the equivalent of three days' unskilled labour in taxes. This gave the vote, it was estimated in 1790, to almost 4.3 million Frenchmen. But all active citizens did in the electoral process was choose one in a hundred of their number as electors, and those eligible for this next level had to be paying taxes to the value of ten days' labour. Only about 50,000 active citizens met this requirement. Electors, in turn, met in departmental assemblies to choose the deputies themselves, who had to be landowners paying at least a 'silver mark' in taxes, the equivalent of 54 days' labour. Although these arrangements gave around 60 per cent of Frenchmen some say in political life, they were considerably more restrictive than the franchise for the elections to the Estates-General, and they appeared profoundly at odds with the principles of civil equality proclaimed in the Declaration of the Rights of Man and the Citizen. From the start they were extremely controversial, the silver-mark provision in particular being denounced by the popular press. 'There is only one voice in the capital,' complained Camille Desmoulins in one of the first issues of his *Révolutions de France et de Brabant*, destined to be one of the most widely read radical papers,[6] 'and soon there will be but one in the provinces against the silver mark. It has turned France into an aristocratic government ... But what is this much repeated word *active citizen* supposed to mean? The active citizens are the ones who took the Bastille.'

But active citizens had more to do than choose assemblies of electors. Under the new regime all public officers, except ministers of the Crown, were to be elective. That meant local administrators, judges, and magistrates, and even parish priests. Power was to emanate, if not from the bottom, then at least from below, and the only entitlement of eligible citizens to positions of authority would be election by their fellow citizens.

All this doomed the old judicial system, already condemned in principle by the abolition of venality and judicial fees. As early as 5 August the suppression of the parlements had been suggested, and on the seventeenth of the same month it became a formal recommendation of the constitutional committee. The political prerogatives of the old sovereign courts violated the principle of the separation of powers, and in any case patriots suspected them as nests of obstructive aristocrats. In November they were put into perpetual vacation, and ten months later abolished outright. The whole structure of lower courts disappeared with them, to be replaced with a system of local justices of the peace, district civil and departmental criminal courts, and a single court of appeal (*tribunal de cassation*) to review the conduct, but not the substance, of cases. No administrative authority was vested in the new courts, and although the deputies committed themselves to an eventual total recodification of the civil and criminal law, and as a start introduced trial by jury, they made no provision for any sort of police to enforce it. Public order was the responsibility of local administrative, not judicial, authorities, and the sole instrument of coercion at their disposal was the National Guard.

Uniformity and decentralization were the keynotes of the administrative organization undertaken by the Constituent Assembly. All the old provinces, generalities, principalities, and municipalities, in all their rich and limitless variety, were swept away. They were replaced by eighty-three departments, roughly equal in size, population and wealth. These in turn were subdivided into districts and communes, all run by elected councils and officials. Nobody was appointed from the centre: the intendants, those instruments of despotism, were still too fresh in everybody's memory. Central government under the new system was to be completely dependent on the zeal and energy of thousands of underpaid (and, at the humblest level, unpaid) local officials, of very variable levels of ability, understanding, or indeed political sympathy, for the implementation throughout France of its entire range of reforms. Most were completely inexperienced. In the earliest elections, it is true, considerable numbers of old regime office-holders and lawyers were returned, but even their experience offered little guidance for the unprecedented duties that revolutionary legislation was to heap upon them. And as time went by they largely disappeared from district and communal office, which became the preserve of merchants, petty tradesmen, and artisans: at this level to be an active citizen was enough. The first local government elections, which took place between May and July 1790, marked, in fact, not only a break with the old order, but in towns at least the end of the interim order that had established itself in the municipal revolutions of July 1789. The latter had produced

MAP 2. The departments of revolutionary France

arrangements almost as diverse as those of the old order itself; but now every commune elected a mayor, a procurator, and a general council. Communes with over 25,000 inhabitants, the great cities in effect, were divided into sections for electoral purposes. Thus Lyons and Marseilles had 32 each, Bordeaux 28, Toulouse 15. Paris had 48, and in thus redividing the capital the deputies congratulated themselves on decimating certain of the 60 electoral districts which had begun to function as centres of popular radicalism. The Cordeliers district, just south of the Pont Neuf, had been among the most prominent, under its ambitious and opportunistic president Georges-Jacques Danton. Desmoulins's newspaper was published from there, as was its older-established rival, Loustalot's *Révolutions de Paris*, and several others. Together they led a vigorous campaign over the spring of 1790 to preserve the Paris districts, but in vain. Yet the legislators underestimated the ingenuity and organization of the political machine Danton had built up. It soon dominated the new section (Théâtre-Français) as it had the old district, and by its activity was to show the other sections the way to continued influence in national as well as purely Parisian affairs.

The National Assembly was also determined to rationalize the various citizens' militias established in the course of the municipal revolution, and it finally did so at the time of the first municipal elections. In August 1789 it had brought them all under the umbrella of the National Guard and placed them at the disposal of local authorities, but left their organization to local initiative. Only in Paris, where a professional soldier like Lafayette was in command, and many of the old French Guards had been drafted in at the initial stage, was it well organized and fully armed and uniformed by the end of the summer. Even then its discipline was uncertain, as Lafayette learned on 4 October when his own men forced him to march to Versailles. Yet the Guard were the only armed force patriots felt they could rely on. The army was officered by nobles known for their unquestioning loyalty to the king; and although the discipline of the ranks had begun to crumble and desertions to soar over the summer, with even the dreaded Flanders Regiment joining Lafayette's force on 4 October, the very idea of calling on the army to maintain public order remained far too dangerous for all but the most conservative of deputies to contemplate. Instead they made their intention to depend on the National Guard crystal clear immediately after the October Days by the passage, on 21 October, of the Martial Law against Tumults. It permitted municipal authorities to proclaim martial law, indicating their decision by deploying red flags. They were then empowered to call out the National Guard and order it to fire on crowds or demonstrators who refused to disperse. Clearly it was essential that this

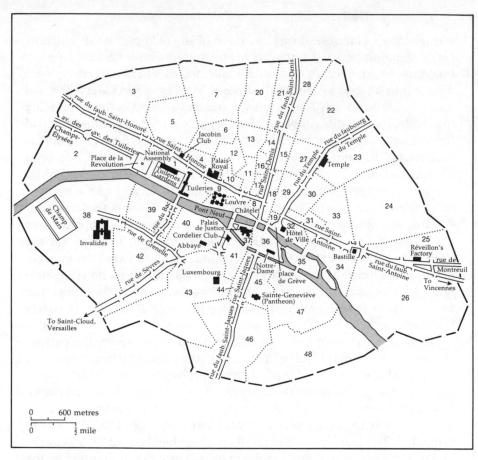

MAP 3. Revolutionary Paris: the sections and main places and streets mentioned in the text    *Source*: G. Rudé, *The Crowd in the French Revolution* (Oxford, 1959).

**Paris Sections:**

| | | |
|---|---|---|
| 1 Tuileries | 17 Marché des Innocents | 33 Place Royale |
| 2 Champs-Élysées | 18 Lombards | 34 Arsenal |
| 3 Roule | 19 Arcis | 35 Île Saint-Louis |
| 4 Palais Royal | 20 Faub. Montmartre | 36 Notre-Dame |
| 5 Place Vendôme | 21 Poissonnière | 37 Henri IV |
| 6 Bibliothèque | 22 Bondy | 38 Invalides |
| 7 Grange Batelière | 23 Temple | 39 Fontaine de Grenelle |
| 8 Louvre | 24 Popincourt | 40 Quatre Nations |
| 9 Oratoire | 25 Montreuil | 41 Théâtre-Français |
| 10 Halle au Blé | 26 Quinze Vingts | 42 Croix Rouge |
| 11 Postes | 27 Gravilliers | 43 Luxembourg |
| 12 Place Louis XIV | 28 Faub. Saint-Denis | 44 Thermes de Julien |
| 13 Fontaine Montmorency | 29 Beaubourg | 45 Sainte-Geneviève |
| 14 Bonne Nouvelle | 30 Enfants Rouges | 46 Observatoire |
| 15 Ponceau | 31 Roi de Sicile | 47 Jardin des Plantes |
| 16 Mauconseil | 32 Hôtel de Ville | 48 Gobelins |

force, at least, should be completely reliable, and over subsequent months uncertain elements were slowly weeded out. A national uniform was introduced, which members had to buy for themselves at a price poorer citizens could not afford. Membership was also confined to active citizens, and repeated oaths of loyalty to the nation, the law, and the constitution were demanded. And although National Guard officers were barred from municipal office, they were positively encouraged to make contact with their counterparts in neighbouring places to develop a common spirit and outlook. Over the spring of 1790 regional rallies of National Guards, or 'federations', began to be held. They culminated on 14 July, the first anniversary of the fall of the Bastille, in a gigantic 'Feast of the Federation' held in the Champ de Mars on the western outskirts of Paris. Here the National Guards from all over France converged, under the eye of their general and the king himself, to renew their oaths and celebrate a year of achievements. The king led the oath-taking in front of an assembly some estimated at 350,000. It rained, but still proved an occasion of genuine enthusiasm, marking perhaps the high-point of national consensus about what the Revolution had achieved, and was achieving. Those who had built the arena expressed their optimism in a new popular song which was to sweep the country in subsequent months: 'Ça ira', things will work out.

And yet by July 1790 there were plenty of signs that things were not always working out. For every patriotic noble like Lafayette, Mirabeau, Duport, the Lameth brothers, or Talleyrand, who as bishop of Autun celebrated mass at the Feast of the Federation, there were many more who deplored the turn of events. More noble deputies followed Mounier's example of abandoning their seats in the Assembly than did clerical or non-noble ones, and emigration became a steady stream. Not a day passed, noted a soldier stationed in Alsace in May 1790, without the passage of a noble carriage *en route* for Switzerland. Few nobles stood for office in the new elections, and even fewer were elected. They were simply opting out of the new order. Gratuitous gestures like the abolition of nobility itself, together with all its trappings like titles, orders, ribbons, and coats of arms (19 June 1790), did nothing to reconcile them. Nor did general popular suspicion, epitomized in the second line soon added to 'Ça ira'—'Let's hang the aristocrats from the lanterns'. Worst of all in the eyes of many nobles was continuing disorder in the countryside, much of it directed against lords who, as the decree of 11 August explicitly authorized, attempted to continue exercising their rights and collecting their dues until redemption. There were endless intrusions into seigneurial woods and game parks, constant refusals to pay dues, and repeated attacks on remaining symbols of lordly power untouched during July and August. Bonfires of seigneurial pews in churchyards were the fashion that autumn. All over the western Massif Central the next spring peasants planted liberty trees on seigneurial land. They called them *Mays*, from a much older tradition, festooned them with symbols of seigneurialism, and claimed that if they stood for a year and a day their lord's rights would be extinguished. For good measure, however, the planting ceremonies often developed into deputations requesting lords to abandon their remaining rights. January 1790 witnessed a new outbreak of château-burning in northern Brittany: twenty-two were destroyed, along with the title-deeds stored in many others. 'In Auvergne', wrote a despairing aristocratic lady towards the end of 1789,[7] 'we suffer a thousand horrors at the hand of our peasants. A whole village refuses to pay unless we produce our title-deeds; others wait the event and do not pay. If we do not show them, they will not pay; if we do, they may burn them.' Further west, in Périgord and Quercy, there were scenes of spectacular violence a few months later when departmental authorities decreed the destruction of newly planted liberty trees. Bands of peasants hundreds strong gathered to protect them, and once assembled sometimes turned to attacking manor houses. Many districts, certainly, escaped such upheavals; but it was the incidents that made news, were reported to the National Assembly, and filled all landlords with dread. And although the National Guard, and occasionally regular troops, were often called out to restore order, they usually arrived too late. Riotous crowds, indeed, often included peasants in National Guard uniform. It was true that, as in July and August, their depredations were seldom indiscriminate; but that did not make them any the less illegal, and the lawyers and men of property in the National Assembly did not distinguish between types of lawlessness. The elaboration over the spring of 1790 of the precise terms for due-redemption only stiffened their determination not to yield to rural direct action. But all too often the authorities on the spot simply lacked the means, and endemic resistance to lords' demands, along with persistent attempts to destroy the titles that legitimized them, continued into 1791.

Even more alarming for legislators trying to keep the State going while they recast its constitution was that popular resistance was not confined to seigneurial burdens. The first year of the Revolution also witnessed massive tax-evasion. The toll-gates and tax-offices sacked during the disturbances of July and August were not rebuilt, and clerks and collectors were reluctant to brave popular fury by trying to reactivate them, even if their superiors were still there urging them to do so. People simply stopped paying, and once the habit was broken it was hard to restore. Officials who tried to collect taxes were physically threatened or had their homes sacked, especially in small places where everybody knew where they lived. In Picardy, where such activities were responsible for an 80 per cent drop in the yield of indirect taxes, resistance was organized in the spring of 1790 into a self-conscious petitioning movement against indirect taxes in general by a land agent thrown out of work by the abolition of feudalism, François-Noël (soon to call himself Gracchus) Babeuf. He was arrested, not for the first or last time; but the irony was that the deputies now reorganizing France shared his distaste for indirect levies. They knew very well how unanimously the *cahiers* had condemned them, and they believed, with the Physiocrats, that only direct taxation of net surplus revenues was not economically harmful. And so, in the course of 1790 and 1791, all the *aides*, *traites*, *octrois*, the salt and tobacco monopolies, and countless other local taxes on trade and consumption were abolished, along with the labyrinth of fiscal jurisdictions which supervised them, and the tax-farms through which private businessmen managed them. The old direct taxes—*taille*, capitation, *vingtièmes*— disappeared too. In place of the old system the Assembly established three direct taxes: a land tax (*contribution foncière*), a tax on movables (*contribution mobilière*) and a commercial profits tax (*patente*). There were no privileges or special exemptions. Citizens would pay according to their capacities; and since all this was patently in accord with the equitable demands of 1789, it was expected that they would pay more than willingly. Accordingly, no machinery of constraint was established. The deputies failed to foresee what every bureaucrat instinctively knows: that direct taxes would be far harder to recover than indirect ones; especially when taxpaying rhythms had been disrupted by years of resistance and administrative upheaval going back to the refusal of the parlements to register the fiscal reforms of 1787 and 1788.

Nor had the financial crisis those far-distant plans had been prepared to deal with gone away. The deputies did not forget that what had forced the convocation of the future National Assembly was the scale of the State's debts. The debt was, as Mirabeau put it, a 'national treasure', and it must be honoured. The nation's representatives did not intend to begin their work by declaring France bankrupt, even if, with more important things on their minds, they had ignored Necker's urgings to address the problem at once at the opening of the Estates-General. But even Necker could not stave off disaster for ever, and in fact by the autumn of 1789 his prestige was on the wane. The peak of his popularity was his triumphant return from his second exile on 29 July, when he stood in tears before an ecstatic Assembly. But his attempt the next day to secure the release of the imprisoned commander of troops on 14 July, Besenval, soured a popular reception organized for him in Paris: and by September his seeming connivance in the king's evasive attitude to the August decrees was attracting widespread censure. Even his old financial wizardry was in doubt: two loans floated in August failed miserably after savage criticism in the Assembly. Late in September he proposed an unprecedented non-recurring 'Patriotic contribution' of a quarter of every citizen's income, payable in cash or valuables. The Assembly glumly accepted the idea, but initially provided no means of checking declarations. Necker launched it with a personal contribution of 100,000 L.; but its yield, over the three years it was supposed to run, came nowhere near its target. Nor did the immediate financial situation allow time to wait. The short-term debt alone was estimated at over 707 millions in November 1789, and by the following summer it was believed to be not far short of two billions as the Assembly continued to decree compensation for one form or another of office or property it had abolished. In these circumstances the deputies turned to a measure far beyond anything ever contemplated by Necker. They decided to nationalize the lands of the Church.

The first threats of such action came with ominous assertions that ecclesiastical property belonged to the Nation during the framing of the 11 August decree. Throughout the financial debates of September, the idea of using church lands in some way to alleviate the burden of the national debt kept recurring. Finally on 10 October Talleyrand lent his authority as a bishop to a formal proposal that the state should take over all clerical property. Two-thirds of it, he argued, should be used to pay the clergy, in place of the tithes lost on 4 August; the remainder should help restore the national finances. Mirabeau, however, moved that the state should have free disposal of the whole, simply recognizing an obligation to maintain the Church out of general national resources. A long and bitter debate on these questions took up much of October. To secular arguments that the Church was merely a trustee administering its lands on behalf of the whole body of the faithful in France, and that since the clergy as an order no longer existed, it could not own property, outraged churchmen, and some laity, replied that clerical entitlement to land was ancient and well attested; that individual institutions, and not the order as a whole, were the true proprietors; and that such a massive expropriation ran clean counter to the property rights guaranteed in the Declaration of the Rights of Man and the Citizen. There was also much disagreement about the likely consequences of selling off so much land once it had been taken over. Some thought it would saturate the market, and so be counter-productive. Others predicted that buyers would constitute a natural and permanent body of supporters for the Revolution. The Parisian press joined vigorously in the discussion on both sides. But few minds seem to have been changed by argument. Most deputies had arrived in Versailles that spring convinced that the Church needed root and branch reform, and they tended to see any clerical opposition to change as self-interested special pleading. The noisy anti-clericalism of the public galleries, which greeted any spirited intervention by a deputy from the clergy with cries of 'Down with skull-caps!', showed that the people shared these suspicions. And besides, no realistic alternative way of honouring the debt was proposed. Consequently on 3 November Mirabeau's original motion was in all essentials accepted. 568 deputies outvoted 346 to place the property of the clergy 'at the disposal of the Nation'.

How the Nation would use this newly acquired facility remained to be decided. At first action looked like being postponed on the initiative, of all people, of the Protestant Necker, who disapproved of the confiscation. He proposed that the first step towards liquidating the short-term debt should be through a limited issue of paper money by a National Bank. The latter would be a nationalized form of the Discount Bank founded in 1776 by a financial consortium, and much used as a source of credit by governments since. But France's previous experience of paper money had not been a happy one. In 1720 the Scottish adventurer John Law had attempted to set up a state bank on the promise of overseas trading profits, and had paid the king's debts in banknotes. After initial runaway success, the whole scheme had collapsed, leaving thousands of families with assets reduced to worthless paper. Subsequent generations were haunted by the memory of this disaster, and there were plenty of deputies prepared to remind their colleagues of it. Nor was there much liking for the 'capitalists' who ran the Discount Bank and who would still be needed after nationalization to make it work. Too many people obscurely believed that in some way they were responsible for the State's financial problems in the first place. And the financial world itself was divided. Catholic financiers, deprived of a livelihood made in manipulating public funds by the abolition of the venal offices through which they did it, did not wish to see their role taken over by a nexus of Protestant and Swiss bankers. Mirabeau made himself the spokesman of all these suspicions, fears, and jealousies when he proposed, against Necker, that the only paper the State should issue should be bonds secured on the value of assets visible to all—the national lands. Surely the credit of the State itself, guaranteed by the National Assembly, was superior to that of any bank? In the course of the debate a name was invented for such bonds: assignats. Eventually this idea won the day. On 19 and 21 December a series of decrees set up an 'Extraordinary Fund' (*Caisse de l'Extraordinaire*) to receive the proceeds of the Patriotic

Contribution and the sale of 400 million *livres'* worth of national lands. On the strength of these prospects, assignats to the same total value would be issued in 1,000-*livre* notes bearing interest at 5 per cent. The State would pay its creditors in them; and they in turn could be used to acquire national lands.

Assignats were, then, not strictly paper money at all at the start. But within months that was what they became. The initial amount had been decided on the expectation of a minimum deficit for 1790, as calculated by Necker, of 80 millions. But by March the fall in tax-revenue forced him to revise the figure to 294 millions. The miscalculation was understandable enough, but it destroyed what was left of Necker's credibility. The Assembly now brushed aside all his warnings about relying too exclusively on issues of paper to meet mounting debts. On 17 April they voted that the assignats should become legal tender, available in denominations of 300 and 200 *livres*, and attract only 3 per cent interest to encourage their conversion into land. But still the deficit mounted, and between April and September no less than six supplementary issues of assignats were authorized to cover it. On the twenty-ninth of the latter month the Assembly formally decided to triple the number in circulation to 1,200 millions. By then, support for the assignats had become a test of commitment to the whole Revolution, irrespective of what the consequences of an immense multiplication of paper might be. The first to fail this test of patriotism was Necker himself. Hounded ever since October 1789 by radical journalists like Marat, spurned and despised by leading deputies like Mirabeau, and forced by the Assembly to carry out policies he had no faith in, on 3 September 1790 he resigned. Twice on his way back to Switzerland he was arrested on suspicion of trying to emigrate, like some disgruntled nobleman. The national hero of the spring of 1789, and the methods and policies he stood for, were now as superseded as the whole *ancien régime* that he had done more than any other man to bring down.

Everyone, in the spring of 1789, had expected France to emerge from the meeting of the Estates-General profoundly changed. Very few foresaw, if the *cahiers* are any guide, quite how profound the changes would be. The deputies claimed to be following the *cahiers* in their reforming work. In the sense that they sought to endow France with a constitutional monarchy, decentralized and representative institutions, civil and fiscal equality, and guarantees for individual liberty, they were broadly true to the instructions of the general *cahiers*, at least. But even these refined and sophisticated documents, from which popular concerns had largely been strained out, contained no mandate for the abolition of provinces, municipalities, nobility, or titles, and only uncertain or ambiguous instructions regarding feudalism, venality, the parlements, or ecclesiastical property. Almost none called for a declaration of rights, and none at all for a national guard or paper money. Most of the reforms carried out or sanctioned by the Constituent Assembly, in other words, were the product of the revolutionary process itself. They were responses to events and situations without any historical precedent, rather than the known desires of the French nation. And yet, once made, the far-reaching changes of the Revolution's first year were mostly well received. Their implementation may have been chaotic and disorganized, but they were carried through with remarkable goodwill and even enthusiasm considering the multitude of vested interests they threatened or damaged. Ex-courtiers might emigrate, and disillusioned deputies abandon their seats; prelates might complain of political plunder, lords of damage to their property, and dispossessed office-holders of under-compensation; but every one of these categories also produced warm partisans of the Revolution. Nobles, clerics, and office-holders all played parts quite disproportionate to their numbers in the Assembly's legislative activity. And in the country at large millions welcomed the end of feudalism and indirect taxes, while hundreds of thousands of bourgeois eagerly seized the opportunity offered by the new regime to participate in public affairs. The work of the Revolution's first twelve months, in fact, had the support of a broad national consensus. The Feast of the Federation which was observed in every commune as well as in Paris, was a celebration of that consensus. But by the time the second anniversary of the overthrow of the Bastille came around, it was rapidly falling apart.

# The Breakdown of the
# Revolutionary Consensus
# 1790—1791

NOBODY had ever expected that, once the reform of France began, the Church would remain untouched. The *cahiers* of all three orders in the spring of 1789 were full of suggestions for improving and rationalizing the organization and conduct of religious life. The clergy, as the first order in the State, expected to play a leading role in the process. And at the start they did play a leading role: it was clerical deputies who first broke the ranks of the 'privileged orders' in June 1789 and so opened the way to the transformation of the Estates-General into the National Assembly. In doing so they were responding to appeals from the third estate in the name of the God of Peace, and hoping to break a deadlock that was preventing emergency action to relieve the sufferings of a hungry populace. There is no evidence that they intended to give up the clergy's status as a separate order in the State, or its veto on action prejudicial to the interests of the Church or religion in general. But within weeks far more than these advantages had been lost. No group, probably, suffered more from the renunciations of the night of 4 August than the clergy. Parish priests lost their tithes, their vestry fees, and their ability to group poor benefices through pluralism. Compensation was mooted, but rejected. Bishops and ecclesiastical corporations, including charitable and educational ones, lost whatever feudal dues they happened to own, which were often substantial. Here compensation was voted, but in the end seldom paid. And the Pope himself lost the Annates, the Peter's Pence that all the faithful contributed towards the upkeep of the Holy See, and whose renunciation had marked the moment, in the sixteenth century, when Protestant kingdoms had made their break with Rome. In the debates over codifying these changes, further threats were uttered, this time against church lands; and Mirabeau declared that all clerics should be content to be salaried servants of the State. The later weeks of August brought yet more blows. The drafters of the Declaration of the Rights of Man and the Citizen refused to declare Catholicism the state religion; refused to restrict freedom of expression and opinion; and declared public office and civil rights available to all, which meant Protestants and Jews as well as Catholics. Clerical speakers in the Assembly were now regularly jeered from the galleries; so that when in October the Assembly returned to the idea of confiscating the estates of the Church for other national purposes, nobody was really surprised. The clergy fought it tooth and nail, not simply to protect what they had left, but also because they saw that the loss of the Church's remaining independent resources would make further action by the Assembly inevitable. Patriotic speakers sought to offer reassurance: the nation would take over the Church's educational and charitable functions, and every parish priest was promised an income of at least 1,200 *livres*. That third of the clergy hitherto dependent on the *portion congrue* could rejoice at the prospect of a massive rise. But for many others, 1,200 *livres* represented a cut; and besides, when would payment begin? The Assembly had ordered the continuance of tithes until that moment, but along with feudal dues and taxes, peasants were no longer paying them in most places, and it was dangerous to try to enforce them. By the end of 1789, in other words, the Revolution that so many priests had greeted with such goodwill and enthusiasm had brought the clergy little but spoliation and promises.

And in 1790 the process continued. On 13 February came the turn of the regular clergy: all monasteries and convents, except those dedicated to educational and charitable work, were dissolved, and new religious vows were forbidden. Previous legislation, of course, had already deprived these institutions of their property and income, but the Assembly's motives went deeper than that. Most deputies, many parish priests among them, believed that contemplatives were useless parasites, unproductive burdens on society whose existence no national church could justify. There were recent precedents elsewhere in Europe for such a wholesale dissolution, notably in the Habsburg lands under the rationalizing Joseph II. France itself had witnessed many monastic closures since the 1760s. But after all the other blows suffered by the Church over the preceding six months, this new one seemed part of a more alarming pattern. On 12 April a worried Carthusian monk, Dom Gerle, who had hitherto voted with the patriots, moved a surprise motion to declare Catholicism the national religion and grant it the monopoly of public worship. Three hundred deputies supported him, but the motion was still lost in an Assembly which a few weeks before had elected a Protestant pastor, Rabaut de Saint-Étienne, as its president.

Some people, indeed, were beginning to wonder if the whole Revolution was a Protestant plot. Although there were only some fifteen known Protestants in the Assembly, they included radical leaders like Barnave and Rabaut himself, who demanded complete equality in every sphere for a group which had enjoyed no civil rights at all before 1787. He and five others represented Nîmes, where determined electoral organization by a Protestant bourgeoisie, enormously enriched by two decades of industrialization in the textile trade, had excluded the complacent Catholic establishment from the third-estate representation. Protestants also played a predominant part in setting up the Nîmes citizens' militia in July. All this constituted a rapid and, to the Catholics, shocking shift of power to a group whose strength had hitherto been solely economic. In Montauban, too, the militia was largely a Protestant creation, arousing similar Catholic apprehensions. The Catholic response was to organize their superior numbers in the municipal elections of the spring of 1790 to ensure that local power remained in their hands. They succeeded, but that left Protestants all the more determined to retain control of the militias and exclude Catholic recruits. In both cities, therefore, sectarian tensions rose over the spring, and on 10 May they broke into an ugly riot at Montauban when crowds led by pious women forcibly prevented officials from taking inventories of confiscated monastic properties. They then turned against the militia, overwhelming them and killing five. Panic-stricken Protestants fled the city, and calm was only restored when militiamen from Bordeaux, with no sectarian associations, arrived in force. A month later far more violent scenes occurred in Nîmes. The term *bagarre* (brawl), by which they were remembered, does no justice to four days of pitched street battles which began on 13 June when Protestant National Guardsmen opened fire on rival companies of Catholics in an atmosphere of rising excitement as both sides organized their vote for the first departmental elections. Reinforced by peasant co-religionaries who poured in from the countryside at the first rumour of the clashes, the two sides fought with no quarter; but the Protestants had more fire-power, and in the end the *bagarre* became a massacre of Catholics. Perhaps 300 died, against barely 20 Protestants, and when it was over the Protestants were in complete control of the city for the first time in their community's history. Subsequently they swept the departmental elections too. Thus it was they, in the Gard department, who represented the revolutionary government and implemented its policies, including its ecclesiastical ones. To pious local Catholics, therefore, the Revolution meant the triumph of an old and feared enemy, the world turned upside-down.

And growing Catholic dismay at the course of events in France extended to the very top—for the Pope himself was soon involved. The end of the Annates proved merely a warning shot. By the end of 1789 many of the 150,000 papal subjects living in the enclaves of Avignon and the Comtat Venaissin were demanding the end of 500 years of rule from Rome and integration into France. In Avignon the annexationists won control of the city council after a long campaign and began to bring local law into line with the changes being made in France. Pius VI refused to accept these changes; and meanwhile, on 29 March, in an address to a secret consistory in Rome, he condemned the Declaration of the Rights of Man and all the policies so far pursued in France on religious matters. Encouraged by their ruler's intransigence, anti-annexationists in Avignon made efforts to recapture power, culminating in a day of riots on 10 June. They were put down with the help of French National Guards, and a number of the Pope's adherents were killed. Immediately afterwards the pro-French party proclaimed Avignon annexed to France, and later in the month several parts of the Comtat did the same. The Assembly, aware of the international ramifications of outright annexation, was in no hurry to accept these declarations, but in its debates on the question there were many who argued that the popular will had settled it. In the Comtat, it certainly had not, and civil war raged throughout the territory for the next twelve months. During that time, the split between the Pope and the Revolution was to become irreparable; but the breaking-point did not come over Avignon or the Comtat. The decisive issue was the Civil Constitution of the Clergy.

Ever since August 1789 an ecclesiastical committee of the Assembly had been working on a comprehensive reform plan to revitalize the Church, bring it into harmony with the principles of the Revolution, and provide a secure financial and organization basis for its future. Only a third of the committee's original fifteen members were clerics; and when, as the full range of their colleagues' ideas became apparent, they began to drag their feet, the Assembly added fifteen more laymen. A handful were freethinkers, steeped in the anti-clerical writings of the *Enlightenment*; but most were sincere Catholics, concerned only to purge the Church of its abuses, making it leaner but fitter. What they proposed, one declared, was 'merely . . . a return to the discipline of the early Church'.[1] But that meant changing many practices centuries old, and observed throughout a Church that far transcended the frontiers of France. And, the committee made clear, it meant doing so without consulting the head of the Church, that foreign monarch, in any way. Nobody disputed the Pope's authority in matters spiritual or doctrinal: but how the French Nation chose to organize the practice of religion within its own frontiers was none of his business.

The most he could expect was the courtesy of notification. As the debates on the proposed Civil Constitution began on 29 May, the king was asked to arrange for the winding up of the Concordat of 1516, which had hitherto governed relations between Rome and the French Church. No replacement was envisaged. The National Assembly, having recast vast areas of French secular life unresisted, and indeed removed the Church's material foundations without much outcry, saw no need to negotiate its policies with anyone. When, at the start of the debates, bishops suggested that the consent of the French Church to the Civil Constitution be obtained through a national council, they were brushed aside. There could be no question of resurrecting the clergy as a separate order in society or the State. Many parish priests in the Assembly endorsed this argument, remembering how before 1789 assemblies of the clergy had been mere mouthpieces of the hierarchy. But the danger of that was past. The danger of not referring the reforms to a national council was that, if the Pope came out against them, no other ecclesiastical authority could challenge his decision.

But was the Pope likely to object? What was proposed was scarcely more radical than changes he had accepted in the Habsburg realms in recent years. And the news from Avignon and the Comtat, coming in when the debate was at its height, suggested that if he did prove recalcitrant a French threat to agree to annexation of these territories would blackmail him into compliance. For all the weeks of debate, therefore, the plan tabled by the ecclesiastical committee was accepted almost without amendment on 12 July. Much of it, too, would probably have been perfectly acceptable to most of the clergy. The salary scales it laid down were generous, although most bishops and many rectors would make less than they had in the days of church lands and tithes. There were stringent residence requirements at every level, but these had been the unanimous demand of the *cahiers*. Even the rationalization of the ecclesiastical map made obvious good sense. Henceforth there were to be only eighty-three bishops, one per department, and ten metropolitans. Parishes, too, were drastically reduced in number: in all towns of less than 6,000 inhabitants there was to be only one. All chapters and other benefices without cure of souls were now abolished. Like monasteries and convents, they were regarded as useless and parasitical. The clergy existed to minister to the faithful, and had no other justification. On these grounds the requirement for bishops to have served fifteen years in a parish, and vicars five as a curate, were also clear improvements. Apart, therefore, from the clerical unemployment bound to result from the reduction and rationalization of benefices, there was little in the reorganization effected under the Civil Constitution to alarm the majority of priests. The real difficulties came with the provisions on appointment. All clerics were to be elected by the laity, just like other public officials. Bishops would be chosen by departmental assemblies, parish priests by district ones. Bishops would exercise their powers in concert with an advisory council. The latter recalled the synods of parish priests long advocated by certain sorts of Jansenists who derived inspiration from the seventeenth-century Sorbonne canonist Edmond Richer. 'Richerists' advocated church government by election—but not lay election, let alone election by a body of active citizens who might even include Protestants, Jews, or atheists. Cure of souls was too serious a business to be left in uninitiated hands. Finally there was the problem of the Pope's role and powers. All French citizens were expressly forbidden to have any contact with any foreign bishop or his agents; without prejudice, it was true, to 'the unity of the faith, and the communion to be maintained with the visible Head of the universal church'. The first draft had called him the bishop of Rome, but that was found too disrespectful. Respect, however, was all he was now to receive. The pontiff who had hitherto confirmed all episcopal appointments was now merely to be notified that they had been made.

The Pope's private reaction anticipated the Assembly's final approval of the Civil Constitution. On 10 July he wrote to Louis XVI urging him not to sanction a document which would drag the whole French Nation into schism. But by the time the letter arrived the king had already given his preliminary sanction, advised by bishops whom the Pope had thought would counsel intransigence. Schism was their fear too, but they thought the initiative for avoiding it lay with Rome. Few of the clerical deputies favoured resisting the new law, whatever their private reservations. But they all believed that it must be accepted by the Church, and since a national council was out of the question, the Pope must pronounce. Unaware that he already had pronounced, over the summer they bombarded Rome with urgings not to condemn the new order, but to seek ways of working with it. When the king formally promulgated the Civil Constitution on 24 August they presumed, erroneously but understandably, that agreement had been reached on abandoning the Concordat, and that a settlement was therefore in the offing. Pius VI, shocked by the pliability of the French episcopate, decided to temporize, consult his cardinals, and belatedly explore ways of avoiding schism. Outwardly he said absolutely nothing; yet so long as he remained silent the French clergy could not feel confident of the acceptability of what was now a law of the French State.

Nor were the French clergy alone in feeling they could not afford to wait. All over the country church lands were now being inventoried prior to sale, monasteries and convents were being closed down, and patriots were proclaiming that support for the Civil Constitution, like the assignats, was a test of commitment to the new order. The whole complex of issues raised by religion, in fact, was soon polarizing opinion in ways not seen since the spring of 1789. The conservative press, disparate and unco-ordinated throughout 1789, came together for the first time to denounce the Civil Constitution with one voice as an attack on the Catholic faith. Patriotic papers responded with by now characteristic anti-clerical vigour. And no stimulus was more important in the proliferation of Jacobin clubs which was such a striking feature of political life in 1790.

When the National Assembly moved to Paris, its radical leaders formed a 'Revolution Club' to discuss and co-ordinate reform policies in the way first pioneered at Versailles by the shadowy 'Breton Club'. It met in a Jacobin convent near the Assembly, and in January 1790 renamed itself the 'Society of the Friends of the Constitution'. A number of provincial centres had also seen the foundation of political clubs in the course of the stirring events of 1789. Some emerged in great cities, like Bordeaux or Dijon, but many sprang up in improbable remote townships. From the earliest stage they sought to correspond with one another, and in the spring of 1790 they began to seek affiliation with the society meeting at the Jacobins in Paris. As the fame of the latter increased new affiliates proliferated. From two dozen in February they grew to 152 in August, and over 200 by November. In these bodies the leisured, educated men of France, recognized by the National Assembly as active citizens, turned their habit of forming circles, associations, and lodges over the preceding two generations to politics. The Paris Jacobins, with a membership of over 200 deputies and, by July 1790, 1,000 others, debated national issues before and even as they were ventilated in the National Assembly itself. The provincial clubs saw their duty as keeping up enthusiasm for the new order. They organized festivals and demonstrations, chivvied lax local authorities, read and distributed patriotic newspapers, and sent endless addresses to their counterparts in other towns. Many figures prominent in the later history of the Revolution gained their first political experience in the clubs. Occasions for their foundation varied, but usually they emerged from some specific event or issue. None was more important than those connected with religion. Thus at Bergerac and Tulle clubs were founded to denounce those deputies who had supported Dom Gerle's ill-fated motion of 13 April. At Nîmes and Montauban they were formed by Protestants in the aftermath of sectarian clashes which marked local Catholic leaders as counter-revolutionary. In September the annexationists of Avignon set up a club as a further sign of their determination to join France, and its appearance was hailed by the Jacobins of neighbouring towns like Aix,

Marseilles, Nîmes, and Tarascon. The clubs of the Midi were also galvanized during the summer by the first armed demonstration of avowed counter-revolutionaries. In August a federation of National Guards met in a remote valley of the northern Gard at Jalès. Unimpeachably patriotic at first in its activities, the meeting was later taken over by the leaders of the Nîmes Catholics defeated in the *bagarre*. They declared themselves to be an insurrection and drafted a petition denouncing Protestant control of the department. 'Exploiting decrees intended for our protection', they complained,[2] 'the Protestants are endeavouring to impose their laws upon us. The department, the districts and the municipalities are all filled with their protégés. They receive the advancements, the offices and the honours . . . the tribunals are deaf to our pleas.' Although the camp then dispersed, it left behind a planning committee to organize further camps and co-ordinate action with agents of the Count d'Artois, who from exile in Turin was now dreaming of armed intervention to rescue the king and reverse the Revolution.

To these groups the Civil Constitution of the Clergy was quite literally a godsend. And the way the Assembly chose to deal with the clergy's persistent hesitations compounded their delight. On 30 October thirty bishops from the Assembly who had voted against the Civil Constitution issued an *Exposition of Principles* to explain why they had. It was no call to arms: they merely declared that they could not connive at such radical changes without consulting the Church through either a council or the Pope. Nevertheless patriots saw it as an incitement to disobey the law, and local authorities, clamorously supported by Jacobin clubs, began to enforce it. Bishops began to be expelled from suppressed sees; chapters were dissolved. In October and early November the first departmental bishops were elected. But this time the clergy did not meekly accept its fate. There were protests. 'I can no more', declared the incumbent of the doomed see of Senez, 'renounce the spiritual contract which binds me to my Church than I can renounce the promises of my baptism . . . I belong to my flock in life and in death . . . If God wishes to test his own, the eighteenth century, like the first century, will have its martyrs.'[3] The first elected bishop, the deputy Expilly, who was chosen by the Finistère department, was refused confirmation by the archbishop of Rennes. In Soissons, the bishop was dismissed by the departmental authorities for denouncing the Civil Constitution. It was impossible to dismiss all the 104 priests of Nantes who did the same, but their salaries were stopped. Evidently there was to be no peaceful transition to a new ecclesiastical order, and indignant local authorities bombarded the Assembly with demands for action. Eventually, on 27 November, action was taken. The deputies decided, after two days of bitter debate, to dismiss at once all clerics who did not accept the new order unequivocally. And to test this acceptance they imposed an oath. All beneficed clergy were to swear after mass on the first available Sunday 'to be faithful to the nation, the king and the law, and to uphold with all their power the constitution declared by the National Assembly and accepted by the king'. All who refused were to be replaced at once through the procedures laid down in the Civil Constitution.

The French Revolution had many turning-points; but the oath of the clergy was, if not the greatest, unquestionably one of them. It was certainly the Constituent Assembly's most serious mistake. For the first time the revolutionaries forced fellow citizens to choose; to declare themselves publicly for or against the new order. And although refusers branded themselves unfit to exercise public office in the regenerated French Nation, paradoxically their freedom to refuse was a recognition of their right to reject the Revolution's work. In seeking to identify dissent, in a sense the revolutionaries legitimized it. That might scarcely have mattered if, as the deputies expected, nonjurors had amounted only to a handful of prelates and their clients. But when, months rather than the expected few weeks later, the overall pattern of oath-taking became clear it was found that around half the clergy of France felt unable to subscribe. With no word from Rome, the king sanctioned the new decree on 26 December, so that oath-taking (or refusal) dominated public life throughout the country in January and February 1791. The clergy in the Assembly themselves set the pattern, in that they were completely divided. Only 109 took the oath, and only two bishops, one of them Talleyrand. As the deadline approached on 4 January the Assembly was surrounded by crowds shouting for nonjurors to be lynched; and the patriots, led unpersuasively by the Protestant Barnave, used every possible argument and procedural ploy to sway waverers. But there were none. And faced with this example from the majority of clerical deputies, it is little wonder that so many clerics in the country at large became refractories (as nonjurors were soon being called). There were, however, spectacular geographical differences. In anti-clerical Paris, few priests braved popular disapproval by refusing.

Last Sunday [wrote one observer on 11 Jaunary] I was at St. Germain l'Auxerrois to watch, since I was curious to see this ceremony, the priests' oath. The church was full up. The vicar and the second curate refused; 15 other priests swore with a good grace and a good heart, to the repeated applause of all the people. On that day there were scandals in almost every parish; at St. Severin, the vicar had fled with his curates . . . The people revile all these runaway priests and dote on those who remain faithful to the new laws. You should hear the things the people say, even in the churches. *How, they say, can there be two consciences? Some swear, others won't swear! Has the Mass changed? No, no, it's the money they miss, it's good cooking, etc. etc. . . .* and all this larded with epithets I would not dare repeat.[4]

Other areas of high oath-taking were the plains around Paris, the Pyrenees, and above all the south-east, Provence and Dauphiné, whose underpaid *congruistes* had been prominent in the clerical revolts of the early 1780s against 'episcopal despotism'. Many big provincial cities, however, saw high levels of refusal, as did most peripheral regions. Less than a quarter of the beneficed clergy took the oath in most districts of Flanders and Alsace, areas culturally distinct from the French heartland. Languedoc, riddled with Protestants who had appropriated the Revolution for their own ends, produced few clergy willing to endorse the new order. Above all, there was a massive refusal of the oath throughout the west. West of a line roughly from Rouen to La Rochelle there were only isolated pockets where more than a quarter of clerics accepted the oath. Here, priests had often lived well on their own tithes and extensive glebe, and they tended to be of local peasant stock, which was even more important than material considerations. Everywhere pressure from the laity seems to have been crucial in the decision priests took. Local authorities and clubs went to great lengths to promote acceptance, and where there was popular support they achieved successes. But in the *bocage* country of the west, where the new local authorities were townsmen already disliked for having done too well out of the Revolution, priests preferred solidarity with their parishioners. In many regions, in fact, the oath acted as a sort of opinion poll on the work of the Revolution so far, and a priest's decision to become a refractory or a 'constitutional' reflected his parishioners' opinion on a far wider range of issues than the Civil Constitution of the Clergy. In the end, about 54 per cent of the parish clergy took the oath. This suggests that well over a third of the country was now prepared to signal that the Revolution had gone far enough.

Not only parish priests were subjected to the oath. All clergy who hoped for election to a benefice in the new constitutional Church had to take it. Their chances of elevation in the hierarchy, non-existent before 1789, were enormously increased by a clean sweep of the episcopate when all but seven bishops refused to swear. Talleyrand, however, was there to assure the apostolic succession, and the constitutional Church opened clerical careers to the talents. Many monks and canons, despite their ejection from the cloister, took the oath in order to qualify themselves for the cure of souls and a salary far better than the meagre pension allotted to ex-regulars. And, despite the Civil Constitution's drastic reduction in the number of parishes, refusal rates meant that there were plenty of benefices to be had.

Too many, in fact: the National Assembly's first humiliation at the hands of the refractories came when it had to ask them to remain in office until suitable replacements could be found. Worse was to come. On 10 March the Pope broke his silence with a private letter to the bishops who had signed the *Exposition of Principles*, criticizing the Civil Constitution at length. On 13 April he asked them formally not to take the oath. On 4 May these texts were made public; and, although they still stopped short of explicit condemnation, all sides now took them for that. Many constitutionals now withdrew their oaths: in the end perhaps 10 per cent. In Paris the Pope was burned in effigy and hostile crowds prevented refractory priests and their congregations from exercising the freedom of worship vouchsafed as one of the Rights of Man and the Citizen. The Assembly returned to debating the annexation of Avignon. At the end of the month, the papal nuncio left the country. The breach between revolutionary France and the Roman Church was complete.

Only now did counter-revolution begin to acquire the makings of a popular base beyond the areas already torn by sectarian strife. Until the spring of 1790, there had indeed been no such thing as counter-revolution outside the over-heated imaginations of the Count d'Artois and his threadbare *émigré* court in Turin. When, after the October Days, Mounier had withdrawn to Dauphiné and attempted to reconvene the Dauphin estates with a view to denouncing the course events were now taking, his co-provincials rebuffed him. It was true that, as early as September 1789, Mirabeau had begun to play a double game. Continuing to boom radicalism from the tribune of the Assembly, he had offered the king and queen his secret services as an adviser. In May 1790, despite their loathing for him personally, they began to pay him for regular secret notes of advice. But Mirabeau wanted to arrest the Revolution, not reverse it. He believed in a strong monarchy, and he believed that the king should be got out of Paris, but he had no time for the plotters of Turin and their schemes of resurrecting aristocratic power. Louis XVI, in any case, took none of Mirabeau's advice, and he died in April 1791 a frustrated man, though with his patriotic reputation still intact. But nor did the king pay much heed to the messages smuggled in from Artois. As the latter told Calonne, whose counsel he was increasingly taking throughout 1790, 'We must serve the king and the queen in spite of themselves'.[5] By then, in fact, his agents were in touch with Catholic leaders in the Gard, and that autumn they felt so encouraged by reports of unrest in the south-east that they began to plan a general insurrection taking in the whole of the Rhône valley. But security was always to prove even less the counter-revolution's strong point than realism, and in December plotters were arrested in Lyons with papers that exposed the whole conspiracy. In February 1791 a second Camp de Jalès failed in its objective of rallying overwhelming numbers of Catholic National Guards to march on Nîmes. A largely Protestant force hunted down the ill-co-ordinated insurgents with considerable bloodshed. By then, Artois's support for such episodes was causing severe embarrassment to the king of Sardinia, who began to make clear that the *émigré* court was no longer welcome in Turin. In January 1791 the affronted exiles decided to leave, and by June they had found themselves a new headquarters in Germany, at Koblenz—the territory, appropriately enough, of a prince of the Church, the archbishop elector of Trier.

Louis XVI, warned of the Lyons plot, had begged his brother not to go through with it. In any case, it had depended for its ultimate success on the co-operation of loyal troops, and by the summer of 1790 it was uncertain whether any units of the army could be completely relied on. Antagonism between aristocratic officers and ranks influenced by unhierarchical National Guard units erupted into a series of mutinies in Lille, Hesdin, Perpignan, and Metz. They culminated in July and August with the rebellion of three regiments stationed at Nancy, energetically supported by the local Jacobin club. General Bouillé, supreme commander in the eastern departments, resolved to make an example of them and took Nancy by storm. Twenty-three mutineers were executed and savage punishments imposed on over a hundred more. Despite uproar in the Assembly at these echoes of *ancien régime* despotism, the example seemed to work. Effervescence in the army diminished over the winter, and the king came to regard Bouillé as someone whom he could perhaps rely on. The queen had been dreaming of flight and/or rescue by her Austrian brother's armies ever since the summer of 1789; but it seems to have been only towards the end of 1790, even as he was urging his exiled brother to drop rescue plans, that the king began to think seriously about escaping on his own initiative.

It was ironic that he should be inclining this way just as the prospects for a popular rallying to the royal cause were beginning to brighten; and doubly so in that both developments could be ascribed to the same cause— the religious schism. It was true that the king had duly sanctioned both the Civil Constitution and the clerical oath, but he had done so with clear misgivings, and when huge numbers of clergy refused the oath, and the Pope remained ominously silent, his personal doubts were reinforced. His confessor took it, but from then on the king refused to consult him. The most important women in his life after the queen, his maiden aunts, also spurned the constitutional clergy. When in February 1791 they begged to be allowed to go to Rome to consult the Pope in person, the king himself supervised arrangements for them to leave prematurely and unmolested. Crowds of women, who were now the mainstay of popular demonstrations in the capital, arrived just too late to prevent them. Encouraged by the Jacobins, the popular press, and the more radical Cordeliers Club (or more formally, 'Society of the Friends of the Rights of Man': pointedly not the Constitution) they mounted menacing demonstrations outside the residences of other members of the royal family, suspecting a plan for piecemeal emigration. Lafayette and his National Guards spent much of the spring of 1791 rushing around Paris dispersing anti-royal and anti-clerical demonstrations. Vilified by the popular press and hated by the popular political societies which the Cordeliers were attempting to foster all over the capital, he won no gratitude, either, from the king or his devotees. Lafayette saw himself as the protector of royalty: they considered him its gaoler. He could not even, they thought, guarantee the security of his charge, for he always seemed to arrive almost too late. On 28 February he was out at Vincennes trying to prevent a militant crowd from demolishing the keep there, a Bastille lookalike. Fearing the king was unprotected, hundreds of nobles armed with knives and pistols converged on the Tuileries. It looked like an escape plot, and Lafayette hurried back to conclude this 'Day of Daggers' by disarming everybody in the palace. The contempt of royalists for this posturing 'mayor of the palace' reached a peak in April, in Easter Week. As in 1790, the royal family intended to spend Easter on the wooded western heights above the city, at Saint-Cloud. But the Sunday before, the king publicly received communion from a refractory priest. Soon the whole city knew, and when, the next morning, the royal family attempted to set out for Saint-Cloud, a huge crowd surrounded their carriage and prevented it from moving. Lafayette, arriving late as usual, ordered National Guardsmen to clear the way. They refused. After almost two hours the king went back into the palace. There is no evidence that the excursion to Saint-Cloud was part of an escape plan; but its abandonment convinced the king that he now really was a prisoner of his Godless capital. From this moment rumours and predictions of his impending flight became self-fulfilling. He began to make concrete preparations for his own emigration.

Meanwhile, popular persecution of refractories intensified. In one incident market women publicly caned a whole convent of nuns who had punished pupils for attending a constitutional mass. Threats of the same treatment prevented refractory congregations from using disused churches they had hired for private worship. And all this lawlessness took place against a background of rising unemployment in the capital, as droves of servants and workers in the luxury trades were thrown on to the streets by noble emigration or retrenchment and the wholesale closure of chapters and monasteries. Public charity workshops, the most famous of which was dismantling the Bastille, took up some of the unemployment. This was where the idea of demolishing the keep at Vincennes came from. With so much labour on the market, wages had not risen much since 1789 but, as depreciating assignats began to drive coin out of circulation, prices were beginning to go up. On 2 March 1791 the National Assembly addressed a problem shelved in August 1789: it abolished trade guilds and corporations as vestiges of a now vanished society based on privilege. But guilds had also been employers' associations, and their disappearance now encouraged various groups of workers to press for higher wages. Most prominent among them were the carpenters and blacksmiths, who by early June were hinting darkly at a 'general coalition' of 80,000 workers determined to force masters into paying more. The carpenters were talking of a minimum wage enforced by strikes, and popular societies were encouraging them. The municipality made increasingly frantic attempts to resist the movement, but at length the National Assembly itself felt obliged to intervene. On 14 June, on the motion of Le Chapelier, it voted to prohibit all organizations of workers, and concerted industrial action of any sort. Local authorities were forbidden to accept representations from such groups or offer any sort of employment to their members. This law was to govern industrial relations in France for the next 73 years.

The fact that it was moved by Le Chapelier was significant. Here was one of the leading radicals of the early Revolution, a founder member of the Jacobin Club, and for long one of the pacemakers of the left in the Assembly. But by 1791 he had become convinced that the Revolution could go no further without imperilling the gains made since 1789. The time had come to consolidate, complete the constitution, and get it working before popular passions undermined it completely. Many hitherto radical deputies were coming to similar conclusions. Sensing the change of mood, in the last weeks of 1790 a group of former *monarchiens* established a Monarchical Club to rival the Jacobins. Soon it had hundreds of members; but it compromised itself with too blatant a bid for popular support when, during the cold winter weather, it began to sell heavily subsidized bread. The Jacobins were able to badger the city authorities into closing it down for disrupting the market. Barnave led this campaign; but by early summer even he had begun to moderate his views, as had his old radical allies Duport and the Lameth brothers. They had begun to realize that, should the king abscond, the keystone of the whole constitution would be lost, with incalculable consequences. Besides, there was also the question of power after the Constituent completed its work, which everyone now expected to be in the summer. Deputies who had taken a lead in national life for two years could hardly view the prospect of a return to provincial obscurity with much enthusiasm. To conciliate the king would open the way to office, especially now that Mirabeau was gone. But the drift of the Barnave, Duport and Lameth 'triumvirate' towards the centre-ground of politics rapidly aroused popular suspicion and brought to favour a number of hitherto obscure deputies on the left whom Mirabeau, in one of his last speeches (28 February 1791), had identified as the 'thirty voices'. The British ambassador was even more explicit about their aims. 'There is a sett of men', he reported on 15 April, 'whose object is the total annihilation of monarchy however limited.'[6] Their leader, he observed, was Robespierre. Whether Robespierre was at this stage republican is doubtful. Certainly he denied it in the Jacobin Club on 10 April. But another British observer saw beyond these professions,

He is [noted W. A. Miles, who had joined the Jacobin Club to report on its activities to London] *in his heart* Republican, honestly so, not to pay court to the multitude, but from an opinion that it is the very best, if not the only, form of government which men ought to admit. Upon this principle he acts, and the public voice is decidedly in favour of his system. He is a stern man, rigid in his principles, plain, unaffected in his manners, no foppery in his dress, certainly above corruption, despising wealth . . . I watch him very closely every night. I read his countenance with eyes steadily fixed on him. He really is a character to be contemplated; he is growing every hour into consequence, and, strange to relate, the whole National Assembly holds him cheap, consider him as insignificant, and, when I mentioned to one of them my suspicions, and said he would be a man of sway in a short time, and govern the million, I was laughed at.[7]

This was on 1 March. Five weeks later, on 7 April, came Robespierre's first tangible achievement. Playing on old suspicions that had blighted Mirabeau's hopes of office in November 1789, he moved that no deputy should be eligible for executive office until four years after the Constituent ended. The motion was carried. So was his next one, on 16 May, which excluded members of the Constituent from the subsequent Legislative Assembly. Both were profoundly important for the subsequent course of the Revolution, but at the time they seemed little more than tactical victories. Right-wingers supported them to spite the triumvirs, gleeful to see the fragmentation of the left.

The fragmentation continued throughout May and early June. When the Assembly returned to debating Avignon, Robespierre and his group called for instant annexation, this time unsuccessfully: the majority were beginning to recognize the risks in further alienating the Pope. Much time was also devoted to colonial questions, which had dogged the history of the Assembly ever since 8 June 1789, when a deputation from Saint-Domingue had demanded recognition. In March 1790 the deputies had voted not to abolish slavery, on the recommendation of a committee chaired by Barnave: evidently the Rights of Man did not extend to blacks. But what about the free coloureds? Whites in Saint-Domingue, where there were almost 40,000 of them, were determined to resist their claims to political rights, and when in October 1790 a small group attempted to assert themselves by force of arms, they were brutally repressed. Others now petitioned the Assembly, where Barnave warned of the dangers of meeting their claims, while Robespierre denounced slavery and called for political rights to be granted regardless of colour. Once more he carried the day. Now, too, he was beginning to dominate the Jacobin Club; and his popularity in Paris was demonstrated when on 11 June he was elected public prosecutor at the criminal court.

None of this was calculated to reassure the royal family, and during all these controversies their plans for flight were gradually elaborated. The king was now indifferent to attempts to conciliate him: he gave all his attention to composing a defiant manifesto which he proposed to leave behind, denouncing all that had been done since October 1789, and much before that. The arrangements were made by the queen's devoted admirer, the Swedish adventurer Count Axel von Fersen. Through him Bouillé was contacted: he promised to provide military escorts when the royal fugitives made the dash for Montmédy, close to the Luxemburg frontier. The troops would think they were being moved up to observe Austrian forces massing on the other side with the co-operation of the Emperor, and in any case the royal party would travel incognito, under a specially prepared passport. On the night of 20 June they slipped out of the Tuileries, past guards which had been doubled at renewed rumours of just such an attempt. Despite delays, they got clean away; but delay meant that the first escort had abandoned its post before the royal coach got there, thinking the enterprise had failed. This was the word that now went up the line of further escorts. At the same time, however, all these troop movements had aroused suspicion at towns along the route, National Guards were called out, and at Sainte-Ménehould, on the evening of 21 June, the king was recognized. Drouet, the local postmaster whose claims to have made the identification launched him into a career in radical politics, made a dash to Varennes, the next town on the route. Here the party was stopped, the whole town turned out, and the troops waiting there could do nothing. On the morning of the twenty-second messengers arrived from Paris with orders to bring the would-be escapers back.

The flight to Varennes was the Revolution's second great turning-point. Like the oath of the clergy, it forced Frenchmen to make choices that most would have preferred not to face. Even if it had succeeded choices would have been unavoidable. Whether the king merely intended, as he claimed, to go to Montmédy and negotiate from that safe distance; or whether, as most suspected (and his brother, Provence, who at the same time did reach the Austrian Netherlands, put about), he intended to emigrate and return at the head of Austrian armies, the achievements of the Revolution up to that moment would have been fundamentally challenged. Diplomats thought war would have been precipitated there and then. The failure of the attempted escape postponed that danger—but demanded choices of a different order. The monarch had renounced the Revolution, and had explained why at great length in the proclamation he left behind. He complained of imprisonment in Paris, violation of property, and 'complete anarchy in all parts of the empire'. He denounced betrayal of the wishes expressed in the *cahiers*, the lack of power accorded to the Crown under the new constitution, the tentacular power usurped by the Jacobin clubs, and, implicitly, the new religious order. How could such a man remain head of State? The blackest suspicions of the Parisian populace and radical leaders were confirmed. Republicans now came into the open. All over the capital symbols of royalty were attacked and defaced, and on 24 June the Cordeliers Club delivered a petition to the National Assembly to depose the king or consult the Nation on his fate in a referendum. A crowd of 30,000 escorted its presenters.

Most members of the National Assembly, however, had been thoroughly frightened by the king's departure. Its very behaviour when the crisis broke, paradoxically, showed that public business could go on perfectly well without a king: ministers were summoned, military dispositions checked, and debate proceeded as if nothing untoward had happened. 'One would never have imagined', marvelled one noble deputy, 'that at this moment there was no longer a King in France.'[8] But to depose the king would mean at best a regency, notorious in French history for their perils; or at worst a complete redrafting of a constitution that was all but completed. Revisions in a republican direction could only lead to a strengthening of those popular forces which increasing numbers of deputies had found so alarming over the spring. Within a day of the news of the flight breaking, however, the Assembly had found a way out of the dilemma. It would pretend, against all the evidence, that the king had been kidnapped. It said so in a proclamation issued on 22 June urging the nation to keep calm. The denunciations he had left behind had been wrested from an unwilling monarch by wicked advisers. Those who objected to such patent fictions were heavily voted down. The king was suspended from his functions: for the rest of its life the Constituent Assembly controlled the executive as well as made laws. But there was never any doubt that the vast majority of deputies were determined to retain the monarchy at the cost of however many fudges and fictions were required. On 15 July the entire blame for the flight was imputed by decree to Bouillé and his subordinates, who were to be prosecuted. By then, however, as the deputies well knew, most of the accused had emigrated, and were safe in Austrian territory.

The sense of emergency at the news of Varennes was nation-wide. There was a general expectation that the Austrians would invade to rescue the royal captive. National Guards were stood to, local authorities organized permanent committees to maintain revolutionary vigilance, and in many places there was renewed persecution of refractory priests and their congregations. The assumption was that they were in league with aristocrats and foreigners in some vast plot. Jacobin clubs were filled to bursting with anxious patriots. The religious turmoil of the spring had revitalized the Jacobin network, with the need to drum up support for oath-taking and promote participation in the election of priests and bishops. By July there were well over 900 affiliated clubs, almost three times as many as at the start of the year; and in his parting manifesto the king had pinpointed them as the source of much of what had gone wrong. But Varennes confronted the clubs with serious problems. Many of their members clearly thought that the king's betrayal of his trust ought to lead to his deposition. At least sixty clubs called for him to be put on trial. But only a handful called openly for a republic, and many others explicitly repudiated the idea. It was soon apparent that the 'mother society' itself was split. Few speakers in its debates seemed to find the Assembly's policy satisfactory, but outright republicanism also found few supporters. Even Robespierre only advocated leaving the decision to the people. But the club felt unable to resist the sense of outrage which swept Paris on 15 July when it became known that the Assembly held the king blameless. That evening its meeting was swamped by a crowd of 4,000 organized by a hitherto obscure radical club called the Social Circle. Before Varennes, the Social Circle had been noted for somewhat Utopian political discussions, but afterwards it had co-operated with the Cordeliers in their call for a republic, and had publicized their petition of 24 June in its newspaper, the *Bouche de fer* (Iron Mouth). The intruders now urged the Jacobins to join them in drawing up a petition against the king's reinstatement. They hoped to attract mass signings by promulgating it on the altar to the Fatherland which had been erected on the Champ de Mars for the celebration of the second anniversary of the fall of the Bastille the day before. A joint committee was set up to draft the petition overnight. Among those elected to it were Danton and Brissot, who had built himself a democratic reputation in Paris through his newspaper, *Le Patriote Français*, and his activities in the Social Circle. But as finally drafted and published in the *Bouche de fer* the next afternoon, the petition declared that the king had abdicated, and should not be replaced unless a majority of the Nation so decided. It was in effect a republican manifesto; and its result was to split the Jacobin Club. Lafayette, the Lameths, and a majority of its active members were committed monarchists, and they now seceded. They took with them every deputy except Robespierre, his close ally Pétion, and one or two others and set themselves up as a rival club meeting in the former convent of the Feuillants. Robespierre was appalled at the fragmentation of his most secure platform, and after a heated debate he persuaded the rump of the Jacobins to withdraw their support for the petition. It was too late. The Feuillants were only too delighted to have shed their radical colleagues. In any case, the Cordeliers had now taken up the petition, and were determined to push ahead with the signing ceremony.

On 17 July, accordingly, perhaps 50,000 people gathered on the Champ de Mars. By late afternoon 6,000 had signed. But long before that two unfortunates found hiding beneath the patriotic altar were lynched by excited and suspicious crowds, and this gave Bailly, as mayor of Paris, an excuse for declaring martial law under the decree of October 1789. Lafayette and the National Guard now marched to the Champ de Mars flying the red warning flag. They were greeted with a hail of stones and some shots. Thereupon they opened fire on the largely unarmed crowd, shooting them down, as one participant put it, 'like chickens'.[9] Perhaps 50 people were killed and several more wounded as the crowd scattered. In the weeks that followed the 'Massacre of the Champ de Mars' another 200 or so known activists in the Parisian popular movement were arrested, although Danton escaped to England, and Desmoulins and Marat went into hiding. It seemed that the nascent republican movement had been broken. Radical newspapers ceased to publish; the Cordeliers and the Social Circle ceased to meet, and the latter never resumed. Even the Jacobins had been shattered, and the Feuillants drafted a confident manifesto to provincial affiliates inviting them to recognize the new club as the only legitimate Society of the Friends of the Constitution. Untroubled, therefore, by further popular pressure, the Constituent Assembly now set about producing a final and definitive version of the Constitution on which it had laboured for two years.

In this process Lafayette and the triumvirate, bitter rivals right down to June 1791, co-operated. Barnave, who, as one of the Assembly's commissioners sent to escort the royal family back from Varennes, had been captivated by the queen, took a lead in trying to secure last-minute amendments that would make the constitution more acceptable to the king. They scored some successes. The Civil Constitution of the Clergy was excluded from the constitution: that meant an oath to the constitution did not imply acceptance of the new ecclesiastical order, and also that the Civil Constitution might be amended or even replaced as an ordinary law without going through the deliberately cumbrous, ten-year process laid down for changing the constitution itself. Meanwhile a proposal that all refractory priests should be ordered not to come within thirty miles of any place where they had been beneficed was thrown out as inflammatory. In a disingenuous gesture, the 'silver-mark' qualification for election as a deputy, which had proved a particularly useful issue for rallying the Parisian popular societies in the spring, was abolished; but qualifications for voting in secondary electoral assemblies, which actually chose deputies, were raised to a level far above the silver mark, to put control of the important levers of power securely in the hands of very rich landowners. In any case, by the time these amendments passed, on 27 August, the elections to the subsequent Legislative Assembly had already been held, and all those chosen had had to pass the silver-mark test. Finally the Feuillants were able to carry a law to restrict the freedom of the press. Holding press licence responsible for much of the popular effervescence curbed (it was hoped finally) in July, the Assembly decreed on 23 August, against the lonely opposition of Robespierre, that any writer who 'deliberately provokes disobedience to the Law, [or] disparagement of the constituted powers and resistance to their acts' might be prosecuted, and that public officials whose probity or honest intentions were impugned might sue for damages. The Lameths, and Malouet (who unlike them had always believed in such safeguards), also dreamed of making the royal veto absolute, allowing deputies to be ministers, and even a second chamber; but it was too late now to revive the *monarchien* programme of 1789. The king was to be asked to accept a constitution the same in all but detail as had been envisaged ever since the laying of its corner-stones in 1789.

Nor was it at all certain that Louis XVI would accept it. Bombarded with conflicting advice from both France and abroad, he seemed undecided until the very last minute. Sometimes he seemed resolved to try to make the constitution work: on 31 July he wrote to Artois asking him to return to the country and abandon his counter-revolutionary plottings. The next day the Assembly provided sterner incentives by passing the first law imposing penalties on *émigrés*. They were summoned to return within a month on pain of subjection to triple taxation. Now for the first time, too, official lists of *émigrés* were to be drawn up. The first proposal for such a law had come the preceding February, but it had been defeated when Mirabeau denounced it. Since that time, however, the stream of emigration had swelled enormously, especially after Varennes. Already alienated by a new oath of loyalty to the nation, the law, and the king (in that order) imposed on 11 June, army officers were outraged by the Varennes débâcle. Bouillé's emigration was followed, over the next six months, by the disappearance of perhaps 6,000 of his fellow officers, well over half the officer corps of the entire army. The flow was not staunched by the abrogation of the new law against emigration on 14 September, as part of a general amnesty to mark the promulgation of the constitution. By this time, discipline throughout the army had all but collapsed amid new mutinies. Many officers who might have been prepared to stay were positively driven out.

In aristocratic circles, in fact, the Feuillants received no credit for their efforts to restore a national consensus around a constitutional king. Every effort was made to block them. In the Assembly nobles, or, as they were now being called, Blacks or *Ci-devants* ('hithertos'), either abstained from voting or took a perverse pleasure in supporting Robespierre and Pétion. Despite its avowedly conservative aims, few right-wingers joined the Feuillant Club; yet it also failed spectacularly to win over most of the provincial clubs. Only seventy-two severed their links with the Jacobins, and many of those had drifted back by the end of the summer. When martial law was lifted early in August, and newspapers began to reappear, no important Parisian journal came out for the Feuillants. Nothing did more to keep politics polarized than rumours of war, which persisted throughout the summer. The left assumed that the flight to Varennes had been part of an international conspiracy to crush the Revolution; and that, indeed, was what the queen and the *émigrés* had hoped to forge. When the flight failed, all sides assumed that the German powers would now redouble their efforts, and that the crumbling French army would not be able to stand up to them. On 10 July, in fact, the 'Padua Circular' issued by the Emperor Leopold invited fellow monarchs to join him in a campaign to restore the liberty of the French royal family. But only the king of Prussia responded positively, and the result was merely a further appeal for concerted action when the two monarchs met at Pillnitz on 27 August.

The Declaration of Pillnitz stated that the situation of the king of France was an object of common interest to all the sovereigns of Europe. It invited the other powers to join in the employment of 'the most effectual means . . . to put the king of France in a state to strengthen, in the most perfect liberty, the bases of a monarchical government equally becoming to the rights of sovereigns and to the wellbeing of the French Nation'. If the other powers agreed, the two kings declared themselves ready to 'act promptly'. Privately the Austrians, at least, recognized that there was no prospect of other powers joining a crusade, and at this very moment they were disbanding regiments. For them the declaration was to satisfy monarchical and family honour, a move that might even promote some moderation within France, but scarcely a serious threat. But in that case it was needlessly provocative to state that it was issued at the request of the *émigré* princes, or to allow the latter to publish it together with an inflammatory letter to Louis XVI urging him to reject the constitution. The Constituent Assembly, therefore, came to an end amid rumours of an *émigré* invasion backed by foreigners; and in the last gesture of defiance towards international opinion, the deputies finally voted on 14 September to annex Avignon and the Comtat.

The princes' appeal to their brother had come too late. On 3 September the constitution was completed and presented to the king for acceptance. On the thirteenth, he signified his acceptance, amid scenes of rejoicing and a general amnesty. The Revolution, the Feuillants were determined to believe, was now complete, and ordinary constitutional life could begin; ushering in, so they hoped, calmer times. But much of the rejoicing was really at the approaching end of the Constituent Assembly, which came on 30 September. Its achievements had been enormous. In twenty-six months it had dismantled the *ancien régime*, the product of centuries of slow evolution. At the same time it had laid down the principles of a new order and established structures whose outlines were to endure down to our own day. When, later in the Revolution, or well into the next century, men spoke approvingly of the principles of 1789, they meant those accepted by Louis XVI in 1791, before the Revolution went to extremes. Yet the seeds of those later extremes had already been sown, and the Constituent Assembly was responsible for them, too. By forcing the clergy to choose between Church and State, it had split the country and given counter-revolutionaries a higher cause than self-interest. In its very last days the Assembly deepened this self-inflicted wound by unilaterally seizing papal territory. The religious schism made it impossible for millions to give the new order their whole-hearted support—beginning with the king himself. Only those who dared not think anything else believed, by September 1791, that his acceptance of the constitution was sincere. He had already shown, and said, what he really thought at the time of what he now chose to call his 'journey' in June. But that created a further split, between constitutional monarchists and a rapidly growing republican movement all the more alarming in that its mainstay was the turbulent populace of Paris. As to the nobles who had done so much to launch the Revolution, most had by now opted out, hiding themselves in rural obscurity or slipping across the Rhine to join the princes. None of this promised well for the Feuillant dream of post-revolutionary life. The British ambassador's prediction of April 1791 was truer than ever by October: 'The present constitution has no friends and cannot last.'[10]

# Europe and the Revolution
## 1788—1791

THE French Revolution took the whole of Europe by surprise. To be sure, all educated Europeans were aware in the 1780s that they lived in an age of upheaval and defiance of authority. America had thrown off British sovereignty, and Ireland had defied it. In the Dutch Republic self-styled patriots were struggling to deprive the prince of Orange of what quasi-monarchical powers he retained. But if any great monarchy seemed destined soon to collapse, it was not that of the French Bourbons, but that of the Habsburgs. Restless and unpredictable, the Emperor Joseph II was turning his German dominions upside-down in a headlong attempt to create a rational, efficient military despotism. By the middle of the decade he was switching his attention to his more outlying territories, Hungary and the southern Netherlands, and soon both were in turmoil.

French diplomats positively encouraged all these developments. Without French help American independence could not have been achieved so rapidly and decisively. The Dutch patriot movement also stood in the way of Orangist attempts to reforge the century-long alliance with the British, ruptured in 1780; so the patriots were promised every support from Versailles. And anything which preoccupied Joseph II domestically was to be welcomed if it curbed his international adventures. But Vergennes, the friend of foreign rebels, was a stern authoritarian at home. Neither he, nor the foreign observers who watched him confidently deploying his master's international influence, discerned that the ground was crumbling beneath him. Yet within six months of his death in February 1787 France, too, was in turmoil.

The first sign that France had been internationally weakened by domestic crisis came in September 1787, when she failed to keep her promises to the Dutch patriots and allowed the Prussians to march into the Republic and crush their movement. The chanceries of Europe registered the change instantly, and not without some gloating. 'If God', wrote the British ambassador to the Hague, 'wished to punish them in the way they have sinned, how I should admire divine justice.'[1] Apparently God did. For the next four years the French became ever more preoccupied with their internal problems, and their international power withered away. Diplomatic relations were conducted, for the first time in centuries, without regard for what the French might think or do. Their apparent inability to restore financial or practical stability amazed and amused the rest of Europe, at least down to the summer of 1789. Until then, few onlookers knew what to make of it all. But with the fall of the Bastille, suddenly and simultaneously throughout the continent the meaning of what was going on in France seemed to fall into place. The Bastille was a state prison. Its storming marked the overthrow of despotism by subjects who until now had known no liberty under kingly rule.

The news was romantic and thrilling. All over Europe people thronged bookshops and reading rooms, clamouring for the latest information. 'I do not know where to turn,' wrote a German lady, 'for the papers contain such great and splendid news that I am hot from reading.'[2] The leaders of German literary life were almost unanimous in welcoming the events in France. Philosophers like Kant and Herder, poets like Klopstock, Hölderin, and Wieland were enraptured by what they heard. Even those, like Goethe and Schiller, who were more sceptical right from the start followed the news avidly. Richer and more adventurous Germans took the road to Paris to observe the new liberty at first hand, and one at least became notorious there—Anacharsis Clootz, a wealthy Prussian nobleman who had left France in 1785 vowing never to return until the Bastille had fallen. He was in Sicily when it did, and hurried back to throw himself into the democratic politics he had hitherto only dreamed of. The impact was similar among the intellectuals of Italy, who rejoiced to see what had seemed the most well established of states shattered by popular uprising and then rededicating itself to national reform. Wholesale reform was not, after all, just for dreamers, or for Americans free to start again in virgin territory: it could take place in the heart of Europe, in the continent's very intellectual capital. That meant it could take place anywhere. As far away as Stockholm the news from France was the talk of the salons and cafés. 'Tell me,' wrote the young Swedish poet Kellgren to his brother, 'was there ever anything more sublime in History, even in Rome or Greece? I wept like a child, like a man, at the story of this great victory.'[3] In St Petersburg, there was jubilation in the streets and a vast expansion in the circulation of news-sheets. Russians were present at the fall of the Bastille, in fact. 'The cry of freedom rings in my ears', rhapsodized one of them, Count

Stroganov, 'and the best day of my life will be that when I see Russia regenerated by such a Revolution.'[4]

One country in Europe felt no such need. In 1788 there were widespread celebrations in Great Britain to mark the centenary of the 'Glorious Revolution' which had thwarted Stuart despotism and finally established parliamentary government and the rule of law. Englishmen revelled in their freedom, and had traditionally regarded the French as slaves to tyranny, superstition, and poverty. They were now benevolently interested to see their neighbour catching up. Fox, leader of the Whig opposition, proclaimed the fall of the Bastille the greatest and best event in history; and while not all British observers went so far, there was little initial hostility. 'It will perhaps surprise you,' one Member of Parliament wrote to a correspondent in France on 28 July 1789, 'but it is certainly true, that the Revolution . . . produced a very sincere and very general joy here. It is the subject of all conversations; and even all the newspapers, without one exception, though they are not conducted by the most liberal or most philosophical of men, join in sounding forth the praises of the Parisians, and in rejoicing at an event so important for mankind.'[5] And meanwhile those who had seen more recent attempts at revolution suppressed or aborted took comfort and encouragement. Many of them were already refugees in France anyway. Genevan democrats, whose attempts to widen the circles of political power in the city-state had been crushed by armed intervention by a league of neighbouring powers, led by France, in 1782, hoped the new regime in Paris would abandon its oligarchic puppets. Shamed at its failure to help the Dutch patriots more tangibly in 1787, the dying absolute monarchy in France had at least extended hospitality to refugees from Orangist and Prussian vengeance. By the end of 1788 perhaps 1,500 Dutch families had been granted residence and small pensions by Louis XVI. When power in France fell into the hands of men who also called themselves patriots and sought to share power more widely, the Dutch exiles were delighted. Largely concentrated in a handful of towns in French Flanders, by 1790 they were forming clubs and setting up National Guard units. The National Assembly, recognizing spiritual allies, continued to subsidize them, too; although its pacific professions and military weakness offered them scant hope at this stage of reversing their defeat of 1787 with French help.

Most of the Dutch exiles, however, did not penetrate as far as France. The vast majority of the 40,000 or so fugitives from the Orangist reaction ended up nearer home, in the Austrian Netherlands or the ecclesiastical principality of Liège. Belgian resistance to Joseph II's rationalizing policies in Church and State was gathering momentum by the time of the Dutch political exodus. The refugees found the atmosphere of defiance, as well as linguistic affinities, congenial; but the issues at stake in Belgium were very different from those preoccupying Dutch patriots. The opponents of William V had sought to change the way things were done. In Belgium it was the distant emperor who sought change: his Flemish and Walloon subjects merely wanted to be left alone. In 1787 and 1788 that brought them closer to the French than to the Dutch; but whereas, by 1789, the French had moved on, and were looking to create a whole new order based on liberty, the Belgian rebels remained largely wedded to protecting existing liberties, that whole complex of customs and prescriptive rights which French patriots were now beginning to denounce as unjust and meaningless privileges. Both conflicts came to a head in the first half of 1789, however, and during the excitement of the struggle few noticed the increasing divergence between the French and what they called the Brabant Revolution. The day after the third estate in Versailles proclaimed themselves the National Assembly and claimed the sole right to authorize taxation, Joseph II demanded that the estates of Brabant grant him a limitless right to tax and legislate (18 June 1789). When they refused, he dissolved them, and renounced the 'Joyous Entry', the charter of liberties which he like all preceding sovereigns had sworn to uphold on his accession. The grain shortage that was so important in France at this moment also affected the crowded cities of the low countries, and as in Paris the hungry populace threw its weight behind the opponents of authority. 'Here as in Paris' in fact became the popular cry in Brussels, and a secret revolutionary society was established to tap anti-Austrian feeling. Using a slogan already favoured by Irish and Dutch para-military reform organizations earlier in the decade, it called itself Pro Aris et Focis—for altars and hearths—and it was generously funded by the Church, which here as elsewhere in the Habsburg Empire had borne the brunt of Joseph II's reforms. No popular uprising came, however, until companies of armed *émigrés* intervened in the autumn. The acknowledged leader of resistance to the emperor, the colourful Brussels lawyer Van der Noot, had been in exile in Holland since August 1788, hoping to interest foreign powers in his compatriots' plight. Spurned by monarchs well content to see Joseph II mired by chaos in Belgium, eventually he turned to armed self-help. In co-operation with the founder of Pro Aris et Focis, his fellow lawyer Vonck, in October 1789 he organized an invasion which overwhelmed the small, over-confident Austrian garrison. The insurgents came not just from across the Dutch frontier, but from Liège in the south, where in mid-August opponents of the prince-bishop had seized power, visibly encouraged by the example of France. By December the Belgian rebels, backed by popular uprisings, were in control of the entire country, and in Brussels everyone was wearing national cockades like the French—but here in black, yellow, and red. On 10 January 1790, at the invitation of the estates of Brabant, representatives of all the provinces met and declared themselves an independent United States of Belgium. The chorus of approval from France was unanimous. But almost at once it became clear how little the two revolutions had in common.

The new 'statist' regime sought only to carry on as before, but without a monarch. Power was to remain with the estates of the various provinces, dominated as they were by great nobles and above all the Church in the form of its traditional representatives, the abbots of the greater monasteries. Van der Noot, now installed as first minister, had no sympathy with a France where the lands of the Church had already been confiscated, monasteries were about to be dissolved, and noble power had been broken. Vonck, however, felt that the moment of establishing a new political order was an opportunity for reform. At the end of January he issued an appeal for constitutional change obviously inspired by the French example. He called for the admission of petty nobles and parish priests to the estates, the doubling of third-estate representation, and the creation of a fourth estate representing small towns. Even this was conservative by the standards now reached in France, but it was bitterly denounced by the statists and the Church as a formula for Frenchified levelling. When Vonck's 'progressives' petitioned for a modification of the Joyous Entry the people of Brussels attacked the houses of their known leaders. When part of the new federation's army mutinied in support of Vonck, thousands of peasants poured into Brussels to protect the statists. Isolated, persecuted, and in a tiny minority amid their deeply conservative countrymen, Vonck and most of the leading progressives fled to France—thus confirming all the worst suspicions of their persecutors.

Yet neither France nor the French example were any real threat to the new Belgian regime. The danger still came from Austria. Joseph II, who had touched off the original revolt, died on 20 February 1790. He was succeeded by his brother Leopold, who initially at least had no despotic ambitions. Grand Duke of Tuscany since 1765, Leopold had sought to rule in Florence with the co-operation and participation of his subjects. He had positively welcomed the first news from France in the spring of 1789. 'The regeneration of France', he wrote on 14 June, 'will be an example which all sovereigns and governments of Europe will be forced, willy-nilly, to copy. Infinite happiness will result from this everywhere, the end of injustice, wars, conflicts and arrests, and it will be one of the most useful fashions introduced by France into Europe.'[6] By 1790 he was less sanguine, but he still had no intention of following Joseph's high-handed policies in Belgium. In fact, in March he offered to confirm the entire new statist regime in return for acknowledgement of his sovereignty. He received no reply. Subsequently he approached Vonck in his French exile, offering to support the progressives if they would work for his restoration. Aware of his liberal reputation, they negotiated for a while; but by now they were being radicalized by the French atmosphere and the contacts lapsed. Only then did Leopold resort to force. First he cleared the diplomatic decks by reaching an accord with Prussia, which had been on the point of war with Joseph when he died. Called in as mediators in the Liège revolution, Prussian troops now straddled the route to Belgium. But when Leopold assured King Frederick William II that his intentions were pacific throughout Europe, Liège was evacuated, and on 27 July 1790 the two German powers concluded the Convention of Reichenbach. Under it Leopold agreed to end Joseph's war against the Turks, going on since 1787, seeking no substantial territorial gains. Thus reassured, Prussia agreed to stop supporting rebels against the Habsburg Crown, whether in Hungary or Belgium. Peace was duly made with the Turks in September, releasing the necessary troops, and the recovery of Belgium began. The new state's army was swept aside; so were irregular companies of peasant volunteers raised in what was known as the 'September Crusade'. By the beginning of December Austrian soldiers had overrun the whole country, and Liège into the bargain, where the bishop returned on their coat-tails. Van der Noot fled once more to Holland. The United States of Belgium had lasted less than a year.

No friends came to their rescue. The British, traditional protectors of the low countries, had actually helped to engineer the Reichenbach agreement. And the French, who were not consulted, looked on with indifference. They had now recognized how little Van der Noot's revolution had in common with their own; and besides, only on 22 May, the National Assembly had elevated France's diplomatic nullity to a point of principle by declaring that the nation renounced offensive warfare. The question arose when a request for diplomatic support arrived from Spain. A year earlier, off Vancouver Island in the far Pacific, Spanish coastguards had tried to arrest British merchantmen in Nootka Sound on the grounds that the entire west coast of America was Spain's. When news of the incident arrived in Europe, the British refused to accept Spanish claims, and both sides began to mobilize for war. Madrid now invoked the Family Compact, the alliance with France repeatedly renewed over the century since its first conclusion in 1733. Louis XVI and his ministers were inclined to send the help requested, even at the risk of war; but the National Assembly, confronting diplomatic questions for the first time, spurned the Spanish request. A national, representative regime did not recognize family ties between ruling houses as fit bases for international agreements, much less action. And so although much traditional Anglophobia surfaced in the Nootka Sound debates, and there was intermittent talk of readying the fleet, the Spaniards were offered no tangible help, and were forced to back down. The revolutionaries felt proud of the way they had refused to perpetuate dynastic diplomacy. Two months later they raged against another specimen of it when Leopold, still nominally France's ally, sought permission for Austrian troops to cross French territory on the way to Belgium. Fears now began to be expressed for the first time of an international plot to attack France and destroy the Revolution. Marie-Antoinette and her circle might dream of it, but nothing could have been further from the truth. As the Turkish war in the east came to an end, the great continental powers were more than happy to leave France wallowing in what they saw as helpless chaos while they turned their predatory attentions to Poland.

In 1772 the Russians, Prussians, and Austrians had combined, in the first partition, to deprive Poland of a third of her territory and population. What was left was little more than a Russian puppet state; but under it many Poles schemed and planned for a national revival when an opportunity should present itself. It did so in 1788, when the Russians became distracted on two fronts by simultaneous war against the Swedes and the Turks. Between October 1788 and January 1789 the Polish diet threw off Russian control and began a massive expansion of the army to protect the country's recovered independence in the future. The advocates of this programme called themselves patriots, and they warmed to the news by then coming from France. Educated Poles knew that France was their country's traditional friend, many read and spoke French, and they felt involved in a common struggle against despotism when they read the French news which flooded the Warsaw news-sheets. But as with Belgium, apart from rebellion against established authority, the situations in Poland and France had nothing in common. Political life in Poland was a noble monopoly, and the diet was outraged when, in November 1789, 141 towns subscribed to a petition calling for non-noble representation. Liberty in Poland meant 'Golden Liberty': the anarchical old constitution in which the king was elected and exercised no real power, legislation could be blocked by a single contrary vote (*liberum veto*), and dissatisfied elements enjoyed a legalized right to rebel. The Russians, for their own reasons, favoured these arrangements, and styled themselves guarantors of the Polish constitution. Patriots, on the contrary, became identified in the course of 1790 with a stronger executive including a hereditary monarchy, majority votes in the diet, and an end to legalized rebellion. Only modernization on this scale, they thought, could give Poland the strength to resist Russia in the future; and with the Convention of Reichenbach signalling the imminent end of the Turkish war the matter became urgent. On 3 May 1791 the king and the patriots combined to push a new constitution through a thinly attended diet surrounded by troops. The phraseology of the 3 May constitution contained many echoes of that being elaborated in France at the same time; and its supporters organized themselves into a club called the Friends of the Constitution. Again the parallel was superficial, but so was the perception of the Polish magnates who had been the mainstay of the old constitution; and so, above all, was that of Catherine II of Russia. The new Polish constitution was in her eyes plainly Jacobinical. Catherine had been determined to recover control in Poland from the moment it was lost. The echoes of France she discerned there made her all the more determined. Paradoxically it would be the actions of the French revolutionaries in 1792 which would enable her finally to do so.

Meanwhile, however, western Europe seemed to be adjusting to the new order in France. Much of the initial enthusiasm had cooled when the fall of the Bastille was followed by continued upheavals. The October Days in particular dismayed many observers of orderly disposition, and hardly anybody outside France thought the first anniversary of the fall of the Bastille worth celebrating. But the full extent of the Revolution's quarrel with the Church to which the vast majority of Europeans belonged was not evident until the spring of 1791; and pity and puzzlement rather than alarm were the predominant attitudes in 1790. People were no longer sure what to think. In November of that year, however, a powerful and persuasive voice began to tell them, with extraordinary success. In that month, Edmund Burke published his *Reflexions on the Revolution in France*.

Initially Burke had been no more sure than anybody else what to make of French events, although he was never swept along by the enthusiasm of some of his fellow Whigs. But what outraged him was the inspiration the Revolution had clearly given to the movement in Great Britain for parliamentary reform. Originating in the late 1760s, agitation for the redistribution of parliamentary seats, shorter parliaments, and extension of the franchise had flagged in the mid-1780s after a ministerial reform bill introduced by Pitt had failed to pass. The centenary celebrations in 1788 revived interest in reform, particularly among dissenters excluded from the franchise by religion. Dissenters proved one of the mainstays of a

'Revolution Society' established to perpetuate these revived aspirations, and it was a leading dissenting minister, Dr Richard Price, who stung Burke into action with a sermon preached under the auspices of the Revolution Society on 4 November (birthday of William III, the hero of 1688) 1789. France, Price implied, had now overtaken Great Britain in the pursuit of liberty. Its religious laws were more liberal, its system of government more representative. And, with news of the October Days still the topic of every conversation, he thanked God that 'I have lived to see THIRTY MILLIONS of people, indignant and resolute, spurning at slavery, and demanding liberty with an irresistible voice; their king led in triumph, and an arbitrary monarch surrendering himself to his subjects.'[7]

Burke's indignation at this interpretation of French events knew no bounds. It triggered an impassioned denunciation of the Revolution in Parliament in February 1790 which left his fellow Whigs dumbfounded. And in the following November it produced his great pamphlet. What had happened in 1688, he protested, was not revolution in the new, French sense, but rather the preservation of hallowed English liberties from the attacks of a monarch bent on subverting them. Reverence for ancient institutions and established practices was the true English way: in fact it was the only way for any self-respecting nation. Yet the French had spurned this principle. Repudiating the wisdom of their ancestors, and heedless of the consequences for their posterity, they were now in the process of renouncing their entire heritage. 'You had', he told them, 'the elements of a constitution very nearly as good as could be wished . . . ; but you chose to act as if you had never been moulded into civil society, and had everything to begin anew. You began ill, because you began by despising everything that belonged to you.' The mildest of monarchs, and the most beautiful of queens, had ruled over a spirited, honourable, and cultivated nobility, a respectable clergy and an independent judiciary. The monarchy had been 'a despotism rather in appearance than in reality', and with a little modest adaptation the Estates-General might have become a body as representative as the British Parliament of the nation's true interests. But the elections of 1789 had brought to power not 'the natural landed interest of the country', but 'country curates' and 'obscure provincial advocates . . . stewards of petty local jurisdictions, country attorneys, notarys, and the whole train of the ministers of municipal litigation, the fomenters and conductors of the petty war of village vexation . . . Was it to be expected that they would attend to the stability of property, whose existence had always depended upon whatever rendered property questionable, ambiguous and insecure?' It was not; and in fact an Assembly dominated by such men had embarked on a confiscation of property unparalleled in history. By the time Burke finished the *Reflexions* the lands of the Church had been nationalized in what he saw as a 'momentum of ignorance, rashness, presumption and lust of plunder, which nothing has been able to resist'. This expropriation had been used to launch a fraudulent paper currency with no possible stable future, and had necessitated a civil constitution which no honourable cleric could submit himself to. 'It seems to me,' he concluded, 'that this new ecclesiastical establishment is intended only to be temporary, and preparatory to the utter abolition, under any of its forms, of the Christian religion.'

These thoughts brought Burke to the causes of the Revolution. Convinced that nothing was fundamentally wrong with the old order, he attributed its subversion to a conspiracy. On the one hand were the 'moneyed interest', resentful at their lack of esteem and greedy for new profits; on the other, and even more important, were the so-called philosophers of the Enlightenment, a 'literary cabal' committed to the destruction of Christianity by any and every available means. The idea of a philosophic conspiracy was not new. It went back to the only one ever conclusively proved to have existed, the plot of the self-styled Illuminati to undermine the Church-dominated government of Bavaria. The Bavarian government published a sensational collection of documents to illustrate its gravity, and Burke had read it. Although he was not the first to attribute events in France to conspiracy of the sort thwarted in Bavaria, the way he included the idea in the most comprehensive denunciation of the Revolution yet to appear lent it unprecedented authority. Nor was the destruction of Christianity and the triumph of atheism the only catastrophe he predicted. Disgusted by the way the 'Republic of Paris' and its 'swinish multitude' held the government captive, the provinces would eventually cut loose and France would fall apart. The assignats would drive out sound coinage and hasten, rather than avert, bankruptcy. The only possible end to France's self-induced anarchy would come when 'some popular general, who understands the art of conciliating the soldiery, and who possesses the true spirit of command, shall draw the eyes of all men upon himself. Armies will obey him on his personal account . . . the moment in which that event shall happen, the person who really commands the army is your master.'

Burke's determination in the *Reflexions* was to persuade his countrymen that the French example was not one to follow. And undoubtedly he articulated what many conservative Englishmen were vaguely feeling about cross-Channel events. But the fury and venom of his attack also focused the minds of France's British admirers, and in so doing paradoxically breathed new life into a domestic reform movement that was once again flagging as Pitt registered yet another victory in the general election of 1790. Burke's intemperate diatribe, reformers felt, must be answered, and several cogent responses appeared in the early months of 1791. All were outshone, however, by Thomas Paine's *Rights of Man*, which was published in February and at once hailed as the definitive reply. An advocate of republican revolution since he had first urged the common sense of it on the American rebels in 1776, Paine had returned to Europe in 1787 and had been looking for an opportunity to announce his views on the French Revolution since visiting Paris over the winter of 1789–90. Burke's outburst provided it.

He began by pouring scorn on Burke's reverence for the past. 'Every age and generation must be as free to act for itself *in all cases* as the ages and generations which preceded it. The variety and presumption of governing beyond the grave is the most ridiculous and insolent of all tyrannies.' He then went on to a detailed refutation of Burke's picture of French affairs, denouncing him as an admirer of power, not principles, and one who, pitying the plumage of the old order, forgot the dying bird. He sought to correct lurid allusions to popular savagery by detailed accounts of the fall of the Bastille (scarcely mentioned by Burke) and the October Days. The overriding purpose of these movements, Paine argued, was to establish the Rights of Man; and he printed a full translated text of the Declaration of the Rights of Man and the Citizen, glossing it at length as a way of refuting Burke's 'pathless wilderness of rhapsodies . . . a sort of descant upon Governments, in which he asserts whatever he pleases'. The French were now in the process of giving themselves a rational, equitable, established constitution, whereas that of Great Britain, so vaunted by Burke, was nothing but a random and arbitrary collection of unjust customs going back to no better title than conquest by a Norman adventurer. Now was the time for all peoples to follow the French example by abolishing nobility and titles, destroying tithes, and proclaiming the regeneration of man. Paine even urged the British to go further, and abandon monarchy itself. 'From what we now see,' he concluded, 'nothing of reform in the political world ought to be held improbable. It is an age of Revolutions, in which everything may be looked for.'

Thus began a great debate which polarized British public life for the rest of the decade. Burke's *Reflexions* were a best-seller (30,000 in two years) but were easily outstripped by sales totalling perhaps 200,000 for *Rights of Man* as hitherto moribund reform societies revitalized themselves to promote its diffusion in London, the provinces, and Scotland and Ireland too. It was, reported the radical young Dublin lawyer Wolfe Tone on his first visit to Ulster in October 1791, the Bible of Belfast. The second anniversary of the Bastille's fall, in contrast to the previous year, was marked with banquets in major provincial towns throughout the British Isles. In London they drank to Burke—for having provoked the debate. Paine by then was in Paris, where he helped to draft the republican petition of the Champ de Mars; but he was back in London by November, bringing Pétion as a guest of honour to the Revolution Society. By then it had become fashionable for radical clubs to exchange fraternal addresses with the Jacobins, and as 1791 closed there was evidence that the debate was awakening groups hitherto dormant politically. December saw the foundation by 'five or six mechanics' of the Sheffield Constitutional Society to press for manhood suffrage and annual parliaments. By March 1792 it had 2,000 members. In January a Scottish shoemaker, Thomas Hardy, founded the London Corresponding Society with similar aims. The appearance of a second part of *Rights of Man* that spring, full less of general principles than of practical British radicalism, provoked the foundation during the year of corresponding societies in most leading provincial cities to promote its distribution. But not all of England was radicalized. In Birmingham a 'Bastille dinner' in July 1791 led to a riot against the dissenters who had been its leading attenders. Crowds cheering for Church and King sacked chapels, meeting houses, and the home of the unitarian scientist Joseph Priestley, while local magistrates stood obligingly aside. Decades of fruitless effort to launch 'God Save the King' as a national song were suddenly crowned with success as respectable people reflected on the flight to Varennes; and in May 1792 the government issued a proclamation against seditious writings and opened proceedings against Paine.

Nor did the British debate begun by Burke go unnoticed elsewhere. As soon as the *Reflexions* appeared they were translated into French, Italian, Spanish, and German. Within four months the French edition had sold 16,000, and sales of the three German editions eventually far exceeded that. Even those who disagreed with Burke's analysis, like his Prussian translator Friedrich Gentz, were profoundly influenced by the comprehensive vigour of his denunciation. Paine struck nothing like the same echoes; for by 1791 most Germans, even those who had been carried away by enthusiasm two years previously, viewed the continuing upheaval in France with mounting horror, and found the Englishman's faith in the rationality of what the French were doing quite incomprehensible. Subjects of benign, unwarlike prince-bishops were shocked by the pillage of the French Church; the teeming bureaucrats well schooled in public law who kept the hundreds of German states going were repelled by the disorder the Revolution seemed to have produced. They therefore took little persuading by Burke, his disciples, and translators that peoples were unwise to abandon their own heritage and traditions in order to start again from scratch. And the attitude of Germany's rulers could be taken completely for granted. The National Assembly, after all, had voted in the course of its attack on feudalism in August 1789 to deprive a number of them of valuable rights guaranteed to them for ever by the Peace of Westphalia. No compensation had been offered. Germany, therefore, was an obvious place for the French *émigrés* to converge on when Artois decided to move his court from Turin in January 1791. After some wandering he settled in Koblenz, the capital of his uncle the prince-archbishop of Trier, a matter of days before the flight to Varennes. There he was joined a few weeks later by his brother Provence, and there the thousands of new *émigrés* who left France after Varennes now gathered, if they did not prefer to join the Prince de Condé further up the Rhine in the territories of another prince-bishop, the elector of Mainz. And as soon as they arrived they organized for war, subsidized by grants from the Emperor and the rulers of Prussia, Russia, and Spain, as well as a number of German princelings. The disruption caused by their preparations, and the general arrogance of their behaviour, scarcely endeared them to the ordinary Rhinelanders; but even this did not create much German sympathy for the Revolution they had turned their backs on. It was one more reason for blaming it.

Yet the war which the Rhinelanders dreaded and the *émigrés* ached for was slow to come. Even after the Declaration of Pillnitz, the only monarch who burned to cross swords with what he called the 'Orang-Outangs of Europe' was Gustavus III of Sweden, who had authorized his subject Fersen to organize the flight to Varennes, and travelled to Aachen in June 1791 in the hope of welcoming Louis XVI to freedom. Disappointed in this, he nevertheless cleared the decks for an attack by offering peace in his three-year war with Russia. Catherine II was delighted, but not because of the opportunity of joining an anti-French crusade. She wanted to fight Jacobinism—but in Poland. While her diplomats were instructed to keep urging the Emperor and the king of Prussia to move against France, she made peace with enemies on both her own flanks: with Sweden in October, with Turkey at the end of December. But Leopold II chose to regard Louis XVI's acceptance of the constitution as rendering any follow-up to Pillnitz unnecessary: the king and the Revolution were reconciled. So Catherine had to bide her time, concentrating her energies meanwhile on suppressing subversion at home.

It is remarkable how slow most governments were to recognize material emanating from France as subversive. Only in Spain, where the Inquisition had retained close control over all expressions of opinion, was French influence combated from the start. As early as May 1789 the official press stopped reporting French events. In September the Holy Office was authorized by the minister Floridablanca, hitherto famous for his enlightened attitudes, to clamp down on all writings which, directly or indirectly, promoted insubordination. In 1791 troops sealed the frontiers and all foreign residents were required to register with local authorities. So successful were these efforts that French *émigrés* in 1792 found villages in Spain where the Revolution had still not been heard of. Few other parts of Europe managed to be so insulated; but by 1791 most governments were beginning to regret earlier openness. Press censorship in Sweden began in 1790, culminating in 1792 in the banning of all imports of written material from France, and prohibition of all reference to French affairs. April 1790 also saw the Russian police authorized to watch out for French propaganda and suspicious-sounding meetings; and two months later the empress herself was thrown into a rage on reading Alexander Radischev's *Journey from St. Petersburg to Moscow*, whose attacks on serfdom and paeans to liberty she regarded as a French-inspired call to overthrow the established order. Radischev was a well-educated civil servant, a dreamer rather than a revolutionary, but his book earned him a death sentence, subsequently commuted. His trial brought his book more fame than it would probably have won by itself, even though most copies were destroyed; but from then on the censorship (which had passed it) became increasingly vigilant.

There can be little doubt that the intellectual debate which first exploded in England was responsible for some of this heightened awareness of the dangerous potency of French principles. But even more important in this process was the flight to Varennes and the subsequent indignities suffered by Louis XVI. Monarchs everywhere saw it as an awful and perhaps portentous example. Their fears were certainly exaggerated, as the subsequent feebleness of non-French revolutionaries, even when everything was in their favour, showed. But they were not to know this, having witnessed the most glorious monarchy in Europe reduced to ignominy by its own subjects. Nor were they reassured by the defiant noises increasingly being heard from Paris in the aftermath of Varennes. In spite of their peaceable professions, the French revolutionaries had always believed that they stood for principles of universal validity. At a famous session on 19 June 1790 the National Assembly had allowed Anacharsis Clootz to bring a self-styled international delegation to its bar to proclaim that the trumpet-call now heard in France was awakening peoples from slavery everywhere. Actors in fancy-dress were among them, occasioning much scorn among more detached observers. But there were also representatives of thousands of genuine political exiles, from Geneva, from Holland, and from Belgium, who hoped that French help might yet enable them to return home to power. The Varennes crisis encouraged them, and they were prominent in urging the French to defy the despots of Europe, whose power could never survive contact with armed apostles of French liberty. Nobody in the dying Constituent Assembly believed it, and nor did the royal family. The army was visibly falling to pieces as its officers decamped in their thousands to join the *émigrés*. Fortunately troops were not required to annex Avignon, so the Constituent Assembly's final defiant gesture came cheap. But the days when Europe could observe events in France with detachment were now over. Increasingly, the revolutionaries would seek to solve their problems by inflicting them on their neighbours.

# The Republican Revolution
# October 1791—January 1793

THE character of the Legislative Assembly which met for the first time on 1
October 1791 was very different from that of the Constituent which had
decreed its existence. Gone were the clerics and nobles who had made up
half the deputies elected in 1789; only a handful of either stood for election
in 1791 or were returned. All the 745 new deputies were comfortably off,
having been elected while the silver-mark requirement was still in force;
but very few had owed their enrichment to trade or industry. Mostly they
were men of property, and above all lawyers. To the departing constituents
who had deliberately debarred themselves from election to the new body,
they seemed obscure, inexperienced, and (given the relative youth of most
of them) callow. In fact they were none of these things. Few, certainly, were
nationally known, although the journalist Brissot and the mathematician
and publicist Condorcet were men of reputation. But most of the new
deputies owed their election to prominence in their home localities, a
prominence won in the new circumstances of revolutionary politics since
1789. In the National Guard, in the Jacobin clubs, and above all in the
innumerable elective offices in the judiciary or the administration which
the new constitution had spawned, they had acquired a range of practical
experience in making the Revolution's reforms work that was denied even
to those who had devised and decreed them. They had also learned who the
Revolution's domestic enemies were. Ever since the beginning of the year
Jacobins, National Guards, and elected local officials had been grappling
with the problem of refractory priests. Over the summer a quarter of the
departments had called for new legislation to authorize closer supervision
of refractories who had been deprived of their benefices. In areas of
widespread refusal of the oath, such as Brittany and the southern Massif
Central, they often introduced their own policy of exiling or imprisoning
notorious refractories. Measures of this sort were intensified after

Varennes, and the elections took place against their background. So it was scarcely surprising that the deputies who convened on 1 October regarded the nonjurors as the most urgent priority confronting them. The issue was first raised on 7 October by Couthon, a crippled deputy from the Auvergne; and two days later the Assembly heard reports of massive resistance to the new ecclesiastical order in the department of the Vendée, where more than nine-tenths of parish priests had rejected the oath.

The other problem obsessing the new national representatives was that of the *émigrés*. The Declaration of Pillnitz was still fresh in their minds when they assembled, and few *émigrés* had taken advantage of the general amnesty declared to mark the promulgation of the constitution by returning. Quite the reverse; the outflow seemed to be increasing. 'There seem to be fewer carriages and fewer fine people about this year than there were last', noted an English visitor. '. . . Since the passage has been left open the emigrations have been amazing.'[1] On 15 October the king issued a formal appeal to those who had gone to return and help make the constitution work; and for once there was no reason to doubt his sincerity. The queen hated and distrusted her scheming brothers-in-law, and the drillings and marchings of professed counter-revolutionaries just across the frontier, people who claimed to understand the king's true interests better than he did himself, helped to perpetuate suspicions which he was trying hard to shake off. By ordering a general illumination of the Tuileries and paying for fireworks to mark the start of constitutional life he had begun to recover popularity, and after some initial misunderstandings he was getting on well with the Assembly. His stand on the *émigrés* maintained this momentum. It also pleased the Feuillant leaders who had remained in Paris after the end of the Constituent, flattered by the royal family's apparent willingness to take their advice and promote reconciliation. Excluded from the Assembly, as former constituents they were also barred from ministerial office for two years; but Barnave and Duport in particular hoped to influence policy privately, and the king and queen encouraged their hopes. Also encouraging was the fact that 345 of the new deputies joined the Feuillant Club, as opposed to only 135 gravitating towards the Jacobins.

But the Feuillants met in private, excluding spectators. There were no oratorical reputations to be made there. Even the founders of the club stayed away, anxious not to be seen too openly politicking. So men of ambition naturally preferred the public sessions of the Jacobins, where they could win applause and acquire demagogic experience and skills valuable in the Legislative Assembly itself. At the Jacobins, too, they could rub shoulders with politicians of established reputation, untainted by the shabby compromises of the summer—men like Robespierre, Pétion, and Brissot. All three had now reaped the rewards of their popularity. Robespierre had been elected public accuser of the Paris criminal court; Brissot had at last been elected to something; and Pétion on 13 November was chosen to succeed Bailly (who had resigned) as mayor of Paris, with almost twice the votes of his only serious rival, Lafayette. The Feuillants could offer no such stars and by early December their membership was melting away. Desperate to revive their support, at last they opened their sittings to the public, only to find their deliberations drowned by heckling from the galleries. The uproar was such that radicals in the Assembly next door were able to complain that the work of the nation's legislators was being interrupted. The club was expelled from the precincts, and not until weeks later was a new, and more distant, meeting place found. By then it was clear that nothing of importance was decided at the Feuillants; whereas at the Jacobins national figures were debating nightly on issues crucial to the whole future of the Revolution.

The pace was made by Brissot, whose first speech in the Assembly on 20 October dealt with the *émigrés*. He proposed confiscating the property of their leaders, including the king's brothers; but if that did not work, then France should strike at those who harboured them. The final solution to the *émigré* problem might have to be war. Though many deputies found such suggestions premature, they were nevertheless determined to confront the *émigrés*. On 9 November they passed a sweeping decree which followed Brissot's suggestion and sequested the revenues of the princes and all other public officials who were abroad without good cause. All French citizens gathered abroad were declared suspected of plotting against their country; and those who had not returned by 1 January 1792 were to be deemed guilty of a capital crime. The king was requested to sanction this decree at once. But on 11 November he refused.

So ended the honeymoon between Louis XVI and the Legislative. The deputies had to recognize that under the constitution the king had a perfect right to his veto. Arguably, even, his motives were respectable, and in a proclamation distributed throughout Paris he set them out. Feuillants had drafted it, and it extolled the virtues of persuasion and gentleness, appealing to the patriotism of the *émigrés* to persuade them to return. The king's very freedom to veto the law showed that he was not the helpless captive they alleged. But to Brissot and his friends royal actions spoke louder than words. Ever since Varennes it had been rumoured that policy was being directed by a secret 'Austrian committee' co-ordinated by the queen, in league with both the *émigrés* and foreign powers to subvert the new order in France by force. Here was concrete evidence of its work!

There certainly was plenty of secret correspondence between the queen and her brother in Vienna—but confrontation rather than conciliation was her objective, and shielding the *émigrés* from vindictive laws had no part to play. Yet why else, deputies asked themselves, should the king wish to protect the Revolution's sworn enemies? Their suspicions were only deepened by the stand he took when they turned to the question of the non-juring priests.

The debate began on 21 October as news came in of massacres in Avignon. When opponents of French annexation lynched an official of the new municipality, annexationists retorted on 16 October by murdering papal supporters incarcerated in the old palace of the popes. Sixty prisoners were reported killed. And stories of nonjuror defiance in the provinces poured in throughout the discussions. 'I maintain', declared the Provençal deputy Isnard on 14 November, 'that as regards refractory priests, there is only one certain course, which is to exile them from the kingdom . . . Do you not see that the priest must be cut off from the people he leads astray?'[2] Eventually, on 29 November, it was decreed that all nonjurors should take a new civic oath, and those who refused should lose the pensions they had been granted on refusing the previous year's oath. Henceforth such double refractories were to be regarded as suspects, and subjected to careful official surveillance. Those resident in places marked by religious disturbances could be exiled; and they were now denied the use of redundant churches for their services. Louis XVI took longer to respond to this decree, and on 5 December, from the unexpected quarter of the directory of the department of Paris, he was urged to veto it. On 19 December he did so.

The moment was well chosen, for temporarily the king seemed to have regained the initiative. Disconcerted by his refusal to act against the *émigrés*, the Assembly decided that at least he could act against their protectors, and on 29 November a deputation urged him to demand that the electors of Trier and Mainz instantly expel the princes' armies from their territory. 'Say to them . . . that if German princes continue to favour preparations directed against the French, we shall carry to them, not fire and the sword, but freedom. It is for them to estimate what might follow from the awakening of nations.'[3] In fact such a course appealed to the king. A war against German princelings might drag in the Emperor, whose seasoned troops were bound to brush aside the shambles which the French army had become. Rescue and reversal of the Revolution would follow. Military men also saw advantages in war: Lafayette, now searching for a new role, thought it would reinvigorate the army, which could then be deployed to restore domestic stability. His opinion was shared by Marshal Narbonne, reputedly a bastard son of Louis XV, who was appointed minister of war early in December. And so there was widespread political support when, on 14 December, the king came to the Assembly and announced that he had issued an ultimatum to the elector of Trier. If, by 15 January, the prince-archbishop had not put a stop to all hostile *émigré* activity within his territories, France would declare war. The Assembly exploded with enthusiasm, and applauded the monarch for minutes on end. All sides were relieved that the time of decision seemed at hand, and only the waning Feuillants were consumed with foreboding.

In these circumstances the king's continuing prevarication over the nonjurors could be overlooked. Once war began, that issue would no doubt resolve itself, for then refractories could be regarded as traitors. Meanwhile Brissot and his most vocal supporters, who included a particularly eloquent group of deputies from Bordeaux (notably Vergniaud, Gensonné, and Guadet) looked forward to a military promenade that would regenerate the nation, restore its honour, discomfit plotters, and show Europe how formidable a free people could be. The king himself would be forced to take sides and reveal his true position, as Brissot declared at the Jacobins on 16 December. Meanwhile Narbonne set about mobilizing three armies, totalling 150,000 men, on the eastern frontier; while Clootz, now calling himself the 'Orator of the Human race' and parading ostentatiously around Paris in a scarlet Phrygian cap of liberty, whipped up war fever among the foreign exile communities by proclaiming that the liberation of all Europe was at hand. But that moment proved to be further off than everybody thought. As soon as he received the French ultimatum, the elector of Trier ordered the *émigrés* to disband and quit his territory. The elector of Mainz did the same. The reason for war was thereby removed, and as 1792 dawned it began to look as if France might have to solve her self-imposed problems by herself after all.

Too many people in French public life, however, had now committed themselves to war as a panacea. Early in December a fierce debate had begun at the Jacobin Club during which Robespierre pointed out all the dangers and uncertainties that war would bring. He feared a dictatorship of generals, particularly the unscrupulous and eternally ambitious Lafayette, if the French forces were successful. And if, as seemed only too likely given the state of the army, they were not, then the Court would call in foreign forces to overthrow the whole Revolution. In any case, the truly dangerous counter-revolutionaries were not the ridiculous, posturing *émigrés*: they were at home, within France, and should be dealt with there. But Robespierre found himself increasingly isolated. Night after night Brissot countered that war was a necessity in the consolidation of the Revolution; it would even serve to restore the flagging value of the assignats! A liberated people had nothing to fear from the despots and aristocrats of feudal Europe. They would be overwhelmed, and their groaning subjects incited to emulate the French example and claim their own liberty. In the Assembly itself, of course, there was no Robespierre to contradict Brissot's optimism and plenty of other voices carried away with the same faith in the regenerative power of war. Moreover, although the Rhenish princes had hurried to comply with Louis XVI's ultimatum, by the time they did so their suzerain in Vienna had decided to intervene on their behalf. Convinced that the Declaration of Pillnitz had resolved the crisis of the previous summer, diplomats in Vienna advised the Emperor Leopold that threats would defuse this one, too. On 21 December, accordingly, he announced that Austrian troops would march if the French followed up their threats against the Rhenish electors. He did not doubt, he added, that other monarchs would join him. When this news arrived in Paris on the last day of 1791 it seemed to confirm all that Brissot and his allies had been claiming about a league of despots determined to crush the Revolution. Advocates of war now forgot the craven electors of the Rhine. France should strike directly at her true enemies, and declare war on the Emperor. In vain Robespierre, from one end of the political spectrum, and the Feuillant leaders from the other, warned that this course was more dangerous than ever. In despair at the queen's obvious indifference to his pacific urgings, in January Barnave went home to Dauphiné. The Assembly, meanwhile, produced scenes of patriotic enthusiasm unparalleled since 1789, with deputies and onlookers swearing to live free or die, in conscious re-enactment of the Tennis Court Oath. The *émigré* princes were now charged in their absence with high treason; and on 25 January the Assembly declared that the Emperor by his plottings with other monarchs had broken the alliance of 1756. The king was told to demand that his brother-in-law renounce all treaties hostile to France and make public declaration of his peaceful intentions. If by 1 March he had offered no satisfaction, war would ensue. In fact, the king replied, he had already done this, since it was his constitutional prerogative, and not the Assembly's, to conduct foreign policy. He was now awaiting the Austrian reply.

The royal note to Vienna was actually a good deal less peremptory than the Assembly would have liked. When it arrived it only confirmed the Austrians' belief that their threats were working. Reassured by the signature of a formal defensive pact with Prussia on 7 February, they replied defiantly; when this exchange of notes was communicated to the deputies in Paris on 1 March there was uproar. Calls were now heard for the dismissal of Delessart, the foreign minister, and they rapidly developed into a general attack on the whole ministry, abetted from within by Narbonne. A royal attempt to resist the pressure by dismissing Narbonne backfired when the Assembly voted to impeach Delessart amid denunciations of treachery and intrigue at the palace. There was even talk of impeaching the queen and suspending the king. At this moment came the quite unexpected news that on 1 March the Emperor had died. Nobody could guess what policies his successor, an untried 24-year-old, might pursue; and in these circumstances the French Court thought it wisest to bow to the Assembly's clamour. On 10 March the king dismissed the entire ministry. They were replaced by a team of outright warmongers, practically Brissot's nominees. They included Clavière, the exiled Swiss financier, once Mirabeau's familiar; Roland, an ageing, unemployed factory inspector, dragged late into revolutionary politics by a vivacious, ambitious wife, and now made interior minister; and above all, to replace Delessart at foreign affairs, Dumouriez, a professional soldier who had hated the Austrians ever since the Seven Years War. Nothing now stood in the way of a formal declaration of war, and Dumouriez appeared at the Jacobins in a red liberty cap to keep patriotic enthusiasm on the boil. Robespierre and Pétion condemned such showy behaviour, but the fashion spread as a way of demonstrating the defiance of freed slaves in the face of threatening despots. These posturings did not prevent Dumouriez from trying to negotiate neutrality at the last minute with the Prussians, which postponed the final step yet again; but by mid-April the Austrians were mobilizing and time was running out. On the twentieth Louis XVI appeared at a delirious Assembly, with all his ministers, to announce that France was now at war with the king of Hungary and Bohemia—for Francis II had not yet been elected Emperor. Only seven deputies voted against the declaration.

It would be, it said, a defensive war of a free people against an aggressive king. There would be no conquests, and French force would never be used against the liberty of any people. Only those guilty of forming a concert against France would suffer; and the French would neglect nothing to soften the impact of the war on the lives and properties of those with whom they had no quarrel. Every one of these pledges would be broken in the course of a war that was destined to end only with the Revolution itself, and engulf much of western Europe.

The aims of the conflict now launched were manifold: to teach the Austrians a lesson and deter foreigners from interfering in France's internal affairs; to destroy the *émigrés*, their bases, and their supporters; to flush out internal traitors and counter-revolutionaries by forcing them to declare themselves. The royal family, and the generals, had their own secret, and very different, hopes about what it would achieve. A further argument often heard in the debates of that winter was that war would heal internal divisions by turning the preoccupations of French citizens outwards, and their antagonisms against the enemy rather than each other; it would distract attention from domestic problems. This it had certainly done ever since the issue came to the fore late in October 1791; but by the time war broke out those problems were multiplying.

One was far away, but it had undoubtedly been precipitated by the Revolution, and would have important consequences for it. In the third week of October 1791 reports began to arrive in France of a slave uprising in Saint-Domingue. It was December before the full scale of the outbreak became clear, but by then it was known that it had begun in the sugar estates in the north of the colony on 14 August, and initial losses were estimated at over 1,000 whites massacred, 200 sugar and 1,200 coffee plantations destroyed, and 15,000 slaves missing. It was to develop into the greatest slave rebellion in the history of the world, and the only successful one. Pessimists had been predicting something like it for a generation, as the colony boomed and demand for slaves grew insatiably. In the confrontations over political rights between whites and coloureds that had marked the years between 1789 and 1791, both sides had drafted slaves into their retinues, heedless of the example it gave; and the failure of the Constituent Assembly to produce a coherent or consistent policy on slavery, the slave-trade, the rights of free 'people of colour', and colonial autonomy itself compounded the confusion both in Saint-Domingue and in France's other West Indian Islands. By the end of 1791 the rebellion had become part of a complex civil war, so fast-moving that any response decided in Paris was never less than three months out of date by the time news of it came through. These events were embarrassing for Brissot, who had been among the founders of the French anti-slavery movement in the 1780s; and for his eloquent friends from Bordeaux, a city whose prosperity was closely tied to the Caribbean slave economy. But apart from shocking stores of rapine and racial massacre, the first consequence of the rebellion was a severe shortage of sugar, which made itself felt in Paris in January 1792 when prices tripled. Throughout that month, and into February, there were outbursts of popular price-fixing in the eastern districts of the capital as largely female crowds raided warehouses and grocers' shops and sold sugar and coffee they found there at the old prices.

For once they were not worried about grain, flour, or bread. But this was because the Paris authorities, remembering 1789, had taken steps to build up good stocks early in the autumn—in the process diminishing the reserves of a wide radius around the city. Accordingly the winter saw repeated outbursts of grain rioting in little market towns all over north-eastern France. In February the mayor of Étampes was lynched when he refused to order a reduction in grain prices, and hundreds of National Guards had to be sent to restore order. An attempt to export grain from Dunkirk in the same month provoked three days of disorder in which many of the port's warehouses were destroyed. What compounded popular worries over the price of foodstuffs was a striking decline in the value of both the French *livre* and the assignats. The *livre* fell by 20 per cent on the foreign exchanges between June 1791 and March 1792. The assignats, still trading in Paris at 82 per cent of their face value in November 1791, had fallen to 63 per cent two months later and continued to decline gently throughout the spring. Both trends inevitably pushed up prices, especially of imported goods. Thus even in a port like Marseilles, with easy access to grain supplies from southern Europe and North Africa, prices climbed steadily throughout the spring; and the municipality darkly threatened merchant hoarders with 'revenge which would not be that of the law'.[4]

Marseilles, in fact, was now a byword for political turbulence. Stung by the Constituent Assembly's decision to make Aix the capital of the new department of Bouches du Rhône, the Marseillais sought to establish their regional primacy by intervention in other cities' affairs. In July 1791, 500 volunteers from Marseilles helped to ensure the triumph of annexationists in Avignon. In September they planned a march by National Guard contingents from all over the department on Arles, now the main regional centre of counter-revolution under the control of a refractory party known as the Chiffon. Only direct orders from Paris stopped them. Nothing, however, prevented them from marching to Aix the following February, disarming its garrison of regulars who were suspected of favouring the Chiffon, and then turning to Arles once again. With politicians in Paris totally absorbed by the impending war, in March a force 6,000 strong was able to lay siege to the city, take it, and expel the Chiffon leaders. Such confrontations could not fail to increase tension generally in a region that had been bitterly polarized already for almost two years; and the drowning of 69 National Guards in the treacherous Rhône at Pont Saint-Esprit on 25 March proved the trigger for a wave of rural violence in the south unparalleled since July 1789. Nobody believed the drownings were accidental; and as rumours of them spread, those who heard them assumed they were part of a counter-revolutionary plot to avenge the dispersal of the second Jalès camp, the Avignon prison massacre, and all the other 'patriotic' triumphs in which National Guardsmen had had a hand. All over the Gard peasants now struck out at suspects and their property—which meant above all non-juring priests and nobles. In that single department in April 1792, 101 incidents were recorded of attacks on castles, ransacking their contents, and removing remaining symbols and records of feudalism. Nor was the outburst confined to the Gard. In neighbouring Ardèche, among properties completely destroyed were those of the most notorious (though long emigrated) co-ordinator of counter-revolutionary schemes, Count d'Antraigues. And down to June the movement spread east into Provence, northward into the Massif, and as far west as the Haute Garonne—although with steadily diminishing intensity. What it signified is hard to decide; but the concentration on the relics of feudalism suggests that southern peasants considered the gains of 1789 to be by no means firmly assured, and indeed in real danger of reversal if the reactionaries of Arles and Avignon were to triumph. The Pont Saint-Esprit disaster suggested that plots might yet succeed where confrontation had failed; and with central government either indifferent to or incapable of imposing order on the lacerated Midi, harassed peasants took the law into their own hands to make sure that the destruction of the old social order would be irreparable. Nothing, however, did more to make that certain than the war which had just begun.

During the first few weeks of war the confidence and enthusiasm which had swept the Legislative Assembly into it seems to have been widely shared. The Austrian alliance, always unpopular, had at last been broken and the Revolution was about to confront its enemies openly. The sense of defiance was well conveyed in the bloodthirsty words of the battle hymn composed for the army of the Rhine at Strasbourg on 25–6 April by Rouget de Lisle, a poetical infantry captain. Impure blood, it exulted, would drench the tracks of the conquering French armies. And the blood of enemies found on the home front would be shed in a way that was also new that month: by the guillotine. The first proposal for a machine to make heads 'fly off in the twinkling of an eye' had been laughed out of the Constituent Assembly in December 1789. But once the deputies had voted (over the protests of Robespierre) to retain the death penalty, something more reliable and humane than previous barbaric techniques seemed desirable; and in the course of 1791 a mechanical decapitator was devised. It was expeditious, egalitarian, and above all (experts agreed) painless. Though not the invention of Dr Guillotin, the original idea had been his and it took his name. Its first victim was a highwayman, who mounted the scaffold on 25 April.

Only a few days later, the war itself claimed its first victim. He was not, however, a hireling of the king of Hungary and Bohemia, but a French general murdered by his own men. The nearest enemy territory was Belgium, and it was assumed that the population there, resentful of the Austrian reconquest of 1790, would welcome freedom-proclaiming French troops with open arms. So the campaign began on 28 April, with a modest advance across the north-east frontier. But at the first resistance French ranks broke, and in their flight from the field the troops turned on a commander whom they suspected of treason. Nor were they the only unit to turn tail; desertion rates in the cavalry doubled, and even troops who remained reliable were unable to advance with their flanks uncertain. Fortunately the Austrians were not well placed to advance either, preferring to wait until a concerted attack could be launched with Prussia—who did not declare war until 21 May, and did not expect to have forces in a position to attack until the end of June.

Meanwhile the shock of the first defeats produced loud recriminations in Paris. Frantic to find scapegoats for reverses their own rhetoric had done nothing to prepare them for, the Brissotins (as the advocates of war in the Assembly and the ministry were now known) turned to denouncing everybody else. 'Everywhere', noted a moderate Jacobin Club member, 'you hear the cry that the king is betraying us, the generals are betraying us, that nobody is to be trusted; that the *Austrian Committee* has been caught in the act; that Paris will be taken in six weeks by the Austrians . . . we are on a volcano ready to spout flames.'[5] New measures to combat treasonable activity were now proposed, and rapidly passed. On 18 May all foreigners in Paris were placed under surveillance. On 27 May the Assembly returned to the question of refractory priests, with a decree which allowed the deportation of any nonjuror denounced by twenty active citizens. On the twenty-ninth it decreed the disbanding of the special bodyguard of 1,800 men allowed to the king under the constitution. Suspected of excessive personal loyalty to a monarch nobody now trusted, they were to be replaced by reliably patriotic National Guardsmen. The king sanctioned the disbandment of his guard with a speed which left his enemies more suspicious than ever, and amid fears of a military coup it was decided to send all regular troops stationed in and around Paris to the front. To replace them the minister of war, Servan, proposed to establish a camp of 20,000 more National Guards, this time provincial ones, just outside the capital. Their arrival was to coincide with the annual Feast of the Federation on 14 July, and for that reason they would be known as *fédérés*. A decree convoking them was passed on 8 June. But in the king's eyes this was too much, and in any case two days later he glimpsed an unexpected opportunity to divide his enemies. Officers of the Paris National Guard, jealous of their pre-eminent role in metropolitan politics, organized a so-called 'petition of 8,000' against the camp. Thereupon the king intimated to his ministers that he proposed to veto the new decree, along with that on refractory priests.

A ministerial crisis now broke into the open. Roland, prompted by his ambitious young wife and supported by Servan and Clavière, wrote a public letter to the king on 10 June denouncing his delays in sanctioning decrees supported by the majority in the Assembly, and blaming the disturbed state of the country on royal behaviour: 'much more delay, and a grieving people will see in its king the friend and accomplice of conspirators'.[6] No monarch could let pass such public criticism from one of his own ministers, and Roland found himself dismissed. Servan and Clavière fell with him on 13 June. Dumouriez, no sympathizer with the ousted trio but no better liked by the king, followed them on the fifteenth. He went to a command on the northern front. The fallen ministers were replaced by Feuillant nonentities—puppets, some said, of Lafayette. This impression was only reinforced when on 16 June the general himself wrote an open letter from the front to the Assembly, in which he denounced the Jacobins as the cause of all the recent troubles and disasters, and welcomed the fall of a ministry foisted on the country by a faction. His intervention merely confirmed suspicions widespread since he had been given a command that he was planning a military coup. To forestall him, however, supporters of the fallen ministers in Paris were now planning a very different sort of coup: popular intervention on a scale not seen since the ill-fated Champ de Mars petition the year before.

The economic shortages of the spring had reinvigorated popular organizations dormant or operating underground since the previous summer. The number of sections with popular societies, where unlike the formal sectional assemblies passive citizens had full rights of participation, probably doubled over the spring. By June most sections in the heavily populated eastern and central districts had them. Renewed popular interest in political demonstrations was shown on 15 April, when thousands attended a celebration to mark the release of those imprisoned after the Nancy mutiny of 1790, with leading Jacobins also present. New leaders were emerging, too, such as the self-named 'Anaxagoras' Chaumette, who led a radical secession from the Cordeliers Club; or Jacques Roux, a constitutional priest with a parish in the Gravilliers section, whose reputation was built on inflammatory sermons calling for price controls and death to hoarders. The early reverses of the war surprised and alarmed sectional patriots, deluded like Jacobins by their own rhetoric; and throughout May they bombarded the Legislative with petitions to allow sectional assemblies to sit continuously (*en permanence*) during the emergency. Nothing united them more, however, than the purge of the ministers; and to demonstrate support for them the sections of the city's east end, co-ordinated from the Cordeliers, planned a vast demonstration to intimidate the king into taking them back. Ostensibly the occasion was to be the planting of a tree of liberty in the Tuileries gardens on the anniversary of the Tennis Court Oath, but everybody knew that, as the American ambassador noted in his diary, 'There is to be a Sort of Riot Tomorrow'.[7] Accordingly, on the morning of 20 June between 10,000 and 20,000 armed demonstrators converged on the Tuileries from the east in menacing silence. The palace guards made no attempt to stop them as they dragged cannon up the grand staircase and made for the king's apartments. Now they began to shout slogans, proclaiming that they were 'sans culottes', ordinary patriots without fine clothes, come to intimidate tyrants. They found the king alone, and for two hours filed past him uttering threats and demanding the ministers' reinstatement. But now for the first time Louis XVI showed the unexpected courage which dignified the last months of his dismal life and reign. He refused to be intimidated. He proclaimed his loyalty to the constitution. He even borrowed one of the fashionable new caps of liberty and wearing it drank to the health of the nation. In the end Pétion arrived from the Hôtel de Ville and persuaded the demonstrators to go home, empty-handed.

In the short term, therefore, the demonstration of 20 June failed. The king kept his ministers, and as the news of the invasion of the palace spread through the country there was a wave of sympathy for the royal family. Many departments sent in condemnatory addresses to the National Assembly, some with thousands of signatures. The king upbraided Pétion in public for neglect of his duties as mayor in not preventing the demonstration, and the department of Paris seized the opportunity to suspend him. Lafayette, too, saw a chance to intensify his campaign against the radicals, and on 28 June appeared in Paris to urge the National Guard to rally round the Crown. Yet none of this deterred those who had organized the *journée* of the twentieth. It merely confirmed their conviction that they would have to try again. Indeed, as early as 23 June they attempted to do so, carrying a petition for the king's deposition. But their organization was not well enough established to mobilize another display of popular strength so soon, and the turnout proved inadequate. It was enough, however, to make them redouble their efforts, and the suspension of Pétion gave them a new cause to rally round. The Assembly's cool reception of Lafayette encouraged them, too. He was accused of deserting his post in time of war and, spurned by the royal family too, returned to the front in despair. At the Tuileries, meanwhile, courtiers were going about armed and preparing defensive positions. All sides were obviously expecting a further, and this time decisive, confrontation; and the precedent of 20 June, together with its lessons, indicated the form it would take. In this sense the American ambassador was right when he wrote, 'The Constitution has this Day I think given its last Groan'.

Anniversaries increasingly dominated the revolutionary calendar, and the greatest of all was now imminent: 14 July. And although the king had vetoed Servan's proposed camp of 20,000 *fédérés*, the usual parade on the Champ de Mars was still planned, with National Guards present from throughout the nation. On the news of the 20 June demonstration, centres of patriotism like Brest or Marseilles decided to increase their contingents, and thus something like the camp would come into existence anyway. On 5 July the Assembly reinforced this trend by elaborating a procedure for declaring the Country in Danger: as soon as this state was proclaimed, all government bodies were placed in permanent session and authorized to raise volunteers from their National Guard units to fight at the front alongside the line army. Less than a week later the decree was invoked. As a result, *fédérés* continued to pour into Paris long after 14 July on their way to the front. Marseilles's volunteers did not arrive until 30 July, when they marched into the capital singing Rouget de Lisle's battle hymn, and thereby gave it the name it has borne ever since. And so throughout July Paris swarmed with the pick of the provincial patriots, and the Jacobins and popular societies made every effort to look after them and draft them into the political struggle. As early as 11 July deputations of *fédérés* were urging the Assembly to impeach Lafayette, annul the royal veto, and reinstate Pétion. Two days later the mayor was restored, as a goodwill gesture for the fourteenth; and the ceremony on the day itself was bigger and more spectacular than ever, with the king insisting on renewing his constitutional oath. But, as a moderate Jacobin noted, it was 'very fine to look at, but not in the hearts of the patriots'.[8] The latter were now openly talking of storming the Tuileries as the Bastille had been stormed, and establishing a republic.

This time, however, they wanted the pressure to mount until it was irresistible. On several occasions newly arrived *fédérés* had to be dissuaded from premature assaults on the palace. To ensure success the sansculottes had to be mobilized, and that could best be done if sectional assemblies were able to admit passive citizens. It was illegal; but on 20 July the Théâtre-Français section voted to ignore the distinction under the leadership of the most resourceful political operator on the left bank, Danton. Within a fortnight six other sections had followed this example, and by the early days of August attendance at sectional assemblies was soaring. From 25 July they were authorized to sit continuously, and by then they were also beginning to co-ordinate their action, and to concert it with the *fédérés*, in a central committee. The Jacobin Club too was now increasingly open in its support for the overthrow of the monarchy by insurrection. On the twenty-ninth even the ever-cautious Robespierre came out for direct action—abandoning the defence of the constitution which had been his watchword throughout the spring. The mounting sense of urgency was only increased by the news that the Austrians had now crossed the north-east frontier. On 25 July the allied commander, the Duke of Brunswick, issued a declaration designed to strike terror into the inhabitants of Paris particularly. The war aims of the Emperor and the king of Prussia, he proclaimed, were to end the anarchy inside France and stop attacks on throne and altar. They intended to liberate the royal family and re-establish the king's 'legitimate' authority. Those who offered no resistance to the allied advance would be protected, and Parisians were explicitly warned to take no action against the Tuileries or its inhabitants. All in the capital were declared answerable for the safety of the king, failing which the city would be subjected to 'exemplary and forever memorable vengeance'. News of these threats, which reached Paris on 28 July, prompted the Assembly to authorize distribution of arms to all citizens, active or otherwise, and to declare all defenders of the country active. Thus the National Guard was opened to all, swamping the cautious men of property who had hitherto dominated its Parisian units. And one by one the sections began to petition openly for the king's immediate deposition. On 3 August Pétion presented the same demand to the Assembly in the name of all 48 sections—although some promptly disavowed it. On the sixth there followed another petition signed by all comers at the symbolic location of the Champ de Mars. Similar calls were now coming in from major provincial cities. Eventually the Assembly agreed to debate the question on 9 August, immediately after hearing a report on Lafayette's earlier desertion of his command.

But events were now slipping beyond the deputies' control, to the alarm of none more than those who had hoped to gain from the fateful demonstration of 20 June: the dismissed ministers and their supporters among the Brissotins and the eloquent deputies from the Gironde. They had hoped that popular discontent would force the king to restore them to power. They had not expected a movement to develop for his total overthrow. But when the Bordeaux deputies Vergniaud, Guadet, and Gensonné pressed the king to appoint ministers 'among the firmest supporters of the Revolution' they received no response. Desperate to impress him with their sincerity, by the first week in August they were openly denouncing calls for dethronement. All they achieved was to attract the suspicion of the sections and their fellow Jacobins, and make the insurrection, when it came, one as much against the Legislative Assembly as against the Crown.

The final signal came when the deputies refused to indict Lafayette on the eighth. From this it was obvious that no clear decision on dethronement could be expected next day, and there was none. Both sides spent 9 August preparing for the long-awaited trial of strength, and the Assembly could only look on helplessly. The ringing of the tocsin, notoriously the call to insurrection since the memorable *journées* of 1789, marked the seizure of power in the small hours of the tenth by the central committee of the sections. Symbolically locking up Pétion, they proclaimed themselves an insurrectionary commune, and ordered the *fédérés* and the newly democratized National Guard of the capital to march on the Tuileries. When these forces arrived there at nine the next morning they found that the king and his family had already fled to the presumed safety of the Assembly across the road. But a garrison remained of 900 well-armed Swiss Guards, between 100 and 200 courtiers and former officers, and 2,000 National Guards. The latter at once defected to the commune's side, which was perhaps 20,000 strong. Nevertheless it was the Swiss who opened fire, and that sealed their fate when the commune's forces gained the upper hand after about an hour. Once the Swiss began to retreat, they were pursued by mobs of bystanders without firearms who hacked them to death with knives, pikes, and hatchets, and tore their uniforms to pieces to make trophies. Altogether 600 of them perished, some in supposed safe custody after the siege was over. Less than half that number fell among the besiegers, 90 of them *fédérés*, and the rest the same sort of shopkeepers, petty tradesmen, and artisans who had been so prominent in the 1789 *journées* and on 20 June. It was the bloodiest day of the Revolution so far, but also one of the most decisive. Though the king and his family remained unscathed, his authority fell with his palace. As crowds rampaged through Paris destroying all symbols and images of royalty down to the very word 'king' in street names, the Legislative Assembly declared the monarchy suspended until a national Convention had met to decide on the future form of government. Only the efforts of Vergniaud averted the abolition of monarchy there and then. But as the king was transferred, under close custody, to the keep of the Temple, a medieval fortress in the north-eastern suburbs, few believed that he would ever sit on the throne again unless with foreign aid.

Power now lay not with the Assembly, but with the new Paris commune.

The Assembly acted as if it was still in charge: for example it appointed a new team of ministers. The three who had fallen on 13 June were at last restored, tainted though they now were by association with the equivocating Brissotins. But the most sensational appointment was the new minister of justice, Danton, who had built a career entirely in the sectional politics of Paris since 1789, and was brought in explicitly to keep the sansculottes happy. The appointments were made by less than 300 deputies. The majority had simply gone to ground over the previous few weeks, thus further diminishing the Assembly's authority. During the six weeks left to it, this rump did almost everything the commune wanted. Such efforts as it made to resist were contemptuously brushed aside.

What the commune wanted most was vengeance—on those who had abetted the king, and those who had resisted the popular will before and during the uprising of 10 August, on refractory priests protected for too long by the deposed tyrant, and on Lafayette, the butcher of the Champ de Mars and would-be military dictator. He at least escaped: after toying briefly with marching his army on Paris, on 17 August, the day the council of ministers decided to dismiss him, he crossed the Prussian lines and gave himself up to the enemy. Even that brought him five years in German prisons. On that same day a special tribunal was set up to try those guilty of political crimes, such as the surviving defenders of the Tuileries. It worked slowly, but on the twenty-first the guillotine despatched its first political victim. Between the nineteenth and the twenty-sixth, the Assembly debated measures against refractories, which many local authorities were taking anyway on their own initiative. Eventually it decreed that all nonjurors were to quit the country within a fortnight, on pain of deportation to Guiana. But so deep had suspicion of priestcraft now gone, that even unbeneficed clergy not subject to the oaths were made liable to deportation on the demand of six citizens. Suspicion was the order of the day, and priests were being arrested by sansculotte vigilantes from 11 August onwards. Nobody was allowed to leave the capital without a passport, and none of these were issued without *certificats de civisme* issued by sectional surveillance committees. The paranoid atmosphere only grew worse when it was learned that the Prussians had invaded French territory; and news arriving on the twenty-sixth of the fall of Longwy, with scarcely any resistance, seemed to confirm that traitors were everywhere. The response of Danton, who increasingly dominated his fellow ministers during these weeks, was to demand a general search of all dwellings in the capital for hidden arms and suspects. These 'domiciliary visits' took place on 30–1 August, resulting in 3,000 further arrests. The result was to cram the prisons of Paris to bursting-point with presumed traitors.

After 10 August Marat, the self-styled friend of the people but hitherto too extreme and bloodthirsty in his opinions to command much support, came into his own. His solution to the crisis was massacre, both of the suspects herded together in the prisons and indeed of selected ministers and deputies. Many sections, and their representatives on the commune, thought the same, and were disgusted by the slow progress made by the 17 August tribunal. When Danton, in response to the fall of Longwy, called for 30,000 volunteers from the capital to go to the front, many sansculottes appeared ready to go, but were reluctant to leave their families at the mercy of a counter-revolutionary prison breakout. Nor were they reassured when, on 30 August, the Assembly attempted to shake off the commune's control by decreeing new elections in Paris. The move was all too obviously inspired by Brissot and his friends, whom Robespierre was beginning to call 'the faction of the Gironde'. It outraged those who regarded the commune as the saviour of the country. The commune refused to be disbanded and, after hints from Robespierre at the Jacobins, tried to have a number of hostile deputies and ministers arrested. It also defiantly drafted Marat on to its committee of *surveillance*, responsible for the prisons. The personal intervention of Danton prevented the arrests, and thereby probably saved the lives of those concerned. For if they had been in prison on 2 September, they would almost certainly have fallen victim to the September Massacres.

The trigger was further bad news from the front. After Longwy, Verdun came under Prussian siege, and on 2 September news came that the enemy had passed it. There were no other fortresses on the road to Paris. Danton, in his most famous speech, urged his compatriots to defiance—'If we are bold, bolder still, and forever bold, then France is saved!'—but the predominant mood in Paris was panic. That afternoon, a convoy of prisoners going from the Hôtel de Ville to the Abbaye prison was stopped and attacked by sansculottes. Seventeen of them were hacked to death. Soon afterwards, a makeshift prison at the old Carmelite convent was attacked and there was more butchery, although most of it was now directed by a kangaroo court. By the end of the afternoon the commune had taken a hand, but only to co-ordinate the massacres, not to stop them. The next day it sent a circular to provincial centres hinting that they might like to follow the Parisian example. By then all except two of the capital's prisons had been broken into, makeshift tribunals established claiming to dispense the people's justice, and vengeance visited on all those deemed from the charges against them to be potential counter-revolutionaries. Extravagant celebrations and cheering marked each acquittal, and there were plenty of them. Even so, about half the the prison population of Paris, between 1,100 and 1,400 people, were killed between 2 September and the last incidents on the seventh; and most of the victims were in no sense politically dangerous. Certainly, they included surviving Swiss defenders of the Tuileries, over 200 priests, and a number of prominent relics of the old order such as the former foreign minister Montmorin, or the queen's notorious favourite the Princess de Lamballe. Forty-five political prisoners were also massacred at Versailles on the ninth, including Delessart. But most of those who died were common criminals, forging assignats being the nearest any of them came to subversive activity. Nevertheless suspicion bred credulity, and society's reprobates could not be presumed unavailable for the purposes of prison plotters. The ordinary Parisian tradesmen and artisans who carried out the killings certainly thought their work both necessary and beneficial, and so did the commune, which voted to pay them for it. But this second great blood-letting within a month horrified most of those who witnessed it, and the lurid details were soon known throughout Europe. Nobody at the Assembly, or the Jacobin Club, was prepared openly to commend what had been done; but the political factions led by Brissot on one side and Robespierre on the other were quick to accuse each other of responsibility or complicity, and these charges and counter-charges would echo on for years. *Septembriseur* became a standard term of political abuse; and fear of a repetition stalked political life for months to come.

Yet this purging of their enemies certainly seemed to reassure the sansculottes. With the threat to their families removed, the men of Paris began to volunteer in droves to go off and face the Prussians. Twenty thousand came forward during the first weeks of September. 'The number of men, for I cannot call them troops', wrote a British agent on 9 September,[9] 'that have left for the army is prodigious . . . and they are still enrolling . . . I have heard today that the multitude of people that are besides this either at or going to Chalons is beyond belief . . . The cause among the lower order of people is more popular than I imagined.' And although he was 'convinced as a military man that they must tend more to create confusion in a regular army than to be of any advantage to it', nevertheless 'I cannot . . . help thinking the Duke of Brunswick ought to get before Paris as quick as he can.' We see here a dim awakening to the fact that the ordered practice of eighteenth-century warfare was perhaps not immutable. And proof positive came only ten days later. On 20 September, at Valmy, just east of Châlons, the French forces at last made a stand. Kellermann and Dumouriez had more men that the Prussians. They had fewer guns, but those they had were superior, and handled by graduates of the outstanding pre-revolutionary gunnery schools. So they outgunned the enemy, and when they followed up their advantage the French charged to cries of *Vive la Nation!* and the singing of 'Ça ira'. They fought with an enthusiasm and determination not seen on European battlefields for generations, and they stopped the invaders in their tracks. Watching all this was Goethe, brought along by the Duke of Weimar to enliven the expected military promenade. In the stunned disappointment of the Prussian camp that damp night he offered Job's comfort to his fellow invaders. 'Here and today,' he told them, 'a new epoch in the history of the world has begun, and you can boast you were present at its birth.'

The Prussians, in fact, at once opened negotiations. King Frederick William was there to authorize them when Dumouriez, who had never believed in their commitment to the Austrian alliance, made the offer. The revolutionary war might almost have ended there and then. But on the day Valmy was fought the national Convention finally met in Paris, and its first act was to declare a republic. The Prussians promptly broke off negotiations and withdrew.

The idea of a Convention predated the Revolution of 10 August. Radicals in the sections and at the Jacobin Club had been talking of the need to produce a new constitution throughout July. Thus on the afternoon of 10 August the Legislative Assembly had little alternative but to 'invite' the French people to form a convention 'to assure the sovereignty of the people and the reign of liberty and equality'. The next day it decreed that the new assembly was to be elected by manhood suffrage, without distinction between citizens. Only servants and the unemployed had no vote. But at least the Legislative resisted the sections' desire that election should be direct, stipulating a two-stage process; and it equally overrode Robespierre's suggestion of another self-denying ordinance, seeing that it would let him in but keep all sitting deputies out. The primary elections took place on 27 August, the secondary on 2 September, at the very height of the national emergency. No doubt this helps to explain the fact that out of seven million electors only about one in five turned up to vote in the primary assemblies. And the patchy and uncertain information that many of the departments had about the Revolution of 10 August and subsequent events in Paris no doubt indicates why no less than 200 of the 749 deputies returned were members of the Legislative and therefore already well known to those who elected them. They included Brissot and his circle and all the most prominent orators from the Gironde. Eighty-three members of the former Constituent Assembly also now reappeared on the national stage, including Orléans (proudly flaunting the new republican name of Philippe-Égalité), Pétion, and Robespierre, all three sitting for Paris.

Danton's election was a foregone conclusion, although it brought his resignation from the ministry. Journalistic notoriety secured almost equally inevitable seats for Marat and Clootz. Frenchmen also recognized their foreign friends by electing Tom Paine and Joseph Priestley. Socially, like its predecessors, the new assembly was dominated by lawyers, professional men, and property owners; and although mercantile, noble, and clerical numbers were smaller than ever, for the first time in the national representation there was a handful of assorted artisans. It was a young body, with two-thirds of deputies under 45. Above all, it brought together a wide range of political experience at both national and local level, experience scarred since the beginning of 1791 by the obstinate, treacherous behaviour of the king.

There was, therefore, never any doubt that the Convention would depose him. Papers found in the Tuileries after 10 August only confirmed suspicions about his treachery. In any case, Paris clearly demanded a republic. And so on 21 September the foundation-stone of the new constitution was laid. Monarchy in France was abolished; and when a year later a new revolutionary calendar was introduced, it was calculated from 22 September 1792, the first day of Year 1 of the Republic. But to abolish the monarchy was one thing. To dispose of Louis XVI was quite another. Much of the autumn was spent deciding what to do with him.

Brissot and the Girondins were attracted by the idea of doing nothing— keeping the king a hostage against future eventualities. Some suspected that, in the light of their equivocations during the fortnight before 10 August, they might even want to keep open the option of restoring him some day. The commune, and the Parisian deputies who sat together on the high benches to the left of the chair and were to become the kernel of a group known as the Mountain or the Montagnards, were determined to close off this option. When on 1 October the vigilance committee of the commune claimed it had evidence that some deputies had been paid collaborators of the fallen monarch, they demanded that he and they be put on trial. A commission was appointed to examine the evidence, which became stronger with the discovery during November of a strong-box (*armoire de fer*) at the Tuileries containing yet more incriminating documents. It was a nice point whether a king, inviolable under the constitution, could legitimately be tried at all, or at least by any court. In response to this some Montagnards began to argue, following the maiden speech of the hitherto unknown young deputy from the Aisne, Saint-Just, on 13 November, that the tyrant had already been tried, and found guilty, on 10 August by the people. All that was needed was to punish him. Robespierre, whom some were already accusing of aspiring to dictatorship, came out for this opinion on 3 December.

Louis cannot be judged, [he argued] he has already been judged. He has been condemned, or else the Republic is not blameless. To suggest putting Louis XVI on trial, in whatever way, is a step back towards royal and constitutional despotism; it is a counter-revolutionary idea; because it puts the Revolution itself in the dock. After all, if Louis can still be put on trial, Louis can be acquitted; he might be innocent. Or rather, he is presumed to be until he is found guilty. But if Louis is acquitted, if Louis can be presumed innocent, what becomes of the Revolution?[10]

Yet the legal training most deputies had received left them reluctant to condemn anyone without a hearing; and on the motion of Pétion, who had steadily been drifting away from Robespierre since the spring, it was overwhelmingly agreed to try the king before the representatives of the sovereign people, the Convention itself. On 11 December he was brought from the Temple through silent, crowded streets to hear his indictment. It covered his entire conduct since the meeting of the Estates-General. But if the deputies hoped to intimidate him they were disappointed. With deliberation and dignity he responded to the heads of accusation with a series of evasions, denials, and outright lies. At the end he called for a defending counsel. As on 20 June onlookers were impressed despite themselves by his resolute bearing in adversity, and this alarmed those who wanted his head, and encouraged those who still hoped to save it.

On the day of the trial it was the same. Reluctantly the deputies had allowed 'Louis Capet' a counsel. 26 December was devoted to the defending speech of Raymond de Sèze, another eloquent Bordelais well known to several of the more prominent Girondins. He portrayed his client as a victim of circumstance rather than a resolute tyrant; a monarch who had given his people all that they asked for, including liberty itself. In his final words the king reiterated that he had never knowingly and willingly shed his subjects' blood. Many seemed moved; but even the king knew that Robespierre had been right in claiming that there could only be one possible verdict. The only real issues were the appropriate punishment and whether it should be subject to review or reprieve. The questions were debated with renewed fury from the moment the king was escorted from the chamber. The Girondins now began to argue that whatever sentence was passed should be subject to confirmation by a referendum: an 'appeal to the people'. Exchanges on this subject were the bitterest so far. Nobody doubted that the Girondins hoped the provinces would reject the death sentence which Paris so obviously wanted—and they might well have. But in that case it was hard to see how civil war could be avoided. In the end these fears triumphed. On 15 January 1793 a roll-call of votes at last took place. On the question of the king's guilt there was near unanimity: 693

deputies voted guilty and none voted for acquittal. On the question of the appeal to the people the true scale of political division within the Convention began to appear: 283 were for, but 424 against. So it was in the knowledge that their sentence would be final that the deputies approached the question of the king's life or death the next day. This time the roll-call went on overnight, as deputies writhed to explain or justify their votes. And it went on amid lurid rumours that any sentence other than death would bring the sansculottes on to the streets to storm the Temple and massacre its prisoners, not to mention the Convention itself. Fear of such consequences perhaps swayed the votes of some. Even so the voting was uncomfortably close. The official result recorded 288 votes against death, and for a variety of forms of imprisonment. A further 72 favoured the death penalty subject to delaying conditions of one sort or another. But still the largest single group, numbering 361, voted for execution. This was the decision announced by Louis XVI on the morning of 17 January.

Still some deputies fought to save him. His counsel issued an appeal to the nation the moment the sentence was announced, but that was ruled angrily out of order. Yet the people, like all sovereigns, had the prerogative of mercy, and on the eighteenth a reprieve was proposed. Another endless noisy session followed, culminating in a fourth roll-call. This time 310 voted against death; but 380 were still for carrying out the sentence. After that there was no more delay. On Monday 21 January 1793 Louis XVI went to the scaffold, in what is now the place de la Concorde, next to the empty pedestal of his grandfather's triumphal statue—his last professions of innocence drowned out by rolling drums.

Thus the republican revolution, brewing since Varennes, and militant since 10 August, reached its logical climax. The destruction of the *ancien régime* was surely now complete, total, irrevocable. Regicide meant there would be no compromise, no going back. But, as a handful of deputies realized when they voted to execute the king only when the war was over, or the entire Bourbon dynasty deposed, the execution of Louis XVI was not so much a victory as a challenge. It satisfied the sansculottes, but throughout Europe, and probably France, too, it made the Revolution far more enemies than friends. It also immeasurably strengthened those who were already its enemies, giving new impetus to their quarrel. The blood of the Most Christian King offered defiance to all who questioned the French Revolution's achievements, or its direction. So the regicide Republic could scarcely complain when, in the course of 1793, these multifarious interests took up its challenge.

# 9

# War against Europe
# 1792−1797

LOUIS XVI was not the first king to be killed by his subjects in the 1790s. In March 1792 Gustavus III of Sweden, fiercest of France's crowned critics, was assassinated at a masked ball in Stockholm. His killers were nobles, outraged at a programme of democratic despotism that made the popular gestures constantly being pressed upon Louis XVI by his secret advisers seem tame. But Gustavus with his last words blamed Jacobinism, and the plotters against him sought to divert responsibility by doing the same. So it was axiomatic even before the revolutionary war began that the French hated kings, and their treatment of Louix XVI seemed to prove it. Monarchs not already at war withdrew their ambassadors from France after 10 August. Even the American ambassador agonized whether he should stay. And, in the euphoria of victory after Valmy, the French proclaimed new war aims calculated to alienate and alarm not only monarchs, but the entire social hierarchies upon which their power rested.

Having helped to check the Prussians at Valmy, Dumouriez allowed them to retreat unimpeded by anything but the weather, while he turned north to attack the Austrian Netherlands. Here was the original front, and the original enemy; and besides, decisive victory there could make the general who achieved it the arbiter of France's future in the political uncertainties of the autumn. On 3 November he crossed the frontier and three days later he routed an Austrian force at Jemappes. In just over a week he was in Brussels and by the end of the month he had overrun the entire Austrian Netherlands, and the bishopric of Liège into the bargain. Meanwhile in the south, Savoy, which had joined the allies the day after Valmy, was invaded by French troops under Montesquiou, and Nice was occupied. On the Rhine, Custine pushed into the ecclesiastical principalities and took Mainz on 21 October, Frankfurt on the twenty-third.

How had the French, seemingly facing defeat in August, managed to turn the tables so dramatically? One obvious advantage was sheer weight of numbers: at both Valmy and Jemappes the enemy was heavily outnumbered. Throughout the decade, in fact, a population rising towards 29 millions would provide far more reserves of able-bodied manpower than any single adversary could muster. The first year of the war, moreover, saw much enthusiastic volunteering, providing 180,000 patriotic recruits determined to defend the new order established since 1789. And although it was true that the old royal army had been severely decimated by desertion, mutiny, and wholesale emigration of officers, those who had remained with the colours were arguably the most committed and professional soldiers France had, and capable NCOs soon filled most of the gaps in the officer corps. And the artillery, the deciding factor in both the key battles, had been the least affected of all the army's units by upheavals since the Revolution had begun, and even at the height of patriotic volunteering had only accepted recruits with previous military experience. All this meant that French forces were not as incompetent or ill prepared as the allies imagined.

Nor were inadequate numbers, over-confidence, poor intelligence, and wishful thinking the only disadvantages of the German powers. They were also increasingly distracted by ominous Russian activity in their rear. In April 1792 Polish nobles discontented with King Stanislas's reforming, centralizing constitution of 3 May 1791 formed themselves, with collusion from St Petersburg, into a confederation at Targowica. They then appealed for help to Russia, recognized since the partition of 1772 as the guarantor of the traditional Polish constitution. A month later, Russian troops invaded the country, and by the end of August, despite a spirited campaign led by the American war veteran Tadeusz Kosciuszko, the country was overrun and the king surrendered. The French viewed the Poles' resistance as a struggle parallel to their own, and on 26 August the Legislative Assembly acclaimed Kosciuszko a French citizen. But the turnabout in their own fortunes might not have been so spectacular had he succeeded. For the Russian triumph brought the virtual withdrawal of Prussian troops from the western front as Frederick William concentrated them in the east in order to secure the prize he had dreamed most of since his reign began: a second partition of Poland that would give him the port of Gdansk, and whatever else Catherine II might be prepared to concede.

So throughout the autumn the French armies surged eastwards, meeting little serious resistance, into enemy territory. The men who had launched the war with claims that the Revolution's principles would make them invincible still dominated French public life in the Convention, and now they saw their predictions justified they were prepared to expand their ambitions. On 19 November, in a famous decree, the Convention declared, 'in the name of the French Nation, that it will accord fraternity and help to all peoples who wish to recover their liberty'. A month later (15 December) generals were authorized in all occupied territories to introduce the full social programme of the French Republic. All existing taxes, tithes, feudal dues, and servitudes were to be abolished. So was nobility, and all types of privilege. The French motto would be, declared some deputies, *War on the castles, peace to the cottages!* In the name of peace, help, fraternity, liberty, and equality, they would assist all peoples to establish 'free and popular' governments, with whom they would then co-operate. But all those connected with, or sympathetic to, the old order would be excluded from power, and the main task of the new authorities would be to see to the provision of 'equipment and supplies necessary to the armies of the Republic, and to cover the expenditure they have incurred or will incur during their stay on their territory'. The meaning was clear: occupied territories, however welcoming and fraternal, would be expected to bear the cost of the French presence, and puppet administrations would be responsible for arranging the unpleasant details. On 15 December it was also decreed that the assignats should be introduced into occupied territories. Nor were these the only ominous signals coming from Paris as 1792 drew to a close. Some territories were not even to be given the option of setting up free and popular governments under French protection. In their case, the nation that had renounced conquest only two years beforehand was increasingly turning its thoughts towards annexations.

Admittedly the idea did not originate in France. The moment French troops crossed the Savoyard frontier in September, calls were heard from local groups for incorporation into France. They cited the precedent of Avignon. Throughout the autumn isolated German voices advocated the annexation of the Rhineland into the Republic, too. The Rhine was France's natural frontier anyway, argued the leader of those who collaborated with the invaders in Mainz, the librarian and publicist Georg Forster. The Convention's initial reaction to such arguments was cautious. Avignon, an enclave deep in French territory, whose distant ruler had no armed forces, was a different proposition from the strategically important lands across the frontier now occupied by the Republic's troops. Annexation might prolong and widen the conflict, and complicate later peacemaking, especially if it was applied to the most spectacular of all the new conquests, Belgium. Some 2,500 exiles driven out by the Austrian reconquest of 1790 followed Dumouriez's advance on Brussels. They expected the French to help them re-establish the independent state snuffed out by Leopold II. Dumouriez, who dreamed of setting up a principality of his own, favoured their plans to elect a national Convention. Support for such independent action, however, was soon on the wane in Paris. 'I can tell you', Brissot wrote to him on 27 November, 'that there is one opinion which is spreading here: namely that the French Republic must have the Rhine as its frontier.'[1] And Danton, who spent December and part of January 1793 on mission to the armies in Belgium, declared on 31 January that: 'The limits of France are marked out by nature. We shall reach them at their four points; at the Ocean, at the Rhine, at the Alps, at the Pyrenees.'[2] Belgium should therefore be incorporated, he argued. But the Rhine was not even the Belgian frontier. Whole stretches of the Dutch Republic lay to the south of it. And any permanent French presence in the Netherlands was bound to be opposed by the British.

Pitt's government undoubtedly disliked the French Revolution and what it stood for. But they had no intention of going to war against it. In February 1792 Pitt declared in Parliament that never had fifteen years of peace seemed more likely. Certainly he wished the allies well once war began on the Continent, but he refused to become actively involved, even after 10 August. No vital British interests seemed at stake, and France's invaders seemed destined for a quick victory. It was the invasion of Belgium that changed matters, for British policy throughout the century had hinged on keeping the low countries out of French hands. And when, on 16 November, the French declared the Scheldt open, they flouted what had been the official policy of the Dutch Republic since its foundation, and breached the Peace of Westphalia into the bargain. The threat was conscious and deliberate; French generals and planners in Paris were now talking openly of reversing the Dutch settlement of 1788, guaranteed by the British and the Prussians, and they were urged on by the 'Batavian Legion' put together over the summer from patriots exiled in France since then. At the end of November the terrified Stadtholder William V appealed formally to London for help, and the British began to mobilize their fleet.

The trial and execution of Louis XVI precipitated the final break. The bloody scenes in Paris on and after 10 August had already done much to alienate even onlookers whose goodwill had survived the shock of royal humiliation after Varennes. Although in England the successes of the French armies encouraged the corresponding societies, who deluged the Convention with congratulatory addresses, exhortations, and even collections of boots (for soldiers presumed still to be clad in wooden shoes), it also sent the propertied classes scurrying into the government-sponsored Association for the Preservation of Liberty and Property against Republicans and Levellers. Founded by John Reeves late in November, within months it had 2,000 branches and far exceeded the corresponding societies in membership. So that when Pitt asked Parliament for funds to organize war against a nation preparing to murder its king, and now publicly committed to helping sympathizers abroad whenever they called for it, he knew he had massive public support and that the legislature would reflect it. His divided Whig opponents were routed. Secret negotiations to avert a final break continued into January, but as soon as Louis XVI was dead the British broke them off. It was the French who actually declared war, by a unanimous vote of the Convention, on 1 February 1793. In the same session, they also declared war on the Dutch Republic.

Carried away by their own success and rhetoric, they now bade defiance to the whole of Europe. 'They threaten you with kings!' roared Danton to the Convention,[3] 'You have thrown down your gauntlet to them, and this gauntlet is a king's head, the signal of their coming death.' 'We cannot be calm', claimed the ever-bombastic Brissot,[4] 'until Europe, all Europe, is in flames.' In token of this defiance, annexations were now vigorously pursued. Savoy was incorporated into the Republic as early as 27 November 1792, following a petition from the self-styled 'Sovereign National Assembly of the Allobroges'. Nice followed on 31 January 1793. In February elections were held on the left bank of the Rine, and although boycotted by most of the population they produced a Convention of beleaguered collaborators with the invader which duly petitioned, under the leadership of Forster, for incorporation into France. Meanwhile the Belgians had also been offered the chance to pronounce on the question in a plebiscite, and throughout February and early March clear majorities for incorporation were recorded among the tiny minorities of the population who could be persuaded to cast their votes in the various occupied territories. One by one throughout March they were annexed. Dumouriez by now had marched into the southern provinces of the Dutch Republic. The French could be forgiven for thinking they were unstoppable.

But they were not. They had, in fact, assumed a hugely expanded range of commitments, and gratuitously taken on new enemies, at the very moment when the old ones were recovering the strength to counter-attack. Two days after Louis XVI's head fell, for example, the Polish question was settled. Rather than fight the Prussians, Catherine of Russia proposed a new partition in which she took the lion's share of territory and population, but Prussia acquired Gdansk and a vast wedge of territory linking up Silesia and the Baltic provinces. Austria was excluded, much to the fury of the Emperor, who dismissed his leading ministers. The Austro-Prussian alliance against France still held together, however, and could now turn its attention again westwards. The Prussians, indeed, recaptured

Frankfurt as early as 2 December 1792, and at the beginning of March 1793 Austrian troops marched once more into the southern Nether-lands. On the eighteenth they met Dumouriez at Neerwinden and defeated him decisively. It was the beginning of a disastrous year for the new Republic.

Even before they formally entered the war, the British had begun to engineer a grand anti-French coalition. In the last days of 1792 they approached Spain for an alliance, knowing that before Valmy the junior branch of the House of Bourbon had already been on the verge of joining the expected Austro-Prussian military promenade to restore Louis XVI to his throne and prerogatives. News of the king's execution produced widespread expressions of revulsion in Spain, and the French envoy was expelled. On 7 March France retaliated by declaring war, and soon afterwards Spain agreed to co-operate in a British blockade of the French Mediterranean coast. On 25 March the British also persuaded Catherine of Russia to commit herself to the anti-French struggle. A month later, a subsidy was offered to the king of Sardinia, while in July Portugal and Naples were also drawn into the conflict by British diplomacy. Minor German states, meanwhile, were more prepared than ever to hire out troops to paymasters in London. No general treaty bound this coalition together. Nevertheless, within months of Louis XVI's execution, most of the states of Europe were openly committed to fighting France.

Nor, by then, did victory seem far off. Neerwinden, when the defeated French troops fled headlong from the field, suggested that after all Valmy and Jemappes had been lucky flukes. Dumouriez made no attempt to regroup. Instead, he asked the Austrians for an armistice, and promised in return to co-operate with the allies by marching what was left of his army on Paris, where he would release the queen and the dauphin from captivity, and proclaim the latter Louis XVII. But when he ordered the march on Paris, his men refused to move, and on 5 April he followed the example of Lafayette and defected to the Austrians. Meanwhile the French had also been driven out of the Rhineland, leaving 20,000 of their men cut off in Mainz; while in France itself armed insurrection had broken out in the Vendée.* In April Danton, the leading voice on foreign policy in the Convention's newly established Committee of Public Safety, began to use the language of conciliation, deflecting a ferocious motion from Robes-pierre that anybody advocating negotiation with the enemy should be executed; and persuading the Convention to abandon its open-ended commitment to help anybody calling for French support. He also made a

---

* See below, pp. 224–6

number of clandestine approaches to coalition powers—which only proved to them how close to defeat France was.

Everything that happened over the summer pointed the same way. By June much of the country was violently rejecting the Convention's apparent subjection to Paris in the 'Federalist' revolt. By July, the French forces had been entirely expelled from Belgium (to great popular jubilation) and the Austrian General Coburg had once more crossed on to French soil, taking the fortress of Condé on the twelfth. A few weeks later, Valenciennes went the same way, and an Anglo-Hanoverian army laid siege to Dunkirk. On the German front, the Mainz garrison capitulated on 23 July, after sustaining 7,000 casualties. In the south, the Spaniards invaded Roussillon and routed its defenders at Mas d'Eu on 18 May. Most humiliating of all, on 27 August rebels at Toulon, the great naval harbour of the Mediterranean coast, turned the port, its arsenal, and fleet over to the British.

The reversal of the French fortunes was spectacular. It caused much paranoia and contributed to momentous political upheavals in Paris. Many attributed it to treason and collusion with the enemy, an impression that Dumouriez's defection did nothing to dispel. And after that even the most patriotic generals were reluctant to take the risk of over-bold action, aware that if they failed they were all too likely to end up on the guillotine. Two (Custine and Houchard) certainly did so. But in some ways the defeats of 1793 stemmed directly from the victories of 1792. The French had become over-confident when the armies of their despotic enemies retreated before them, and in fact by the end of the year thousands of volunteers who had enlisted for a single campaign to meet the emergencies of 1792 were returning home, and being allowed to return, in the belief that the job was done. By February there were only about 230,000 men under arms; so that diminishing forces had to confront the explosive growth in the number and resources of the Republic's enemies, external and internal, during the first half of 1793. It is scarcely surprising that things went so badly.

Even more surprising, however, is how little relative advantage her enemies took of France's weakness. Their incursions into French territory never penetrated far beyond the periphery, and there was next to no concerted action by the coalition as a whole, or even groups of its members. Nor did most of them even share common aims. All were notionally committed to the restoration of the French monarchy, but with the king a sickly child in republican hands the project was harder to focus on than when wronged Louis XVI still lived. The British wanted Belgium back in Austrian hands—although they were quite happy to commit troops to seizing France's troubled Caribbean islands while a state of war gave them the opportunity. The Austrians wanted Belgium back, too, and yet were again toying with an old idea of exchanging it for Bavaria once it was securely theirs again. It had, after all, brought them nothing but trouble since 1786, and as soon as they were re-established they found their Belgian subjects just as awkward to deal with as before, and unwilling to make any extra sacrifices to the war effort. Besides, the new Austrian minister, Thugut, was determined to reserve his strength for intervention in Poland in case of further upheavals there. He did not intend to be excluded from any further share-out. Prussia and Russia too were uncertain that the latest partition would hold, so that Prussian armies on the French front moved sluggishly and were not reinforced, and Russia confined her coalition contribution to harassing such French trade as got to the Baltic past the blockade, which was the first British action in any war with France. When the British declined to pay her a subsidy, Catherine bluntly refused to commit any troops at all to the coalition. Many coalition statesmen clearly expected France to collapse without any special effort on their part. As Pitt wrote: 'If we distress the enemy on more sides than one, while their internal distraction continues, it seems hardly possible that they can long oppose any effectual resistance.'[5]

But resist they did, and with increasing success. Between 6 and 8 September a muddled, indecisive battle at Hondschoote raised the siege of Dunkirk and forced its British besiegers, under the (Grand Old) Duke of York, to withdraw. More spectacularly, at another three-day battle, between 15 and 17 October Jourdan defeated the main Austrian army on French territory at Wattignies, despite inferior numbers, and pursued it across the frontier. Jourdan, a 31-year-old veteran of the American war whose republicanism was far more sincere than that of Dumouriez or Custine, fought the battle under the eye of Lazare Carnot, the member of the Committee of Public Safety now most concerned with military matters. Carnot's efforts over the subsequent year would earn him enduring fame as the organizer of victory.

Already on 24 February a levy of 300,000 conscripts had been decreed. It triggered off the Vendée revolt and met with massive resistance throughout the west and north of the country, but by the summer the official number of men under arms had risen to 645,000. And in August the Convention went on to declare a programme of national mobilization on a scale never before seen anywhere: the *levée en masse*. Originating among the sansculottes of the Paris sections, the idea of putting the entire resources of the nation at the disposal of the war effort was urged in a series of petitions lodged between 12 and 16 August. Practically Carnot's first act on joining the Committee of Public Safety was to draft the decree promulgated on the twenty-third, under which, until the moment 'when enemies have been driven from the Republic's territory, all Frenchmen are permanently requisitioned for the service of the armies'. All unmarried men between 18 and 25 were to present themselves for military service; others were to serve in manufacture, food production, and transport; women were to make clothes and staff hospitals, children make bandages, and even old men should 'have themselves carried to public places to excite courage in the warriors, hatred of kings, and the unity of the Republic'. All horses and publicly owned buildings were to be drafted into service, a massive expansion of munitions manufacture was proclaimed, and the government generally given powers to do whatever it thought necessary to win the war. These measures produced an army of 1,169,000 by September 1794. It was true that only about 750,000 were fully equipped and trained for battle, but that still made the Republic's armed forces the largest ever seen in the history of Europe.

Unprecedented size demanded unprecedented organization, support, and tactics. Throughout 1792 the French armies had consisted of the diminishing remnants of the old line army, National Guard units assigned to the front, and, sometimes overlapping with the latter, battalions of volunteers. Each tended to hold the others in some suspicion and contempt, and they were differently paid, organized, clothed, and equipped. On 21 February the Convention voted to end this situation by introducing the principle of amalgamation (*amalgame*). The idea was to blend each line battalion into two volunteer units to form a demi-brigade, a principle already tried in the field, with considerable success, by Dumouriez. The new formations were to have identical pay, procedures, uniforms, and equipment. Implementation proved slow, and did not become general until after a new decree in January 1794. Even then it was a two-year process. But the end result was to streamline and simplify the Republic's military organization, expunge the chaos of its beginnings, and increase the whole army's sense of being a new, superior force—a citizen army utterly unlike the mixture of mercenaries and reluctant serf conscripts sent against them by the German despots. It was unlike them too in being much harder to equip and supply. For most of the war food and shelter were found by pitiless requisitioning and billeting, and until the Republic's armies began to operate once more on foreign territory in the latter half of 1794, the burden was mostly borne by France's own frontier districts. Provision of arms and munitions was expanded by thirty new workshops established between August 1793 and July 1794, and metal supplies were supplemented by melting down railings, church bells, and ornaments. A massive drive was implemented to recover saltpetre from cellars and caves, and thus avoid dependence on imports from the east for the main component of gunpowder. The French war effort of 1793–4 was a triumph for ruthless makeshift action, meeting demands, however roughly and readily, never before seen; and showing incidentally how much proper, more formalized organization might achieve later. Equally suggestive of the future were the tactics deployed by the young Republic's monster armies. There was no possibility of quickly training so many new recruits in the precise and formal drill and manoeuvres of the eighteenth-century battlefield. But weight of numbers, driven on by the patriotic enthusiasm first seen at Valmy and Jemappes, also made that unnecessary. The French could overwhelm their enemies with human waves; and although commanders facing them were at first appalled by their disregard for human life, they soon learned how effective it was. Citizen soldiers felt no restraints, particularly when defending their homeland, as in 1793. They reintroduced into warfare a ferocity and lack of restraint unknown, in western Europe at least, for well over a century.

Even so it took some time before the full force of these efforts was brought to bear. Much of the autumn of 1793 was absorbed in quelling and mopping up the various centres of revolt within France. The only striking success after Wattignies was partly such an operation. On 19 December Toulon was recaptured and the British fleet driven out, the key role in their expulsion being played by the 25-year-old commander of the artillery, Napoleon Bonaparte. His rise began here, and within two months he was a general, planning a march into Italy. But the main front was still in Flanders, and here the coalition hoped to advance along the whole line for the spring campaign of 1794. Emperor Francis II even made the journey from Vienna to inspire his troops and flatter his Belgian subjects, who had never before been visited by their Austrian sovereign. But he did not impress them, nor they him, and he had gone back east, alarmed by news from Poland, when the first major battle occurred. At Tourcoing on 17–18 May the French stopped a numerically superior coalition army from threatening key fortresses. Six weeks later, on 26 June, the Austrians retreated after a bitterly fought confrontation at Fleurus. Even on the sea, against the reputedly invincible British, the French held their own. Over the winter Carnot's colleague on the Committee of Public Safety, the ex-Protestant pastor Jeanbon Saint-André, had worked to restore the debilitated and demoralized Brest fleet. In mid-May it put to sea in order to escort a major grain convoy from America into port. In what the British chose to call the 'Glorious First of June' the French were seriously mauled, losing 13 ships; but the victors themselves were so exhausted that the convoy eluded them unharmed. Fleurus, however, was much the most important engagement. In fact it marked the turning-point of the whole war. From that moment the French went on to the offensive, and they scarcely looked back until all their continental opponents had been knocked out of the conflict, and even the British were desperate to make peace.

Thus they began to reap the rewards of a year of desperate, frenzied activity. Yet, as in 1792, not all their success was attributable to their own efforts. Once again the Poles distracted enemies at the crucial moment. Encouraged by the sympathy with which his campaign against the Russians had been viewed in 1792, Kosciuszko made his way to Paris in January 1793 and spent six months trying to interest the new Republic in supporting a renewed Polish insurrection. He received little more than fair words, and in August rejoined his fellow *émigrés* massing in Leipzig and plotting a rising. Even though the French were offering no tangible help, their enemies were the same, their apparent ability to generate mass enthusiasm was an inspiration, and the language of liberty, national rights, and representative government still had seductive echoes in traditional Polish political rhetoric. Kosciuszko was anxious to avoid a premature rising, but resentment at the Russian occupation within what was left of Poland was growing. In the spring of 1794 his hand was forced by a mutiny within the army, which the Russians were attempting to cut down from the 50,000 to which it had grown during the Four Years Diet, to a mere 15,000. The Russians could not be allowed, in putting the mutiny down, to decimate the force on which the plotters planned to rely. On 24 March, accordingly, Kosciuszko arrived in Cracow and proclaimed an insurrection. A fortnight later he defeated a Russian force sent against him at Raclawice (4 April) and news of this success triggered uprisings against occupying garrisons in Vilno and, above all, Warsaw. Tricolour cockades sprouted everywhere, Polish translations of the 'Marseillaise' and 'Ça ira' appeared, and a 'Society of Friends of the National Insurrection', which everyone recognized as a Jacobin club, was established. The Russians withdrew from the capital after losing half their men to popular fury in an episode twice as bloody as the Paris September Massacres of 1792. There were also popular reprisals against those associated with national betrayal in the Targowica confederation. Kosciuszko dreamed of a Polish *levée en masse* to drive out foreign invaders and, fearing 'lest the noble ardour of the people grow cold',[6] on 7 May he issued a proclamation granting peasants personal freedom, diminishing the burdens owed to lords, and hinting at further freedoms to come.

Not all the insurgent leaders, most of whom belonged to Poland's teeming nobility, thought such promises wise. Certainly they only confirmed the most visceral prejudices of the partitioning monarchs and their advisers. Poland was clearly in the grip of international Jacobinism, and the influence of what Frederick William I called 'that diabolical sect' would not be stamped out until the whole of Poland was completely controlled by the forces of order. Determined to take a lead in this, and make further gains into the bargain, the Prussians marched into Poland in May with the encouragement of Catherine II. They did not know that she was also secretly urging the Austrians to intervene in the south. They beat the Austrians to Cracow, and joined forces with the Russians to besiege Warsaw; but in September they were forced to withdraw to deal with a revolt in former Polish territory annexed in 1793. The Austrians now took the opportunity to occupy large stretches of south Poland, while the Russians decided to reduce Warsaw single-handed. To do this they sent general Alexander Suvorov, a veteran campaigner from savage Balkan wars, who, having defeated Kosciuszko at Maciejowice at the beginning of October, advanced on the capital with overwhelming force. On 4 November he stormed Praga, its suburb beyond the Vistula, where the Russian troops took pitiless revenge for their treatment six months previously. Anything between 10,000 and 20,000 Poles died that day, when, as Suvorov proudly reported, 'The whole of Praga was strewn with dead bodies, blood was flowing in streams'.[7] Watching the most destructive one-day massacre in this entire decade of appalling carnage, the inhabitants of Warsaw realized that their only hope was to negotiate surrender. Within days it was agreed. By the end of 1794 the last convulsion of independent Poland was over, and Kosciuszko was a prisoner in St Petersburg. The surrounding powers had decided to partition the country out of existence long before the fighting was over. They spent much of 1795, however, haggling over precisely how the spoils were to be carved up, and for several months in the spring it looked as if Prussia would fight the other two for a larger share. In preparation for this eventuality, she concluded an armistice with France in November 1794 and began to negotiate a definitive peace. In practice she had already played no part in the war in the west for over eighteen months.

It was ironic that, until it was almost over, the French refused to think of helping a Polish uprising that looked to France for inspiration, copied the French revolutionary style and language, was identified by its opponents as plainly Jacobinical, and did so much to take pressure off France while she confronted her internal problems. But fraternity and assistance to foreign sympathizers was a Girondin policy. The Montagnards who held power in 1793 and 1794 were more interested in securing the Revolution in France than exporting it to others. Thus it was not until November

1794, when Warsaw had already fallen (although they did not yet know that), that policy-makers in France began to think seriously about the Poles; and by then the success of the French armies was exporting the Revolution anyway.

After Fleurus the Austrians abandoned Belgium, and by the end of the summer the French had reoccupied the whole of it. Thugut declared openly that recovering it was not worth the effort. Once more, too, the French moved into the southern provinces of the Dutch Republic, reawakening in the defeated patriots of 1787 all the hopes and expectations so abruptly dashed in 1793. Clubs of patriots, thinly disguised as 'reading societies', mushroomed north of the Rhine mouths, and as the Prussians began to negotiate with the French the Stadtholder saw his chief bulwark since 1787 begin to melt away. He remained strong enough in the autumn to destroy a premature pro-French conspiracy, but with the onset of one of the coldest winters of the century the rivers froze and thereby destroyed Holland's main line of defence. The French poured across, and such were the depredations of what was left of York's British army retreating before them, that it was not only long-standing Dutch patriots who welcomed them. On 18 January William V embarked for England as groups of patriots ousted his minions from power in town after town across the country. The transfer of power was remarkably bloodless, perhaps because it happened before, rather than after, the invaders actually arrived. The patriots believed, and encouraged others to believe, the sincerity of French promises before the invasion that once that stooge of the British and Prussians, William V, had been dislodged from power, the Dutch would be left free to organize themselves and pursue policies as they wished. In this, however, they deluded themselves. The true French view was trenchantly expressed by one of their generals:

Holland has done nothing to avoid being classed among the general order of our conquests. It was the ice, the indefatigable courage of our troops and the talents of the generals which delivered her and not any revolution. It follows from this that there can be no reason to treat her any differently from a conquered country. With very few exceptions the patriots of this country are all timid adventurers led by ambitious intriguers, avid speculators who never dared to take up arms in our favour.[8]

Throughout the century the French had always believed the Dutch to be fabulously rich, and the temptation to mulct their assets for French purposes was irresistible. So the peace treaty signed at The Hague in May was punitive. The Batavian Republic (as it now officially became) was required to pay a war indemnity of 100 million florins, and lend France

100 million more at concessionary rates of interest. It was compelled to cede various southern territories, including control of the mouth of the Scheldt, and pay for the upkeep of a French occupying army of 25,000 men. Finally it was forced to conclude an alliance with the French Republic whose chief attraction was to place the supposedly formidable Dutch navy in the balance against Great Britain. This, then, was what the fraternity and help of the French Republic actually meant: total subordination to French needs and purposes. It was an awful warning to other French sympathizers elsewhere in Europe—although entirely confirming the expectations of their far more numerous opponents. Nor did the full implications for the Dutch become apparent at once. What was very clear by May 1795, however, was that the coalition of 1793 was rapidly breaking up.

A month before the Dutch accepted the French terms, Prussia had finally withdrawn. By the treaty of Basle signed on 5 April, she left France a free hand along the entire length of the Rhine's left bank (including occupation of Prussian territories) in return for a recognition of Prussian hegemony in north Germany and that region's neutralization. The agreement came too late to free Prussia to pursue all she wanted with her full strength in Poland, but it left the Rhenish princes and electors at the Republic's mercy. French occupying troops set about systematically exploiting this hitherto prosperous region to fund the French war effort. Then in July peace was also made (again at Basle) with Spain. By the end of 1794 the Spanish forces had been driven out of Roussillon and the French were advancing into Catalonia and the Basque provinces. They met a population far more resolute in its resistance to the Godless invaders than on other fronts, but the court of Madrid was obsessed by fears of pro-French subversion. 'In the taverns and in the fashionable salons . . .', wrote a Madrid priest, 'all one hears is battles, revolution, convention, national representation, liberty, equality. Even the whores ask you about Robespierre.'[9] In February 1795 plans for a republican uprising were uncovered. The conspirators, a group of teachers and lawyers led by an educational theorist called Picornell, were condemned to death but reprieved on French insistence when peace was concluded. This plot, and rumours of others, had been enough to scare Godoy, the queen's feckless favourite who dominated the government, into seeking terms. And France, not really threatened by Spain but anxious to transfer troops east for use against the Austrians, was prepared to be magnanimous. In Europe, she demanded nothing more than Spanish good offices in bringing Portugal and minor Italian states to the conference table. Overseas, Spain ceded the eastern part of Saint-Domingue, but with the French west in chaos and the Caribbean dominated by the British,

France was in no position to take much immediate advantage of the gain. The real importance of peace with Prussia and Spain was to free French resources for a knock-out blow against what was left of the coalition. By August 1795 that meant Portugal, Sardinia, a number of minor Italian states, and above all Great Britain and Austria.

Austria looked by far the most vulnerable. Distracted in the east, abandoned even by the grand duke of Tuscany, the Emperor's own brother, in February, she sustained her war effort only by borrowing from a suspicious Great Britain. She also had her own internal dissidents. Amid a general and increasing war-weariness and a wave of public sympathy for the beleaguered Poles, especially in Hungary, police spies identified a group of 'Jacobins' who had sent a peace mission to Paris and who held regular meetings to discuss the overthrow of the government. Between July and September 1794, 25 conspirators were arrested in Vienna and 34 in Hungary. The treasonable activities revealed at the trials of the Viennese amounted to little more than planting a liberty tree and taking rash oaths; but the leader of the Hungarian plotters, the ex-priest Martinovics, had plans for a republic, an attack on the Church, and concessions to the serfs similar to those proclaimed by Kosciuszko in May 1794. These ideas cost Martinovics his life in May 1795, along with six other convicted plotters. All except six of the rest were given long terms of imprisonment after show trials designed to deter further toyings with Jacobinism. But the inspiration of the conspirators had been far more the memory of the reforming emperors Joseph and Leopold than a desire to ape France, and what they most feared—the abandonment of the changes introduced since 1780—now came about much more quickly thanks to the fright they had given Emperor Francis. Aware that, despite thwarting internal enemies, the threat from France was growing ever more serious he sanctioned discreet peace feelers over the summer of 1795; but on 1 October France showed its disdain for anything short of total victory when it declared once again that occupied Belgium was now French territory. Its former ruler was offered no compensation, and so resolved to fight on. The same uncompromising annexation guaranteed continued commitment to the war on the part of the British.

Pitt, too, in fact, had been putting out peace overtures after the breakup of the coalition. He continued to hope until the spring of 1796 that a new and uncertain government in France might yet offer concessions on Belgium. That would enable him to withdraw honourably from a struggle which was proving more costly, in every sense, than he had ever dreamed. Since the end of 1793 almost everything had gone wrong. Toulon had been lost, York's army in the Netherlands had performed dismally, and the coalition had come apart. In June 1795 an ambitious amphibious operation to land 3,300 men, mostly *émigrés*, on the Brittany coast at Quiberon Bay, there to link up with thousands more royalist *chouan* guerrillas, ended in fiasco.* After that Pitt concentrated British efforts on the West Indies. French planters in Saint-Domingue were desperate for British protection against rebellious blacks, and a small force had been sent there in 1793. When the Spaniards gave up their part of the island to France, the attractions of a more sustained British occupation grew. Imitative slave uprisings swept the British West Indies, too, early in 1795, while republican privateers operated from Guadeloupe. Besides, there were obvious commercial advantages in trying to make the Caribbean a British lake. Thus a huge expedition was sent there in November 1795, and eventually it made the British islands secure and captured others. But it never subdued Guadeloupe or Saint-Domingue, and in 1795, meanwhile, Pitt had to content himself with vaunting consolation prizes, like taking the Cape of Good Hope after the Dutch changed sides, as triumphs.

It was not even as if all was well at home. The massive surge of loyalism that had helped to carry the country into war lost momentum as the prospects of a swift victory dimmed. By the end of 1793 the corresponding societies, stunned into silence momentarily when their French inspiration became the enemy, had recovered their verve and were campaigning against the war in favour once more of radical parliamentary reform. In Scotland two national conventions of reform societies had been held despite the onset of war, while in Ireland an unprecedented convention of representatives of the majority Catholic population called for full civil and political equality with Protestants. Aware that the Irish Catholics, who knew what had happened to their Church in France, were worth conciliating, Pitt forced a reluctant Irish Parliament to concede them all except seats in the legislature early in 1793. But after that there were no more concessions to reformers. One did not, declared Pitt, try to mend the roof in a hurricane. An overwhelming majority in Parliament agreed with him. Ever since Burke had come out against the Revolution in 1790 the opposition Whigs had been falling apart, and in the summer of 1794, urged on by Burke, a number of leading Whigs joined the administration. Fox and the opponents of the war were left in a helpless minority, protesting in vain as publishers of Painite propaganda were prosecuted for sedition. Scottish judges were soon sending organizers of conventions to Botany Bay, and the Irish Parliament banned them entirely. The very name 'convention' now smacked of treason, and in 1794 treason was the charge brought in England against Hardy and other leading British

* See below, pp. 312–14

'Jacobins'. The move followed the revelation that that spring the French had sent an agent through England to Ireland in order to report on the prospects for a pro-French uprising. Before his arrest in Dublin he had made contact with leaders of the United Irishmen, a non-sectarian group of parliamentary reformers founded in Belfast in 1791 and dedicated to weakening British control over Ireland. The English, on the other hand (he had reported), were not ripe for pro-French rebellion; but Pitt feared otherwise. When, in a triumph for the jury system, all those accused of treason were acquitted (December 1794), he turned to outright alteration of the laws. Habeas Corpus had already been suspended in May 1794, and in November the next year, in the notorious 'Two Acts', the scope of treasonable practices was widened, while magistrates were empowered to prevent the monster meetings which the reform societies had come to favour over the summer. An attack on George III's coach as he drove to open Parliament in October triggered these new measures, whose application those affected soon labelled Pitt's reign of terror. In Ireland, meanwhile, the United Irishmen had been dissolved and their founder Wolfe Tone, suspected of encouraging French intervention, went into exile rather than face prosecution. He made his way to France, where from the spring of 1796 he began a lonely but persistent campaign to persuade the Directory that a French invasion of Ireland would bring an uprising so serious that Great Britain would be knocked out of the war.

The Directory's prime target for 1796, however, was Austria, now facing France without the support of any major continental ally. The plan was to strike through Germany in massive numbers at the Austrian heartland, distracting her meanwhile in the rear by a smaller force sent against her territories in northern Italy. At the last minute Bonaparte, the victor of Toulon and since then remarkably sure-footed in domestic politics, was appointed to command the army of Italy. Compelled to improvise for lack of adequate supplies and equipment, he moved with quite unexpected speed, forced the Austrians to retreat, and during their confusion knocked Sardinia out of the war in a series of lightning battles. This was just a month after he had taken command. In the subsequent peace a few weeks later (15 May) Victor Amadeus III accepted the loss of Savoy and Nice. But by then Bonaparte had descended from the Alps into the Lombard plains and had reached Milan. In all this time the armies in Germany had scarcely advanced at all. The Italian theatre had become the main one, and there was talk of dividing the command. Bonaparte made it clear that he would not tolerate such an affront, and his victorious troops were already so loyal to him personally that the Directory shrank from testing their authority. Yet it failed to reinforce him, too; while the

Austrians, holding their own on the Rhine with surprising ease, were able to renew their Italian armies from their reserves. Thus although the French, by a threatening southward march, were able to scare Naples and Parma into abandoning the coalition, they were too weak to take Mantua. Between August and January 1797 the Austrians sent no less than four armies down the Alpine passes to relieve it, each repulsed by Bonaparte in brilliant but increasingly desperate manoeuvres. But after the last of these relief columns had been turned back at Rivoli (14 January 1797), Mantua at last surrendered. Soon afterwards the long-promised reinforcements arrived and, unthreatened from the rear, Bonaparte turned north and began to advance towards Vienna.

His position was not as strong as it looked. His lines of communication were dangerously extended; and there was unrest behind him in Venetian territory where, despite the republic's neutrality, much of the campaign had been fought and the French forces, as everywhere, were now living off the land. Nevertheless, he was now within a hundred miles of Vienna and there was panic in the imperial capital. Unknown to him, the French forces in Germany had at last crossed the Rhine. So that when he offered peace talks, the Austrians were ready to accept almost any terms he might suggest. To their surprise, the preliminaries of Leoben, which they accepted on 18 April, were not as demanding or as damaging as they might have expected. That they were asked to accept the loss of Belgium came as no surprise. They had already written it off three years beforehand in practice. They also willingly recognized whatever French frontiers the laws of the Republic laid down, since whether that meant the left bank of the Rhine remained unclear. And although Bonaparte was not willing to give back Milan, he was prepared to acknowledge that Austria was entitled to some compensation for her losses, and he now proposed that she should take it at the expense of Venice. The revolts in Venetian territory proved the ideal excuse, and so now the ancient republic was carved up like Poland. The city itself, and all its territory east of the Adige, went to Austria, giving her an extensive Adriatic coastline. The French held on to the rest, which Bonaparte incorporated a few months later into a puppet Lombard state, the Cisalpine Republic.

None of these terms was authorized from Paris. They came to the Directory, and to the generals now at last making progress along the Rhine, as a *fait accompli*. And in fact they totally contravened the instructions Bonaparte had been given at the start of the Italian campaign, and the clear war aims that the Directors had been pursuing. He had been told to take Austrian territory and hold it as a bargaining counter for ultimate peacemaking. Opinion in the Directory was divided about what it should be bargained for: most favoured an Austrian recognition of a French frontier along the Rhine, although others, including Carnot, thought that a formula for endless future conflict. But nobody had foreseen, much less authorized, the carve-up of neutral states, or indeed the creation from French conquests of new 'sister republics'. Such arrangements left nothing to bargain with, whereas on the matter of the Rhine frontier the Leoben terms were extremely ambiguous. The generals on the Rhine, no less than the Directory, were understandably furious; but the conclusion of peace preliminaries on his own authority was only the culmination of months of independent action by Bonaparte. In December 1796 he had prompted French sympathizers in cities freed by French arms from Modenese and papal rule to form themselves into a Cispadane* Republic, itself absorbed in June 1797 into the equally factitious Cisalpine one. By January the civil commissioners normally attached to commanders in the field to ensure their compliance with government policy had been recalled, leaving him a completely free hand. After the fall of Mantua he had, as the Directors had long hoped, invaded the Papal States and extracted territorial concessions from the Pope. But so far from treating Pius VI as the irreconcilable enemy of the Republic and seeking to dethrone him, in the treaty of Tolentino (19 February) he merely underwrote the secession of the Cispadane cities, assuring the pontiff otherwise that he would find the French Republic, of all places, 'among the truest friends of Rome'. Successful generals had dreamed of pursuing their own aims and ambitions ever since Dumouriez: but now one of them had won the entire war, and he felt perfectly entitled to dictate the terms of peace as well.

Only Great Britain was now left fighting, and long before Leoben she too had been exploring the possibilities of peace. There were no victories in 1796, merely mounting difficulties met by rising war taxation and ever-extending impressment and conscription. In October, after months of provocation from both sides, Spain joined France and declared war on the tyrant of the seas; Catherine of Russia, a stalwart anti-Jacobin even if an inactive one beyond eastern Europe, died in November; and the defeat of Austria was now acknowledged even by Pitt and George III to be merely a matter of time. An official peace mission was sent to Paris. The Directory strung it along, but by now France was putting together a plan even bolder than the thrust into Italy. Jealous of Bonaparte's meteoric success, another young military prodigy, Lazare Hoche, who had pacified the Vendée and destroyed the Quiberon invasion force, was desperate for some further triumph to sustain his own prestige. He was thus ready to be persuaded by

* i.e. south of the Po. See below, pp. 359–60.

Wolfe Tone's repeated assurances that Ireland would rise against British rule if the French invaded in reasonable force. The Directory, too, particularly Carnot, relished the idea of stirring up domestic subversion in the British Isles in the way the British had done in the rebellious French west. Accordingly, in December 1796, peace overtures were suddenly rebuffed and a major expedition of 46 ships and almost 15,000 men set sail for Ireland. By the time they sighted their destination, however, Hoche's ship had been blown far out into the Atlantic, and they limped back to France without making a landing. Nor was it likely that, despite feverish preparations by the now underground organization of the United Irishmen, the sort of mass rising the French had been led to hope for on landing would have occurred. They arrived too soon, and at the wrong end of the country. Nevertheless the landlords of the Anglo-Irish Ascendancy were terrified, as was the government in London. February 1797 saw a serious run on the Bank of England, reflecting market anxieties about years of lending huge sums to unsuccessful allies like the Austrians, but triggered by an emergency loan to Dublin for the strengthening of Irish defences. With the combined naval strength of Spain and the Dutch to support them, it seemed certain that the French would soon be back. The panic subsided—although payments from the Bank in gold remained suspended—with the news at the end of the month that the Spanish fleet had been crippled at St Vincent. But only a few weeks later the country was faced with the ultimate catastrophe: mutiny in the Royal Navy. Between March and June the fleets at Spithead and the Nore were immobilized by sailors demanding better pay, conditions, and rations. The Nore mutineers even blockaded the mouth of the Thames. They swore that should the French put to sea they would happily put aside their dispute to fight them, and indeed no serious evidence of subversion in the fleet has ever been found. As soon as the government conceded the sailors' main demands the trouble subsided, and less than two dozen ringleaders were hanged. But many suspected the influence of French agents or—worse—United Irishmen; and faith in the willingness and ability of the navy to protect the country was only fully restored in October, when the Dutch fleet was destroyed at Camperdown, largely by vessels and crews involved in the mutinies.

But long before that happened the setbacks and narrow escapes of the spring had led Pitt to renew peace proposals to the French. Britannia might more or less rule the waves, but the Republic, however Godless and Jacobinical, undoubtedly dominated the land. The war was plainly stalemated. Subversion might be under control in England, but Ireland, where the appearance of the French boosted United Irish hopes and recruitment, was a different matter; and everywhere there was obvious war-weariness. Accordingly, in June 1797 plenipotentiaries from the two sides began peace talks in Lille. Pitt was agreeably surprised by the polite welcome his approaches received; but the spring elections in France had returned many royalists, who hoped an equitable settlement with the Bourbons' most determined supporters might smooth the way to a restoration. They pressed for similar give-and-take in the negotiations for a final settlement with the Austrians. Carnot, never a believer in immoderate gains, was prepared to go along with them. Bonaparte, however, was not; and he willingly co-operated in a plot to purge the ruling councils (and the Directory) of royalists and moderates. On 4 September troops commanded by Bonaparte's envoy Augereau stood by while Carnot and the leaders of the new batch of deputies were expelled from public life in the coup of Fructidor.* The French stance in negotiations with both Austria and Great Britain immediately hardened. The Austrians recognized that there was little point now in prolonging discussions about the finer points of their capitulation. By the peace of Campo Formio, therefore (18 October), the war begun in 1792 was at last brought to an end. The terms were roughly those of Leoben, and as then Bonaparte largely dictated them. Venice disappeared, partitioned between the Austrians and the Cisalpine Republic. France took her Ionian islands: the general was already dreaming of imperial schemes in the eastern Mediterranean. Austria now also explicitly recognized France's Rhine frontier, but pointed out that this action could not commit the Holy Roman Empire, at whose expense most of the Rhineland conquests had been made. To secure agreement there, there would have to be massive compensatory redistributions of territory, and the complexities were left to a later congress fixed to meet in Rastadt. The 'sister republics' of Italy (the Cisalpine had now been joined by the Ligurian, formerly Genoa) were also recognized, and the loss of Belgium once more acknowledged.

Belgium had brought Great Britain into the war: but so hopeless did the continental situation now appear that she, too, was prepared to acknowledge it as part of France. In fact Pitt was ready to recognize all France's conquests in Europe, and to secure peace he was even willing to surrender gains made from France overseas. But the French demanded that he also restore overseas territories won from their Dutch and Spanish allies, including that key to India, the Cape. No compensations whatsoever were offered. The Directors, masters of the Continent, wanted nothing less than total surrender; but Pitt, desperate as he was for peace, was not yet that desperate. Negotiations were broken off, and a few weeks later

* See below, pp. 330–1.

Camperdown emphasized continuing British strength. The ink was not yet dry on the treaty of Campo Formio, in fact, before Thugut was investigating the possibilities of a second coalition based on Austro-British co-operation. But for the moment, the Continent was at peace for the first time in five years, and Great Britain was left to fight on alone.

The main aim of the French politicians who had launched this great struggle in 1792 had been to force their compatriots to come out clearly for or against the Revolution. In this they succeeded far more thoroughly than they could ever have calculated. But the war also forced that choice on the rest of Europe, belligerent or not, especially after the French began to achieve victories. The withdrawal of the Republic's open-ended offer of fraternity and help to all sympathizers only four months after it was made passed unnoticed, or unbelieved, abroad. The French seemed intent on revolutionizing and republicanizing all Europe, if necessary by force of arms. Whatever their government said, Frenchmen abroad who were not *émigrés* openly encouraged their hosts to follow French examples. The ostentatious contempt of French residents in Spain for Church and king throughout 1792, for instance, did much to predispose the government in Madrid towards the war that broke out early the next year; and Jacobins in Naples only came to the surface after a French fleet docked for repairs in the early days of 1793. They advertised their sympathies by founding a club, as did the few Mainzers around Forster who had welcomed the French invaders of the Rhineland several weeks earlier, or the Poles of Warsaw and Vilno who defied the Russians in 1794, or the patriots of the Dutch 'reading societies' who eagerly assembled to greet the oncoming liberators the following winter. By 1797, in fact, the year Burke died, still railing against the perils of a 'regicide peace', clubs had become the key to a new denunciation of the Revolution that was to become every bit as influential as his great tract of 1790. It was embodied in the *Memoirs to Serve for the History of Jacobinism* by the ex-Jesuit Augustin de Barruel. An opponent of the anti-clerical Enlightenment since long before 1789, Barruel argued that the whole Revolution had been a conspiracy of anti-Christian, anti-royal, and anti-social freemasons bent on reducing civilization to chaos. The Bavarian Illuminati plot had merely been a rehearsal for the greater conspiracy that followed. Had not the masonic slogan always been *Liberty, Equality?* The clubs now plaguing Europe were obviously masonic lodges at last openly proclaiming their true purpose. In this way Burke's hints about philosophic machinations were expanded to cover not just the origins of the Revolution, but its whole, ever more radical course down to the very moment of Barruel's publication. Those who had hitherto felt baffled to understand the bewildering rush of events since 1789 found deep satisfaction in seeing it thus so comprehensively explained. The popularity of Barruel's ideas proved ominous for all freemasons. They had already been under suspicion everywhere since the upheavals had begun, and the fact that masons were to be found among the leading revolutionaries in France, and among the clubists who welcomed French successes abroad, now seemed more than the coincidence it was. Barruel's allegations never won widespread acceptance in England, where freemasonry had begun; but elsewhere they led to determined repression of masonic activity, and panicky abandonment of the lodges by the respectable, educated members of society who had flocked to join them in the quieter days of the *ancien régime*.

If masonry was the cause of the French Revolution, that was bad enough. If it was also responsible for its course, even worse. For not only had the revolutionaries visited war and destruction on their neighbours; they had also fought and persecuted each other with vindictive savagery, and allowed the Parisian mob to dictate to the rest of the country, and set about the systematic elimination of everybody who stood in their way through the cold machinery of the guillotine. The prospect of all this drove kings and queens, particularly, to distraction: 'I should like this infamous nation to be cut to pieces,' raved Maria Carolina of Naples, the sister of Marie-Antoinette, 'annihilated, dishonoured, reduced to nothing for at least fifty years. I hope that divine chastisement will fall visibly on France.'[10] Some argued that it already had. But the scenes which so shocked the rest of Europe in 1793 and 1794 were not the result of a masonic conspiracy, or indeed any other sort. Very largely they were the consequence of the war so thoughtlessly launched in 1792, at a time when the triumphs of 1797 could never have been foreseen.

# 10

# The Revolt of the Provinces

ALTHOUGH many provincial *fédérés* had taken part in the storming of the Tuileries, the fall of the French monarchy had very largely been the work of the insurrectionary commune of Paris. The very idea of a national Convention to give France a republican constitution also originated in the Paris sections. It was therefore understandable that the sansculottes should regard themselves as the guardians and watchdogs of the new republic, and the arbiters of what it should stand for. And of course they were very well placed to enforce their will. The Convention sat in Paris, it had no forces to defend itself from popular pressure. All available troops in 1792 and 1793 were occupied at the front, and the Paris National Guard was no longer the force that had shot down republican petitioners on the Champ de Mars. Since the end of July it had been open to all citizens and was little more than a sansculotte militia, commanded from 10 August by Santerre, a rich brewer but long a popular activist in the city's east end. The Legislative Assembly had been forced to recognize its own helplessness in the face of Parisian power during its last weeks. Its only attempt to assert itself, the decree dissolving the commune and ordering new elections on 30 August, was ostentatiously ignored and rapidly rescinded. And the deputies had had to sit powerless while the same sansculottes who claimed to be the nation's conscience massacred half the capital's prison population during the following week. The nation's representatives were clearly in the clutches of a capricious and bloodthirsty mob, and in this respect the Convention was no more secure than its predecessor. 'Never forget', the ex-monk Chabot warned his fellow deputies, 'that you were sent here by the sansculottes.'[1] None of them was likely to; but they were deeply divided over whether that committed them to continue to do Paris's bidding. The role of the capital in national affairs was to be the most hotly debated issue during the first nine months of the Convention's existence.

Leading the attack on Paris were those who had sought to avert the insurrection of 10 August, and whom Robespierre had tried to have arrested by the commune just as the prison massacres were beginning—men like Brissot, Vergniaud, and the 'faction of the Gironde'. They had been deputies in the previous assembly, but they were supported by a number of newcomers, too. They were not a party, and never would be, except in the wishful imagination of their opponents; but they all sat for provincial constituencies, and the more prominent among them had grown used to informal co-operation with each other throughout the Legislative. They tended to meet, as they had then, at the house of Roland, still minister of the interior. There his pretty and ambitious wife, though a Parisienne herself, railed constantly against Marat, Danton, Robespierre, and the whole Parisian delegation in the Convention. These men, the Girondins were convinced, had been deeply implicated in the September Massacres, and intended to use their Parisian support to seize national power. Within days of the Convention's first meeting the challenge was thrown down. The ex-constituent Buzot, soon to become Mme Roland's lover, proposed the establishment of a 'departmental guard' recruited outside Paris, to protect the Convention. 'Do you suppose', he asked,[2] 'we are to be enslaved by certain deputies of Paris?' The Montagnard response was to denounce the idea as 'Federalism'—an attempt to dissipate the unity of the nation. They proposed, and carried, a declaration that the Republic was one and indivisible. Most deputies were happy to vote for both proposals, reluctant as they were to become involved in the faction fights of extremists whose antagonisms seemed as much personal as principled. But the uncommitted deputies of the 'Plain', as they soon became known from their tendency to sit in the middle of the house, between Montagnards on the left of the chair and Girondins on the right, were quickly to find that the antagonism between the two factions coloured every issue. For much of October the object of Girondin attack was Marat, and the shame Paris had brought upon itself by electing one who had constantly advocated massacres. He had also regularly called for a dictator, and to the Girondins it seemed obvious whom he had in mind: Robespierre. On 29 October Louvet openly accused this 'insolent demagogue' of aspiring to dictatorship. On 4 December the attack was turned on Philippe-Égalité, when Buzot moved that anybody advocating a restoration of monarchy should suffer the death penalty. The inference was that the Montagnards planned to make this former prince of notorious ambition king once Louis XVI was dead. Everything to do with the king's fate, in fact, drove the factions even wider apart. The Montagnards suspected their opponents of seeking reconciliation with him before 10

August. They were right, but they had no proof. When Roland announced the discovery of the *armoire de fer*, they accused him of removing documents from it that implicated his friends, just as those it did contain revealed the earlier treachery of Mirabeau. On 3 January, amid the voting on the king's trial, they again insisted on debating rumours of secret correspondence between the Bordeaux deputies and the Tuileries the previous July. The aim now was to discredit the Girondin-sponsored idea of an appeal to the people over the death sentence. This in its turn was designed to thwart the obvious determination of Paris and its sections that the king should be executed without delay. Montagnards argued that the appeal would be a call to civil war; Girondins responded that not to allow the departments to pronounce on the king's fate would in itself provoke such a war. The Girondin idea of clemency was debated in similar terms. And the way a deputy had voted in these two contentious divisions was to mark him politically for ever, both in the subsequent public affairs of revolutionary France and in the analyses of its historians.

All these clashes had taken place at a time of victory in the war, but even foreign policy was not unmarked by them. Dumouriez had always been associated with those now called Girondins, and they revelled in his successes. It was they who proposed offering fraternity and assistance to foreign sympathizers, but Robespierre who warned of the futility of trying to establish liberty in foreign countries by force. Yet when Brissot quite uncharacteristically became the advocate of caution, and argued for reprieving the king so as not to antagonize more foreign powers, the Montagnards scorned his cowardice and were in the van of the movement to declare war on Great Britain, Holland, and Spain. Then, having dispatched the king and challenged most of Europe to a fight to the death, the factions returned to their vendetta. The Montagnards now had a martyr to their cause: on 20 January the former nobleman and judge in the Paris parlement Le Peletier de Saint-Fargeau was assassinated by a fellow noble who blamed him for voting for the king's execution. His remains were placed in the Pantheon as men began to talk of removing those of Mirabeau. The Jacobin Club also now became a Montagnard monopoly: Brissot had been expelled from this scene of his former triumphs as early as October; and on 1 March all deputies who had voted for the appeal to the people on the king's execution were likewise excluded. The Montagnards failed to capture the ministry of the interior when Roland, wearied by their repeated attacks, resigned on 22 January; but they did defeat a renewed proposal for a departmental guard, and they tore to pieces a projected constitution brought forward by Condorcet on 15 February on the grounds that it was a charter for Federalism and executive paralysis.

In all this they felt confident of popular support in Paris; but in fact, now the great drama of the king's trial and execution was over, the people of the capital were turning their attention to more everyday matters. On 12 February the Convention received a deputation from the sections of Paris calling for comprehensive price controls on basic commodities. The petitioners called their proposal a 'maximum'. With rare unanimity the deputies rejected the idea. They believed that attempts to interfere with the free exchange of goods did more to distort markets than supply them, and they had in fact renounced all economic controls as recently as December 1792. Even Marat, who believed the only solution to scarcity was to guillotine hoarders and speculators, denounced the petitioners as dangerously misguided. They were reacting, however, to a serious deterioration in the economic situation in the capital.

Throughout the upheavals of 1792, the value of the assignats had continued to decline. By January 1793 they were down to 51 per cent of their face value, despite the decision to make them legal tender in occupied territories. Coinage, on the other hand, was becoming increasingly rare. Requisitioning and bulk-purchasing for the armies over the autumn had disrupted the supply of many basic commodities, and war against the maritime powers had brought a blockade on seaborne imports. And particularly hard-hit were the products of the West Indies, where deepening chaos was devastating the economy of the French islands and leaving all reliable production in the hands of the British. Such disruptions were reflected in commodity prices. By February sugar had doubled or trebled since 1790, and soap had more than doubled. Other items, like coffee and candles, were also rising steadily. These increases provided the impetus behind calls for a maximum, which were renewed in petitions to the Convention and the Jacobin Club between 22 and 24 February. When they remained unanswered, the city was swept by a wave of attacks on grocery shops and warehouses throughout the twenty-fifth. Mostly the crowds, led as usual by women, behaved traditionally, fixing prices at levels they considered just, selling the stocks they found at those, and handing the proceeds to the hapless shopkeepers. But there was more outright pillage and pilfering than the previous year, and crude and brutal threats were more overt. The summer's bloodshed had clearly lowered the threshold of acceptable violence. On the twenty-sixth Santerre's National Guards restored order, but the whole Convention was visibly shaken by the outburst. The Girondins, predictably, blamed the incitements of Marat. The Montagnards suspected a plot organized by Roux, who since the autumn had been calling for hoarders and speculators to be treated the same way as 'Louis the Last'. They began to call Roux and his associates, such as Jean

Varlet, who ranted daily to passers-by from a soap-box just outside the Convention hall, the rabids (*enragés*). There had probably been no plot on 25 February, but the outbreak certainly seems to have engendered the idea of one. It developed rapidly in the crucible of the new crisis which broke in March.

Determined to build on the autumn's victories and replace the one-year volunteers who were now leaving the army, the Convention decided that the newly expanded war would require more than volunteers. On 24 February it decreed a new levy of 300,000 men to be raised by volunteering, if possible, but conscription if necessary, with each department allotted a quota. Local authorities would be free, if they saw fit, to find their recruits among eligible young males by the well-tried technique used for raising the pre-revolutionary militia: drawing lots. Such a return to hated practice only abolished four years previously was bound to be unpopular, and in fact only half the 300,000 men were ever raised. But in some parts it was more than unpopular; and in the department of the Vendée the first attempts to conscript in the early days of March met with violent resistance which within weeks had flared up into an open rebellion against the entire course the Revolution had taken. The Vendéan peasants resented their able-bodied young men being taken off to fight distant enemies, with whom they had no quarrel, by authorities with whom their quarrel was limitless. They resented the fact that the conscription decree was implemented by bourgeois from the local towns who were themselves exempt because of the public offices they held. The National Guard, who were merely these bourgeois and their friends in uniform, were deemed mobilized 'on the spot', which meant that they did not have to go to the front either, yet were the main force needed to compel others to go. The disturbances began with clashes between peasant youths and National Guards. And who were these uniformed self-styled patriots forcing others to fight their battles? The same people who had ejected non-juring priests in 1791 and forced in intrusive newcomers; the same people who had bought up the best church lands when they had come on the market; townsmen who had done consistently well out of the Revolution at the expense, so it seemed, of surrounding peasant communities and the Church upon which loyalties had focused in the calmer, remoter days when the king had reigned undisputed. These resentments had been simmering and spluttering throughout western France for over a year in innumerable clashes between peasants and local authorities over recruiting drives and measures against non-juring priests. The zeal of both sides intensified after 10 August, and the declaration of a republic made the king a new rallying-point for those opposed to the patriots. Down with the

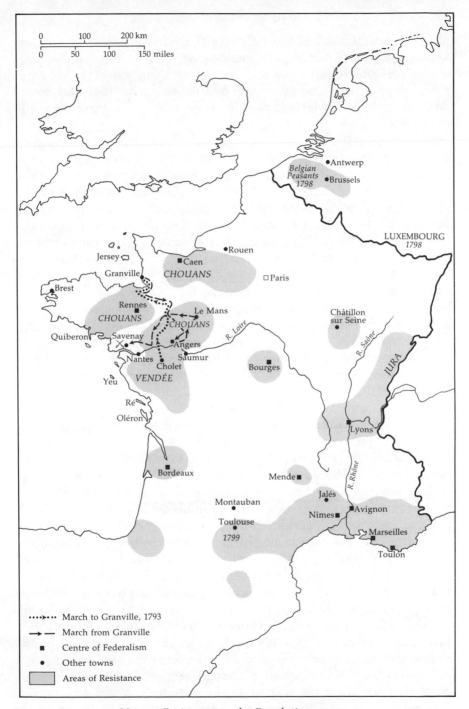

MAP 4. Resistance to the Revolution, 1793–9

national cockade, shouted malcontents who gathered in thousands in the Vendée late in August 1792; long live the king, up with the nobles. Nobles, in fact, played little part in these outbreaks, and only joined the western rebels in 1793 after the insurgents had made it clear that they were anxious to have noble leaders: but in patriotic eyes they were all aristocrats.

Much of rural Brittany also rose in March 1793, and not only against conscription. Pay no more taxes, urged one Breton agitator, 'since there's no more king there are no more laws ... be fucked to the nation'.[3] But Brittany was better garrisoned and the garrisons better armed than south of the Loire. Within a month the Breton risings had been suppressed and districts were meeting their quotas under the February decree. Resistance continued, with great determination, but in the form of guerrilla warfare, *chouannerie*, which was to plague the departments along the Channel coast for the rest of the decade and beyond. In the Vendée, however, peasant hordes stormed the little towns where patriot power was based, and the local authorities collapsed. Military reinforcements were unable to penetrate the labyrinthine *bocage* countryside. By 13 March recognizable leaders had begun to emerge, including the ex-soldier Stofflet, whose 10,000 men could overwhelm regular troops sent against them by sheer weight of numbers. Soon, too, the rebels were wearing sacred hearts, crosses, and the white cockade of royalism. 'Long live the king and our good priests', was their cry. 'We want our king, our priests and the old regime.' 'And they wanted', noted a terrified republican who observed this, 'to kill off all the Patriots.'[4]

Reports of this unprecedented resistance to revolutionary authority began to reach Paris during the second week in March. They coincided with increasingly bad news from Belgium, where the Austrians had counter-attacked on the first and turned the flank of Dumouriez's advance into Holland. Yet Dumouriez had refused to draw back until explicitly ordered to do so, and some deputies began to sniff treachery. The Girondins had been keen to adopt Dumouriez when he was driving the enemy before him, and the taint he now began to acquire rubbed off on them. By 8 March it was being alleged in the Convention that the armies were in headlong retreat, and panic swept the capital. Danton, who knew the situation in Belgium at first hand, called for volunteers from Paris to march north and save the campaign, which did nothing to restore calm. Everybody remembered how the previous September the departure of volunteers had occasioned the prison massacres. Certain elements in Paris evidently believed that this was the moment to eliminate the city's enemies in the Convention. Some sections began to demand the establishment of a revolutionary tribunal to try traitors, and the Jacobin Club took up the call. The Convention accepted the proposal on the ninth and decreed in the same session that deputies should be sent out to all departments, as 'representatives on mission', to explain and expedite war emergency measures. That night, armed bands toured the print shops where the leading Girondin journals were produced, smashing the presses and destroying copy. They were in disguise, but seem to have been organized by a radical club calling itself the Defenders of the One and Indivisible Republic, whose leading light was himself a journalist, Jacques-René Hébert, producer of the increasingly popular *Père Duchesne*. The next day these same elements tried to organize a full-scale insurrection which would force the Convention to arrest all suspect generals, ministers, and the leading Girondin deputies. *Enragés* like Varlet joined in. The tocsin was rung and the city gates closed. But the commune refused to become involved, and Santerre put together 9,000 National Guards to maintain order. The insurgents melted away. Yet a precedent had been set, and all sides recognized it. Popular action might be used to purge the Convention of unpopular elements. The Montagnards as yet shrank from such an assault on the nation's elected representatives; although the Girondins were quite prepared to believe, and say, that the hated deputies of Paris had been implicated once again in a plot to massacre them. Understandably, but fatally, their worries about the threat from Paris were developing into an all-consuming obsession.

For weeks afterwards they raked over the murky details of the abortive *journée*, while the bad news both from the Vendée and Belgium got worse. On 12 March Dumouriez openly denounced French policy in Belgium, sowing new suspicions. His defeat at Neerwinden a week later intensified them. Treason was not its cause, but it was its result, and only the refusal of his army to co-operate prevented him from marching on Paris to restore the constitution of 1791 with the infant Louis XVII as king. His perfidy was generally recognized a fortnight before his flight across the Austrian lines on 6 April. Nobody came well out of the crisis. Girondins fell under suspicion from their previous association with the traitor; but leading Montagnards like Danton suffered from their last-minute attempts to strike deals which might prevent his defection. Yet it was the Montagnards who produced all the constructive proposals for dealing with the crisis, and most of the votes in the Convention went their way even though many of their sympathizers were now heading off to the departments as representatives on mission. The new measures included the establishment of watch committees (*comités de surveillance*) throughout the country to scrutinize the activities of foreigners and suspects (21 March); and an attempt to bring the war effort under more decisive legislative control through a new co-ordinating committee. Ever since the fall of the monarchy executive power had nominally been vested in a council of ministers, but each minister was shadowed by a specialist committee of the Convention. On 1 January a Committee of General Defence was set up to co-ordinate these bodies, but it proved cumbersome and ineffective, and the crisis of March led to a search for something stronger. On the twenty-fifth, accordingly, on the suggestion of a deputy now making a name for himself as a deviser of ingenious compromises, Bertrand Barère, a 25-member Committee of Public Safety was created to take over its role. By the time it began to function on 7 April its membership had been reduced to nine, renewable monthly. Barère was elected, and would prove its longest serving member, but Robespierre declined election because he doubted the Committee's value. The dominant voice for its first two months would be that of Danton, and for much of that time he preached union and reconciliation in the face of the dangers confronting the nation. His urgings, however, fell on deaf ears.

The Montagnards had hoped, in setting up the Revolutionary Tribunal, to use it against those whom they saw as impeding the war effort by their vendetta against Paris. Girondins, however, saw that this sword was double-edged, and it was from them that a proposal came on 1 April to abolish deputies' immunity from arrest. Success in this cleared the way for an attack on the most exposed figure in the Montagnard ranks, recognized even by his own side in their cooler moments as a liability—Marat. As president of the Jacobins, on 5 April he had signed a circular appealing to the provinces to defend Paris against a 'sacrilegious cabal' in the Convention, attempting thus to steal what the Girondins regarded as their own constituency. Alleging an insult to the Convention, they called on 12 April for Marat to be impeached; and, with normal Montagnard support depleted by the absence of many of their normal allies on mission, the motion passed overwhelmingly. Thirty-three sections of Paris responded to this attack on their hero by calling for the expulsion from the Convention of 22 named deputies including Brissot, all the Bordelais, and Pétion, who had drifted away from his earlier radicalism since the fall of the monarchy. Both the Jacobins and the commune endorsed the demand, but withdrew their approval when Robespierre, reluctant to see the nation's representatives coerced, condemned it. In any case they had their revenge on 24 April, when Marat was acquitted by the Revolutionary Tribunal and carried shoulder-high from the court back to the Convention by exultant sansculottes.

Among the charges brought against him had been that he had incited the populace to take the law into its own hands against hoarders and speculators in his paper (renamed *Journal de le République française* since the previous September) on the morning after the February grocery riots. His acquittal now encouraged the sections to renew their pressure on economic questions. Even before his trial they had begun to call again for controls on the price of bread and grain, amid Girondin denunciations of their economic illiteracy. Ominously the Montagnards, who had joined in the defence of free markets in February, were silent. By the end of the month, in fact, they had changed tack completely and were supporting demands for controls, cheered on by the Convention's public galleries. On 30 April Girondins began to declare that the assembly was no longer safe in Paris and called for its sittings to be transferred to Versailles, predicting economic disaster if price controls were forced upon it. But that was what happened on 1 May. The Convention was mobbed by 8,000 demonstrators from the faubourg Saint-Antoine who declared themselves in a state of insurrection until price controls on bread were introduced. Nothing was conceded that day, but fear of a less-controlled recurrence led to the passing, on the next, of a law (formally promulgated on the third) stipulating a maximum price for grain and bread, and giving local authorities wide powers of search and requisition. Overt Montagnard advocacy of such a measure marked a turning-point, a recognition that Parisian support could not be taken for granted, even against the Girondins. As a police spy reported to the interior minister: 'The Jacobins know only too well that the people cannot be resisted when one needs them.'[5]

They may have been alarmed that even in Paris there were signs of resistance to conscription, since it was this that had plunged the provinces into turmoil; and not only in the west. There were reports of riots against the 300,000 levy from places as far apart as Franche Comté, western Languedoc, and Normandy. More alarming still, in the course of the spring some of the major provincial cities began to break away from central authority.

First to waver was Marseilles, all the more shockingly in that the great Mediterranean port had been a watchword for radicalism ever since 1789. The sansculottes remembered with admiration the arrival of the militant Marseillais *fédérés* in July 1792. But Marseilles's radicalism was in many ways the response of a vigorous minority of activists to a conservative hinterland and a mercantile community clearly reluctant to commit either its energies or its wealth to the patriotic struggle. This detachment had allowed the militants of the local Jacobin club to seize political control of the city and even, in defiance of the Legislative Assembly, to transfer the seat of departmental administration from Aix in August 1792. From this position they sniped constantly at 'the rich', and continued to do so even when the upheavals in the West Indies and deteriorating relations with the maritime powers began to threaten the whole basis of the city's commerce. Uneasy in the absence of so many of their most stalwart sympathizers as volunteers in the armies, and obsessed by rumours of royalist plots, which experience had shown were often more than figments in the Midi, the Marseilles Jacobins took the news of the establishment of a Revolutionary Tribunal in Paris as a licence to establish one of their own. They also decreed a general disarmament and a forced loan on the rich to fund measures of revolutionary vigilance, and they carried this policy to the surrounding countryside in expeditions sent out to support the often embattled clubs of little towns inland. 'After the former nobility', declared representatives of the Marseilles Jacobins, 'the bourgeoisie is the class which weighs heaviest on the people'[6] but in fact it soon became clear that the people were prepared to rally behind their supposed oppressors in resisting the Jacobin militants. Resistance coalesced in the city's 32 sections. Once themselves a bastion of Jacobinism, their meetings had been gradually packed over the winter with port workers whose livelihoods were as threatened by economic disruption as those of the great merchants. The two groups now made common cause against the Jacobinism which they saw as the true source of the city's misfortunes both locally and nationally. The arrival of the Montagnard representatives on mission from the Convention in March, endorsing all that the local Jacobins had done, finally provoked the sections into outright resistance. Forming a central committee (on the Parisian pattern of the previous summer), they resisted further militancy so successfully with the cry that 'it is time for the anarchy of a few men of blood to stop'[7] that on 27 April the deputies on mission fled the city and left their allies in the club to their fate. From the safety of Montélimar they proclaimed that Marseilles was in a state of counter-revolution. In fact it was in a state of faction-torn chaos, and it took three more weeks before members of the club were arrested by the central committee: but from Paris Marseilles seemed to be in revolt, espousing 'Federalism' against the one and indivisible Republic.

Certainly news of the downfall of the Marseilles Jacobins promoted unrest against their satellites elsewhere in the Midi. Resistance to the militants who had dominated local affairs since the previous summer began to revive in Aix, Arles, and Avignon. In Nîmes a long-standing rivalry between two clubs led the less extreme one to appeal for support to the city's sections against a rival increasingly committed to the radicalism of the Paris mother society, and on 20 May the 12 sections of Nîmes declared themselves to be in permanent session. All over the south, in fact, the extremism with which Jacobin club members responded to the renewed national crisis of the spring provoked a backlash of protest even among many who had accepted the declaration of the republic and the execution of the king. And nowhere was this process more spectacular, and more menacing for the future of the young republic, than in the nation's second city, Lyons.

The silk industry which was the basis of Lyons's economy had been in crisis when the Revolution broke out, but events after 1789 only worsened its problems. Silk was a luxury product, but those who had normally bought silk goods before the Revolution quickly learned that ostentation could be dangerous in the new times, and demand slumped. War brought a shrinkage in foreign markets, too, and disruptions in the supply of raw materials from Savoy. Nor did the austere republicans who took control in Paris in 1792 have much sympathy for distress in the luxury trades. Montagnard attacks on Roland, who had lived in Lyons and been a vocal defender of its interests between 1784 and 1791, also did little to endear the militants of Paris to most Lyonnais. And yet, as in Marseilles, the reluctance of the city's notables to involve themselves in the turbulent new world of electoral politics meant that in November 1792 Jacobin activists, led by the unbalanced former manufacturer Joseph Chalier, were able to take over local government, especially after previous elected officials had been discredited by a week of food riots and popular price-fixing during September. But in fact Chalier and his friends had nothing to offer beyond parroting the resolutions and policies of the Paris Jacobin Club, and their attempts to ensure plentiful supplies of cheap bread were vitiated by lack of money, disruption of supply networks far from the city, and competing claims for provisioning the armies manning the south-eastern frontiers. The maximum decreed in Paris on 3 May simply could not be implemented under Lyonnais conditions, bread in Lyons cost almost a third more than in Paris, and the whole month was marked by acute anxieties over essential supplies. They culminated on the twenty-fourth in the ransacking of a warehouse full of provisions destined for the armies; crowds of women sold them off at what they deemed fair prices. The response of the Convention's representatives on mission was to order troops from the Alpine front to march on Lyons, but news of this brought on a confrontation between the city's sections and the municipality. The sections knew that the troops would place in the hands of the local Jacobins a coercive power they had hitherto lacked. They feared a massacre if that happened, and in the circumstances they demanded that the National Guard, which the sections controlled, be mobilized. On the twenty-eighth the departmental authorities overrode municipal objections and called them to arms, and the next day this force stormed the town hall and overthrew the Jacobin commune. Lyons, too, was now in open revolt against the Convention.

And meanwhile the rural uprising in the west was growing ever more serious. The Convention's decree of 19 March, that all rebels captured with arms in their hands should be put to death, did nothing to deter the rebels, who captured town after town in the uplands of the Vendée and with every success expanded their numbers. As many as 45,000 men seem to have joined the Catholic and royal armies (as they were now openly calling themselves) in the course of the spring. Against them the Republic was scarcely able at this stage to field more that 15,000 or 16,000, and even the minority of seasoned troops among them had no experience of the type of war they were now compelled to fight. The Vendéan armies materialized suddenly and supplied themselves from their own country. They melted away just as rapidly when checked, whereas the only safety for the 'blues' (as the republican troops soon became known) lay in keeping together in large units. They were quite unable to garrison potential strong points adequately before the rebels stormed them, and down into June rebel-controlled territory continued to expand. On 5 May they took Thouars; on the twenty-fifth, Fontenay, threatening to break out to the sea, where they could get access to British support. On 7 June they took Doué, pushing north towards the Loire; and on the ninth they reached it when they occupied Saumur, driving out Santerre, commander of the Paris National Guard, who had reached the Vendée with a battalion of patriotic volunteers only three weeks beforehand.

By May 1793, therefore, the new crisis for the Republic that had erupted in March had grown spectacularly worse. As the armies fell back along every frontier, a new, internal war zone established itself in what would soon be called the 'military Vendée'; and the Convention even began to lose control of major provincial cities. The response of politicians in Paris was destined to make these problems even worse before they got better.

Immediately after the voting of the maximum there were unexpected signs of support for the Girondins in Paris. On 1 May the commune had decreed that a special extra levy of conscripts to fight in the Vendée would be made by popular societies designating recruits. It terrified better-off elements, who already considered their property threatened by a special war tax on the rich, decreed on 9 March but not yet implemented, not to mention the price controls involved in the maximum. Encouraged by Pétion from the Convention, young Muscadins (as well-pomaded rejectors of the shaggy sansculotte political style were coming to be known) seized control of several sectional assemblies and denounced the 'popular despotism' of the commune. They also paraded in the Champs-Élysées, calling for Marat to be guillotined. Steps taken against them were noisily denounced by the Girondin speakers in the Convention. With ever more Montagnards or deputies who normally voted their way now absent on mission, the Mountain's usual ability to defeat Girondin eloquence with solid votes seemed threatened. These were the circumstances which finally swung them round to the idea of purging the Convention.

It went back at least to the failed *journée* of 10 March; and delegates from 27 sections had begun meetings to co-ordinate action to 'save the country and liberty' at the former archbishop's palace (*évêché*) on 29 March. A list of the most obvious candidates for purging had been endorsed by 33 sections on 15 April. It was not, however, until a month later that positive plans began to be laid, and the Girondins knew all about them within hours. On 16 May they denounced them in the Convention. Two days later, amid calls for a 'shadow Convention' to convene at Bourges to assume power if that in Paris were deprived of its freedom, it was agreed to establish a Commission of Twelve to investigate insurrectionary activity in Paris. The idea came from Barère, no Girondin, but the members elected in a thin house on 20 May included several of them, and not a single Montagnard. Within four days it had the evidence it was looking for, after questioning Pache, the mayor, and scrutinizing sectional registers. Recommending a strengthening of the National Guard around the Convention, and the closure of all sectional meetings by ten in the evening, it ordered the arrest of those it had identified as the main plotters of insurrection. They included Varlet and, following a ferocious issue of *Père Duchesne* in which he urged the sansculottes to annihilate the Girondin 'traitors who conspired against the Republic', Hébert. When the commune sent a deputation to object, Isnard, one of the more intemperate Girondins, who was currently president of the Convention, brushed it aside. 'If,' he declared,[8] 'by these constantly recurring insurrections it were to happen that the Nation's representatives should suffer harm, I tell you, in the name of all France, that Paris would be annihilated.' Brushing aside Marat too, who protested that he was dishonouring the assembly, he went on: 'Soon they would search along the banks of the Seine to see if Paris had ever existed.'

It was an empty threat: but its echoes of Brunswick's crude menaces the previous August outraged Parisians. For some weeks the Girondins had been hinting at departmental vengeance for any attack Paris might make on the Convention, and immediately before Isnard's outburst a deputation from Marseilles had been heard, denouncing the Montagnards. Ominous rumblings from other provincial cities, such as the Girondins' own Bordeaux, not to mention Lyons, were also now coming in. The Girondins had done nothing practical to organize such protests, but along with the struggles still going on in certain of the Parisian sections themselves, they convinced the insurrectionaries that their time was limited. Even Robespierre, who saw well enough the dangers of coercing the Nation's representatives, now recognized that the deadlock in the Convention must be broken by outside force. At the Jacobins on 26 May, he 'invited the people' to rise up against the Convention's 'corrupt deputies' and declared himself in insurrection against them. The first step was to get rid of the Commission of Twelve; and late that same night, after a tumultuous session in which members of rival sections had spilled into the Convention hall and fought each other, the few deputies who had not gone home exhausted voted to dissolve the Commission. Those it had arrested were automatically released. Two days later, it was reinstated, but promptly resigned when it was unable to get a hearing for its president. The deputies were still debating whether or not it existed, and what it should do next if it did, when they were finally overtaken by the long-dreaded insurrection.

It began in the small hours of 31 May when Varlet, in the name of the insurrectionary committee sitting at the archbishop's palace, ordered the ringing of the tocsin. Soon after dawn the insurrectionaries formally deposed the commune and reinstated it under their own orders. The gates were closed, a round-up of suspects ordered, and Hanriot, a former clerk who had been made commander of the National Guard (in the absence of Santerre) the night before, was confirmed in office. But, on this working day, the sansculottes were slow to respond to the call to arms, and it soon became clear that, however much prior collusion there had been between the insurrectionary committee and the commune, there were divisions within both about how to proceed. Varlet wanted to dissolve the whole Convention. Others sought the arrest of the 22 deputies named on 15 April. Still others, including the commune's procurator Chaumette, urged caution; and seemed simply to want to force the abandonment of the Commission of Twelve, and to scare the Girondins into more moderate conduct. But the threatened deputies' reaction to the crowds who gathered all day around the Convention soon showed there was no prospect of that, at least. They demanded an inquiry into the insurrection, and they had no trouble in getting a petition for their own arrest sidestepped by referring it to the Committee of Public Safety. Clearly sensing the disarray of their antagonists, they refused to be intimidated, and kept on uttering threats of departmental vengeance. By the time Robespierre moved the impeachment of those named in the petition, the crowds were melting away, and the crisis seemed to have passed. All the insurrectionaries achieved was the final abandonment of the Commission of Twelve.

Frustration, however, only increased the determination of the insurrectionary committee to oust its enemies from the Convention once and for all. It was aided by the arrival of news on 1 June of the overthrow of the Jacobin commune in Lyons, a new uprising in the Lozère, and further defeats in the Vendée. The departmental revenge so long evoked by the Girondins seemed to be beginning. There was no time to waste, the Montagnards concluded, if civil war was to be avoided: those seeking to foment it must be removed from the national representation. It was therefore agreed to renew the pressure on the Convention on the second, a Sunday, when the sansculottes would not be at work. That morning a deputation from the commune presented a new petition for the arrest of 30 deputies. When it, in turn, was referred to the Committee of Public Safety, the cry went up for a report on the previous petition. This time the petitioners were taking no chances. The previous evening Hanriot had posted his men in key positions all around the Convention. Estimates of the number of National Guardsmen on duty vary between 75,000 and 100,000, and they were reinforced by thousands more onlookers. No deputy stood a chance of leaving the chamber, and when one group tried, they were turned back by Hanriot and Guardsmen with drawn sabres. Barère, in the name of the Committee, refused to recommend the arrest of the named deputies; but by now it was clear that the surrounding forces would not go until the Convention surrendered. They no longer had any choice. Before the day ended, therefore, they had decreed the arrest of 29 deputies—all but two of the 15 April list, and most of the Commission of Twelve. Two ministers were arrested under the same decree; and in the meantime Roland and his wife had also been picked up on the authority of the commune. Most deputies present abstained from the vote, visibly unwilling to violate the national representation under duress. The Montagnards, as always, were more realistic. Knowing they had no choice, they voted for the arrests in the hope of saving the Convention from an even worse fate. They also saw that it would leave their own domination of the Convention undisputed.

The expulsion of the Girondins was neither the destruction of a party nor the overthrow of a government. Onlookers then and since, certainly, have often seen it in these ways as they groped to make sense of complex events and issues through a fog of rhetoric and recrimination. But the very idea of political parties was abhorrent to a generation whom Rousseau had taught to seek the general will which is always for the best and never wrong. Even in Pitt's England, with its long parliamentary tradition, Fox was finding it difficult to convince most fellow MPs that party was in any way respectable or distinguishable from selfish and power-hungry faction. Girondins and Montagnards called each other factions, but as terms of abuse. Both vehemently denied the charge. There were certainly overlapping circles and groups of friends among those called Girondins—around Brissot, around Roland, around the deputies from Bordeaux—but they never concerted their action in any sustained way, and they often voted divergently. Only when 22 of them were named as candidates for purging did they begin to respond to events with something like co-ordination. What made a Girondin was revolutionary intransigence: an attitude of mind that was not prepared to compromise the principles of 1789, whatever happened. This was the spirit that offered defiance to the whole of Europe as the war spread, and resisted the call for price controls which all men of education believed to be economically disastrous. This was the spirit, too, which insisted that all France must be consulted on an issue as momentous as the death of the former king. Above all, this was the spirit that resisted the dictatorship of a capital apparently in the grip of men who had organized or at least connived at the September Massacres. The representatives of the sovereign Nation must not be subjected to the fickle and murderous whims of the sansculottes and the bloodthirsty and irresponsible demagogues, like Marat or Hébert, who pandered to them.

All these were attitudes widely shared in the Convention. In calmer times very few of the deputies would have repudiated any of them. But the times were not calm, and there were certain realities which the Girondins refused to face. Without Paris, the Republic would not have been established and the Convention itself would not have existed. And however abhorrent the forces in control of the capital, it was only sensible for an assembly sitting there (and where else could it credibly sit?) to try to work with them. This was the Montagnard position. To Girondin intransigence they opposed prudence and practicality. And although the kernel of the Montagnards was the 24 deputies representing Paris itself, who acted more like a party than the Girondins ever did, it is striking how often they were able to carry a majority in the Convention on major questions like the fate of the king, the emergency measures of March, the establishment of the maximum, and even the toning-down of the previously open-ended offer of fraternity and help to foreign peoples seeking their liberty. Girondin successes only came when many deputies were absent, and were not hard to reverse later. Their oratory outshone that of the Montagnards, but they were clearly far from dominating or controlling the Convention.

They were not therefore a government. France had no government in a

normally recognized sense between August 1792 and June 1793.
Executive action emerged from the interplay between the council of
ministers and a number of committees of the Convention, and none of
these bodies was clearly dominated by Girondins or Montagnards. Yet
there was also a real extension of governmental power, or at least
pretensions, over the same period; and especially from March 1793. It was
shown by the decree on conscription, the establishment of the Revolutionary Tribunal, the law of the maximum, and the creation of an embryonic
war cabinet in the form of the Committee of Public Safety. Above all it was
shown by the institution of the representatives on mission, who from being
occasional special emissaries to troubled areas in the autumn of 1792, had
by the following spring become a permanent presence in each of 41 pairs of
departments, omnicompetent agents of the central power charged by their
fellow deputies with the implementation of laws to deal with the wartime
emergency. Sometimes as many as 130 deputies at a time might be absent
from the Convention in this capacity. These men were the real governors of
France during these months, in the sense that they were invested with the
full authority of the national Convention to use as they saw fit. And in
the sense, too, that when in Paris they tended to vote the same way as the
Montagnards, a tendency which their provincial experience only reinforced, the Republic had something like a Montagnard government by the
early spring of 1793. Only the absence of these same deputies on mission
enabled the Girondins in the Convention to look as strong as they did. The
removal of their leading spokesmen did not hand control of the Convention
to the Montagnards: it merely made clear and explicit where control had
already lain since the king's trial.

Why then purge them at all? No single motive united all those involved
in the *journées* of 31 May and 2 June. The sansculottes wanted their
enemies silenced at whatever cost. No compromise seemed possible with
men who denounced patriotic Parisians as anarchists, blood-drinkers,
*septembriseurs*, and repeatedly invited the provinces to march on the
capital and destroy it. The Montagnard fear was that Paris would pursue
the quarrel at the expense of the Convention itself. Varlet, Roux, and the
*enragés* had no trust in any representative form of government, and
repeatedly said so. Accordingly, until the very last minute leading
Montagnards such as Danton pleaded with the Girondins to stop attacking
Paris and provoking the power in whose shadow they all sat. Besides, there
was a war to fight, and it was not going well. It was no moment to be
inciting civil war with inflammatory threats of departmental vengeance. If
the Girondins had resigned themselves to the abolition of the Commission
of Twelve, many clearly believed, and most probably hoped, that the

insurrectionary impetus would have died. But Girondin intransigence was complete. Their quarrel with Paris was paralysing the entire course of public affairs, if not endangering the very existence of the Convention. Faced with such dangers, the practical, experienced men who made up its majority agreed, with anguished reluctance, to sacrifice a handful of their colleagues. Whether that would create as many problems as it solved was another matter.

Nowhere was the news of the purge of the Girondins likely to have more effect than in Bordeaux. Reeling from the impact of upheavals in the Caribbean and British blockade, what only a few years beforehand had been the second busiest port in Europe had no cause to welcome the course the Revolution had taken. Yet in 1791 the department of the Gironde had sent eloquent radicals like Vergniaud, Gensonné, and Guadet to the National Assembly, and it had returned them a year later to the Convention. Bordeaux was not without Montagnard sympathizers, congregating in the National Club, which had close links with the Paris Jacobins. But the city's political life was dominated by the rival Friends of Liberty, where the Girondin deputies took their first steps in politics, and whose rules dedicated it to 'the maintenance and strengthening of the Constitution, and of liberty, and discussion of all questions relating to public welfare and general tranquility'.[9] Members of this club dominated most of Bordeaux's 28 sections, and throughout the winter of 1792–3 they took their cues from their deputies in Paris. In March they even succeeded in having the National Club closed, and as early as January they were talking about sending a departmental force to Paris to protect the Convention from violation. On 5 May, after being compelled to swallow the maximum, Vergniaud decided that the time had come for more positive action. 'Men of the Gironde', he wrote,[10] 'rise up! The Convention has only been weak because it has been abandoned. Support it against all the furies threatening it . . . there is not a moment to lose. If you develop great energy, you will impose peace on men who are provoking civil war. Your generous example will be followed, and virtue will triumph at last.' The Bordeaux sections responded with blood-curdling threats against the Convention; but they took no action, unlike Marseilles or Lyons, until news arrived of the purge of 2 June, which involved five of the Gironde's deputies. Even then it took reports and urgings to collective action from elsewhere to push them beyond mere verbal protest. But on 7 June a 'Popular Commission of Public Safety' was set up, declaring the city in insurrection against a faction-dominated Convention until the purged deputies were restored. Bombarding its own citizens with anti-Montagnard propaganda, it also sent out representatives to other cities it deemed ripe for resistance, including those known already to have rejected Parisian dominance. Their message was twofold. They urged that the departments should unite to elect the shadow Convention at Bourges which Girondin deputies had been proposing before they were silenced; and more important, they pressed all areas which rejected the purged Convention's authority to raise volunteers to march on Paris and restore constitutional government. They spoke optimistically of 80,000 men, hinted at support from the army, and on 14 June announced the formation of a departmental force of 1,200 as the Gironde's contribution.

Marseilles and Lyons, already in revolt, were much encouraged by this response to an event that anti-Jacobins in both cities had long been predicting. They were already co-operating between themselves: one of the first steps of the Lyons insurrectionaries had been to send fraternal delegates down the Rhône to co-ordinate with the Marseillais, and they arrived just as the news from Paris broke. In Marseilles a popular tribunal was re-established in defiance of a decree from the Convention on 15 May suppressing a previous version: it was used to persecute Montagnard sympathizers throughout the Bouches du Rhône department. On 12 June Marseilles formally declared itself 'in a legal state of resistance against oppression' and announced the formation of a 'departmental army' which would march on Paris under the slogan *One and Indivisible Republic; respect for persons and properties*. By early July it was advancing on Avignon, which it occupied. Meanwhile at the other end of the Rhône Lyons had followed Bordeaux in establishing a Popular Commission (24 June), which ordered the raising of a departmental force intended to number 10,000. Eventually, it did reach about 4,000. When, in mid-July, the Convention proclaimed Lyons a city in rebellion and advised all loyal citizens to leave, the new authorities responded by executing Chalier, whom it took four falls of a blunt guillotine blade to despatch.

Other southern cities were now drawn in. On 11 June in Montpellier the departmental council of the Hérault ordered the raising of a force to march on Paris. In Toulouse and Grenoble, both near to frontiers where the enemy was on the offensive, the authorities agonized before eventually drawing back from endorsing the Bourges Convention or the idea of departmental armies. But at Toulon, which had at first taken the news of 2 June calmly, mid-July witnessed the beginning of what was to be perhaps the most dangerous and certainly the longest-lasting attempt to repudiate the authority of the Convention. Like Marseilles, Toulon had been ruled by pro-Montagnard Jacobins since the summer of 1792, although it had taken a massacre of local officials in July to open their way to power. Their position owed nothing to the city's sections, which during the autumn ceased to meet. But seeing how the sections of nearby Marseilles over the following spring spearheaded the overthrow of Jacobinism there, anti-Jacobins in Toulon began campaigning for the sections to be reopened. Disillusion with the Convention was now widespread among the workers of the naval dockyard as the war with Great Britain and Spain increased their workload and swamped them with migrant workers, while at the same time their wages began to be paid in depreciating assignats. Like the dockers of Marseilles, they proved ready recruits in the struggle of the local notables against Jacobin levelling. The Jacobins tried to block the campaign for reopening the sections with armed demonstrations intended to remind their opponents of the previous summer's bloodshed. But all they achieved was their own overthrow. On 13 July the sections began to meet again of their own accord, and on the fourteenth a general committee was elected to co-ordinate their activity. Three days later this committee dissolved the town council, after closing the Jacobin club and arresting its leaders. A popular tribunal was set up as at Marseilles, and over the summer it handed down 30 death sentences, mostly against known Jacobin supporters and activists. On 15 July it even arrested and imprisoned two representatives on mission. In contrast with the other southern cities in revolt, Toulon saw a revival of religious activity under municipal auspices. Yet the social orientation of the rebel authorities was much the same as elsewhere. 'We want to enjoy our goods, our property, the fruits of our toil and industry in peace', declared the revived sections in August,[11] 'yet we see them incessantly exposed to threats from those who have nothing themselves.'

Not all the anti-Montagnard revolts occurred south of the Loire. The remote department of the Jura, for instance, on the Swiss frontier, was one of those which set up a departmental army. Neighbouring departments followed suit, although their projected march on distant Paris never began. Far more serious, because far closer to the capital and to the royalist rebels of the Vendée, were outbreaks of defiance in Brittany and Normandy. As late as 25 May the general council of the department of Île-et-Vilaine, meeting in Rennes, declared that it wanted republican unity, 'neither Robespierre nor Guadet, Danton or Gensonné, neither Mountain nor Valley, or any of those lines of demarcation which degrade the dignity of the people's Representatives'.[12] But one of those purged from the Convention a week earlier was their own deputy Lanjuinais, and within a week they had committed themselves to the formation of a departmental army to march on Paris and liberate him and his colleagues. Other Breton departments rallied in support. From Finistère, Quimper called for the suppression of the Revolutionary Tribunal, co-ordinated action, and the convocation of the Bourges shadow Convention. And all sought from the start to link up with protesters in the Norman department of Calvados, where Caen had denounced the Convention on 31 May, on hearing of the first dissolution of the Commission of Twelve. On 9 June Caen declared itself in a state of insurrection and resistance to oppression and arrested two deputies on mission who were in the department supervising coastal defences. The leaders also approached the local military commander, Wimpffen, with requests for help. Unknown to them, Wimpffen was a royalist and possibly in English pay; he proved very responsive. When, on 30 June, Caen became the headquarters of a 'Central Assembly of Resistance to Oppression' claiming to represent six Breton departments as well as Calvados, Wimpffen accepted command of its armed forces, whose notional numbers now exceeded 3,000. By then the rebels were also encouraged by the arrival, in the days following 9 June, of a number of the proscribed Girondin deputies themselves, who had escaped from the lax house arrest under which they had been placed on 2 June. They included Buzot, Louvet, and Pétion, and at first they were lionized by the richest inhabitants of Caen. But, noted Pétion, it did not last. When their hosts discovered that the Girondins had not been turned royalist by their treatment, their attitude rapidly cooled. 'They detested the Mountain most cordially,' he recalled,[13] 'but they liked republicans no better.'

Thus surfaced one of the many divisions that were to bedevil and ultimately doom what Parisians called the 'Federalist revolt'. But these weaknesses were not visible at the start, and certainly not from the viewpoint of the capital. From there, it looked to many in June 1793 as if much of France was in revolt against the Convention, and there was wild talk (too often repeated uncritically by historians) of 60 or 70 out of the 83 departments repudiating central authority. Centres of revolt, of course, had every interest in making similar claims. More sober observers, even at the time, refused to be panicked. On 31 July the administrator of nationalized property, whose office was naturally sensitive to the slightest tremor of anti-revolutionary activity, noted serious resistance in only eight departments. Nevertheless, the country's second, third, and fourth cities lay in these recalcitrant districts, so the 'Federalist' challenge could scarcely be brushed aside. What was easier was to misunderstand it.

It was not an attempt, however it might look, to break up the one and indivisible Republic. In the eyes of the rebels, wherever they arose, it was Paris which was sowing division in the Republic by dictating to and then tampering with the deputies elected by the rest of the nation. The Revolution of 1789 had been against centralization, that tool of Bourbon despotism. The failure of the constitution of 1791 to guarantee the disappearance of despotism had produced the Convention, but its purpose was supposedly to strengthen rather than abandon the principles of 1789; and not least local autonomy. Yet instead new intendants, the representatives on mission, had been sent out to the provinces with limitless powers; and although they came on behalf of the sovereign Nation incarnated in the Convention, that body itself was now hostage to the 'anarchists' and 'blood-drinkers' of the Paris sections. Nor were the leaders of 'Federalism' royalists, although royalists were happy to lend them support if it would foment division in republican ranks. As the commanding general in the south-west reported of the Bordelais on 5 June: 'They appeared to me determined not to involve themselves in Parisian affairs, but more determined still to retain their liberty, their property, their opulence . . . They don't want a king; they want a republic, but a rich and tranquil republic.'[14] That, however, could scarcely mean a republic at war; and what the 'Federalists' appear to have resented if anything even more than the grip of the sansculottes on other deputies was the range of emergency measures any government would have felt obliged to take to cope with the downturn in French fortunes that spring. Conscription, enhanced police powers, market controls, and forced loans, actual or threatened, were now coming on top of years of upheaval tolerated only because of the promise of calmer times to come. For ports there was the added blow of enemy activity. Whatever their losses, men of property doubtless rode out these tribulations better than those with little or none; but the disappearance over the summer of 1792 of the distinction between active and other citizens seemed to place the power to exercise authority enhanced by the emergency in the hands of those with least to lose. Embattled Jacobins in Marseilles, Lyons, and Toulon were reckless in their reliance on threats against property to retain power seized in the aftermath of the fall of the monarchy. Inevitably they expected support from the Montagnards, and inevitably they got it. But just as inevitably those who turned against one turned against the other. Nor was it just the rich, although they certainly gave the lead. 'Federalism' could never have got the grip it did (however transitory it proved) without support from many ordinary people who feared and resented what Jacobinism meant for them in the form of instability, inflation, and shortages—similar preoccupations, ironically enough, to those of the sansculottes in Paris. And they no more wished to be conscripted to fight distant enemies than the peasants of the Vendée or Brittany. This attitude proved (more irony!) fatal for the very resistance they supported. For the most striking failure of 'Federalism' was the dismal record of its departmental armies. If Marseilles was able to make up a force

15. The Festival of the Federation, 14 July 1790

16. Brissot: a journalist in power

17. Robespierre in 1789

18. Dumouriez, patriotic general and traitor

19. Danton at the height of his revolutionary prestige

20. The overthrow of the monarchy, 10 August 1792

21. Louis XVI in the Temple, shortly
before his execution

22. Sketch by David of Marie-
Antoinette on the way to the
scaffold

23. Marat, the 'People's Friend'

24. Carnot, 'Organizer of Victory' and Director

25. Vendéan generals: Stofflet

26. Vendéan generals: Charette

27. The contrast between the old and new France, as seen by Gillray, whose anti-French cartoons aroused deep resentment among revolutionaries

28. A little-known David. Outraged by Gillray, the artist responded with a number of anti-coalition cartoons of his own

29. The first public audience of the Directory, November 1795

30. (*left*) Barras in directorial robes

31. (*bottom left*) La Révellière-Lépeaux, depicted as a republican intransigent

32. (*bottom right*) Bonaparte in 1799

which at its largest seems to have reached 3,500 men, Bordeaux only put together a third of its 1,200 target. When the first Breton volunteers arrived in Caen they paraded through the town expecting to be joined by swarms of Norman recruits. Only seventeen came forward, and the Finistère battalions almost went home there and then. Nor did those who did volunteer show much willingness to march far from home. The Marseillais never got beyond Avignon. The Bordelais marched south rather than towards Paris, and ended up encamped in vineyards a mere 20 miles up the Garonne. A combined Breton and Norman force did better: leaving Caen on 8 July, about 2,000 men passed Evreux on the twelfth making for the Seine. But the next day they turned tail and ran at the first shots from forces sent against them by the Convention at Brécourt. They did not stop running until they were back in the Calvados.

Reluctance to leave their home territory was also to bedevil the Catholic and royal armies of the Vendée; but in June 1793 this weakness had not yet emerged as they continued to drive republican troops before them. On 10 June a hitherto unknown leader, a petty nobleman of some military experience called Charette, retook Machecoul from 'blues' who had captured it in April. On the nineteenth, the rebels crossed the Loire and entered Angers, which the republicans had evacuated. On the twenty-ninth they appeared before the greatest prize of all, the Atlantic port of Nantes. Throughout the spring Nantes had been one of the foremost centres of support for the Girondins against Parisian and Montagnard extremism, but as the forces of counter-revolution approached, the city authorities recognized that it was no moment to renounce the Convention. Appeals from other Breton cities to provide a contingent for the departmental army assembling at Caen were rebuffed. So was a call to surrender from the Vendéan army. The attack, when it came, was ill co-ordinated, and the city resisted with more determination than its besiegers had ever expected. After two days of assault, the attackers withdrew. Nantes, however grudgingly, had held firm for the Jacobin Republic against its enemies of both types. The worst moment in the Montagnards' struggle to keep control of France had passed.

It was fortunate for them that their opponents were so divided and unco-ordinated, because even in Paris itself the weeks after the purge of 2 June were chaotic. Few deputies positively welcomed the purge of national representatives, and a number who had no special links with the proscribed deputies went out of their way to condemn the deed openly in letters to their constituents. Seventy-five signed a secret protest between 6 and 19 June; it would later be used to condemn the signatories in their turn as Girondins. The loose conditions of arrest imposed on the twenty-nine, while the Convention decided what to do next with them, also showed how reluctant their colleagues were to treat them as criminals. Only when a number of them escaped from Paris were those remaining confined more closely. To the radicals who had launched the insurrection on 31 May such laxity smacked of treachery—all the more so as the Montagnards had shown themselves determined from the moment of their triumph on 2 June to dissociate themselves from the allies who had made it possible. From 3 June onwards the Committee of Public Safety began a relentless campaign to whittle away the independence of the central committee of the sections which had organized the insurrection, and on the eighth it was merged into a body firmly under the control of the constituted departmental authorities. At the same time the Montagnards sought through popular questions to cut the ground from under the feet of those who expected a radical new dawn, such as the *enragés*. Already on 2 June itself, before proscribing the Girondins, the Convention had voted in principle to establish a 'Revolutionary Army'. There was nothing military about this idea, which had first surfaced in April, and become a staple of discussion in the sections over succeeding weeks. This sort of army would be a band of patriotic vigilantes, solid sansculottes, who would march into the countryside, or anywhere else their services might be required, to root out and punish traitors, hoarders, moderates, the indifferent, and suspects of all sorts. On the same day the Convention also voted to discuss the constitution every afternoon until a draft was ready. Moving with determined speed, it had produced by 10 June one which was deliberately designed to win popular approval, in both Paris and the country at large. Gone, in this project, were the checks, balances, and elaborate electoral limitations proposed by Condorcet in February and hotly debated since then. The separation of powers and extreme decentralization deemed so essential in 1789 were also largely abandoned. The constitution of 1793 provided for a unicameral legislature elected annually by direct manhood suffrage, and the legislature would choose the executive council. It was prefaced by a declaration of rights twice as long as that of 1789 which guaranteed to all citizens, in addition to the rights proclaimed then, public assistance when in need, state education, and the right to resist oppression by insurrection. On 24 June the project was ratified, and copies were sent out to all the primary assemblies which had elected the Convention for their approval in a sort of referendum. The aim was to secure this approval by the first anniversary of the fall of the monarchy on 10 August. Mean-while the Convention also moved to appease the peasantry. On 3 June the sale of *émigré* property in small, affordable lots was ordered. On the tenth it was decreed that all common lands might be redistributed among inhabitants of the communities where they were situated. On 17 July all remaining feudal rights still notionally in existence until bought out were abolished outright without compensation. All documents relating to them were to be collected and officially burned.

But none of this meant much to the sansculottes who, with their Girondin enemies out of the way, were now preoccupied once more with the supply of foodstuffs and other basic commodities. By the second week in June Paris was full of complaints against butchers and the price of meat. By the third week there were renewed fears for the bread supply as rumours came in from Normandy that the rebels in the Calvados would attempt to blockade the Seine. Roux, Varlet, and the *enragés*, frustrated in their desire for a more radical purge on 2 June, now sought to capitalize on this continuing unrest. Roux proposed at the Cordeliers that the new constitution should include a mandatory death sentence for usurers and speculators. 'Liberty', he declared, 'does not consist in starving your fellow men.' On the twenty-fifth he led a deputation from the more radical sections to the Convention, where he denounced the deputies for their inaction on hoarding and speculation and suggested that they, and the Montagnards in particular, were scarcely better in such matters than the despots of old. The outraged deputies threw him out; but attacks by women that very day on soap suppliers, whose stocks they sold at their own prices, showed that he was articulating real grievances. The Montagnards made a determined attempt to break Roux and destroy his influence. They were able to dislodge him from office as editor of the commune's news sheet, and engineer his expulsion from one of his power bases at the Cordeliers. Marat, the vehement friend of the people, though now debilitated by a skin disease only relieved by constant bathing, was persuaded to denounce the *enragés* and all they stood for. But such infighting among the victors of 2 June was brought to an abrupt halt in mid-July when 'Federalism' struck its first (and, as it turned out, only) blow in Paris. Rumours of tens of thousands of Marseillais, Lyonnais, and Bordelais marching on the capital had been current for weeks. But it was a single, determined emissary from Caen, acting on her own, who visited Girondin revenge on their most ferocious adversary. On the thirteenth, Charlotte Corday stabbed Marat to death in his bath.

Here was a new Montagnard martyr, and a much greater one than Le Peletier, or Chalier, news of whose grisly end came in from Lyons a few days later. For all his ferocity, Marat had only been influential since the previous summer, and thanks to his illness his great days were already over. But loss of his counterweight against the *enragés* seemed serious, even if the initial impact of his murder was to stun the sansculottes. It

seems to have galvanized the Montagnards into more positive action. They
made the most of their martyr, of course. On 8 August they even paraded
his widow before the Convention to denounce the *enragés* as agents of
Austria and England. But the realization was now dawning, as disaster
upon disaster was reported from the war fronts and from rebel
departments, that much more ruthless and determined action would be
required if the crisis facing the Republic was to be overcome. Problems of
government would have to be taken more seriously. Danton, suspected of
excessive trimming, had already been voted off the Committee of Public
Safety on 10 July. So had his right-hand man Delacroix. Two weeks later
(26 July), convinced at last of its value, Robespierre accepted nomination
to the Committee, noting to himself that its priorities must be 'food supplies
and popular laws'. A law against hoarding passed that very day, making it
a capital offence, seemed just what was needed. The new constitution, too,
appeared to have achieved its purpose. The primary assemblies endorsed it
by 1,801,918 votes against 11,610—not a brilliant turnout, but
respectable enough at a time of civil war. The promulgation ceremony on
10 August, therefore, went ahead as planned, with a huge procession
wending its way through Paris to where eighty-three pikes, one brought
from each department by a patriot ripe in years, were bound into a huge
fasces symbolizing republican unity. The constitution itself was deposited
in a cedar box and suspended from the roof of the Convention hall.

Theoretically, the Convention's work was now done. Like the Constituent Assembly before it, it could dissolve itself and make way for regular,
constitutional government. Delacroix proposed just this on the eleventh.
That same night, however, Robespierre denounced a proposal which could
only bring to power 'the envoys of Pitt and Coburg'. The current
emergency, when the very survival of the Republic was at stake, was not
the time to increase political uncertainties. The constitution could not
safely be brought into force in time of war. So long as the emergency lasted
it would remain suspended, in every sense.

# Government by Terror
## 1793–1794

JULY 1793 was the low point in the Jacobin Republic's struggle against its enemies. All the military news was bad. The forces of the coalition were established on French soil in Flanders and along the Pyrenees. Thousands of French troops surrendered when Mainz fell; while a British fleet cruised off Marseilles hoping to link up with the 'Federalist' rebels there. Nor was news from the interior much better. The Vendéans' retreat from Nantes only seemed to consolidate their grip on the heartland of the rebellion. The only general successful against them, Biron, retook Saumur, but was dismissed on 12 July under suspicion as a former duke. He was replaced by his sansculotte deputy Rossignol, politically sound but a drunken incompetent. And whereas the Federalist revolt in Normandy rapidly collapsed after Brécourt, Lyons proclaimed its continued defiance with the execution of Chalier; and Toulon, hitherto loyal, became a new centre of resistance. Charlotte Corday was denounced as the agent of a far-flung Girondin plot; and after her execution on 17 July she was adopted as a martyr by a whole spectrum of anti-Montagnards from moderates to royalists. It was feared that she was one of thousands operating in the capital, suspicions fanned by political struggles in some of the sections. Not all of them were in the grip of solid sansculottes. Control of some at the western end of the city changed hands almost nightly, and when elections were held for the post of commander of the Paris National Guard, Hanriot was only confirmed after massive gerrymandering againt a candidate who had fired on the republican petitioners in the Champ de Mars.

'The evil which besets us', declared Jeanbon Saint-André on 1 August,[1] 'is that we have no government.' As a member of the Committee of Public Safety, he ought to have known. But when Danton proposed, in the same session, that the Committee be recognized formally as France's provisional government, the Convention would not agree. The Committee seemed adequate for its purpose without taking new powers; and, with the addition to its ranks on 11 August of two experienced military technocrats, Carnot and Prieur de la Côte d'Or (the latter just released from Federalist clutches in Caen), it now set about vindicating the Convention's confidence. It never did become the government, or enjoy undisputed executive authority. But in the course of the next twelve months it was to give the country the leadership to mobilize its resources with unprecedented assurance, and put the crisis of 1793 behind it.

The first step was to defeat the 'Federalists'—or rather, those who were not already managing to defeat themselves. No further military operations were necessary in Calvados after Brécourt. The disgusted Bretons marched out of Caen on 25 July, along with the fugitive Girondin deputies, leaving the city to its fate. By 3 August a representative on mission and member of the Committee of Public Safety, Robert Lindet, was in control again. Nor did the Bretons hold out long. In mid-August they issued public retractions of their earlier defiant proclamations, and the fugitive deputies moved on again, making their way south to what they imagined would be the safety of Bordeaux. Bitter disappointment awaited them: resistance was collapsing in the Gironde, too. In the last week of July the Popular Commission still seemed very much in charge, seizing all the coinage in the local mint to defray its mounting expenses. Then, on 2 August, alarmed by threats of military vengeance issuing from Paris, and mounting problems of food supply, it abruptly dissolved itself and recalled its volunteer army. If it hoped to fend off Montagnard vengeance it was to be disappointed. Although none of the money was used, the raid on the mint was viewed as theft of national property. Besides, ever since its establishment the Commission had been the source of much virulent anti-Parisian propaganda, and had dispatched emissaries to foment Federalism all over the south and west. Its contribution, in fact, to the national crisis was regarded as far more damaging than that of Caen or Rennes, and retribution was accordingly going to be far more drastic. On 6 August all members of the Popular Commission were declared traitors and outlawed. Representatives on mission arrived on 19 August, to restore legitimate authority, but they did not find the cowed and contrite city they expected. Jostled and threatened by ugly crowds of Muscadins, they felt safer withdrawing the next day to the republican safety of La Réole, thirty miles up river. From there they reported their reception to the Convention, and called for troops to accompany their next entry to the city. Not until 17 October did they feel secure enough to attempt it. By then Bordeaux had been bracing itself for several weeks. On 27 August the National Club reopened, and three weeks later a new Jacobin-dominated municipal council was elected. A festival in honour of Marat had even been held. But, remarked Tallien, the deputy now sent from the Vendée to deal with Bordeaux, 'this is pure face-saving. Hunger and fear alone have brought the twenty-eight sections together for even a minute.'[2]

Similar pressures also precipitated the surrender of Marseilles. Detachments from the army in the Alps were ordered in July to march against both Marseilles and Lyons. By the beginning of August Lyons was surrounded but seemed bent on resistance. Marseilles, however, now cut off from sympathizers further up the Rhône, began to panic. The departmental army of the Bouches du Rhône withdrew from Avignon, pursued by regular troops under Carteaux. With the port blockaded and the new harvest not yet in, bread riots broke out in the city in the early days of August. The Popular Tribunal began to execute known Jacobins, and priests reappeared in public praying for divine aid to save the rebels. Finally, as Carteaux's army closed in, the rebels appealed to the British admiral Hood to allow grain ships from Italy to pass his blockade. This was treason, and it proved too much for some of Marseilles's sections to follow. Fighting broke out on 23 August between advocates of surrender to Carteaux and partisans of collaboration with the British. Two days later, Carteaux arrived. Those who could, made their escape to Toulon, where they had a dramatic effect on the situation. The Toulon Federalists had had no previous thoughts of collaboration with the enemy, even though they knew that if Carteaux took Marseilles their own turn must come. But, surprised by the approach from Marseilles, Hood concluded that Toulon might be ripe for negotiation, too. On 23 August, accordingly, he formally offered Toulon military protection if the port would proclaim Louis XVII. Many were outraged, but others were equally appalled by atrocity stories spread by refugees from Marseilles. After agonized debate, the sections decided to accept Hood's offer. It took another three days to persuade the sailors of the Mediterranean fleet that resistance at this stage would be futile, but on 27 August the British fleet sailed into France's Mediterranean naval base and coalition forces occupied the town. They met with no resistance.

The fall of Toulon to the British precipitated a new crisis in Paris. Ever since the death of Marat various factions in the capital had been jostling to appropriate his mantle and his following; hence the venom and persistence of the Montagnard attack on the *enragés*. But no sooner had Roux been dislodged from influence at the commune than others came forward to appropriate his programme. The new populists had until now been orthodox spokesmen for Montagnard policies in the commune (in the person of Chaumette, its procurator, and Hébert, his deputy) and at the war ministry. They also dominated the Cordeliers Club. Hébert's *Père Duchesne*, written in the oath-strewn vernacular, became the undisputed best-selling paper in Paris once Marat was silenced. It also began, soon after that, to call for sterner measures against hoarders and speculators, the extension of the maximum to all goods of first necessity along with stricter enforcement, faster progress in the organization of the Revolutionary Armies decreed on 2 June, and greater efforts to marshal the people's revolutionary enthusiasm through mass effort. These demands were barely distinguishable from those still being made by Roux and his journalist ally Leclerc, who had even given his own paper Marat's old name of *L'Ami du Peuple*. Both groups believed that only ruthless use of the guillotine would eliminate traitors, backsliders, suspects, speculators, and 'egoists'. The answer to the nation's problems lay in Terror.

Even in the Convention this cry was increasingly being heard. Deputies like the ferocious Billaud-Varenne, who had moved the death penalty for hoarding, and his close ally Collot d'Herbois, former actor and already known as a ruthlessly efficient representative on mission, increasingly stood out from their fellow Montagnards in spurning caution and conciliation. And the Committee of Public Safety did authorize some popular gestures: the *levée en masse* proclaimed on 23 August was a response to a petitioning campaign from the sections. But stirringly as Carnot's prose read and spectacularly effective as his implementation of the decree was to be, the conscription it authorized fell far short of the universal national enlistment dreamed of in the sections. The Nation's resolve, Leclerc proclaimed, was being sapped by a 'spirit of moderation' in the Convention that needed to be expunged, if necessary, by the sort of popular action already seen on 2 June. Hébert, defeated to his great surprise in a bid to be elected minister of the interior on 20 August, seized on the same theme, and began to work the Jacobin Club up to accepting it. Economic circumstances favoured him. Over the summer the assignat had continued to decline, reaching a mere 22 per cent of its face value in August—a loss of 14 per cent since the purge of the Girondins alone. Weeks of hot weather had produced a good harvest, but many watermills were becalmed by drought, so flour remained scarce. All basic goods had risen in price since June, and some quite spectacularly: soap was up threefold. For all this moderates and dozers (*endormeurs*) in the Convention were blamed: and when on 2 September news arrived of the loss of Toulon it was easy to focus popular anger on them. Billaud-Varenne had already come close to condemning the incompetence of the Committee of Public Safety with a proposal for a new committee to supervise ministers.

So when what appears to have originated as a spontaneous demonstration by manual workers for higher wages and more bread broke out on 4 September, Hébert and his allies at the commune and in the clubs were quick to turn it to their advantage. Confronted by crowds in the place de Grève, they persuaded them to reassemble on the fifth for a march on the Convention. They used their official powers to close all workplaces the next day, and that evening they persuaded the Jacobins to back their initiative, brushing aside the temporizings of Robespierre, who as current president of the Convention would have the task of confronting the morning's demonstration. There was certainly no hope of resisting it. Chaumette, at the head of thousands of sansculottes, denounced the shortages, the failure to implement existing laws to deal with them, and those who caused them: 'Legislators, the immense gathering of citizens come together yesterday and this morning ... has formed but one wish; brought to you by a deputation, it is this: Our subsistence, and to get it, apply the law!'[3] That meant first of all organizing the Revolutionary Armies and launching them against the hoarders and greedy, unpatriotic inhabitants of the countryside. The Convention voted to do it on the spot—although it did not authorize the guillotines on wheels which Chaumette thought every detachment of the new force ought to have. The motion was moved by Billaud-Varenne and seconded by Danton. Danton also moved that arms production be stepped up until every patriot had a musket, that the Revolutionary Tribunal be divided so as to get through more business; and that, as he put it, to permit 'hardworking men, who live by the price of their sweat', to attend their sectional assemblies, these assemblies should take place twice weekly and attendance at them be paid at 40 *sous* a time. It was all carried by acclamation, amid scenes, in Barère's words, of delirium.

Terror, he observed, was now the order of the day. The sansculottes appeared to have coerced the Convention for the second time in three months and to be set to dictate its policies without resistance. Over the next few weeks the legislature certainly committed itself to radical and energetic action on a scale not seen since the emergency of March. Billaud-Varenne and Collot d'Herbois were now added to the Committee of Public Safety, although Danton refused nomination. On 17 September a comprehensive Law of Suspects was passed, which empowered the watch committees set up the previous March to arrest anyone who 'either by their conduct, their contacts, their words or their writings, showed themselves to be supporters of tyranny, of federalism, or to be enemies of liberty', as well as a number of more specific categories such as former nobles 'who have not constantly manifested their attachment to the revolution.'[4] Practically anybody might fall foul of such a sweeping law. In the weeks following even everyday speech acquired a sansculotte style. Those who refused to call each other 'citizen' rather than the deferential 'Monsieur', and to use the familiar form of address (*tutoiement*), fell under automatic suspicion. Then on 29 September the Convention passed a General Maximum Law which imposed price controls on a wide range of goods defined as of first necessity from food and drink to fuel, clothing, and even tobacco. Those who sold them above the maximum would be fined and placed on the list of suspects. The Revolutionary Army was at last set on foot, and command of it went not, as the Committee of Public Safety would have liked, to Hanriot, but to Ronsin, one of the fiercest allies of Hébert. Ever since June many sections had also been calling for the Girondins still in captivity to be put on trial, along with Marie-Antoinette. Such gestures were bloody (since acquittal was inconceivable) but empty, as Robespierre saw. He campaigned against them and sought to impede them as long as he could. But on 9 September news broke of a plot to free the former queen from the solitary confinement in which she was now kept, and after that her fate was inevitable. She was sent for trial on 3 October, the same day as the Girondins. All Robespierre could do was dissuade the Convention from the roll-call demanded by Billaud-Varenne to identify those favouring mercy for traitors.

The first well-known victims of the reign of terror, however, came from the other end of the political spectrum. The radicals used their triumph to eliminate the rivals whose policies they had stolen. In the course of September the leading *enragés* were all arrested. Roux, first imprisoned as early as 22 August, then released, was rearrested on 5 September. Varlet, who with some prescience denounced Danton's idea of payment for attendance at fixed weekly sectional meetings, followed him into custody on the eighteenth. Leclerc stopped publishing and disappeared. No more was now heard of the call, periodically taken up by the *enragés*, for the constitution to be brought into force, with all its democratic practices and implicit renewal of the national representation. Quite the reverse. On 10 October the Convention formally accepted that it was impossible to activate it as things were. At a time of emergency the processes it enshrined were too cumbersome and slow. 'It is impossible', declared Saint-Just in the name of the Committee of Public Safety,'[5] for revolutionary laws to be executed if the government itself is not constituted in a revolutionary way.' He therefore proposed that the Committee itself should take on the central direction of the entire state apparatus, subject only to the oversight of the Convention. Such 'Revolutionary Government' would be temporary; but the government of France was declared revolutionary until the peace.

Thus began the most famous stage of the French Revolution, when in the course of nine months around 16,000 people perished under the blade of the guillotine. The cold, mechanical efficiency of the method had all Europe watching with fascinated horror. The Terror began—and ended far into 1794—with famous victims. Marie-Antoinette went to the scaffold, her defiant appearance in the tumbril memorably sketched by David, on 17 October. Two weeks later (31 October) 21 Girondins, including Brissot and Vergniaud, followed her, after a show trial cut short when the eloquence and debating skills of the accused threatened to prolong it indefinitely. They went to their deaths defiantly singing the 'Marseillaise'. Those who had signed the secret protest against their purging in June were imprisoned as Girondins after its existence was revealed in the preparations for the trial; but Robespierre always blocked moves to have them too put on trial. Of those who had escaped in June, four went to the guillotine in Bordeaux, while Pétion and Buzot shot themselves. Their bodies were later found, half-eaten by wolves. Roland too committed suicide when he heard of his wife's execution in November. November also saw the execution of Égalité, no Girondin, but a prince of royal blood with an *émigré* son; and suspect figures from the past like Barnave, arrested a year previously when his 1791 intrigues with the queen were revealed; and Bailly, still hated by the sansculottes for his part in the massacre of the Champ de Mars. For him a special guillotine was erected at the scene of the crime. The others all met their deaths where the guillotine now permanently stood, close to where Louis XVI's head had fallen in the place de la Révolution.

Even so, only 177 people were executed in Paris between October and the end of 1793. The pathetic spectacle of the once mighty and famous now brought low distracted attention from the thousands of less well-known provincials who made up the bulk of the Terror's victims. Just as the show trials in Paris were beginning, Lyons finally surrendered to the besieging armies after two months of bombardment and resistance during which its defence was increasingly reliant on royalist volunteers commanded by a returned *émigré*. Hoping to be relieved by a Piedmontese invasion from the east, the starving city had held out over the summer. But when in the first few days of October the invaders were thrown back, defeat became inevitable and Lyons surrendered to the representative on mission Couthon. His inclination was to adopt the policy of conciliation and clemency that had worked so effectively in Caen over the summer. But Lyons was different. The country's second city had defied the Convention for a third of the year, when the Republic was in mortal peril. It had murdered Chalier and not hesitated to make common cause with other rebels, not to mention royalists and foreign enemies. The city's name was reviled in Paris far more than those of the other 'Federalist' centres, and the

Committee of Public Safety was resolved to make Lyons an example. On receipt of the news of its fall, on 12 October, the Committee moved a decree that Lyons should be destroyed. Its very name was to disappear, except on a monument among the ruins which would proclaim 'Lyons made war on Liberty. Lyons is no more'. 'The collection of houses left standing'—for the destruction of the city was glossed later in the decree as the destruction of the houses of the rich—was to be renamed Freed-Town (*Ville Affranchie*). Couthon had no stomach for such comprehensive vengeance. He set up special courts and began to demolish some of the city's richest dwellings, but at the same time he asked to be transferred elsewhere. He was replaced at the beginning of November by Collot d'Herbois and Fouché, the latter previously on mission in Nevers. They came determined to exact the exemplary vengeance decreed from Paris, and to help them they brought units of the Paris Revolutionary Army, now fully organized under the direct authority of the Committee of Public Safety. Thousands of suspects were imprisoned as parties of sansculottes swept the city with 'domiciliary visits', but by the end of November scarcely more than 200 'Federalists' had been condemned by the special courts. Collot thought a mere twenty deaths a day not enough. On 27 November a special 'Tribunal of Seven' was established to speed matters up, and within days had handed down capital sentences on almost 300 convicted rebels. This was too much for the local guillotine: in the *mitraillades* of 4–8 December, condemned men were blown into open graves by cannon-fire and grape-shot. Even so executions continued into the spring. By April, 1,880 Lyonnais had been condemned. Arriving in the city with a detachment of the Paris Revolutionary Army on 22 January, a German adventurer who had joined them gazed in horror at:

whole ranges of houses, always the most handsome, burnt. The churches, convents, and all the dwellings of the former patricians were in ruins. When I came to the guillotine, the blood of those who had been executed a few hours beforehand was still running in the street . . . I said to a group of sansculottes . . . that it would be decent to clear away all this human blood. —Why should it be cleared? one of them said to me. It's the blood of aristocrats and rebels. The dogs should lick it up.[6]

The troops who had taken Lyons had meanwhile moved on south to join the armies encircling Toulon. The coalition forces occupying the port were not reinforced, and so had done little to enlarge their bridgehead. But they could keep supplied from the sea so long as they occupied the heights around the harbour. Thus the siege of Toulon went on for $3\frac{1}{2}$ months. But when, on 17 December, Captain Bonaparte's gunners drove the British and Spanish troops from the key forts on those heights, Admiral Hood saw that he must evacuate the port immediately or have his fleet shot to matchwood. Perhaps 7,000 refugees crowded on to the warships which sailed out over the next three days under republican fire, including most of the leaders of Toulon's original revolt. Nevertheless the Jacobins released from imprisonment were able to identify plenty of remaining rebels. 800 were shot without trial as French citizens caught in armed rebellion. A Revolutionary Commission set up by the representatives Barras (a former noble) and Fréron condemned 282 more to the guillotine over the next month for conniving at a revolt that had not only proclaimed Louis XVII, but also allowed the enemy to tow off or destroy over two-thirds of the French Mediterranean fleet as the occupation ended. 'Mountain-Port' (Port-de-la-Montagne), as it was now renamed, therefore suffered second only to Lyons in the Terror which purged the centres of 'Federalism'. Only its vital strategic importance as a naval base cushioned it from further reprisals.

Repression at Marseilles and Bordeaux, in comparison, was relatively mild. Well controlled and formally meticulous, the Revolutionary Tribunal which sat at Marseilles between August 1793 and April 1794 tried 975 suspects and acquitted 476 of them. 289 of those convicted were executed—although of course many of the most guilty must have escaped to Toulon before Carteaux's forces marched in. Even the attempt to give the city the new name of Nameless (*Sansnom*) was half-hearted. Bordeaux kept its own name throughout, although the Gironde department where it lay was redesignated Bec d'Ambès (from the point where Garonne and Dordogne meet). Despite bloodthirsty language from the representatives Tallien and Ysabeau, the Military Commission they established acquitted more suspects than it condemned, and between October 1793 and June 1794 only 104 were sentenced to the guillotine. So moderate had the repression been that the representatives themselves fell under suspicion. Ysabeau seemed too fond of the company of rich merchants, while Tallien was under the thumb of his beautiful, pleasure-loving mistress, Thérèse Cabarrus, the wife of a noble and herself daughter of a dubious Spanish financier. They were supplemented in June 1794 by a young, austere acolyte of Robespierre, Jullien, and in the two months of his rule 198 more heads rolled at Bordeaux. By then, the Terror was tailing off everywhere else except in Paris.

Jullien was chosen to go to Bordeaux on the strength of his success in uncovering terroristic abuses in Nantes under the representative sent there in October 1793, Carrier. Nantes by then was the main centre of operations against the Vendée, and bursting with prisoners as the war began to turn against the rebels. After their failure to take the great port in the first days of July the 'whites' melted back into the countryside. A republican counter-offensive began, spearheaded by regular troops who had surrendered at Mainz and been repatriated by the coalition on condition of not being put back in the line. They, and a legion of sansculotte volunteers from Paris under Rossignol, now carried a deliberate policy of terror and devastation into the Vendéan heartland. The rebels rapidly abandoned Saumur and Angers, and their leaders fell to quarrelling about who should have overall command. Reactivated by messages from London that the British would send them aid if they could capture a port, they regrouped and defeated the Parisian army at Coron on 18 September and the Mainz veterans at Torfou the next day. But characteristically afterwards most of the rebels went home to sing *te Deums* instead of pursuing their advantage. Early in October the Committee of Public Safety launched a new drive to crush the 'inexplicable Vendée', as Barère called it. Command of the various republican armies was unified, and by mid-October four columns were converging on the very headquarters of rebel territory, the *bocage* around Cholet. There, on 17 October, they defeated the rebels decisively and killed several of their leaders. Only now, pursued by triumphant republicans, did the Vendéans break out of their home country in a bold and desperate bid to link up with the British. They crossed the Loire and struck north under Stofflet, making for the nearest port to British territory, Granville, on the Cotentin peninsula opposite Jersey. As they went they were joined by *chouans* from the disaffected countryside of upper Brittany, and by the time they reached Granville on 14 November they may have been 60,000 strong. But the British were not there. There were plenty of troops and supplies in Jersey, but news of the march only reached their commander, via London, on 26 November, and even then he did not know that Granville was their destination. The port was well fortified and defended, whereas the Vendéans had no siege train. By the time British warships appeared off Granville on 2 December the rebel army was in retreat, far to the south. By the fourth they were once more at Angers, but this time the republican garrison held firm, and they were unable to get back across the Loire. They turned north again, and on 12 December republican forces at last caught up with them at Le Mans, where they were routed in a night battle fought in pouring winter rain. Many escaped, but in complete disorder. Westermann, in command of the blues pursuing them westwards back into Brittany, ordered no quarter to be given. 'The road to Laval is strewn with corpses', reported one of his men.[7] 'Women, priests, monks, children, all have been put to death. I have spared nobody.' Perhaps 10,000 died during this retreat. On 23 December, finally, the remnant of the Catholic and royal army turned to face its pursuers at

Savenay. Only 4,000 or 5,000 were left in any state to fight, although twice that number were crammed into the little town. Two-thirds of them were destroyed in the battle and the mass shootings which followed. The 'Great War of the Vendée' was over.

Alongside casualties on this scale, even the number of victims who perished in the Terror of Nantes seems modest. Yet nowhere else was the Terror so destructive. Forty-two per cent of the death sentences during the entire Terror were passed in the three departments most affected by the Vendée rebellion, and the various special courts established in the Loire-Inférieure, Nantes's department, accounted for 3,548 capital sentences. Carrier, whose previous record at Rennes, dealing with mere Federalists, had been moderate and conciliatory, believed that fanatical royalist counter-revolutionaries deserved far harsher treatment. As at Lyons, the guillotine could scarcely cope with the flood of victims: yet the prisons were overflowing, ravaged by epidemics, and there was not enough food to feed innocent citizens, let alone condemned traitors and rebels. These considerations led Carrier to approve perhaps the most notorious expedient of the whole Terror: the *noyades*. On 19 November some 90 priests were executed by sinking them, hog-tied, in a holed barge in the Loire. In the six weeks that followed six other batches of victims, many though not all of them non-juring priests convicted (or sometimes just suspected) of exciting the fanaticism of devout rebels, were disposed of in the same way. Perhaps 1,800 perished altogether in the *noyades*, and their bodies were washed up on the tidal banks of the Loire for weeks afterwards. But the citizens of Nantes, repeatedly threatened by insurgents who reputedly gave no quarter, raised little objection to such methods, or to the hundreds of shootings of armed rebels that Carrier also authorized. They believed they would have been massacred if the whites had triumphed: the Vendée rebellion had begun, after all, with massacres of good republicans. And hardly any Nantais were executed under Carrier. What brought him down, and precipitated his recall to Paris on 8 February, was rumours of the sheer scale of his operations in Nantes at a time when the Committee of Public Safety was beginning to wonder—however temporarily—whether ferocity was not now making the Republic more enemies than it eliminated. In this climate subordinate terrorists in Nantes were anxious to blame the representative on mission for as much excess as possible; and Jullien, as the confidant of the always-suspicious Robespierre, was a willing recipient of their denunciations. Repression under Carrier, Jullien reported, had been indiscriminate, and too often the letter of the law had been ignored. Official policy was now to set severe limits to the independent initiative of representatives on mission, and Carrier was the first, and most spectacular, casualty of the changed atmosphere.

Throughout the autumn of 1793, however, representatives on mission had been free to interpret their role much as they wished. This phase of the Terror was anarchic, unco-ordinated, and little subject to central direction. Its characteristic instruments were the Revolutionary Armies, which mushroomed throughout the provinces in imitation of that of Paris, and whose numbers may have reached 40,000 men at their height. Terroristic jacks-of-all-trades, their purpose was to intimidate and punish, arrest and repress, anyone suspected of activities that could be deemed hostile to the Revolution. Representatives arriving in districts suspected of disaffection tended to establish such forces as a matter of priority, as rallying-points for active and reliable patriots. Overwhelmingly they were recruited in towns, among married artisans, and they tended to operate locally: the Paris battalions sent to Lyons were exceptional. Local knowledge, in fact, was essential to their functioning. They knew who the suspects were, and where to find them; and, recruited as they were, it was not surprising that they spent much of their time foraging in surrounding countryside, hunting down hoarders and speculators whose greed threatened to starve hungry patriot families in the towns and flouted the Law of the Maximum. The same local knowledge underpinned the powers of the watch committees sitting in most localities since the spring. On to them devolved the responsibility of implementing the Law of Suspects passed in September, as well as a whole range of other duties such as issuing certificates of *civisme*—identity cards and testimonials of public reliability all in one. Originally only foreigners had been required to carry these documents, but the Law of Suspects made the requirement general. Those without them were liable to arrest and imprisonment; and in fact up to half a million people may have been imprisoned as suspects of one sort or another during the Terror. Up to 10,000 may have died in custody, crowded into prisons never intended for such numbers, or makeshift quarters no better equipped. These too, deserve to be numbered among the victims of the Terror, although not formally condemned. So do those who were murdered or lynched without trial or official record during the chaotic, violent autumn of 1793, when the supreme law of public safety seemed to override more conventional and cumbersome procedures. Altogether the true total of those who died under the Terror may have been twice the official figure—around 30,000 people in just under a year. Even so it was far from the bloodiest episode in a murderous decade for Europe: the same number died in a matter of weeks in Ireland in 1798, in a country with only one-sixth of France's population; while two-thirds of that number may have been slaughtered in a single day in Warsaw on 4 November 1794. Nor is it true that most of those killed in the Terror were members of the former 'privileged orders', whatever the Revolution's anti-aristocratic rhetoric might suggest. Of the official death sentences passed, less than 9 per cent fell upon nobles, and less than 7 per cent on the clergy. Disproportionately high as these figures may have been relative to the numbers of these groups in the population as a whole, they were not as high as the quarter of the Terror's victims who came from the middle classes. And the vast majority of those who lost their lives in the proscriptions of 1793–4—two-thirds of those officially condemned and doubtless a far higher proportion of those who disappeared unofficially—were ordinary people caught up in tragic circumstances not of their own making, who made wrong choices in lethal times, when indifference itself counted as a crime. It is scarcely a coincidence that most death sentences were passed in areas of 'Federalist' or royalist rebellion, or in frontier districts where the repeated passage of opposed armies demanded rapid but ultimately unconvincing changes of allegiance from those who lived there.

Other districts, meanwhile, particularly in the centre of the country, remained almost untouched by the Terror. Here even more than in disturbed areas the personal whims and idiosyncracies of representatives on mission could be decisive. Sometimes they could even set an example that would be widely followed. The Nièvre, for example, deep in central France, had given the Convention no cause for worry. But the arrival there in September 1793 of the representative Fouché transformed it into a beacon of religious terror. Fouché, himself a former priest, came from the Vendée, where he had witnessed the ability of the clergy to inspire fanatical resistance to the Republic's authority. Christianity, he concluded, could not coexist in any form with the Revolution and, brushing aside what was left of the 'constitutional' Church, he inaugurated a civic religion of his own devising with a 'Feast of Brutus' on 22 September at which he denounced 'religious sophistry'. Fouché particularly deplored clerical celibacy: it set the clergy apart, and in any case made no contribution to society's need for children. Clerics who refused to marry were ordered to adopt and support orphans or aged citizens. The French people, Fouché declared in a manifesto published on 10 October, recognized no other cult but that of universal morality; and although the exercise of all creeds was proclaimed as free and equal, none might henceforth be practised in public. Graveyards should exhibit no religious symbols, and at the gate of each would be an inscription proclaiming *Death is an eternal sleep*. Thus began the movement known as dechristianization. Soon afterwards Fouché moved on to Lyons; but during his weeks in Nevers his work had been watched by Chaumette, visiting his native town from Paris. He was to carry the idea back to the capital, where it was energetically taken up by his colleagues at the commune.

Other representatives on mission, meanwhile, had also taken to attacking the outward manifestations of the Catholic religion. At Abbeville, on the edge of priest-ridden Flanders, Dumont favoured forced public abjuration of orders, preferably by constitutional clergy whose continued loyalty to the Revolution could only now be proved by such gestures. On 7 October in Rheims, Ruhl personally supervised the smashing of the phial holding the sacred oil of Clovis used to anoint French kings. None of this was authorized by the Convention; on the other hand the adoption on 5 October of a new republican calendar marked a further stage in the divorce between the French State and any sort of religion. Years would no longer be numbered from the birth of Christ, but from the inauguration of the French Republic on 22 September 1792. Thus it was already the Year II. There would be twelve thirty-day months with evocative, seasonal names; each month would have three ten-day weeks (*décades*) ending in a rest-day (*décadi*). Sundays therefore disappeared and could not be observed unless they coincided with the less-frequent *décadis*. The introduction of the system at this moment only encouraged representatives on mission to intensify their lead; and dechristianization became an important feature of the Terror in all the former centres of rebellion when they were brought to heel. Once launched it was eminently democratic. Anybody could join in smashing images, vandalizing churches (the very word was coined to describe this outburst of iconoclasm), and theft of vestments to wear in blasphemous mock ceremonies. Those needing pretexts could preach national necessity when they tore down bells or walked off with plate that could be recast into guns or coinage. Such activities were particular favourites among the Revolutionary Armies. The Parisian detachments marching to Lyons left a trail of pillaged and closed churches, and smouldering bonfires of ornaments, vestments, and holy pictures all along their route. Other contributions took more organization, but Jacobin clubs and popular societies, not to mention local authorities, were quite happy to orchestrate festivals of reason, harmony, wisdom, and other such worthy attributes in former churches; and to recruit parties of priests who, at climactic moments in these ceremonies, would renounce their vows and declare themselves ready to marry. If their choice fell on a former nun, so much the better.

When Chaumette returned from Nevers, the Paris Commune made dechristianization its official policy. On 23 October the images of kings on the front of Notre-Dame were ordered to be removed: the royal tombs at

Saint-Denis had already been emptied and desecrated by order of the Convention in August. The word *Saint* began to be removed from street names, and busts of Marat replaced religious statues. Again the Convention appeared to be encouraging the trend when it decreed, on 20 October, that any priest (constitutional or refractory) denounced for lack of *civisme* by six citizens would be subject to deportation, and any previously sentenced to deportation but found in France should be executed. Clerical dress was now forbidden in Paris; and on 7 November Gobel, the elected constitutional bishop, who had already sanctioned clerical marriage for his clergy, came with eleven of them to the Convention and ceremonially resigned his see. Removing the episcopal insignia, he put on a cap of liberty and declared that the only religion of a free people should be that of Liberty and Equality. In the next few days the handful of priests who were deputies followed his example. Soon Grégoire, constitutional bishop of Blois, was the only deputy left clinging to his priesthood and clerical dress. The sections meanwhile were passing anti-clerical motions, and on 12 November that of Gravilliers, whose idol had so recently been Jacques Roux, sent a deputation to the Convention draped in 'ornaments from churches in their district, spoils taken from the superstitious credulity of our forefathers and repossessed by the reason of free men'[8] to announce that all churches in the section had been closed. This display followed a great public ceremony held in Notre-Dame, or the 'Temple of Reason', as it was now redesignated, on the tenth. On this occasion relays of patriotic maidens in virginal white paraded reverently before a temple of philosophy erected where the high altar had stood. From it emerged, at the climax of the ceremony, a red-capped female figure representing Liberty. Appreciatively described by an official recorder of the scene as 'a masterpiece of nature', in daily life she was an actress; but in her symbolic role she led the officials of the commune to the Convention, where she received the fraternal embrace of the president and secretaries.

However carefully choreographed, there was not much dignity about these posturings; and attacks on parish churches and their incumbents (who were mostly now popularly elected) risked making the Revolution more enemies than friends. Small-town anti-religious Jacobin zeal, for example, provoked a minor revolt in the Brie in the second week in December. To shouts of *Long live the Catholic Religion, we want our priests, we want the Mass on Sundays and Holy Days*, crowds of peasants sacked the local club. Several thousands took up arms and joined the movement, and only a force of National Guards and sansculottes from the Revolutionary Army restored order in a district whose tranquillity was vital to the regular passage of food supplies to the capital from southern Champagne. But even before this the Committee of Public Safety was growing anxious about the counter-productive effects of dechristianization. Robespierre in particular, who believed that religious faith was indispensable to orderly, civilized society, sounded the alarm. On 21 November he denounced anti-religious excesses at the Jacobin Club. They smacked of more fanaticism than they extinguished. The people believed in a Supreme Being, he warned, whereas atheism was aristocratic. At the same time he persuaded the Committee to circularize popular societies warning them not to fan superstition and fanaticism by persecution. On 6 December, finally, the Convention agreed to reiterate the principle of religious freedom in a decree which formally prohibited all violence or threats against the 'liberty of cults'. But by then it was too late. The example of Paris had encouraged Jacobin zealots everywhere, and with the repression of revolt in full swing and the role of priests in the Vendée particularly notorious, the remaining trappings of religion were too tempting a target to ignore. The commune's response to Robespierre on 23 November had been to decree the closing of all churches in the capital; and soon local authorities were shutting them wholesale throughout the country. By the spring, churches were open for public worship only in the remotest corners of France, such as the Jura mountains. By then, perhaps 20,000 priests had been bullied into giving up their status, and 6,000 had given their renunciation the ultimate confirmation by marrying. In some areas, such as Provence, dechristianization only reached its peak in March or April 1794. On the other hand it was scarcely a movement that could go on indefinitely. When most churches had been closed, and stripped of their furnishings and relics, and had no incumbents, what more could be done? All that remained was vigilance against continued religious practice behind closed doors; but the Committee of Public Safety, and the law itself as enunciated in the decree on the freedom of cults, were against such harassment; and the reach of both, from the end of 1793, was growing ever closer and more sure.

The dangerous chaos of dechristianization, in fact, seems to have been one of the most important factors pushing the Committee of Public Safety towards taking a firmer grip on the government of the country. It was certainly when the anti-religious paroxysm was at its height in Paris that the 'Revolutionary Government' proclaimed in October was given a structure and a chain of authority under a 'decree constituting Revolutionary Government' first proposed on 18 November, passed on 4 December, and known, from the latter date under the republican calendar, as the Law of 14 Frimaire. The principle animating it was extreme centralization. Executive power, subject always to the overriding authority of the Convention, was vested in the Committee of Public Safety in matters of internal administration and police. An executive council of ministers was still maintained, although Billaud-Varenne in the course of debates on the proposal repeated Danton's earlier call for its abolition; but it was now down-graded to a passive channel for transmitting the orders of the two committees. And all subordinate authorities, at whatever level, were expressly forbidden to alter, gloss, or interpret the law in any way. The obvious targets of this provision were the representatives on mission, who for much of 1793 had ruled their assigned territories subject to hardly any central control. They were, it is true, to be entrusted with the first application of the Law of 14 Frimaire, but it was to be their last great assignment. Subsequently, the execution of revolutionary laws at local level was to be the responsibility of district and commune councils, who would report directly, every ten days, to the governing committees. The departments, a consistently conservative force since their creation and motors of 'Federalism' in many areas since the spring, were bypassed for all except routine administrative functions such as tax-collection and public works. But to ensure that the districts and communes discharged their new and wider responsibilities properly, each was assigned a 'national agent' appointed by and reporting independently to the central committees. Meanwhile all unofficial local bodies set up in the course of the emergency since March including any local Revolutionary Armies, were abolished as 'subversive of the government's unity of action, and tending to federalism'. Only the watch committees, established uniformly everywhere in March and now reporting to the Committee of General Security, retained a role, no doubt because the operation of the Law of Suspects depended on them. Plainly the committees were now aiming at uniform, obedient administration, responding rapidly to central initiatives, and incapable of resisting, adapting, or varying government policy in any substantial way. The spirit of the Law of 14 Frimaire was the very opposite of that aspired to by the constitution-makers of 1791, or even, in the main, that of the Convention's own suspended constitution. But decentralization and separation of powers were ideals for calmer times, as Robespierre explained in moving a supplementary measure to reorganize the Revolutionary Tribunal on 25 December. 'The goal of constitutional government', he declared,[9] 'is to preserve the Republic; that of revolutionary government is to found it. The revolution is the war of liberty against its enemies: the constitution is the regime of liberty victorious and peaceful. Revolutionary government requires extraordinary activity, precisely because it is at war.'

Thus the Law of 14 Frimaire heralded the end of the anarchic Terror. It heralded the end of the depredations of the Revolutionary Armies, now reduced to a single force under close central supervision; and the end, by implication, of dechristianization. Above all it heralded the end of the proconsular autonomy hitherto enjoyed by the representatives on mission. It established the first strong central government that France had enjoyed since 1787. But although it aimed at a regime of instant obedience, the new law certainly did not take instantaneous effect. It was some months before the last provincial Revolutionary Armies were wound up, or dechristianization began to flag. And this was above all because many representatives on mission found the trimming of their powers hard to accept. 'Yes,' declared Javogues,[10] representative in the new department of the Loire, created to dismember the old Lyons-dominated Saône-et-Loire, 'there exists a plan for Counter-Revolution in the Committee of Public Safety; I have seen signs of it developing wherever I have been. They have tried to turn the Revolution back by sending out men who paralysed vigorous measures.' The Law of 14 Frimaire was not applicable, he argued, to a department like his, still in rebellion. Only after two months of defiance was he recalled. By then accusations of abuse of power and resistance to central authority by representatives had become a main plank in a campaign led by Danton and his friends to abandon government by terror. It was in this atmosphere that Robespierre sanctioned the missions of Jullien to Nantes and Bordeaux which led to the recall, in turn, of Carrier and Tallien. Ultimately, the Dantonists' campaign for 'indulgence' failed. But by the time it was over the power once wielded by the representatives on mission had been broken.

Yet the Law of 14 Frimaire was not the first attempt to impose uniform practice on the embattled Republic. The Law of the General Maximum had theoretically done so ever since 29 September 1793. It, too, had encountered initial difficulties. For most commodities the price it fixed was one-third above the local price of 1790, but in many cases that was more than the current price, and the days before the law took effect were marked by disorderly runs on shops stocking such goods. Local variations in price made supplies extremely uneven as producers preferred to sell their stocks where prices were higher. In any case it took far longer for local authorities, harassed by a myriad of other problems, to draw up comprehensive scales of prices than the week allowed between the promulgation of the decree and its implementation. Within a month the crude guideline of 1790 prices plus a third had had to be modified to take account of transport costs and reasonable levels of profit for those who handled the goods. And the provision of the Maximum Law which limited the level of wages was scarcely implemented at all; it would have required a whole extra apparatus of investigation and control, and in a place like

Paris the commune knew that its power ultimately depended on the support of the wage-earners who made up the majority of the sansculottes, and that the wages many of them were earning were already in excess of the maximum laid down. Nevertheless by November district authorities were beginning to control prices, at least, over much of France, and on 27 October supply of provisions on a national scale was placed under the supervision of a 'Subsistence Commission' answerable directly to the Committee of Public Safety, and more particularly to its longest-serving member, Robert Lindet. Lindet soon became the Carnot of economic organization as the commission took powers to direct bulk purchases, distribute grants, and regulate exports and imports. Above all it addressed itself to establishing a nationwide schedule of maximum prices for necessities, which was promulgated on 21 February 1794. Despite the draconian penalties of the law against hoarding, the less severe but still serious ones laid down in the Maximum Law itself, and the informal terror exercised against rural producers over the autumn by the Revolutionary Armies, the black market flourished behind the spreading apparatus of economic controls. The market was also disrupted by bulk-purchasing for the armed forces, when payments were made in cash and if necessary at rates above the maximum. Nevertheless by the spring of 1794 France was obviously making substantial progress towards a controlled economy. The most vivid evidence came from the value of the assignats. Controlled prices diminished the demand for a paper currency which had been legal tender since April 1793. Consequently fewer need be printed. Standing at 22 per cent of their face value in August 1793, they rose to 33 per cent in November and 48 per cent in December. Although from then on they began to decline again, the fall was nothing like as steep as in the spring of 1793 until economic controls began once more to be abandoned in the autumn of 1794.

Another factor in arresting the decline of the assignat had been a forced loan on the rich. The principle was first adopted in response to sansculotte pressure on 20 May 1793 but, despite the urgings of the *enragés*, nothing was done to implement it until the crisis of September. On the third of that month, however, it was decreed that all income over 6,000 *livres* for the unmarried and 10,000 *livres* for families should be taxed on a sliding scale which at the top end took everything. It looked punitive, but those subject to it were able to discharge their obligations in depreciated assignats, and millions therefore were taken out of circulation. In any case many local authorities were slow to identify those liable, although in the commercial centres of 'Federalism' terror against its now-vanquished paymasters produced substantial results. France's wealthy were certainly to look back on the forced loan as one of the most shocking expedients of the year of terror, a time they would remember as one of vindictive class legislation. Another example was the decrees passed in the spring of 1794 on the disposal of lands confiscated from enemies of the Revolution, and known as the Laws of Ventôse. On 26 February (8 Ventôse) Saint-Just moved on behalf of the Committee of Public Safety that the goods of 'persons recognized as enemies of the Revolution' should be 'sequestered'. On 3 March (13 Ventôse) he moved that watch committees should draw up lists of all those detained since 1 May 1789 with a view to their property being redistributed to approved 'indigent patriots'. Ten days later a further decree established 'popular commissions' to decide which of those listed should be declared enemies of the Revolution and thus suffer confiscation and redistribution of their goods. In practice little was done to implement these decrees, and what was done was chaotic. However much Saint-Just personally may have been committed to the principle they represented, most of his colleagues on the governing committees were distinctly lukewarm. They supported such populist measures only in order to outbid the Parisian radicals in a new political crisis which reached its climax in this same revolutionary month of Ventôse.

'Nobody', recalled one deputy later,[11] 'had dreamed of establishing a system of terror. It established itself by force of circumstances.' But that meant that nobody had control of it either, even among those with a vested interest in its continuance. And nobody, above all, seemed to have the power to end it, even when its purpose and achievements came to seem less and less self-evident. To criticize the Terror was to risk suspicion of sympathizing with its victims, and thereby become one of them. Yet many deputies, probably most, were deeply uneasy about terror as a basis for government from the start; and as soon as the emergency began to lift, with the first victories over the Austrians in October, the recovery of the centres of 'Federalism' in the weeks after that, and the defeat of the Vendéans, pressure began to mount for a less savage way of running the country.

Among those sympathetic to this viewpoint was Robespierre, very conscious that needless excesses would discredit the Revolution at home and make enemies abroad more intransigent. His attempts to save the queen and the Girondins, his denunciation of dechristianization, and his strong support for extending the powers of central government in the Law of 14 Frimaire were all evidence of his concern. And in this he had the vocal support of Danton, who called on 22 November for less bloodshed, and played a constructive role in the elaboration of the 14 Frimaire Law. When attacked in the Jacobin Club for advocating moderation, he was vigorously defended by Robespierre. Two days later the friend of both, the veteran revolutionary journalist Desmoulins, launched a new paper with Robespierre's blessing, the *Vieux Cordelier*. Its title proclaimed its approach, one critical of the new masters of the Cordeliers Club and leading advocates of continuing terror and dechristianization. By now Robespierre suspected that a number of Hébert's allies, if not the man himself, might be more or less willing agents of Pitt, recruited to the counter-revolutionary cause by the notorious royalist intriguer the Baron de Batz. Their persistent attacks on Danton and his associates ever since the summer fell into place when it was suggested to Robespierre in mid-November by Chabot, ex-monk, ex-representative on mission, and ex-member of the Committee of General Security (until voted off late in September under Hébert's pressure), that there existed a plot of breath-taking proportions to discredit the Revolution and set its supporters at each other's throats. While a clutch of corrupt deputies had sought to make illicit profits by manipulating the winding-up of the former Indies Company, they had worked to entangle others, this time good patriots like (as he naturally claimed) Chabot himself, so that Hébert and his friends could then denounce them.

It sounded less implausible to the suspicious mind of Robespierre than it does today. After all, Batz certainly existed, and his subversive activities were well known; and the allegations of shady dealing in Indies Company shares soon proved only too well founded. The Committee of General Security, suspecting that Chabot was only intent on saving his own corrupt skin, imprisoned him when he took his denunciation to them. Robespierre meanwhile continued to encourage Desmoulins in his attacks on terrorists and dechristianizers, and on 12 December stood by when an attempt was made to alter the membership of the Committee of Public Safety itself, seemingly designed to remove extremists like Billaud and Collot, and bring back Danton. Although it failed, the campaign went on. On 15 December the *Vieux Cordelier* compared conditions in France to the bloodiest times of imperial Rome, and made pointed allusions to the massacres at Lyons. On the twentieth Robespierre persuaded the Convention to establish a 'committee of justice' to investigate cases of wrongful arrest. By then, what Desmoulins and his friends considered some rightful arrests had been made: Ronsin, commander of the Paris Revolutionary Army, just back in the capital from Lyons, and Vincent, secretary general of the war ministry, who had been hinting at a new purge to silence the so-called 'Indulgents'. Leading the attack on this occasion (17 December) was Danton's friend the poet Fabre d'Eglantine.

The so-called 'Hébertists' were at first too stunned to fight back. Those still at liberty were reduced to babbling protestations of innocence. What put new heart into them was the sudden appearance of Collot d'Herbois in the capital on 21 December. Alarmed by news of the arrest of Ronsin, his close collaborator in the repression at Lyons, Collot rushed back to Paris determined to vindicate their methods before he too came under attack. He did so by proceeding straight to the Jacobin Club, where he delivered a rousing defence of those arrested. Urged on by Hébert, the club rallied to him, and demanded that the accusers substantiate their charges. The effect of Collot's intervention was to reinvigorate defenders of terror as an instrument of government and thereby to polarize politics in a way not seen since the purge of the Girondins. The polarization extended at first into the Committee of Public Safety itself, when Billaud and Collot were able, on 26 December, to have Robespierre's committee of justice abolished. It might have continued had it not been for the revelation, during the first week in January, that Fabre d'Eglantine had been deeply involved in the Indies Company scandal. Robespierre was devastated. Desmoulins by now (in *Vieux Cordelier*, no. 5) was denouncing Hébert for corruption, yet here was the indulgents' main spokesman in the Convention himself deeply tainted by speculation and fraud. A bitter denunciation of Fabre at the Jacobin Club on 8 January marked the end of Robespierre's flirtation with the Indulgents, and on 12 January Fabre was arrested. The only deputy to speak up for him was a personal friend, hitherto little involved in the factional strife of that winter: Danton.

Uneasy calm now descended after six bitter and noisy weeks. Desmoulins abandoned the *Vieux Cordelier*, but in any case repression in the provinces had now passed its peak, renegade representatives on mission were being brought to heel under the Law of 14 Frimaire, and Jullien was investigating their more questionable previous activities on behalf of Robespierre. Leading figures were now denouncing the faction fighting between Indulgents and Hébertists as the greatest problem faced by the Republic; and when, on 1 February, Vincent and Rosin were released by the Committee of General Security for lack of evidence to their alleged crimes, Danton applauded the move. But he also called for the release of Fabre as well, which cast doubt on his motives. Vincent and Ronsin were certainly unimpressed. They emerged from prison determined to revenge themselves on those who had put them there, and so the factional strife was rekindled. The committees did all they could to lower the temperature: Desmoulins claimed that he was prevented from bringing out further issues of the *Vieux Cordelier*. But their attempts to stifle dissension only turned the fury of the Hébertists against them as much as against the Indulgents, whom they were now accused of protecting. Urged on by returning provincial terrorists like Carrier and Javogues, who were anxious to deflect any punitive action from their own heads, they began to proclaim that a new insurrection was necessary to cleanse the Convention of what they called 'the faction'. From their base in the Cordeliers Club they began to try to stir up the sansculottes, and by the end of February addresses were trickling in from sympathetic sectional societies denouncing 'disloyal' deputies. On 4 March the club resolved to launch a new popular journal, taking Marat's old title *L'Ami du peuple*; and meanwhile it decreed that the Declaration of Rights in its meeting hall should be draped in black until the 'faction' was destroyed. Hébert denounced Desmoulins as an enemy agent, accused him of misleading Robespierre himself, and joined in the cry for an insurrection, a 'new 31 May'. On 6 March section Marat, where the Cordeliers were located, declared itself in a state of uprising (*debout*) 'until the people's murderers are exterminated', and marched to the Hôtel de Ville to demand action. No other section followed its lead, and Chaumette accordingly received the demonstrators guardedly: but nobody mistook the echoes of the previous September.

The committees, whose mandate was due for renewal the next week, were now thoroughly alarmed. Paris was restive under a malfunctioning maximum, and every market day saw scuffles around stalls selling basic commodities, while black marketeers flourished. 'A fine liberty we have', an unemployed labourer was arrested for yelling at a grocer on 19 March.[12] 'It's all for the rich. The only war they're fighting is against the poor.' In such conditions calls for insurrection might be all too readily answered. The committees began to close ranks. Even Collot d'Herbois, having saved his own position, now began urging the Jacobins to rally to the established order and invite the Cordeliers to join them. In one of those curious, aberrant waves of fraternal emotion which sometimes carried away revolutionary assemblies even at the tensest times, they agreed, and sent the black veil from the Declaration as a token of their goodwill. But Vincent and Ronsin denounced the gesture, and kept on calling for purges. Hébert, somewhat more equivocally, supported them. The Committee of Public Safety waited until its renewal was safely past, on 11 March; then, stiffened by the return of Robespierre after a month's illness, it struck. On 13 March Saint-Just on its behalf denounced a far-reaching plot by 'factions of foreign inspiration' to 'destroy representative government by corruption, and to starve Paris'. Thousands of copies of his speech were promptly distributed in the capital. In contained much grandiloquent rhetoric in which factions were denounced as divisive of the national will, and insurrection condemned as resistance to the people themselves, who now held power. It contained no specific charges against anybody. But on the strength of it Hébert, Vincent, Ronsin, and a number of their followers or presumed sympathizers, twenty in all, were arrested on the fourteenth and during the days following and sent before the Revolutionary Tribunal. Fouquier-Tinville, the public prosecutor, was ordered by the Committee of Public Safety to secure a conviction at all costs in what would be a blatantly political trial. Accordingly, they were accused of fomenting insurrection, attempting to create an artificial famine by sabotaging food supplies, and plotting a prison massacre. The trial took place on 21–4 March, its result a foregone conclusion. Among those who went to the scaffold with Père Duchesne on the afternoon of the twenty-fourth were Vincent, Ronsin, and the leader of section Marat, Momoro. To substantiate the charge of a foreign plot, a clutch of colourful aliens perished with them too, including Clootz, who bade farewell to his beloved human race in front of the biggest crowd ever to surround the guillotine.

It was a largely hostile crowd, too. In the end the sansculottes abandoned those who claimed to be their champions and most faithful spokesmen. Police reports make it clear that ordinary people in Paris were only too ready to believe the allegations cobbled together by Fouquier-Tinville. The Committee of Public Safety must have been relieved. The charge of trying to create famine, the simultaneous introduction of the Laws of Ventôse, and the wide distribution of Saint-Just's speech of 13 March all showed how anxious it was to deprive the accused of popular support. So did a special grant made by the Subsistence Commission to steady the price of bread in the capital. But they need not have worried. The failure of the other 47 sections to follow the lead of Momoro's section Marat on 6 March showed that those who had called so emotionally for insurrection two days before had taken no trouble to organize forces outside their own neighbourhood, any more than they had during their opportunistic triumph the previous September. And even if they had done so, it is by no means certain that their call would have evoked a response. After almost two years of revolutionary vigilance and tension, the sansculottes were showing signs of nervous exhaustion. Much of their programme had now been achieved—the law against hoarding, the *levée en masse*, the general maximum, a comprehensive policy on suspects, and a government prepared to enforce all these policies with terror. Patriots who had campaigned for all these things over the previous summer thought a government prepared to enforce them deserved support against factions of whatever sort. Many former 'blood-drinkers' were now in effect government employees in any case, as members of watch committees interning suspects and issuing *civisme* certificates, answerable ultimately to the Convention's committees under the Law of 14 Frimaire; or simply as paid attenders at sectional meetings under Danton's double-edged resolution of 4 September 1793. Purists might scoff at such '40-*sou* patriots', who had given up the vital right to permanent sessions for a pittance; in many sections unofficial alternative assemblies, 'sectional societies', sprang up over the autumn. But the most energetic, practical, and experienced sansculottes had been creamed off into the state apparatus, and from that perspective were prepared to see Hébert and his friends as suspicious and ambitious trouble-makers, stabbing in the back a government which was winning the war both at home and abroad.

Yet it proved the end of the sansculottes as a political force, and the end of the Paris commune as their independent mouthpiece. Chaumette, though not arrested with Hébert and the others, was picked up four days after their execution; and he and a group of presumed sympathizers, including ex-bishop Gobel, went to the guillotine in their turn on 13 April. The presumption of sympathy came from the fact that it had taken the commune almost a week to congratulate the Convention on thwarting the alleged Hébertist plot. On this pretext too the Convention decreed a general purge of the commune's personnel which left it, by the end of April, the docile tool of the Committee of Public Safety. The same charge of guilt through silence condemned the stunned Revolutionary Army, which Ronsin was supposed to have been preparing to lend force to the alleged insurrection. On 27 March it was dissolved, to the general relief of the peasants, priests, and comfortably-off citizens it had so spectacularly terrorized. The end of the Terror, foisted on the country by the bloodthirsty populace of Paris, seemed to be at hand. Few foresaw how long it had to run; or that, firmly in the hands of the government rather than the sansculottes, it was destined to get worse before it got better.

# Thermidor, 1794—1795

IT was only natural, as the architects and original advocates of terror were themselves destroyed by it, or reduced to silence or impotence, that Frenchmen should begin to wonder what terror was for, and where the Revolution was going. 'I don't know', a police spy heard someone say late in March 1794,[1] 'what it's all coming to; people have railed against the revolutionary committees, and now we have come to think them suspect; they have railed against the revolutionary army, and now it's been dissolved; there seems to be something against everything that carries the name revolutionary.' But there was one powerful and eloquent voice who certainly did not agree: Robespierre. Throughout the autumn and early winter he too had agonized about the direction and meaning of the Revolution, as his flirtation with the Indulgents and their policies showed. But by February his vision was beginning to clear, and on the fifth of that month he came to the Convention to deliver a profession of revolutionary faith. 'What', he asked,[2] 'is the end towards which we are striving? The peaceful enjoyment of liberty and equality; the reign of that eternal justice whose laws are engraved, not on marble and on stone, but in the heart of all men . . . What sort of government can realise these prodigies? Only democratic or republican government: these two words are synonyms.' But democracy was not, said Robespierre, implicitly rejecting the claims of the sansculottes to interfere in government, the sovereign people in constant action.

Democracy is a state where the sovereign people, guided by laws which are its own work, does by itself all that it can do well, and by delegates all that it cannot do for itself. So it is in the principles of democratic government that you must look for the rules of your political conduct . . . What then is the fundamental principle of democratic or popular government, that is to say the essential underpinning which sustains it and makes it work? It is virtue . . . which is nothing other than the love of the land of your birth and its laws . . . this sublime sentiment supposes a preference for the public interests above all particular interests . . . The first rule of your political conduct must be to relate all you do to maintaining equality and developing virtue . . . In the system of the French Revolution, what is immoral is impolitic, and what corrupts is counter-revolutionary. Weakness, vices and prejudices are the high-road to monarchy.

Coming from anyone else, these ideas would be one more example of the vapid rhetoric which the French Revolution produced so readily. Robespierre, however, was a figure of authority and power, and he took his own ideas extremely seriously. Throughout the spring and early summer of 1794 he became increasingly obsessed with cleansing the Republic of the corrupt and all who fell short of his exacting standard of virtue.

The first casualty of his obsession was Fabre d'Eglantine, whom he denounced in bitter terms at the Jacobins on 8 January. But in Robespierre's eyes Fabre's greed, duplicity, and corruption threw suspicion on his known associates, including leading Indulgents like Desmoulins; and loud-mouthed trimmers like Danton, whose persistent defence of Fabre suggested that he put his friends before patriotic principles. Shortly after outlining his ideal republic of virtue, Robespierre was taken ill and did not reappear in public for almost a month. During this time Hébertist machinations dominated the political agenda; and Amar, the member of the Committee of General Security deputed to report on the Indies Company scandal so that the accused could be brought to trial, proved curiously dilatory in reporting his conclusions. It is possible that he was even involved himself. Under mounting pressure from his colleagues, eventually he did report on 16 March, indicting Fabre, Chabot, and a number of others. In the Convention he was openly denounced by Robespierre and Billaud-Varenne for over-concentrating on financial details to the exclusion of the alleged plot's political ramifications. Widening his scope somewhat, Amar reported again on 19 March, and this time Fabre and his associates were sent for trial. As soon as the Hébertists were dispatched, the timing and preparation of this trial became the central preoccupation of the governing committees.

It appears that both were split. Some, like Billaud-Varenne, seem to have thought that the Indulgents, having goaded the Hébertists into destroying themselves, now deserved to perish in their turn, whether involved in the Indies Company scandal or not. Vadier, of the Committee of General Security, was of the same opinion. The case offered a convenient pretext, since Fabre before his arrest had been a leading opponent of continuing terror. This would eliminate people like Desmoulins, and Danton, too, although he had played little role in the Indulgents' campaign. His notorious opportunism made him too dangerous to leave at liberty while his friends stood trial. Other members thought widening a trial for corruption into a political showpiece was far too dangerous. The balance was held by Robespierre, and the thought of trying Danton put even his increasingly rigid political principles to the test. The first proposal to arrest Danton and the Indulgents appears to have come while the Hébertists were on trial, but Robespierre wavered for another week. It was not until 30 March, after two mysterious meetings with Danton, that Robespierre seems to have decided to abandon him. But when he did, he did so totally. No sooner was the arrest warrant issued that day than he began to assemble materials for Danton's indictment. His notes form the basis of Saint-Just's speech of the thirty-first in the Convention when, in the name of both committees, he announced the arrests of 'the last partisans of royalism, who, for five years, have served factions, and have only followed liberty as a tiger follows its prey'.[3] He called for them to be put on trial. The motion, perhaps because Saint-Just emphasized that this was likely to be a final cleansing of the body politic, passed virtually unopposed.

The vagueness of Saint-Just's denunciation was echoed in the charges made between 2 and 5 April when the East Indies conspirators, Desmoulins, Danton, and others—sixteen in all, including nine deputies— came on trial. Danton himself was not even accused of corruption, which would have been very easy. The charges against him were all generalities based on his political record since 1789. Through sheer eloquence, he was soon dominating the courtroom, to Fouquier-Tinville's alarm. Only when the Convention, acting on a deliberately misleading report that the prisoners were in revolt against the Revolutionary Tribunal, decreed that the trial should continue in their absence, could a verdict of guilty be secured. Their 'revolt' had merely been a noisy demand that witnesses be called—but now they were deemed superfluous. On 5 April Danton, Desmoulins, Fabre, Chabot, and the others went to the guillotine.

Few episodes in the Revolution are harder to interpret than the fall of Danton and Desmoulins, for reliable evidence about the motivation of those involved is almost completely lacking. At least Hébert and his associates had been openly calling for an insurrection. Desmoulins had merely been advocating (and by now he had stopped) a less bloody regime; and Danton had not been calling with any vehemence or consistency for anything. It seems that they were struck down more for what they might do than for what they had done. Their execution, in fact, marked the beginning of a new phase in the Terror, when people would die for their potential as much as for specific crimes, and sometimes merely for their failure to match some ideal moral standard. 'The word virtue made Danton laugh,' Robespierre grimly noted.[4] 'How could a man, to whom all idea of morality was foreign, be the defender of liberty?' Danton's death marked the inauguration of a Republic of Virtue.

It was characterized by continued concentration of power at the centre. On 1 April the council of ministers was at last abolished. Departments of state were all put into commission, each one supervised by a member of the governing committees. Two weeks later (16 April) it was decreed that all conspiracy cases should henceforth be tried only by the Revolutionary Tribunal in Paris, and over the ensuing weeks most of the various special courts which had enforced the Terror in the provinces were closed down. The effect was to cram the prisons of the capital with suspects, and to cope with them the procedure of the tribunal was simplified and speeded up. By the Law of 22 Prairial (10 June) the number of judges and jurors was increased, witnesses were virtually dispensed with, and accused persons were deprived of defending counsel. The purpose of the tribunal was redefined as the punishment of enemies of the people, and the only penalty it was allowed to impose was death. But enemies of the people were so widely defined that, as with the Law of Suspects, almost anybody was vulnerable to the charge. The effect on the character of the Terror was immediate. Executions, which had declined sharply between January and March, and risen again in April with a new burst of repression in the Vendée, fell back somewhat in May; but from early June began to climb markedly once more. Most of the victims of the renewed rise perished in Paris. Of the 2,639 people guillotined in the place de la Révolution between March 1793 and August 1794, over half, 1,515, died during June and July 1794. A far higher proportion of them, too, were from the upper ranks of society than in the Terror as a whole: 38 per cent of its noble victims and 26 per cent of its clerical ones were dispatched during this short phase, and almost half of those from the richer bourgeoisie. Never was the Terror closer to being an instrument of social discrimination rather than one punishing specific counter-revolutionary acts than in these months; and although most of those who died were doubtless as guilty as many another of subversive or traitorous activity, the abrupt change in the Terror's pattern suggests that some at least of those it now struck down died as much for what they were (or had been before 1789) as for what they had done.

The dead Hébertists might have approved of such a policy: but little else the governing committees did once they were gone would have pleased them. After the fall of Chaumette, for example, the Paris commune was placed under the direct authority of the Committee of Public Safety, and its membership remodelled to produce a majority that could be relied upon to take its orders from above rather than below. At once it turned its attention to the maximum—but to the aspect which the Hébertists had deliberately neglected: wage control. It took some months to gather the material and draw up the tables they had always refused to contemplate, but wage-earners meanwhile were given plenty of warning of what was coming. In April the Le Chapelier Law was invoked to punish the ringleaders of tobacco workers who had petitioned for a wage rise. Other groups were threatened with conscription as war-workers, subject to military discipline, if they pressed such demands; but the very occurrence of these incidents showed that inflationary pressures were far from contained. Yet the new rates, when they were finally published on 23 July, imposed substantial cuts in the earnings of most workers. During the early 1790s many had seen their wages double or treble as the value of the assignat plummeted, and the 50 per cent above 1790 levels permitted under the maximum fell far short of what they were now making. Nor did they have any effective vehicles of protest by then. The sections had been absorbed into the governmental machine, and throughout April and May the commune had harried the popular societies into oblivion. By the beginning of June most had announced their own dissolution.

Even dechristianization was now being reversed. There seems to have been general agreement in the governing committees that it had been a disaster, and on 7 April Couthon announced that new proposals would shortly be brought forward for channelling the spiritual leanings of the nation in more patriotic directions. The result was the cult of the Supreme Being, launched by a speech from Robespierre to the Convention on 7 May. Designed as the first of a series of republican festivals to be held on each official rest-day (*décadi*), it would proclaim that the French people recognized the existence of a Supreme Being and the immortality of the soul. These principles, declared Robespierre to applause, were a continual reminder of justice, and were therefore social and republican. While denouncing priestcraft, he recurred to his heartfelt theme that the purpose of the Republic was to promote virtue, he deplored the excesses (though not in so many words) of dechristianization, and sang the praises of Rousseau, himself the architect of a civic religion. On 20 Prairial (8 June), he moved, the nation should celebrate the Supreme Being. Thus every locality was given a month to make its preparations. The fact that 8 June was also Whit Sunday may or may not have been a coincidence; if not, it could have been conceived either as a challenge or as an olive branch to Christianity. In the event little direction was given to the localities on how to organize the festival. Some adapted the props of all-too-recent festivals of reason, merely painting out old slogans with new ones. Others used the opportunity to allow mass to be said publicly for the first time in months. But in Paris the organization of the occasion was entrusted to the experienced hands of the painter David, himself a member of the Committee of General Security. He built an artificial mountain in the Champ de Mars, surmounted by a tree of liberty, and thither a mass procession made its way from the Tuileries. At its head marched the members of the Convention, led by their president, who happened that week to be Robespierre. He used the opportunity to deliver two more eulogies of virtue and republican religion, pointedly ignoring, though not failing to notice, the smirks of some of his fellow deputies at the posturings of this pseudo-Pope. Others found it no laughing matter. 'Look at the bugger,' muttered Thuriot, an old associate of Danton.[5] 'It's not enough for him to be master, he has to be God.'

It was a feeling that increasing numbers of deputies, and members of the governing committees too, were coming to share. Ever since the autumn of 1792 Robespierre had been subject to periodic charges of aspiring to personal dictatorship, but now it seemed more credible than ever. He seemed to be speaking for the Committee of Public Safety more and more, and was certainly better known in the country at large than any of his colleagues. At Orléans, as well as in Paris, the Festival of the Supreme Being took place to cries of *Vive Robespierre*. Two weeks beforehand he had been pursued by two would-be assassins. One of them eventually attacked Collot d'Herbois, but the other got as far as the door of the man she called a tyrant. Both were executed, along with 52 others suspected of involvement in the machinations of Batz, dressed in red, the colour of parricide. The law under which they died was that of 22 Prairial, whose provisions Robespierre largely drafted and, with Couthon, sprang upon an unsuspecting Committee of Public Safety with no prior consultation. Yet the fact that they chose to do it in this way reflected uncertainty about this support. Ever since April, indeed, the Committee had been the scene of increasingly heated quarrels setting Robespierre, Saint-Just, and to a lesser extent Couthon against the rest. At one point they threatened Carnot, who riposted that they were 'ridiculous dictators'. Yet when on 16 April a special 'Bureau of General Police' was established within the Committee to supervise the conduct of public officials, the three were appointed to it— perhaps in the hope of sidelining them. They threw themselves into their new task with characteristic zeal, however, and this served to alarm the Committee of General Security, which regarded the Bureau as trespassing on its own territory, already seriously infringed since the show trials of the spring. All this multiplied Robespierre's enemies, and the Law of 22 Prairial added even more. Many deputies in the Convention, not to mention members of the two committees, were alarmed by its sweeping terms. They were not reassured when in the debate on the law, Robespierre denounced those who sought to sow division. Remembering how the Dantonists had been arrested without a prior decree from the Convention, they were particularly frightened by a clause overriding all conflicting legislation: they were afraid it might destroy their normal immunity from arrest. Accordingly, on 23 Prairial, a number of those who had scoffed at Robespierre's prominence at the Festival of the Supreme Being moved a specific guarantee of deputies' immunity under the new law. It was carried. From that moment onwards, the anti-Robespierre forces began to coalesce.

He was well aware of what was happening, although he was at a loss to understand it. 'Why come to me?', he asked one of the petitioners who were always at his door these days.[6] 'Why not apply to the Comité? Every one applies to me, as if I had omnipotent power.' He concluded, like the good disciple of Rousseau he was, that the purity and rectitude of his intentions were being deliberately vilified and obstructed by a corrupt faction of unpatriotic intriguers. Among them were deputies recalled from provincial missions on account of their excesses—men like Fouché and Tallien—and Dantonists like Thuriot and the ex-butcher Legendre. But when the Committee of Public Safety refused, on 12 June, to be browbeaten into giving him the 'nine heads' he believed to be at the heart of the conspiracy against him, he ceased to attend their meetings, confining his public appearances increasingly to the one forum where he knew he could always command support, the Jacobin Club. But the Jacobins were not the power they had been. To take a stand there and not in the Convention was to provoke suspicions of insurrectionary intentions. Suspicion, in fact, suffused the whole of public life during these terrible weeks when there were executions by twenties and thirties almost daily. As many as sixty deputies, it was said, were afraid to sleep in their own beds at night. And yet it was becoming increasingly clear that terror was no longer necessary in order to win the day. The British had failed on 1 June to prevent a major grain convey from arriving from America, and the sinking of the ship of the line *Vengeur* was turned, in the report made on it to the Convention by Barère, into an epic of republican heroism and defiance. Even more important, on 26 June came the great victory of Fleurus, which opened the way for a renewed invasion of Belgium and removed the last threat from the Austrians. After that everybody was longing to breathe more easily; yet with the governing committees torn apart by mutual suspicions, and dark hints and threats being thrown out by all sides, nobody knew how to end the slaughter, except by annihilating their opponents before they were themselves destroyed.

In mid-July one last attempt was made to restore unity, if not exactly harmony. Barère, always the trimmer, arranged a joint meeting of the governing committees on the twenty-second at which it was agreed to speed up the implementation of the Laws of Ventôse. The Convention and the Jacobin Club were assured afterwards that, notwithstanding previous appearances to the contrary, France still had a united government. But at another joint meeting the next day, Robespierre reappeared for the first time in almost a month and made bitter personal attacks on Billaud, Collot, Amar, and Vadier. He did endorse the new joint policies, but after his earlier outburst any truce could scarcely be expected to last. Deputies outside the committees were, however, terrified that the newly trumpeted unity might be real, and lead to a purge of those on Robespierre's proscription list. Fouché and Tallien now launched themselves into feverish lobbying among the uncommitted deputies of what had once been known, in contradistinction to the Mountain, as the Plain, but whose inertia as the rhythm of the Terror increased again had won them the less flattering description of the 'Marsh'. But Robespierre, too, thought he could swing the Convention, and on 26 July he reappeared there to deliver a long, rambling speech, naming few names but full of threats against seemingly everybody. After extolling his own probity and love of virtue in now characteristic fashion, he declared that there existed a 'conspiracy against public liberty' involving unspecified numbers of deputies, the Committee of General Security, and even some members of the Committee of Public Safety. These 'traitors' must be punished, their 'factions' crushed. Both committees must be purged, for 'defenders of liberty will always be proscribed so long as power lies with a horde of knaves'.

It was a declaration of war; and, realizing now that their lives might depend on a rapid counter-attack, Robespierre's enemies took up the challenge. First there was a noisy debate over whether his speech should be printed, and if so in what quantity. Accusations of dictatorship were now renewed by those whom he had attacked, amid clear signs of sympathy from the deputies as a whole. That night Robespierre read his speech again to the Jacobins, who tumultuously refused to allow Billaud and Collot to reply to it. On Couthon's motion they voted to expel all deputies who had been against printing the speech, and there was vague talk of a new purge of the Convention. Billaud and Collot, both shaking with fury, went straight to the committees, and they seem to have spent most of the night preparing for the inevitable confrontation next morning. Among deputies outside the committees, Tallien was doing the same, aware that Collot, currently president of the Convention, could choose who spoke and when. The strength of feeling became clear on the morning of 27 July—9 Thermidor—when Saint-Just, who had been little involved in the growing factionalism of the preceding weeks, unexpectedly came out for Robespierre. Billaud denounced him in the name of the Committee of Public

Safety, and Tallien from the floor. They were cheered; but when Robespierre demanded the right to speak, he was drowned out by cries of *Down with the tyrant!* Collot consistently refused him the floor, while attack after attack whipped the deputies into a frenzy. Eventually his arrest was proposed. His brother Augustin demanded to be arrested with him, and the Convention obliged. Others proposed the arrest of Couthon, who had also stood by him, and Saint-Just. All were decreed. So was that of Hanriot, commander of the Paris National Guard.

It was a parliamentary rout. Robespierre, shut away in his rue Saint-Honoré lodgings for most of the preceding month, had fatally overestimated his support among the deputies, while in his speech of 27 July he had attacked so many of them directly or indirectly that none could feel entirely safe. But repudiation by the Convention was not quite the end of Robespierre. The evening of the twenty-sixth had shown that he still commanded support from the Jacobin Club and its public galleries; and the commune, remodelled after the fall of the Hébertists, was largely packed by his nominees. There was still, therefore, a chance that Paris, where his popular reputation had been consistently high since the spring of 1791, would rally to him. And initially the commune did not fail him. On the afternoon of the twenty-eighth it ordered all gaolers in the capital to refuse to accept the prisoners, and Hanriot was allowed to escape. While he tried to marshal his National Guards for an insurrection, the arrested deputies were taken into the commune's protection at the Hôtel de Ville. But only 17 out of 48 sectional National Guard companies responded to Hanriot's call and assembled on the place de Grève. Some of the others wavered, but when the Convention took decisive action they quickly fell into line. On the proposal of Barère, the prisoners, presumed to have escaped, were outlawed. Under a provision ironically first moved by Saint-Just, that meant they could be executed without trial. And forces loyal to the Convention were given a commander in Barras, who had distinguished himself at the siege of Toulon. Faced by such determination, and its inability to arouse most of the sections from hostility or indifference, the commune wavered. Over the evening, its assembled forces drifted away home. So that when Barras and his troops arrived at the Hôtel de Ville at two in the morning on 29 July, it was undefended. Robespierre had tried to shoot himself, but had only broken his jaw; but it was in this maimed state that he went to the guillotine the next afternoon.

His brother, Couthon, Saint-Just, and eighty other 'Robespierrists' from the commune followed him over the next 24 hours. 'About sixty persons', noted the Irish political exile Hamilton Rowan,[7] who watched the spectacle, 'were guillotined in less than one hour and a half, in the Place de la Revolution; and though I was standing above a hundred paces from the place of execution, the blood of the victims streamed beneath my feet. What surprised me was, as each head fell into the basket, the cry of the people was no other than a repetition of "*A bas le Maximum!*" ' The new tariff for wages published earlier that week was certainly not the only reason why the sections did not respond to the commune's insurrectionary call. The crisis had arisen too suddenly, and there had been no prior planning. And, told by the Convention that Robespierre had been aiming at tyranny and dictatorship, a populace that had meekly accepted what it had been told about the machinations of the Hébertists and Dantonists was unlikely to stir to save yet another idol shown to have feet of clay. Even so, the imposition of the wage maximum by the Robespierrist commune only a few days before the crisis broke alienated ordinary Parisians at a crucial moment, and their notorious taste for scapegoats was satisfied by the destruction of Robespierre and his municipal henchmen. As to Robespierre himself, he never was a dictator, and there is no reliable evidence to suggest that it was his aim. But he was suspicious by nature, and over the spring the stresses of government drove him to the verge of paranoia. Surrounded by rumours of plots, not to mention assassination attempts, yet completely sure of his own rectitude, he took contradiction for bad faith and independence for opportunism. In the end he seems to have concluded that hardly anybody in public life could be relied on, and by saying so openly he ensured that they could not. And by implying that those of whom he disapproved or with whom he disagreed deserved execution, he forced them into destroying him before he destroyed them. Men called him a dictator because they feared moral inflexibility in one who had power. After they had destroyed him they used the charge to justify what they had done. It also enabled them to blame him for acts they themselves had helped to commit, but which became increasingly a subject for shame, recrimination, and revenge during the months of retreat from terror and ruthless government which now began.

The ninth of Thermidor marked not so much the overthrow of one man or group of men as the rejection of a form of government. Those who thought otherwise were swiftly disillusioned. When Barère, who tried on 29 July to dismiss the whole episode as 'a disturbance which leaves the government unaffected', proposed nominees to replace the three executed members of the Committee of Public Safety, his motion was defeated. Instead the Convention accepted Tallien's proposal that a quarter of the Committee should retire every month, and not be eligible for immediate re-election. It did for the moment reject a motion to abolish the Revolutionary Tribunal, but that anybody should so much as dare to propose it showed how totally the atmosphere had changed. Soon all the Convention's committees were subjected to the same renewal rule, and among the first new members of that of Public Safety was Tallien himself. Former friends of Danton joined him there, and on the Committee of General Security. On 1 August the remodelled committees carried the repeal of the Law of 22 Prairial, and on the tenth they purged the membership of the Revolutionary Tribunal, arresting Fouquier-Tinville. As a result the Terror collapsed. Only 6 people were guillotined in Paris in August, and only 40 more over the rest of the year. Counter-revolutionary intent now had to be proved to secure a conviction. The difficulties of that rendered superfluous much of the work and powers of the watch committees, which on 24 August were reduced from 48 to 12 in Paris, and one per district elsewhere. In all this the initiative increasingly came from the Convention floor, and on 11 August the Committee of Public Safety was deprived, against its own advice tendered by Barère, of its overall superintending role in government. All its duties except war and foreign relations were redistributed to other committees. Thus, within a month of Robespierre's fall, the central institutions of Terror and Revolutionary Government had been dismantled by a Convention increasingly certain that they were no longer necessary.

There was an outburst of relief throughout the country. The second anniversary of the revolution of 10 August was celebrated with now uncharacteristic abandon. But the most spectacular evidence of changed times, apart from the drop in executions, was the release of suspects from prison. From the start it was generally expected, and excited crowds gathered daily outside prison gates and the doors of the Committee of General Security. In Paris it began early in August, and by the end of the month 3,500 prisoners had been set free. They emerged from custody bitter and resentful against those who had put them there—for the most part fellow citizens on the watch committees, now stigmatized as terrorists. They wanted revenge. When on 31 August a gunpowder factory at Grenelle, in the south-western suburbs, blew up with around 400 casualties, nervous terrorists saw it as the first act of vengeance. It seems in fact to have been an accident. What was not accidental was the emergence around the same time of squads of anti-sansculotte vigilantes, the so-called 'Gilded Youth'. Some were released prisoners themselves; some were draft-dodgers; many were clerks and petty bureaucrats, and all were looking for trouble. Affecting expensive clothes and hairstyles of a sort few would have dared to wear only a few weeks earlier, they came to number two or three thousand. They made it their business to harass known terrorists, disrupt their meetings, and break up public occasions of which they did not approve. One of the leading plotters against Robespierre, the ex-representative on mission at Toulon, Fréron, gave them open encouragement in his newspaper, *L'Orateur du peuple*, which began to appear early in September, and soon was co-ordinating the marauding of this private street army. But his was far from the only voice now denouncing the excesses of the Terror and those who had perpetrated them. A whole range of right-wing papers mushroomed in Paris throughout August and September, leading to calls in the Convention and the Jacobin Club for a curb on their incitements. The 'Thermidorians', as Tallien, Fréron, and the others who had triumphed in that revolutionary month were now coming to be known, responded with a loud defence of press freedom. Those wishing to limit it were, they said (in the title of a pamphlet published late in August), *Robespierre's Tail*, blood-drinkers who wanted a return of government by terror. On 29 August an open attack was launched in the Convention on leading terrorists in the committees who had only turned against Robespierre at the last moment: the impeachment of Barère, Billaud, Collot, Vadier, Amar, and David was proposed. Once again this was going too far, too fast, for the Convention. It refused to indict them and, to demonstrate its continuing commitment to radicalism, it ordered the remains of Mirabeau to be removed from the Pantheon, and those of Marat to replace them. Rousseau's body was also ordered to be exhumed and deposited there. Encouraged by these signs, the Jacobin Club took the offensive. On 4 September it expelled Tallien and Fréron. A few days later Tallien was attacked in the street.

All this, the Thermidorians claimed, was the beginning of a return to terror. The Grenelle explosion was Jacobin work! Fréron now turned his gangs against the club, and for the first time in France (though not of course abroad) the term 'Jacobin' became one of general opprobrium, associated indelibly with terror and the 'dictator' who had so long dominated the club's platform. Sectional assemblies which supported the Jacobin line were mobbed by well-dressed rowdies who roughed up their leaders. And at this point, if any reminder was needed of what terror had been like, a group of alleged Federalists from Nantes came before the Revolutionary Tribunal and were acquitted. During their examination lurid details of the drownings at Nantes under Carrier emerged, enough to indict the members of the Nantes revolutionary committee who had been his collaborators and induce the Convention to establish an investigation of Carrier himself—who, as a deputy, remained immune from arrest unless on the Convention's explicit decree. Such developments were a godsend to the Thermidorians, who now stepped up their anti-Jacobin pressure. Early in October Tallien founded a paper of his own, *L'Ami du citoyen*, while in the

Convention Legendre once more moved the impeachment of Barère, Billaud, and Collot. Again they were saved, this time by colleagues on the former Committee of Public Safety whom nobody yet wished to attack, including Carnot, who testified that all members had endorsed the reign of terror. But the pressure was working for all that. On 16 October it was decreed that all clubs and societies should publish lists of their members, and all correspondence between them was forbidden. Everybody knew that the measure was intended to destroy the national network of affiliates which gave the Jacobin Club such authority, and lists of members identified whom to attack. When early in November Billaud uttered threats against the club's enemies from the rostrum where he and Robespierre had so often dictated national policy, a crowd of Muscadins marched from their usual meeting place at the Palais Égalité (formerly Royal) and broke every window of the building with showers of stones. Two day later (12 November) they returned in their hundreds, stormed the hall, and beat up both men and women they found inside. The Convention, which had just decreed Carrier's arrest, was in no mood to sympathize. Instead of punishing the attackers, it ordered the closure of the Jacobin Club as an incitement to public disorder, and a potential rival to itself. But, in effect, street violence had triumphed. Within days, noted a police spy, it was 'enough simply to have the look of a Jacobin to be called after, insulted and even beaten up'.[8]

In the provinces reaction to the fall of Revolutionary Government was slower. Not all special courts disappeared when revolutionary justice was centralized in Paris. Some of the most notorious were set up after that, such as the Popular Commission at Orange, whose rules were the model for the Law of 22 Prairial, and which accounted for 332 victims between June and August. It and several others, notably in the west, continued to function for five or six weeks after 9 Thermidor and continued to hand down death sentences. But soon new representatives on mission were sent out to the departments to supervise the dismantling of the Terror, and with the decree of 24 August reducing the watch committees to one per district, thousands of provincial terrorists were thrust from public office. Soon afterwards those they had imprisoned began to be released. Many of them, or their friends or relatives, now took power in remodelled popular societies and municipal councils, and at once began to imprison their former persecutors. By the first week in September, for instance, the members of the Orange Commission were behind bars. And when it became clear, during the autumn, that the tide in Paris had set against the former terrorists, provincials were quick enough to take the hint. Suddenly, noted a British prisoner aboard the warship *Marat* at Brest, early in December, the sailors had stopped shouting *Vive la Montagne!* and *Vivent les Jacobins!* That was now forbidden, a cabin-boy told him. Now they were to shout *The Mountain to the devil!* and *Down with the Jacobins!* But the ultimate symbol of reaction, for both capital and departments, was not so much the closure of the Jacobins as the fate of that supreme provincial terrorist, Carrier. On 23 November he was sent to the Revolutionary Tribunal, protesting to the last that he had only been obeying the Convention's own orders at Nantes, and that the whole body was guilty 'down to the president's bell'. It availed him nothing. He was condemned and, on 16 December, guillotined. His defence was perhaps fair enough, and he was certainly not responsible for all the atrocities attributed to him. But in sacrificing him the Convention set an ominous example. A week before he died the 71 Girondin sympathizers saved by Robespierre from the guillotine in October 1793 were reinstated as full members of the Convention. The political turnabout was now complete; but the return of the Girondins and the elimination of the most notorious of terrorists were not harbingers of a return to restraint and consensus. So far from reconciliation, 1795 was to be a year of revenge.

None of these developments appear to have been unpopular. Police reports suggest a general approval in Paris for the closure of the Jacobins and the execution of Carrier. The main source of discontent in the capital during the second half of 1794 was economic. On 7 September, as the brief Jacobin revival was beginning, the Convention extended the Law of the Maximum for another year, signalling its intention of keeping the economy under control. But during the crisis of the summer the fall in the value of the assignat had once more accelerated: between August and December it fell from 34 to 20 per cent. Accordingly, although on 9 August the post-Robespierrist commune abandoned the draconian wage controls that had turned Paris against the 'tyrant', fixing far more generous rates, there was agitation for higher wages throughout the autumn. Government munitions workshops led the way; but, rather than yield to their demands, in January the Convention simply closed them down. Even more serious was the scarcity of basic commodities, which ensured that when available they sold at prices far higher than those authorized under the maximum. 'Everything', noted a police report in October,[9] 'is selling in the markets above the maximum'; adding, more surprisingly, that 'the people are saying that this law is unenforceable, and that unlimited freedom of trade is the only remedy for its ills'. The deputies of the Convention, of course, had always believed this. They had only accepted the maximum under popular pressure, and their recognition that it had worked in the year since its imposition was never more than grudging. When they began to hear that, even among the populace, support for it was waning, they once more allowed their convictions to guide them. Price controls, they thought, had worsened the very scarcity and hoarding they had been intended to curtail. Only a free market would restore abundance, not to mention reanimating foreign trade, which had languished under a controlled economy. A report on the whole issue was commissioned, and early in December the result was a recommendation that the maximum should be abolished. On 24 December the recommendation was accepted.

That night there was a savage frost. It marked the onset of a winter colder even than 1788; in fact, the worst of the whole century. And the conditions which permitted the Republic's armies to swarm across the frozen Rhine into Holland brought acute hardship to its citizens remaining at home. Rivers froze and supplies of coal and firewood, already scarce over the autumn, were immobilized. The whole country was affected. In the south olive-trees just recovering after the disaster of 1788 were blighted again, and even the Rhône was full of ice. The harvest of 1794 had been indifferent, and the armies had had first claims on its product. Grain had been bought abroad, as far afield as the Baltic and North Africa, but on arrival it could neither be transported nor milled because of the ice, and the floods which followed when it thawed. Some cities, such as Lyons and Paris itself, supplemented grain supplies with rice, but there was often not enough fuel to cook it. Consequently by the spring bread was being rationed and its price subsidized by local authorities who borrowed heavily to do so. That still gave Parisians a pound of bread per day in the depth of the crisis, February and March 1795; but in the provinces the ration was often much less and not as frequent. Most other prices, meanwhile, rocketed once the maximum was abolished. Meat went up by 300 per cent between December and April in Paris; butter more than doubled. Hungry people froze to death in the streets in January 1795. Others killed themselves before it came to that: suicide rates rose markedly in Paris and other northern cities like Rouen and Le Havre. And to add to all this, the bottom finally fell out of the assignats. With the abolition of price controls, the government itself was forced to pay market prices for the massive supplies it still needed to sustain the war effort. Taxes came in sluggishly as the agencies of government were paralysed by political uncertainties and farmers' incomes were shorn by harvest shortfalls. Nobody paid them in anything but assignats. The only way to meet the State's commitments was to print yet more assignats, and in May 1795 the number in circulation was approaching double that of a year beforehand. By then their value had fallen to a mere 8 per cent.

Against this background the anti-Jacobin campaign in Paris continued.

Fréron's Muscadins policed the theatres, wrecking performances they did not like by howling choruses of their new battle song, 'The People's Awakening'. They also tried to drown the 'Marseillaise' when it was sung, claiming that it was a mere Jacobin anthem. People in red caps were attacked, trees of liberty cut down, terroristic wall slogans painted out. And the first weeks of 1795 saw a sustained campaign against the cult of Marat. The plaster busts of the People's Friend which had proliferated throughout 1793 and 1794 were systematically sought out and smashed. Various attempts were made to demolish a memorial erected to him outside the Convention hall, while the right-wing press began to call for the removal of his remains from the Pantheon. The remnants of the sansculotte movement bitterly resented these attacks on a figure who was a saint to circles far wider than paid-up Jacobins. In the handful of sections, mostly in the eastern districts of the city, which were still dominated by veterans of the year of terror, popular societies raised noisy protests. Their efforts were encouraged by a new journal, *Le Tribun du peuple*, published clandestinely by the hitherto obscure extreme democrat and former feudal lawyer Babeuf. At the end of January he called for a new popular insurrection to secure the introduction of the still suspended constitution of 1793, with all its democratic forms. As a rallying cry it proved completely counter-productive. A week later an intensive police search ended in Babeuf's arrest, and the Convention ordered the closure of the popular societies. On 8 February, barely five months after placing him there, it yielded to the Muscadin campaign and decreed that Marat should be removed from the Pantheon. Nobody, it declared, should lie there until at least ten years after death. On this pretext, the bones of a number of other martyrs of the Year II were also ejected.

By now, in fact, the tide of reaction was flowing too strongly for the Convention to make any further pretence of standing against it. December and January saw the first relaxation of the laws against emigration, with sailors, manual workers, and artisans being allowed to return to the country subject to certain provisos. On April 11 outlawed Federalists, too, were allowed to return. Meanwhile a commission was established to look into the charges still being persistently levelled at the former members of the governing committees, and on 2 March it reported against them. Barère, Billaud, and Collot were put under house arrest pending trial. Vadier, also indicted, was already in hiding. A week later occurred perhaps the most vivid sign of how far reaction from the Jacobin regime of the Year II had gone. Churches reopened for public worship. During its last, fleeting endorsement of Jacobinism, on 18 September 1794, the Convention had carried the drift of the Revolution since 1790 to a logical conclusion when it finally renounced the constitutional Church. The Republic, it decreed, would no longer pay the costs or wages of any cult— not that it had been paying them in practice for a considerable time already. It meant the end of state recognition for the Supreme Being, a cult too closely identified with Robespierre. But above all it marked the abandonment of the Revolution's own creation, the constitutional Church. For the first time ever in France, Church and State were now formally separated. To some this decree looked like a return to dechristianization, and here and there in the provinces there were renewed bursts of persecution against refractories. But most read it, correctly, as an attempt to deflect the hostility of those still faithful to the Church from the Republic. The natural corollary came with the decree of 21 February 1795 which proclaimed the freedom of all cults to worship as they liked. The tone of the law was grudging, and it was introduced with much gratuitous denigration of priestcraft and superstition. Religion was defined as a private affair, and local authorities were forbidden to lend it any recognition or support. All outward signs of religious affiliation in the form of priestly dress, ceremonies, or church bells remained strictly forbidden. The faithful would have to buy or rent their own places of worship and pay their own priests or ministers. But they found them readily enough as soon as the decree was passed. 'Today, Sunday 8 March 1795', noted a Parisian in his diary,[10] 'they began to say mass publicly everywhere in Paris in rooms, in apartments, in halls and in some monastic chapels. Everybody everywhere went to hear it . . . There were places where masses were said from six in the morning until midday and where there are many people who took communion . . . Mass has not been said since Sunday 13 October 1793.' A week earlier, in devout Brittany, a British prisoner was drawn by the sound of the organ into the devastated and pillaged cathedral of Quimper, where he found 'rows of people on their knees', while 'a fine grey-headed, respectable-looking priest, habited in his pontificals, officiated at the altar.'[11] The congregation were mostly 'poor people from the country, with a few of the higher ranks, many more of whom, I was assured, would have been there, could they have believed themselves secure from reproach'.

Much of the impetus for the new religious policy came from the deputies' awareness of the need to bring permanent peace to the Vendée, where religious grievances had turned opponents of the Revolution royalist. Although the rebels' defeat at Savenay in December 1793 had ended the 'Great War' of the Vendée, resistance continued in guerrilla form throughout 1794. During the spring the official response was terror, when the so-called 'infernal columns' of General Turreau ravaged and burned their way across the rebel heartland. But the effect of such a policy was to embitter the whole region yet more rather than to pacify it. Further north in Brittany, meanwhile, resolute enforcement of conscription had driven many more young men than previously into the arms of the *chouans*, and organized bands of some size began to appear under the co-ordination of regional leaders. By May there were perhaps 22,000 *chouans* operating throughout Brittany, although most were not armed; and before the summer was over they had reduced government outside the larger towns to chaos with murder, threats, disruption of communications, and attacks on constitutional priests and buyers of national lands. A new Breton Catholic and royal army was even announced in July 1794; and although this was wishful thinking on the part of its progenitor, the royalist adventurer Puisaye, the Convention was naturally alarmed. Rural insurgency had put much of the west beyond the Republic's control, and only well-garrisoned ports seemed to be preventing the British from coming to help the rebels. So after Robespierre's fall a new and more conciliatory policy began to emerge. Republican troops were ordered to cease provocative operations and withdraw from billets into camps, while peace feelers were sent out to identifiable guerrilla leaders—Stofflet and Charette in the Vendée, Puisaye in Brittany. General Hoche was brought back from the German front to take overall command of troops north of the Loire, and he proclaimed an amnesty and bounty for all rebels who handed in their arms. News of the trial of Carrier reassured the insurgents that the Republic had now renounced terror, and on 1 December the Convention itself decreed an amnesty for all who would surrender within a month. Many did so, and by January 1795 serious negotiations were under way for a general cease-fire. Early in February Charette, whose bands dominated the Vendée lowlands, concluded the pacification of Lajaunye, under which the rebels agreed to stop their operations in return for a guarantee of religious freedom, no reprisals, and exemption of the region from conscription laws. The Republic would return all confiscated private property, grant indemnities for losses, and allow the rebels to keep their arms and maintain law and order in their districts in the Republic's name. All the Republic did not, and could not, concede to the rebels was the restoration of monarchy in the state within the state that it now recognized. No doubt the 'blues' believed that such generous terms were responsible for the previously intransigent Stofflet's acceptance of similar ones for the Vendée *bocage* early in May, and their extension to the *chouans* of Brittany under the treaty of La Mabilais on 20 April. If so, they were seriously mistaken. Charette had signed only because he believed himself dangerously isolated; the other two armistices represented mere playing for time by the rebels, who by then had received secret assurances that Puisaye had persuaded the British to mount a major expedition against the Breton coast. When Charette was alerted, he assured the others that he, too, would co-operate with the expedition.

Before that crisis broke, however, the Convention had to surmount a spectacular challenge on its own doorstep—the last attempt of the people of Paris to coerce the nation's deputies in the now legendary manner of 1793. For ordinary Parisians, all that had made the terrible winter of 1795 endurable had been the regular bread ration which the Convention had been determined to maintain. But by the beginning of March its ability to guarantee even this was crumbling. With it crumbled the remarkable popular confidence which the deputies had been able to retain in the depth of the winter's misery. Queues at bakers' shops began to lengthen, rations were cut, and on some days some districts had no supplies of bread at all. For the first time since 1792 royalists began to come into the open to argue that the shortages showed that the Republic had failed. But the initial instinct of the women who were the first to experience empty food shops was not to dream of taking the sickly Louis XVII from his lonely confinement in the Temple and setting him on the throne. It was to remember the controlled economy of the Terror. 'There is talk', reported a police spy on 16 March,[12] 'of the regime of before 9 Thermidor, when goods were not as dear and money and assignats were worth the same.' Talk began to be heard at the same time, especially in the city's east end, of a new uprising. Yet at the same moment the Convention was reintegrating surviving Girondins now out of hiding, such as Lanjuinais, Isnard, and Louvet, who had made their names denouncing the sansculottes. It was also trying the leading survivors of the government of the Terror: the impeachment of Barère, Billaud, Collot, and Vadier opened on 22 March. And when bands of women petitioned the Convention for better bread supplies, they had to push their way through crowds of aggressive, smirking Muscadins who mocked their distress. Yet the deputies were not unconcerned. They voted to requisition two-thirds of available grain from normal supplying areas as a forced loan (24 March) and for bread rations to be delivered to the door to eliminate queueing (28 March). Meanwhile they had also taken steps to defend themselves by decreeing savage punishments for attacks on the Convention. Fréron began to organize his Gilded Youth into an informal legislative guard. He was not a moment too soon. On 27 and 28 March there were attempts to march on the Convention amid several days of bread riots in former radical sections like Gravilliers, Jacques Roux's old centre of operations. Those involved had now taken up Babeuf's cry for the constitution of 1793, which, whatever else it meant, would bring the end of the Convention. There was no organization such as had characterized sansculotte action in 1792 or 1793. The institutions necessary for that had been pulverized twelve months previously, and their lack would eventually doom the movement now gathering momentum. But on 1 April (12 Germinal) days of disturbance culminated in about 10,000 people, mostly from eastern Paris, marching on the Convention and swamping the Muscadins who had been assembled to stop them. They poured into the hall calling for bread and the constitution of 1793, milling about, and impeding all debate for about four hours. But they had no clearer programme of demands, they were not co-ordinated, and the deputies from whom they expected support, the handful of Montagnard remnants known now as the 'Crest', took the lead in urging them to leave. As National Guardsmen with Muscadin reinforcements began to arrive from western districts towards evening, the crowd melted away empty-handed. The Convention appointed General Pichegru, fresh from victories in the Netherlands, to co-ordinate all forces of law and order in the capital. Then, to emphasize its defiance and no doubt give vent to pent-up tensions, it delivered its verdict on the four impeached terrorists. By acclamation Barère, Billaud, and Collot (and Vadier in his absence) were condemned to deportation. At least they avoided Carrier's fate; but not, their colleagues thought, for long. The place of their exile was to be Guiana, later to be known as Devil's Island but in 1795 more familiarly (if inaccurately) called the 'dry guillotine'.

In the Parisian context the gesture was merely provocative, and over the next few days the city remained very unsettled, with talk of new marches and demonstrations. Pichegru's response was to disperse large gatherings and order the arrest of anybody with a suspicious record. On 10 April the Convention backed him up by authorizing the disarmament of all those 'known' in their sections as activists during the Terror. Throughout Paris that meant 1,600 people were rendered officially defenceless against any sort of reprisals. By this time sixteen ex-Montagnard deputies had been placed under cautionary arrest, too. Those who had conducted and collaborated with revolutionary government in the Year II, most of whom by now no longer occupied any public office, were in effect identified by these measures as public enemies. Nor was their impact confined to Paris. In the provinces, as the spring weather thawed the paralysis of that ice-bound winter, the new measures proved the signal for an outburst of counter-terror.

It was called 'White', implying that its inspiration was royalist. Some of it undoubtedly was: outside Paris, the disillusionment brought by the Convention's inability to handle the famine conditions of the first half of

1795 produced a surge of nostalgic sentiment for days when kings had seen to their subjects' basic needs. In the department of the Gard, around that original centre of counter-revolution Nîmes, 'Companies of the Sun' emerged to terrorize former terrorists under the direction of men who had never been anything but royalists and were in touch with agents of the Count d'Artois. The 'Companies of Jesus' in the Lyons area were similar. But mostly the White Terror was motivated by little more than vengeance for the cruelties and tragedies inflicted by its victims when they had been in power the year before. It was closer to the anarchic terror of 1793 than to the well-organized machine of the subsequent spring. Nor was the guillotine, that symbol of all the counter-terrorists abhorred in their enemies, a feature. White Terror operated through lynch mobs and murder gangs, abductions and ambushes. Its first manifestations predated the Germinal uprising and the crackdown which followed. The first victims at Nîmes, for example—former officers of the Terror butchered by National Guards supposedly escorting them to prison—died late in February. A former judge of the Popular Commission of Orange was lynched at Avignon around the same time. But the real trigger for widespread counter-terror was the Law of 10 April, under which more zealous local authorities, themselves often nominated by resolutely Thermidorian representatives on mission, not only disarmed suspects but imprisoned them into the bargain. As many as 80,000 or 90,000 people may have spent several weeks or months in custody over the summer of 1795. In most parts of the country they emerged no later than the autumn relatively unscathed. But in the Rhône valley, Provence, and eastern Languedoc, where the Terror had been particularly bloody and traditions of vendetta flourished, the imprisonment of former terrorists proved an invitation to massacre them. Thus on 4 May in blood-drenched Lyons, the prisons were systematically attacked by huge crowds and between 100 and 120 of their inmates hacked to death. A week later 60 prisoners perished similarly in Aix, 24 in Tarascon on 25 May, and on 5 June a further 100 were dispatched in Marseilles, with the open connivance of a representative on mission. At Toulon, whose naval activity soon restored patriotic zeal after its recapture from the British, rumours of reactionary anarchy further west led the arsenal workers to organize a pro-Jacobin march on Marseilles to cries of *Vive la Montagne!* Thousands set out on 17 May, but a week later they were dispersed by a mixed force of regular troops and National Guards, and in addition to the 40 or 50 killed then another 52 were sent to the guillotine by a special military commission established to try those involved. And these were only the most spectacular incidents. Isolated murders, beatings, and other atrocities became commonplace throughout the south-east over the summer, perpetrated mostly by gangs of young men much like the Parisian Gilded Youth in their elaborate and ostentatious clothing, arrays of offensive weapons, and determination to evade conscription. Altogether they accounted for perhaps 2,000 victims throughout the south-east in 1795. Nor did their activities stop after the initial explosion of May. In June, in fact, they were spurred on by news of further unheavals in Paris.

Warned by the great demonstration in Germinal, the Convention decreed the supplementation of bread rations in Paris with rice and biscuits when it was deficient: but the still chronic shortage of fuel meant that rice remained uncookable, and meanwhile the bread shortage got worse. There were simply no untapped reserves of grain anywhere in France, and British control of the sea kept supplies from abroad completely uncertain. Thus rations in Paris continued to diminish in April and May, and only the weather improved. 'All Paris', noted a diarist on 22 April,[13] 'has been reduced today to a quarter pound of bread each. Never has Paris found itself in such distress'; but by the beginning of May it was down to two ounces. Populist gestures like the execution of Fouquier-Tinville and other personnel of the Revolutionary Tribunal on 7 May failed to divert the starving populace. As news came in of victorious peace signed with Holland, with Prussia, and with Spain all people asked was why the nation which could dictate to Europe was unable to feed its own citizens. Frantic women threw accusations of cowardice at their menfolk for not storming the Convention and insisting on more bread at whatever cost, while royalists continued to fish in these troubled waters by insinuating that only a king could restore abundance. As before the Germinal demonstration, however, it was the remnants of the sansculottes who were most listened to, and this time they began to organize themselves for a *journée* that would succeed. Sectional assemblies began to meet regularly, as in the old days, some declared themselves to be in permanent session, and by 15 May rumours were rife that a new explosion was imminent. On the nineteenth the signal was given by the publication of an anonymous pamphlet entitled *People's Insurrection to Obtain Bread and Recover our Rights*, and the next morning the familiar sound of the tocsin was heard in the eastern working districts north and south of the river. In the revolutionary calendar it was 1 Prairial.

Urged on by frenzied women, men left their workshops and began marching on the Convention hall. 'Everybody', the same diarist noted,[14] 'was in a massacring mood', and it was not improved when the first groups to arrive were driven out of the public galleries by attendants with whips. But by early afternoon the Convention was surrounded by armed National

Guards from the Saint-Antoine and Saint-Marcel districts, and when the deputy Feraud and a group of colleagues tried to stop them entering the hall, he was shot. The crowd then hacked off his head and burst through the doors carrying it on a pike, to the sound of more shots and cries of *Bread and the Constitution of 1793!* And once inside, the insurgents demanded more: the release of imprisoned patriots, permanent sessions in the sections, reintegration of an independent Paris commune, compulsory food searches, the arrest of returned *émigrés* and of deputies who persecuted Jacobins. *Vive la Montagne!* they cried, and this time their force seemed so overwhelming that the deputies of the 'Crest', so far from asking them to leave, publicly took up their demands. But earlier in the day the governing committees had issued a general appeal for troops and armed citizens to come to the Convention's rescue, and while excited Montagnards were compromising themselves inside the hall loyal forces were massing outside. When motions to remodel or disband the committees began to be put, these forces were called in, and around midnight they at last drove the sansculottes from the hall with some violence, although no further shots were fired. But the crisis was still far from over. Throughout the small hours the insurgents issued appeals for reinforcements to the sansculottes of Saint-Antoine, and the National Guards of the eastern sections responded by bringing out their artillery. By mid-afternoon on 21 May they were drawn up outside the Convention with a crowd of 20,000 in support. Perhaps twice that number confronted them, but they were not all reliable: at one point some of their gunners defected to the other side. Yet nobody was keen to open fire. Although there were plenty of regular troops on the Convention's side there were also thousands of ordinary citizens barely distinguishable from those who faced them, and just as hungry. So that when the Convention declared itself willing to receive a petition the insurgents seized the opportunity with obvious relief. It asked once more for bread and the constitution of 1793, and the former at least was solemnly promised. The rebels dispersed.

They had lost the initiative, and they never regained it. The Convention had already shown in the early hours, once the hall had been cleared of intruders, what it really thought of the sansculottes' demands by burning the record of all the votes taken under popular duress, and decreeing the arrest of the eleven Montagnard deputies who had moved them. Many thought (and some historians still think) that the governing committees deliberately allowed the Crest time to incriminate itself before unleashing their own forces. But once they had done so the Montagnards' fate was certain. Accused not merely of taking advantage of the attempted insurrection but also (quite unjustifiably) of planning it, they were sent for trial before a special commission on 12 June. One of them killed himself beforehand, and his example gave the others a lead when the inevitable conviction was pronounced on 17 June. Six were condemned to death, but four cheated the guillotine by stabbing themselves as they were led from the court, in what they appear to have planned in advance as an ultimate act of exemplary patriotic defiance. By then, too, they knew about the vengeance visited on those they had sought to lead on 1 Prairial. The very day after the confrontation of 21 May, the Convention gave orders to surround the entire Saint-Antoine district. As regular troops moved slowly up, some sections hesitated to commit their National Guards to a plainly punitive action, especially in concert with jubilant Muscadins now massing outside the barricades thrown up by the district's inhabitants. A first attempt by the Muscadins to invade the area was repulsed. But as the ring tightened, outside sections came into line behind the Convention's demand that the murderers of Feraud should be given up, along with all arms. The next morning the three surrounded sections recognized that there could be no successful resistance. They surrendered, and within days Feraud's assassins had been guillotined. Nor did repression end there. The commission which condemned the Montagnard deputies also executed 36 others, among them the gunners who had gone over to the rebels on 21 May; perhaps 3,000 suspects were arrested by the Convention's decree; and all the sections obediently disarmed or arrested dubious individuals whom they were invited to identify—almost another 3,000 persons in all. For years afterwards, whenever the political pendulum swung to the right, these same individuals would be rearrested as potentially dangerous characters. But most of them had only been dangerous in the context of an organized popular movement: and that, emasculated in 1794, was finally destroyed for ever by the failure of this last sansculotte insurrection in 1795.

Naturally there was no question now of implementing the constitution of 1793—if indeed there ever had been. Already in February leading deputies had agreed that it would be completely unworkable and needed total revision—and now it was also a standard of rebellion. Yet the Convention remained aware that, like the Constituent before it, its basic reason for existence was to present France with a constitution that would give stable and enduring expression to the Revolution's ideals. But did that aspiration exclude monarchy? Monarchist sentiment had clearly burgeoned during the economic distress of the spring, and perhaps some more conservative deputies hoped that Louis XVII, brought up by sound constitutionalists, might yet become an acceptable monarch. But on 8 June the 10-year-old orphan died of scrofula, the very disease so many in

1775 had still beiieved his father's touch could cure. The Count de Provence, who ever since the execution of Louis XVI had styled himself regent of France, at once proclaimed himself Louis XVIII; and on 25 June, from his exile in Verona, he issued a declaration which completely destroyed any hope of agreement with the men who ruled the kingdom he claimed. In it he announced that once restored he would bring back the three orders in society, the Church, and in fact the whole old regime with the exception of certain unspecified 'abuses'. There would be no taxation without the consent of the Estates-General, but he made no promises about how often they would meet. Nor did he mention the crucial issue of the national lands. He did offer an amnesty to his erring subjects, but not to regicide deputies. In short he did nothing to reassure anybody whose support would be essential for a successful restoration, and cut the ground even from under constitutional monarchists who hoped for a return to something like the constitution of 1791. He made a Bourbon restoration by agreement impossible. Yet in June 1795 that scarcely seemed to matter. Confident counter-revolutionaries were about to attempt it by force.

# 13

# Counter—Revolution
# 1789—1795

In its intransigence and blindness to political realities, even favourable ones, the Declaration of Verona typified the whole history of the counter-revolution. As a movement, counter-revolution began as soon as there was a revolution to counter. Once launched, of course, it sought and found justification from a wide range of conservative ideas current before 1789; but it took the creation of a new regime, itself appealing to new justifications, to focus these strains into a counter-revolutionary outlook. It was not, therefore, until the third week in June 1789, when the third estate and a few country priests had laid claim to sovereignty in the name of the Nation, that anything properly deserving the name of counter-revolution came into existence. The Royal Session of 23 June, when populist concessions devised by Necker were amended without his knowledge by the queen, Artois, and sympathetic fellow ministers, was the first serious attempt to halt the Revolution and reverse some of its achievements. The programme announced then by Louis XVI was not without concessions to the revolutionary spirit, in granting no taxation without consent, regular meetings of the Estates-General, abrogation of binding mandates, individual and press freedom, and a number of their fiscal, administrative, and legal reforms. But the smirks of the noble deputies as they heard these proposals expounded in the context of the continued separation of the three orders, maintenance of honorific privileges and feudal rights, and rejection of the momentous claims made over the preceding week by the third estate to national sovereignty showed clearly enough that they thought the revolutionary drift had been stemmed. For the rest of the revolutionary decade the programme of 23 June would represent the most that the princes who led the forces of counter-revolution were prepared to concede should they regain power. Many of their followers proved unwilling to go even that far, dreaming of a complete restoration of the old regime, and they in turn would bitterly resent the arrival in counter-revolutionary ranks of men whose break with the hated movement came later, sometimes much later, and who until the moment of defection had accepted its work or tried to arrest its course from within, From the start, counter-revolution was no more of a unity than the revolution it opposed.

Although defeated by the third estate's defiance and the king's weakness after the Royal Session, the party of the queen and Artois did not give up hope of recapturing control until after 14 July. Indeed, it was they who engineered the dismissal of Necker which triggered off the popular explosion culminating in the fall of the Bastille. But once that happened they saw no further hope of achieving their aims from within France. On the night of 17 July Artois and a handful of friends stole out of Versailles and made their way with the help of a royal passport to the Austrian Netherlands. They did not expect to be away long, although characteristically they do not seem to have thought at all clearly about what circumstances it might be acceptable to return in, or how they would be brought about. But their example proved infectious. By early August, many of the greater courtiers had also left the country, along with a number of lesser nobles alarmed by the castle-burning and threats of personal violence that marked those panic-stricken weeks in the countryside. The failure of the *monarchiens* to lay the foundations of a British-style constitution of checks and balances induced yet more to go; and the renewed popular violence of the October Days produced a massive surge in applications for passports. By then, committees of French *émigrés* were established just beyond the whole length of the French frontier—in Brussels, in Trier, in Mainz, in Basle, in Geneva, in Nice. Artois, finding the Austrian Netherlands scarcely less disturbed than France and his brother-in-law Joseph II less than warm about his presence there, made his way in September to Turin, where his wife's father ruled. There he established a committee of great lords and other nobles to co-ordinate counter-revolutionary activity. At first it merely petitioned crowned heads for support, but was politely brushed off. Nobody had much experience of public or international affairs. But soon Artois secured the help of somebody who had: Calonne, who, after fleeing to . England in 1787 to escape prosecution by the parlement of Paris, had married a rich heiress and was now prepared to put his wealth and expertise at the service of the monarchy he had vainly sought to save from the difficulties it was now in. After initial resistance from Victor Amadeus III, who feared French reprisals in the form of attacks on Savoy or Nice, Calonne was eventually brought to Turin in November 1790, having already advised the *émigré* princes and served as their plenipotentiary in London for the best part of a year.

By then the first signs of counter-revolution had begun to appear within France. In December 1789 the Marquis de Favras, a former soldier with no contacts in Turin but ambiguous links with Provence, the royal brother who had not emigrated, was arrested as he conspired to rescue Louis XVI from Paris with an armed band who would spirit him to the frontier. Favras was hanged for treason in February 1790—incidentally the first noble to suffer the commoners' capital penalty. During the trial the king felt it prudent to make a public avowal before the Assembly of his loyalty to the constitution, much to the fury of the *émigrés* when they heard about it.

Although we had long been prepared for it [wrote the Prince de Condé to Calonne] we were as sensitive as you may imagine to this excessive humiliation of the head of our house. A step such as this, whatever effort may be made to give it the appearance of a liberty which does not exist, manifests to such a degree a character of constraint, of prison, and consequently of nullity, that both our patriotism and our attachment to the king's person engage us not to slacken our efforts, but on the contrary to redouble them, to preserve the kingdom from the annihilation of the monarch and the monarchy . . .[1]

Nor was this ambition confined to them. In Paris, Mirabeau, after the rejection of his transparently self-interested proposal to allow deputies to be ministers, put himself forward as secret adviser to the king and queen. Overcoming initial incredulity and long-standing revulsion for this raddled adventurer, from March 1790 the royal couple paid Mirabeau for support in the Assembly and regular advice. Mirabeau was not a counter-revolutionary, and had no links or sympathy with the *émigrés*. He believed in a strong constitutional monarchy, which he thought perfectly compatible with the principles of 1789. But in practice there was little to distinguish his schemes for the king to escape from Paris, or appoint a special bodyguard, or mount a vast campaign of royalist propaganda in the provinces, from those being plotted in Turin. In any case the king ignored them all. But so long as he seemed so inert in the face of his revolutionary subjects there was no hope of winning foreign support for his cause. As a Spanish minister told the Prussian ambassador in Madrid early in 1790: 'It is for the king of France to show himself worthy of support. It would be as senseless as it is impossible to make him a monarch in spite of himself.'[2]

Yet throughout 1790 evidence of widespread dissatisfaction with the Revolution's drift continued to accumulate. Emigration went steadily on. The abolition of nobility was the last straw for many, and the military mutinies of that year produced an exodus of disgusted officers. Magistrates deprived of their positions by the abolition of the parlements were also among those leaving, and there was talk of establishing a parlement in exile. Prelates and priests, meanwhile, appalled by the Assembly's radical religious policy, began to appear in the more faithful Catholic countries surrounding France. And it caused a sensation on both sides of the frontier when one of the foremost radicals of 1789, Mounier, crossed into Switzerland in May. Nor was disenchantment confined to the upper ranks of society. It was increasingly clear that many of the popular disturbances that went on throughout 1790 were, if not counter-, then at least anti-revolutionary. The most spectacular was undoubtedly the *bagarre* at Nîmes, in June, when pro-revolutionary Protestants defeated with massacre an attempt by Catholic National Guardsmen to take over the city. Both sides were driven on by traditional sectarian antagonisms destabilized and sharpened by the Revolution's reforms, but the Catholic leader Froment was in touch with Turin and had been commended for his counter-revolutionary fervour by Artois himself. His most reliable men openly sported the white cockade of the Bourbons and made no secret of their contempt for the National Assembly. For them the *bagarre* was a defeat; but in the longer term the massacre reinforced Catholic royalist sentiment throughout the Midi by providing martyrs. The 20,000 armed men who convened at the first Jalès camp two months later seemed evidence of what reserves of strength might be available, and lent support to rumours of royalist plots about to reach fruition from places as far apart as Toulouse and Lyons. When they heard them the princes in Turin assured their contacts that any uprisings would receive immediate support in money and troops from sympathetic foreign powers. This was wishful thinking, but those anxious to believe it were not put off when no such support materialized for anti-revolutionary riots in July. Undeterred, the Lyons counter-revolutionaries promised that they could deliver the city to a flying column marching from Switzerland, and over the autumn a grandiose plan was elaborated to abduct the king and bring him to the second city while the whole of the Midi rose in support. Louis XVI was warned, and a date set in December for the uprising. But the king refused to co-operate, and even asked Victor Amadeus III to prevent his brother and cousins from leaving Turin to set the plan in motion. He thought it too dangerous: and certainly in the course of December the whole plot was discovered, amid a renewed round of arrests and executions in Lyons. The furious princes vented their frustration on their host and, full of recriminations, in January 1791 they left Turin in search of more congenial quarters further north.

Yet Louis XVI had not given up hope of escape. At this very moment, in fact, he was beginning to consider a new project devised by Mirabeau involving a royalist grouping in the Assembly, a nation-wide network of secret agents, and, at a ripe moment, a dash by the royal family for the eastern frontier. It was shelved when Mirabeau died early in April, but not for long. And in the meantime counter-revolution had begun to affect the Assembly itself. A number of noble deputies had already emigrated, including the leading *monarchiens*, Mirabeau's brother (the obese 'Mirabeau-Tonneau'), and Count d'Antraigues, a bitter enemy of absolute monarchy in 1788 but soon to be the main co-ordinator of royalist secret agents. Others chose to stay and try to discredit the Assembly by fomenting extremism and confusion. Among the latter were Cazalès, a magistrate of recent nobility who believed that every step taken since (and including) the merger of the three orders had been retrograde; and Maury, a self-made cleric who was particularly outraged by the Assembly's ecclesiastical policy, whose dire consequences were only fully revealing themselves that spring. With grim masochism such deputies were welcoming and even voting for the most radical measures by the spring of 1791, increasingly convinced that the worse things got the sooner the new order would collapse. 'Let this decree pass,' Maury called to Cazalès during a contentious debate in January,[3] 'we need it; two or three more like that and all will be over.'

Nobody was surprised when Louis XVI himself attempted to join the emigration in the flight to Varennes. It had been rumoured for months, and the escape of the king's aunts to Rome in February was seen as a first step which the monarch himself soon intended to follow. The *émigrés*, for their part, had been urging him to flee from the start. But the timing of the escape attempt was set by the royal family alone. Artois had no prior warning, and even the Emperor Leopold, whose troops were expected to mass along the frontier in Belgium to receive the royal fugitives, only learned of the plan just over a week in advance. But the flight transformed the prospects for counter-revolution, even though it failed. In the first place it was no longer possible to believe that the king of France was not an unwilling prisoner in Paris. However desperately the deputies of the Constituent Assembly subscribed to tales of kidnap and abduction, it was obvious that Louis XVI had renounced (and indeed denounced) the Revolution and all its works. It was now obvious, too, that there was a substantial republican movement in Paris, even if it was momentarily tamed—silenced by the Champ de Mars massacre. All this lent urgency to the priority of rescuing the king. At the same time it gave a massive boost to emigration, above all among army officers who considered their oath of loyalty to the king dissolved by his loss of liberty.

The first *émigrés* had not envisaged taking military action on their own. Throughout his sojourn in Turin, Artois had placed his hopes of armed support in uprisings inside France and intervention by the great powers. But by the spring of 1791 certain *émigré* communities had begun to organize themselves militarily. Mirabeau-Tonneau had established a 'Black Legion' of former officers in Switzerland, while other groups drilled in the forests of the Ardennes. After Varennes, with the arrival from France of so many serving officers, counter-revolution began to militarize itself in earnest. Koblenz, where after some months Artois finally established his court in mid-June, soon took on the character of a military headquarters as fugitive officers organized themselves into regiments and undertook manoeuvres. At its peak during the autumn the *émigré* army stood at almost 20,000 men. Even so it never envisaged itself as much more than an auxiliary force to the armies of Prussia and Austria. For another result of the Varennes crisis had been to induce the powers for the first time to take seriously the prospect of intervention in France. The Padua Circular sent to fellow monarchs on 10 July, and the Convention of Reichenbach with the Prussians two weeks later, showed that Leopold II was at last being stirred by the fate of his sister and brother-in-law. Whether, after an initial wave of emotion, his intention was to do anything very positive seems doubtful; but the *émigrés*, cheered by the arrival in their ranks of Artois's elder brother Provence (who fled at the same time as the king, and evaded capture), were enormously encouraged by this imperial show of action. And when Artois heard that the Prussian king and the emperor were to meet late in August at Pillnitz, he noisily demanded an invitation. Receiving none, he and Calonne turned up anyway. The declaration that resulted from the meeting, accordingly, stated explicitly that it had been issued in consultation with the *émigré* princes. Not only that. The sovereigns handed their statement over to Artois to use as he saw fit, and he and Provence annexed it to a long open letter which they addressed to Louis XVI on 10 September, urging him not to accept the now completed constitution.

In this it failed, and they knew it would. The queen had already told them that her husband would accept the constitution despite private abhorrence. But the princes' letter is interesting as the first explicit manifesto of the expatriate counter-revolution. The constitution, they argued, had no legitimacy, since it was the work of an assembly that was not the Estates-General. And any sanction the king might give was also invalid, since it would be patently given under duress. Illegitimate, too, were the culpable, appalling, abusive, ruinous, and outrageous policies the Assembly had pursued: its destruction of the orders of society, its attack on the Church, its subversion of the army, its devastation of the economy, its attacks on property. The king was sworn, since his coronation, to uphold the 'fundamental maxims' of the kingdom. 'How could you, sire, give sincere and valid approval to the pretended Constitution which has produced so many evils? Holder in trust of the Throne which you have inherited from your ancestors; you may not either alienate its primordial rights, or destroy the constitutional base on which it rests . . .'[4] Should such a betrayal occur, the princes would know their brother was not a free agent, and would refuse to accept it as sincere. And they would be supported in this, they (quite unjustifiably) claimed, by the armed forces of the whole of monarchical Europe. Thus articulated, the aim of the princes seemed to be something less liberal even than the 23 June programme. They did admit the legitimacy of the Estates-General, and they seemed to allow that there had been abuses needing remedy under the old order since they castigated the National Assembly for going beyond the demands of the *cahiers*. But their main concern was to see a free king with his own legislative power, and loyal and obedient forces at his disposal to enforce it. The society he would rule over would be, apparently, a complete restoration of the old regime.

That this was the *émigrés'* dream can also be seen in the way they led their life in exile. The innumerable nuances and petty snobberies of noble life before 1789 were reproduced and magnified in the princely courts of Turin and then Koblenz. Quarrels of precedence were loudly pursued. When they began to arm themselves, some regiments excluded nobles of recent lineage; and when newcomers arrived they were exhaustively scrutinized for their nobility, their political record since the 1780s, and their reasons for not leaving earlier. 'I was worn out', wrote one seasoned officer,[5] 'with a string of silly questions like an interrogation . . . I confess that this beginning displeased me greatly and made me regret all the efforts I had made to come thus far.' Cazalès, who went to Koblenz after Varennes, returned home in disgust. So did François Suleau, a journalist of impeccable right-wing credentials. And towards their Italian and German hosts the *émigrés* often behaved with lofty indifference, leaving a trail of unpaid bills once the monies they brought out with them were exhausted, pushing up local prices, and disrupting everyday life with their routs and military exercises. Yet they were not all petulant, posturing egotists, concerned only for their lost powers and privileges. Many had taken considerable risks, and abandoned their families and property, to join the princes—and the late-comers so despised by more hardened exiles found the process of emigration far more hazardous than the first affluent semi-tourists expecting an early, painless return. Many were sincerely moved by the fate of the king after Varennes, and had their course dictated by a romantic, irrational loyalty. 'The Bourbons', recalled Chateaubriand,[6] 'had no need for a younger son of Brittany to return from beyond the seas to offer them his obscure devotion', yet on hearing of Varennes in America he at once took ship back to Europe, passed through a France that confirmed all his worst fears, and joined the exile army. And he and many like him, former officers all, were content to serve in the ranks of *émigré* regiments, since at this stage relatively few commoners had joined the emigration, and those who did seldom directed their tracks to Mainz or Koblenz.

Whatever their motivation, the commitment of the overwhelming majority of *émigrés* to the course they had chosen was vividly demonstrated by the failure of the amnesty announced to mark the inauguration of the constitution. In combination with the threatening and belligerent attitude of the princes, it did much to fuel the violent anti-*émigré* attitude of the Legislative Assembly during the autumn of 1791. But the princes and their followers really believed that their moment was at hand. In addition to the Declaration of Pillnitz, they had begun to receive subsidies from most of the greater German rulers, from Spain, and from Russia. In all they received $6\frac{1}{2}$ million *livres*, with which they bought arms and equipment and hired mercenaries to strengthen their forces. The paranoia in Paris about their activities could only increase their sense of their own importance and military value. But over the autumn disappointment once more set in. The subsidies dried up, and the powers did not move. When threatened with French military action if they did not remove the *émigré* armies from their territories, the Rhenish prince-bishops hastened to comply, and ordered the regiments to disband. They were already falling apart anyway for lack of equipment, arms, shelter, and even food. Some degenerated into little more than bands of marauders, living off the country. These developments were all the more dispiriting in that the *émigrés* were convinced that more and more people within France were being alienated by the continued radical impetus of the Revolution; and that the moment royalist forces invaded the kingdom there would be spontaneous uprisings to support them.

Unfortunately the two propositions were not necessarily linked. There is no doubt that disenchantment with the Revolution's achievements within France was widespread and growing. To all the administrative, institutional, fiscal, and professional upheavals brought about by the reforms of its first two years, the clerical oath of November 1790 had added religious schism, as those opposed to the new church policy were forced to declare themselves against the whole Revolution. The Pope's subsequent condemnation of the Civil Constitution of the Clergy put the Roman Church into official opposition to the Revolution, so that the *émigrés* could now claim that God himself was on their side. But as yet the transmutation of anti-revolution into counter-revolution had only occurred in the sectarian south. Even there the paradoxical effect was to strengthen patriotic zeal. Thus when Pascalis, the mayor of Aix, urged resistance to the abolition of the local parlement and the traditional constitution of Provence at the end of 1790, he was lynched by a patriotic crowd. And when, after the ubiquitous Froment had travelled to Koblenz in January 1792 and secured princely support for a 'Catholic Army of the Midi' to be put together at a new Jalès encampment, a premature rising early in July attracted only a few hundred adherents, many of whom were killed by National Guards and regular troops sent out by the departmental authorities of the Gard to disperse them. It was true that by this time the princes had promising contacts in other regions. A Breton nobleman unreconciled from the start to the loss of his native province's independent character, the Marquis de la Rouërie, appeared at Koblenz in May 1791 claiming to represent a counter-revolutionary 'Breton association' of which he proposed to establish branches or at least link-men in all the coastal towns of Brittany. The remarkable scale of oath-refusal among the Breton clergy, and the support these refractories were receiving from the laity, was already well known to the exiles. Accordingly La Rouërie was encouraged, and reported regularly throughout the autumn and spring. There was plenty of support for his organization, he constantly averred. His chief problem was to persuade his most trusty contacts to remain in Brittany rather than taking the 'honourable road' into emigration. By the beginning of 1792, his adherents had a considerable stock of arms, if no very clear plan about how to make use of them. But within months this and all other counter-revolutionary projects were transformed by what the *émigrés* had dreamed of from the start and, it is fair to say, played their own modest part in precipitating in the end: the outbreak of war between France and the great powers of Germany.

Once again their hopes soared. It seemed inconceivable that the demoralized and disorganized remnants of the French army could hold out against the well-equipped and seasoned professionals of the king of Prussia and the new emperor. Or indeed, some thought, against the self-confident regiments of their own former officers, who now quickly regrouped across the Rhine. 'It will be a walk-over', one exiled nobleman called to his wife as he rode off to join the colours. Artois even doubted whether the help of the Prussian army would be needed. But elation soon gave way to suspicion and frustration. The Prussians, to whom most of the *émigré* regiments attached themselves, moved forward very slowly, insisted on keeping their counter-revolutionary allies in the rear, and starved them of supplies and equipment. They even talked of making political compromises once they reached Paris with the Feuillants, whom, as with the *monarchiens* before them, the *émigrés* hated even more than Jacobins and 'demagogues'. Worst of all, the invaders were stunned to find that the population along their route did not rally to them with open arms. 'The . . . enemy', noted one,[7] 'has formidable artillery, and is not as contemptible as we thought. Nobody is coming over to us as had been hoped, and we have not noticed that opinions have changed in the territory we have taken.' In such an atmosphere the ferocious threats of the Brunswick Manifesto were bound to be counter-productive, yet the *émigrés* welcomed it as the best way to deter the Parisians from attacking the royal family. In the event it helped to precipitate just such an attack, but the overthrow of the monarchy on 10 August left *émigré* circles largely unmoved. In their eyes it had long been overthrown already, and the priority was to rescue the king whether he still sat on the throne or not. The bloody scenes which marked the storming of the Tuileries, and the September Massacres a month later, were positively seen by some as serving their longer-term purpose by highlighting the iniquity of the movement they were seeking to destroy. The real blow to the *émigré* cause was, therefore, Valmy. None of them were present at the famous cannonade, but their main forces were certainly caught up in the rain-soaked and disease-ravaged retreat which followed. With the exception of the regiments of the Prince de Condé, which had remained in Baden throughout the invasion, the *émigré* armies fell to pieces, fleeing headlong before the republican forces as they now overran the old refuges in Belgium and the Rhenish electorates. On 23 November Provence and Artois formally disbanded their forces. A diaspora began, which carried French exiles to every corner of unconquered Europe—except Prussia, which gave Provence and Artois modest hospitality in the little town of Hamm but firmly closed its territory to their followers. It was, therefore, in a state of dispersion and deep demoralization that the *émigrés* heard, in the early weeks of 1793, about their estranged compatriots' ultimate act of defiance, representing the failure of all they had worked for for $3\frac{1}{2}$ years—the execution of Louis XVI.

It was counter-revolution's low point. So far from rescuing and restoring the powers of the Bourbon monarchy, the war the *émigrés* had helped to foment had destroyed it. The forces they had assembled were scattered, their German protectors were in disarray, and their links with counter-revolutionary hopefuls inside France completely disrupted. By now over 40,000 French citizens had turned their backs on the Revolution through emigration, but apart from Condé's army of some 5,500, now being absorbed into the imperial forces, they lacked all organization and co-ordination. Provence, on hearing news of the execution, at once proclaimed his dead brother's son Louis XVII, and declared himself Regent of the Kingdom. At the same time Artois, whom nevertheless he disliked and mistrusted, received the title of Lieutenant-General of the Kingdom. A defiant proclamation was also issued, largely reiterating the terms of the letter sent to Louis XVI in September 1791. The regent would lend all his efforts, he declared, to rescuing the remnants of his family and re-establishing the French monarchy 'on the unalterable basis of its constitution'. Unspecified 'abuses' would be remedied when that happened, but the main business would be the restoration of the Church, the orders, the old judicial system, and all confiscated properties. If anything this marked a hardening of the princes' position. But nobody any longer believed they had any prospect of making their pledges a reality. So insignificant had they become that all the powers of Europe except one refused even to recognize Provence as regent. The exception was Russia, and hearing the news Provence dispatched his brother to St Petersburg to discover what other support Catherine II was prepared to offer. After a month of fair words Artois came away in April 1793 with a jewelled sword inscribed *With God, for the King* but no more tangible support. The Bourbon cause in France, as far as the courts of Europe were concerned, seemed lost.

Yet in fact at this very moment the foundations for a new phase of counter-revolution were being laid, without any initiative from the *émigrés*. The entry of Great Britain into the war brought an ally whom the princes had long sought to recruit, and one whose sea power laid the whole coast of France open to royalist penetration. Eventually the British would be counter-revolution's most consistent foreign mainstay. But in the spring of 1793 they remained extremely wary of commitment to any programme for France's political future. Their aim was simply to limit French power, whoever exercised it, and in the process to boost their own. In any case they did not believe that the Republic could long survive against a European coalition, so there was little to be gained in cultivating its French enemies with commitments which might prove inconvenient once the collapse came. Such indifference infuriated the princes; especially when, in the early days of March, a mass movement of counter-revolution at last appeared in the Republic's western departments, when no less than fourteen of them exploded into violent resistance to conscription.

Conscription was of course only the trigger, igniting far more deep-seated resentments among a peasantry which had gained much less than those of most regions from the Revolution. Even the great gains of 4 August 1789 had scarcely affected them. The abolition of seigneurial dues was of little consequence in areas where their burden was light, and lords distant, as in the Vendée or Sarthe departments; and the end of the tithe chiefly benefited proprietors, whereas most peasant farmers in western Brittany were tenants, who found in 1790 that their landlords were to be allowed to raise their rents by the amount hitherto paid out for tithes. The opposition of such regions to the Revolution's work as a whole was made plain in the massive refusal among their clergy to take the oath to the constitution. Many clearly refused it under strong pressure from their parishioners, who wished thereby to send a strong hostile signal to Paris—and the agents of Paris in the form of the new authorities in local administrative centres. But Paris ignored them. And, determined to treat refractory priests like counter-revolutionaries, it eventually made them just that, especially after the draconian measures facilitating deportation passed in the wake of the Revolution of 10 August. The fall of the monarchy merely gave western opponents of Paris one more cause to identify with, a way of advertising hostility to the Revolution. Under the king's rule, it seemed in retrospect, people had been left to run their own affairs, and had prospered. Revolutionary governments, by contrast, interfered in everyday life to an unprecedented degree, and the result had been disruption and a rise in the demands of landlords and tax-collectors that made the once-resented burdens of the old regime seem mild. In some areas the increases in outgoings may have been as high as 40 per cent. Conscription, in these circumstances, was simply the last straw. But resistance to authority in time of war, especially when it was trying to raise troops, was tantamount to treason, to be met with all the severity normal for such a crime. There was therefore little to lose in taking resistance all the way and proclaiming the king. Within weeks of the first incidents, accordingly, the Vendéan rebels were calling themselves a Catholic and royal army, adopting white cockades and sashes, and sacred heart badges, and looking for noblemen to lead them as would only have been natural under the old monarchy. The *chouan* guerrillas of Brittany too made no secret of their allegiance to Church and king, although they never coalesced like the Vendéans. Much energy and effort would be spent over the years by royalist agents trying to get them to do so.

Over the spring and summer of 1793, however, their potential was largely ignored by the new Republic's enemies as they watched the great provincial capitals come out against Paris in the 'Federalist' revolt. Counter-revolutionaries assumed, over-hastily, that those who rejected the authority of the Convention must favour royalism. Royalists certainly were involved in some of the episodes, and sought to exploit all of them. Puisaye, for example, struck his first blow for the king in Wimpffen's ill-fated march from Caen in mid-July. Lyons, in the desperate final stages of its resistance in September, relied increasingly for defence on an army riddled with royalists and their sympathizers. And, of course, Toulon, at the end of August, actually called in the British fleet and proclaimed the king. In response to an invitation from the rebels in the great naval port, and with encouragement from the Spaniards who shared the occupation with the British, late in November Provence set out from Hamm with the intention of going there. But he had got no further than Verona when news came of Toulon's fall. He made little effort to conceal his relief, and with good reason. Toulon had only invited the British in out of fear of the Convention's vengeance, and after much agonizing. To reassure the inhabitants, Admiral Hood had declared for a restoration of the constitution of 1791, which was not at all to the prince's taste. Yet that was the extent of such royalism as emerged during the Federalist revolt. Hardly anybody dreamed of restoring the old regime along with the king. When, in still occupied Toulon, refractory priests reappeared in the streets and former nobles began to demand deference as of old, there were bitter complaints. Such behaviour was a sobering warning to the only city to proclaim the king, of what his rule would really be like.

Thus, it was only the peasant rebels of the west who were true and determined counter-revolutionaries, and by late summer this was at last beginning to dawn on the Republic's overseas enemies. Only in August do the British seem to have begun to think seriously of sending them help, and even then it was extremely difficult to decide their true strength, and who, if anybody, spoke for them. Arms and ammunition were stockpiled in Jersey, agents sent to sound out the insurgents, and *émigrés* encouraged to concentrate in the Channel Islands in the hope of being put ashore in royalist territory. An expedition commander was even named—Lord Moira. It was to meet such an expedition that the Vendéans crossed the Loire on their epic march to Granville. But by the time orders had been given to link up with the Catholic and royal army it was already in retreat, and Moira's ships cruising and signalling offshore in the first days of December received no response. Yet a pattern had been set. Moira's force remained in being for several more months, hoping for another opportunity; and the Vendéans, even after their movement dissolved once more into banditry and opportunism following the destruction of their army at Le Mans and Savenay, were led to expect further British help. From the spring of 1794, however, the British proved increasingly inclined to send it not south of the Loire, but to the *chouans* of Brittany, whom Puisaye succeeded in persuading them he spoke for, with fateful consequences.

All these manoeuvres took place with no reference to Provence or Artois. The British, unlike the Spaniards, opposed the self-styled regent's plan to go to Toulon, and outraged both the royal brothers with the statement of intent they issued in November 1793. In declaring that 'the acknowledgement of an hereditary monarchy and of Louis XVII as lawful sovereign, affords the only probable ground for restoring regular government in France,'[8] and that a restored monarchy would doubtless be subject to various unspecified 'modifications', they showed themselves seemingly less than totally committed to monarchy and agnostic on its precise constitution. But then, there was no consensus about such matters in counter-revolutionary ranks either. While the princes felt most at home with 'pures' who had left France early and refused to contemplate a restoration of anything beyond what Louis XVI had offered on 23 June 1789, after 1792 the ranks of the *émigrés* were increasingly swelled by men who had helped to construct the constitution of 1791, and still believed it could have worked, with certain changes. These 'constitutionals' were in their turn an uneasy combination of former *monarchiens* (like Mounier and Lally-Tollendal), Feuillants (like the Lameth brothers and Duport), and more consistent, right-wing ex-deputies (Montlosier, Malouet). All were monarchists, but some believed still in the unicameral legislature and separation of powers of 1791, while others, naturally choosing exile in Great Britain, preferred two chambers and minister-deputies. But they were united in believing that the clock could not be put back to a time before France had a written, representative constitution. There was no future for the allies, argued the Swiss journalist Mallet du Pan, whose *Mercure de France* had provided an invariably acute right-wing commentary on French affairs until he emigrated in 1792, in trying to reverse the Revolution as the *émigrés* were urging. He even doubted by the time he published his *Considerations on the Nature of the Revolution in France and the Causes which Prolong it* in August 1793 whether war alone could defeat such a movement. What was needed was intensive propaganda to assure the French that, along with suppression of the disorder and mob rule that had engulfed them, an allied victory would guarantee the basic gains so many of them had made in the Revolution. The British were impressed by Mallet's analysis, and retained him as an intelligence-gatherer on French affairs, based between 1793 and 1797 in Berne. The 'purer' *émigrés*, predictably, were incensed by both his views and the credence the powers seemed to give them. They were not even interested in the intelligence he commanded. They preferred to rely upon the network set up late in 1793 by d'Antraigues. Establishing himself in Venice, not far from Provence's new base in Verona, until 1797 d'Antraigues collected information from trusted correspondents all over France and subsequently sold it to interested allied powers. None of these correspondents, who often wrote in cipher or invisible ink, were without their own political views; that was why d'Antraigues, the title of whose 1792 pamphlet *No Compromise* made clear his own position, used them. Nor was he afraid to amend or load the reports he based on their letters yet further in order to persuade those he wrote for that a restoration of the old regime was both desirable and feasible. The problem he faced, like Mallet du Pan, was that the allies refused to rely on him alone for their information and political analysis. Not only were they writing against each other; they were also in competition with more direct contacts maintained by the powers in France, and particularly the links to the western rebels which the British thought they had established through the indefatigable Puisaye.

In the course of 1794 counter-revolutionary hopes were fixed more and more on the British as the war on land turned again in France's favour, the Austrians were driven once more from the southern Netherlands, and Prussia stood increasingly aside. The British in turn, devastated by the disasters in Belgium, were at least encouraged by the apparent drift to the right which followed the fall of Robespierre, and the persistence of royalist guerrilla activity in Brittany and the Vendée. But they were themselves undecided about whether to commit their resources now against the French West Indies or in support of the western royalists within the country; and it took the arrival of Puisaye in London in September to persuade them that an expedition to western France would be worthwhile. Puisaye spoke, he claimed, for 30,000 organized *chouans*, and could draw on 40,000 more with British help in money, arms, and ammunition. In actual fact the *chouans* probably numbered less than 22,000 in all, and Puisaye could in no real sense speak for such a fluctuating, spontaneous, and scattered movement. He did have sporadic contact with the chiefs of some of the larger bands, but the 'Catholic and royal army of Brittany' which he confidently claimed to represent from July 1794 existed largely in his own imagination. The *chouans* were undoubtedly proving enormously disruptive, as only guerrillas can. Few parts of the Breton countryside were safe from their depredations, and outside the towns orderly government had largely broken down amid murder of officials, resistance to taxation and conscription, and attacks on official and patriot-owned property. But none of this was militarily useful, and the *chouans* never showed any sign of being able to capture and hold a port, which ever since the fiasco at Granville the British navy had insisted must be the essential pre-condition for any amphibious operation. Yet Puisaye was persuasive, and impressed Pitt. As the triumphant republican armies systematically removed every other possibility of a firm continental foothold over the winter of 1794–5, the British government found the idea of a major initiative in Brittany increasingly attractive, and began to build up supplies once again in the Channel Islands. Artois, when he heard how much progress Puisaye had apparently made, and despite suspicions that this new figure in the counter-revolution was less than 'pure', gave his projects a royal blessing and named Puisaye a lieutenant-general.

Yet long before an expedition finally set sail late in June, the odds against its succeeding were mounting. Within France, the rightward drift of politics over the spring of 1795 brought the final abandonment of all vestiges of terror as a method of government, and the harassment and even arrest of its leading perpetrators at both national and local level. In the west in particular, the restoration of open religious practice eliminated one of the most persistent of popular grievances inclining the peasants to support *chouans* and Vendéan guerrillas. At the same time the insurgents themselves came under mounting pressure. As their always inadequate supplies dwindled and were not replaced from abroad (the British now putting all their efforts into building up stocks for the projected expedition), the new counter-insurgency tactics of General Hoche broke up guerrilla bands and scattered them. A number of important *chouan* leaders were killed, others defected to the 'blues', and neither were easily replaced. Nor were warnings that a landing was imminent taken as seriously as they would have been if so many previous rumours had not proved false. Such factors were responsible for the series of treaties made between blues and whites throughout the west between February and May. Despair brought the royalist leaders to the negotiating table. But in their secret messages to London they disclaimed any sincere intention to live at peace with the Republic.

Tell the British government and the Princes [Charette instructed their emissary] that I signed the peace simply because I feared that my party, given its total lack of powder, would be destroyed in an assault that was being prepared by superior forces; but assure them that I will never make a genuine peace with those who have murdered my king and my country . . . I am entirely ready to take up arms again. My soldiers are battle-hardened and eager to fight; it is simply prudence which leads me to hold them back until I can fight with advantage.[9]

Similar messages were received from the Breton *chouans*, and in fact by no means all of their chiefs had subscribed to the treaty of La Mabilais which ostensibly ended hostilities in the peninsula.

In the light of these assurances an expedition was finally launched. The destination chosen was the narrow, rocky Quiberon peninsula in southern Brittany. The British even gave up their insistence on a port, so thoroughly persuaded were they by now that the local *chouans* could easily take and defend what was almost a natural harbour. In the last days of June, accordingly, 3,000 men were embarked for Quiberon, with arms and supplies for 70,000. No British troops were to land, at least until a firm bridgehead was established, but Pitt's counter-revolutionary protégés happily accepted that. Too many *émigrés* were aching for action throughout southern England, and it seemed better all round that the king of France should be restored by loyal Frenchmen. Thus the spearhead of the force was a mixture of exiles and drafted French prisoners. When they landed, 10,000 *chouans* converged on Quiberon and the local blues were swamped. But the *chouans* were ill disciplined, and the euphoric *émigrés* scarcely better; the chain of command was not clear, and the invaders failed to advance from their bridgehead. Hoche was soon on the scene, but he took care to build up strong forces before attacking. When he did so, on 3 July, he had 10,000 regulars under his command, and within a week he had recaptured the peninsula and taken 6,000 prisoners. Over 1,000 of these were *émigrés*, and they were subjected to the full severity of renewed laws (first passed when the war had begun) concerning *émigrés* captured with arms in their hands: 640 of them were shot, along with 108 *chouans*. When the first, optimistic reports of the landing had reached London, the British hurriedly brought Artois from Bremen, where he had been negotiating for months for a passage to England but had been deterred by fears of arrest for unpaid debts incurred there the last time his prospects had seemed bright. The plan now was to send him to take command in Brittany. But by the time he reached Portsmouth early in August the world knew that the Quiberon expedition had failed disastrously, and that the bravest and most loyal of the counter-revolution's warriors had lost their lives either in the fighting or facing Hoche's firing squads.

It was not the end of British attempts to land *émigrés* in the west in the hope of linking up with guerrillas there. Their efforts now switched southwards, to the Vendée, where Charette as he had promised had taken the field again, and was indicating that he would be there to welcome an allied force ashore. In fact he had shot hundreds of republican prisoners when he heard of the reprisals after Quiberon. As soon as he arrived in Portsmouth, Artois demanded to be taken to join his brother's loyal subjects, and early in September he duly sailed with a new expedition partly made up of the remnants of the old. On the thirtieth he landed opposite the Vendée on the Île d'Yeu. But by then Hoche had been able to concentrate fresh troops released from the Pyrenean front by peace with Spain. He lined the coast with them, and Charette was unable to break through. In mid-November the British recalled the expedition and Artois returned with them, not to set foot again on French soil until 1814.

The events of the summer of 1795 traumatized the counter-revolution. Even as the Quiberon expedition was about to set sail, on 8 June, Louis XVII died. The intransigent proclamation issued by his uncle from Verona on assuming the title Louis XVIII not only cut off all hope of co-operation with influential right-wingers inside France: it was also a snub to *émigré* moderates and constitutionalists, and was so intended by those like d'Antraigues who had a hand in its drafting. Most of those who sailed with the expeditions to Quiberon and Yeu were 'pures', too: the catastrophe which befell them left those who survived looking for scapegoats, and they were soon blaming everybody but themselves. Puisaye was an obvious target. He had not even been incompetent, argued some of his more extreme critics: the expedition had been designed to fail, and in its failure immolate the finest flower of intransigent counter-revolutionaries, so opening the way for a 'constitutional' takeover. With such tales about, Puisaye was wise not to return to England, though he survived the rout. By early in September he was back with his beloved *chouans* in Brittany—only to find that there too his reputation and authority had been irreparably damaged. If *chouannerie* had anyone who could be called a leader, it was now one of the chiefs, who had spurned the treaty of La Mabilais, and waited in vain for Artois to arrive at Quiberon with reinforcements—the redoubtable, inflexible Georges Cadoudal. The one party all shades of French counter-revolutionary could agree on blaming was the British. Ancestral suspicion of perfidious Albion had always anyway been as deep among royalists as among their republican opponents, although more recent grievances differed. England had been late to join the war, had not recognized Provence as regent, had taken Toulon only to pillage it. Then she had used the war as an excuse to seize French territories in Corsica and the West Indies rather than establish legitimate government there. Finally she had under-equipped and then let down the Quiberon expedition and its 'pure' participants. Nobody was therefore surprised when in 1796 Pitt once more began to concentrate his efforts in the Caribbean. And yet the counter-revolutionaries needed Great Britain more than ever as the coalition fell apart. More and more *émigrés* found that the island state was their only safe refuge—even if Artois himself had to be accommodated in Scotland to avoid his still insistent English creditors. And where else could the *chouans* and Vendéans hope to be supplied from?

Few supplies, however, reached them as the winter drew on. And meanwhile Hoche, his 'Army of the Ocean Coasts' reinforced by yet more regulars from victorious fronts, saturated Catholic and royal territory on both sides of the Loire with search and destroy missions. In February 1796 he captured Stofflet and executed him. A month later he caught Charette, too, and treated him similarly. This, combined with religious toleration and strict control over the depredations of 'blue' troops, reduced the Vendée at last to a precarious peace. By midsummer, Hoche was able to declare the insurrection finally at an end, and be proclaimed 'Pacifier of the Vendée' by a grateful Directory. By then, too, so many troops had been drafted into Brittany that the *chouans* could scarcely make a move. Puisaye was reduced to hiding in underground dugouts, like some hunted fox.

Indeed, by then Louis XVIII himself was in full flight from those he regarded as his subjects. As soon as Bonaparte's army of Italy crossed the Alps the terrified Venetian authorities ordered the hapless pretender to leave Verona. He made his way, unauthorized, across Switzerland to join the Prince de Condé's forces in Austrian service along the Rhine. Much had been hoped of Condé's thousand or so *émigrés* the previous spring. As the White Terror swept along the Rhône and scores of Jacobins were massacred in Lyons there were plans for the Austrians, spearheaded by Condé's *émigrés*, to make a lightning strike into Franche Comté and then south to link up with the Lyonnais royalists. The British provided money to retain agents throughout the region, and both they and the Austrians were intrigued to hear that the French commander on the Rhine, Pichegru, the conqueror of Holland and the avenger of the Prairial uprising in Paris, was considered susceptible to royalist advances. In the end he was, but in the summer of 1795 attempts to win him paralysed any further action. The year concluded with a formal truce along the Rhine and no help for the plotters in Lyons. With the resumption of campaigning in the spring of 1796 Condé hoped to reactivate the plan, and the arrival of the king himself (who donned uniform and reviewed the troops) was greeted with enthusiasm. But not in Vienna, where the presence of the pretender was viewed as inviting a French attack. The Emperor, who like most other rulers had not yet even recognized him as Louis XVIII, ordered him to leave. Shortly afterwards an unidentified gunman tried to shoot him. Was nowhere safe? The only host he could find for the moment was a grudging Duke of Brunswick, whose army in 1792 had failed to rescue his brother. So it was from Blankenburg, 'in a nasty little town, in a nasty house, tiny, badly furnished, if at all',[10] that he watched the French Republic's armies sweep to victory over their last continental enemy during the ensuing months.

Counter-revolution, therefore, in the sense of the armed overthrow of the French Republic and many of the innovations it stood for, was defeated by the time the land war came to an end at Leoben in April 1797. Three days after those preliminaries were signed, French troops arrested d'Antraigues as he fled from Venice. Under questioning, on one occasion by Bonaparte himself, he revealed a good deal about his spy network, including information that damned Pichegru. Subsequently he was allowed to escape, but the effect of what remains an exceedingly murky episode was to ruin his credit with Louis XVIII and his fellow *émigrés*. But what was one more quarrel among so many others? Counter-revolution was bedevilled from start to finish by vicious feuding and factionalism between groups who hated and mistrusted one another—often, it seemed, more than the Revolution itself. By their own efforts, the bickering *émigrés* never had any chance of arresting or moderating, much less reversing, the march of events in France. All they sometimes succeeded in doing, by their antics, was to help push things to greater extremes—which only the more crass among them expected to advance their cause. They needed help: but neither of the sources they looked to was necessarily much interested in seeing them succeed.

The great powers sought at first simply the weakening of France, and only went to war when it became clear that she had not achieved that for herself. Most *émigrés*, however, dreamed of recovering power over a strong kingdom, with intact resources. Only the Revolution itself, in their eyes, had brought weakness, and they deeply resented the rumours they heard about victorious powers partitioning France, like Poland, not to mention the use of British sea power to capture French overseas possessions. Subsequently the powers concluded that a stable France was more desirable than a weak one; but even then they remained open-minded about the sort of regime most likely to restore and maintain order. Their commitment to monarchy, of whatever type, was never more than conditional, and even in 1797 Louis XVIII was only recognized by Russia and Sweden. Only sporadically did the great powers, always pursuing their own interests, regard French counter-revolutionaries as more than a nuisance, a complication, or at best a catspaw.

As to internal counter-revolutionaries, most of them sought little more than to be left alone. Their quarrel was with a Revolution that had disrupted their communities and their religious and social certainties, and brought outside interference in every aspect of their lives, without producing enough compensatory benefits. Men in power in Paris, and those who sought to implement their orders in the localities, were too inclined to call any resistance counter-revolutionary. Much of it, however, like the so-called 'Federalist' revolt of 1793, merely sought to stop the Revolution going further. It was only in the Gard, the Vendée, and rural Brittany that mass movements developed, fighting openly for the Church and king they remembered from before 1789. Even then their resistance had no national dimension. It was significant that what triggered the revolts in the west was conscription, which threatened to take young men away to distant frontiers to fight unknown enemies. Popular counter-revolutionaries infinitely preferred to fight patriots, constitutional priests, and Protestants on their own doorstep. Their one sortie outside home territory, the Vendéans' march to Granville, was a desperate bid to attract foreign help as the tide began to turn against them. Resistance would probably not have continued after Savenay without the unrelieved brutality of republican reprisals over the spring of 1794. Leaving aside the bungling, misunderstandings, and plain bad luck which blighted the one major attempt of *émigrés*, foreign powers, and royalist rebels to act together in the summer of 1795, and even if, as the popular leaders constantly urged, Artois had come to the mainland and raised his standard, it seems doubtful whether the peasant counter-revolutionaries of the west, however numerous on their own ground, would have willingly set out to march as far as Paris. And if they had, they would surely have been stopped on the way by the most seasoned and successful soldiers in Europe.

Nor would they have made many converts to their nostalgic creed of restoring a golden past if they had broken out. As Mallet du Pan, most clear-eyed of royalists, wrote to Louis XVIII after the Declaration of Verona, 'The great majority of the French will never willingly give in to the former authority and those who wielded it'.[11] That did not mean there was no support for a limited, constitutional monarchy, repugnant though the new king and his entourage might find it. The Verona Declaration might have killed the prospect for the legislators of the Convention; but in the country at large, in the aftermath of the last sansculotte convulsions in Germinal and Prairial, monarchy seemed increasingly to offer the best prospects for stability. And with the approaching end of the Convention it might even hope to triumph: not through foreign invasion or internal insurrection, but through the normal political process of elections.

# The Directory
## 1795—1799

THE problem facing the Convention in the summer of 1795 was now very clear. Having routed the forces of both terrorism and royalism, it had to devise a constitution for the country which would prevent the recovery of either. All the deputies agreed that what France needed most was stability. But they also believed that stability could and should be achieved without sacrificing the principles of 1789, the ideals which their countrymen had endured so many years of torment and turmoil to establish and preserve. The principles of 1789 were not to be confused with those of 1793. The constitution of that year, declared Boissy d'Anglas, introducing the report of the drafting committee on 23 June,[1] had been 'Drafted by schemers, dictated by tyranny, and accepted through terror . . . nothing other than the organization of anarchy'. It had no redeeming features.

Civil equality, in fact [he went on], is all that a reasonable man can claim. Absolute equality is a chimera; for it to exist, there would have to be absolute equality in intelligence, virtue, physical strength, education and fortune for all men . . . We must be governed by the best; the best are those who are best educated and most interested in the maintenance of the laws: now, with very few exceptions, you find such men only among those who, owning a piece of property, are devoted to the country that contains it, to the laws that protect it, to the tranquillity that maintains it, and who owe to this property and to the economic security it provides the education that has made them capable of discussing with wisdom and exactitude the advantages and inconveniences of the laws that determine the fate of their native land. The man without property, on the other hand, requires a constant exercise of virtue to interest himself in a social order that preserves nothing for him, and to resist actions and movements that hold out hope to him . . . A country governed by non proprietors is in a state of nature.

These principles underlay the new constitution finally approved by the Convention on 22 August. It was headed by a declaration of rights, like its predecessors; but there was no mention of equality of birth or entitlement to social services, and the 22 rights enunciated were balanced by 9 specific duties. All male taxpayers over 21 were declared citizens, with voting rights. But deputies would be chosen by electoral assemblies to which only citizens owning or renting (according to constituency size) property worth between 100 and 200 days' labour were eligible. This produced a notional electorate of about 30,000—barely half that of 1791. Elections would be annual, renewing a third of the deputies each time; but the legislature, for the first time, would be bicameral. Experience since 1789 had borne out all the warnings of the *monarchiens*, so heedlessly brushed aside then, about the dangers of a single chamber. A constitution of elaborate checks and balances was now the aim. Thus there would be two 'Councils'. The lower, or Council of Five Hundred, would initiate all legislation. The upper, the Council of Elders (*Anciens*), with 250 members, married or widowed, over 40, could merely pass or reject legislation coming from the Five Hundred. Executive power, now that the restoration of a king was out of the question, would be vested in five Directors chosen by the Elders from a list presented by the Five Hundred. One of them would retire each year, by lot. Neither they nor the ministers they appointed could sit in the legislature: here was a principle of 1789 that the experience of the Year II seemed to underline the wisdom of. Finally, the constitution of the Year III was deliberately made very difficult to change. The procedures envisaged could not take less than nine years. The aim, again, was to maximize the stability of the new regime, and make any changes in the direction of either extreme *ipso facto* illegal. But even this was not enough entirely to reassure the members of the Convention that their intentions would be observed. The transition to the new order needed some continuity. They looked back on the self-denying ordinance of 1791 (moved, of course, by Robespierre) as one of the Constituent Assembly's crowning mistakes. They therefore accompanied the Constitution with decrees stipulating that two-thirds of the members of the first Councils to be elected under it should be drawn from their own ranks.

The Two Thirds Law came as a shock to public opinion. By now there was a general weariness with the Convention and its posturings. Shortages of basic commodities and inflation of the assignats continued throughout the summer, and the deputies were (not entirely unreasonably) blamed. When on 10 August a festival was held to commemorate the third anniversary of the overthrow of the monarchy, it was coldly received. 'Market women', noted a police spy,[2] 'said it would have been better to do something about bringing down the price of things instead of holding useless and expensive festivals.' But at least the drafting of a constitution meant that the country would soon be rid of the Convention. The Two Thirds Law blighted these hopes. It also deprived monarchists, who hoped to show their strength in the elections, of the prospect of an early victory. The extent of the disappointment was shown when, early in September, the constitution and the Two Thirds Law were submitted for ratification to the primary electoral assemblies. The constitution was accepted by 1,057,000 votes to 49,000. Almost four million electors cast no vote, but the acceptance was convincing enough. The Two Thirds Law, however, was only approved by 205,498 votes to 108,754. Nineteen departments opposed it, and in Paris all but one of the 48 sections were against. Metropolitan hostility reflected the thorough purging of the sections that had gone on since Prairial, in which all suspected 'terrorists' had been arrested, leaving conservatives in uncontested control. The vote against the law followed a noisy campaign by right-wing newspapers which alerted the Convention to the danger: and early in September it began to take countervailing action by releasing Jacobin suspects and summoning troops to Paris. These moves were taken as evidence that the constitution was to be imposed by force, and possibly with terrorist support. The hostile clamour only increased. When the results of the votes were announced on 23 September (1 Vendémiaire) a number of unanimous Parisian returns were discounted on the grounds that precise figures had not been stated. After that several of the city's western sections began to organize for an insurrection, their primary assemblies refusing the Convention's instructions to disband, and concerting defiant denunciations of its ballot-rigging.

On 3 October a royalist riot at Dreux, 40 miles to the west, was dispersed with violence. When news of the incident reached the capital the next day, a call was issued for representatives of all the sections to meet to plan joint action. Only fifteen appeared, an ominously tepid turnout, and even then no action was agreed. The Convention hurriedly outlawed such meetings and stationed troops with cannon at strong points throughout the city. Even so, on the morning of 4 October (12 Vendémiaire) seven sections declared themselves to be in insurrection and mobilized their National Guard units. Regular soldiers sent that evening against section Le Peletier, the centre of resistance, accepted promises of disarmament and withdrew. The promises were not kept. The next morning, therefore, 25,000 insurgents converged on the Convention, mostly from south of the river. They were stopped by troops who had invested the main bridges on the orders of the deputy Barras—advised in turn by the 26-year-old artillery general Bonaparte. All afternoon the two sides faced each other, but at 4.30 the Convention's cannon opened fire. The insurgents had no cannon; indeed, so effectively had Paris been disarmed after Prairial that even those who had rifles were short of powder and shot. Nevertheless, the Convention had only 6,000 troops, and once the fighting had begun, rebel sections north of the river threw their forces into the balance, and the battle lasted $6\frac{1}{2}$ hours. Isolated skirmishes continued until the morning of the sixth. It took more than Bonaparte's vaunted 'whiff of grape shot' to win the day for the Convention, and when it was over hundreds lay dead.

It was the last time Paris attempted to impose its will on the national representatives. And although troops had been prominent in mopping up after Prairial, it was the first time the army had been unleashed against unrest in the capital since the Reveillon riots of April 1789. The Vendémiaire uprising was therefore much more of a turning-point than the end of the Convention and inauguration of the constitution of the Year III, which took place three weeks later, on 27 October. The one clear aim of the rebels had been to prevent the operation of the Two Thirds Law in the elections scheduled for the second week in October. Their failure meant that 500 members of the Convention duly took their seats (although only 394 by election) in the new Councils, from where they could prolong the spirit and policies of the Thermidorian Convention until reduced to a minority in the spring elections of 1797. The first Directors chosen were not surprisingly from their ranks, too. Barras, a slippery ex-noble, was a natural choice after his role in Vendémiaire. Sieyès now resurfaced after years of prudent silence, but refused to preside over a system not of his own devising. His place was taken by Carnot, whose prestige as a military organizer outweighed his terroristic record. La Revellière-Lépeaux, Reubell, and Letourneur were as yet unknown quantities, chosen for their republicanism—thus far more proven than their abilities. The policy they would pursue remained that which had emerged over the summer of 1795. When Jacobinism threatened, clubs would be closed and suspected terrorists rounded up, as after Prairial. When royalism seemed the danger curbs would be imposed on the well-funded right-wing press, while Jacobin papers would receive subsidies. Sansculottes in detention would be released and encouraged to open clubs. Clemency to the recently execrated terrorists marked the Convention's response to the Vendémiaire crisis, both in the build-up to the insurrection and in its aftermath. Indeed, rumours of the renewed favour enjoyed by Jacobins did much to help precipitate the rising, and some newly released veterans of Prairial served as volunteers alongside Barras's soldiers. Yet the repression after Vendémiaire did not match that after Prairial. No efforts were made to prevent known ringleaders fleeing the city, and only two of those arrested were executed. For, despite the Convention's propaganda, it was far from certain that most of those involved were royalists. Much clearer was that they included many people of property and substance, who might be wooed from their leanings towards monarchy if the new constitution could provide the security they craved. The most resolute steps taken after Vendémiaire, therefore, struck not at those involved but at the apparatus which both they and their sansculotte predecessors had used to mount insurrections ever since 1792. Thus on 10 October sectional assemblies were abolished, along with the National Guard organization which they had controlled. A new, centrally controlled Parisian Guard took its place, designed to be an instrument of the government rather than the governed. It was now clear above all, however, that the supreme instrument of government, at home as well as abroad, was the army. True, the constitution excluded all regular troops from a radius of 60 kilometres round the capital. But the Directory could not have begun as its architects intended without military help, and it was soon to recognize that it needed that help to survive, too.

The most pressing problems facing the Directors as they installed themselves in the chilly, dilapidated, and unfurnished Luxembourg palace on 1 November were economic. The harvest of 1795 brought little relief to the famine conditions of the spring. The savage winter had meant grain was sown late, and it failed to swell during the unusually dry summer. While the British blockade disrupted imports from overseas, the best of domestic produce continued to be requisitioned for the armies. All basic foodstuffs, candles, and firewood were strictly rationed (although the black market flourished) and the first frosts of what was to be another exceptionally cold winter arrived early, at the beginning of November. On top of all this came the final, catastrophic collapse of the assignats. They had reached 1 per cent of their face value by the time the Directory began. A month later in Paris bread was costing 50 *livres* a pound, butter 100, coffee 250, soap 170. 'The price of everything is excessive', noted a Parisian diarist.[3] 'No more order, no more supervision, everybody free to sell what he has for whatever he wants . . . It really seems as if the time has come at last to die of hunger and cold, lacking everything. Great God, what a Republic! And the worst of it is, one can't tell when or how it will end. Everybody is dying of hunger.'

On 19 October the floor of the printing house where assignats were produced collapsed with the activity of the presses, which were turning out 2,000 millions worth of paper money per month. Specie had completely disappeared. On arriving in Normandy in February 1796 the Irish revolutionary Wolfe Tone noticed that coinage was actually refused on the presumption that it could not be genuine. Landlords had in any case been authorized to take half their rents in kind since the summer, and the salaries of the Directors themselves and other public officials were expressed in the constitution in measures of grain rather than money. Debtors did well in these circumstances, paying off their creditors in currency worth quite literally less than the paper it was printed on. The greatest debtor of all was the government itself, simply meeting its commitments by printing what was required. But the government was also a creditor, receiving only its own worthless paper back in taxes, despite attempts to make taxpayers account for half in cash or kind. Even a 'war rate' (25 October) designed simply to mop up surplus assignats by demanding a paper contribution twenty times the value of assessed taxes made no impact on the problem, while a forced loan in specie decreed six weeks later (6 December), in order to draw hoarded coinage back into circulation to the tune of 600 millions, had only yielded 116 millions four months later. Much of that had come in in the end in the form of discounted assignats which were at once reissued. There were over 34,000,000,000 *livres* worth still in circulation when, in February 1796, it was finally decided to print no more. On the nineteenth, a solemn public bonfire of the broken plates used to produce them was lit in the place Vendôme.

Yet even supposing this gesture succeeded, returning to specie would take time. To bridge the gap, it was at first proposed to establish a land bank issuing notes on the credit of still unsold national lands. Ramel, the newly appointed finance minister, had been well connected in banking circles since before 1789, and now tried to put together a consortium of financiers to launch the new institution. But the suspicion of banks which had kept France without one since the great crash of 1720 was still virulent, especially in Jacobin circles eternally hostile to speculators. A furious journalistic campaign led by Lindet, who had managed the controlled economy of the Year II and now ran a newspaper, *L'Ami des lois*, led to the scheme's rejection by the Councils. Instead they adopted what were in effect the assignats by another name, the 'territorial mandates' redeemable in national lands or in assignats still in circulation, at the rate of 30: 1. But their value in relation to land was fixed at the levels of 1790, long undermined by the unprecedented amount of property thrown on to the market during the intervening years. Moreover, three times as many were issued as the entire face value of the assignats still in circulation. The result was that even on their first day of issue they were being discounted at 18 per cent of their face value, and by midsummer they were as worthless as the assignats. Ceasing to be legal tender on 17 July, in four months they had run the course which took the assignats five years. But those months proved a remarkable opportunity for speculators in national property, who bought in worthless paper and resold or leased for cash: far more of a profiteers' paradise than the bank which deputies as yet refused to countenance. Enormous profits were also made by the private company which contracted to withdraw the remaining paper from circulation over the winter of 1796–7. But by 4 February 1797, when the mandates were officially demonetized, the revolutionary experiment with paper money was at an end.

The speculative fortunes being made in these chaotic conditions could only reinforce resentment at the privations ordinary people were forced to endure for a second exceptionally lean year. Such popular discontents in turn were fertile soil for the Jacobins, whose fortunes continued to revive rapidly in the aftermath of Vendémiaire. Although 68 'terrorist' deputies suspected of being too left-wing had on 22 August been declared ineligible for the directorial Councils, they were not excluded from other political activity. Others joined them when an amnesty proclaimed to mark the start of the Directory brought the release from prison of the remainder of those arrested after Prairial. They were soon meeting regularly, and Jacobin journalists like Lindet, or Duval, publisher of the *Journal des hommes libres*, found that discreet governmental subsidies were available They were even allowed to establish a club: the Pantheon Club was founded on 16 November, and was soon able to boast over a thousand members.

The next day the most eloquent journalistic agitator of the previous year, Babeuf, began once more to produce his *Tribun du peuple*. But whereas many Jacobins were prepared to accept favours from a government that seemed at least firmly republican, Babeuf was intransigent from the very moment of hisrelease under the amnesty. 'What', he asked,[4] 'is the French Revolution? An open war between patricians and plebeians, between rich and poor.' Until the fall of Robespierre the poor had made considerable progress in this struggle. Since then it had been one long retreat. But now Babeuf went even further. During his months in prison he had come to the conclusion that there would be no true equality among men until property itself was abolished. Common ownership and equal distribution of goods should be the proper aim of the State, which it should pursue if necessary by terroristic methods far more fierce than any seen in France so far. Meanwhile the first step would be to implement the constitution of 1793. And it was this now classic demand, rather than the full-blooded communism of which he was the first active exponent in modern times, that struck the most immediate chords with Babeuf's contemporaries. Within weeks the *Tribun du peuple* was selling 2,000 copies, and was being read not only in Paris clubs and cafés, but in circles composed of former terrorists in provincial towns all over northern France, and some much further afield. After only two issues the government tried to arrest the author, but sansculotte sympathizers spirited him into hiding, from where he continued to produce the journal. As much of his fury was directed against the fickleness of his fellow Jacobins as against the Directory, and for a time that cut him off from the Pantheon Club and other groups prepared to rub along with the new regime. But when his wife was arrested for distributing the paper, Jacobin opinion in general swung his way, and her release after three weeks failed to reopen the division. By the middle of February 1796 the Pantheon Club was giving thunderous applause to readings of Babeuf's journal which denounced the Directors as tyrants. At the theatres, fierce patriotic pieces sustained these sentiments. 'I never knew what enthusiasm was before',[5] noted the newly arrived Wolfe Tone, moved to tears. Understanding no French, he little knew that the ballets he was attending were a form of Jacobin rally. Lindet's campaign against the proposed bank, along with vocal popular resentment against steadily diminishing bread and meat rations, began to look like a co-ordinated challenge to government. 'It's a fine bugger of a republic for robbers,' shouted women queueing outside a wine shop on 10 February,[6] 'first they guillotine us, now they make us die of hunger. What's more, Robespierre didn't let us waste away, he only brought death to the rich; this lot are letting people die every day!'

In fact the policy of conciliating the Jacobins to keep the monarchists at bay seemed to be getting beyond control; and on 27 February it was brusquely reversed. Five clubs and a theatre were closed, including the Pantheon, cleared by soldiers under the command of Bonaparte. A few days later a purge began to clear Jacobin suspects from posts of authority. On 16 April, advocacy of the constitution of 1793 was made a capital crime. Faced with renewed persecution from a regime some had hoped they could live with, the Jacobins now turned instinctively to insurrection. But a classic sansculotte *journée* was out of the question. The machinery through which such mass demonstrations had been put together no longer existed. Even the 48 sections had now been replaced by twelve more amorphous *arrondissements*. During his months in prison, however, Babeuf had become increasingly attracted by the idea of seizing power by a *coup d'état* rather than mass confrontation. In the course of March and April he and a group of victims of the Year II (including Buonarroti, once a middle-ranking official of the Terror, later to achieve fame as the chronicler of this conspiracy) established an insurrectional committee. Its aim was to co-ordinate the energies of 'democrats' throughout the capital, and secretly to subvert the Police Legion, which had now replaced the National Guard as the main force of law and order in the city. Approaches were also planned to military units. The idea was that when the signal was given for a rising, there could be no resistance, since the forces of order would join it. An 'Insurrectionary Act' was prepared, and even printed. It proclaimed, in the name of Equality, Liberty, and the Common Happiness, that sovereignty had been usurped by a faction of conspirators (the members of the Convention who still dominated the Councils) whom French democrats now intended to overthrow and 'judge'. Once in power, the 'Equals' would bring into effect the constitution of 1793, organize free distributions of bread, and implement the Laws of Ventôse Year II to distribute national lands to needy patriots. There would be no mercy to the usurpers. Heads, gloated one veteran of the Terror, would 'fall like hail [with] tripes and bowels scattered about the pavement'.[7] But before these vengeful fantasies could be fulfilled, the conspiracy was betrayed by one of its own members, along with the hiding place of Babeuf and other leading Equals. They had already lost perhaps their best opportunity to strike. When on 28 April certain units of the Police Legion mutinied, they insisted that their 'Day of the People' must remain 19 May. So the mutiny was put down (eventually with 17 executions), and on 10 May Babeuf and Buonarroti were arrested. Other Equals were brought in on subsequent days. Altogether there were 10 arrests, 48 of them in the provinces. The ringleaders were imprisoned, like the 'tyrant' whose memory they so much execrated, in the Temple.

It was the spring of 1797 before they were brought to trial. Carnot, the Director responsible for smashing the conspiracy, was determined to secure convictions at all costs, and the excuse that one of the conspirators was a deputy (Drouet, the man who had recognized Louis XVI at Varennes) was used to send all of them before a specially constituted high court. Drouet escaped in August, but arrangements went ahead for the court to sit at Vendôme, far from the Paris populace the plotters had hoped to propel into action. In the meantime the exposure of the conspiracy brought further anti-Jacobin repression. The subscription-list of the *Tribun du peuple* found among Babeuf's papers provided an obvious roll-call of suspects, who were duly harassed and removed from any positions of influence they might hold. The suspect Police Legion was dissolved—another step towards making the government completely dependent on the army. But was the army reliable? Babeuf and his fellow conspirators had always believed the troops could be subverted, and that belief continued in Jacobin circles even after the conspiracy's collapse. Ten thousand bored and underpaid troops were encamped at Grenelle, near the Champ de Mars, dreaming enviously of comrades now winning spectacular and glorious victories in Italy, and being paid by their general in plundered coin. Rumours of mutiny among them circulated throughout the summer, and dubious elements were periodically discharged. But when on 9 September several hundred Jacobins marched to Grenelle expecting a dragoon regiment to defect to them, informers in their ranks had alerted the authorities, and the soldiers charged the marchers with drawn swords. Twenty were cut to pieces, and another thirty of those arrested then or subsequently were shot after military trials. By then Babeuf and his co-conspirators, secure in iron cages on wheels, had been transported to Vendôme to face less summary but—the Directors hoped—just as inevitable justice.

The rout of the Jacobins could not fail to encourage monarchists of every stripe. They certainly had little enough to cheer them on other fronts. Their foreign friends were either deserting them—like the British, who were putting out peace feelers—or being defeated in the field, like the Austrians in Italy. The royalist rebellions in the Vendée and Brittany were now in the final stages of being stifled by Hoche. It was true that White Terror continued to make life unsafe for those with Jacobin pasts throughout the south-east, and that the British spymaster Wickham in Switzerland, and d'Antraigues in Italy, entertained high hopes that some movement might come together out of the random vengeance killings that went on all the time in a region where vendetta had long been a way of life. Mallet du Pan, characteristically, saw more clearly. 'The south', he wrote,[8] 'is in ferment, but its agitation is vague, without ends or means.' The people of Arles, noted a local observer in January 1796, 'taken up entirely with themselves and little indeed with the public interest have contracted the habit of concentrating great national concerns in their personal passions and feelings. For them, revolutionary crises have not been this or that event favourable or disastrous to liberty, but ways of letting one party prevail over another.'[9]

In such circumstances, monarchists hoping to recapture the State increasingly pinned their hopes on winning elections. The next ones were scheduled for the spring of 1797, and already a number of deputies who were not ex-members of the Convention were discussing how the reduction of the latter to a minority could be turned to monarchist advantage. They met regularly in the prosperous suburb of Clichy. First emerging in Thermidorian times, this 'Clichy Club' was understandably quiescent in the aftermath of Vendémiaire, but now it took on new life. A well-funded and outspoken right-wing press, several of whose editors were regular attenders at Clichy, used renewed government complaisance to emphasize the coming opportunity. It was true that there was no real unity on the right, or even within the Clichy Club. Absolute monarchists hated constitutionalists, and only co-operated with them in order to use them. Constitutionalists in turn could be subdivided into those hoping for concessions from Louis XVIII, and Orleanists, who placed more hope in the junior branch of the royal house represented by Louis-Philippe, the *émigré* son of Philippe-Égalité. A king who was himself the son of a regicide might, legitimists feared, be an attractive prospect to the regicides who still dominated politics, if their republic should fail. Even so, all royalists believed by the autumn of 1796 that events were moving their way, and most were content to co-operate in winning the elections, leaving decisions about subsequent policy until later. While newspapers and pamphleteers hammered home the inadequacies of the Republic—its contempt for the law and above all its economic and financial incompetence—something like a party organization grew up with the establishment of semi-secret royalist clubs calling themselves the 'Philanthropic Institute'. Beginning in Bordeaux, they soon spread throughout the south, and at their height were active in perhaps 70 departments, some of them receiving secret British funds. The self-styled 'friends of order' who made up their membership played assiduously upon the fears of the men of substance who would be casting their votes in April 1797; but their efforts were undermined by the activities of an inner circle of 'legitimate sons' who still toyed with more violent means. The futility of that was, however, demonstrated as the year began when a royalist version of the Grenelle plot to subvert troops stationed near Paris was revealed by informers. Brottier, the chief agent of d'Antraigues's network in the capital, was arrested, along with several key members of his organization, at the end of January. They were at once subjected to a show trial, running concurrently with that of Babeuf which finally began in Vendôme on 20 February.

The twin dangers facing the Republic were thus graphically displayed side by side; and in addition for the first time during the revolution the government resorted to systematic electioneering on its own behalf. Under the constitution, each department was administered by a five-man elected administration, subject in turn to the surveillance of a centrally appointed 'directorial commissioner' modelled on the national agent employed under the Revolutionary Government of the Year II. In disturbed departments of the west, or along the Rhône valley, departmental administrations had never been elected from the start, and were regularly remodelled according to each swing of the pendulum in Paris. In the first three months of 1796 eleven departments had their personnel totally or partially renewed to remove Jacobinical influences. During the spring of the subsequent year this network of officials was directed to use all its influence to see that the electoral assemblies returned solid, middle-of-the-road republicans. On 25 February it was decreed that only *émigrés* whose names had been removed from the official list might vote, scotching plans for a mass return to participate in the elections: while in March an oath to defend the constitution against both monarchists and anarchists was imposed on all members of electoral assemblies. The right was alarmed at these confident directorial ploys. As well as denouncing them furiously in the press, its leaders begged Louis XVIII to make some gesture to reassure propertied waverers before the assemblies met. Eventually, on 10 March, he issued a grudging declaration from Blankenburg, full of ambiguity, urging Frenchmen to vote decisively against Jacobinism, and holding out the vaguest hope that the Declaration of Verona had not after all been his last word.

Despite all these unprecedented manoeuvres, the elections of the Year V, between 21 March and 9 April, took place amid the same public indifference that had characterized every election since 1791. Most of those qualified to vote in replacing the 234 or so former members of the Convention now to retire by lot did not bother to do so. But the verdict of the electoral assemblies was nevertheless clear. They voted heavily against the Convention and its legacy: only 11 of the retiring deputies were re-elected. They voted, too, against Jacobinism. No clearly identifiable left-wing candidates were returned. Above all they voted against the Directory. Of those elected, 228 were without any previous political experience, but were still preferred to the trusted hacks the authorities had tried to favour. And 182 of them were royalists. That did not mean that they constituted a united party. They ranged from the most gradualist believers in a constitutional restoration, to General Pichegru, who had been in sporadic contact with Louis XVIII's agents for almost two years over the prospects of a restoration by military coup. But their arrival destroyed the more-or-less stable majority on which the Directors had been able to rely since the inauguration of the constitution. For this reason alone Reubell at once proposed the annulment of the elections. His colleagues felt, however, that the complexion of the new majority was by no means clear; and the first test of opinion confirmed the uncertainty. When it fell to Letourneur's lot to retire, the new Councils elected Barthélemy, a career diplomat best known for negotiating the Peace of Basle in 1795. His constitutional convictions were unclear. He seems to have been chosen on the presumption that he would help to bring an end to the war.

All these domestic convolutions took place, of course, against the background of Bonaparte's victories in Italy and even (at last) progress on the German front. The preliminaries of Leoben were signed on 18 April. The new Councils convened on 20 May under their shadow, and the nature of the peace they were to produce became at once one of the central issues in politics. The desire for peace was general after five years of battling against the whole of Europe. When in July the British offered to negotiate, the prospects for a general settlement seemed bright. Royalists believed that it would smooth the way towards a restoration, and to hasten the moment, they favoured a conciliatory approach to both Austria and Great Britain. Pragmatists like Carnot and Barthélemy also realized that a peace without

significant concessions was bound to be unstable. In any case they believed
that a working relationship must be developed with the new majority. But
the other three Directors, after characteristic initial wavering by Barras,
feared that co-operation could only lead to a monarchist triumph. Pichegru
had been elected president of the Five Hundred, and by this time the
Directors, though not the deputies, had received damning evidence from
Bonaparte of his treasons. Nor did the Republic's more successful generals
wish to see their conquests bartered away to bring in a king. That meant not
only Bonaparte, but Hoche, who as commander in the Netherlands hoped
to restore a prestige dented by the Irish débâcle of the previous winter.
Encouraged by Barras, Hoche moved troops within the constitutional belt
around the capital in July, and under their eye on the fourteenth the
Directory, outvoting Carnot and Barthélemy, carried out a ministerial
reshuffle which deliberately challenged the Councils by removing the most
prominent right-wingers. The 'triumvirs', as the right-wing press now
dubbed Barras, Reubell, and La Revellière, also began to make gestures
towards Jacobinism. Babeuf had been finally convicted at Vendôme, and
he and one other conspirator had gone to the guillotine on 27 May. They
would be remembered as Jacobin martyrs (having, like those of Prairial,
tried to kill themselves as soon as the verdict was pronounced), but most of
the other accused had been acquitted, so it was possible now to close the
episode and quietly rehabilitate less extreme forms of Jacobinism. But any
such gestures naturally alarmed the Councils, who were busy discussing
ways to circumscribe the Directory's financial powers, and measures
favourable to nonjuror priests. Thus tension between executive and
legislature mounted over the summer, while the majority of a clearly
divided Directory steadily drafted more and more troops into the Paris
region. Late July, in fact, was marked by a surge of patriotic addresses from
the armies professing loyalty to the Republic, and neither the Directory nor
the generals did anything to discourage such overt partisanship. Bonaparte
even told his men they would cross the Alps 'with an eagle's swiftness' if the
Republic should be threatened. Meanwhile he dispatched one of his
deputies, Augereau, to command the forces being assembled by the
triumvirs. Desperately, royalist leaders spent August trying to put together
a counter-force. While the Councils debated measures to revitalize the
National Guard, irregular bands of street fighters were recruited, and there
were clashes with Augereau's troops. But in the face of so much
accumulating force, the Councils could do little but bluster. Thus, at the end
of August, they finally approved the abrogation of all laws against
refractory priests.

The triumvirs took up the challenge. On the night of 3–4 September

(17–18 Fructidor, Year V) they ordered the troops they had assembled to seize all strong points in Paris and surround the legislative chambers. They then issued orders for the arrest of Carnot, Barthélemy, 53 deputies (including Pichegru), and several other prominent members of the right. They also closed down some 30 newspapers. These measures were confirmed by a handpicked quorum of deputies from both Councils meeting under military surveillance. Meanwhile the city was plastered with a proclamation denouncing royalist machinations and publicizing for the first time the treason of Pichegru. There was no resistance. The coup was practically bloodless. As soon as it was over the purged Councils annulled the results of the spring elections in 49 departments, leaving 177 vacant seats. The vacant posts on the Directory were filled by François de Neufchâteau, a noted anti-clerical, and Merlin de Douai, one of the chief architects of the constitution which the coup of Fructidor had in effect destroyed.

Whether it saved France from a restoration seems improbable. Although it undoubtedly thwarted the 'grand design' of certain British-backed royalist agents like the ex-magistrate and deputy d'André, who hoped to achieve a peaceful recall of the pretender by a legislative majority built up over several elections and tireless cultivation of moderate opinion, the very number of its victims shows that no sort of royalist majority yet existed. It is quite likely, as Carnot had hoped, that a working relationship could have been established between the Directory and a moderate, republican majority. But the triumvirs dreaded a conspiracy, and the generals feared and despised all moderates. They combined, therefore, to destroy the constitution before it had weathered its first real test. From now on, although legal forms would continue to be observed, the 'Second Directory' would not hesitate to rig or set aside any results that proved inconvenient. They thereby proclaimed that they had no confidence in the system by which they ruled. They could scarcely, then, expect their fellow citizens to trust it either, or to come to its defence when it was under threat from forces outside the Directory two years later.

Meanwhile, however, Fructidor ushered in a period of decisive government. The whole of the Year V (October 1796–September 1797) had been a time of paralysis and suspended action. During its first half the coming election had dominated all preoccupations; its second was stalemated by the results. But now, with a united Directory and a subservient legislature, the government could turn to the problems shelved over the previous twelve months.

First the international situation was clarified. Both the Austrians and the

British had been happy to spin out peace negotiations in the hope of wringing concessions from a divided France. They now saw no further prospect of that. Within six weeks the Austrians had signed the peace of Campo Formio, accepting conditions much like those agreed at Leoben the previous spring. The British, meanwhile, were offered terms amounting to little more than complete surrender, and broke off their negotiations within a week of the Fructidor coup. The whole French war effort was now to be marshalled against the island state, and Bonaparte was summoned back from Italy to command an army of invasion being encamped along the Channel coasts. Hoche, who had always regarded the British Isles as his destined prey, died suddenly late in September, removing the Corsican's last credible rival. Yet failure on the northern seas had almost destroyed Hoche in 1796, and the victor of Italy did not want to risk his own reputation. The Dutch fleet, an indispensable auxiliary, had been destroyed at Camperdown in October; and inspection of the northern ports quickly convinced him that no adequate expedition could be launched against England before the end of 1798. But did Great Britain need to be attacked frontally? As early as the summer of 1797, when he was still in Italy, Bonaparte had begun to dream of striking at a major source of British wealth, India, through Egypt. In September, while still in Italy, he had formally suggested the idea, and it appealed to Talleyrand, who, after a period of emigration, had re-emerged in July to become foreign minister. It appealed to the Directors, too, when the general and the minister formally proposed the idea of an Egyptian expedition on 5 March 1798. Bonaparte had behaved modestly since his return and refused to put on military airs except when inspecting the troops in Normandy; but the presence at home of so successful a general, who had more than once forced the pace of the Republic's policies against the instructions of its Directors, unnerved them. They would feel happier with him far away in Egypt, and the expedition he proposed was smaller and less expensive than a full-scale descent on England would have been. If he succeeded, the British would surely be knocked out of the war: they seemed too dependent on the wealth of India, and French control of the Suez isthmus would turn their control of the route round the Cape from an asset into a burden. If he failed, they would be rid of him. Accordingly, the Directory welcomed the Egyptian project warmly. A fleet was equipped at Toulon over the spring of 1798, and on 19 May it sailed, carrying an army of 35,000 men.

Fructidor also cleared the way for resolving the Republic's financial difficulties. Ramel, the finance minister, had survived in office throughout all the Year V's political upheavals, but the collapse of paper money confronted him with problems scarcely less difficult that those it had caused.

The disappearance of inflated paper provoked a massive deflation as still scarce coinage became once more the only legal tender. Debtors who had not already cleared their obligations in paper now found themselves overwhelmed as prices plummeted and interest rates soared. In many districts a natural economy of barter proved the only viable means of exchange. Taxes, now payable in cash, practically dried up for a time, just at the moment when the government was brought face to face with the true scale of the debt it had run up to finance the war. The early months of 1797 witnessed desperate attempts to raise coinage from any source. Future revenues were mortgaged against advances at usurious rates, and the State's assets were recklessly sold off—from former church lands in now annexed Belgium, right down to the crown jewels of the former kings. The main source of funds proved to be windfall income from the war— indemnity payments from the Batavian Republic, or plunder from other conquered territories. Germany yielded 16 millions, Italy (all told) perhaps 200 millions. It all re-emphasized how dependent the Republic had now become on its generals. Yet it was still not enough, and in the build-up to the Fructidor coup Ramel's administration and the speculators on whom he relied to put together some of his more bizarre financial expedients were ferociously denounced in the Councils. The main critics were among those purged. Within a week of their elimination Ramel had radical and decisive remedies to propose, and the Directory adopted them. On 30 September two-thirds of the State's debts were renounced by a one-off payment in paper valid for the purchase in national lands. The other third was 'consolidated'. Not since 1770 (except momentarily in August 1788) had the French government declared bankruptcy; and throughout the Revolution a rare consensus had survived that the national debt should be sacrosanct. Without it, the Revolution itself might not have come about, and it was a symbol of confidence in the new order. In Fructidor, the abandonment of the Revolution's longest-held principle looked like one more admission of failure. Bitter debt-holders found in subsequent months that the bonds in which they had been paid off lost 60 per cent of their face value within a year, and soon afterwards a decision no longer to accept them in payment for national lands completely destroyed them. But the 'Two Thirds Bankruptcy' relieved the State of debts which cost it 160 millions a year, and paved the way for durable financial reconstruction. The process began only a few weeks later (12 November) with the establishment of an 'Agency for Direct Contributions', to orchestrate the recovery of direct taxes at local level via the directorial commissioners—the first centralized fiscal apparatus since the old regime, largely staffed too with officials who had learned their trade then. And their methods: taxpayers in arrears would find troops billeted on them. In 1798 another principle of the Revolution was abandoned with the reintroduction of the indirect taxes so universally execrated in the *cahiers*. It had been their very effectiveness that had made them unpopular, and which now constituted their appeal. They were now imposed on tobacco, on road traffic, on legal documents, and on doors and windows—although the Councils balked at a proposal to tax salt, with its echoes of the most hated of all the pre-revolutionary levies, the *gabelle*. None of these measures gave spectacularly rapid results. It took years to draw as much coinage back into circulation as had been available in 1789, and although the last years of the century were marked by good harvests, business confidence was slow to revive. The most immediate effect of the bankruptcy and the State's reviving capacity for taxing its citizens was to increase its unpopularity among the very propertied groups on which it claimed to base its support.

Nor were the latter reassured by the politics of the Directors after Fructidor. The purge of the Councils and annulment of the elections proved only the beginning of a 'Directorial Terror' (as some called it) lasting many months. Laws against *émigrés* were reactivated, and those who had returned with the revived royalist hopes of the spring were given two weeks to leave the country, on pain of death. Over the next few months 160 were put to death under this, or older, unrepealed laws. Now for the first time in the whole Revolution nobles as a category were condemned by a law which deprived them of French citizenship merely for being noble. Little was done to implement this draconian measure, which would have made Barras and Bonaparte, to mention no others, legally into foreigners. But laws against refractory priests, on the verge of abrogation before the coup, were now reactivated; and any cleric who refused to swear a new oath of hatred for royalty, passed the day after the coup, made himself liable to summary deportation to Guiana. The revival of organized religion had made steady progress since the breakthrough of the spring of 1795, and even during leftward swings such as that after Vendémiaire the central government had not enough authority in the localities to arrest the recovery. With the royalist surge of the Year V many priests who had emigrated returned, and there were plenty of congregations ready to welcome them and provide them with a living. Fructidor proved a rude blow to them. Many who did not leave the country once more were rounded up, and of these only a small number took the oath of hatred. Ten thousand refused it, thus making themselves liable to deportation—although four-fifths of these were in Belgian departments. In these newly annexed territories, it was seen as too dangerous to provoke a sullen population with mass deportations; nevertheless 1,400 nonjurors in all were sent to the western islands of Ré and

Oléron prior to embarkation for Guiana. British ships rescued some of those sent on to the penal colony, so that eventually only 230 arrived there. But those interned included many who had been too old or ill to evade arrest, and they died on Ré or Oléron. Meanwhile the Directors sought to encourage less subversive cults. While the relics of the ill-starred constitutional Church were left to wither away (which, however, they refused to do, largely thanks to the organizing energy of Grégoire), the anti-clerical La Revelliére gave his support to Theophilanthropy. Originating late in 1796, this movement of intellectual, republican deism prospered in towns where dechristianization had been popular. After Fructidor it was allocated former churches for its services, and La Revellière saw to it that the best and most prominent ones in Paris (including for a time Notre-Dame) came its way. But it never commanded much popular support, any more than it proved possible to stamp out the observation of Sundays in favour of the *décadis* of the republican calendar.

The renewed official anti-Catholicism, however, was warmly welcomed by Jacobins who, after eighteen months in the wilderness, suddenly found themselves once more in modest favour. Although a small band of self-styled sansculottes from eastern Paris presenting themselves for service on 18 Fructidor had been sternly told to disperse, with royalism perceived as the main danger it was inevitable that the triumvirate should now look again leftwards for support. New elections were after all due in April 1798, when the last of the Convention's 'Perpetuals' would retire. If another royalist triumph was to be avoided proven anti-royalists would have to be mobilized. So, immediately after the coup, clubs were once more allowed to meet, and within weeks 'constitutional circles' were being formed in most of the departments. Not all by any means could be described as Jacobin: the Directors saw them as rallying-points for all sound republican opinion. But inevitably, with suspicion of royalism so prevalent, most of those prepared to take a public stand had pasts tainted with terrorism, dechristianization, or democracy. Inevitably, too, with their ranks decimated by repeated persecution since 1794, they sought to win new converts among working men. Thus, for example, although the circle set up at Evreux in February 1798 committed itself only 'to demonstrate the advantages of a free and popular government . . . to develop the wise and immutable principles of the Constitution [and] to confer public office only on upright, virtuous, modest, patriotic and enlightened men',[10] a local official reported of it to the minister of the interior: 'I recognize among them good republicans, but also persons whom I have heard declare in front of over a hundred people that Babeuf was murdered at Vendôme.' The language of social resentment so instinctively used by the democratic press, which revived in the new atmosphere, was also closely watched. As the elections approached, the more outspoken constitutional circles and neo-Jacobin journals began to be closed down. In Paris that included the left-bank Rue du Bac Club, which was calling for electoral reform which would radically widen the franchise established in 1795.

For the Second Directory had no interest in enlarging the electorate. It still sought to base itself on 'decent folk' (*honnêtes gens*) and substantial men of property. The problem was that too many of such people remained attracted by royalism. Yet no less than 437 seats (including those left vacant after Fructidor) had now to be filled, so if anything even more was at stake than in 1797. Blatant steps were therefore taken to rig the outcome at every stage. While lists of official candidates were established, the outgoing Councils declared their intention to 'verify' the results. Careful steps were taken to monitor the political complexion of every department, and government supporters and local officials were encouraged to foment splits in electoral assemblies whose inclinations looked dubious, so as to allow the Councils to decide on the legitimacy of the rival factions and their candidates. Such splits had taken place in every election since 1789 somewhere or other, but in 1798 they occurred in over a quarter of the departmental electoral assemblies, 27 in all, and in even more of the primary ones. The results showed that attempts to damp down the Jacobin revival had come too late. In many districts the constitutional circles packed the primary assemblies and secured the defeat of directorial candidates, notably in Paris and a number of major cities. Not surprisingly, then, former members of the Convention did much better than in the previous year: 162 were elected, 71 of them regicides. Electors were not deterred by directorial talk of an unholy pact between the two political extremes—'royalism in a red cap'. Royalism made no significant showing. Government supporters carried 43 departments, but it was not considered enough. As soon as all the results were in, accordingly, the process of checking began, and deciding on split returns. But there were so many difficult cases that the elaborate process of scrutiny promised to last beyond the meeting date of the new legislature, set for 20 May (1 Prairial, Year VI). The Law of 22 Floréal (11 May) therefore imposed a guillotine: 127 deputies were purged from the legislature before even taking their seats. The results from 8 departments were completely quashed, and only those in 47 (out of 96) were allowed to stand untouched. Nineteen secessionist minorities had their candidates accepted, and runners-up were declared elected in other instances. Eighty-six identifiable Jacobin winners were 'Floréalized', along with a number of newly chosen local officials. The effect was to maintain firm directorial control on the Councils, and chance helped sustain their authority too: François de Neufchâteau, the least forceful of the Directors, drew the lot to retire. He was replaced by Treilhard, a noted anti-clerical who reinforced the solidarity of the other four.

The coup of Floréal was less spectacular than that of Fructidor, and less decisive too—within a year significant numbers of those admitted as reliable had turned against the Directors. But for the moment it perpetuated the executive's control of the legislature asserted in Fructidor—if only by denying, for the second time in a year, the electorate's right to choose its own representatives. Some historians think that a viable parliamentary opposition might have developed in an unpurged legislature in 1798–9, seeing little evidence that the Jacobins still aimed (in contrast to the royalists the year before) at the overthrow of the constitution itself. But they were men with a bloody record, which inspired no trust in those they now denounced as oligarchs. To allow them a central power base seemed to imperil the republican middle way which the Directors saw as their overriding duty to uphold.

Nor, as two unresisted coups had now shown, did they have much difficulty in doing so. An electorate largely disinclined to vote in the first place raised little protest when the results of votes were overridden. The relaxation of the central grip on the localities between 1794 and 1798 had restored some of the local autonomy whose loss had caused such resentment in the Year II, and peace with victory met a deep-felt aspiration. In the aftermath of Floréal, therefore, a triumphant Directory faced the future with some confidence. Too much confidence in fact: within twelve months, sated with success, it would deliberately throw away most of these advantages.

The most fateful mistakes occurred in foreign affairs. Nowhere was the arrogance of the Directory more flagrantly displayed. Having routed all continental enemies, the French now increasingly spoke of themselves as the 'Great Nation', superior in kind to all the others, and entitled for that reason to behave according to their own rules. Bonaparte, in announcing the terms of Campo Formio to the Directory, was preaching to the convinced when he condemned the Italians as 'unworthy peoples who have little love for liberty and whose tradition, character and religion cause them to hate us profoundly'.[11] 'You have succeeded', he later declared to the Directors, 'in organising the great nation whose vast territory is circumscribed only because nature herself has imposed limits to it.' They believed it; and the way in which others rushed to do their will after the fighting was over only confirmed their arrogance. At the Congress of Rastadt, convened to settle peace terms between France and the Holy Roman Empire, matters moved slowly because of the sheer complexity of the Empire, but by April 1798 the Germans had been browbeaten into agreeing to allow the left bank of the Rhine to be incorporated within France's self-proclaimed 'natural' frontiers, and condoning the secularization of ecclesiastical states to provide compensation for those who lost by that process. In January 1798, meanwhile, a French-backed coup had overthrown the age-old government of the Swiss Confederation, substituting yet another 'sister republic', the Helvetic. In August a treaty of alliance gave France perpetual free access to the Alpine passes. In Italy, too, there were French advances. Bonaparte had shown that reputations could be made there, and lesser generals left behind were keen to emulate him. They were encouraged by the renewed anti-clericalism of the Directory after Fructidor to bully the Pope and infiltrate Italian Jacobins from the north into his territories. A riot in Rome on 28 December 1797 accidentally led to the death of a French general. It was used as a pretext for invading the Papal States, and on 15 February, in a Holy City occupied by French troops, a group of Jacobins proclaimed the Roman Republic and were at once recognized. The Pope was taken prisoner, that same Pius VI whose condemnation of the Civil Constitution of the Clergy had precipitated France's religious troubles. In increasingly delicate health, he spent the next eighteen months being bundled from one place of captivity to another, before dying on French soil at Valence in August 1799.

Such displays of power could only alarm the rest of Europe—especially Austria, whose Italian gains at Campo Formio seemed already threatened by continued French expansion in the peninsula. But nothing did more to turn alarm into resistance than the Egyptian expedition. Conceived as a project without cost, its initial military record was indeed impressive. Sailing on 17 May, on 12 June Bonaparte took Malta, dissolved the order of the Knights of St John, and garrisoned it with French troops. On 2 July he arrived in Egypt and took Alexandria by storm. On the twenty-first he defeated the Mameluke army at the battle of the Pyramids, and a few days later was in Cairo, the master of Egypt. Another campaign of lightning brilliance; but it was reduced to nothing on 1 August when the fleet which had conveyed the expedition was smashed to pieces by Nelson in what the British remember as the battle of the Nile. The British had withdrawn from the Mediterranean in 1797. To send a fleet back there was a gamble, and it took Nelson weeks to find the French. But when he did, he showed that not even their greatest commander was invulnerable. He cut off thousands of their best troops in the east, and provided the vital impulse for the formation of a new European coalition against France.

Outraged by the unprovoked invasion of what was, however nominally, Ottoman territory, the Turks declared war on France as soon as they heard about Nelson's victory. Militarily this meant little, but so great was the fury in Constantinople that the hitherto unthinkable was allowed. A Russian fleet passed through the Bosporus, sailing to attack Corfu, a French possession since Campo Formio. For all Catherine II's posturings, Russia had never yet taken the field against revolutionary France. But after she died in 1796, her unstable son Paul I looked for opportunities to make his counter-revolutionary mark. Already incensed by being ignored at the Congress of Rastadt, which was redrawing the map of Germany without consulting him, in violation of rights recognized since 1779, he boiled over with fury at the seizure of Malta, of which he had declared himself the protector in 1797. He was also concerned at reports that the French were making trouble in Poland. So he, too, rushed to declare his hand when news broke of Nelson's victory. So did the Neapolitans. Deeply shocked by the French takeover of the Papal States, and a series of threats which followed it, the Bourbon government in Naples was elated by the arrival of the victorious Nelson in September. He urged them to join the rapidly coalescing new alliance. Noting the weakness of the French garrison in Rome, they were anxious to strike before reinforcements arrived, and in November their troops marched north against the new sister republic. They reached Rome and occupied it, led by an Austrian general. They signed an offensive alliance with the Russians. But at the first clash with French troops they turned and fled. Championnet, the French commander, saw Bonaparte-like opportunities opening up, and pursued them back to Naples, which the royal family abandoned on 23 December, sailing off to Sicily with Nelson. On 26 January 1799, Championnet proclaimed the Parthenopean Republic. He proved to be no Bonaparte, and he was not dealing with the divided Directory of 1796. They had not wanted to take on yet another unstable and rootless puppet state. He was relieved of his command. But the damage was done. By this time Russia had sought, and received, permission for her troops to cross Austrian territory going to the aid of their southern ally. By the end of the year an army of 11,000 Russians was on Austrian soil. Not unnaturally, the French regarded their presence as a hostile sign, and on 2 January 1799 they issued an ultimatum for their removal. The Austrians did not respond, and in March war was formally declared. The emperor joined the network of treaties which over the preceding months had pulled most of the still independent powers of Europe together into a second anti-French coalition. At Rastadt, where negotiations to settle the last details of the peace of Campo Formio still meandered on, two French delegates were hacked to death by Austrian soldiers on 22 April. A new war to destroy the French Revolution had clearly begun.

The renewal of continental warfare after barely a year's respite received no welcome in France. The shattering naval defeat which announced the general resumption of the struggle signalled that the time of apparently effortless victory was over. The scale of the renewed effort likely to be required was spelled out with the passage on 5 September 1798, as the international horizon darkened, of the Jourdan Law on conscription—a new word with a long future. The numbers in the armies had fallen steadily since the Year II. By 1798 there were only 270,000 Frenchmen under arms. It had taken well over a million to fend off the previous coalition. The new law, devised by the victor of Wattignies and Fleurus, reiterated the principle of the *levée en masse* that all citizens were at the Republic's disposition in times of emergency. Army numbers were to be made up by volunteers in the first instance, but if they proved insufficient, young men between 20 and 25 were to be drafted to make up the numbers. From registers drawn up by local authorities, an annual 'class' would be called to arms.

The last time military service had been imposed, it had triggered off the uprising in the Vendée and civil war. Then as now, the government imposing it had been violently anti-clerical, scorning popular religious feelings. And its response to defiance and defeat had been one of terror. The Directory seemed to be bringing the Revolution full circle; with no prospect of a stable and durable settlement of the problems which for the best part of a decade had torn France, and much of Europe too, apart. In the course of the ensuing year even the army, which had hitherto sustained and defended the Directory, would come to this dispiriting conclusion. Then the end of the Revolution would at last be in sight.

# Occupied Europe
## 1794−1799

PITT's decision to send a squadron to the Mediterranean in the spring of 1798 was a bold gamble. In involved depleting the Channel fleet by eight capital ships, leaving it with far from overwhelming superiority to the known strength of the French navy in the western ports. And when the order was sent out, on 29 April, the British cabinet had known for six weeks that an uprising was imminent in Ireland, and that its leaders expected French help. The French had proved in December 1796 that they could mount a major expedition against Ireland and elude the British fleet. Only bad luck had prevented them from landing. Three months later they actually did land a small force of released convicts and desperadoes on the coast of Pembrokeshire in the hope that they might launch a British *chouannerie*. They were soon rounded up—but the fragility of British command of the seas stood exposed.

All this immeasurably encouraged Irish revolutionaries. Since 1795 the United Irishmen had worked to establish a country-wide organization by integrating themselves with the network of agrarian secret societies, the Defenders, which had grown up over the preceding decade. The Defenders were not much interested in politics. Originating in sectarian rivalry for land in Ulster, they had become general redressers of rural grievances, with overwhelmingly local concerns. But they inherited age-old traditions of French help; and as soaring population, poor harvests, and economic disruption resulting from the war brought increasing hardship to the Irish countryside, they seemed ripe for integration into the insurrectionary plans of Ireland's urban radicals, who were now dreaming of national independence. Though the failure of Hoche's expedition disappointed them, it fired their hopes for the future. Numbers taking the United Irish oath soared in 1797, and as the British fleet mutinied they impatiently awaited a new French landing. In fact there was little hope of that, especially after Hoche died in September. Remembering how Ireland had failed to stir even when the 1796 expedition had appeared in Bantry Bay, French strategists wanted tangible evidence of a rebellion, rather than promises, before even thinking of a further attempt. And while such mutual misunderstandings bedevilled hopes for an Irish revolution, the Dublin government took vigorous measures to pre-empt any uprising by disarming the most suspect areas. Starting with Ulster in the spring of 1797, it allowed an undisciplined soldiery to terrorize the countryside with floggings, burnings, and torture. The yield of hidden arms was so encouraging that these methods began to be applied further south. The United leaders began to fear that their organization would be broken before it could act. On the vaguest of rumours that the French were planning to come again in 1798, they resolved to rise. But informers had leaked their plans to the government, and on 12 March their Dublin leaders were arrested. When second-rank members precipitated a rising in Leinster in May it was squashed within days. So was another outbreak a few weeks later in Ulster. But by then sectarian panic had spread south to Wexford, a hitherto tranquil area, where no activity had been expected. There Catholic bands, whose numbers soon reached 20,000, massacred Protestants and repelled inadequate millitary units sent against them. A ragged rebel army marched north, but, instead of breaking out of the locality, encamped on Vinegar Hill. There, just three weeks after the Wexford outbreak began, they were pounded to pieces by heavy artillery. By the end of June the rebellion was over—or almost. News of its early success, however, had by now reached Paris, and desperate attempts were made to cobble together new task forces to help the rebels. Eventually just over a thousand men landed at Killala, in remote Mayo, on 22 August. Hundreds flocked to join them, although the Godless French were bemused to find themselves identified as soldiers of the Blessed Virgin. Some skirmishes were even won as the force marched inland to where United Irishmen (thin on the ground in Connacht) were reputedly massing. But by September there were 30,000 government troops in Ireland, and a third of them confronted General Humbert on 8 September at Ballinamuck. After token resistance, he surrendered. Other, smaller expeditions sent from France in the meantime fared no better. One of them contained Wolfe Tone, who was brought in chains to Dublin, and only evaded execution by cutting his own throat.

The Irish uprising of 1798 never had any real chance of success. Most of Ireland was untouched by it, and many of those involved had only the vaguest notion of what their French allies stood for. The latter had neither the resources nor the commitment, by 1798, to support it as it would have required for Ireland to be detached from the British Crown or merely become, as so many of them dreamed, a British Vendée. But (unless the Polish struggle of 1794 against the partitioning powers is counted) it was the largest pro-French uprising of the revolutionary decade. It terrified both the Protestant Ascendancy who ruled Ireland and their backers in London, who had little to cheer them until news of Nelson's victory arrived at the beginning of October. And, although not comparable in concentrated savagery with the carnage in Warsaw on 4 November 1794, it produced 30,000 victims in $3\frac{1}{2}$ months—a similar number to the Terror in France, but over a shorter period, and from a population barely one-sixth the size. And if, at this or some lesser cost, it had succeeded, the objectives of the peasant rebels, their educated urban leaders, and their French allies were far from clear or mutually compatible. The United Irish conspirators liked to imagine that, having helped them to freedom, their French liberators would leave them alone to seek their own destiny. 'Undoubtedly,' Wolfe Tone told a French general in July 1796,[1] 'the French must have a very great influence on the measures of our Government, in case we succeed, but ... if they were wise, they would not expect any direct interference.' Optimistic to the last, Tone discounted the general's ominous response: 'It might be necessary, as it was actually in Holland, where, if it were not for the continual superintendence of the French, they would suffer their throats to be cut again by the Stadtholder.'

The Dutch Republic was the only region reached by the French armies where sympathizers with the revolutionary cause were at all common. Patriots driven underground since 1787, and ordinary people outraged at the undisciplined behaviour of British and Prussian soldiers brought in to prop up William V, welcomed the French armies initially as liberators. The punitive peace treaty of 1795 came as a shock, but one whose impact those who now took power in Holland hoped would pass. Adopting the slogan *Liberty, Equality, Fraternity* at a time when it was being washed off buildings all over France, the first sister republic set about endowing itself with a more rational and democratic constitution than the age-old Union of Utrecht. But it took almost a year to decide how this should be done, and when eventually it was agreed (under mounting French pressure) that the means should be a national Convention rather than the traditional Estates-General, the body elected in March 1796 was soon immobilized by quarrels between advocates of a unitary state and Federalists. More radical elements favoured unity, and when the objections of more traditionally minded deputies brought discussion to an impasse, patriot clubs tried to bring pressure on the Convention in the well-tried Parisian manner. One of the

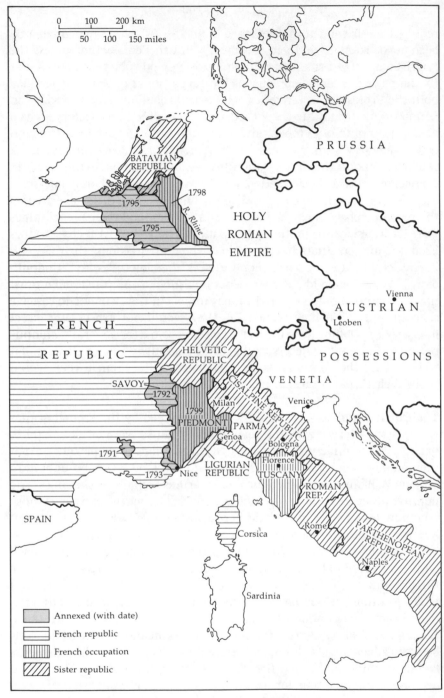

MAP 5. The expansion of revolutionary France

most spectacular of these episodes was the mutiny of certain Amsterdam National Guard units against the conservative city authorities early in May. It was thwarted without loss of life, but coinciding as it did with the exposure of Babeuf's conspiracy in France, it alerted the occupying army to the dangers of Dutch radicalism. Closer French control of the Batavian Republic, as Wolfe Tone was told a few weeks later, was evidently necessary. From then on the French applied steady pressure in favour of a unitary solution, and their troops were increasingly conspicuous on the streets of the major cities. Yet the eventual draft constitution, finalized in May 1797, fudged the federal issue. Submitted to a plebiscite the following August, it pleased nobody, and public endorsement by the French ambassador sealed its fate. It was rejected by 108,761 votes to 27,955. A new Convention was therefore elected, to begin the task afresh; but once more it was soon stalemated. But by now the Fructidor coup in France had removed the men of caution from the Directory and the Councils, and the Great Nation was more inclined than ever to assert its authority over its clients. The destruction of the Dutch fleet at Camperdown only confirmed the contempt felt in Paris for the ineffectiveness of the Batavians. Fructidor itself offered a model for how to get out of a political impasse, and it was eventually followed. On 22 January 1798, 22 Federalists were expelled from a Convention surrounded by troops under French orchestration. Others resigned in protest. A provisional Directory was proclaimed to handle the Republic's affairs until a constitution took effect. A draft of such a constitution had in fact already been prepared, and over the next few weeks only a few minor amendments were made. In April it was put to another referendum, and this time it was accepted by 153,913 to 11,587.

Two years after the French conquest, therefore, the Dutch *ancien régime* was at last swept away. The Estates-General, and the provinces they represented, went the same way as the Stadtholderate. So did the once-powerful guilds, the oligarchical, self-perpetuating city councils, and the established Church. The Batavian Republic was now to be one and indivisible, organized into eight roughly equal departments. A bicameral legislature, elected by all male citizens earning a living, would make the laws. In turn, the legislature would select an executive of five Directors. It was a far more democratic constitution than any adopted in France during the 1790s—but then the Dutch had practised representative government (of a sort) for centuries before 1789, and the constitution's drafters felt confident in leapfrogging the relative novices who had given them the chance to build on their traditions. What they did not feel confident of was the continuing support of their fellow citizens. Those purged in January were kept in prison, and their supporters throughout the country were now systematically ejected from all posts of influence. And in May, with French support, they decided to guarantee their constitution by the same means the Convention in Paris had used to launch the constitution of the Year III: by perpetuating themselves. They decreed that the first elections would only choose one-third of the new legislature. The other deputies would be made up of themselves, to be deemed already elected. The result was uproar. The press, enjoying a freedom also long established in Dutch tradition, denounced the cynicism of the new Directory. From Paris it began to look as if once more the Dutch had failed to establish revolutionary stability. Having dealt with resurgent Jacobinism at home in the coup of Floréal, the French government was now keen to curb radical excesses elsewhere. Abandoning Delacroix, the ambassador who had orchestrated a year of French intrigue at The Hague, they raised no objection when Daendels, an ambitious Dutch general, launched a coup against the Batavian Directory. Having quarrelled publicly with his political masters on 16 May, Daendels ostentatiously travelled to Paris to lobby higher authority. He returned on 10 June a popular hero, cheered by all the regime's now multifarious opponents. And, while a new French commander, Joubert, stood obligingly aside, on 12 June Daendels and his men cashiered the Directory and arrested the most vocal members of the legislature. Amazingly, Daendels did not seize power for himself. He handed it over at once to those imprisoned since January. They disclaimed all desire to perpetuate themselves, too. Instead, they called elections, and by the end of July a new legislature was in session. The constitutional life of the Batavian Republic began at last to function normally: and it did so, with regular elections, until yet another new regime in Paris decided it was unsatisfactory in the spring of 1800.

Whether it would have gone on unmolested for even that long without the difficulties France was now experiencing elsewhere, with the renewal of war, seems doubtful. Dutch political life remained volatile, and the Republic persistently failed to live up to the standards of support and subservience expected by the Great Nation of its little sisters. For their part, fewer and fewer Dutchmen felt much benefit from the association. 'What fruits, until now', asked a moderately patriotic newspaper founded in the summer of 1798,[2] 'have the people plucked from the liberty tree, planted in the Winter of 1795? To tell the truth, not much.' The intervening years had brought heavier taxation, and added defeat on the sea to that already sustained on land. In August 1799 an Anglo-Russian force landed in the north after the mutinous remnants of the Dutch navy surrendered to a British squadron with William V's son on board. Only 10,000 French troops were by then stationed in the Republic, although it was still paying under the 1795 treaty for 25,000. A joint force eventually defeated the invaders, and compelled their withdrawal—but only after two months of fighting in which the British confirmed their reputation as pitiless marauders. And war against the island state had meanwhile brought ruin to Dutch trade. Overseas colonies were ruthlessly picked off, and the Republic's ports were blockaded. Colonial goods so basic to many of the industries built up in the Republic over two centuries were either cut off or only got through at exorbitant cost. Shipbuilding and all the trades connected with it languished. Such was the price of alliance with a power bent on war to the finish with Great Britain. Nor did France offer any compensatory advantages. The army of occupation, frequently undisciplined and always demanding, paid for its requisitions until 1797 in worthless assignats. And for commercial purposes the sister republic was treated anything but fraternally. High tariff barriers excluded Dutch manufactures from what was now Europe's largest area of free exchange, and they cut off Dutch territories lost in 1795 from economic partners of immemorial standing. The unemployment resulting from these disruptions placed intolerable strains in turn on a system of poor relief that had once been the envy of Europe. A disestablished Church now demanded funds for its upkeep that had hitherto gone, partly at least, to charity, and the role of pastors in co-ordinating relief was no longer unquestioned. In the greater cities, between a quarter and a half of the population found itself demanding relief, and municipalities went deeply into debt to provide it. Even then it was never enough. In a once-flourishing fishing port, an English traveller observed nothing but 'impoverishment and decay. The harbour was crowded with fishing vessels no longer employed . . . the quay was covered in long grass and a melancholy assemblage of beggars importuned us for relief wherever we walked.'[3]

By the turn of the century these tribulations had brought widespread disillusionment with the friendship and protection of France, yet no serious movement to break the link ever took shape. Even if it had been possible to renounce treaty obligations to so overwhelming a partner, there was no practical alternative. Neutrality was unsustainable without armed forces of unimaginable size and loyalty. Recalling the prince of Orange, for so long the natural response when republicanism failed, meant subservience to Great Britain, from where William V was issuing manifestos even more intransigent than those of Louis XVIII. British commanders during the invasion of 1799 reported that there was no natural groundswell of support for a prince likely to be even more of a foreign puppet than the Directors in The Hague. Pehaps this was because, despite repeated interference at every turn of the political roundabout in Paris, for much of the time the Dutch were left to run their internal affairs in their own way. This could hardly be said of other territories overrun by the French.

The first conquests of the revolutionary armies had been in Belgium, and during the first occupation in 1792–3 the armies of Dumouriez looked on it as enemy territory to be used and exploited to the full. The decrees annexing it to France in the spring of 1793 came too close to the Austrian reconquest to bring about any change in treatment. When the French returned, in June 1794, Belgium was once more dealt with as occupied enemy territory rather than a reconquered part of the Republic. Debate was certainly reopened in Paris on the drawbacks and advantages of reannexation, but while it went on Belgium was exploited for all it was worth. War taxes were levied, requisitions imposed to feed and supply the occupying armies, and as usual any compensation, if paid at all, came in assignats. In Belgium, declared Carnot on 11 July,[4] the French must 'take all we can . . . strip it . . . because it is a country devoted to the Emperor, with plenty of restitution to make to France'. Everything useful to the French war effort was to be removed, and targets totalling 109 millions in cash were set, though far from achieved, for military levies. A euphemistically named 'commercial agency' (*agence de commerce*) was established to co-ordinate the pillage, and its rapacity soon embarrassed even the representatives on mission. The chorus of complaint—in a language, too, that the French could understand—was deafening, and as 1794 drew to a close policy-makers in Paris began to realize that the long-term repercussions of such a policy might seriously outweigh its short-term advantages. In February 1795 the commercial agency was dissolved, and in August nine territorial departments were established as the channels for all governmental action. The palimpsest of territories and jurisdictions which had survived a decade of attempts, whether Austrian or 'patriot', to reform it was thus finally rationalized. Complaints were numerous as the proposed new boundaries and jurisdictions were revealed, but anything seemed better than the anarchy and extortion of the preceding twelve months, and the common sense of the organization was soon widely acknowledged. But nobody could doubt, after the introduction of a French pattern of administration, what the next step would be. France had by now gained a slice of Dutch territory south of the Rhine mouths, and forced the Batavian Republic to recognize the reopening of the Scheldt. It was unthinkable to leave a no man's land behind these gains, for all the warnings of respected figures like Carnot that the natural frontiers proclaimed in 1793 were a formula for interminable war. And so, on 1 October 1795, in one of its last acts, the Convention decreed the incorporation of Belgium into the French Republic.

Requisitions and extraordinary taxation now stopped. The Belgians had become citizens of the land of liberty, and were to enjoy all its benefits. Patriots soon overcame their disappointment at not being allowed to re-establish their independence, and threw themselves into making the new order work. But, as the more controversial laws of the Republic were progressively introduced, they found themselves increasingly isolated as the tools of a state bent on more than administrative reorganization. Above all, administrators in Belgium were charged with introducing French religious policy. The French had not been heedless of the notorious devotion of the Belgian population during the conquest, and although blasphemous outrages inevitably occurred and churches, particularly monastic ones, were sometimes stripped of their more lavish ornaments, official policy was one of restraint. The Belgians felt reassured when the Republic officially turned its back on both dechristianization and factitious deistic cults to declare itself religiously neutral. Yet with a paper money nominally backed by ecclesiastical properties spiralling downwards out of control, the rulers of France looked with growing greed at the still intact church lands of Belgium. In September 1796, therefore, most monasteries were dissolved and their lands put on the market. Ten thousand of their inmates were turned out. At the same time parish priests lost the function of registering births, marriages, and deaths. But buyers for confiscated church lands were not easily found, and in the first French elections in which the new departments participated, those of 1797, Belgian hostility to these policies was reflected in the return of right-wing candidates. After the Fructidor coup neutralized these results, the Belgian clergy were further traumatized by the oath of hatred for royalty, which met with a massive refusal, particularly in Flemish-speaking areas. The post-Fructidorian Directory had no patience with such resistance, and a special effort was made to purge the presumed leaders of this movement. Almost 600 Belgian non-jurors were condemned to deportation and thereby, of course, lost their benefices. The mistakes of the Vendée were being repeated in a territory where the prestige and authority of parish priests was just as strong. The Jourdan Law on conscription of September 1798 completed the familiar picture. The first attempts to apply it, drafting able-bodied young Flemish peasants into the French army, provoked riots early in October, and by the end of the month they had blossomed into a full-scale revolt.

With a tame sister republic to the north, the Belgian departments were lightly garrisoned by troops not expecting to be used to keep domestic order. So no sooner had the initial outbreak been contained at the end of October than there were new disturbances further west, perilously close to the coast off which the British were cruising. Further inland, a peasant army had assembled, 10,000 strong at its height, marching under white flags bearing red crosses. They were very poorly armed—although the British hurriedly attempted to smuggle supplies in to them—and attracted few leaders from the upper ranks of society. Nor did many townsmen join them, and when they took towns they scarcely had time to burn archives, cut down trees of liberty, and sack the homes of public officials before hurriedly withdrawing again at the first approach of troops. Modelling themselves quite consciously on the Vendéans, they also shared their lack of long-term objectives. Though some shouted *Long live the Emperor*, most adopted the slogan *For land and religion*, merely wanting to be left alone with their familiar priests and their sons not being butchered on distant battlefields for the benefit of a Republic once more exulting in its own Godlessness. But they had none of the Vendéan savagery, and caused little bloodshed. The same was true of a contemporaneous uprising which took place further south in Luxembourg. The response of the French, however, was not so gentle. Flying columns harried rebel territory throughout late November, and on 5 December the remnants of the peasant army were surrounded at Hasselt. Lacking cavalry themselves, over 700 were hacked to death by French horsemen. Others scattered and went to ground, imitating the *chouans*. But by July 1799 the last of them had been caught, and open resistance was over. Harsh repression followed. Rebels found with arms in their hands were shot, and the mass deportation of the entire Belgian clergy—7,500 priests in all—was decreed. In the event not more than 500 were rounded up, but the drive against them did nothing to conciliate those who had rebelled. And passive resistance to conscription continued. Of the 22,000 recruits expected from the Belgian departments, only just over 5,000 had materialized by the end of 1799, and these came overwhelmingly from the towns.

Rural Belgium, therefore, remained unreconciled to French rule. The urban response was more pragmatic. Despite a 50 per cent rise in taxes since the time of Austrian rule, and considerable economic disruption, free access to the French national market promised opportunities for recovery in calmer times. Within a few years they materialized, and Belgian industry, undisturbed by the ravages of armies again until 1814, was able to take profitable advantage of them. Nor were the Belgian bourgeoisie as reluctant as the peasantry to buy nationalized church lands. In Flemish areas they even embraced the French language as never before. Yet they showed little interest in public affairs, and were content to be administered by French officials as they previously had been, until the reforms of Joseph II, by imperial ones. They no more felt French than they had previously felt Austrian. It might have been different if the calm times of rule from Paris after 1799 had not been preceded by six years of rapine and exploitation from the same quarter.

When the annexation of Belgium was decreed on 1 October 1795 the mover of the proposal, Merlin de Douai, also recommended the annexation of the entire left bank of the Rhine. After all, it too lay within the natural frontiers, and French armies were in occupation of it. Much of it had been annexed once before, in 1793, just like Belgium. But those who were unhappy about even Belgian annexation on the grounds that it would prolong the war indefinitely saw greater disadvantages still in incorporating the Rhineland. The Austrians had already written Belgium off, so only Great Britain would now oppose its annexation to France, and with no footholds left on the Continent she could be ignored. But innumerable states had territorial interests and claims in the Rhineland, and to brush them aside would create countless perpetual enmities. Far better to use the occupied territory as a bargaining counter to secure a lasting peace. Besides, French agents on the spot were uncertain about the likely benefits of annexation. 'All these people', wrote a civil commissioner with the occupying army of the Sambre-et-Meuse,[5] 'detest us most cordially, they love only their priests, their princes and their emperor. Let us deal with them as we deal with a vanquished enemy . . . Besides, what purpose would be served by joining the country to France?' Such arguments prevailed in 1795, and the Rhineland remained outside the Republic's frontiers. In the spring of 1797, it was even briefly suggested that a 'Cis-Rhenan' sister republic be created. The idea came from Hoche, now commanding on the Rhine and looking for any opportunity to offset the ever-growing personal empire of Bonaparte in Italy by creating a puppet state of his own to rival the Cisalpine Republic. The idea died with Hoche in September 1797, the same month that saw the removal of Carnot, the main opponent of the natural frontiers, from the Directory. Among those remaining was Reubell, himself from Alsace and a long-standing advocate of Rhineland annexation. But even he could not secure immediate satisfaction. While at the peace of Campo Formio the next month the Austrians recognized that the left bank should be French, the consent of the Holy Roman Empire (including Prussia, which also had left-bank territories) was left to be worked out at the Congress of Rastadt. It was only obtained, and then under threat, in December 1798. It remained provisional until France had overcome the second coalition in 1801. But long before then practical assimilation had begun: in January 1798 the occupied territory was divided into four departments, and thenceforward the region was governed to all intents and purposes as part of France.

The Rhineland, however, was very different from Belgium. It had no history of resistance to established authorities before the French arrived, and there were hardly any local Jacobins or self-styled patriots sympathetic to the Revolution on whose collaboration they could rely. None of the inhabitants spoke French as a native tongue, and few understood it. Above all, the Rhineland was front-line territory for as long as hostilities lasted, and expected to sustain huge French armies long after the garrison of Belgium had been reduced to a few thousands. Consequently the military exploitation which in Belgium lasted for scarcely three years in all went on in Germany for at least twice that length of time. It reduced an area that had been prosperous and flourishing before the 1790s to an enfeebled shadow, systematically stripped and re-stripped of its wealth and assets in order to sustain armies that the home government could not pay and positively urged to live off the country.

We had no kind of financial resources whatsoever [reminisced one veteran of Rhineland campaigns] . . . we had no kind of administrative organisation to deal with requisitions; we had to live as best we could, and off the resources of the region in which we found ourselves—resources which were soon exhausted, especially as the armies had crossed and recrossed this territory several times . . . one can imagine the distress of the army; it could exist only by plundering.[6]

Everything useful to an army on the move was taken—horses, fodder, carts, grain, livestock. Troops were billeted on households and pillaged and abused their hosts without compunction. Able-bodied men and boys were requisitioned for forced labour to dig fortifications and establish camps. The arrival of more ordered conditions simply meant that exploitation became more systematic. Forced loans and military taxes were now imposed, and requisitions were now paid for—in assignats. Attempts to pay the new levies in assignats, however, were understandably not welcomed. And moves towards incorporating the Rhineland into the Republic, the salvation of Belgium, only compounded the problems of France's German subjects. In July 1798 French customs posts were established along the Rhine. They transformed it at a blow from an artery of commerce holding together an economic region comprising both banks, into a frontier—as in the southern Netherlands. Nothing, noted observers of the Rhineland scene, had done more to alienate the Rhinelanders from French rule, and only smugglers made any gains. But a large portion of the riverbank population now fell into this category, and constant clashes with customs officers almost institutionalized their hostility to the new order.

Much of the economic life of the pre-revolutionary Rhineland had revolved around servicing the lavish courts of ecclesiastical princes, such as the archbishops of Trier and Cologne, and the 'residential towns' where they were located. The French invasion shattered this pattern forever. The prince-bishops, their courtiers, and their chapters fled beyond the Rhine, and their goods and lands were confiscated by the invaders. Overnight thousands were deprived of employment in the luxury and service trades that were the lifeblood of these little capitals. Even those who might have hoped to benefit from the secularization of so much church property were disappointed. The French maintained the feudal dues payable to former lords until the spring of 1798—a source of revenue too valuable to be sacrificed to universal principles. The same applied to the tithe, levied no longer for the upkeep of priests, but for that of the French armies. As in France, when it was abolished in March 1798 an equivalent sum was added to rents. Thus there were no compensations for the sacrilege visited on the Church, its buildings, and its customs by the invading armies—always the last bastions of a dechristianization long burnt out in France. Even when local laws were brought into harmony with those of France, from 1797 onwards, it was at a time when directorial policy was fiercely anti-clerical and parades of devotion, so characteristic of Rhenish Catholicism, were prohibited. Priests naturally bore the brunt of these policies, and French suspicions that they were the main ringleaders of resistance were entirely justified. Throughout the occupation, therefore, German priests were expelled, exiled, and arrested—not, certainly, on the scale attempted in Belgium, but quite enough to keep the resentment of their pious congregations bubbling.

Yet the Rhineland experienced no mass uprising of the sort seen in Belgium and Luxembourg. Rumours of these outbreaks spread into Germany rapidly enough in the autumn of 1798, and led to an upsurge in lawlessness and defiance of French authority. Liberty trees were cut down, officials intimidated, and inflammatory leaflets were circulated urging all good Germans to rise up against the oppressors. The authorities were genuinely alarmed. But no general movement emerged. There were too many French soldiers in occupation, and the last straw in the Belgian case—conscription—was not introduced in a territory not yet fully part of France. Passive resistance was the German way, but even that was effective enough to make French officials compare parts of the Rhineland to the Vendée. 'I have not yet found one district', reported a French general on his arrival in 1792,[7] 'which really wants to be free.' Five years later nothing had changed. 'Never expect any affection', warned a civil official, 'from people who yearn for slavery.' Clearly the Revolution had even cast a blight on language; if the German experience of French rule was freedom, words were losing their accepted meaning.

For the Great Nation, however, staggering though she was from one coup against representative institutions to another, liberty could only be French. Particular problems arose when she confronted peoples with their own traditions and rhetoric of freedom. The Dutch were one such case. The Swiss were another. The Swiss Confederation was a loose association of sovereign territories unequal in every way. Its complexity almost beggared description, and it had no central authority to lend it coherence. Any such authority would have set unacceptable limits to the vaunted freedoms of each constituent part. Nor had external threats led the Swiss to think within living memory that such an authority was desirable for other reasons. No great power coveted this mountainous heart of Europe, and it had no great strategic significance—until 1796. It was French conquests in northern Italy that transformed the situation. Switzerland now bestrode the Alpine passes which linked France most conveniently with her client states and major sources of foreign booty in the plains of the Po. More perceptive Swiss saw at once that this would mean increased French interference in their affairs. In order not to be overwhelmed, thought Peter Ochs, a leading member of the Basle patriciate, the Confederation must transform itself into a unitary state. Inevitably that would mean adopting many French-style institutions and principles, and abandoning many hallowed traditions and liberties; but if Switzerland did not to some degree imitate France, she would remain the helpless prey not only of France itself but equally probably of her Austrian rival. No sooner had the peace of Campo Formio been signed, in fact, when the Directory turned its attention to Switzerland. La Harpe, an exile in Paris for long-standing advocacy of French intervention to emancipate the francophone Vaud district from the tutelage of German-speaking Berne, urged Reubell to invite Ochs to Paris to discuss the reform of what the Director already regarded as a 'crazy formless assemblage of governments without any connection, some oligarchic, others democratic, all despotic and all enemies of the French Republic'.[8] When Ochs arrived in December 1797 he found that Bonaparte was also party to the discussions. He was asked to draft a constitution for a 'one and indivisible' Swiss republic which would come into being when the Swiss themselves, on a signal from France, rose up to overthrow the old order. That signal would be the annexation by France of outlying northern and western parts of the confederation, the cities of Mulhouse and Geneva.

On 28 January 1798 Mulhouse was duly annexed: Geneva followed on 26 March. Rural revolts against urban domination broke out in the hinterlands of Basle and Zurich, while in the Vaud patriots proclaimed the independence of Berne. But none of these outbreaks, except in the Basle district, had as much to do with establishing a unitary republic as with pursuing far older antagonisms. The Vaud rebels proclaimed their own tiny

'Leman Republic', oblivious of wider loyalties. And, again with the exception of Basle, the urban patriciates showed unexpected vigour in moving to repress the rebels. The French had to intervene directly, and in February General Brune was ordered to occupy Berne. Confusion followed. Brune was at first ordered to establish no less than three separate sister republics, conforming roughtly to linguistic divisions. In Catholic mountain districts, peasants led by their priests now rose against the invading French and were cut down in their hundreds. The appalled Swiss patriots in Paris protested that only a single, centralized sister republic could hope to contain such outbreaks in the long term, and the Directory yielded to their calls. On 22 March Brune proclaimed the Helvetic Republic and declared its constitution to be that drafted by Ochs and French collaborators. No convention was called to ratify it—the Dutch example had demonstrated the perils of that. With its 23 equal cantons, bicameral legislature, and executive of five Directors, it was simply imposed. When the legislature first met a month later, with Ochs as president of the Senate, only ten cantons were represented, the others refusing to condone a system on which they had not been consulted. Once more French troops had to intervene to coerce them. And the first international act of the new state, the treaty with France of 2 August which granted her perpetual access to the Alpine passes, guaranteed the presence of such troops for the foreseeable future.

The Helvetic Republic was not even a conquered enemy, like the Dutch, but that did not save it from the depredations which a French army of occupation always brought. Under pressure from Ochs and La Harpe, the Directory promised not to impose requisitions; but the well-stocked treasuries of the main Swiss cities were impounded to pay the army of Italy and to equip the Egyptian expedition being fitted out at Toulon. War taxes were imposed, and pillaging, as everywhere, only sporadically controlled. As early as June 1798 two of the new Swiss Directory were replaced on French insistence because they had not proved co-operative enough towards their protectors. But as 1798 drew to a close, the French proved unable even to guarantee protection. In November, Austrian troops occupied the eastern cantons, making Switzerland for the first time in centuries a theatre of war. Soon the Russians in their turn would be campaigning there. The French now demanded that the Helvetic Republic conscript 18,000 men into a militia to act as auxiliaries to the French armies; but despite the support of Ochs and other leading architects of the new Republic, the legislature refused the demand. All it would authorize was a volunteer army, whose members never reached a quarter of those required. The Swiss still remembered the grisly fate of the last Swiss regiments in French service, butchered at the Tuileries in August 1792. In other respects, however, the new authorities showed themselves eager to follow the French lead. A massive programme of rationalization was announced for the Republic, including abolition of internal tolls and customs barriers, guilds and corporations, the tithe, and feudal dues. Church lands were taken into national possession, and monasteries forbidden to recruit new novices. In Protestant areas, such measures were applauded but had little impact. In Catholic ones, which included some of the remotest valleys whose traditions of self-government were among the most democratic in Europe, they caused deep resentment. The new constitution, declared one mountain priest,[9] 'seeks to rob us of our holy religion, our freedom enjoyed undisturbed for hundreds of years, and our democratic constitution inherited from our blessed ancestors'. And while French troops made short work of the small rebel army assembled by the peasants of the Valais in May 1798, guerrilla resistance continued, and was not so easy to deal with especially when war engulfed the country and gave the French more pressing priorities. When that happened, too, the initial ban on requisitioning soon broke down, making the Republic's French defenders barely distinguishable from the Austrian and Russian enemies who throughout 1799 poured across its borders from the Tyrol in the east, and up the Alpine passes from Italy.

It was Bonaparte's conquests in Italy that had sealed Switzerland's fate. From Italy, too, came the model for her reorganization. Yet although the first sister republic, the Batavian, was already in existence when the French crossed the Alps in the spring of 1796 nobody, not even Bonaparte, seems to have yet thought of establishing parallel client states in other conquered territories. When in his initial march across the Alps, Bonaparte swept aside the army of Victor Amadeus III of Piedmont, a small group of the latter's subjects sympathetic to French ideas proclaimed a republic at Alba. They were ignored. Anxious only to remove the Piedmontese army from the military balance, Bonaparte signed an armistice with the defeated king and left him a free hand to deal with the rebels against his authority. It was true that over the winter of 1795–6 various Italian political exiles in France, co-ordinated by Buonarroti, extolled the prospects for 'liberating' Italy and tried to convince the Directory that they could organize an uprising in Piedmont to facilitate the advance of the Republic's armies. But Buonarroti's involvement in the Babeuf plot uncovered in May 1796 discredited him and his friends in directorial eyes. His radical social and political ideas would be just as dangerous in occupied territories as they were in France. Suspicions, far from groundless, that the true sympathies of Italian Francophiles lay with Jacobinism and the ideals of the Year II rather than directorial moderation would hamper their prospects through-out the three years of the first French occupation. Equally well founded was the French belief that Italian Jacobins enjoyed scant popular support. 'There can be no question of republicanising Italy', reported one consul on the eve of Bonaparte's triumphs.[10] 'The people are not at all inclined to accept liberty, neither are they worthy of this boon. In view of their degradation, all we can hope for is the silence born of cowardice and the respect born of fear; they execrate our principles as contrary to their passions and their prejudices.' In any case, the Directory's strategy in invading Italy was merely to occupy and exploit it, exchanging it for the Rhineland at the final peace.

Yet the French were welcomed by more people in Lombardy than in any other territory they invaded except the Dutch Republic. Especially in the cities, middle-class intellectuals welcomed outside intervention as a means of breaking the recently reinforced clerical and aristocratic stranglehold on Italian life. During an unprecedented half-century of peace and relative prosperity since 1748, intellectual life had flourished in northern Italy, and the activities of reforming monarchs like Leopold of Tuscany and his elder brother the Emperor Joseph II (ruling the duchy of Milan) had convinced many thinking Italians that Enlightenment would soon triumph through-out the peninsula. But in the early 1790s these hopes were shattered. Joseph died and Leopold went back to Vienna to succeed him, dying himself soon afterwards. And, as horror stories rolled in from France, reforms were abandoned and governments clamped fierce controls on independent intellectual life. The Bourbon monarchies of Parma and Naples were swept by hysteria, and the Pope anathematized reform as a threat to faith itself. More ominously still from the viewpoint of bourgeois radicals, this tide of reaction enjoyed some obvious popular support: when Leopold II left Tuscany, exultant rioters, to cries of *Viva Maria!*, drove the Jansenistic priests he had installed from their churches and put back the images, relics, and pious trappings that the reformers had tried to banish.

But in 1796, as the French poured into the Lombard plains and smashed every Austrian army sent against them, hitherto frustrated Italian intellectuals were overcome with excitement. They could not believe the invaders would not favour them, and while refugees from Piedmontese persecution of the Alba republicans trailed after Bonaparte on his triumphal march, Jacobins in his path unceremoniously deposed their local rulers and proclaimed the rule of Liberty and Equality. On arrival in Milan Bonaparte found a club of 800 members, mostly lawyers and merchants, waiting to greet him; and within a week this 'Society of the Friends of Liberty and Equality' was producing its own journal. A few more weeks and

it was advocating an ideal most people had thought Utopian until then—
Italian unity. Bonaparte in turn recognized how these sentiments, and those
expressing them, could be used. In a proclamation issued on 19 May he
denounced kings, the rich, and the privileged, and spoke vaguely of
achieving 'the independence of Lombardy, which should bring its
happiness'.[11] But, he added, the French army could not achieve these lofty
ends without supplies, supplies which France could not provide. So the
former Austrian provinces would be required to make 'a very small
contribution' to their expenses, and the new men now in power in Milan
would be entrusted with the task of raising it.

So began the inevitable exploitation of Italy, and of France's Italian
friends. A general who had promised his ragged army unlimited booty when
they descended into the richest plains in the world was now about to keep
his word—to them, at least. A war tax of 20 millions was the 'very small
contribution' announced in the proclamation. Meanwhile requisitioning of
foodstuffs proceeded ruthlessly in the army's wake. Stockpiles were
established for plundered grain and wine, and plans were made to corral
4,000 cattle. Municipal treasuries were everywhere impounded, as were
the contents of the public pawnshops so characteristic of Italian cities.
Tuscan neutrality was cheerfully violated on the excuse that massive British
supplies were stockpiled at Leghorn. When the forewarned islanders
evacuated most of them in a remarkable amphibious scratch operation, the
city was stripped of all its other resources. Works of art were systematically
removed from churches and palaces, and shipped to France by the cartload.
Bullion too: in 1796 alone Bonaparte remitted something like 45 millions to
Paris. Thanks to the Milanese authorities compounding for irregular
exactions to the tune of a million per month, he was also able to pay his
soldiers mostly in cash at a time when it was completely unavailable in
France, and when requisitions, if paid for at all, were settled up in the ill-
fated territorial mandates at face value. Needless to say the commander-in-
chief and his main lieutenants made personal fortunes. But scarcely had
these depredations begun before they ran into resistance. At Pavia on
25 May, a Jacobin administration, set up by the French army as it passed
through like a swarm of locusts, was overthrown as soon as the front had
moved on by riotous peasants outraged by anti-religious excesses.
Bonaparte himself had to turn aside to deal with the rising, doing so by
delivering the city to twenty-four hours of unrestrained sack. Other
resistance was less spectacular, but harder to deal with since most of it was
rural. Whereas most towns had their kernels of Jacobins ready to greet
and—initially at least—co-operate with the invaders in organizing the
exploitation of their fellow citizens, in the countryside the French were seen

simply as Godless foreign marauders, to be resisted, ambushed, and harassed whenever opportunities occurred. Thus there were peasant uprisings throughout the Lombard plains over the summer of 1796, some of them resulting in massacres of isolated French units. Essentially local, however, they never came together, and the ebb and flow of the war zone made soldiers of all sides the peasants' enemy.

Even in towns the Jacobin honeymoon did not always last long. In papal Bologna and Ferrara, occupied in June, crackdowns on subversives over the previous two years had left an atmosphere of anti-clerical resentment: the last execution in Bologna had taken place only two months before the French arrived. Bolognese Jacobins, therefore, were encouraged to draw up an independent constitution for their territory, which kept them busy, and grateful, for the rest of the year. Not surprisingly, the end product was based closely on the Constitution of the Year III. But no such freedom was allowed to the turbulent radicals of Milan. By the end of May, their two-week old club had been dissolved, and only began cautiously meeting again, as a 'patriotic society', two months later. In September it was reborn yet again, as an 'Academy of Literature and Public Instruction', with the sanction of Bonaparte, but as soon as it began agitating for a national convention to regenerate the whole of Italy, adopting a distinctive tricolour cockade of red, white, and green, it met renewed French resistance. Neither the Directory in Paris nor Bonaparte had any interest in uniting Italy. So that when, in November, a renewed Austrian offensive threatened to expel the French, the club prepared to seize power the moment they withdrew. A demonstration was organized to plant a liberty tree in the city centre and proclaim, with legal formalities, the independence of the Lombard nation. But the Austrians were once more defeated and the French, more firmly in control than ever, crushed the movement and the club which had sponsored it.

Yet Bonaparte realized that to spurn such aspirations was to turn his back on France's surest source of support. The energies of Italian patriots should be harnessed, if possible, rather than rejected. It was for this reason that, in the autumn, he encouraged those whom French power had placed in control at Bologna and Ferrara, and at Modena (a duchy also swamped by the French tide), to concert their action against local conservative resistance. Nor did he demur when, at the end of December, their representatives meeting at Reggio declared themselves a single one and indivisible Cispadane Republic. In fact, he intervened personally to expedite the drafting of the new state's constitution, which was eventually proclaimed on 27 March 1797. Thus the first of the Italian sister republics was born, and it was recognized by the Pope, at whose expense it had largely been created, in the treaty of Tolentino in February.

Lombard radicals watched these moves with mounting excitement, although Bonaparte refused to allow them to send representatives to the Reggio congress. When the Cispadanes adopted the new tricolour and, following an example set in Milan the previous autumn, set up a national guard or 'Italian Legion' to give armed support to the new state, they saw clear signs of common aspirations. Accordingly, the results of the first elections, held in April 1797 under a constitution once more closely modelled on that of France, came as a shock. Large numbers of conservatives were returned, under the influence of the clergy. Bonaparte too was shocked. Occupied since February with his final pursuit of the Austrians up the Alpine valleys towards Vienna, he had been in no position to control this first free expression of Italian opinion. 'Like Lombardy,' he complained,[12] 'the Cispadane Republic needs a provisional government for three or four years, during which the influence of the priests can be lessened; otherwise, you will have done nothing by giving liberty . . . However . . . I shall start by joining Lombardy and the Cispadane, under a single provisional government.' This was on 1 May. Within a few weeks (29 June) the Cisalpine Republic had been created, and the short-lived Cispadane had been incorporated into it.

From Paris it looked like the deliberate creation of a personal client state, and the imperious way in which the general went on to dictate its constitution, and rule it by decree all that summer from lordly surroundings in the palace of Mombello, suggested long-meditated ambitions in this direction. In fact the concept seems to have emerged much more haphazardly, and at every stage strategic considerations seem to have been paramount. The Cispadane Republic was a buffer against attack from the south, with viable natural frontiers. Nothing comparable ·could have been created in Lombardy until the Austrians were expelled from Mantua; and Venetian territory marched with the eastern and northern limits of French occupation along purely jurisdictional lines of no strategic logic. Venice had remained neutral in the conflict but, straddling as it did all the main Austrian lines of communication with Italy, its territory was a major theatre of war throughout the campaign. When Bonaparte disappeared northwards towards Leoben, there were vicious outbreaks of hostility to the garrisons he had left to guard his lines of communication through the *terraferma*, culminating on 17 April with the massacre of 400 French soldiers in Verona. In response he issued blood-curdling threats against the Doge and Senate of Venice. But when the Austrians, at Leoben, asked for compensation for their losses in Belgium and Lombardy, the outrages offered a perfect occasion for a diplomatic deal. Venetia would be given to the Habsburgs, shorn of a number of outlying territories which would consolidate French conquests further west. When, therefore, two months later, the Cisalpine Republic came into being, it had a coherent frontier to the west, at least, along the Adige; which the Austrians accepted, along with their own acquisition of the rest of Venetia, at Campo Formio the following October.

In these circumstances the creation of a consolidated north Italian sister republic was logical. The alternative—to incorporate the conquered territories into France—would have made little sense and would have outraged all her Italian friends. As it was they were outraged enough. Expecting to draft their own constitution in the Cispadane manner, they found it dictated to them by Bonaparte. And all but the most moderate found themselves excluded from positions of authority in the new state. Although the new constitution, promulgated on 9 July, was elective, Bonaparte decreed that, so that the passage from a military to a constitutional regime should occur 'without shocks, without anarchy', he would nominate all members of executive and legislature for the first year of its operation. In the event the constitution only lasted fourteen months, and the republic itself only seven more. But during that time it became a byword both for French exploitation of allies ('We do not wish to allow ourselves to be *cisalpinised*', complained a Swiss official,[13] as French requisitions began) and for radical turbulence. Milan rapidly became a centre for Jacobin refugees fleeing from Venice, from Piedmont, from the Papal States, and from Naples. They agitated constantly for an Italian republic, freedom of the press, and anti-noble and anti-clerical legislation. So long as Bonaparte remained in Italy, he acted decisively against such activity. The constitution made no explicit provision for clubs, and when, imitating post-Fructidorian France, a constitutional circle was set up in November 1797, it was closed within a few days as a hotbed of 'anarchists'. Not until he had left, a month later, was it allowed to reopen, and then it became an organ for all the views and opinions he had feared. Only too clearly the Jacobins of Milan dreamed of an Italian Year II to sweep away all obstacles: one female enthusiast even offered to marry the man who would bring her the Pope's head. The terms which France imposed on her latest sister republic were further grist to their mill. In February 1798 a treaty of alliance was signed. It stipulated that a French Army of 25,000 would be stationed in the Republic and maintained at its expense. It was also required to raise and maintain an army of its own of 22,000 men— which it had no prospect of doing without resort to the always-explosive conscription. Preferential tariffs were to be extended to French goods, while British ones were to be totally excluded. Given that the republic was a

French creation, and depended utterly on France for its survival, these terms were perhaps not excessively onerous, but they shocked a wide range of opinion. While clubs, in Milan and other cities, denounced the treaty, the legislature refused to confirm it. Eventually they yielded, but not before orders had gone out from Paris, at the suggestion of the Cisalpine ambassador there, for a 'Cisalpine Fructidor'. In April 1798, accordingly, the legislative councils and the Directory were purged, removing the most conservative of Bonaparte's nominees (much to his fury), and leaving in control elements much more sympathetic to the radicals of the clubs.

Calls for Italian unity were now loudly renewed. The issue was becoming more urgent as separate sister republics appeared all over the peninsula. The ancient city-republic of Genoa, quite unable to resist French power, had been transformed into the Ligurian Republic in June 1797, following the crushing of an uprising of Genoese patriots and their French collaborators. The new republic's constitution, drafted locally, was approved in a plebiscite in December—in striking contrast with Cisalpine experience. At the end of the same month a riot in Rome resulted in the accidental death of a French general, and the ambassador, Bonaparte's brother Joseph, fled in panic to Florence. The Directory, in renewed anti-clerical mood since Fructidor, ordered an invasion of what was left of the Papal States after the surrender at Tolentino. The Pope had no army, and Rome was occupied without resistance on 10 February 1798. Five days later a small group of Jacobins, most of whom were not native Romans but adventurers from the sister republics of the north, proclaimed a Roman Republic. It was recognized on the spot by the French commander. The Pope was deported. But not until a popular uprising, the so-called 'Roman Vespers', was put down on 25 February was the new state securely established. Echoes of it continued for days afterwards in the Alban hills, and hundreds were shot in the mopping-up which followed. Nor was there any question here of native Italians drafting their own constitution. A commission of jurists was sent from Paris. They produced a structure full of ancient Roman terminology, with Consuls, a Senate, and a Tribunate, but modern and Parisian in form. Like the Cisalpine constitution it was to be operated by nominees, not elected officials, for its first year. And nothing was to be enacted without the consent of the French commandant, who was for good measure authorized to make whatever laws he saw fit. Nothing could have stated more explicitly that the new Italian republics existed primarily for the convenience of the Great Nation.

And the way these latest additions to the constellation of sister republics were treated emphasized the point. The first demand made on the Ligurian Republic, presumed inheritor of the traditional Genoese role as international banker, was for a loan of 800,000 francs. When the legislature refused, the French ambassador engineered a coup (31 August 1798) which purged the leading resisters. Similarly, the continued fermentation at Milan, positively encouraged by the more radical elements left in control after the April purge, led to renewed pressure from Paris for French agents to assert themselves. The purpose of the Cisalpine Republic, a new ambassador was told in June 1798,[14] was 'to serve the exclusive interests of the French Republic, and to help it become, over the entire peninsula, the arbiter of all political contests. It must become powerful enough to be useful to us, but never so much that we are damaged.' More conservative elements, hostile to ideas of Italian unification, should therefore be brought to power. A new constitution, modelled on that of the Roman Republic and with a restricted franchise based on the highest taxpayers, was proposed. Leaked in advance by General Brune, who had been ordered against his will to support its imposition with military force, it raised a furore both in Milan and Paris, where resurgent Jacobins feared that it would be a trial run for constitutional remodelling in France itself. Nevertheless it was imposed on 30 August, and Brune was ordered to ensure that the changes were ratified by primary assemblies. Instead, he secured ratification for the mass expulsion of moderates from the government, deliberately defying orders from Paris in what was effectively the third Cisalpine *coup d'état* in a year. A fourth followed his inevitable recall, with the 30 August constitution finally being imposed, and Jacobins once more being expelled, in December. This time the response was more muted, for the war of the second coalition had begun, on whose outcome the fate of all the sister republics would depend.

The first shots, in fact, had been fired in Italy. On 12 November the Neapolitan army invaded the Roman Republic, and within two weeks it had taken its capital, to be welcomed by excited crowds disgusted by the anti-religious excesses of ten months of republican rule. During this time churches had been plundered, pious fraternities dissolved, new monastic vows forbidden, and many religious houses closed down. In a state whose sole resources were religion and tourism, and whose swarming poor relied on clerical charities, these reforms were catastrophic. Paper money issued by the new authorities had plummeted in value almost at once, exacerbating the problems. Even worse was to follow a few weeks later, when the regrouped French forces returned to chase the invaders back to Naples. The Roman Jacobins resurfaced more militant than ever, now banning all public signs of religious practice, restricting ordinations, and imposing forced loans. French exactions were renewed, their total value reaching perhaps 70 millions.

There was scarcely time to extend this pattern to the last of the sister republics, and the shortest-lived—the Parthenopean Republic proclaimed at Naples by Championnet on 26 January 1799. By this time the Directors wanted no more of such satellites. As the Austrians and Russians prepared to march into Switzerland and Italy, the French armies were already dangerously stretched, and the poor, remote Neapolitan kingdom had limited strategic value. Championnet knew this, and after the flight of Ferdinand IV's forces was at first content to conclude an armistice under which he occupied the northern provinces but not the city of Naples—by far Italy's largest. All he demanded there was that Nelson and his British squadron should be denied a landing. But the panic-stricken king and queen abandoned Naples, sailing off to Sicily with Nelson. Chaos gripped the city as the volatile Neapolitan poor, the notorious *lazzaroni*, armed to confront the French and ended up lynching noblemen and sacking the empty royal palace. The city's Jacobins, emerging from three years of prudent obscurity since the breakup of their clubs in 1795, appealed to Championnet to intervene. He could not resist this opportunity to emulate Bonaparte, but a thousand Frenchmen and three times that number of *lazzaroni* lay dead or wounded before the blue, red, and yellow tricolour of the Parthenopean Republic flew over Naples. A provisional government of Jacobins now set about drafting a constitution, while a club dedicated to 'public instruction' elaborated a whole range of Utopian reform projects. Championnet, however, was recalled in disgrace after expelling a critical civil commissioner from Naples in true Bonapartist style. His dismissal was the last triumph under the Directory of the civil arm over the military, and even that rebounded in June when a court-martial failed to convict him. And by then the Republic he had created in southern Italy had disappeared. The Russians had arrived in Lombardy, and in order to avoid being cut off the new French commander in Naples, MacDonald, abandoned the city in a desperate march northwards. His collaborators were left with no force to rely on but a few hundred French troops garrisoning strong points. This might be enough to contain the *lazzaroni*, but it was certainly no match for the royalist forces now making for Naples from the south—the 'Christian Army of the Holy Faith' led by a fighting prince of the Church, Cardinal Ruffo.

Ruffo was a Calabrian who had served in the papal curia but had found more favour at the Neapolitan court. Sailing with the royal family to Sicily, he offered to raise his native province for the king before the French got there. Feeling he had nothing to lose, Ferdinand IV accepted the offer, and Ruffo landed in Calabria with a handful of companions and a banner bearing the cross and the royal arms on 7 February. Within weeks his followers had swelled to an army of 17,000 and were in control of the whole toe of Italy. Soon the neighbouring provinces of Apulia and Basilicata had fallen to them as well. Ruffo's technique was to appeal pointedly to social antagonisms in an area recently ravaged by natural disasters, over-populated, deeply impoverished, and groaning under heavy indirect taxes and feudal burdens. He proclaimed the latter abolished while the Jacobins in Naples were merely toying with the idea, thus inferring that the French and their friends represented the rich and powerful. He also whipped up the deep-rooted antagonism of peasants for the towns, knowing that if all townsmen were not Jacobins, all Jacobins were certainly townsmen. As everywhere, political labels were stuck on innumerable long-standing local antagonisms and vendettas and provided new justifications for pursuing them. The march of the 'Sanfedist' army was a peasants' revolt which in other circumstances might just as easily have been against the Bourbon government. Like other such revolts, it was chaotic, undisciplined, and largely local in its impetus and effects. Law and order in Calabria did not recover from it for decades. Even so, enough of those involved were prepared to march with Ruffo up to defenceless Naples, where they arrived on June 13 as British ships threatened the city from the bay. A week of confused siege and renewed anarchy followed.

The populace [reported Ruffo, appalled at the savagery now unleashed], and many outlaws who have come to fight for the King . . . are robbing and plundering without let or hindrance. All respectable folk are fleeing to the country. Our better soldiers are guarding the houses against pillage, but to little purpose. Often the pretext is Jacobinism: that is what they call it, but in fact it is plunder that often produces Jacobin proprietors. I find the same in small places. To the cry of 'Long live the King!' they dare anything with impunity.[15]

He could see no point in further draconian reprisals once calm returned; but his royal master, his fearsome Habsburg queen, and their British advisers thought otherwise. They demanded victims, and show trials followed the royal return to Naples. In consequence, 120 Jacobins were hanged and over 1,100 more imprisoned.

By now the whole of Italy was in revolt against the French and their protégés. Briefly, as the forces of the coalition massed, the invaders attempted to seize control of the whole peninsula. Piedmont, surrounded as a result of the previous war by French, or French-controlled, territory, had been browbeaten into a treaty of alliance in October 1797. The following June the Republic's troops were allowed to garrison the citadel at Turin, from where they encouraged local sympathizers to demonstrate against the monarchy. Matters came to a crisis when the French demanded that the lands of dissolved Cisalpine monasteries on Piedmontese territory should be sold. King Charles Emmanuel IV refused, unless the citadel was returned. The French response was to demand yet more military facilities, and when the king held out, they occupied the whole country (December 1798) and forced him to abdicate. Exhorting his former subjects to obey the French, he left for the island kingdom of Sardinia that was still his. Piedmontese patriots rejoiced, but not for long. In February 1798 a carefully rigged referendum approved the annexation of Piedmont to France. Such a solution was not contemplated in Tuscany, further south, but as war resumed in the spring the French decided they needed to occupy it and draw on its still untouched resources. In March 1799 they marched in, packing the Grand Duke Ferdinand off to his brother in Vienna. But no sooner was this control asserted that it was challenged—by the Austro-Russian invasion from outside, and by indigenous revolts from within.

All over the peninsula there were anti-French outbreaks, especially as the Republic's overstretched forces withdrew to concentrate in the north. Taken together they probably represented the greatest and most spectacular repudiation of the French Revolution and its principles that this turbulent decade had produced. For the Italian peasants who were the mainstay of the revolts, the French stood for military marauding and looting, and heavy impositions. All too often, despite grandiloquent denunciations of feudalism, they prolonged the exactions of landlords as a convenient source of revenue. Worse, the French stood for impiety, with their plunder of churches and contempt for religious customs and superstitions. Bonaparte was not alone among their generals in seeing what damage such behaviour could do. They eagerly curried support among the quite numerous prelates and clerics who were ready to establish a working relationship with them, and distributed copies of sermons proclaiming that Liberty, Equality, and Christianity were perfectly compatible. But they could not control the everyday behaviour of soldiers who knew from years of experience, at home and abroad, that priestcraft was the most persistent and insidious enemy of the Revolution. Producing acts of casual blasphemy and sacrilege, such beliefs were self-confirming. Finally the French stood for the rule of Jacobins: rich, educated townsmen more intent, in peasant eyes, on seizing power for themselves, often again with a show of gratuitous anti-religious excess, than in addressing the problems country people thought important. Peasants knew that these people owed their power to the French, and kept it by doing the foreign invaders' bidding, and used it to enrich themselves by expropriating the Church and buying up the proceeds. Frenchmen often compared rural revolts in Italy to the Vendée, or called the rebels *chouans*; and in the mixture of religious and material resentments, and country versus town antagonisms, there was a good deal in common between Italian insurgents and France's own archetypal anti-revolutionaries.

But not all those who rejected the rule of the French were peasants. French occupation, looting, and exactions brought severe disruption to urban life, too. The anti-French rallying cry of *Vive Maria!* was heard most loudly in Rome in 1798 or Florence in 1799. Here again, however, local conflicts often underlay the resistance—resentment at attacks on the Church which in Tuscany went back to the 1760s, outrage that the French and their clients did not revoke the free-trade policies that had pushed up the price of subsistence in the swollen cities, again since the 1760s. Jews, too, whose ambiguous status all Jacobins vowed to improve, came under popular attack when the French withdrew. By 1799, in fact, increasing numbers of the Italian Jacobins themselves were turning against their benefactors. They had never been united. Everywhere moderates who hoped only for a resumption of the steady, ordered reforms of the 1780s in the individual territories of the peninsula struggled with radicals who sought its prompt unification, if necessary by methods of terror. Consistently thwarted once French control was well established, the latter by 1798 had begun to hatch ambitious plots, sometimes in concert with anti-directorial Jacobins in France itself. 'There can be no doubt', wrote a well-informed directorial agent in October 1798,[16] 'that at this moment a vast plot is being hatched to assassinate Frenchmen . . . Scoundrels are planning a new Sicilian vespers against the Italian governments. They have been listened to by many people, and mystery still shrouds part of the horrors that have been prepared to make the war more deadly for the hated nation, if fighting should start again.' In Piedmont the conspirators actually managed to enlist peasant sympathies, and in February 1799, although their plot was uncovered, peasants in the Langhe district rose in protest at impending French annexation, carrying not (ultimate irony) pious objects and symbols, but miniatures of the Jacobin martyrs Le Peletier and Marat.

The Year VII, therefore, beginning in September 1798, was marked by popular uprisings against the French and their Revolution in most of the areas where they had penetrated—Belgium, Luxembourg, Switzerland, and Italy. Although a new wave of unrest swept the distant Russian steppes in 1796–8, and may have owed something to garbled rumours of upheaval far to the west, the only pro-French uprising of any significance occurred in a place Frenchmen never reached until it was over. Even there it was obvious that Irish peasants had no idea what they stood for. 'God help these simpletons', remarked one of Humbert's officers.[17] 'If they knew how little we cared for the Pope or his religion, they would not be so hot in expecting help from us.' By the late 1790s, the fact is that whereas the friends of revolutionary France beyond her borders still ran into thousands, their numbers were rapidly diminishing. Her enemies, on the other hand, ran into millions, and were increasing all the time. Combined with the organized forces of the second coalition, who on paper at least could muster between them armies of over 400,000, they constituted a threat to the revolutionary Republic more mortal than any it had faced since the Year II. And although the outbreaks of resistance had been contained or reduced to a sustainable level of defiance by the time military campaigning began in earnest in the spring of 1799, in Italy they completely outran French resources.

Yet the arrogance born of four years of uninterrupted success died hard. It was the French who declared war on Austria, and they began it by taking the offensive on all fronts. In Germany Jourdan crossed the Rhine and marched towards Vienna. Despite being outnumbered three to one, he gave battle to the Archduke Charles at Stockach on 25 March and suffered a paralysing defeat. Armies that had advanced from Switzerland now had to fall back, pursued by Austrian and Russian forces. Equally outnumbered in Italy, and confronted by the redoubtable Suvorov, the French fought a bloody rearguard campaign. By the end of June they were penned into a coastal strip around Genoa. The sister republics collapsed in a welter of revenge and reprisal, and Suvorov proclaimed the restoration of Charles Emmanuel IV in Turin. Only in distant Egypt did the general who, more than any other single person, had precipitated this new crisis continue to win victories. But nobody in Europe knew this, and Bonaparte in turn was unaware of French disasters in the new war. Late in June he was writing to Paris asking for more troops to be sent. It was not until the beginning of August that, by courtesy of a British admiral, he received newspapers already two months old announcing defeat upon defeat. Already disillusioned about what might be achieved in Egypt, he now foresaw nothing but ultimate surrender. The Directory took the same view. On 25 May, in fact, it had ordered him to evacuate Egypt. But these orders had still not arrived when, on 24 August, he sailed secretly for France of his own accord, leaving the army he had taken to the east to shift for itself. Two years later, depleted by two-thirds, its diseased and demoralized remnants surrendered to the British, who transported them back at last to a France now ruled by the general who had abandoned them.

# An End to Revolution
## 1799—1802

As 1799 began, amid renewed foreign war and continued political strife, the stability that alone could ensure permanence for the Revolution's achievements seemed as far away as ever. Yet vast reserves of potential support awaited any regime that could achieve that stability, and that permanence. The peasants of the Seine-et-Oise to the west of Paris, wrote a directorial commissioner,

are not in the least partisans of royalty, the memory of tithes and rents being odious to them. They are quite satisfied that their harvests should have doubled since the extinction of game rights, they recognise and greatly value the possession of equality. Many of them have bought national lands and all have improved their position, so that when they compare the old order to the new they give their preference to the latter. But the evils of the old order are far away, and they remember only the evils that have been brought upon them by the revolutionary turmoil. French victories appeal to a section of them, but do not touch them greatly, because they are purchased at the cost of their sons' blood, and the peasantry are not sufficiently committed to accept such sacrifices. They neglect the exercise of civic rights because exercising these rights has exhausted them. They still give themselves to the priests more out of stubbornness than any other sentiment. This picture proves that it only requires peace, tranquility and a certain period of calm to make them like the Revolution again.[1]

But could the Revolution—meaning the directorial regime—ever hope to achieve this peace, tranquillity, and calm? Fewer and fewer people seemed to think so.

Apart from the renewal of warfare, and the Directory's obvious intention to create armies to fight it by conscription, which had already brought the Belgian departments out in revolt, it was clear that once again they were intending to rig the annual elections. While the ministry of the interior issued the usual proclamations denouncing the twin evils of royalism and 'anarchy', electoral assemblies were tacitly invited once more to split, and individual Directors endorsed acceptable candidates in regions where they believed themselves influential. The apathy of the electors themselves was more obvious than ever—derisory numbers turned up to vote everywhere in March 1799. But those who did returned electoral assemblies which refused to accept the directorial lead. Only 66 of 187 endorsed candidates were elected. Twenty-seven assemblies split, producing rival lists of candidates as in 1798. But this time it was the turn of the outgoing Councils to spurn the executive line. Deputies returned as reliable in Floréal now showed themselves narrowly constitutionalist, and in all but two cases they accepted the elections made by the larger faction in split assemblies. This let in some 50 Jacobins or fellow-travellers, including some purged in Floréal. Without the support of other deputies they were nowhere near a majority, but there were plenty of more moderate deputies discontented for their own reasons with the Directory. By the time the new Councils convened on 20 May news of military defeat was pouring in from all fronts. And their predecessors had ended their sittings with a final gesture of no confidence. When lots were drawn for the Director to retire, Reubell, the most self-confident among them, lost his place. Elected to succeed him on 16 May was a long-time critic of the constitution, Sieyès, currently ambassador to Berlin. In contrast to 1795, he did not refuse to serve. Apparently he believed that the moment was now ripe to make the sort of changes he had long believed necessary.

The opening of the new Councils therefore precipitated a political crisis, with a divided executive, a volatile legislature, and a military emergency potentially as serious as that of 1793. Almost at once a savage attack was launched on the Directory, with the newly nominated Sieyès standing ostentatiously aside. On 6 June the Five Hundred summoned the executive to explain the defeats suffered by the armies. Corrupt and profiteering contractors, Jacobins alleged, had kept the Republic's forces undersupplied, and Directors no less corrupt had connived at the malversations of these 'dilapidators'. The Directory, its unity gone, stood paralysed before the onslaught, and made no response. A week later the Five Hundred resolved to go into permanent session until it replied, and the Elders followed their lead. It was now claimed, too, that Treilhard had come to office illegally the year before, twelve months not having elapsed since he had ceased to be a deputy. The issue had been thoroughly ventilated when he had been chosen, and the same rule should now have excluded Sieyès. But Treilhard chose not to fight and resigned. Elected to succeed him was Gohier, a left-leaning bureaucratic nonentity who sided with Sieyès. Barras, always the trimmer, did the same. La Revellière and Merlin had been reduced to a minority on the executive, therefore, when the Councils turned their fire on them, accusing them of violating the constitution in organizing the Floréal purge. Their three colleagues now urged them to resign to avoid the impeachment which seemed destined otherwise to follow, unless the military intervened first. Sieyès's favourite general, Joubert, made appropriately fierce noises. After hours of agonizing, they agreed to resign, and more relative nonentities, the regicide Ducos, and Moulin, an untested general, were installed in their places on 18 June. This was the coup of Prairial: the first and only occasion on which the Councils purged the Directory and not the other way round. The legislature, exulted Lucien Bonaparte, the conqueror of Italy's younger brother and now a leftwardly inclined deputy, had resumed its rightful leading place in the constitution. And certainly the Councils' attack had been fuelled by resentment across a wide spectrum of opinion at the gerrymanderings of the previous year. But what gave it impact was the co-ordinating role of Sieyès. It placed the executive power effectively in his hands, a degree of concentration not seen since the days of Robespierre. And Sieyès's aim was to diminish the power of the legislature, not increase it.

First to realize how they had been misled were the Jacobins. As the main victims of Floréal, they saw themselves as the main beneficiaries now it was avenged. Suppressed for over a year, their newspapers began to appear once more, and freedom of the press was declared on 1 August. On 6 July a new club was announced, the Manège Club, meeting in the historic and heroic surroundings of the old Convention hall in the Tuileries, and presided over by members of the surviving Jacobin old guard like Drouet, now chiefly known as a former Babeuf collaborator. Jacobins reappeared in public office, too: Ramel was replaced at the financial ministry by Lindet. Above all, as the news from the front continued to get worse, a stream of Jacobin-inspired legislation was passed by the Councils. On 28 June the Jourdan conscription law was activated in its fullest form: all those between 20 and 25 eligible for military service were to be conscripted at once, and nobody was to be allowed to buy a substitute. Jourdan himself, as a deputy, moved this measure, which he described in so many words as a new *levée en masse*. At the same time he proposed a forced loan on the rich, designed to raise 100 millions for waging the war. By this time the armies no longer occupied much foreign territory off which they could live as they had done since 1794, so the Republic was inevitably thrust back on to her own resources. The rates of the loan would be punitive for the richest citizens. Both these measures evoked haunting memories of the Year II. Even worse was the Law of Hostages, passed on 12 July. Under it, resistance to the new measures, or indeed any other, could lead to a department or district being declared 'disturbed'. In such places, the authorities were empowered to arrest relatives of *émigrés* or nobles, imprison them at their own expense, and fine them and impound their property to pay for any damage done by those causing disturbances. No proven links with those responsible were required. Taken together, these laws seemed to announce a return to sansculotte terror, threatening the rich and the propertied above all. Previous forced loans in 1793 and 1796 had certainly been targeted on them, while the Law of Hostages recalled the Law of Suspects, but gave those implementing it even wider powers. Emboldened by their success in pushing these laws through, the Jacobins went on to move the impeachment of the fallen Directors and their minister of war, General Schérer, who was accused of massive corruption. But under the constitution such indictments required thirty days and three readings to be enacted, and this gave time for Sieyès to orchestrate measures to curb the Jacobin momentum. As president of the Directory, he used the anniversaries of the Revolution's great moments—14 July, 27 July (9 Thermidor), and 10 August—to issue public warnings against the bloody perils of extremism. A press campaign was also orchestrated against the Manège Club, which was accused of seeking to bring in the constitution of 1793. With a membership of 3,000, including perhaps 250 deputies, its stirring sessions certainly awoke memories of headier times. But it also encountered much barracking and harassment from royalist gangs, which in turn evoked post-Thermidorian clashes. It was therefore very easy to portray the club as a threat to public order, and on 26 July the Elders were persuaded on these grounds to expel it (like the Feuillants in 1791) from the legislature's precincts. It moved to another historic site in the rue du Bac, across the river, resentment making its members even shriller. On 13 August, finally, it was closed down by the new minister of police, a man who knew more about Jacobinism than most: Fouché. This was the lead the Councils needed. Most deputies had never been Jacobin, and they were now anxious not to be carried further down the paths of extremism. Five days later, although by only three votes, the Five Hundred threw out the indictments against Merlin, La Revellière, and Schérer.

It was not quite the end of the Jacobin resurgence, however. The emergency which had done so much to fuel it was far from over. For some weeks, in fact, it continued to worsen. Joubert, sent to Italy to establish himself as the Republic's leading general, was killed on 15 August and his army catastrophically defeated at Novi. No sooner had this news reached Paris than it was announced that the British and Russians had landed in Holland and the Dutch fleet had gone over to them. Internal insurrection had also broken out, for the first time since 1797. Encouraged by the formation of an international coalition and its initial successes, monarchist organizations which had lain low throughout 1798 now hurriedly put together plans for risings to coincide with the expected invasions. In the south-west, they planned to engulf the Jacobin stronghold of Toulouse with a peasant army swollen by refugees from the new conscription law. Throughout the spring politically motivated lawlessness mounted around Toulouse. In July the local directorial agent reported, 'Several republicans assassinated, the properties of a greater number burned or destroyed, Liberty trees chopped down or uprooted in more than 40 communes.'[2] Three weeks later, on 5 August, the countryside rose. Ten thousand men flocked to the white Bourbon flag now raised, although most of them were unarmed. For a month civil war raged along the upper Garonne, claiming over 4,000 casualties. But, despite the absence of regular troops, the rebels never captured Toulouse, and National Guards from surrounding departments rushed in to reinforce it. Supporting uprisings in neighbouring cities like Bordeaux, Dax, or Agen never went beyond a few scuffles. The defeat of this outbreak by Toulouse, the only major city to stay consistently in Jacobin hands throughout all the vicissitudes of the Directory, was an embarrassment for Sieyès, who at this very moment was trying to clamp down on the left-wing press in Paris. His enemies in the Councils saw the opportunity to recover their momentum: and on 13 September Jourdan moved in the Five Hundred that the country should be declared in danger, under the law of 5 July 1792 which gave emergency powers to all authorities. An impassioned debate followed, Jacobins urging that the revolutionary enthusiasm of former days needed to be rekindled if the Republic was to survive, their opponents arguing that to declare the Country in Danger was a makeshift expedient no longer appropriate in a better-organized state, while others warned that to suspend normal procedures would open the way, as it had before, to 1793. This was the argument which counted. On a vote, the motion was defeated by 245 votes to 171, a clear signal of confidence in the new Directory and its anti-Jacobin policy.

Within days, moreover, this confidence proved justified. Suddenly the armies began to win. In the Batavian Republic, the Anglo-Russian invaders were turned back by Brune and Daendels on 19 September and within a month had been forced to evacuate the country. In Switzerland the Russians, abandoned by the main Austrian army which Thugut now diverted to secure objectives in the Rhineland, were caught divided, severely mauled, and by the end of September had evacuated the Helvetic Republic. Sieyès saw that, with the armies once more achieving victories and the Councils in confusion, a ripe moment had come to make changes.

Now was the time to strengthen the executive permanently. Nor could it be done in any constitutional way—the procedures were too long and complex. It had to be by *coup d'état*, and the changes would be so profound that military support would be essential. The problem was to find a reliable general. Joubert, his original preference, was dead. Jourdan was a Jacobin. Moreau, when approached early in October, was visibly reluctant. It was at precisely this moment that Bonaparte landed. 'There is your man,' declared Moreau. He was right, but only in the short run.

Landing on 10 October, Bonaparte took another six days to reach Paris. His progress north was one long triumph, with deputations, addresses, and jubilant crowds gathered to greet the peacemaker of 1797, the Republic's one undefeated general. In the capital, too, everybody sought him out—his record aroused hopes right across the political spectrum. As in the winter of 1797–8, he behaved modestly, but he needed time to appraise a situation much changed since May 1798. Nevertheless nobody could afford to wait long. The crisis in the Republic's affairs was far from over. The Austrians were still in control of Italy, threatening the Alpine frontier, and in the west, the last fortnight in October saw a renewed outburst of *chouannerie*. Alarmed by the sweeping new law on conscription, the leaders of the various *chouan* bands had agreed in mid-September to resume their activities on behalf of the king. On 14 October they engulfed Le Mans, 3,000 strong, and spent four days ransacking it for arms and supplies. Other major cities, such as Nantes, were also briefly occupied. Not only Jacobinism, therefore, threatened the Republic in the autumn of 1799. Both the extremes between which the Directory had endlessly see-sawed seemed as alive as ever, further underlining its inadequacies. Sieyès, accordingly, was soon in touch with Bonaparte, first indirectly, then face to face. The general did not like him, but he saw that he could use him. Sieyès for his part underestimated this soldier without experience in the labyrinthine world of Parisian politics, a man who had always projected himself as direct and simple. But, each for his own reasons, they agreed to co-operate in enforcing constitutional change. Bonaparte's brother, now president of the Five Hundred, was also closely involved; as were Fouché, and Talleyrand, once more out of office and looking for a way back in.

The coup was dressed up as a final blow against Jacobinism. Alleging a plot, on 9 November Lucien Bonaparte induced the Councils to agree to transfer their sessions to the suburban security of the former royal palace of Saint-Cloud, far away from the influence of the Parisian populace: not that the populace had lifted a finger in politics since 1795. Bonaparte, who had saved the legislature from mass attack in that year, was appointed commander of all the troops available in the metropolitan area. Meanwhile the whole Directory, including Sieyès, resigned—although Gohier and Moulin only did so under pressure. France was now without an executive. The aim was to induce the Councils to establish a provisional government at Saint-Cloud, the next day, 18 Brumaire, Year VIII. But matters there did not go smoothly. Despite a massive show of military strength Bonaparte was coldly received by the Elders when he demanded constitutional changes, while in the Five Hundred, always the stronghold of the Jacobins, he was mobbed and manhandled to cries of 'Outlaw him!' Bleeding from a scratch received in the tumult, he was carried from the chamber. His brother, emerging subsequently, declared to the troops outside that Jacobins had tried to assassinate him. In the highly charged atmosphere this was enough to induce them to obey orders to clear the hall. Some hours later a compliant quorum was reassembled to vote, as the Elders had already done, to adjourn the legislature for six weeks while a joint committee of 50 deputies worked out a complete constitutional revision. Executive power during that time was vested in a provisional government of three Consuls—Ducos, Sieyès, and Bonaparte. The Directory was over.

Why had it failed? The Brumaire conspirators blamed the impossible structure of the constitution, which made the legislature too strong, and the executive too weak. In practice the Directory had controlled and dominated the Councils throughout most of the existence of the constitution of the Year III; but only by electoral manipulations and purges. 'It is a great tragedy', Bonaparte confided to Talleyrand after the Fructidor coup,[3] 'for a nation of 30 million inhabitants in the eighteenth century to have to call on bayonets to save the state.' But he did not see the solution in a mere technical readjustment of the balance. He wanted a complete reversal. 'The power of the government,' he wrote in the same letter, 'in all the latitude I would give it, ought to be considered as the true representative of the nation.' The legislature would be part of the government, empowered to make general or (a favourite word) 'organic' laws. 'Circumstantial' laws would be the executive's province. Sieyès, a self-proclaimed political genius, favoured no such open-ended executive power. He retained an Enlightened fear of despotism, and he dreamed of an elaborate system of checks and balances to keep the executive under the restraint of legality. The real problem in his view was elections. The nation was of course sovereign, as he himself had proclaimed in the Revolution's distant springtime of 1789, but elections of the Directory type were not necessarily the best means of expressing that sovereignty. Those in authority, at every level, should certainly be people deemed worthy to exercise it by responsible fellow citizens; but should not be dependent on those over whom they held sway. 'Confidence', he declared,[4] 'comes from below, power comes from above.'

These were drastic solutions for a problem which arguably was more political than constitutional. The constitution of the Year III was never in fact given the chance to work properly. Its first elections were meaningless thanks to the Two Thirds Law, and all subsequent ones were sooner or later discounted. No wonder decreasing numbers of citizens bothered to vote, knowing that after this empty ritual the Directory would exclude those of whom it disapproved anyway. After 1792, for all their talk of national or popular sovereignty, the men who ruled France never accepted the verdict of the electorate. Nor did they accept what all representative regimes sooner or later must: the inevitability of party politics. Imbued still with a Rousseauistic belief in a general will which all honest citizens share, they regarded political organizations as factions, illegitimate conspiracies against the constitution, designed to sow division rather than promote consensus. Thus neither neo-Jacobin clubs nor monarchist philanthropic institutes were ever given time to develop into the party organizations they might have become. They were tolerated from time to time, but only to the exclusion of each other. No serious attempt was made by the Directors, either, to create an organized centre or moderate party to concentrate their own support—although the endorsement of acceptable candidates in the 1799 elections perhaps showed them groping towards the idea. They seem to have considered the virtues of the Thermidorian republic self-evident to all right-thinking men; who would accordingly support them without further organization. They did so, but without conviction. Bonaparte was right when he declared in the Elders on 10 November that the constitution no longer had anyone's respect. Even its self-appointed guardians had never trusted it to function freely.

Yet that stance, too, was not without some justification. The royalists in 1796 and 1797 may have been prepared to operate like a political party within the constitution, but their long-term aim was undoubtedly to overthrow it and bring in the king. That king in turn was explicitly committed to the reversal of everything done since June 1789. As for the Jacobins, they may have been sincere in professions, increasingly heard in 1799, that they were merely a party of honest democrats, legitimately organized to oppose those in power by constitutional means. If so, they were rash in the extreme to revert constantly to the rhetoric of the Year II, to keep green the memory of Babeuf, and lend vocal support to more radical elements in the sister republics. All this raised understandable fears that their true loyalty was still to the levelling constitution of 1793. And nothing in their attitude, or that of the royalists, suggests that once in power either would have been more tolerant of opposition than the Directory was. Neither had any interest in compromise or conciliation. Neither was prepared to recognize the good faith and legitimate interest of opponents.

The difficulties plaguing the Directory, then, were far from simply constitutional, and the constitution of the Year VIII, drafted within a month under relentless pressure from Bonaparte, did little to address them. What it did was give a plenitude of power to the executive which left no excuse for not confronting the deep and still unsolved problems created by the Revolution. At the base of the political system, all citizens were now allowed to vote for 'those among them whom they believed most suitable to conduct public affairs'. But this merely meant a tenth of their own number who would then constitute a 'communal list'. The latter in turn chose a tenth of themselves to constitute a departmental list. From them, a further tenth were chosen for the national list of 'citizens eligible for national office'. This included membership of the legislature. The choice of members would be made by a new institution, the Senate, whose powers were not otherwise defined in the 95 articles of this laconic constitution. But Sieyès had long believed in the desirability of a 'conservative power' to vet the legality of the State's activities. In 1795 he had proposed a 'constitutional jury' to perform these functions, but without success. Now, with the Senate, the idea was adopted, and he became the body's first president. The legislature itself would remain bicameral, but whereas the lower house, the 100-member Tribunate, was to discuss all proposed legislation, it could not vote it. The upper house, the 300-member Legislative Body, did the voting—but could not discuss. Neither had any initiative in legislation. Draft laws came from the government alone, and were to be elaborated in a Council of State, a revival of a key institution of the old monarchy. Most of these provisions emanated from Sieyès. His ideas on the executive, however, were not adopted. Here at last General Bonaparte showed his true hand. Sieyès's initial proposal was for an executive of two Consuls, one for internal and one for external affairs. They would be appointed, along with other members of the state apparatus, by a supreme officer, the 'Grand Elector', holding office for life but exercising no other authority—a sort of constitutional monarch in effect. Bonaparte was envisaged in this role. But from the start he made it clear that he had no intention of being what he called a 'fatted pig'. He wanted real power, and in the final version he got it. There would be three Consuls, as since 10 November, but the first among them would have the overriding authority. Nobody doubted who it would be.

Completion of the new constitution was announced on 15 December. There was no referring back, as originally promised, to the former legislative Councils. It was to be approved by plebiscite, and for the revolutionary month of Nivôse (21 December 1799–20 January 1800) registers were open in every commune for citizens to record their approval or opposition. The result, announced early in February, gave 3,011,007 in favour and 1,562 against. Some six million did not vote at all, and creative methods were used to swell the numbers accepting. Yet it scarcely mattered. The constitution was brought into force in anticipation of popular acceptance on 25 December. It was, claimed its authors,[5] 'based on the true principle of representative government and on the sacred rights of property, equality and liberty. The powers which it sets up will be strong and stable, as they must be in order to guarantee the rights of citizen and the interests of the State. Citizens, the revolution is established on the principles with which it began. It is over.'

The effrontery in this statement was to become all too familiar over the fifteen years during which Bonaparte was to rule France. Only a handful of mutilated relics of the principles of 1789 could be discerned in the terse and ambiguous clauses of the consular constitution. And the First Consul was certainly not the first person to declare that the Revolution was over. But this time it was—or would be once the stability also promised became a reality. That depended on a satisfactory resolution of the issues which for a decade had torn France apart. Within two years they had been resolved: and for years afterwards most of the citizens of France thought a little effrontery, and the sacrifice of most of the principles of 1789, a small price to pay.

Many of the most serious problems of revolutionary France arose from the fact that for most of the 1790s it was a country at war. Even the peace of 1797 had not included the most dogged enemy of all, Great Britain. Few experienced statesmen expected continental peace to last long, either. Eventually, renewed war had brought a soldier to power. The most important task facing him was to end it, and end it victoriously. If France was defeated, he could hardly hope to survive to do anything else.

As 1799 came to an end, matters were already drifting his way. The greed and duplicity of the Austrians had placed intolerable strains on a coalition whose armies, by any rational calculation, ought now to have been marching deep into France. But instead of supporting his Russian allies in Switzerland, Thugut diverted the Archduke Charles with the best Austrian troops north to the Rhine; while in Italy his aim was to establish Austrian control of territories Suvorov had won rather than drive the last of the French back over the Alps. Suvorov's impressive but strategically disastrous retreat through Switzerland in the autumn of 1799, combined with the failure of the Anglo-Russian invasion of the Batavian Republic, left the volatile Paul I believing he had been betrayed by both his main allies in the coalition. By the beginning of 1800 he had resolved to withdraw, and ordered his troops home. The First Consul used the opportunity to propose peace to Francis II and George III—but only on the terms of Campo Formio, that brilliant but unstable triumph. Spurned, as he must have known he would be, he prepared to resume the campaign with a blow against Austria similar to that planned in 1796, with armies striking towards Vienna simultaneously from the Rhine and northern Italy. This time in overall control, like the Directors before him he realized that the Italian theatre should be secondary. But Moreau, commanding on the Rhine, thought the thrust proposed there too bold, and Bonaparte was still not secure enough in power to override him. He therefore decided to stake everything on repeating his own triumphs of 1796 and 1797 in Italy. After building up troops and supplies in eastern France in great secrecy, at the end of April 1800 he crossed the Alps from Switzerland. On 2 June he re-entered Milan, a few days after the French besieged in Genoa since the previous summer surrendered. This meant that when he confronted the Austrians at Marengo on the fourteenth, they had no distractions elsewhere, and he was outnumbered and outgunned. Accordingly he nearly lost the battle. Only fresh reserves at the last minute saved him. But instead of regrouping to fight another day his opponents promptly sued for an armistice, under which they evacuated the whole of Lombardy and Liguria. So the First Consul was able to claim another triumph, and an armistice was soon concluded on the Rhine as well. Once more France offered peace; but the terms were the same, and the Austrians believed themselves strong enough to achieve better ones. In November, fighting resumed, and this time the First Consul was strong enough to insist on a knock-out blow through Germany. It was delivered by Moreau at Hohenlinden, just outside Munich, on 3 December. By Christmas, the fighting was over, and negotiations in earnest began.

The result was the treaty of Lunéville, expedited by the fall of Thugut after the defeats of the summer. It was signed on 9 February 1801. Not only did it confirm the settlement of Campo Formio, with its recognition of Belgium and the left bank of the Rhine as French, and the establishment of French sister republics in northern Italy. It also, while confirming the Austrian hold in Venetia, expelled the Habsburgs from Tuscany. Once more under French occupation, the grand duchy now became a kingdom, Etruria. And its monarch was to be a Bourbon, Louis I, son of the duke of

Parma and son-in-law of the king of Spain. When the triumphant Republic began creating kingdoms, and for Bourbons of all people, the end of revolution really must be in sight. Nor was the Parthenopean Republic resurrected further south. The Bourbons of Naples, who also made peace with France in March 1801, lost certain outlying territories and accepted French garrisons in key ports, but in return had their legitimacy recognized. France took more in 1801 from her longest-standing ally than from her enemies. Spain, her client since 1796, ceded her the vast, untracked territory of Louisiana. Spanish ministers thought the price well worth paying for re-establishing their influence (as they hoped) in Italy.

The effect of all these settlements was to leave Great Britain isolated once again. At sea she was still unchallenged, and unchallengeable. In the Mediterranean British squadrons thwarted all attempts to relieve or reinforce the French garrison left in Egypt, and in January 1800 Kléber, its commander, agreed to evacuate. But nothing was done before the European successes of the spring, which encouraged the French to hold out. The First Consul never quite abandoned the dream which had taken him to Egypt, even after the British landed an expedition which in March 1801 forced the surrender of the last French troops there. In September 1800, meanwhile, they had also expelled the French from Malta. Its capture completed the alienation of Paul I from his former coalition allies. As Grand Master of the Knights of St John, he still regarded the island as his by right. He now offered full co-operation to Bonaparte, and began by organizing an 'armed neutrality' of Baltic powers to deny the tyrant of the seas access to the ports of northern Europe. But when Denmark, controlling access to the Baltic with its vital naval supplies, joined this new league, Nelson appeared with a squadron which destroyed the Danish fleet in Copenhagen itself on 2 April 1801. Just over a week earlier, Paul I had been assassinated in St Petersburg, and within days Anglo-Russian contacts resumed. By then, however, nobody in London was looking for yet another coalition. When Bonaparte had proposed peace in December 1799, the lofty British response had been to demand a prior restoration of the Bourbons. A year on, they could no longer afford such disdain. France was once more in complete control of the Continent, and intense war-weariness was compounded by economic difficulties to create a new wave of domestic discontent. Ireland, legally united with England in 1801, was still very uncertainly pacified, yet George III had set his face against the measure Pitt thought most likely to expedite that pacification, the admission of Catholics to Parliament. On this pretext Pitt, the most tenacious of all the French Revolution's enemies, resigned in February 1801. Within days his successor, Addington, was sending out peace feelers to Paris. Bonaparte responded at once, and a summer of negotiations was concluded in preliminaries signed in October.

The terms which at last brought the wars of the French Revolution to an end were an unqualified triumph for France. The Republic made no substantial concessions at all. Of gains made through her control of the seas, Great Britain retained only Ceylon and Trinidad, the first at the expense of the Dutch, the second at that of Spain. The Cape was returned to the Batavian Republic, and the evacuation of Malta promised. It was true that the French agreed to evacuate Egypt, but the British even provided the ships for that. British attempts to secure a follow-up commercial agreement or compensation for the deposed Stadtholder and the king of Piedmont, were brushed aside. There was no explicit British recognition of the Swiss or Italian sister-republics, or the annexation of Belgium, which they had originally gone to war to prevent. But the very act of negotiation was a tacit acknowledgement. The explosion of jubilation throughout England when the preliminaries were announced muted most criticism of these humiliating terms. Accordingly they were enshrined in the final peace signed at Amiens on 25 March 1802.

It was a month short of ten years since revolutionary France had turned to war as an instrument of policy. The vicissitudes of that decade of conflict had transformed the country far more radically than the principles of 1789 had promised to do, and they had transformed much of the rest of western Europe, too. Few could have dreamed in April 1792 that at the end of it all France would have extended her frontiers to the Rhine and the crest of the Alps, and would be in complete control of a blanket of client territories stretching from the North Sea to the Adriatic. Whether or not the effort had been worth while, or even necessary, the outcome was certainly glorious; and Bonaparte made sure that he got most of the credit. 'It is not sufficiently realised', he told a Prussian diplomat in July 1800,[6] 'that the French Revolution is not finished so long as the scourge of war lasts . . . this Revolution could still disturb, upset, and overthrow many states in its course. I want peace, as much to settle the present French government, as to save the world from chaos.' In the event this peace did not last long, and chaos would soon be extended to areas of Europe scarcely touched in the 1790s. But that was largely the work of the Emperor Napoleon, rather than the Revolution through which he had climbed to power.

Even before war had engulfed the Revolution, French opinion had been polarized over the question of the king. The first major consequence of the war was the creation of a republic, but that proved just as contentious as the rule of Louis XVI. Within weeks of the king's execution, monarchist rebels began a civil war in the west which was never fully won and seemed on the verge of breaking out afresh in 1799. When allowed to express themselves freely, as in the elections of 1797, massive numbers of French citizens indicated that they preferred a king to the Republic. Many more would willingly have accepted a restoration if it would bring calmer times, or if the king would recognize and guarantee some of the earlier achievements of the Revolution. Much of France, therefore, hoped and expected at the end of 1799 that the First Consul would be the Bourbons' General Monck, standing aside once his military authority had stabilized the government in favour of the legitimate ruler. The pretender himself cherished such hopes. On 20 February 1800 Louis XVIII wrote in flattering terms to 'the victor of Lodi, of Castiglione, of Arcoli, the conqueror of Italy and Egypt', urging him to seize the ultimate glory by restoring the dynasty which alone could ensure France's tranquillity. Bonaparte proved in no hurry to reply. Until military victory had consolidated his power he had every interest in neutralizing monarchist opinion by keeping up its hopes. But at the same time he moved resolutely to cut off the sources of royalism's strength.

The greatest immediate threat came from the *chouans*, who had become active again only weeks before he took power. Yet his very arrival in power disconcerted them, and one by one the various *chouan* leaders began to make peace. He in turn was prepared to be generous, reminding the western departments in a proclamation of 28 December that freedom of worship was guaranteed under the new constitution, and that the notorious Law of Hostages of the previous summer had been repealed. He also arranged to meet some of the most prominent *chouan* leaders and urged them to rally to him. 'The Bourbons no longer have a chance,' he told them.[7] 'You have done everything you ought to have for them, you are good men, ally yourselves with the side of glory.' A few remained unconvinced, including Cadoudal, who continued to plot with the British. But most had come to terms by the spring of 1800, and those who had not were ruthlessly tracked down. The Marengo campaign could scarcely have been fought without drawing on the 40,000 troops who only a few months before had been required to garrison the disturbed departments of the west. Success in that campaign in turn secured the First Consul's own position within France. By 8 September he felt ready to reply to Louis XVIII's overtures. Addressing the son of St Louis merely as *Monsieur*, he told him frankly,[8] 'You must not hope for your return to France; you would have to walk over a hundred thousand corpses. Sacrifice your interest to the peace and happiness of France ... I shall contribute with pleasure to the sweetness and tranquility of your retirement.'

Meanwhile he was conciliating the *émigrés*. Although the new constitution forbade their return in any circumstances, the importance of this clause lay in its last sentence: 'The property of the *émigrés* is irrevocably vested in the Republic.' Acquirers of such property were thereby assured that their rights were secure, a commitment that Louis XVIII had never yet made. Provided they accepted these losses, it was soon made clear to the *émigrés* that they were welcome to return. In March 1800 the list of *émigrés* was formally closed. In October a general amnesty was declared for all who had taken up arms against the Republic. By now many who had done even this had returned, but no action was taken against them. Simultaneously those whom monarchists, or those attracted by monarchy, feared the most were systematically persecuted—the Jacobins. The pretext for the Brumaire coup had been the prevention of a Jacobin plot, and in the course of it 62 left-wing deputies were excluded from the national representation. No conciliatory gestures were made in their direction, and the new constitution offered them no hope of ever repeating their electoral success of 1799. By the summer of 1800 Jacobin survivors, denounced by the First Consul as 'terrorists, wretches in perpetual revolt against every form of government . . . assassins of 3 September, the authors of 31 May, the conspirators of Prairial',[9] were reduced to plotting in cafés, invariably eavesdropped on by Fouché's ubiquitous agents. But their talk was bloodthirsty enough, and always revolved around assassinating the new ruler of France. Thus the government, at least, was not wholly surprised when, on 24 December 1800, a huge 'infernal machine' was exploded in central Paris only moments after the First Consul's carriage had passed. There were many dead and injured. Bonaparte was convinced that Jacobin plotters were responsible. In fact it was quite the contrary. Fouché was soon able to prove that the bomb was the work of *chouans* sent to Paris by Cadoudal. His master, however, was not interested. This was a heaven-sent opportunity to strike at the Jacobins: there must be blood. And so there was. Sweeping aside legal formalities, Fouché rounded up 130 Jacobins whose names had been well known to the police for years, and who had grown used to arrest whenever since 1795 the directorial pendulum had swung to the right. Four were guillotined, five shot: most of the rest were deported either to Guiana or (a new penal depository) the Seychelles. None of the real culprits suffered at all for the moment, apart from those blown up in the attempt.

Along with vengeance on men he hated and who hated him, however, Bonaparte had a more calculated motive. 'This is an opportunity', he declared to the Council of State,[10] 'of which the government must take advantage . . . A great example is necessary to reconcile the middle classes to the Republic.' He meant, of course, a republic headed by himself, and he knew that the surest way of defeating royalism was to make his own rule appear more likely than that of a king to guarantee stability and the security of property. Thus he struck ruthlessly against the levelling heirs of Babeuf, having already cleared away the alarming legislation passed when they had last been influential. The Law of Hostages was abrogated within four days of the Brumaire coup; the forced loan within nine, to be replaced by a small proportional surtax. The State's creditors were also reassured: in February 1800, 80 years of suspicion and prejudice were jettisoned with the establishment of a state bank, the Bank of France. The following August it was announced that all the State's debts would henceforth be paid on time, and in cash: over that summer, stock in the 'consolidated third' of the debt reorganized by Ramel in 1797 doubled in value. Tax-revenues improved dramatically as a regular system of collection, reviving many effective pre-revolutionary practices, were instituted. In 1802, the year of peace, the First Consul was able to proclaim a balanced budget. The underpinnings of these achievements were as yet uncertain, but they were self-reinforcing. The finances of the State appeared every day to be under firmer and more responsible control.

Law and order took on the same appearance. The authority of the central government in the localities was firmly established by the creation of prefects in each department, recalling the intendants swept away in 1789, and with far wider powers than the directorial commissioners who had linked central to local authority between 1795 and 1799. They confronted a situation of disorder and crime which had reached almost epidemic proportions ever since the promulgation of the Jourdan conscription law, which drove thousands of able-bodied young men into lives of banditry and crime as they fled from recruiting officers. In the south, inevitably, they joined royalist gangs harassing local officials, tax-collectors, buyers of national lands, National Guardsmen off duty, former Jacobin activists, and other hate-figures. Elsewhere they blended into roving bands of criminals, known from the way some of them tortured rich victims into sumbission as 'warmers' (*chauffeurs*). In the first year of the Consulate, as all available troops were drafted to the Rhine and Italy to confront foreign enemies, this crime wave continued unchecked. With the return of peace, not only did the pressure of conscription ease, but returning soldiers were available to enforce the will of the new, centrally appointed local authorities against criminal elements. In February 1801 special criminal courts with wide powers were created to deal with brigandage. Disorder began to subside. And, despite the First Consul's brazen contempt for legal procedures at the level of high politics, in everyday terms he made careful efforts to present himself as the apostle of the rule of law. Talk of endowing France with a uniform, comprehensive law code had gone on since at least the 1770s. Successive revolutionary assemblies set up commissions to work on the project, but none had brought it to fruition. Bonaparte was determined to do so. In 1800 he set up his own commission, lodged with it the papers and plans of previous ones, and pressed it ceaselessly to produce quick results. He was present himself at 57 of the 102 sessions which produced its first fruit, the Civil Code. Although not formally promulgated until 1804, preliminary drafts were circulating by the end of 1801. In all this, French citizens could admire, as they were meant to, the drive and activity which were elaborating for them a clear set of rules binding the holding and transfer of property. Neither kings nor representative assemblies had been capable of achieving so much, so quickly. And by the time the Code appeared, the last great doubt about the legitimacy and longevity of titles to land acquired during the Revolution had been removed, by a settlement with its oldest and most implacable enemy, the Church.

Nothing had done more to shatter the early revolutionary consensus than the National Assembly's inept attempt to regenerate the nation's religious life and organization. No wound of the revolutionary years went deeper, or was reopened more persistently by all parties. And despite a massive, swelling revival of everyday religious practice in France from 1795 onwards, the last phase of the Directory was marked by renewed official anti-clericalism. When Pius VI died a captive in France on 29 August 1799, his traditional capital lost to him and turned into a French sister republic, it was widely assumed in Paris that he would have no successor. The Catholic Church had challenged the Great Nation, and had lost; and, though the ignorant populace might remain mired in credulity and mindless superstition, the Church as an institution was rapidly crumbling away, to the general benefit of humanity.

Bonaparte, however, had never made the mistake of underestimating either the power of religion or the resilience of the Church. Under orders in the spring of 1796 to march on Rome to avenge the murder by a Roman mob of a French envoy, he was confronted by a Spanish emissary from the pontiff.

I told him [the Spaniard reported], if you people take it into your heads to make the pope say the slightest thing against dogma or anything touching on it, you are deceiving yourselves, for he will never do it. You might, in revenge, sack, burn and destroy Rome, St. Peter's etc. but religion will remain standing in spite of your attacks. If all you wish is that the pope urge peace in general, and obedience to legitimate power, he will willingly do it. He appeared to me captivated by this reasoning . . .[11]

Certainly he continued while in Italy to treat the Pope with more restraint than the Directory had ordered; and when, early the next year, the Cispadane Republic was established in territories largely taken from the Holy See, he advised its founders that: 'Everything is to be done by degrees and with gentleness. Religion is to be treated like property.'[12] Devoid of any personal faith, in Egypt he even made parade of following Islam in the conviction that it would strengthen French rule. By the time he returned to Europe, it was already clear that Pope Pius VI would not after all be the last. A conclave of the scattered cardinals had been summoned, and the Austrians allowed it to meet on their new territory in Venice. There, in March 1800, a surprise candidate emerged successful: Chiaramonti, bishop of Imola, who took the name of Pius VII. His chief claim to fame was that in a Christmas sermon of 1797, subsequently (and understandably) printed and distributed by the French invaders, he had declared that Christianity was not necessarily incompatible with either democracy or equality, even quoting Rousseau to reinforce his argument. Here, then, was a pope whose pragmatism might match that of France's new ruler to produce a solution to the most intractable of all problems thrown up by the Revolution.

Even before the conclave had begun to vote, the First Consul was sending out conciliatory signals. The Directory's insistence on the observation of the revolutionary calendar's *décadi*, rather than Sunday, was quietly dropped. In December 1799 he ordered full funeral honours for Pius VI. The next month he was hinting to representatives of the *chouans* that their religious grievances would soon be met. And once the cardinals' choice was made, he lost no time in speaking his mind. On his second entry into Milan, in June 1800, he convoked the city's clergy to the great cathedral, and declared, even before Marengo was fought:

It is my firm intention that the Christian, Catholic and Roman religion shall be preserved in its entirety, that it shall be publicly performed . . . No society can exist without morality; there is no good morality without religion. It is religion alone, therefore, that gives to the State a firm and durable support . . . As soon as I am able to confer with the new Pope, I hope to have the happiness of removing every obstacle which will hinder complete reconciliation between France and the head of the Church.[13]

Immediately after the battle, he contacted Pius VII with an offer to open negotiations for a new concordat to re-establish the Church in France.

The stakes were high. If the altars of France could be restored, the chief source of popular discontent with the new order would be eliminated. And if the enmity between Paris and Rome could be ended, the alliance between religion and counter-revolution, which had given such obduracy to both, could be prised apart. The inhabitants of sister republics would be conciliated, and new French citizens in Belgium and the Rhineland could embrace the change with relief. On the other hand the whole enterprise bristled with difficulties. Which church was to be restored? There were now two, both claiming legitimacy, both with bodies of apostolically consecrated bishops. How would bishops be appointed in the future? Would the restored church be Gallican, with all the liberties and traditions accumulated since the sixteenth century, and a rich institutional outgrowth of agencies, assemblies, chapters, monasteries, and hospitals? Or would it be more like the spare, utilitarian body the National Assembly had hoped to create in 1790? Above all, who would pay for it? The First Consul ruled out one potential solution to this problem as a pre-condition for even starting negotiations. There could be no question of returning any of the church lands confiscated in 1790 and since sold off. The Pope accepted this readily enough, although he was never to concede the legality of the confiscation, any more than that of the annexation of Avignon. With that understood, negotiations could begin in earnest, which they did in November 1800.

Success was by no means certain. Not until July 1801 was agreement reached, and then only after several near-breakdowns, angry ultimatums from the First Consul, and foot dragging by French ministers who included the arch-apostate and ex-bishop Talleyrand, and the priest turned fervent dechristianizer Fouché. There were also serious misgivings within the college of cardinals. Yet the Concordat as eventually agreed was far from the dictated peace which Bonaparte was able to impose in that year on France's secular adversaries. It began by facing facts. Catholicism was the religion of the majority of the French. Papal negotiators had wished it to be accepted as dominant, the religion of the State; and when a parallel agreement covering France's Italian satellites was worked out in subsequent years that was agreed. But in France there were hundreds of thousands of Protestants, and who knew how many sceptical disciples of Voltaire? To them the freedom of belief and worship proclaimed by the Revolution was fundamental, and the First Consul thought so too. It was reiterated in the Concordat's first article. Even so, a state Church was set up, the Catholic clergy would be paid out of the public purse and appointed, via the bishops, by the government. Bishops, as under the old order, would be designated by the head of state, and invested only with their spiritual authority by the Pope. They and their clergy would take an oath of obedience to the government. In this way, by an agreement with the Pope, the Consulate secured what the National Assembly had been unable to achieve unilaterally and without consultation: a Church organized according to the same principles as the State. In 1790, clergy were to be elected like secular officials: in 1801, bishops became clerical prefects. Under both regimes, there was a close (though not entirely identical) correspondence between civil and ecclesiastical geography.

A defeat, then, for royalist dreams of restoring the full panoply of the old-regime Church; and equally a defeat for the Jacobin doctrine of complete separation between Church and State. The survivors of the much-maligned constitutional Church, who convened a council of 40 bishops in Notre-Dame in June 1801 to show their strength, could believe themselves vindicated. From the exile in which all but a handful of them still lived, refractory prelates feared that Bonaparte, in restoring the altars, would prefer to hand them over to a clergy which had never renounced the Revolution. But in fact, at the same time as he had refused to discuss challenging the land settlement, the First Consul had demanded another pre-condition from the Pope. All existing bishops, constitutional or refractory, must be deprived. Any settlement must have a completely fresh beginning. The Pope made no objection; for to make such a request was to acknowledge that he had powers which no secular ruler had ever before recognized. Once agreement was reached, they were invoked. By the Brief *Tam multa*, he appealed to all refractory bishops to surrender their powers to him. Of the 93 surviving, 55 obeyed, as they had obeyed his predecessor's injunction to reject the Civil Constitution of the Clergy. Those refusing, he deprived. Since Rome had never recognized the legitimacy of constitutional ordinations, no such measures were required in the case of the constitutional Church. Bonaparte did what was necessary, ordering their council to disperse unacknowledged. The Pope was shocked, however, when he went on to nominate 12 constitutionals to the new bench, all but two of whom refused to retract the oath they had taken in 1790. And greater shocks were still to come. By the 77 'Organic Articles' added unilaterally to the Concordat just prior to its promulgation in April 1802, the power of the Pope to communicate with the French clergy was circumscribed even more closely than under the Gallican days before 1789. Louis XIV's four anti-papal 'Gallican Articles' of 1682 were once more to be taught in all schools and seminaries. But by now, as the First Consul had calculated, Pius VII recognized that it was too late to imperil the whole settlement by quibbling, however important the issues. No doubt many of them could be cleared up later. Other provisions, anyway, were positively welcome, such as the final abandonment of the *décadi* in favour of Sunday. All, in any case, paled into insignificance beside the fact that free exercise of the faith in France had been restored, the hierarchy was back in place, and the authority of the papacy had received far more fulsome recognition from the heirs of a Godless revolution than ever it had won from the Most Christian Kings of the old regime.

Nothing the First Consul had done was more controversial. To many, the re-establishment of the Church seemed a renunciation of all that the Revolution had stood for or, as one disgusted general put it, all that 100,000 men had died for. But yet a further revolutionary legacy would be cast aside before the Law on Cults of 18 Germinal, Year X, which comprised both the Concordat and the Organic Articles, was passed. The last vestiges of free parliamentary life were stifled in the purge of the Tribunate and Legislative Body of January 1801. Nominated by Sieyès and the Senate in December 1799, the members of these bodies were chosen for their likely pliancy, but they were not nonentities. Only 47 out of 400 had not sat before in any of the various revolutionary assemblies, so they were familiar with deliberative procedures and the ways of legislatures, and found it hard to accept that their only function was to endorse what the First Consul had decided. Nor had this been the intention of Sieyès in drafting the constitution. Now, disgruntled at the turn of events, he encouraged his friends in the Tribunate to criticize proposed legislation openly, to Bonaparte's increasing irritation. His critics in the Tribunate, the First Consul declared, were abstract 'metaphysicians' who deserved drowning. He would not, he warned, let himself be defied like Louis XVI—a pregnant comparison. Even the consolidation of his position after Marengo, or the wave of obvious public relief when he survived the 'infernal machine' assassination attempt, failed to mute their criticisms. By the spring of 1801, it is true, only six bills had been rejected, and another six withdrawn, but much more vigorous opposition was feared in the session of the Year X (1801–2), when the Concordat would need to be enacted as a law of the State. When the houses convened in November, even some of the victorious peace treaties laid before them attracted carping, while measures to expedite the drafting of the Civil Code ran into what the head of state regarded as malicious obstruction. When the Tribunate nominated for the Senate Daunou, a constitutional authority who had led opposition to a bill to set up special tribunals to deal with rural brigandage, he took it as a deliberate challenge. He felt he must act before the Concordat was discussed. The studied obscurity of the constitution was now invoked to good effect. It stipulated that the membership of the two houses should be renewed in the Year X, but neither how nor precisely when. This was therefore declared as good a moment as any, and the Senate was ordered to conduct the operation by naming those who would remain members. Sixty names were by this means dropped from the Legislative Body, and 20 from the Tribunate. There was no resistance, and within a few months many of those eliminated had been found official positions elsewhere. Public reaction to this first legislative purge since Brumaire is hard to gauge. By this time the independent press had largely disappeared. But police reports suggested that all café talk in Paris was on the First Consul's side, and contemptuous of functionaries who represented nobody and yet constantly bit the hand that fed them. The main source of public concern was now reported to be the safety of the First Consul's life, a far surer guarantee of stability and order than the antics of politicians, whose incapacity more than a decade of upheaval and uncertainty had vividly demonstrated.

In this atmosphere the Concordat was at last presented to the legislature between 5 and 8 April, as news of the Peace of Amiens was trumpeted throughout the country. It was not quite unopposed, but it passed overwhelmingly. Over the next two months, a whole series of new measures would also be presented—to reorganize education, to create a new Legion of Honour, and to extend the First Consul's term of office. Before the year was out, Bonaparte would be Consul for life, and France would almost have a king again.

Meanwhile, however, April 1802 was to be a month of celebration. It culminated on the eighteenth, Easter Day, with a solemn mass to mark the resurrection of the Catholic Church in France. It was held in Notre-Dame in the presence of the First Consul, the entire government, and the diplomatic corps. The preacher was the 70-year-old Boisgelin, once archbishop of Aix, now of Tours. A nobleman of old stock, he had delivered the sermon at the coronation of Louis XVI. As then, he celebrated a new beginning; but the jubilant crowds who thronged Paris that day, thrilled by the boom of cannon and the ringing of bells silent since 1793, and the people of quality who lit their windows when night fell, were not thinking about what the future might bring. With the end of the war, the elimination of political strife, and the restoration of religious freedom, they were celebrating the burial of the Revolution.

# 17

# The Revolution
# in Perspective

THE revolutionary war terminated by the treaties of Lunéville and Amiens had been a far more total conflict than anything previously known. Among other things, polite travellers were shocked to discover that they could no longer go freely to countries with which their own was at war. None felt the change more keenly than the British, who for much of the 1790s found themselves cut off by French power from most of western Europe. The conclusion of the peace reopened the Continent to them, and in 1802 thousands of them swarmed across the Channel to visit the scene of the Revolution and see for themselves what George III and his ministers had been fighting against. 'I had conceived an horrific idea of the populace of this country,' wrote Fanny Burney (married it is true to an *émigré*) when she arrived at Calais in April, 'imagining them all transformed into bloody monsters.'[1] She found them nothing of the sort: but then, the economy of Calais had been devastated by the interruption of the Dover ferries, and the inhabitants were glad to see rich British tourists passing through again. Posting towards Paris in the hope of catching a glimpse of the fascinating hero who had brought the Revolution to an end (he was not yet the 'Corsican Ogre' he was to become in British demonology) the first thing these sightseers noticed was the roads. The highways that in 1787 had left Arthur Young awestruck were now pitted and neglected. Everywhere, too, were ruins and boarded-up buildings: defunct monasteries and convents, and abandoned aristocratic châteaux. Although, passing as they were through devout Flanders and Picardy, travellers noticed congregations flocking to mass on Sunday in their best linen, they often found larger churches pillaged and dilapidated. Rouen cathedral, noted one gentleman arriving from Le Havre, was 'blackened and dingy' from being used as a gunpowder factory. The tricolour was everywhere, and few people were seen without the national cockade; but evidence of changing orthodoxies could be seen on public buildings, where the slogan *Liberty, Equality, Humanity, Fraternity, or Death* was inscribed—with the last two thinly painted out. Royal arms and insignia, needless to say, were everywhere defaced or obscured, and at Versailles the palace was deserted. 'Who could, without emotion', wrote one visitor,[2] 'behold the windows broken and barred up, the doors falling off their hinges, the grass waving in the courtyards, where formerly a weed was never seen, and where all was gaiety and splendour.' Arriving in Paris, however, those who had known it before the great upheaval found it less changed than they expected. The Bastille had gone, its site converted into a woodyard. Those who visited the Tuileries, in the hope of seeing the First Consul now installed there, could hire guides who would point out the bloodstains left when the Swiss Guards had been massacred in 1792. There were far fewer rich private carriages in the streets, and any number of bits of furniture or other battered relics of aristocratic or pious living could be bought from street dealers. But the great city was as animated as ever, and the Palais Royal was if anything even more crowded than when Arthur Young had visited it during the ferment of 1789. Nobody, though, was talking politics there. It had become a rather frenetic pleasure garden, and was only one among several. Rich, fashionable society was on parade again, as in monarchical times, and the well-policed streets were agreed to be a good deal safer. Military parades and reviews, not surprisingly in a country ruled by a general, were an almost daily spectacle.

Such were the visible fruits of thirteen years of turmoil; symptoms, some of temporary disruption, others of permanent and irrevocable change. Almost none, however, reflected what reformers had aimed for and dreamed of as they set about national regeneration in the heady spring of 1789. For at the beginning, the impetus of the French Revolution had been intellectual far more than social or economic. Enriched and enormously expanded by three generations of widening prosperity, the leisured classes of France had invested their gains in culture—which meant above all education. And while the clergymen at whose feet they all sat tried hard to mould their minds into habits of orthodoxy and obedience, even by denouncing it they introduced their charges to the progress which independent thinking had achieved since the Reformation. By the mid-eighteenth century an educated, critical public opinion was emerging, an expanding market for ideas which writers of all shades of opinion sought to engage, and which government itself was increasingly to court. Loss of public confidence underlay the financial and political crisis which precipitated the downfall of a system of government too little changed in its habits and priorities since the days of Louis XIV. Surprise at the rapid collapse of a state whose ambitions had outstripped its means was universal. Nobody had expected it, or prepared for it, for all their disillusionment with existing ways and institutions. But once the crumbling away of the old absolute monarchy began to look irreversible, in the course of 1788, men began to turn their minds towards what to put in its place. With the calling of the Estates-General, and the drafting of *cahiers* that preceded it, the whole of France, far beyond the educated élite, was invited to consider this question, too. Suddenly anything seemed possible. Any abuse seemed remediable, any grievance capable of redress—any old score within reach of settlement. The message was change, and it thrilled men of education far beyond the borders of France. Here was an opportunity for enlightened men to bring about a more rational, just, and humane organization of the affairs of mankind. And enlightened men seized it. The National Assembly which launched the Revolution included the cream of the country's intelligentsia, who consciously saw themselves as the products, and the instruments, of the triumph of Enlightenment. All over France, men of similar background rallied to them, inspired by the same ideals. The spontaneous proliferation of the Jacobin clubs, with their high-minded commitment to the rights of man and the citizen, reflected this inspiration. Among some of them, although a dwindling minority as the revolutionary years went on, it never died.

And in many respects, the labours of France's revolutionaries did introduce greater rationality and logic into the country's affairs on a permanent basis. The administrative reorganization into departments, sweeping away the jurisdictional jungle grown up over a millennium, survives not much altered to this day. The metric and decimal system, superseding another prescriptive nightmare, was introduced after five years of elaboration in April 1795. It has swept the world since. Scarcely less successful has been the Civil Code, that succinct, lucid compendium dreamed and talked of for generations before 1789. Although it took the authority and determination of the First Consul to bring it to fruition, drafting had begun during the Revolution's first impulse in 1790. The barbarities and inequities of the old criminal law also disappeared permanently. The guillotine proved less of a success, although it might have won more recognition as the humane refinement it was meant to be—quick, reliable, and by all calculation painless—had it not become the main public instrument of terror. Yet in some ways it was curiously appropriate that it should. For most of those it dispatched were deemed to be resisting, for reasons no rational man could accept as valid, other changes equally dictated by logic, equity, and humanity.

It was resistance that made the Revolution violent. It was naïve of the men of 1789 to think that they could regenerate the nation without opposition, and imagine that the honesty and benevolence of their intentions would be as obvious to others as to themselves. But the Enlightenment had never been afraid to impute ignorance, superstition, and selfishness to its opponents, and its disciples entirely shared this cast of mind. Critics who traced the spirit of terror back to 1789, because even then the patriots had not hesitated to use intimidation to get their way, were therefore not entirely wrong. 'Shut up, bad citizen!' yelled a spectator who threw himself upon Malouet from the gallery on 15 June 1789 as he criticized proposals to declare a National Assembly.[3] A month later, Barnave was publicly defending the lynching of Foulon and Bertier. It was true that in 1789 royal resistance to the formation of a National Assembly could probably not have been overcome without the threat of bloodshed; but the very success of patriotic defiance set an example of how to deal with future challenges. Even after the nation had been sickened with public carnage, politicians still found it impossible to accept the legitimacy and good faith of their opponents. In the end it took a general who openly despised intellectuals to make them sink their differences in the interests of stability.

First resistance to change came from the nobility. Their powers and prerogatives thrown into relief by resort to an Estates-General where their representatives sat as a separate order, by the end of 1788 they found themselves isolated and under attack. This attack had been launched by an intellectual coterie, the Society of Thirty, who deliberately exploited social tensions within the educated élite to marshal overwhelming public support for an undivided legislature. Frightened, many nobles took refuge in their privileges, thus exacerbating the antagonism and mistrust towards them now rampant among the bourgeoisie. The original issue was still unresolved when the Estates convened, and by the time it was settled, months of anti-noble rhetoric had cast a whole social category into intransigent opponents of national regeneration. This they had certainly never been until then. Their *cahiers* showed an impressive willingness to contemplate reform and surrender many of their most valuable privileges. But by now nothing would satisfy patriots but the surrender of them all. Aristocracy became the Revolution's most telling term of abuse and disapproval, describing all who opposed it. Equality, a situation where nobody enjoyed any privileges based on unfair criteria such as birth or ancestry, became one of its driving aspirations. Even Napoleon paid it constant lip-service and, though of noble birth himself and educated in a military academy reserved for the sons of poor gentry, always gloried in being a product of the Revolution's opening careers to talent.

Nobles were therefore the first, and greatest, losers from the Revolution. Even before it began they had agreed to sacrifice their tax-exemptions and fiscal privileges. Almost from the start they lost the deference and preference to which they had been accustomed since time immemorial. Years later it would creep back, and it still lingers today; but never since 1789 has it been automatic or unchallengeable. In June of that year they lost the right to separate political representation and corporate powers—a fleeting enough advantage, it is true, since with the exception of a few *pays d'états* it had only existed when the Estates-General were in being. In August their material losses began with the abolition of feudalism. They were by no means the only beneficiaries from feudal rights, dues, honours, and prerogatives, but their stake in the system was indisputably the greatest. Relics of feudal levies lingered on in remote corners far into the nineteenth century, but to all intents and purposes feudalism, and the profits lords made from it, had disappeared forever by 1794. The night of 4 August also transformed the character of the French nobility. Hitherto an open élite within the élite, accessible to new money invested in ennobling offices, the abolition of venal office turned it for the first time into a caste. Ennoblement ceased. Within a year nobility itself had ceased to be recognized, and the display of arms and insignia was forbidden.

But nobility itself could not be abolished. Defined as a hereditary quality, it was in the blood, or at least in the minds of those who thought they possessed it—another instance though this seemed, to enlightened men, of human ignorance and superstition. Revolutionary policies drove many nobles from a country they no longer recognized as their own. At least 16,500 emigrated during the Revolution, and probably several thousand more, lost to statistics through various anomalies. The property of those who refused to return, or who were executed, was confiscated, depriving perhaps 12,500 families of all or some of their land. Many, however, managed to buy some of it back, immediately or later by gradual stages, and long before 1799 *émigrés* were cautiously returning. Soon enough the Emperor Napoleon would create a new nobility, and to give it tone was anxious to leaven it with as many *ci-devants* as possible. All he demanded was solid landed wealth in addition, but they had no difficulty in showing evidence of that. In most departments under the Empire, the ranks of the highest taxpayers were completely noble-dominated.

The material losses of the nobility, therefore, were neither as great nor as irrevocable as might be imagined. But they were still traumatic enough, and the process by which they occurred was truly harrowing. As triumph persistently eluded the counter-revolution, emigration proved a life of disappointment, bitterness, and poverty. 'Separated perhaps forever from my family,' lamented the Marquise de Falaiseau as 1793 dawned,[4] 'proscribed, a wanderer outlawed from my country, no longer possessing anything, far from all I knew and loved in my childhood, from my days of happiness, I saw around me nothing but distress and no hope for the future at all.' Hundreds of the menfolk of such ladies perished when they attempted to return in force at Quiberon, or on other battlefields. For those who never left there was constant suspicion. Although only 1,200 or so nobles were executed in the Terror, many more were imprisoned for months on end as suspects, and in 1797, just when circumstances seemed to be easing, they were deprived of civil rights merely for being nobles, and almost found themselves deported *en masse* for the same reason. Such tribulations bred a bitter hatred and contempt for the Revolution and all it stood for in noble circles. Although former nobles were to be found active in the public life of France during every phase of the revolutionary years, it was a far cry from the monopoly they had enjoyed before 1789, and nothing like those days would ever return. Many nobles now ostentatiously turned their backs on public life, as beneath their dignity. The psychological impact, in other words, was far more serious than the material one, for nobles and non-nobles alike. 'The bonds of subordination are so loosened everywhere', complained the Count de Villèle, minister of a restored monarchy, in 1826,[5] '. . . the evil is in our mores, so influenced are we still by the Revolution.'

The first attacks of the Revolution on the clergy passed almost unresisted. In the more sober debates following the euphoric night of 4 August some clerical disillusionment was expressed at the National Assembly's refusal to allot compensation for the loss of the tithe; but priestly goodwill had played a major part in the fusion of the orders into a National Assembly, and most ecclesiastics found it hard to believe that the spiritual life of the nation would not be promisingly regenerated by the Revolution along with everything else. In the event, the clergy were to suffer even more cataclysmically than the nobility. The damage of 4 August went beyond the tithe: many ecclesiastical institutions lost extensive feudal rights, and only complete dispossession of their lands a few months later eclipsed these previous losses. Meanwhile, those who gained most from the Revolution, the acquirers of national lands, largely did so at the clergy's expense.

Even before the oath of 1790 further irreparable losses had been sustained, not all of them material. The old corporate organization of the Gallican Church, self-governing and self-taxing, had disappeared in effect

well before the Civil Constitution of the Clergy pronounced its death-
warrant. Nothing like it was restored by the Concordat. Monasticism was
also doomed by 1790; and although many monks seemed to have
welcomed release from their vows, France's 45,000 nuns were almost
unanimous in opposing the dissolution of their convents. 'In the world,'
complained the Carmelites of the diocese of Paris,[6] 'people like to say that
the monasteries are full of victims, slowly consumed by regrets, but we
protest before God that if there is true happiness on earth, we enjoy it, in the
shelter of the sanctuary.' The Concordat made no provision for the
restoration of the cloistered life, and although monastic orders did
reappear, they never proliferated as they had under the old order. And
meanwhile the oath, and its various successors, had torn the clergy apart.
Those who refused it and therefore resisted the Revolution, suffered most.
Deprived of their benefices, refractories soon became pariahs in the eyes of
patriots, a subversive influence wherever they operated, and once war
began a treasonable one. Priests were the first victims of the September
Massacres of 1792. In addition to the 223 slaughtered then, almost 1,000
were condemned in the Terror, while nearly 25,000, almost one-sixth of
the whole clergy, emigrated or were deported. Since 90 per cent of clerical
*émigrés* were seculars, the loss of parish clergy was not far short of a half. By
1794 even the constitutional clergy were under suspicion, having faced
repudiation by Rome and the majority of the French population apparently
for nothing. Some found belated vindication under the Concordat, but for
others the break with Rome that their oath-taking signified could not be
healed and they soldiered on into the nineteenth century in an ever-
dwindling 'little church'. The French clergy had been forced by the
Revolution into a bitter, tragic schism, its pain only compounded by the
outrages of dechristianization. The depth of the trauma was vividly
expressed by an Italian cardinal[7] as the Sacred College discussed the last
details of the Concordat.

Oh, God, [he agonized] . . . what will a government do which, after having
proscribed the Catholic religion, after having persecuted it by the most scandalous
laws, after staining itself with the blood of so many martyrs, today reopens the door
to it not as the dominant religion, but as the religious opinion of the majority of the
people, not out of love, but out of fear, not from respect but from policy? Meanwhile
it desires it stripped and naked, with rare ministers, ministers in its pay, ministers
appointed by the government itself, ministers who, in the past, have fed the flames,
ministers who are supposed to pass for Catholics yet are the authors of schism,
neither repentant nor reconciled. And in contrast we see legitimate pastors,
confessors of the faith of Jesus Christ exiled from their homeland . . . separated from
their flocks . . . religious hounded out from the whole of that great empire; holy

virgins without refuge, chapters and seminaries without the means to subsist; temples which, after profanation, remain soiled and ruinous; foundations, pious works, prerogatives and immunities abolished and destroyed; in a word, a soulless, bloodless, powerless skeleton. That is the shadow of a religion being re-established in France, and those who thought up this sorry project are glorying in it and usurping the title of restorers of the altars . . .

And yet Cardinal Antonelli still voted for the Concordat. Its saving grace was that it restored free worship in France, a properly constituted clergy, and papal power. Despite serious material losses, in fact, the papacy was one of the great gainers from the work of the Revolution. In the 1780s it had appeared an institution in perhaps terminal decline, scorned by secularizing monarchs and defied in Germany and Italy by Jansenizing bishops. Its apparent helplessness did much to mislead the drafters of the Civil Constitution. But before the end of the 1790s the Holy Father himself was sharing in the glory of martyrdom visited on his fellow priests by a Godless republic and its sympathizers abroad. Throughout France and the areas of Europe it dominated, meanwhile, the vast majority of the population was showing itself loyal to a clergy which had rejected the Revolution on his instructions. These were facts which the First Consul of France had the perception and the courage to recognize, against the advice and inclination of most of those who had tried to manage France's affairs throughout the 1790s. Instant harmony did not follow. Within a few years he would find himself as exasperated as any Jacobin at priestly wiles. But he never tried to undo the basic settlement of 1801; and the clergy restored then, stripped of indefensible excrescences and abuses, now for the first time ever devoted almost all of its energies to the cure of souls, under Rome's unchallengeable doctrinal and spiritual authority. Not that they thanked the Revolution for all this. As in the case of the nobility, the experience from which it had arisen was altogether too painful. Throughout the nineteenth century the Roman Catholic Church would anathematize the French Revolution and all its works as an outburst of atheistical excess fomented by malignant philosophers and scheming freemasons, lending its full authority to the unhistorical ravings of Barruel. Republicans in turn, whose convictions were rooted in the Revolution, would see the Church as their most formidable foe, and join masonic lodges to express their antagonism. Nothing but the complete separation of Church and State, as between 1794 and 1802, would allay their suspicions. In 1905 it was eventually brought about, after decades of mounting extremism on both sides, all traceable back ultimately, to 1790.

Also traceable back to that fateful divide was the breaking of the Church's hold on the two social services it had controlled throughout the old order—education and poor relief. The men of 1789 saw education as yet another area to be regenerated on rational lines. Grandiose schemes were mooted throughout the 1790s, including one drafted by the last of the *philosophes*, Condorcet, in 1792. But other priorities repeatedly postponed practical action. Meanwhile, the existing system fell to pieces. Although lands owned by educational institutions were at first exempted from nationalization, other sources of support, such as impropriated tithes and standard donations from chapters and monasteries, dried up. Clerical teachers refusing the oath were dismissed; those who took it were often called away to become parish priests. Teaching orders (such as the Oratorians) at first escaped the Revolution's attack on monasticism, but in August 1792 suspicion of all priests in positions of influence was such that they were dissolved. Finally even lands owned by schools and colleges were swallowed up as national property by a Republic desperate for resources in March 1793. Not until 1802 were comprehensive measures taken to fill the vacuum thus created, even though the constitution of 1793 had declared education to be among basic human rights. That of 1795 made no such rash commitment, and although the Directory set up a central school in each department and established a number of higher schools in Paris to replace the universities abolished by the Convention as bastions of corporatism, it left primary education to local initiative and made no public financial provision for it. Bedevilled at every level by a shortage of trained teachers (clerics being too dangerous to entrust with the education of republican youth), the Revolution, itself the fruit of unprecedented educational advance, created chaos in education, and a marked drop in numbers undergoing it. Whereas 50,000 pupils were attending colleges in 1789, only 12,000 or 14,000 were in the central schools a decade later. Basic literacy fell from 37 per cent in 1789 to more like 30 per cent in 1815.

In the field of poor relief the record was even bleaker. Again, there was no shortage of reforming intentions and bold projects to tackle a problem which everybody could see in the 1780s was getting worse. The Constituent Assembly set up a committee on mendicity which collected impressive information on the scale of the problem. The Legislative established its own committee, and in its brief existence passed no less than 56 decrees in the area of poor relief. Every citizen in need, declared the constitution of 1793, had a right to public support, and in May 1794 a 'Great Book of National Benevolence' was instituted where deserving cases could register their needs. Two months earlier, a comprehensive law on poor relief had been passed, which among other things forbade private alms giving on the grounds that the State would now provide. In October came the corollary: begging too was forbidden. Some of these measures would have been rashly ambitious at the best of times. In a country desperately at war and diverting all available resources towards fighting it, they were practically meaningless. In some districts, local authorities made heroic efforts to establish the Great Book, but under the Directory the project was abandoned. Yet by then the problem was far worse than it had been in 1789. The poor were far more numerous thanks to the economic disruption which six years of upheaval had brought about, and previous provision, inadequate though it obviously was, had been shattered by the attack on the Church. Monastic charity dried up when church lands were nationalized and houses dissolved. Parish-based relief, largely derived from endowments and pious donations, was disrupted by the schism among parish priests over the oath, and those with money to give closed their purses for fear of drawing envious attention to themselves. And the last resorts of the indigent, hospitals and poor houses, had their already overstretched resources pitilessly blighted by almost every wave of revolutionary legislation. Like schools and colleges, many lost important sources of income in the reforms of 4 August 1789. Fiscal changes which abolished municipal tolls took away others. The value of investments was slashed by the inflation which had taken hold by 1792, and institutions which depended on direct grants from the Crown found the National Assembly unwilling to continue them. Like teaching orders, the charitable ones who were the backbone of nursing in the hospitals were at first exempted from dissolution and from the oath. But as in teaching, too, it did not last, and by 1792 the piety with which nuns ministered to the poor was viewed with suspicion by patriots. They were not allowed to recruit novices, and in October 1793 they were at last subjected to a clerical oath. Those who refused were arrested and imprisoned, despite the clear impossibility of obtaining adequate replacements. A final blow came when in July 1794 hospital property was nationalized.

In this way the old structure of charity was pulled apart and, for all the talk, nothing constructive put in its place. Under the Directory, all thought of national provision was abandoned. Nevertheless, after 1794, some recovery began. The sale of hospital lands was halted, and those still unsold returned. Imprisoned nuns were released and resumed their ministrations. Rich laymen, who had played a crucial part in fund-raising and management before 1789, re-emerged gingerly to take on something like their old co-ordinating roles. Local taxes and surcharges on luxuries like theatre tickets were also reintroduced as a means of subsidizing hospitals. In Napoleonic France all these trends would be officially fostered, and charitable giving would revive. But pre-revolutionary levels were not restored. Even by 1847, the number of hospitals in France, for a population seven millions higher, was still almost 42 per cent less than in 1789. Nobody, therefore, suffered more than the poor and the sick, over several generations, from the blind destruction of established institutions before viable alternatives had been devised and funded. In no sphere was more human damage done by the French revolutionaries' failure to match rhetoric with reality.

It is true that their difficulties, here and elsewhere, were compounded by severe economic problems. In fact, the Revolution was an economic disaster for France. But much of that was the revolutionaries' own doing, too.

The Revolution broke out at a moment of rare economic crisis, and this circumstance was to affect its whole subsequent character. Much of the boundless, unrealistic hope invested in the Estates-General by all classes in the spring of 1789, which did so much to ensure the success of the third estate, sprang from anxieties aroused by the harvest failure of 1788, a harsh winter, rising prices, and the slump in demand for manufactures. Popular support for the patriotic cause in Paris in July was based on the assumption that under the new regime there would be guaranteed supplies of cheap bread. In the eyes of the sansculottes, failure to achieve this would mean betrayal of the Revolution. Their determination to maintain it would constrain the economic policies of successive revolutionary assemblies down to 1795. Even when their power was broken, no government was unpragmatic enough to leave the provisioning of Paris to the free market forces in which almost all men of education believed in principle. Finally, the concessions made on 4 August 1789 to appease a peasantry paranoid with fear for the safety of the harvest would become, despite the Assembly's initial misgivings, central to the Revolution's anti-feudal ideology. Left to itself, once the good harvest of 1789 was in the economy might have been expected to improve. But almost at once its development began to be affected by revolutionary legislation.

The first series of disruptions resulted from the losses sustained by the nobility and the clergy. The destruction of a privileged society setting a high value on services could scarcely be brought about without serious shock waves which reached far beyond the immediate sufferers. Faced with the loss of feudal revenues, which in some regions might constitute as much as 20 per cent of landlords' income, their immediate reaction was to raise rents. In December 1790 proprietors were specifically authorized to add the equivalent of the abolished tithe to the rents they charged. On some estates by 1791 the notional rental had risen by a quarter. It was no coincidence that the most persistent peasant resistance to the Revolution came in areas where leaseholders predominated. The disappearance of the aristocratic lifestyle also had serious repercussions. For a town like Versailles the shock was brutal and irreparable, as the English visitors haunting its abandoned, crumbling glories found in 1802. Formerly fashionable parts of Paris suffered a similar fate. 'The Fauxbourg St. Germain can never recover,' wrote an unduly pessimistic diplomatic visitor in 1796.[8] It was 'quite depopulated; its hotels almost all seized by Government, and the streets near the Boulevard are choked with weeds.' And every city where a parlement had sat, or provincial estates regularly convened, found its economy rocked when these institutions disappeared and their rich and noble members emigrated, or shrank into unostentatious obscurity. The spoliation of the Church compounded such problems. Monasteries, chapters, and cathedrals provided innumerable jobs for the laity, directly or indirectly, from builders and painters all the way to washerwomen keeping surplices clean. All were now lost as these institutions were deprived of their property, their revenues, and ultimately their very existence. Servants were dismissed wholesale. In Bayeux, for example, the nobility and clergy had employed 467 between them in 1787: nine years later they only gave employment to 76. The luxury trades were also devastated by the disappearance of their main customers and the introduction of simpler fashions that went with it. The silk capital of Lyons, already in difficulties before the Revolution, found the 1790s as disturbed economically as they were politically. Between 1790 and 1806 its population fell by almost a third, from 146,000 to 100,000. Between 1789 and 1799, the number of silk workshops fell by more than half.

Many of these convulsions were the consequence, ultimately, of the massive land transfer which proved one of the Revolution's most enduring achievements. But the use to which nationalized property was put created its own range of difficulties in the form of the inflation of the assignats. Convinced by the Physiocratic nostrum that land was the only true source of wealth, the members of the National Assembly were only too willing to believe that a paper money based on land was more secure than the disastrous, still remembered notes issued by John Law in 1720. And so it might have been if the assignats had not been massively over-issued, and had been withdrawn in an orderly way as originally envisaged. But, their minds set firmly against any forced reduction of the debt inherited from the monarchy on the one hand, and lacking both the power and the will to raise taxes and enforce their collection firmly on the other, the revolutionaries found the temptation to print money too strong. Already by January 1792 over-issue had brought down the value of the assignat by

28 per cent; and once war began, financed as it had to be until 1794 largely by France's own resources, there was little alternative but to go on. In all, a nominal 45,000,000,000 *livres* worth of paper were issued between 1790 and 1797, but its total real value (at 1790 prices) was less than a seventh of that. And three-quarters of the depreciation over that time can be convincingly attributed to over-issue. The consequences affected every area of the economy. Thanks to the inflation, even the sale of national lands which was supposed to underpin the whole operation only realized 25 per cent of these lands' true value. Until the deflation of 1798, revolutionary France was a debtor's paradise, since assignats were legal tender at face value. As one of their earliest opponents had predicted, 'Every man in France who owes nothing, and to whom everything is owing, will be ruined by paper-money.'[9] Paradise for debtors was a hell for creditors. It was no atmosphere for business confidence, and outside the black market and the enforced activity of war industries, normal production and exchange stagnated for much of the 1790s. Credit was tight, interest rates usuriously high. Cash was hoarded, and what little could be extracted had to be spent on dealings with foreigners who refused to accept French paper. Wage-earners and all those on fixed incomes found their resources catastrophically eroded; and although wages eventually had to rise in the face of four-figure increases in the cost of living, they seldom caught up. Few rises equalled the 3,000 per cent achieved by government employees between 1790 and 1797. Government was the only employer whose demand for labour grew steadily throughout the Revolution. Others, faced with shrinking markets and spiralling costs, cut back and laid their workers off. By 1798 there were 60,000 unemployed in Paris, a tenth of the city's population. There were clear links between such unemployment and the rise in crime which everybody commented on under the Directory—not to mention a marked increase in urban suicides. There was no longer, after all, even the former network of charitable institutions to fall back on.

It was the war, of course, which finally made the country hostage to the assignats, although the preposterous Brissot had actually claimed on the last day of 1791 that war would eliminate the depreciation that had already occurred. And war was also responsible for perhaps the most permanent damage suffered by the French economy under the Revolution—the destruction of overseas trade. Before 1789, it had been the most glitteringly successful sector. Unlike the others, it felt few shocks in the Revolution's early stages. The trade of Bordeaux and Marseilles peaked in 1791. But that year also saw the outbreak of the great slave rebellion in Saint-Domingue, where an increasing proportion of the colonial trade of

Bordeaux, at least, was concentrated. It developed into a full-scale civil war which could not have failed to disrupt trade to the Caribbean whatever happened. Then, in 1793, came war against most of Europe and, most ominously of all, against Great Britain. The French coast was now blockaded, and to compound the chaos, in August the Convention banned the export of all goods of first necessity and embargoed all neutral ships. By the time these restrictions were lifted a year later, the British had tightened their grip, and they dominated the Atlantic approaches, at least, for the rest of the decade. The trade of the ports was not reduced to nothing, and in privateering they found a new resource; but their colonial business was largely destroyed, and the boom times of before 1789 were lost for ever. Foreign trade shrank from 25 per cent of the country's economic activity to just 9 per cent in seven years: the population of Marseilles fell between 1790 and 1806 from 120,000 to 99,000, that of Bordeaux from 110,000 to 92,000, that of Nantes from perhaps 90,000 to 77,000.

This collapse of what had been the unchallenged leading sector of the old-regime economy proved a permanent structural shift. It was accentuated by the captive continental markets conquered by France in the later 1790s and retained, in various guises, until 1814. International commerce reorientated itself away from the sea towards continental markets, where French power was increasingly successful in excluding British competition, too. For those able to take advantage of such changing circumstances the revolutionary years were not without their opportunities. War industries of course did well—munitions, metallurgy, and even woollen textiles, meeting an unprecedented demand for uniforms. The mines and woollen towns of Belgium, incorporated into the French national market after 1794, boomed at the expense of older centres in France proper. And the revival of the French cotton industry was almost a success story. Mortally challenged in the late 1780s by the cheaper, better-quality products of a technologically more advanced Lancashire, which flooded into the country under the ill-conceived commercial treaty of 1786, French cottons were saved from annihilation by renewed conflict with Great Britain. The population of Rouen, the cotton capital, actually grew despite the loss of a parlement, important ecclesiastical institutions, and maritime trade. After 1796 much new machinery was introduced, although only of a sort used across the Channel for decades and already being superseded there; and in the first decade of the nineteenth century French cottons would boom under the impetus of a revival of luxurious fashions and continued exclusion of British competition.

In fact, traumatic though it was for those who had to live through it, much of the economic upheaval of the 1790s proved transitory. Lyons recovered when silk came back into fashion. Even overseas trade clawed itself back to the volume of 1789. But in both these areas pre-revolutionary levels were not reached again until the 1830s, and that was typical. The revolutionary years had set French economic expansion back by at least a generation, and had done little to make structures more dynamic. Certain pre-conditions for later progress had indeed been established. Internal customs barriers had been eliminated, standardized weights and measures introduced, guild restrictive practices abolished, and labour organizations restricted by the Le Chapelier Law. But none of this released entrepreneur-ial energy of itself. The hideous uncertainties of the 1790s did quite the reverse. Spectacular fortunes were made by shrewd speculators and military supply contractors, particularly under the Directory. But most of those with money to invest hastened to sink it into the one security that was no risk—land. It was very much the pattern of pre-revolutionary times, and the Revolution accentuated it by removing what before had been a uniquely French alternative, venal office. At the same time it placed unprecedented amounts of new land on the market when it offered the property of the Church and the *émigrés* for sale, and on bargain terms. Thus the long-standing tendency of the French bourgeoisie to shun commercial investment or get out of it as soon as possible was reinforced, and would persist far into the nineteenth century.

Nor did the Revolution bring any marked changes in the cultivation of the land. Benefits derived from the abolition of feudal burdens were largely offset by higher rents and taxes. Revolutionary legislation reinforced rather than inhibited the division of properties on inheritance, ensuring that most holdings remained small. Inflation increased the appeal of share-cropping, already so well established. Military requirements were a constant drain on livestock, wasting its precious manure; while conscrip-tion (or its evasion: the effect was the same) decimated the most able-bodied of the work-force. By 1802, it is true, French agriculture was managing to feed over a million more mouths, a substantial achievement, especially given the deterioration in transport networks. But apart from an acceleration in the spread of potatoes, no innovations underlay this increase in capacity. The reliability of an expanding market might even have discouraged risky experiments. Even in the 1840s, the patterns and basic productivity of French agriculture were much what they had been a century beforehand. Only with the advent of the railways did fundamental change begin, here as in much of the rest of the French economy.

Was, then, the Revolution worth it in material terms? For most ordinary French subjects turned by it into citizens, it cannot have been. It had made their lives infinitely more precarious, when they had expected the reverse. It had bidden fair to destroy the religious, cultural, and moral underpinnings of the communities in which they lived. The *cahiers* of 1789 make overwhelmingly clear that most French people wanted less state interference in their lives, yet it brought far more, and fiercer. Government by terror scarcely outlasted the Year II, but nothing like it had ever occurred before. When it ebbed, the power of the State remained, permanently augmented and disposing of coercive powers not dreamed of by the old monarchy. It was no wonder therefore, that the most persistent and massive resistance that the Revolution encountered came not from the former so-called 'privileged orders' but from ordinary people who simply wanted to call a halt. In alienating so many of their fellow citizens, the revolutionaries furnished counter-revolutionaries with constant hope and encouragement. But most popular resistance was anti- rather than counter-revolutionary. Though they might mouth slogans about restoring Church and king, all most anti-revolutionaries wanted was stability and autonomy after years of upheaval and intrusion by outsiders. Their resistance, however, only too often pushed France's new authorities to further extremes of repression, gouging existing wounds yet wider and deeper.

Popular rejection of what the Revolution had become was not confined to the open rebellion of the Vendée, or even to the recurrent *chouannerie* of Brittany, Maine, and western Normandy, where the bonds of village communities had been severed by the impact of the new religious policy on regions where even the abolition of feudalism had brought few gains to peasants who were predominantly renters. It was endemic throughout the south, where the Revolution was perceived as designed to benefit rich Protestants; and broke out periodically in rioting on local issues in many other areas. The statistics of emigration and terror are also suggestive. Almost 32,000, a third of all registered *émigrés*, were peasants or workers turning their backs on the land of liberty. Of the official victims of the Terror, 8,350, or almost 60 per cent, were from the same groups, dying for their resistance. Deserters or draft-dodgers, tellingly defined as 'insubordinate' (*insoumis*), were another gauge. In 1789 drawing for the militia, one of the most hated institutions of the old order, had been abolished. By 1793 it was back, and in 1798 conscription assumed a far more systematic character. Evasion of military service was universally agreed to be a major ingredient in the rural crime wave which marked the directorial period. 'Many deserters are lurking about the woods', wrote an English traveller through Chantilly in 1796,[10] 'and there are continual robberies and murders. We have not travelled half an hour in the dark.' Banditti, he called them later on: bandits—a category social scientists have learned to recognize as a classic form of protest against an established order.

Anti-revolution, in other words, was a popular movement—far more so than that of the sansculottes who have usually monopolized this description; yet there is a sense in which the sansculottes were anti-revolutionary, too. They shared none of the economic liberalism of the men of 1789, and none of their extreme commitment to the rights of property. Their belief was in a moral, not a market, economy, and they were prepared to offer armed resistance to those, like the Girondins, who were overt in rejecting these ideals. Their belief in popular democracy, and mistrust for the rich and over-educated, paralleled peasant antagonism towards well-off urban patriots who intruded into largely self-governing village communities with their purchases of national lands and client constitutional priests. Sansculottes welcomed the Revolution because they knew that in its last years the monarchy had begun to turn its back on time-honoured moral commitments towards its subjects. So long as their energies could be usefully harnessed, those in power accepted and paid lip-service to their support. But most deputies never accepted the legitimacy of the sansculottes' claim to dictate the course of national policy, and they sanctioned the popular savagery of terror and dechristianization with ill-concealed reluctance. As soon as they could they shrugged off popular tutelage, and by 1795 were openly treating the remaining militants of Paris as anti-revolutionaries. By then the latter had one more thing in common with others elsewhere who opposed it: they had no gains to show, either, for all the upheaval and disruption.

Yet some groups undoubtedly gained. In any list of them, pride of place must go to the owners of land. Freed in August 1789 from the burdens of feudalism and the tithe, they were able to proclaim property as the supreme social and political commodity. The Civil Code, when it was completed, consolidated and clarified their rights, and the means of transmitting them. Successive constitutions, in one way or another, made the effective exercise of political rights dependent in turn on property. Property would define the class of Notables who ruled France, as electors, from the Consulate down to the late nineteenth century. The social profile of property owners was little altered by the Revolution. The amount of land held by the nobility inevitably fell, although in the 1800s they still dominated the ranks of the largest and richest proprietors. At the other end of the scale the sale of national lands, especially in the mid-1790s when they had been marketed in small lots, had produced an increase in the number of petty peasant owners, though their overall share scarcely rose.

The great gainers from the redistribution of church and noble property were the bourgeoisie. More than anything else, their fears about the security of their gains finally pushed the Revolution into the hands of a dictator who imposed stability and offered all property owners unconditional recognition of their title. By the time he fell, their grip on their gains was beyond challenge, and the restored Bourbons, though they returned *émigré* lands still unsold and organized a fund to compensate those whose property had gone, never seriously thought of undoing the land settlement bequeathed by the Revolution.

The bourgeoisie also gained by the Revolution, in the end, as the group from which the professions were recruited. The men of 1789 had proclaimed careers open to the talents, believing that neither birth nor wealth should give privileged access to any employment. At first the implementation of this principle looked like developing into a disaster for the professions. When venal offices were abolished, compensation was decreed for the property rights thereby suppressed; but it was calculated on the basis of values declared for tax (and therefore considerably underestimated) in 1770, before the great inflation of office prices which marked the last twenty years of the old order. It was also paid largely in depreciating assignats. The dispossessed officers understandably felt cheated. Equally alarming was the Revolution's early hostility to professional associations in general, interpreting their commitment to maintaining standards as a hangover from the now abandoned world of corporatism and privilege. 'This was one of the first abuses of freedom', recalled a distinguished lawyer,[11] 'that the right was left to anyone, without scrutiny, or any apprenticeship, to practise the liberal professions.' Medicine, the bar, and the law in general were thrown open to the market, with minimal qualifications required from practitioners. Most of the former validating bodies, like universities, were abolished in any case. Revolutionary France was therefore a happy hunting ground for quacks and charlatans of every sort—most of them, to be sure, members of the bourgeoisie too. Not until Napoleonic times did the State take the situation in hand and reintroduce a rigorous system of licensing to restore professional standards. The solution was more bureaucratic than before 1789—but then so was France.

Although hostility to the power of royal administrators had been one of the most universal grievances expressed in the *cahiers* of 1789, and the constitution of 1791 placed almost all responsibility in the hands of elected officials, dispensing with the intendants and their professional staffs, as soon as France went to war this trend was reversed. Central administration, employing less than 700 in the 1780s, was 6,000 strong by 1794. The overall number of administrators expanded fivefold, to about a quarter of a million, perhaps 10 per cent of the entire bourgeoisie. These numbers fell somewhat in the later, chaotic days of the Directory, when the ranks of bureaucrats were regularly purged, but they stabilized not far below their 1790s peak under the Empire, that supreme administrative government. By then this apparatus had clearer qualifications and rules for entry, a well-established career structure, and even the rudiments of a contributory pension system—a source of livelihood as safe and secure as any investment in landed property.

Another group who did well out of the Revolution were soldiers. In no sphere were careers thrown more open to the talents, as the most successful careerist of them all was always ready to testify. Although military careers continued to attract high numbers of nobles still throughout the nineteenth century, the aristocratic monopoly of the officer corps had gone for ever. Proclaimed in 1789, equal opportunity in the army became a reality far more suddenly than could have been naturally expected when discipline collapsed and a large proportion of officers emigrated over the next two years. By 1793, accordingly, 70 per cent of officers in service had risen from the ranks. Even the officer-entry nobles who were left had their promotional chances improved by the departure of so many of their fellows. And for more than two decades after this, the vastly expanded army, first of the Great Nation, then of the Napoleonic Empire, would offer glory and good prospects to those who joined it and stayed with the colours. It was, of course, dangerous. By 1802 400,000 French men had fallen in battle, and another million, perhaps, would follow them before night fell on the field of Waterloo. The thousands of draft-dodgers and deserters who evaded each call-up showed clearly enough that the army's appeal was far from universal. Yet there was no mistaking the enthusiasm, commitment, and revolutionary arrogance of the Republic's armies. From the start soldiers were among the most fervent and extreme revolutionaries, scorning officers who still behaved like aristocrats, lynching generals suspected of treachery, cheering on dechristianization, and vigorously imposing the bracing discipline of liberty on defeated enemies. By 1795 and 1796, the opportunities for looting and plunder were limitless, and those lucky enough to be in the army of Italy had the unique privilege of being paid in coin. By 1797 the armies saw themselves in the former sansculotte mantle as guardians of the Revolution's purity, standing ready to intervene in domestic politics under any successful general who would mouth slogans about saving the Republic from feckless babblers. When eventually the luckiest of such generals took power, military style was imposed on the State. When Lord Cornwallis, the British peace negotiator and an experienced soldier himself, visited a sitting of the Legislative Body in 1801, he was embarrassed to find his entry and departure marked by a roll of drums. And throughout Napoleon's rule, whether as members of the Legion of Honour or of the imperial nobility, soldiers would stand first in the consular and then imperial hierarchy. The ease with which the returned emperor put together a new army in 1815 shows how much soldiers felt they owed to the new order.

Landowners, the bourgeoisie, bureaucrats, soldiers—all these groups did well out of the Revolution, taking advantage of the circumstances it had brought about. Certain others benefited from deliberate and conscious acts of emancipation. Most prominent among them were the Protestants. Although the monarchy had been moving towards a more tolerant attitude with its grant of civil status in 1787, French Protestants welcomed the Revolution almost unanimously as their true benefactor, proclaiming as it did freedom of thought and worship and full equality of civil rights between all French citizens. They were quick to lay claim to these rights, too—with inflammatory results in the cities of the south where old Catholic élites lost power as a result. Their triumph there merely confirmed their age-old reputation in Catholic eyes as subversives and trouble-makers. Their early commitment did not save them in 1793 from the ravages of terror and dechristianization. Many became involved in the Federalist revolt in the Gard, and 46 were condemned in the reprisals which followed. In the cities churches opened only a couple of years earlier (often in premises formerly the property of the Catholic Church) were closed or transformed into temples of reason, while in the Cévennes, Calvinism's rural heartland, the ranks of pastors were decimated by renunciation of orders. But there were no Protestant martyrs, and under the Directory practice revived more slowly than among Catholics. Post-Fructidorian laws against public worship affected Protestants more severely than Catholics, too, since they outlawed their traditional open-air worship 'in the desert'; while disproportionate numbers were seduced from their faith by the pale rationalities of Theophilanthropy. Yet the annexation of Geneva in 1798 added the most famous Calvinist centre of all to French territory, and consular realism refused to countenance any return to Catholic legal dominance. In fact, under Bonaparte, the Protestant churches were established on a parallel basis to the Catholic, with salaried pastors. In the process many of their more democratic traditions were lost, and isolated communities left uncatered for. The return of the Bourbons in 1815 sparked a new White Terror, too, in the Gard, where Catholic triumphalism took revenge on Protestants for tribulations reaching back to 1790. But by then there was no going back on the rights and status accorded to Protestants at the start of the Revolution, and confirmed by Bonaparte when he ended it.

The Revolution also brought emancipation to France's 39,000 Jews. Here again there had been signs of change before 1789. The name of Grégoire first came to public notice when in 1784 he won the Academy of Metz's essay competition on the theme of how the lot of Jews could be improved. In the same year a number of legal disadvantages borne by the Jews of Alsace were lifted, and when the Revolution began the government was planning further concessions in what it, and Jewish leaders too, regarded as a natural corollary to the moves in favour of Protestants. Yet the National Assembly proved in much less of a hurry to grant Jews the full rights of French citizens. When the issue was debated (which it was not until the last days of 1789) it became clear that many did not regard them as French at all, or at least not the unassimilated Yiddish-speaking Ashkenazim of Alsace who made up nine-tenths of the Jewish population. Accordingly the latter did not benefit from the first emancipation decree of January 1790. Not until the very end of the Constituent, 27 September 1791, were they admitted to full citizenship, against the vocal opposition of the Alsatian future Director, Reubell. Strictly speaking, dechristianization could not be applied to Jews; but the practice of their religion was still persecuted in 1793 and 1794 by the Montagnard zealots of Alsace, who remembered that Jewish fanaticism and superstition were as much condemned by Voltaire and other prophets of progress as by undiminished popular prejudice. Prejudice remained when terror ended. In fact it was exacerbated by the arrival, in the late 1790s, of a new wave of Ashkenazim from Germany, attracted by the superior status their fellows in France now enjoyed. Not, however, until 1805 did the government intervene again in Jewish affairs, and then Napoleon's aim was to consolidate their position as citizens, if only by imposing closer state control on their activities. There was to be no return to the marginal status of before the 1780s—much to the disgust of the anti-Semites who continued to be found throughout French society.

Finally, reluctantly and belatedly, the Revolution also abolished slavery. In contrast to the case of Protestants and Jews, there was little expectation of change in this sphere before 1789. Although most of the *philosophes* had condemned slavery and the trade which sustained it, the first French abolition society, the Amis des Noirs, was not founded by Brissot until 1788. Only a handful of *cahiers* mentioned the issue, and the defenders of slavery were well organized and funded by the wealth of the colonial trade. They dominated the colonial committee of the National Assembly. But when the Assembly voted, in July 1789, to admit unconvoked deputies from Saint-Domingue it did so only after a long and bitter debate about whom they represented. It had raised the question of the political rights of the numerous and increasingly well-organized free coloured population, not to mention the black slaves. And whereas, its decision made, the Assembly passed on to pressing metropolitan business, the impact on the colony itself was volcanic. Struggles for political control now began there between whites and free coloureds, culminating in an uprising of the latter in October 1790 which the whites put down with great brutality, breaking its leader, Ogé, on the wheel. News of these clashes provoked a new debate in Paris, and in May 1791 the Assembly, at the urging of deputies like Grégoire and Robespierre, granted civil rights to coloureds born of two free parents. It was the Revolution's first gesture towards racial equality; but before news of it could reach Saint-Domingue, the slaves, stirred up by the ferocity of the political conflicts around them, had risen in the great rebellion of August 1791. It was the progress of this uprising that forced the pace on racial issues. In April 1791 the Legislative, of which Brissot was the most prominent member, granted full rights to all free coloureds regardless of parentage. But when commissioners sent out to enforce the new law arrived in the colony, they found the situation so envenomed that it made little impact. Within months of their arrival, France was at war with Great Britain, and communications with home perilous. Willy-nilly the commissioners were forced to use their own initiative in responding to a complex and shifting situation. Thus, while on arrival they loudly reaffirmed the commitment of what was now the French Republic to slavery, by the beginning of February 1793 Commissioner Sonthonax was beginning to denounce 'aristocrats of the skin'. The latter responded by trying to drive the commissioners from the colony by force. Only non-whites defended Sonthonax; and in recognition of this in June 1793 he offered freedom to all blacks who would fight for the Republic. 'It is', he declared,[12] 'with the natives of the country, that is, the Africans, that we will save Saint-Domingue for France.' Two months later, as Spaniards from the other part of the island invaded the troubled colony, he took the final step. On 29 August, slavery itself was abolished in the northern province. In October general freedom was proclaimed for all Saint-Domingue. None of this had been authorized by the Convention. In fact in July, after the purge of the Girondins, the commissioners had been recalled as associates of the now-discredited Brissot. But when news of the emancipation arrived in Paris in January 1794 the Convention greeted it with enthusiasm, if only because, like Sonthonax, the deputies saw it as a way to defeat the Republic's British and Spanish enemies in the Caribbean. On 4 February, accordingly, the Convention framed its own decree: Negro slavery was abolished in all French colonies, and all men living there were citizens with full rights.

The effect was dramatic. As soon as the news arrived in the colony, late in April, black rebel leaders began to rally to the Republic. The free black Toussaint L'Ouverture, who had joined the Spanish invaders, switched sides. The Spaniards were driven out by black forces, who proceeded to massacre whites who had welcomed the invaders. Under the peace of 1795 Spain ceded all of Hispaniola to France. Terrified whites now appealed to the British, who with slave unrest spreading to their own islands were anxious to stamp it out at its source. There had been British troops in Saint-Domingue since 1793, and now they were reinforced. But, newly drafted in from Europe for the most part, they died like flies in the pestiferous climate. They withdrew in 1798 with nothing to show but 13,000 dead. Many ex-slaves, meanwhile, had been militarized under Toussaint, and they used their power to persecute and terrorize the coloureds. Toussaint remained loyal to France, but beyond French control until peace with England reopened the seas. As soon as it did so, Bonaparte took characteristically vigorous steps to reassert metropolitan authority, dispatching an army which captured Toussaint and sent him a prisoner to Europe. But the French troops were soon as ravaged by disease as their British predecessors, and when word arrived that the First Consul had decreed the re-establishment of slavery in May 1802, black leaders who had been only too willing to betray Toussaint resumed their resistance, and the renewal of war between Great Britain and France cut communications once more. Slavery lasted, restored, in French colonies down to 1848. But it was never re-established in Saint-Domingue, which proclaimed itself, on 1 January 1804, the Republic of Haiti.

Years of bloody vicissitudes lay ahead for the new state. Within 18 months of Toussaint's death in a prison in the Jura mountains in 1803, one of his former lieutenants, Dessalines, was proclaiming himself an emperor and decreeing a new massacre of whites. Yet French control over the former richest colony in the world was never regained. Haiti was thus the only truly independent state to come into being as a result of the French Revolution. Within a few years, of course, much of Latin America would be proclaiming its independence from a Spain made impotent by French invasion; but it was the Revolution's heir, and not the movement itself, who precipitated the break when he deposed the legitimate dynasty in Madrid.

Even so, much of the imagery and language employed by the founders of Latin-American independence was derived from the Revolution, with their declarations of rights, constitutions, and tricolours. At least one of their leaders, Miranda, had served the Republic as a general and had been dreaming of revolutionizing his native continent since the 1780s. And by the time they came into the open the ideas of national freedom and independence which they proclaimed were well established among France's European neighbours. The impact and influence of the Revolution on Europe beyond France were far from exhausted by the mid-1800s, but already the old landscape was scarcely recognizable.

Whole states had been permanently swept away. French power had obliterated famous city-republics like Geneva, Genoa, and, most spectacular of all, Venice. When the Revolution had apparently reduced France to helplessness, predatory neighbours had carved up her old ally Poland. The basis of other states, like the Dutch Republic or Switzerland, had been radically transformed and would be again when the Emperor Napoleon decided to set up satellite kingdoms. Even beyond French reach, the pro-French uprising in Ireland in 1798 had precipitated the end of Irish legislative independence from Great Britain. The Holy Roman Empire would limp on until 1806, finally destroyed by yet another Austrian defeat at French hands. From 1797, however, from the moment the Peace of Campo Formio conceded the left bank of the Rhine to France, it was clear that the Empire's traditional composition could not survive. Princes dispossessed there would have to be compensated with territory elsewhere in Germany taken from ecclesiastical rulers. And so they were, when the settlement of Campo Formio was confirmed after the Peace of Lunéville. The states of Germany were completely secularized just three years before the Empire itself finally crumbled.

Imposed on Europe by French power, these changes outlasted it. After the defeat of Napoleon, however, France lost most of the gains she had made for herself, even within her self-proclaimed 'natural frontiers'. Belgium became part of a new kingdom of the Netherlands and then, after 1831, a separate realm in her own right; Luxembourg became an independent grand duchy. Austria, more than content with gains in Italy, wanted neither back. Prussia inherited most of the Rhenish left bank, for nobody dreamed of reinstating the ecclesiastical princes. Even Savoy was restored to a reconstituted Piedmontese kingdom of Sardinia. Of these losses, France only recovered Savoy, in 1860. The long-term gainers from the wars launched by the French revolutionaries against Europe, in fact, were the enemies they were so confident of destroying. The Austrians, having shown an almost miraculous ability to recover in the face of repeated apparently decisive defeats, emerged hugely expanded in territory and would dominate central Europe for half a century. The Prussians, when they faced French armies squarely for the first time since Valmy, in 1806, were shatteringly defeated—but they emerged with the hegemony of northern Germany first forged by Frederick the Great enormously strengthened, and far more extensive territories. Russia and Spain, for their part, demonstrated the practical limitations of even French military power. Napoleon's failure to subdue either marked the beginning of the French Empire's decline. Above all, the British remained invulnerable beyond the Channel, even in the face of an attempt to exclude their merchandise from Europe, first experimented with by the Directory and developed into a full-blown system by Napoleon. Meanwhile they subsidized France's continental enemies, and used their sea-power to strengthen their already formidable trading links with the rest of the world and systematically destroy or appropriate the assets of their rivals. French occupation completed the economic decline of the Dutch, long overtaken by England but still a substantial power in the 1780s in trade, colonies, finance, and banking. Most of this power drained away to London while Amsterdam was governed from Paris. But Great Britain's greatest economic competitor throughout the eighteenth century had been France herself. It seems unlikely that she could have kept up economically even if the Revolution had not occurred. From the early 1780s the British were showing signs of moving decisively ahead in volume of trade and industrial production. But the Revolution widened the gap irrecoverably, the British appropriating the overseas markets and resources that France lost. Militarily, when France became bogged down in the Iberian peninsula, British sea power at last found a way of directly influencing the continental struggle by transporting an army there, under the general who would eventually impose the decisive military defeat on Napoleon. Appropriately, Wellington's victory took place in Belgium, the territory for which Great Britain had entered the war in the first place. Intervention in the same cause in 1914 would herald the end for Great Britain of the century of world power which opened with the defeat of France.

The French Empire defeated in 1815 was no longer, of course, the country which had begun the war. But then the victorious powers had changed extraordinarily too. Every state which survived confrontation with revolutionary France was deeply marked by the effort. The Republic from 1793 onwards had committed itself to mobilizing the entire resources of Europe's most populous country (Russia excepted). The monarchies against whom this drive was directed could only hope to defeat it if they did the same. Mass warfare resulted, involving huge armies and whole populations no longer insulated, as they had been during a century and a half of contained warfare for limited objectives, from the full impact of military demands. As Clausewitz, whose whole great theory of war was based upon analysis of the conflicts between 1792 and 1815, put it:[13]

In 1793 such a force as no one had any conception of made its appearance. War had again suddenly become an affair of the people, and that of a people numbering thirty millions, every one of whom regarded himself as a citizen of the State . . . By this participation of the people in the war . . . a whole Nation with its natural weight came into the scale. Henceforward, the means available—the efforts which might be called forth—had no longer any definite limits . . . the element of War, freed from all conventional restrictions, broke loose, with all its natural force. The cause was the participation of the people in this great affair of State, and this participation arose partly from the effects of the French Revolution on the internal affairs of countries, partly from the threatening attitude of the French towards all Nations.

But these changes needed to be organized, and nothing could be done if government did not take extensive new powers. Everywhere, for example, conscription of some sort became the norm. Introduced into the Austrian hereditary lands under Maria Theresia, in 1802 it was extended to Hungary. After the defeat of the old Prussian professional and half-mercenary army in 1806, a new *Landwehr* began to be organized, based for the first time largely on the state's own citizens, while the spirit of the *levée en masse* was sought in the creation of a popular force of resistance to invasion, the *Landsturm*. In Great Britain balloting for the militia and other auxiliary forces were extended. There were riots throughout Ireland when a militia was introduced for the first time in 1793, the same in Scotland in 1797, and the activities of the press-gang in the ports of the British Isles were a source of constant tension. These governments seldom made the French mistake of equating resistance to conscription with treason and sympathy with the enemy; but fears that genuine Jacobins would exploit the resentments it caused, among other popular grievances, led to a general increase in police activities and numbers, and spies and informers proliferated. The burden of taxation, of course, rose spectacularly, and much ingenuity was displayed everywhere in finding new commodities to impose levies on. The first self-confessed income tax was introduced in Great Britain in 1799, and soon afterwards a similar levy was introduced in Austria. Nor were the assignats the only paper money to be issued—and depreciate. By 1800, 200 million *Bankozettel* were circulating in Austria, and by 1804 had lost 35 per cent.

And yet, except in Ireland in 1798, resistance to more burdensome government in states fighting France never attained the scale and persistence witnessed there. This was because, in the end, the subjects of Europe's beleaguered kings and emperors feared and hated the French more than they did their own rulers. What they learned of French behaviour in occupied territories did nothing to reassure them. An exuberant, uncompromising nationalism lay behind France's revolutionary expansion in the 1790s: but what the French found, after this first impact of a nation in arms on its neighbours, was that the neighbours responded in kind. They found that the doctrine of the sovereignty of the nation, proclaimed by them at the outset of the Revolution in 1789, could be turned against them by other peoples claiming their own national sovereignty. In states long united by custom and language, such as the Dutch Republic, all the French example did was to reinforce patriotic sentiments already strong. In areas never before united, like Italy, it created a powerful national sentiment for the first time by showing that archaic barriers and divisions could be swept away. The first Italian nationalists placed their hopes in French power to secure their ends, but from the start their attitude was double-edged. 'Italy', declared the winning entry for an essay competition on the best form of Italian government, sponsored by the new French regime in Milan in 1796,[14] 'has almost always been the patrimony of foreigners who, under the pretext of protecting us, have consistently violated our rights, and, while giving us flags and fine-sounding names, have made themselves masters of our estate. France, Germany and Spain have held lordship over us in turn . . . it is therefore best to provide . . . the sort of government capable of opposing the maximum of resistance to invasion.' The tragedy for nationalistic Italian Jacobins was that, when popular revulsion against the French invaders swept the peninsula in 1798 and 1799, they found themselves identified with the hated foreigners. Elsewhere, peoples and intellectual nationalists found themselves more at one; and not the least of the reasons why France's most inveterate enemies were able to resist her so successfully was the strength of volunteering. An Austrian call for volunteers against the French produced 150,000 men in 1809. Three years later the Russians were able to supplement their normal armed forces with over 420,000 more or less willing recruits to drive out the alien invader. Only nationalism could successfully fight nationalism: and when it did, as Clausewitz again saw, it would be a fight to the death. Wars of peoples could admit of none of the old limited, bargained conclusions of pomaded dynasts. But these would be the wars of the future, and the French Revolution had pioneered them.

It was ironic that a movement that so fired and hardened national antagonisms should have been launched in the name of the universal Rights of Man. It was even more surprising that these values should have remained associated with the French cause when revolutionary France herself had turned away from most of them. But apart from French puppets, no other European state dreamed of espousing the revolutionary ideology. They knew that, whereas French power threatened their existence, French principles challenged their legitimacy. Yet for all their efforts, and Napoleon's too, sooner or later much of this ideology still triumphed.

The message of the French Revolution was that the people are sovereign; and in the two centuries since it was first proclaimed it has conquered the world. What it means in practice is subject to constant disagreement, and was from the start. Representative government after properly held elections was one thing—but the deputy who declared on 15 June 1789, as he pointed to the screaming public galleries,[15] 'Learn . . . that we are deliberating here in front of our masters and we are answerable to them for our opinions', was asking for trouble. In 1792 it arrived, when the much-feared tumultuous democracy, warned against by men of order ever since the beginning, triumphed amid the bloodshed of the storming of the Tuileries and the September Massacres. The people were now in power, or so the sansculottes and their Montagnard allies claimed, for the first time since antiquity. Later democrats have looked back on those months as the first triumph of their beliefs. Yet at the time most men of property and education were horrified, and they continued to be haunted by the memory down the generations. In the end the activities of the sansculottes probably retarded rather than advanced the cause of mass democracy. Nevertheless, prescription and hereditary right would never again command unchallenged consent as a basis for legitimate political authority. Sooner or later, even the most absolute monarchs or dictators would feel the need to confirm their right to power with a show of popular endorsement. More often than not, perhaps, elections or plebiscites would be rigged. The French revolutionaries pioneered that technique too. But since 1789 ever-dwindling numbers of regimes have felt it wise to do without any token of consent from those over whom they rule.

If asked to sum up their cause in one word, the men of 1789, and perhaps most of their compatriots down to 1802, even, would have responded: liberty. In revolutionary France, and in the countries France overran, the imagery of liberty was everywhere—Phrygian caps, allegorical statues, and above all liberty trees, planted by triumphant Jacobins and as often as not hacked down later by counter-revolutionaries—60,000 had been planted by 1792. After 1792 the trappings of Roman republicanism became fashionable, with fasces and axes; and stern ancient patriots like Brutus, Scaevola, and Cato, familiar to all men of education, were much invoked. But what did 'liberty' mean? In everyday practice it appeared to mean whatever those in power wanted. For them, Rousseau's statement that legitimate authorities should force men to be free was wonderfully convenient, and in the Year II sophistries of this sort littered the speeches of more speculative rhetoricians like Robespierre and Saint-Just. Abroad, liberty simply meant French rule. Yet less equivocal definitions were available, and had been offered by the revolutionaries at the outset. It was defined in the Declaration of the Rights of Man and the Citizen as the right to do anything that did not harm others, limited only by others' enjoyment of the same right. It also meant freedom from arbitrary power, which by 1792 was being routinely identified as the power of any king. Finally it meant freedom to think, write, and worship as one chose. Although it was soon limiting them in practice, the Revolution never ceased to pay copious lip-service to these values. They would remain inseparable from the creed of all those subsequently inspired by the French revolutionary myth.

The same was true of the second key to the Rights of Man, equality. If we know nothing else about the French Revolution, we know that it spawned the famous motto adopted for the state by the Third Republic and never abandoned since, except by the Vichy regime: *Liberty, Equality, Fraternity*. In historical fact, fraternity came late, appearing only in 1793, and went soon, being largely abandoned by the end of 1794 as a now-redundant sop to the sansculottes. Equality, however, was there from the beginning. All men, proclaimed the Declaration, are born and remain free and equal in rights, social distinctions can only be based on common utility, the law should be the same for everybody. By these tokens a society based on privilege, hereditary superiority, or feudal prerogatives was renounced, and the revolutionaries of France offered a complete programme for other societies wishing to do the same. Yet the equality aimed at by the men of 1789 had very clear limits. Equality of opportunity, expressed as careers open to the talents, was one thing. Equality of fortunes or property, which alone could make true equality of opportunity a reality, was quite another, and never espoused by more than a tiny handful of political activists in the 1790s. Property, indeed (and the security that went with it), was proclaimed as one of the natural and imprescriptible Rights of Man. In March 1793 the Convention, amid scenes of general enthusiasm, decreed the death penalty for anybody proposing an agrarian law—a forcible redistribution of property of the sort familiar to all the deputies from reading at school about the ill-fated Gracchi in republican Rome. Equality of political rights commanded more support, especially in 1793–4, but it is hard to decide how much of the democratic talk heard then was intended more to impress the sansculottes than as an expression of real conviction. Certain it is that the only constitution of the 1790s to fix no property qualifications for voting or eligibility at any level, that of 1793, was never brought into force and abandoned as impractical as soon as popular pressure on the Convention eased. The constitution-makers of 1795 did not resurrect the category of active citizen elaborated in 1790, but they put effective voting power, that of the secondary assemblies, squarely in the hands of substantial property owners. The consular lists would observe the same principles, defining the political nation in effect as the Notables. Not until 1848 was this principle challenged again.

Equality between men and women, meanwhile, was brushed aside as scarcely worthy of consideration, despite the unprecedented part women had played in public affairs in and after 1789. Whether marching to Versailles to bring back the royal family in October 1789, or urging on their menfolk to take more decisive action in most of the subsequent *journées* down to Prairial 1795; or whether forming, as nuns, the most solid block of clergy to refuse the clerical oath, or leading the steady drift back to religious observance over the late 1790s, women at crucial points were of decisive importance in the Revolution. Invariably their intervention pushed matters to extremes. Grégoire, despairing at popular refusal to patronize his rump constitutional Church, cannot have been the only one to lament the influence of 'crapulous and seditious women'.[16] Meanwhile, whereas at the highest level the closet influence of political wives like Mme Roland and Mme Tallien, or Necker's busybody daughter Mme de Staël, continued the well-established traditions of the old regime, the unprecedented atmosphere of early revolutionary Paris threw up new and unusual figures. There was Théroigne de Méricourt, sitting among the men at the Jacobin Club in her National Guard uniform, rallying the faint-hearted at the Tuileries on 10 August, and perhaps spying for the emperor; or Claire Lacombe, actress and *enragée*, who organized a club of 'revolutionary republican citizenesses' which fought pitched battles with market women. They were so disorderly that on 30 October 1793 the Convention formally banned women's organizations. Or there was Olympe de Gouges, playwright and pamphleteer, who attacked Robespierre and offered to defend the king, and failed to avoid the guillotine by feigning pregnancy (at 45) after being arrested for demanding government by plebiscite. In 1791 she had written a pamphlet, *The Rights of Women and the Citizen*, in which she laid claim to equal political rights with men. But there was never any hope of that. The men of the French Revolution saw women's role exclusively as that of wife and mother, bearing children for the homeland, but leaving politics to men. In this respect Napoleon was entirely typical, and many of his interventions during the drafting of the Civil Code were directed at restricting women's property rights. He would not have dissented from the advice offered to women by the Jacobin journalist Prudhomme in 1793:

Be honest and diligent girls, tender and modest wives, wise mothers, and you will be good patriots. True patriotism consists of fulfilling one's duties and valuing only rights appropriate to each according to sex and age, and not wearing the [liberty] cap and pantaloons and not carrying pike and pistol. Leave those to men who are born to protect you and make you happy.[17]

The practical egalitarianism of the French Revolution was, therefore, quite narrow. Even so, the Revolution also produced the most radical and imaginative attempt to achieve equality yet seen in history, Babeuf's Conspiracy of Equals. Designed to achieve one of the fundamental Rights of Man, it drew its inspiration from another, endorsed by the declarations both of 1789 and 1793: resistance to oppression. For one thing revolutionaries could never do was proclaim revolution itself illegitimate. Every regime down to 1814 could trace its title back no further than the seizure of sovereignty by the representatives of the nation in June 1789, confirmed by the popular action of mid-July. Thus, declared the 1793 Declaration of Rights, 'When the government violates the rights of the people, insurrection is for the people and for each portion of the people the most sacred of rights and the most indispensable of duties.' Exercising this right, a second revolution within the Revolution had overthrown the monarchy in August 1792; and discontented elements for the whole span of the First French Republic regarded rebellion as a legitimate, if final, recourse against regimes they believed to be violating the Rights of Man. It was a reflex that would become permanently entrenched in French history; and, soon enough, in that of the whole world. The modern idea of revolution goes back no further than 1789. But once it had occurred in France, the idea that it was possible, and right, to overthrow an existing order by force, and on grounds of general principles rather than existing law, was launched. Simultaneously a new figure appeared on the stage of history: the revolutionary. There had been no revolutionaries before 1789. Nobody expected, foresaw, or planned for the catastrophe that began then. The revolutionaries of France were created by the Revolution. But that never happened again. Afterwards, revolutions would be consciously prepared for; and even when their form or occasion was unexpected (as in 1917) there were always revolutionaries there, with plans laid, to take advantage of them. Henceforth it was recognized that revolutions which were more than just sudden or violent changes at the top could be engineered, and succeed. For this new breed, the French Revolution was the classic political and social experience. It provided an inspiration: proof that revolution could occur. It provided a model: what techniques to use, what mistakes to avoid. It provided a style and a language. Self-conscious revolutionaries would adopt a tricolour as the flag of liberty, imitate French uniforms (Wolfe Tone dreamed of clothing a United Irish 'national guard' in 1792 in green-striped trousers: no culottes), rename streets after the dates of revolutionary events, and institute public holidays and ceremonies on the anniversaries. As late as 1956 crowds in Poland sang the 'Marseillaise' in the momentary conviction that Soviet power in their country was being overthrown. Marx, Lenin, and Trotsky all studied the 1790s as a guide to revolution, and what happened (or is thought to have happened) then occupies a crucial place in the theory of history which underpins Marxism.

But the later political influence of the Revolution reached far beyond the ranks of revolutionaries. The vocabulary of all politics was permanently changed. The categories of Left and Right go back to the Constituent Assembly, where radicals soon fell into the habit of sitting together to the left of the chair, while their opponents congregated on the right. Only later did socialists, seeing their own antecedents in the outlook and ideas of the more extreme revolutionaries, appropriate the left-wing label and (it has sometimes seemed) lay exclusive claim to the revolutionary heritage. Yet what enabled them to do so was the total rejection of that heritage by the Right.

Before 1789 conservatism, as a positive, self-conscious political outlook, was unknown. No established order was under the comprehensive threat that the French Revolution later posed. By 1793, however, a new, revolutionary ideology had led to attacks on all the principal pillars of stability—property, social hierarchy, religion, monarchy. None of these, or their justification in the nature of things, could any longer be taken for granted. They now needed to be defended, both in theory and in practice. The theoretical task was undertaken by men like Burke, Gentz, or the Savoyard refugee from French invasion Joseph de Maistre, who began his denunciations with *Considerations on France* in 1797. The history of the Revolution showed, he believed, that too much striving after abstract freedom and rationality led to chaos and anarchy. In fact, as with later Marxists, the whole political outlook of the early right was based on a theory of history—though theirs was confined much more narrowly to the Revolution itself. The key, thought Maistre, to restoring the order and stability destroyed by the Revolution was to restore the other things it had overthrown—aristocracy, throne, and above all altar. But once restored, these institutions would need to guard against being subverted once again by the corrosive of free thought and revolutionary inspiration. This was the lesson most remembered when the much-bruised remnants of the old order emerged from the cataclysm: no compromise. If the Revolution was God's punishment on the old regime for countenancing creeping laxity and infidelity, then the best hope for lasting stability in the future was to support religion, avoid representative institutions, control opinion, and maintain vigilance against subversive plots. A whole right-wing political outlook had been born, and like its revolutionary antithesis it transcended frontiers. It would dominate many nineteenth-century governments; but in the end they would find that intransigence merely provoked what it hoped to prevent. Reformers were driven to plotting revolution because there was no hope of change in any other way; while hostility to religion and the social order was all the more virulent when, in the end, it did break out again.

Moderate conservatives feared as much. In every state there would be those who believed that reform rather than intransigence was the best way to prevent revolution. They were not always successful, but at least they were prepared to look reality in the face. For good or ill, the Revolution had happened, and the ideals, aspirations, and myths it had inspired could not be expunged from human memory. And the world of acceptance which it had shattered could never be artificially re-created.

The shadow of the Revolution, therefore, fell across the whole of the nineteenth century and beyond. Until 1917 few would have disputed that it was the greatest revolution in the history of the world; and even after that its claims to primacy remain strong. It was the first modern revolution, the archetypal one. After it, nothing in the European world remained the same, and we are all heirs to its influence. And yet, it can be argued, much that was attributed to it would in all probability have come about in any case. Before 1789 there were plenty of signs that the structure of French society was evolving towards domination by a single élite in which property counted for more than birth. The century-long expansion of the bourgeoisie which underlay this trend already looked irreversible; and greater participation by men of property in government, as constant experiments with provincial assemblies showed, seemed bound to come. Meanwhile many of the reforms the Revolution brought in were already being tried or thought about by the absolute monarchy—law codification, fiscal rationalization, diminution of venality, free trade, religious toleration. With all these changes under way or in contemplation, the power of government looked set for steady growth, too—which ironically was one of the complaints of the despotism-obsessed men of 1789. In the Church, the monastic ideal was already shrivelling and the status of parish priests commanding more and more public sympathy. Economically, the colonial trade had already peaked, and failure to compete industrially with Great Britain was increasingly manifest. In other structural areas, meanwhile, the great upheaval appears to have made no difference at all. Conservative investment habits still characterized the early nineteenth century, agricultural inertia and unentrepreneurial business likewise. And in international affairs, it is hard to believe that Great Britain would not have dominated the world's seas and trade throughout the nineteenth century, that Austro-Prussian rivalry would not have run much the course it did, or that Latin America would not have asserted its independence in some form or other, if the French Revolution had never happened. In all these fields, the effect was to accelerate or retard certain trends, but not to change their general drift.

Against all this, it is equally hard to believe that the specifically anti-aristocratic, anti-feudal revolutionary ideology of the Rights of Man would have emerged as it did without the jumble of accident, miscalculation, and misunderstanding which coalesced into a revolution in specifically French circumstances. It is equally hard to believe that anything as extraordinary as dechristianization would have occurred without the monumental misjudgement which produced the Revolution's quarrel with the Catholic Church. Without that quarrel, the dramatic revival in the authority of the papacy also seems inconceivable. Representative government may well have been on the horizon, but how long would the ideal of popular democracy have taken to establish itself without the example of the sansculotte movement? It certainly transformed and widened out of all recognition the cause of parliamentary reform in England—although the blood-stained figure of the sansculotte probably galvanized conservative resistance on the other side. Above all, the revolutionaries' decision to go to war, which all historians agree revolutionized the Revolution, destroyed an established pattern of warfare in a way no old regime government would otherwise have promoted. Arming the people was the last thing they would have dreamed of. The emergencies of that war in turn produced the scenes which have indelibly marked our memory of the Revolution: the Terror. Massacres were nothing new, and the worst ones of the 1790s occurred outside France. But there was something horribly new and unimaginable in the prospect of a government systematically executing its opponents by the cartload for months on end, and by a device which, however humane in concept, made the streets run with blood. And this occurred in what had passed for the most civilized country in Europe, whose writers had taught the eighteenth century to pride itself on its increasing mildness, good sense, and humanity. This great drama transformed the whole meaning of political change, and the contemporary world would be inconceivable if it had not happened.

In other words it transformed men's outlook. The writers of the Enlightenment, so revered by the intelligentsia who made the Revolution, had always believed it could be done if men dared to seize control of their own destiny. The men of 1789 did so, in a rare moment of courage, altruism, and idealism which took away the breath of educated Europe. What they failed to see, as their inspirers had not foreseen, was that reason and good intentions were not enough by themselves to transform the lot of their fellow men. Mistakes would be made when the accumulated experience of generations was pushed aside as so much routine, prejudice, fanaticism, and superstition. The generation forced to live through the upheavals of the next twenty-six years paid the price. Already by 1802 a million French citizens lay dead; a million more would perish under Napoleon, and untold more abroad. How many millions more still had their lives ruined? Inspiring and ennobling, the prospect of the French Revolution is also moving and appalling: in every sense a tragedy.

# Notes

## Chapter 1. France under Louis XVI

1. *Travels in France during the Years 1787, 1788 and 1789*, ed. C. Maxwell (Cambridge, 1929), 275–6.
2. Quoted in W. Scott, *Terror and Repression in Revolutionary Marseilles* (London, 1973), 10.
3. *Travels*, 180.
4. *Travels*, 10 June 1787 (p. 23).
5. Quoted in F. Bluche, *La Vie quotidienne au temps de Louis XVI* (Paris, 1980), 275.
6. Quoted in O. H. Hufton, *The Poor of Eighteenth Century France 1750–1789* (Oxford, 1974), 11.
7. Quoted in Hufton, *The Poor*, 69.
8. Quoted in O. H. Hufton 'Towards an Understanding of the Poor of Eighteenth Century France', in J. F. Bosher (ed.), *French Government and Society 1500–1850: Essays in Memory of Alfred Cobban* (London, 1973), 152.
9. *Journal de ma vie: Jacques-Louis Ménétra compagnon vitrier au 18ᵉ siècle*, ed. D. Roche (Paris, 1982).
10. *Tableau de Paris* (12 vols. Amsterdam, 1783) quoted in S. L. Kaplan, 'Réflexions sur la police du monde de travail 1700–1815', *Revue historique*, 329 (1979), 70.
11. Quoted in Y. Durand, *Les Fermiers Généraux au XVIIIᵉ siècle* (Paris, 1971), 190.
12. *Travels*, 26 Aug. 1787 (p. 60).
13. Quoted in M. Garden, *Lyon et les Lyonnais au XVIIIᵉ siècle* (Paris, 1970), 534–5.
14. *Travels through France and Italy* (London, 1763), Letter IV.
15. *Memoirs of Louis-Philippe Comte de Ségur*, ed. E. Cruikshanks (London, 1960), 41.
16. *Maximes et pensées: Caractères et anecdotes*, ed. C. Roy (Paris, 1963), 76.
17. Quoted in M. Marion, *Dictionnaire des institutions de la France aux XVIIᵉ et XVIIIᵉ siècles* (Paris, 1923), 314.
18. *Travels*, 23 Oct. 1787 (p. 89).
19. Mme Campan, *Mémoires sur la vie de Marie-Antoinette, reine de France et de Navarre*, ch. 4.
20. Diary of Lord Herbert, 7 May 1780, in *The Pembroke Papers*, ed. Ld. Herbert (London, 1942), 473.
21. Quoted in S. K. Padover, *The Life and Death of Louis XVI* (NY, 1963 edn.), 50–1.

## Chapter 2. Enlightened Opinion

1. Quoted in L. Réau, *L'Europe française au siècle des lumières* (Paris, 1938), 47.
2. Quoted in D. Mornet, *Les Origines intellectuelles de la Révolution française 1715–1787* (Paris, 1933), 311.

3. Quoted ibid. 307.
4. Quoted in R. Darnton, *The Business of Enlightenment: A Publishing History of the Encyclopédie 1775–1800* (Cambridge, Mass., 1979), 295–6.
5. *De l'esprit des lois* (Geneva, 1748), bk. XI, ch. VI.
6. Quoted in M. Cranston, *Jean-Jacques: The Early Life and Work of Jean-Jacques Rousseau, 1712–1754* (London, 1983), 228.
7. Quoted in J. Lough, *France on the Eve of Revolution: British Travellers' Observations 1763–1788* (London, 1987), 160–1.
8. Quoted by M. Ozouf in K. M. Baker (ed.), *The French Revolution and the Creation of Modern Political Culture*, i: *The Political Culture of the Old Regime* (Oxford, 1987), 422.
9. Quoted in T. Besterman, *Voltaire* (London, 1969), 427.
10. Mme d'Epinay to Galiani, in *L'Abbé F. Galiani: Correspondance*, ed. L. Perey and G. Maugras (2 vols., Paris, 1890), i. 375.
11. Quoted in W. Doyle, *The Parlement of Bordeaux and the End of the Old Regime 1771–90* (London, 1974), 205.
12. Quoted in J. Lough, *An Introduction to Eighteenth Century France* (London, 1960), 192.
13. Quoted in *Correspondance de Félix Faulcon*, ed. G. Debien (2 vols., Poitiers, 1939), i. 180.
14. Quoted in B. S. Stone, *The French Parlements and the Crisis of the Old Regime* (Chapel Hill, 1986), 147–8.
15. *The Adams Papers: Series I*, ed. L. H. Butterfield (4 vols., Cambridge, Mass., 1961), iv. 35.
16. Quoted in D. Echeverria, *Mirage in the West: A History of the French Image of American Society to 1815* (Princeton, 1957), 152–3.
17. *Adolphe, ou Principes élémentaires de politique* (London, 1795), 91.

## Chapter 3. Crisis and Collapse, 1776–1788

1. Quoted in Orville T. Murphy, *Charles Gravier, Comte de Vergennes* (Albany, 1982), 235.
2. Quoted in D. Dakin, *Turgot and the Ancien Regime in France* (London, 1939), 131.
3. *Despatches from Paris 1784–1790*, ed. O. Browning (2 vols., London, 1909–10) i. 134.
4. Quoted in W. Doyle, *Origins of the French Revolution* (2nd edn., Oxford, 1988), 51.
5. Quoted ibid. 97.
6. Quoted ibid. 98.
7. 5 May 1787. *The Letters of Lafayette to Washington 1777–1799*, ed. L. Gottschalk (Philadelphia, 1976), 322.
8. *Avertissement* in Calonne, *De l'état de la France, présent et à venir* (London, 1790), 439.
9. Quoted in J. Egret, *La Pré-Révolution française 1787–1788* (Paris, 1962), 59.
10. Quoted ibid. 60.
11. Quoted in *Journal de l'Assemblée des Notables de 1787*, ed. P. Chevallier (Paris, 1960), 79.
12. H. Swinburne, *The Courts of Europe at the Close of the Last Century* (2 vols., London, 1895), ii. 22.

13. *Travels*, 75.
14. Ibid. 80.
15. *Les Remontrances du parlement de Paris au XVIII$^e$ siècle* ed. J. Flammermont (3 vols. Paris, 1888–1908), iii. 738–9.
16. *Despatches from Paris*, ii. 44, 8 May 1788.
17. A. F. Bertrand de Molleville, *Private Memoirs Relative to the Last Years of Lewis the Sixteenth, Late King of France* (3 vols., London, 1797), i. 108.

## Chapter 4. The Estates-General, September 1788–July 1789

1. *Despatches from Paris*, ii. 140.
2. Quoted in Egret, *La Pré-Révolution*, 334.
3. *Correspondance secrète sur Louis XVI, Marie Antoinette, la cour et la ville de 1777 à 1792*, ed. A. de Lescure (2 vols., Paris, 1866), ii. 305.
4. Quoted in M. Gresset, *Gens de justice à Besançon (1674–1789)* (2 vols., Paris, 1978), ii. 756.
5. *Despatches from Paris*, ii. 161, 19 Feb. 1789.
6. *Travels*, 134.
7. *Despatches from Paris*, ii. 217.
8. J. A. Creuzé-Latouche, *Journal des États Généraux et du début de l'Assemblée Nationale (18 mai–29 juillet 1789)*, ed. J. Marchand (Paris, 1946), 130.
9. *Travels*, 154.
10. Nicolas Ruault, *Gazette d'un Parisien sous la Révolution* (Paris, 1976), 142.
11. *Travels*, 159.
12. Ruault, *Gazette*, 154.

## Chapter 5. The Principles of 1789 and the Reform of France

1. Quoted in G. Lefebvre, *The Great Fear of 1789* (Eng. trans. London, 1973), 102.
2. Quoted in J. P Hirsh, *La Nuit du 4 août* (Paris, 1978), 128–9.
3. *Marquis de Ferrières: Correspondance inédite 1789, 1790, 1791*, ed. H. Carré (Paris, 1932), 114.
4. Ruault, *Gazette*, 170 (16 Sept. 1789).
5. *Despatches from Paris*, ii. 268. Fitzgerald to Duke of Leeds, 15 Oct. 1789.
6. Quoted in L. G. Wickham Legg, *Select Documents Illustrative of the History of the French Revolution: The Constituent Assembly* (2 vols., Oxford, 1905), i. 173–4.
7. Quoted in S. Herbert, *The Fall of Feudalism in France* (London, 1921), 121–2.

## Chapter 6. The Breakdown of the Revolutionary Consensus, 1790–1791

1. Quoted in A. Aulard, *Christianity and the French Revolution* (London, 1927), 59.
2. Quoted in G. Lewis, *The Second Vendée: The Continuity of Counter-Revolution in the Department of the Gard 1789–1815* (Oxford, 1978), 28.
3. Quoted in P. de la Gorce, *Histoire religieuse de la Révolution française* (5 vols., Paris, 1902–23), i. 303.
4. Ruault, *Gazette*, 217.
5. 8 Aug. 1790. Quoted in R. Lacour-Gayet, *Calonne: Financier, réformateur, contre-révolutionnaire 1734–1802* (Paris, 1963), 290.

6. *The Despatches of Earl Gower*, ed. O. Browning (Cambridge, 1885), 79.
7. *The Correspondence of William Augustus Miles on the French Revolution 1789–1817*, ed. C. P. Miles (2 vols., London, 1890), i. 245.
8. Ferrières, *Correspondance*, 362–3.
9. G. Rudé, *The Crowd in the French Revolution* (Oxford, 1959), 89 and 91.
10. *Despatches of Gower*, 79–80.

## Chapter 7. Europe and the Revolution, 1788–1791

1. Quoted in A. Cobban, *Ambassadors and Secret Agents* (London, 1954), 212.
2. Quoted in G. P. Gooch, *Germany and the French Revolution* (London, 1920), 39–40.
3. Quoted in C. Nordmann, *Grandeur et liberté de la Suède (1660–1792)* (Paris/Louvain, 1971), 430–1.
4. Quoted in P. Dukes, 'Russia and the Eighteenth Century Revolution', *History* (1971), 380.
5. Romilly to Dumont, quoted in A. Cobban (ed.), *The Debate on the French Revolution 1789–1800* (London, 1950), 39–40.
6. Quoted in C. A. Macartney, *The Habsburg Empire 1790–1918* (London, 1969), 134.
7. Quoted in Cobban, *The Debate*, 64.

## Chapter 8. The Republican Revolution, October 1791–January 1793

1. Quoted in J. M. Thompson, *English Witnesses of the French Revolution* (Oxford, 1938), 146.
2. Quoted in de la Gorce, *Histoire religieuse*, ii. 30.
3. Quoted in J. M. Thompson, *French Revolution Documents* (Oxford, 1933), 161.
4. Quoted in Scott, *Terror and Repression in Revolutionary Marseilles*, 33.
5. Ruault, *Gazette*, 284 (24 May 1792).
6. Quoted in Thompson, *Documents*, 177.
7. *A Diary of the French Revolution by Gouverneur Morris 1752–1816*, ed. B. C. Davenport (2 vols., London, 1939), ii. 453.
8. Ruault, *Gazette*, 295 (17 July 1792).
9. *Despatches of Gower*, 238.
10. H. Morse Stephens, *The Principal speeches of the Statesmen and Orators of the French Revolution* (2 vols., Oxford, 1892), ii. 359.

## Chapter 9. War against Europe, 1792–1797

1. Quoted in T. C. W. Blanning, *The Origins of the French Revolutionary Wars* (London, 1986), 137.
2. Stephens, *Orators*, ii. 189.
3. Ibid.
4. Quoted in Blanning, *Origins*, 137.
5. 19 July 1793. Quoted in J. H. Rose, *William Pitt and the Great War* (London, 1914), 144.

6. Quoted in B. Lesnodorski, *Les Jacobins polonais* (Paris, 1965), 88.
7. Quoted in I. de Madariaga, *Russia in the Age of Catherine the Great* (London, 1981), 446.
8. Quoted in S. Schama, *Patriots and Liberators: Revolution in the Netherlands, 1780–1813* (London, 1977), 201.
9. Quoted in R. Herr, *The Eighteenth Century Revolution in Spain* (Princeton, 1958), 325.
10. Quoted in H. Acton, *The Bourbons of Naples (1734–1825)* (London, 1956), 254.

## Chapter 10. The Revolt of the Provinces

1. Quoted in J. Hardman (ed.), *French Revolution Documents*, ii (Oxford, 1973), 23.
2. Quoted in M. J. Sydenham, *The Girondins* (London, 1961), 126.
3. Quoted in D. Sutherland, *The Chouans: The Social Origins of Popular Counter-Revolution in Upper Brittany 1770–1796* (Oxford, 1982), 260.
4. Quoted in C. Tilly, *The Vendée* (Cambridge, Mass., and London, 1964), 317.
5. Quoted in A. Schmidt, *Tableaux de la Révolution française* (3 vols., Leipzig, 1867), i. 174.
6. Quoted in Scott, *Terror and Repression in Revolutionary Marseilles*, 55.
7. Quoted ibid. 84.
8. Quoted in Hardman, *Documents*, ii. 67.
9. Quoted in A. Forrest, *Society and Politics in Revolutionary Bordeaux* (Oxford, 1975), 67.
10. Quoted ibid. 99.
11. Quoted in M. H. Crook, 'Federalism and the French Revolution: The Revolt of Toulon in 1793', *History*, 65 (1980), 393.
12. Quoted in D. Stone, 'La Révolte Fédéraliste à Rennes', *Annales historiques de la Révolution française*, 43 (1971) 368–9.
13. Quoted in Hardman, *Documents*, ii. 102.
14. Quoted in Forrest, *Bordeaux*, 111.

## Chapter 11. Government by Terror, 1793–1794

1. Quoted in Hardman, *Documents*, ii. 149.
2. Quoted in Forrest, *Bordeaux*, 226.
3. Quoted in Hardman, *Documents*, ii. 357.
4. Quoted in Thompson, *Documents*, 258–9.
5. Quoted in Hardman, *Documents*, ii. 157.
6. *Un Allemand en France sous la terreur: Souvenirs de Frédéric-Christian Laukhard*, ed. W. Bauer (Paris, 1915), 272–3.
7. Quoted in de la Gorce, *Histoire religieuse*, iii. 246.
8. W. Markov and A. Soboul, *Die Sansculotten von Paris* (Berlin, 1957), 206.
9. Quoted in *Robespierre: Textes choisis*, ed. J. Poperen (3 vols. Paris, 1958), iii. 99.
10. Quoted in C. Lucas, *The Structure of the Terror: The Example of Javogues and the Loire* (Oxford, 1973), 357.

11. Quoted in N. Hampson, *A Concise History of the French Revolution* (London, 1975), 139.
12. Quoted in Rudé, *The Crowd in the French Revolution*, 133.

## Chapter 12. Thermidor, 1794–1795

1. Quoted in R. Cobb, *Les Armées révolutionnaires* (2 vols., Paris, 1963), ii. 856.
2. Quoted in *Robespierre: Textes choisis*, iii. 112–15.
3. Quoted in Stephens, *Orators*, ii. 508.
4. Quoted ibid. ii. 563.
5. Quoted in de la Gorce, *Histoire religieuse*, iii. 503.
6. Quoted in Thompson, *English Witnesses*, 254.
7. Quoted ibid. 248.
8. Quoted in Schmidt, *Tableaux*, ii. 244.
9. Quoted ibid. 240.
10. *Journal de Celestin Guittard de Floriban, bourgeois de Paris sous la Révolution*, ed. R. Aubert (Paris, 1974), 495.
11. Thompson, *English Witnesses*, 257–8.
12. Schmidt, *Tableaux*, ii. 302.
13. *Journal de Guittard*, 506.
14. Ibid. 514.

## Chapter 13. Counter-Revolution, 1789–1795

1. Quoted in Lacour-Gayet, *Calonne*, 283–4.
2. Quoted ibid. 283.
3. Quoted by N. Hampson in F. Lebrun and R. Dupuy (eds.), *Les Résistances à la Révolution* (Paris, 1987), 446.
4. Quoted in Legg, *Select Documents*, ii. 135.
5. Quoted in J. Vidalenc, *Les Émigrés français 1789–1825* (Caen, 1963), 77.
6. *Mémoires d'outre-Tombe* (Paris, 1961 edn.), 282.
7. Quoted in Vidalenc, *Les Émigrés*, 156.
8. Quoted in H. Mitchell, *The Underground War Against Revolutionary France* (Oxford, 1965), 34.
9. Quoted in M. G. Hutt, *Chouannerie and Counter-Revolution: Puisaye, The Princes and the British Government in the 1790s* (2 vols., Cambridge, 1983), ii. 227.
10. Quoted in P. Mansell, *Louis XVIII* (London, 1981), 79.
11. Quoted in W. R. Fryer, *Republic or Restoration in France? 1794–97* (Manchester, 1965), 36.

## Chapter 14. The Directory, 1795–1799

1. Quoted in P. H. Beik (ed.), *The French Revolution* (London, 1970), 317–18.
2. Schmidt, *Tableaux*, ii. 338.
3. *Journal de Guittard*, 575.
4. Quoted in A. Soboul, *Le Directoire et le Consulat* (Paris, 1967), 25.
5. *Memoirs of Theobald Wolfe Tone*, ed. W. T. W. Tone (2 vols., London, 1827), i. 214, 216.

6. Schmidt, *Tableaux*, iii. 95.
7. Quoted in R. B. Rose, *Gracchus Babeuf: The First Revolutionary Communist* (London, 1978), 239.
8. Quoted by M. Lyons, *France under the Directory* (Cambridge, 1975), 47.
9. Quoted by C. Lucas in G. Lewis and C. Lucas (eds.), *Beyond the Terror* (Cambridge, 1983), 183.
10. Quoted in I. Woloch, *Jacobin Legacy: The Democratic Movement under the Directory* (Princeton, 1970), 197.
11. Quoted in *Letters and Documents of Napoleon*, ed. J. E. Howard (London, 1961), 205, 210.

## Chapter 15. Occupied Europe, 1794–1799

1. *Memoirs*, ii. 25–6.
2. Quoted in Schama, *Patriots and Liberators*, 354.
3. Quoted ibid. 370.
4. Quoted in J. Godechot, *La Grande Nation* (2 vols., Paris, 1956), ii. 541.
5. Quoted ibid. i. 91.
6. Quoted in T. C. W. Blanning, *The French Revolution in Germany* (Oxford, 1983), 87.
7. Quoted ibid. 304.
8. Quoted in R. R. Palmer, *The Age of the Democratic Revolution*, ii: *The Struggle* (Princeton, 1964), 413.
9. Quoted ibid. 417.
10. Quoted in Blanning, *French Revolution in Germany*, 330.
11. *Letters and Documents of Napoleon*, 122.
12. Ibid. 186.
13. Quoted in Godechot, *La Grande Nation*, ii. 563.
14. Quoted ibid. ii. 465.
15. Quoted in Acton, *Bourbons of Naples*, 389.
16. Quoted in S. J. Woolf, *A History of Italy 1700–1860* (London, 1979), 186.
17. Quoted in T. Pakenham, *The Year of Liberty* (London, 1969), 351.

## Chapter 16. An End to Revolution, 1799–1802

1. Quoted by C. H. Church, 'In Search of the Directory', in Bosher, *French Government and Society*, 286.
2. Quoted in J. Godechot, *The Counter-Revolution: Doctrine and Action 1789–1804* (London, 1971), 344.
3. *Letters and Documents of Napoleon*, 203.
4. Quoted in J. Godechot, *Les Institutions de la France sous la Révolution et l'Empire* (Paris, 1968), 555.
5. Adapted from *Letters and Documents of Napoleon*, 323.
6. Quoted in A. Fugier, *Histoire des relations internationales*, iv: *La Révolution française et l'empire Napoléonien* (Paris, 1954), 153.
7. Quoted in Godechot, *Counter-Revolution*, 365–6.
8. Quoted ibid. 364.

9. Quoted by M. J. Sydenham, 'The Crime of 3 Nîvose (24 December 1800)', in Bosher, *French Government and Society*, 300.
10. Quoted ibid. 306.
11. Quoted in A. Latreille, *L'Église catholique et la Révolution française* (2 vols., Paris, 1946), i. 229.
12. Quoted in Blanning, *French Revolution in Germany*, 224–5.
13. Quoted in F. M. H. Markham, *Napoleon* (London, 1963), 92–3.

## Chapter 17. The Revolution in Perspective

1. *The Diary of Fanny Burney: A Selection*, ed. L. Gibbs (London, 1940), 347–8.
2. Quoted in C. Maxwell, *The English Traveller in France, 1698–1815* (London, 1932), 219.
3. *Mémoires de Malouet* (2 vols., Paris, 1874), ii. 10.
4. Quoted in M. Wiener, *The French Exiles, 1789–1815* (London, 1960), 44–5.
5. Quoted by R. Forster, 'The Survival of the Nobility during the French Revolution', *Past and Present*, 37 (1967), 83.
6. Quoted in J. McManners, *The French Revolution and the Church* (London, 1969), 33.
7. Quoted in Latreille, *L'Église catholique et la Révolution*, ii. 38–9.
8. Swinburne, *Courts of Europe*, ii. 114–15.
9. Quoted in F. Aftalion, *L'Économie de la Révolution française* (Paris, 1987), 247.
10. Swinburne, *Courts of Europe*, ii. 105–6.
11. Quoted in M. P. Fitzsimmons, *The Parisian Order of Barristers and the French Revolution* (Cambridge, Mass., 1987), 65.
12. Quoted in R. L. Stein, *Leger Félicité Sonthonax: The Lost Sentinel of the Republic* (London, 1985), 76.
13. *Clausewitz: On War*, ed. A. Rapoport (London, 1968), 384–6.
14. Quoted in D. Mack Smith (ed.), *The Making of Italy, 1796–1870* (New York, 1968), 15.
15. Malouet, *Memoires*, ii. 11.
16. Quoted by O. H. Hufton, 'The Reconstruction of a Church 1796–1801', in Lewis and Lucas, *Beyond the Terror*, 48.
17. Quoted by H. B. Applewhite and D. G. Levy, 'Women, Democracy and Revolution in Paris, 1789–1794', In S. A. Spencer (ed.), *French Women and the Age of Enlightenment* (Bloomington, 1984), 75.

# APPENDIX 1

# Chronology of the French Revolution

| | |
|---|---|
| 1756–1763 | Seven Years War. |
| 1762 | Publication of Rousseau's *Emile* and *Du contrat social*. |
| 1764 | Expulsion of Jesuits. |
| 1768 | Corsica annexed. |
| 1770 | Marriage of dauphin (future Louis XVI) to Marie Antoinette. Partial bankruptcy of Terray. |
| 1771 | Remodelling of parlements by Maupeou. |
| 1774 | |
| 10 May | Accession of Louis XVI. |
| 24 Aug. | Dismissal of Maupeou and Terray. Reintegration of parlements follows. |
| 1775 | |
| Apr.–May | 'Flour War'. |
| 11 June | Coronation of Louis XVI. |
| 1776 | |
| 4 July | American Declaration of Independence. |
| 22 Oct. | Necker joins government. |
| 1778 | Franco-American alliance. War with Great Britain. Death of Voltaire and Rousseau. Necker establishes two 'provincial administrations'. |
| 1781 | |
| 19 Feb. | Necker's *Compte rendu*. |
| 19 May | Necker resigns from government. |
| 1783 | Peace of Paris. |
| 3 Nov. | Calonne appointed Comptroller-General of Finances. |
| 1784 | Death of Diderot. |
| 1785 | Necker's *Administration of the Finances*. |
| 1786 | Anglo-French commercial treaty. |
| 20 Aug. | Calonne presents reform proposals to Louis XVI. |
| 1787 | |
| 22 Feb. | Assembly of Notables convenes. |
| 8 Apr. | Calonne dismissed. Brienne joins government (30th). |
| 25 May | Assembly of Notables dissolved. |

| | |
|---|---|
| Aug. | Exile of parlements of Paris and Bordeaux. |
| 13 Sept. | Prussian invasion of Dutch Republic. |
| 19 Nov. | Royal Session in parlement of Paris. |

**1788**

| | |
|---|---|
| 8 May | Lamoignon remodels parlements. |
| June/July | Noble revolt. Day of Tiles in Grenoble (7 June). Assembly of the three orders of Dauphiné at Vizille (21 July). |
| Aug. | Estates-General convoked for May 1789 (8th). Payments from treasury suspended (16th). Brienne resigns; Necker reappointed (24th–26th). |
| Sept. | Parlements restored. Paris parlement demands 'forms of 1614' (25th). |
| 5 Oct.–12 Dec. | Second Assembly of Notables. |
| 27 Dec. | Doubling of third estate. |

**1789**

| | |
|---|---|
| 24 Jan. | Estates-General formally summoned. |
| Feb–June | Elections to Estates-General. |
| Feb. | Publication of Sieyès's *What is the Third Estate?* |
| 27–8 Apr. | Reveillon riots. |
| 5 May | Estates-General convene. |
| June | Third estate votes for common verification of credentials (10th). First parish priests break ranks (13th). National Assembly proclaimed (17th). Tennis Court Oath (20th). Royal Session (23rd). Orders unite (27th). |
| July | Necker dismissed (11th). Bastille falls (14th). Necker recalled; troops withdrawn (16th). Foulon and Bertier murdered (22nd). |
| Late July | Great Fear. |
| Aug. | Abolition of feudalism and privileges (4th). Renunciations of 4th codified (11th). Declaration of Rights of Man and the Citizen (26th). |
| Sept. | Second chamber rejected (10th). Suspensive veto (11th). |
| Oct. | October Days; Louis XVI and National Assembly move to Paris (5th–6th). Martial Law against Tumults (21st). |
| Nov. | Church property nationalized (2nd). Deputies excluded from government (7th). |
| 12 Dec. | Assignats introduced. |

**1790**

| | |
|---|---|
| Feb. | Monastic vows forbidden (13th). Execution of Favras (19th). |
| 12 Apr. | Dom Gerle's motion on established religion. |
| May | Sections of Paris established (21st). Foreign conquests renounced (22nd). |
| June | *Bagarre* at Nîmes (13th). Nobility abolished (19th). |
| July | Civil Constitution of the Clergy (12th). Feast of the Federation (14th). |

| | |
|---|---|
| Aug. | Judiciary reorganized: parlements abolished (16th). Mutiny at Nancy (31st). |
| 27 Nov. | Oath of the clergy. |

1791

| | |
|---|---|
| 3 Jan. | Roll-call on clerical oath. |
| Feb. | Emigration of king's aunts (19th). 'Day of Daggers' (28th). |
| 2 Mar. | Guilds dissolved. |
| Apr. | Death of Mirabeau (2nd). Pope condemns Civil Constitution (13th). Louis XVI prevented from spending Easter at Saint-Cloud (18th). |
| May | Debates on colonies and civil status of free coloureds (7th–15th). Self-denying law (16th). |
| June | Voltaire's ashes placed in Pantheon (11th). Le Chapelier Law (14th). Flight to Varennes (20th). |
| July | Leopold II's Padua Circular (10th). Reinstatement of Louis XVI (16th). Champ de Mars massacre (17th). |
| Aug. | Slave rebellion in Saint-Domingue (14th). Declaration of Pillnitz (27th). |
| Sept. | Annexation of Avignon. Louis XVI accepts constitution (14th). National Assembly dissolved (30th). |
| Oct. | Legislative Assembly convenes (1st). Brissot's first call for war (20th). |
| Nov. | Decree against *émigrés* (9th). Louis XVI vetoes *émigré* decree (12th). Decree against refractory priests (29th). |
| 19 Dec. | Louis XVI vetoes decree against priests. |

1792

| | |
|---|---|
| 25 Jan. | French ultimatum to Austria. |
| 10 Mar. | Dumouriez joins government. |
| Apr. | War declared on Austria (20th). First use of guillotine (25th). |
| 27 May | New decree against refractories. |
| June | Dismissal of Brissotin ministry; Prussia declares war (13th). Sansculottes invade Tuileries (20th). Lafayette denounces Jacobins (29th). |
| July | Petition of 20,000 (1st). Decree of 'Country in Danger' (11th). 'Country in Danger' proclaimed (22nd). Paris sections in permanent session; Brunswick Manifesto (25th). Marseilles *fédérés* enter Paris (30th). |
| Aug. | Paris sections demand dethronement (3rd). Vindication of Lafayette (8th). Storming of Tuileries; overthrow of the monarchy (10th). Extraordinary tribunal established (17th). Defection of Lafayette; Prussians cross the frontier (19th). Fall of Longwy (20th). |
| Sept. | Fall of Verdun (2nd). September Massacres (2nd–6th). Battle of Valmy (20th). Convention meets (21st). Republic proclaimed (22nd). Nice occupied (29th). |

| 10 Oct. | Brissot expelled from Jacobins. |
| Nov. | Battle of Jemappes (6th). Decree of fraternity and help to foreign peoples (19th). *Armoire de fer* discovered (20th). Annexation of Savoy (27th). |
| Dec. | Decision to try Louis XVI (3rd). Interrogation of Louis XVI (11th). Decree on treatment of occupied territories (15th). Defence of Louis XVI (26th). |

**1793**

| Jan. | Condemnation of Louis XVI (7th). Death sentence on Louis XVI (16th). Vote against reprieve (18th). Le Peletier assassinated (20th). Execution of Louis XVI (21st). Second partition of Poland (23rd). |
| Feb. | War declared on Great Britain and Dutch Republic (1st). Amalgamation of volunteer and line regiments (21st). Decree conscripting 300,000 men (24th). Food riots in Paris (25th–27th). |
| Mar. | War declared on Spain (7th). Revolutionary Tribunal created (10th). Revolt in the Vendée (11th). Battle of Neerwinden (18th). Revolutionary Armies decreed; revolutionary committees created (21st). |
| Apr. | Dumouriez defects (5th). Committee of Public Safety created (6th). Assignats made sole legal tender (11th). Marat sent for trial (13th). Marat acquitted (24th). 'Federalist' uprising in Marseilles (29th). |
| May | First maximum decreed (4th). Forced loan on the rich; Commission of Twelve appointed (20th). Chalier overthrown in Lyons (30th). First anti-Girondin uprising in Paris (31st). |
| June | Purge of Girondins from Convention (2nd). Spread of 'Federalist revolt' to Bordeaux and Caen (7th). Vendéans capture Saumur (9th). Constitution of 1793 accepted (24th). |
| July | Danton leaves Committee of Public Safety (10th). Marat assassinated (13th). Final abolition of feudalism (17th). Fall of Mainz (23rd). Death penalty for hoarding (26th). Robespierre joins Committee of Public Safety (27th). |
| Aug. | Decree of *levée en masse* (23rd). Marseilles recaptured (25th). Toulon surrenders to the British (27th). |
| Sept. | Convention forced to implement government by terror (5th). Battle of Hondschoote; first French victory in 1793 (8th). Law of Suspects (17th). Year II begins (22nd). General maximum introduced (29th). |
| Oct. | Girondins sent for trial (3rd). Revolutionary calendar introduced (5th). Fall of Lyons (9th). Revolutionary Government declared (10th; 19th vendémiaire). Battle of Wattignies; Marie Antoinette executed (16th). Vendéans |

defeated at Cholet (17th). Trial of Girondins (24th–30th). Execution of Girondins (31st).

Nov.    Festival of reason in Notre-Dame (10th; 20 brumaire). Vendéans retreat from Granville (13th). All Parisian churches closed (22nd).

Dec.    Law constituting Revolutionary Government (4th; 14 frimaire). First issue of *Vieux Cordelier* (5th). Vendéans defeated at Le Mans (12th). Fall of Toulon after British evacuation (19th). Vendéans defeated at Savenay (23rd).

## 1794

12 Jan. (23 nivôse)  Fabre d'Eglantine arrested.

Feb.    Abolition of slavery (4th). Price controls revised (21st). First Law of Ventôse (26th; 8 ventôse).

Mar.    Second Law of Ventôse (3rd; 13 ventôse). Arrest of Hébertists (13th). Hébertists executed (24th). Revolutionary Armies disbanded (27th).

Apr.    Danton and Desmoulins executed (5th; 16 germinal). Rousseau's ashes moved to Pantheon (14th).

June    British naval victory, 'Glorious First of June' (1st; 13 prairial). Festival of the Supreme Being (8th; 20 prairial). Law of 22 prairial (10th). Battle of Fleurus (26th).

July    Wage controls introduced in Paris (5th; 17 messidor). Fall of Robespierre (27th–28th; 9–10 thermidor).

Aug.    Law of 22 Prairial repealed (1st; 14 thermidor). Revolutionary Tribunal reorganized (10th). Reorganization of government (24th).

Sept.    Trial of Nantes Federalists (8th). State renounces all subsidies to religion (18th; 2nd complementary day). Year III begins (22nd).

Nov.    Jacobin Club closed (12th; 22 brumaire). Carrier sent for trial (23rd).

Dec.    Reinstatement of surviving Girondins (8th; 18 frimaire). Execution of Carrier (16th). Maximum abolished; invasion of Holland (24th).

## 1795

20 Jan. (1 pluviôse)  Amsterdam occupied.

Feb.    Pacification of Lajaunye in Vendée (17th; 29 pluviôse). Freedom of worship restored (21st).

Mar.    Arrest of Barère, Billaud-Varenne, Collot d'Herbois (2nd; 12 ventôse). Fouquier-Tinville sent for trial (28th).

Apr.    Uprising of Germinal (1st–2nd; 12–13 germinal). Treaty of Basle concluded with Prussia (5th). Disarmament of 'terrorists' (10th). Peace concluded with *chouans* at La Prévalaye (20th).

May    Prison massacre at Lyons (4th; 15 floréal). Fouquier-Tinville executed (6th). Treaty of The Hague concluded with Batavian Republic (16th). Uprising of Prairial (20th–23rd; 1–4 prairial). Revolutionary Tribunal abolished (31st).

June          Death of Louis XVII (8th; 20 prairial). Declaration of Verona (24th). Royalists land at Quiberon (27th).

July           Quiberon invasion defeated (21st; 3 thermidor). Treaty of Basle concluded with Spain (22nd).

22 Aug. (5 fructidor)   Constitution of the Year III and Two Thirds Law approved.

23 Sept. (I vendémiaire)   Year IV begins; constitution and Two Thirds Law promulgated.

Oct.           Annexation of Belgium (1st; 9 vendémiaire). Uprising of Vendémiaire (5th). End of Convention (26th).

Nov.          Directory constituted (2nd; 11 brumaire). Pantheon Club opened (16th).

10 Dec. (19 frimaire)   Forced loan.

## 1796

Feb.          Abolition of assignats (19th; 30 pluviôse). Stofflet executed (25th). Pantheon Club closed (27th).

Mar.         Bonaparte appointed commander in Italy (2nd; 12 ventôse). Territorial mandates issued (18th). Charette executed (29th).

Apr.          Invasion of Italy (11th; 22 germinal). Armistice with Piedmont; Police Legion mutiny (28th).

May          Battle of Lodi; Arrest of Babeuf (10th; 21 floréal). Anti-French rising in Pavia (23rd).

12 June (24 prairial)   Papal territory invaded.

5 Aug. (18 thermidor)   Battle of Castiglione; alliance with Spain.

Sept.         Grenelle uprising (9th; 23 fructidor). Year V begins (22nd).

Oct.          Peace overtures from Great Britain. Cispadane Republic created (16th; 25 vendémiaire).

15–18 Nov. (25–7 brumaire)   Battle of Arcole.

15 Dec. (25 frimaire)   Irish expedition sails.

## 1797

Jan.          Withdrawal of Irish expedition (6th; 18 nivôse). Battle of Rivoli (14th).

Feb.          Mantua falls (2nd; 14 pluviôse). Return to metallic currency (4th). British naval victory at St Vincent (14th). Treaty of Tolentino with the Pope; Babeuf's trial begins at Vendôme (19th).

18 Apr. (29 germinal)   Preliminaries of Leoben; elections of Year V.

May          Venetian Republic occupied (15th; 27 floréal). Councils convene; Barthélemy enters Directory (20th). Execution of Babeuf (27th).

29 June (11 messidor)   Cisalpine Republic created.

July                  Ministries reshuffled (16th; 28 messidor). Political clubs
                      closed. (25th).
24 Aug.               Laws against clergy repealed.
Sept.                 Coup d'état of Fructidor (4th; 18 fructidor). Carnot and
                      Barthélemy removed from Directory (5th). British peace
                      overtures rejected (17th). Year VI begins (22nd).
                      Consolidation of Two Thirds Debt (30th).
Oct.                  British naval victory at Camperdown (11th; 20
                      vendémiaire). Peace of Campo Formio (18th; 26
                      vendémiaire).
28 Nov. (8 frimaire)  Congress of Rastadt opens.
8 Dec.                Ochs meets Bonaparte and Reubell.

1798
Jan.                  Dutch Convention purged (22nd; 3 pluviôse). Annexation
                      of Mulhouse (28th). Law on elections (31st; 21 pluviôse).
Feb.                  Roman Republic proclaimed (15th; 27 pluviôse). Alliance
                      with Cisalpine Republic (21st).
Mar.                  Egyptian expedition approved (5th). Helvetic Republic
                      proclaimed; elections of Year VI (22nd).
May                   Coup d'état of Floréal (11th; 22 floréal). Treilhard joins
                      Directory. (16th). Egyptian expedition leaves (19th).
                      Uprising in Ireland (21st).
10 June (22 prairial) Fall of Malta.
1 July (13 messidor)  Bonaparte lands in Egypt.
Aug.                  Battle of the Nile (1st; 14 thermidor). Humbert lands in
                      Ireland (22nd).
Sept.                 Jourdan Law on conscription (5th; 19 fructidor). Turkish
                      declaration of war; Surrender of Humbert at Ballinamuck
                      (9th). Year VII begins (22nd).
12 Oct. (21 vendemiaire)  Peasants' War in Belgium begins.
25 Nov. (5 frimaire)  Neapolitans take Rome.

1799
Jan.                  French take Naples (23rd; 4 pluviôse). Parthenopean
                      Republic proclaimed (26th).
Mar.                  Austria declares war (12th; 22 ventôse). Battle of Stokach
                      (25th).
Apr.                  Elections of Year VII. Pope brought to France (10th).
                      Suvorov takes Milan (28th).
9 May (20 floréal)    Reubell retires from Directory.
June                  Sieyès assumes power as a Director (9th; 21 prairial). Coup
                      d'état of 30 Prairial (18th). Forced loan (27th).
July                  Manège Club founded (6th; 18 messidor). Law of Hostages
                      (12th).
Aug.                  Royalist uprising around Toulouse (5th; 18 thermidor).
                      Manège Club closed (13th). Joubert killed at Novi (15th).

|  | Bonaparte leaves Egypt (22nd). Anglo-Russian force lands in Holland (27th). |
| Sept. | Rejection of Jourdan's 'Country in Danger' motion (13th; 27 fructidor). Year VIII begins (23rd). |
| Oct. | Bonaparte lands in France (9th; 17 vendémiaire). Bonaparte reaches Paris (16th). Anglo-Russian invaders evacuate Holland (18th). |
| Nov. | Bonaparte overthrows the Directory (9th–10th; 18–19 brumaire). Law of Hostages repealed (13th). |
| 25 Dec. | Constitution of Year VIII comes into force. |

**1800**

| 13 Jan. (23 nivôse) | Bank of France established. |
| Feb. | Referendum results published (7th; 18 pluviôse). Prefects established (17th). |
| 15–23 May (25 floréal) | Bonaparte crosses the Alps. |
| 14 June (25 prairial) | Battle of Marengo. |
| 2 July (13 messidor) | Bonaparte returns to Paris. |
| 23 Sept. | Year IX begins. |
| Dec. | Battle of Hohenlinden (3rd; 12 frimaire). Attempted assassination of Bonaparte (24th; 3 nivôse). |

**1801**

| 5 Jan. (15 nivôse) | Proscription of Jacobins. |
| Feb. | Peace of Lunéville (9th; 20 pluviôse). British peace overtures (21st). |
| 23 Mar. | Assassination of Paul I. |
| 2 Apr. | Battle of Copenhagen. |
| 16 July (17 messidor) | Concordat signed. |
| 23 Sept. | Year X begins. |

**1802**

| 27 Mar. | Peace of Amiens. |
| Apr. | Purge of Tribunate and Legislative Body (1st; 10 germinal). Organic Articles added to Concordat (8th). Promulgation of Concordat (18th). |

# APPENDIX 2

# The Revolutionary Calendar

INTRODUCED in October 1793 and dating from 22 September, the anniversary of the declaration of the Republic, the calendar remained in official use until 1806. The names of its months, invented by Fabre d'Eglantine, were intended to evoke the seasons, but defy easy translation. Scornful British contemporaries, however, rendered them: Slippy, Nippy, Drippy; Freezy, Wheezy, Sneezy; Showery, Flowery, Bowery; Heaty, Wheaty, Sweety. Twelve thirty-day months left five days over. These days were originally called *sansculottides*, but under the Directory were re-labelled complementary days. A concordance between the revolutionary and Gregorian calendars appears on the following page.

| Month | Revolutionary year | | | | | | | |
|---|---|---|---|---|---|---|---|---|
| | II | III | IV | V | VI | VII | VIII | IX |
| 1 vendémiaire | 22 Sept. 1793 | 22 Sept. 1794 | 23 Sept. 1795 | 22 Sept. 1796 | 22 Sept. 1797 | 22 Sept. 1798 | 23 Sept. 1799 | 23 Sept. 1800 |
| 10 | 1 Oct. 1793 | 1 Oct. 1794 | 2 Oct. 1795 | 1 Oct. 1796 | Oct. 1797 | 1 Oct. 1798 | 2 Oct. 1799 | 2 Oct. 1800 |
| 20 | 11 | 11 | 12 | 11 | 11 | 11 | 12 | 12 |
| 1 brumaire | 22 | 22 | 23 | 22 | 22 | 22 | 23 | 23 |
| 10 | 31 | 31 | 1Nov. 1795 | 31 | 31 | 31 | 1 Nov. 1799 | 1 Nov. 1800 |
| 20 | 10 Nov. 1793 | 10 Nov. 1794 | 11 | 10 Nov. 1796 | 10 Nov. 1797 | 10 Nov. 1798 | 11 | 11 |
| 1 frimaire | 21 | 21 | 22 | 21 | 21 | 21 | 22 | 22 |
| 10 | 30 | 30 | 1 Dec. 1795 | 30 | 30 | 30 | 1 Dec. 1799 | 1 Dec. 1800 |
| 20 | 10 Dec. 1793 | 10 Dec. 1794 | 11 | 10 Dec. 1796 | 10 Dec. 1797 | 10 Dec. 1798 | 11 | 11 |
| 1 nivôse | 21 | 21 | 22 | 21 | 21 | 21 | 22 | 22 |
| 10 | 30 | 30 | 31 | 30 | 30 | 30 | 31 | 31 |
| 20 | 9 Jan. 1794 | 9 Jan. 1795 | 10 Jan. 1796 | 9 Jan. 1797 | 9 Jan. 1798 | 9 Jan. 1799 | 10 Jan. 1800 | 10 Jan. 1801 |
| 1 pluviôse | 20 | 20 | 21 | 20 | 20 | 20 | 21 | 21 |
| 10 | 29 | 29 | 30 | 29 | 29 | 29 | 30 | 30 |
| 20 | 8 Feb. 1974 | 8 Feb. 1795 | 9 Feb. 1796 | 8 Feb. 1797 | 8 Feb. 1798 | 8 Feb. 1799 | 9 Feb. 1800 | 9 Feb. 1801 |
| 1 ventôse | 19 | 19 | 20 | 19 | 19 | 19 | 20 | 20 |
| 10 | 28 | 28 | 29 | 28 | 28 | 28 | Mar. 1800 | 1 Mar. 1801 |
| 20 | 10 Mar. 1794 | 10 Mar. 1795 | 10 Mar. 1796 | 10 Mar. 1797 | 10 Mar. 1798 | 10 Mar. 1799 | 11 | 11 |
| 1 germinal | 21 | 21 | 21 | 21 | 21 | 21 | 22 | 22 |
| 10 | 30 | 30 | 30 | 30 | 30 | 30 | 31 | 31 |
| 20 | 9 Apr. 1794 | 9 Apr. 1795 | 9 Apr. 1796 | 9 Apr. 1797 | 9 Apr. 1798 | 9 Apr. 1799 | 10 Apr. 1800 | 10 Apr. 1801 |
| 1 floréal | 20 | 20 | 20 | 20 | 20 | 20 | 21 | 21 |
| 10 | 29 | 29 | 29 | 29 | 29 | 29 | 30 | 30 |
| 20 | 9 May 1794 | 9 May 1795 | 9 May 1796 | May 1797 | 9 May 1798 | 9 May 1799 | 10 May 1800 | 10 May 1801 |
| 1 prairial | 20 | 20 | 20 | 20 | 20 | 20 | 21 | 21 |
| 10 | 29 | 29 | 29 | 29 | 29 | 29 | 30 | 30 |
| 20 | 8 June 1794 | 8 June 1795 | 8 June 1796 | 8 June 1797 | 8 June 1798 | 8 June 1799 | 9 June 1800 | 9 June 1801 |
| 1 messidor | 19 | 19 | 19 | 19 | 19 | 19 | 20 | 20 |
| 10 | 28 | 28 | 28 | 28 | 28 | 28 | 29 | 29 |
| 20 | 8 July 1794 | 8 July 1795 | 8 July 1796 | 8 July 1797 | 8 July 1798 | 8 July 1799 | 9 July 1800 | 9 July 1801 |
| 1 thermidor | 19 | 19 | 19 | 19 | 19 | 19 | 20 | 20 |
| 10 | 28 | 28 | 28 | 28 | 28 | 28 | 29 | 29 |
| 20 | 7 Aug. 1794 | 7 Aug. 1795 | 7 Aug. 1796 | 7 Aug. 1797 | 7 Aug. 1798 | 7 Aug. 1799 | 8 Aug. 1800 | 8 Aug. 1801 |
| 1 fructidor | 18 | 18 | 18 | 18 | 18 | 18 | 19 | 19 |
| 10 | 27 | 27 | 27 | 27 | 27 | 27 | 28 | 28 |
| 20 | 6 Sept. 1794 | 6 Sept. 1795 | 6 Sept. 1796 | 6 Sept. 1797 | 6 Sept. 1798 | 6 Sept. 1799 | 7 Sept. 1800 | 7 Sept. 1801 |
| 1st complementary day | 17 | 17 | 17 | 17 | 17 | 17 | 18 | 18 |
| 5th | 21 | 21 | 21 | 21 | 21 | 21 | 22 | 22 |
| 6th | | 22 | | | | 22 | | |

# Bibliography

EVERY aspect of the French Revolution has aroused controversy. Most of the statements in this book represent judgements made between interpretations often wildly at odds, but to justify them all in academic terms would have demanded a different sort of book. In any case there is no shortage of readily available works through which the full range of issues raised by the Revolution can be followed. The main problem, in fact, is their sheer quantity. It is said that more is published every year on this subject than on the rest of early modern French history put together, and the bicentenary in 1989 has produced a new surge. All that can be attempted here is to indicate some of the more significant contributions to the study of the Revolution, many of which have important bibliographies of their own, or indicate their sources in learned footnotes.

The most up-to-date, well-researched, and stimulating general survey is at present D. M. G. Sutherland, *France 1789–1815: Revolution and Counter-Revolution* (London, 1985). Its bibliography is also extensive and excellent. It takes full account of the extraordinary outburst of research among English-speaking scholars which over the last generation has transformed the contours of the subject. How it looked before that can be studied in A. Soboul, *The French Revolution, 1787–1799* (2 vols., London, 1974), where the last great left-wing French master of the subject distilled a lifetime's learning and conviction. The greatest treatment in that classic tradition remains A. Mathiez, *The French Revolution* (London, 1928), and its sequel *After Robespierre* (New York, 1929)— wonderful polemical writing by a passionate admirer of Robespierre. Dominating French work on the subject for much of this century, the left-wing view had, however, begun to be challenged in France even before the work of 'Anglo-Saxons' made its impact. The book which did so, in 1965, was F. Furet and D. Richet, *The French Revolution* (abridged, London, 1970). A brief, thoughtful, and still stimulating overview of changing perceptions of the subject is J. M. Roberts, *The French Revolution* (Oxford, 1978).

The origins of the Revolution are a field in themselves. The classic treatment is G. Lefebvre, *The Coming of the French Revolution* (Princeton, 1947), the best general work by the other great twentieth-century master whose detailed researches underlie much of what subsequent scholars have achieved. His conclusions have dated, however. W. Doyle, *Origins of the French Revolution* (2nd edn., Oxford, 1988), offers a more recent interpretation, prefaced by a full account of how and why the classic picture came to be modified. Intellectual aspects of the origins of the Revolution are currently commanding renewed attention. The leading pioneer of this revival is R. Darnton, whose most seminal writings are collected in *The Literary Underground of the Old Regime* (Cambridge, Mass., 1982).

For the politics of 1787–8, J. Egret, *The French Pre-Revolution, 1787–88* (Chicago, 1977), remains definitive, but the first phase of the Revolution down to

1792 is ripe for reappraisal. There are no reasonable, up-to-date surveys, but N. Hampson's reflective *Prelude to Terror* (Oxford, 1988) should rekindle interest. The story is taken up with critical detachment from the fall of the monarchy, by M. J. Sydenham, *The First French Republic 1792–1804* (London, 1974). Lefebvre covered the period 1794–9 magisterially in *The Thermidoreans* and *The Directory* (New York, 1964), but again his views have dated. M. Lyons, *France under the Directory* (Cambridge, 1975), drew on much subsequent research in what is still a fast-expanding field. The directions in which it is moving may be sampled in G. Lewis and C. Lucas (eds.), *Beyond the Terror: Essays in French Regional and Social History 1794–1815* (Cambridge, 1983). The Consulate forms part of *France under Napoleon* by L. Bergeron (Princeton, 1981), while questions of current interest are indicated in the excellent bibliography of the otherwise ordinary J. Tulard, *Napoleon: The Myth of the Saviour* (London, 1984).

The debate on the Revolution in our own day was begun by Alfred Cobban. His many shorter contributions to the subject are collected in *Aspects of the French Revolution* (London, 1968). The full sweep of his attack on orthodoxy appeared, however, only with *The Social Interpretation of the French Revolution* (Cambridge, 1964). Essential reading for French historical polemics is F. Furet, *Interpreting the French Revolution* (Cambridge, 1981). The most up-to-date brief appraisal of what these debates have established is T. C. W. Blanning, *The French Revolution: Aristocrats versus Bourgeois?* (London, 1988). The theoretical issues are discussed in the difficult but rewarding G. Comninel, *Rethinking the French Revolution: Marxism and the Revisionist Challenge* (London, 1987). Some of the most important articles are collected in D. Johnson (ed.), *French Society and the Revolution* (Cambridge, 1976), but unanthologized as yet is the crucial G. V. Taylor, 'Noncapitalist Wealth and the Origins of the French Revolution', *American Historical Review*, 79 (1967), 469–96.

The best short introduction to the religious history of the Revolution is J. McManners, *The French Revolution and the Church* (London, 1969). But this area is now being renewed, beginning with an outstanding discussion of the great divide by T. Tackett, *Religion, Revolution and Regional Culture in Eighteenth Century France: The Ecclesiastical Oath of 1791* (Princeton, 1986). Wider repercussions are chronicled in O. Chadwick, *The Popes and European Revolution* (Oxford, 1981). A now classic analysis of how religion shaded into counter-revolution is C. Tilly, *The Vendée* (Cambridge, Mass., and London, 1964), but doubt was thrown on some of its suggestions by D. M. G. Sutherland's investigation of a parallel phenomenon, *The Chouans* (Oxford, 1982). The French, too, are now looking again at these once-taboo subjects, but still untranslated are C. Petitfrère, *Les Vendéens d'Anjou* (Paris, 1981), and R. Dupuy, *De la Révolution à la Chouannerie* (Paris, 1988). They make J. Godechot, *The Counter-Revolution: Doctrine and Action 1789–1804* (London, 1971), seem superficial, but the amount of information collected there remains both impressive and convenient.

The most extreme phase of the Revolution has always been well-tilled ground. The easiest introduction to it is N. Hampson's short pamphlet *The Terror in the French Revolution* (London, 1981). There are two translations of A. Soboul's classic treatise on the sansculottes. The fuller, simply entitled *The Sans-Culottes*, came out in New York in 1972. For an overall survey of the so-called popular movement,

G. Rudé, *The Crowd in the French Revolution* (Oxford, 1959), has still to be bettered. To see the sansculottes in action against their enemies, R. Cobb, *The People's Armies* (London, 1987), is incomparable. A brilliantly written essay which sets them alongside their English counterparts is G. A. Williams, *Artisans and Sansculottes* (London, 1968). The political alignments of this period, long deemed self-evident, were fundamentally reappraised in 1961 by M. J. Sydenham, *The Girondins* (London). Even more radical, hard to absorb, but in the end entirely convincing, was the analysis of A. Patrick, *The Men of the First French Republic: Political Alignments and the National Convention of 1792* (Baltimore, 1972). Provincial politics, meanwhile, have been restored to life by the pupils of Richard Cobb. They include W. Scott, *Terror and Repression in Revolutionary Marseilles* (London, 1973), A. Forrest, *Society and Politics in Revolutionary Bordeaux* (Oxford, 1975), C. Lucas, *The Structure of the Terror: The Example of Javogues and the Loire* (Oxford, 1973), G. Lewis, *The Second Vendée: The Continuity of Counter-Revolution in the Department of the Gard 1789–1815* (Oxford, 1978), and M. Lyons, *Revolution in Toulouse: An Essay on Provincial Terrorism* (Berne, 1978).

The economic and social history of the Revolution has always been hard to disentangle from its politics. Nobody has ever translated the greatest work in this field, E. Labrousse, *La Crise de l'économie française à la fin de l'Ancien Régime et au début de la Révolution* (2 vols., Paris, 1944), but there is a new edition (1984). There is still much to be learned, too, from A. Mathiez, *La Vie chère et le mouvement social sous la Terreur* (Paris, 1927). The question of the assignments has recently been reopened by F. Aftalion, *L'Economie de la Révolution française* (Paris, 1987) and of the government's financial agents by M. Bruguière, *Gestionnaires et profiteurs de la Révolution* (Paris, 1986). Economic data also bulk large in a thought-provoking, non-academic analysis of 1987, R. Sédillot, *Le Coût de la Révolution française* (Paris). The most distinguished of all studies of peasants, G. Lefebvre, *Les Paysans du Nord pendant la Révolution française* (Bari, 1959), also remains untranslated, but that brilliant essay, *The Great Fear of 1789: Rural Panic in Revolutionary France* (London, 1973), is available in English. P. Jones, *The Peasantry in the French Revolution* (Cambridge, 1988), summarizes two generations' work in this huge area, while despite some of its questionable assumptions, A. Forrest, *The French Revolution and the Poor* (Oxford, 1981), has reopened a field too long left to Catholic propagandists.

The greatest radicalizing force in the whole Revolution was of course the war. T. C. W. Blanning, *The Origins of the French Revolutionary Wars* (London, 1986), shows convincingly why it began, and was resumed in 1798. Its impact on the French armed forces is assessed in S. F. Scott, *The Response of the Royal Army to the French Revolution: The Role and Development of the Line Army during 1789–93* (Oxford, 1978), and J. A. Lynn, *The Bayonets of the Republic: Motivation and Tactics in the Army of Revolutionary France, 1791–4* (Champaign, Ill., 1984). The French authority on this topic is now J. P. Bertaud, and *The Army of the French Revolution: From Citizen-Soldiers to Instruments of Power* (Princeton, 1988) is perhaps his best work. On French expansion in general J. Godechot, *La Grande Nation: L'Expansion révolutionnaire de la France dans le monde* (2 vols., Paris, 1956), is still irreplaceable. It may be supplemented by volume ii of R. R. Palmer, *The Age of the Democratic Revolution: The Struggle* (Princeton, 1964), despite its curious biases. An epic portrait of the state engulfed by the revolutionary tide is S. Schama, *Patriots and Liberators: Revolution in the Netherlands, 1780–1813* (London, 1977), while T. C. W. Blanning, *The French Revolution in Germany: Occupation and Resistance in the Rhineland, 1792–1802* (Oxford, 1983), is far more widely relevant than its title suggests, with an invaluable synoptic final chapter. Similarly despite its title, D. P. Geggus, *Slavery, War and Revolution: The British Occupation of Saint-Domingue* (Oxford, 1982), is by far the fullest introduction now available to the Revolution's impact on the Caribbean. The best recent study in detail of the relations between France and admirers beyond her military reach is M. Elliott, *Partners in Revolution: The United Irishmen and France* (New Haven, 1982). C. Emsley, *British Society and the French Wars, 1793–1815* (London, 1979), summarizes a wide range of work, and enables striking parallels to be drawn with the French wartime experience.

Most of the great figures of the Revolution have been the subject of biographies, although this approach is no longer as fashionable as it was among professional historians. Yet there is still no good, reliable life of Louis XVI. His last months are better served. D. P. Jordan, *The King's Trial: The French Revolution vs Louis XVI* (Berkeley, 1979), is readable and trustworthy. The biases in P. Girault de Coursac, *Enquête sur le procès de Louis XVI* (Paris, 1982), need constant attention behind the ample documentation. The greatest recent biographical enterprise for a figure of the period is L. Gottschalk's multi-volume *Lafayette* (Chicago, 1950–73). It remains unfinished at mid-1790, and it seems legitimate to ask whether that self-important figure is worth such attention. There is still no good biography of Mirabeau (though several mediocre ones), nothing on Barnave since E. D. Bradby's two volumes (Oxford, 1915), and nothing worthwhile on any of the leading Girondins, apart from G. May, *Madame Roland and the Age of Revolution* (New York, 1970). L. Gershoy, *Bertrand Barère, a Reluctant Terrorist* (Princeton, 1962), tackles an interesting subject. Unusually useful, too, are two volumes of collective biography: R. R. Palmer, *Twelve who Ruled* (Princeton, 1941), on the members of the great Committee of Public Safety, and N. Hampson, *Will and circumstance: Montesquieu, Rousseau and the French Revolution* (London, 1983), which is mostly about the intellectual development of various revolutionaries, and is the most sensible treatment on, among others, Brissot and Marat. M. Reinhard, *Le Grand Carnot* (2 vols., Paris, 1950–2), and G. Walter, *Hébert et le Père Duchesne* (Paris, 1946), are authoritative on their subjects, while N. Hampson, *Danton* (London, 1978), summarizes what little reliable evidence there is on that enigmatic figure. Decent books on Robespierre abound. Among them, the fullest is by J. M. Thompson (2 vols., Oxford, 1939), and the most stimulating, N. Hampson's masterpiece *The Life and Opinions of Maximilien Robespierre* (London, 1974). Napoleon's life has been even more fully chronicled, and continues to be analysed from every conceivable angle. By far the best brief summary is still F. M. H. Markham, *Napoleon* (London, 1963).

The obsession of historians over the last generation with the social interpretation of the Revolution appears to be running out of steam. Whether any dominant issue will come to replace it is far from clear as yet. A number of scholars have grown interested recently in the language and rhetoric of the Revolution. W. H. Sewell, *Work and Revolution in France* (Cambridge, 1980), explores these themes. So does one of the essays in L. A. Hunt, *Politics, Culture and Class in the French*

*Revolution* (Berkeley, 1984), but the author looks at symbolism and electoral behaviour, too, drawing important conclusions about both. Perhaps the most comprehensive guide to how the study of the Revolution stands at present among scholars is to be found in the published proceedings of two conferences marking the bicentenary on the theme of *The French Revolution and the Creation of Modern Political Culture.* Volume i, edited by K. M. Baker, covers the political culture of the old regime (Oxford, 1987). Volume ii, edited by Colin Lucas, discusses the political culture of the Revolution proper (Oxford, 1988). Both have contributions from many of the leading historians in the field, and mark a new level of communication and co-operation between French scholars and those writing in English.

The most comprehensive work of reference is S. F. Scott and B. Rothaus (eds.), *Historical Dictionary of the French Revolution* (2 vols., Westport, Conn., 1985), although the quality of the entries is uneven and there are some strange omissions. More compact is C. Jones, *The Longman Companion to the French Revolution* (London, 1989). The biographical glossary to Sydenham's *First French Republic* is also useful, and there is much revolutionary material in J. Tulard (ed.), *Dictionnaire Napoléon* (Paris, 1987). The historiography of the subject is a subject in itself. J. Godechot, *Un jury pour la Révolution* (Paris, 1974), is sound on French works but does less than justice to what has been written in English. P. Farmer, *France Reviews its Revolutionary Origins: Social Politics and Historical Opinion in the Third Republic* (New York, 1944), puts historical debates in context. G. Rudé, *Interpretations of the French Revolution* (London, 1961), is a convenient distillation down to the moment when the great debate of the 1960s and 1970s was about to open. The first chapter of Doyle, *Origins of the French Revolution*, covers writing on those origins since 1939.

As noted earlier, most of these works are rich in references and bibliography. An attempt is made to collect most significant titles in English by W. Doyle, *The French Revolution: A Bibliography of Works in English* (London, 1988). A fuller survey is R. J. Caldwell, *The Era of the French Revolution: A Bibliography of Western Civilisation* (New York and London, 1985).

# Index

Aachen 171
Abbaye 191
Abbeville 12, 260
Académie française 30, 47, 50
academies 15, 25, 47–8, 411
active citizens 124, 129, 142, 420
Adams, John (1735–1826) 63
Addington, Henry (1757–1844) 380–1
Adige 214, 361
Adriatic 214, 381
Africa 13, 182, 286
Agen 373
Agrarian law 419
Agriculture 5, 6, 9–12, 57–8, 70, 405, 424
Aiguillon, Armand Desiré du Plessis—
    Richelieu d'Agenois, Duke d' (1761–1800)
    116
Aisne 194
Aix 7, 72, 142, 182, 230, 292, 305, 390
Alba 356, 357
Alembert, Jean Le Rond d' (1717–83) 51
Alexandria 338
Alfieri, Vittorio (1749–1803) 44
Alps 200, 213, 231, 249, 315, 338, 354,
    355, 356, 360, 374, 379, 381
Alsace 2, 8, 9, 10, 115, 129, 145, 351, 411
amalgamation 205
Amar, André (1755–1816) 273, 279, 283
America 2, 32, 46, 62–4, 66, 118, 159,
    160, 164, 169, 206, 278, 304, 424
Amiens 12, 381, 389, 391
Amsterdam 345
André, Antoine Balthazar Joseph d'
    (1759–1825) 331
Angers 36, 243, 256
Anglophobia 165
Anjou 5
Annates 136, 139
Anticipations 69, 79, 84–5
Antonelli, Leonardo, Cardinal 398
Antraigues, Emile Louis Henri Alexandre de
    Launay, Count d' (1754–1812) 183, 301,
    310–11, 315–16, 327, 328
Apulia 365
Arc, Chevalier d' (1721–95) 30
Arcoli 382
Ardèche 183
Ardennes 302

aristocracy see nobility 81, 120, 125, 156,
    226, 254, 357, 394, 424
Aristotle (384–322 BC) 49
Arles 182, 183, 230, 327
armed neutrality 380
armoire de fer 194, 222
army 30–2, 36, 48, 79, 83, 100, 108, 110,
    147, 156, 168, 173, 177, 183, 184, 187,
    190, 192, 198, 199, 203, 205, 210, 213,
    223, 224, 230, 231, 232, 239, 286, 301,
    304, 320–1, 322, 326, 330, 340, 347,
    352, 353, 355, 356, 357, 361, 364, 368,
    370, 409, 410, 415–6
Arras 25
Artois 25, 93, 95, 109
Artois, Count d' (Charles X) (1757–1836)
    74, 102, 105, 111, 112, 143, 146, 147,
    155, 171, 292, 297, 298, 300, 301, 302,
    305, 306, 307, 309, 312, 313, 314, 317
assignats 133–4, 135, 142, 149, 168, 179,
    182, 192, 199, 223, 240, 265, 276,
    285–6, 290, 319, 322–3, 349, 352,
    402–3, 408, 416
ateliers de charité 15
atheism 51, 141, 168
Atlantic 5, 7, 13, 51, 216, 243, 404
Augereau, Pierre François Charles
    (1757–1816) 217, 330
Aunis 6
Austria 43, 57, 58, 60, 147, 151, 152,
    153, 157, 162, 165, 179, 180, 183, 188,
    193, 197, 201, 202, 204, 206, 208, 211,
    213, 214, 215, 216, 217, 218, 226, 246,
    266, 278, 298, 302, 311, 315, 327, 329,
    331, 338, 346, 351, 354, 355, 356, 357,
    359, 360, 361, 364, 366, 368, 373, 374,
    378, 379, 386, 414, 416, 417, 424
Austrian committee 176–7, 184
Autun 34, 90, 129
Auvergne 16, 130, 175
Avignon 2, 45, 46, 47, 139, 140, 146,
    150, 157, 173, 177, 182, 183, 199, 230,
    243, 249, 292, 387


Babeuf, François Noël (Gracchus) (1760–97)
    131, 287, 290, 324–6, 327, 328, 330,
    335, 345, 356, 371, 376, 384, 421

Bac, rue du 336, 372
Bacon, Francis (1561–1626) 50
Baden 306
Bailly, Jean Sylvain (1736–93) 101, 103, 112, 122, 154, 176, 253
Ballinamuck 342
balloons 64
Baltic 201, 204, 286, 380
banking 24, 62, 216, 323, 325, 384
*Bankozettel* 416
bankruptcy 15, 32, 59, 66, 84–5, 131, 168, 333, 334
Bantry Bay 342
Barère, Bertrand (1755–1841) 228, 233, 235, 251, 256, 278, 280, 281, 283, 284, 287, 290
Barnave, Antoine Pierre (1761–93) 26, 89, 95, 101, 113, 120, 138, 144, 149, 150, 151, 154, 175, 179, 253, 394
Barras, Paul, Viscount de (1755–1825) 255, 280, 320, 321, 330, 334, 370
Barruel, Augustin de (1741–1820) 218–19, 398
Barthélemy, François, Marquis de (1750–1830) 329, 330, 331
Basilicata 365
Basle 210, 298, 329, 354, 355
Basque provinces 210
Bastille 45, 83, 110, 111, 112, 124, 129, 135, 148, 149, 153, 160, 161, 166, 169, 170, 187, 298, 392
Batavian Republic 209–10, 332, 335, 343–8, 348, 355, 356, 373, 379, 381
Batz, Jean Pierre, Baron de (1754–1822) 267, 277
Bavaria 65, 168, 204, 218
Bayeux 16, 33, 47, 402
Bayonne 6
Béarn 6
Beauce 6
Beaumont-sur-Oise 22
Beauvais 20
Beccaria, Cesare, Marchese di (1738–94) 55
Bec d'Ambès 255
begging 14, 15, 19, 22, 27
Belfast 169, 213
Bergerac 142
Berlin 97, 370
Berne 310, 354, 355
Bernis, François Joachim de Pierre, Cardinal de (1715–94) 35
Berry 61
Bertier de Sauvigny, Louis Bénigne François (1737–89) 112, 394
Besançon 8, 18, 36, 61, 83, 95
Besenval, Pierre Victor, Baron de (1722–91) 131

Billaud-Varenne, Jean Nicolas (1756–1819) 250, 251, 263, 267, 268, 273, 279, 282, 284, 287, 290, 291
Birmingham 170
Biron, Armand-Louis de Gontaut, Duke de (1747–94) 247
bishops 7, 29, 34, 36, 54, 72, 99, 116, 136, 140, 141, 143, 144, 145, 153, 162, 170, 261, 353, 387, 388
blacksmiths 149
Blankenburg 315, 329
Blois 261
blue library 47
*bocage* 5, 145, 256, 289
Bohemia 180, 183
Boisgelin, Raymond, Cardinal de (1732–1804) 390
Boissy d'Anglas, François Antoine (1756–1826) 318
Bologna 359
Bonaparte, Joseph (1768–1844) 362
Bonaparte, Lucien (1775–1840) 371, 374, 375
Bonaparte, Napoleon (1769–1821) 30, 206, 213, 214, 217, 254, 315, 316, 320, 321, 325, 329, 330, 332, 334, 337, 338, 339, 351, 354, 356, 357, 358, 359, 360, 361, 362, 364, 366, 368, 371, 374–90, 391–2, 393, 394, 395, 398, 410, 411, 413, 414, 415, 417, 420–1, 425
books 23, 46–7
Bordeaux 5, 6, 8, 13, 21, 22–3, 50, 57, 63, 76, 77, 78, 80, 83, 127, 138, 142, 178, 181, 188, 195, 222, 228, 234, 236, 238–9, 242, 243, 245, 248, 249, 253, 255, 264, 328, 373, 403, 404
Bosporus 339
Botany Bay 212
*Bouche de fer* 153, 154
Bouches du Rhône 182, 239, 249
Bouillé, François Claude, Marquis de (1739–1800) 147, 151, 153, 156
Bouillon 45
Boulogne 29, 61
Bourbons 196, 202, 217, 241, 296, 300, 303, 306, 307, 357, 365, 373, 379, 380, 382, 408, 410
bourgeoisie 22–7, 28, 29, 30, 48, 90, 91, 93–4, 95, 135, 138, 224, 230, 275, 350, 357, 383, 394, 405, 408, 409, 410, 423
Bourges 233, 239, 241
Brabant 124, 162
bread 21, 22, 58, 61, 86, 88, 95, 98, 109, 112, 113, 121, 122, 149, 181, 229, 231, 245, 270, 286, 290, 293, 294, 322, 325, 401
Brécourt 243, 247, 248

Bremen 313
Brest 5, 32, 187, 206, 284
Breteuil, Louis Auguste Le Tonnelier, Baron de (1730–1807) 108, 113
Breton Club 116, 142
Brie 261
Brienne 30; *see also* Loménie de Brienne
Brissot, Jacques-Pierre (1754–93) 27, 64, 154, 174, 176, 178, 179, 180, 181, 184, 188, 191, 192, 193, 194, 200, 201, 221, 222, 228, 236, 253, 403, 411, 412
Brissotins 188, 190
Brittany 2, 4, 6, 11, 29, 61, 83, 92, 94–5, 96, 100, 102, 115, 130, 212, 226, 240, 242, 243, 248, 256, 288–90, 304, 305, 308, 311, 313, 314, 315, 316, 327, 406
Broglie, Victor François, Marshal de (1718–1804) 108, 110
Brottier, André Charles (1751–98) 328
Brumaire, coup of 374–5, 383, 384, 389
Brune, Guillaume (1763–1815) 355, 363, 373
Brunswick, Karl Wilhelm, duke of (1735–1806) 188, 192, 233, 315; declaration of 188, 306
Brussels 162, 163, 197, 199, 298
Brutus, Lucius Junius (d. 508 BC) 259, 418
Buonarroti, Philippe Michel (1761–1837) 325, 326, 356
Burgundy 8, 11, 115
Burke, Edmund (1729–97) 166–9, 170, 171, 212, 218, 422
Burney, Fanny (1752–1840) 391
Buzot, François (1760–94) 221, 241, 253

Cadoudal, Georges (1771–1804) 314, 382, 383
Caen 241, 243, 248, 253, 308
*cahiers* 97, 98, 99, 100, 114, 118, 131, 134–5, 136, 140, 152, 303, 334, 393, 394, 406, 408, 411
'Ça ira' 129, 193, 207
Cairo 338
Calabria 364–5
Calais 390
Calas, Jean (d. 1762) 7, 55, 56, 59
calendar 194, 260, 335
Calonne, Charles Alexandre de (1734–1802) 68–73, 74, 75, 77, 78, 79, 80, 81, 87, 90, 108, 146, 298, 299, 302
Calvados 241, 243, 245, 248
Camisards 7
Camperdown 216, 218, 332, 345
Campo Formio 217, 218, 332, 337, 338, 339, 351, 354, 361, 379, 414
Canada 13
canals 11

Cape of Good Hope 2, 13, 212, 217, 332, 381
capitation 27, 131
Caribbean 13, 181, 203, 210, 212, 238, 404, 412
Carmelites 397
Carnot, Lazare (1753–1823) 204, 206, 215, 217, 248, 250, 265, 277, 284, 321, 326, 329, 330, 331, 348, 351
carpenters 149
Carrier, Jean Baptiste (1756–94) 255, 257–8, 264, 268, 283, 284, 285, 289, 291
Carteaux, Jean François (1751–1813) 249, 255
Carthusians 137
Caserta 44
Castiglione 382
Catalonia 210
Catherine II (1729–96) 44, 166, 171, 198, 201, 202, 204, 208, 215, 307, 339
Cato, Marcus Porcius (237–142 BC) 418
cattle 12, 16, 61
Cazalès, Jacques de (1758–1805) 301, 303
censorship 36, 46, 56, 89, 99, 172
*certificats de civisme* 190, 258, 270
Cévennes 7, 410
Ceylon 381
Chabot, François (1759–94) 220, 267, 273, 274
Chalier, Joseph (1747–93) 231, 239, 245, 247, 253
Châlons 192
Chamfort, Nicolas Sébastien Roche *called* (1741–94) 30
Champagne 1, 261
Champ de Mars 129, 153, 154, 170, 185, 187, 188, 190, 277, 326; Massacre of 129, 154, 190, 247, 253, 301
Championnet, Jean Antoine Étienne (1762–1800) 339, 364
Champs Élysées 233
Channel, English 5, 391, 404, 415
Channel Islands *see* Jersey 309, 312
Chantilly 406
Charette, François (1763–96) 243, 289, 290, 312, 313, 314
charity 15, 309
Charlemagne (742–814) 1
Charles, Archduke (1771–1847) 368, 378
Charles Emmanuel IV (1751–1819) 366, 368
Chartres 33, 90
Châteaubriand, François René, Viscount de (1768–1848) 29, 303–4
Chaumette, Anaxagoras (1763–94) 185, 234, 250, 251, 260, 269, 271, 275

Cherbourg 32
chestnuts 6
Chiaramonti *see* Pius VII
Chiffon 182
Choiseul, Étienne François de Stainville, Duke
    de (1719–85) 42, 59
Cholet 256
Chouans 226, 256, 289, 308, 309,
    311–13, 314, 315, 340, 350, 366, 374,
    382, 383, 386, 406
Christ 260
Church 1, 2, 9, 17, 28, 29, 33–6, 45, 50,
    51, 52, 53, 54, 72, 97, 99, 117, 132,
    133, 136–46, 147, 157, 161, 162, 163,
    166, 170, 211, 212, 218, 224, 254, 259,
    287, 296, 302, 304, 307, 316, 333, 345,
    347, 349, 353, 357, 358, 363, 366, 367,
    385–90, 396–8, 406, 410, 420, 424;
    constitutional 145, 259, 288, 335, 420;
    lands of 132–3, 136–7, 140, 167, 224,
    349, 350, 353, 387, 396, 399, 405, 408
Cincinnati 64
Cisalpine Republic 214, 215, 217, 360,
    361–2, 363, 366
Cispadane Republic 215, 359–60, 361, 386
Cis-Rhenan Republic 351
Civil Code 385, 389, 393, 407, 421
Civil Constitution of the Clergy 139–43,
    144, 145, 146, 147, 155, 168, 304, 338,
    388, 398
Clausewitz, Karl von (1780–1831) 416,
    417
Clavière, Étienne (1735–93) 180, 185
clergy 22, 33–6, 48, 70, 71, 72, 73, 83, 88,
    91, 92, 94, 96, 97, 99, 100, 101, 102,
    103, 104, 106, 107, 109, 113, 114, 117,
    119, 132, 133, 135, 136–46, 157, 174,
    259, 275, 350, 386, 387–8, 392, 396,
    401, 420; Assembly of 72, 83, 140;
    constitutional 260, 261, 289, 317, 388,
    397; refractory 147, 148, 153, 155,
    174–5, 177, 178, 183, 184, 185, 190,
    224, 257, 261, 288, 308, 309, 330, 334,
    388, 397
Clermont de Lodève 12
Clermont-Tonnerre, Stanislas, Count de
    (1757–92) 119
Cleves 45
Clichy 327
climate 7, 84–5, 86–7, 98, 114, 121, 286,
    291, 322
Clootz, Anacharsis (1755–94) 160, 172,
    178, 194, 270
clover 10
Clovis (466–511) 1, 260
clubs 76, 77, 90, 91, 142–3, 145, 153,

185, 230, 238, 248, 251, 321, 324, 352,
    327, 335, 336, 357, 359, 361, 362, 364,
    371, 372, 393, 420
Cobourg, Friedrich, Prince of Saxe–
    (1737–1815) 203, 246
coffee 13, 23, 181, 223, 322
Colbert, Jean-Baptiste (1619–83) 32
Collot d'Herbois, Jean Marie (1750–96) 250,
    251, 254, 267, 268, 269, 277, 279, 280,
    283, 284, 287, 290, 291
Cologne 352
colonies 13, 150–1, 411–13, 424 *see also*
    West Indies
*comités de surveillance* 227, 251
Commission of Regulars 35
Commission of Twelve 233, 234, 235, 237,
    241
Committee of General Defence 228
Committee of General Security 263, 267,
    268, 273, 277, 279, 282
Committe of Public Safety 202, 204, 206,
    228, 234, 235, 237, 244, 246, 247–8,
    250, 251, 252, 254, 256, 257, 262, 263,
    265, 266, 267, 268, 269, 270, 271, 275,
    277, 278, 281, 282, 285
Common Rights 11, 16, 245
Commune of Paris 189–90, 191, 192, 194,
    220, 221, 227, 232, 235, 245, 249, 251,
    260, 262, 264, 271, 275, 276, 280, 281,
    285, 294
*compagnonnages* 19
Comtat Venaissin 139, 140, 157
Concordat, of 1516 34, 140, 141; of 1801
    386–90, 397, 398
Concorde, Place de la 196
Condé 202; Louis Joseph de Bourbon, Prince
    de (1736–181) 171, 299, 306, 315
Condorcet, Antoine Nicolas de Caritat,
    Marquis de (1743–94) 90, 174, 222,
    244, 399
Connacht 342
conscription 27, 31, 32, 204, 215, 224,
    229, 237, 242, 276, 293, 307, 308, 311,
    317, 340, 349, 350, 353, 355, 361, 369,
    371, 373, 374, 385, 405, 406, 416
conservatism 422–3
Constantinople 59, 339
Constituent Assembly 135, 144, 149, 150,
    153, 154, 157, 173, 174, 175, 181, 182,
    183, 193; 246, 289, 295, 301, 319, 399,
    411, 422 *see also* National Assembly
Constitution 81, 105, 118–20, 123–4, 129,
    134, 144, 148, 149, 154, 155, 156, 158,
    166, 167, 174, 175, 186, 187, 188, 194,
    227, 238, 244, 298, 302, 303, 304, 310,
    317, 345, 355, 356, 360, 361, 363, 365,

371, 374, 414; of 1791 227, 242, 263, 296, 309, 310, 408; of 1793 244, 246, 252, 263, 287, 290, 291, 294, 295, 324, 325, 326, 372, 376, 399, 420; of 1795 319, 320, 321, 322, 328, 332, 335, 359, 372, 376, 399, 420; of 1800 377–8, 382, 383, 388
Consulate 362, 377–90, 391–2, 407, 410, 420
*contribution foncière* 131
*contribution mobilière* 131
Convention 189, 193, 194–6, 198, 199, 200, 201, 202, 203, 204, 205, 220, 221, 223, 224, 226, 227, 228, 229, 231, 232, 233, 234, 235, 237, 238, 239, 240, 241, 242, 243, 244, 245, 246, 247, 248, 250, 251, 252, 253, 259, 260, 261, 262, 267, 268, 270, 271, 272, 273, 274, 276, 277, 278, 279, 280, 281, 283, 284, 285, 287, 289, 290, 291, 293, 294, 295, 309, 317, 318–22, 327, 329, 335, 336, 343, 345, 346, 348, 355, 371, 399, 404, 412, 419, 420
Copenhagen 380
Corday, Charlotte (1768–94) 245, 247
Cordeliers, district 127; Club 148, 152, 153, 154, 185, 186, 245, 250, 267, 269
Corfu 339
Cornwallis, Charles, Marquis (1738–1805) 409
Coron 256
coronation 1, 302, 390
corresponding societies 170, 200–1, 212
Corsica 2, 30, 58, 391
*corvée* 11, 27, 69, 76, 106
Contentin 256
cotton 5, 12, 13, 404
Council of State 377, 383
councils, Directorial 321, 323, 324, 326, 329, 330, 331, 334, 336, 370, 371, 373, 374, 375, 378; of Five Hundred 319, 330, 370, 372, 373, 374, 375; of Elders 319, 370, 372, 375, 376
counter-revolution 146–7, 155, 171, 178, 180, 182, 191, 195, 243, 273, 275, 282, 292, 296, 297–317, 339, 387, 396, 406, 418
Country in Danger 187, 373
Court 28, 29, 41–2, 44, 60, 63, 68, 102, 108, 111, 135, 178
Court of Aids 61
Couthon, Georges (1756–94) 175, 253, 254, 276, 277, 279, 280
Coyer, Gabriel François (1707–82) 30
Cracow 207
craftsmen 19

Crevecoeur, Saint John de (1735–1812) 64
crime 15–16, 18, 19, 125, 130, 384, 403, 406
Cults, Law on 389
Custine, Adam Philippe, Count de (1740–93) 197, 203
customs 4, 15, 57, 69, 352, 356, 405

Daendels, Herman Willem (1762–1818) 346, 373
Daggers, Day of 148
Damiens, Robert François (1714–57) 55
Danton, George Jacques (1759–94) 26, 127, 154, 187, 190, 191, 194, 200, 201, 202, 221, 226, 227, 228, 237, 240, 246, 247, 251, 252, 263, 264, 266, 267, 268, 270, 273, 274–5, 277, 281, 282
Daunou, Pierre Claude François (1761–1840) 388
dauphin 122 *see also* Louis XVII
Dauphiné 2, 8, 83, 88–9, 92, 93, 96, 101, 102, 105, 115, 145, 146, 179
David, Jacques Louis (1748–1825) 253, 277, 282
Dax 373
*décadis* 260, 276, 335, 386, 388
Declaration of the Rights of Man and the Citizen 118–19, 121, 123, 124, 132, 137, 139, 169, 244, 269, 318–19, 414, 417–19, 421, 424
dechristianization 259–62, 264, 266, 267, 276, 288, 335, 349, 353, 387, 397, 407, 409, 410, 411, 424
defenders 341
Delacroix, Charles (1754–1808) 346
Delacroix, Jean François (1753–94) 246
Delessart, Antoine-Nicolas Valdec (1744–92) 179, 180, 192
democracy 272, 386, 407, 418, 424
Denmark 380
departments 125, 140, 143, 393
*dépôts de mendicité* 15
*dérogeance* 28
Desmoulins, Camille (1760–94) 124, 127, 154, 266, 267, 268, 269, 273, 274
despotism 39, 45, 50, 51, 57, 59, 60, 61, 63, 72, 80, 81, 84, 93, 94, 105, 113, 123, 125, 145, 147, 159, 160, 161, 173, 179, 197, 205, 233, 242, 245, 354, 375, 424
Dessalines, Jean Jacques (1758–1806) 413
Devil's Island 291
diamond necklace 60
Diderot, Denis (1713–84) 46, 51, 52, 59, 63

Dijon 8, 47, 48, 52, 83, 114, 142
Directory 213, 214, 215, 216, 217, 315,
  318–40, 345, 346, 347, 349, 351, 353,
  354, 355, 356, 357, 359, 361, 362, 364,
  367, 368, 369–78,383, 384, 385, 386,
  399, 400, 403, 405, 409, 410, 411, 415
Discount Bank 133
Dissenters 166–7
districts of Paris 98, 127
Dol 4
domain, royal 69
*domaine congéable* 11–12
*don gratuit* 83
Dordogne 255
Dorset, John Frederick Sackville, Duke of
  (1745–99) 89, 99
Douai 2
Doué 232
Dover 391
Dreux 320
Drottningholm 44
Drouet, Jean Baptiste (1763–1824) 151,
  326, 371
Du Barry, Jeanne Bécu, Countess (1743–94)
  42, 59
Dublin 169, 213, 216, 342
Ducos, Roger (1754–1816) 371, 375
Dumont, André (1764–1838) 260
Dumouriez, Charles François (1739–1824)
  180, 185, 192, 193, 197, 199–200, 201,
  202, 203, 204, 205, 215, 222, 226, 227,
  348
Dunkirk 188, 203, 204
Dupont de Nemours, Pierre Samuel
  (1739–1817) 57, 61, 69
Duport, Adrien Jean François (1759–98) 90,
  91, 94, 95, 100, 120, 149, 150, 175, 210
Dutch Republic 75–6, 77–8, 159–60, 161,
  162, 200, 201, 209–10, 216, 218, 343,
  354, 357, 414, 415, 417 *see also* Holland
Duval d'Eprémesnil, Jean Jacques (1746–94)
  79, 81, 82, 91, 100


Economists 57–8 *see also* Physiocrats
education 23, 24, 29, 30, 33, 36, 48–9, 99,
  101, 137, 244, 318, 389, 392, 393, 399,
  418
Egypt 332, 338–9, 355, 368, 380, 381,
  382, 386
Elbeuf 12
elections 124, 125, 129, 138, 141, 143,
  153, 169, 201, 244, 317, 319, 320, 327,
  331, 336, 346, 360, 375, 377, 418; of
  1789 93, 96–8, 102, 104, 113, 336; of
  1791 155, 174, 329; of 1792 193–4; of

  1797 327, 328, 329, 332, 349, 376,
  382; of 1798 335, 336, 337; of 1799
  369–70, 376
emigration, *émigrés* 112, 123, 129, 134,
  135, 146, 147, 148, 149, 152, 153, 155,
  156, 157, 172, 173, 175, 176, 177, 178,
  179, 180, 198, 207, 244, 253, 297, 294,
  298, 299, 301, 302, 303, 304, 305, 306,
  310, 313, 314, 315, 316, 317, 328, 332,
  334, 372, 383, 391, 395, 396, 397, 402,
  405, 406, 407, 409
enclosure 16
*Encyclopédie* 48, 51–2, 56, 57
England 8, 9, 44, 50, 51, 64, 66, 77, 170,
  172, 212–13, 216, 219, 236, 246, 298,
  313, 314, 332, 381, 402, 406, 413, 415,
  424 *see also* Great Britain
Enlightenment 49–55, 99, 139, 168, 218,
  357, 393, 394, 425
*enragés* 224, 227, 237, 244, 245, 246, 249,
  252, 265, 420
entail 9
estates, of Artois 93, 95; of Brabant 163; of
  Brittany 5, 92, 94–5, 96, 100; of
  Dauphiné 8, 88, 89, 92, 93, 96; of
  Franche Comté 93; of Languedoc 7, 88;
  of Navarre 96; of Provence 7, 93;
  provincial 61, 76, 83, 92, 96, 402
Estates-General 59, 70, 72, 75, 76, 79, 80,
  81, 83, 84, 85, 88, 89, 91, 92, 93, 95,
  96, 99, 100, 110, 124, 131, 134, 136,
  167, 195, 296, 297, 302, 303, 343, 393,
  394, 395, 401
Étampes 182
Etruria 379
Evreux 243, 335
Expilly, Louis Alexandre (1742–94) 143

Fabre d'Eglantine (1750–94) 267, 268,
  273, 274
Falaiseau, Marquise de 396
Family Compact 164
famine 10, 14, 17, 291, 322
'famine pact' 21
Farmers-General 40, 41, 131
Favras, Thomas de Mahy, Marquis de
  (1744–90) 299
Federalism 203, 221, 222, 230, 238–43,
  245, 247, 248, 249, 251, 253–4, 255,
  257, 259, 263, 265, 266, 283, 287,
  308–9, 316, 343
Federation 129; Feast of 129, 135, 184
*fédérés* 184, 187, 188, 189, 220, 229
Feraud, Jean Bertrand (1759–95) 294, 295
Ferdinand III, Grand Duke of Tuscany
  (1771–1824) 366

Ferdinand IV, of Naples (1751–1825) 364, 365
Ferney 50
Ferrara 359
Fersen, Hans Axel, Count von (1755–1810) 151, 171
feudalism 11–12, 16, 17, 29, 33, 57, 106, 114, 115, 116–17, 129–30, 131, 135, 136, 137, 171, 179, 183, 199, 245, 297, 307, 353, 356, 365, 366, 395, 401, 405, 406, 407, 410, 419, 424
Feuillants 154, 155, 156, 157, 158, 175, 176, 178, 179, 185, 306, 310, 372
*feuille des bénéfices* 34
financiers 26, 28, 29, 40–1, 67, 79, 85, 180, 323
Finistère 143, 240, 243
Flanders 2, 5, 10, 68, 109, 145, 161, 206, 246, 349, 350, 391; Regiment 121, 127
Flesselles, Jacques de (1721–89) 112
Fleurus 206, 209, 278
Fleury, André Hercule, Cardinal de (1653–1743) 35
Floréal, purge of 336–7, 346, 370, 371
Florence 163, 362, 367
Floridablanca, Franco Antonio, Count de (1728–1828) 172
'Flour War' 1, 21–2, 62
Foix 2
Fontenay 232
forms of 1614 88, 89, 90, 91
Forster, Georg (1754–94) 199, 201, 218
Fouché, Joseph (1759–1820) 254, 259–60, 278, 279, 372, 374, 383, 387
Foulon, Joseph François (1715–89) 112–13, 394
foundlings 16
Fouquier-Tinville, Antoine Quentin (1746–95) 270, 274, 282, 293
Four Years Diet 207
Fox, Charles James (1749–1806) 161, 212, 236
*franc-fief* 27
Franche Comté 2, 4, 8–9, 93, 95, 115, 229, 315
Francis I (1494–1547) 34
Francis II (1768–1835) 180, 188, 201, 206, 211, 305, 315, 339, 348, 349, 351, 379, 420
Frankfurt 197, 202
Franklin, Benjamin (1706–90) 63–4, 65
Frederick II (1712–86) 31, 44, 415
Frederick William II (1744–97) 164, 188, 193, 198, 208
freemasonry 15, 25, 64–5, 218–19, 398
French Guards 36, 98, 107, 108, 110, 127

Fréron, Élie (1718–76) 45
Fréron, Louis Marie Stanislas (1754–1802) 255, 283, 287, 290
Fréteau, Emmanuel Marie Michel Phillippe (1745–94) 80, 100
Frimaire, Law of 14 262–3, 264, 266, 268, 270
Froment, François (1756–1825) 300, 305
Fructidor, coup of 217, 331, 332, 333, 334, 335, 337, 338, 345, 349, 361, 362, 375, 410

gabelle 4, 27, 131, 334
Gard 138, 143, 146, 182, 183, 292, 305, 316, 410
Garonne 6, 243, 255, 373
Gascony 6
Gdansk 198, 201
generalities 2, 61
general will 53, 118, 235, 376
Geneva 46, 50, 52, 161, 173, 298, 354, 410, 414
Genoa 217, 362, 368, 379, 414
Gensonné, Armand (1758–93) 178, 188, 238, 240
Gentz, Friedrich (1764–1832) 170, 422
George III (1738–1820) 213, 215, 379, 380, 391
Gerle, Dom (1736–1805) 137, 142
Germany 9, 147, 160, 164, 170–1, 177, 199, 210, 213, 214, 289, 303, 304, 305, 306, 333, 338, 339, 351–3, 368, 398, 411, 414, 415, 417
Germinal, uprising of 291, 293, 294, 317
Gilded Youth 282–3, 290, 293 *see also* Muscadins
Gironde 6, 188, 191, 193, 239, 248, 255
Girondins 193, 194, 195, 208, 221, 222, 223, 226, 227, 228, 229, 232, 233, 234, 235–8, 239, 241, 243, 244, 245, 247, 248, 250, 253, 266, 268, 285, 290, 407, 412
Gobel, Jean Baptiste Joseph (1727–94) 261, 271
Godoy, Manuel (1767–1851) 210
Goethe, Wolfgang (1749–1832) 160, 193
Gohier, Louis-Jérôme (1746–1830) 370, 375
Gouges, Olympe de (1748–93) 420
governors 2, 37, 70
Gracchi 419
grain 10, 21, 57, 58, 62, 69, 76, 86, 98, 109, 113, 114, 121, 162, 181, 182, 229, 249, 278, 286, 290, 293, 323, 352, 358
*grands bailliages* 82, 84

Granville 256, 309, 311, 317
Great Britain 13, 30, 62, 66, 70, 75, 77,
  87, 159, 161, 164, 166, 167, 169,
  200–1, 202, 203, 206, 207, 210,
  211–12, 213, 215–16, 217, 218, 222,
  232, 240, 254, 278, 307, 309, 310, 311,
  312, 314, 316, 322, 327, 329, 332, 334,
  346–7, 349, 350, 351, 358, 361, 365,
  368, 372, 378, 379, 381–1, 382, 392,
  404, 413, 414, 415, 416, 424
Great Fear 114–15
Great Nation 337, 345, 346, 353, 362,
  385, 409
Greece 160
Grégoire, Henri (1750–1831) 261, 335,
  411, 412, 420
Grenelle 282, 283, 326–7, 328
Grenoble 22, 26, 83, 89, 239
Grève, Place de 55, 110, 251, 280
Grimm, Frederic Melchior, Baron de
  (1723–1807) 45
*gros fermiers* 10, 11, 17
Guadeloupe 13, 212
Guadet, Marguérite-Élie (1758–94) 178,
  188, 238, 240
Guiana 190, 291, 334, 335, 383
Guilds 19, 20, 57, 149, 355
Guillotin, Joseph Ignace (1738–1814) 183
Guillotine 183, 190, 203, 219, 223, 233,
  239, 250, 251, 253, 254, 255, 270, 271,
  274, 275, 280, 282, 285, 291, 292, 295,
  330, 336, 383, 393, 420, 424
Gustavus III (1746–92) 171, 197
Guyenne 61, 76


Habeas Corpus 213
Habsburgs 137, 140, 159, 162, 164, 361,
  365, 379
Hague, The 160, 209, 346, 347
Hainault 115
Haiti 413
Hamm 306, 309
Hanover 203
Hanriot, François (1761–94) 234, 235,
  247, 252, 280
Hardy, Thomas (1752–1832) 170, 212
harvests 12, 14, 20, 21, 22, 58, 69, 84–5,
  86, 98, 109, 114, 117, 121, 250, 286,
  322, 334, 341, 401
Hasselt 350
Haute-Garonne 183
Hébert, Jacques-René (1757–94) 227, 233,
  236, 250, 251, 252, 267, 268, 269, 270,
  273, 274, 275, 280, 281
Helvetic Republic 338, 373
Henriot 98

Henry IV (1553–1610) 59, 87
Hérault 239
Herder, Johan-Gottfried (1744–1803) 44,
  160
Hesdin 147
Hispaniola 413
hoarding 21, 98, 182, 185, 223, 229, 244,
  245, 246, 250, 258, 270, 286, 403
Hoche, Lazare (1768–97) 215–16, 289,
  312, 313, 314, 315, 327, 330, 332, 341,
  342, 351
Hohenlinden 379
Hohenzollerns 77
Hölderin 160
Holland 45, 46, 78, 79, 162, 164, 173,
  209, 222, 226, 286, 293, 315, 343, 372
Holy Office 172
Holy Roman Empire 217, 338, 351, 414
Holy Spirit, Order of 1
Hondschoote 204
Honours of the Court 41
Hood, Samuel (1735–1816) 249, 254–5,
  309
hospitals 15, 16, 18, 35, 387, 400, 401
Hostages, Law of 371–2, 382, 384
Hôtel de Ville 55, 112, 121, 122, 186, 191,
  280
Houchard, Jean Nicolas (1738–93) 203
Huguenots 45 *see also* Protestants
Humbert, Joseph Amable (1767–1823) 342,
  368
Hungary 159, 164, 180, 183, 211, 416


Île de France 22, 32
Île-et-Vilaine 240
Illuminati 65, 168, 218
Imola 386
Independence, Declaration of 63
India 4, 13
Indies Company 267, 268, 273
Indulgents 267–9, 272–5
industry 8, 12–13, 19–20, 23, 28, 87, 101,
  174, 350
infernal machine 384, 389
intendants 2, 28, 37, 40, 60–1, 69, 72, 83,
  112, 242, 384, 408
Invalides 110
Ionian Islands 217
Islam 386
Isnard, Maximin (1755–1825) 177, 233,
  290
Ireland 14, 159, 162, 169, 212, 213, 216,
  258, 330, 341–3, 367–8, 380, 414, 416
Italy 44, 160, 206, 210, 211, 213, 214,
  217, 249, 303, 315, 326, 327, 329, 332,
  333, 337, 351, 354, 355, 356–67, 371,

372, 374, 378, 379, 380, 381, 384, 387, 398, 409, 414, 417

Jacobins 142–3, 147, 148, 149, 150, 151, 152, 153, 154, 156, 170, 174, 175, 178, 180, 184, 185, 187, 188, 189, 192, 193, 197, 207, 208, 211, 213, 218, 222, 223, 227, 228, 229, 230, 231, 235, 239, 240, 242, 243, 246, 248, 250, 251, 255, 260, 261, 262, 266, 268, 269, 273, 278, 279, 280, 283, 284, 285, 286–7, 292, 294, 306, 315, 320, 321, 323, 324, 325, 326, 327, 328, 329, 330, 335, 336, 337, 338, 346, 352, 356, 357, 358, 359, 361, 362, 363, 364, 365, 366, 367, 370, 371, 372, 373, 374, 375, 376, 383, 384, 388, 393, 398, 416, 417, 418, 420, 421
Jalès 143, 147, 182, 300, 305
Jansenism 45, 53–4, 56, 141, 357, 398
Javogues, Claude (1759–96) 264, 268
Jeanbon Saint-André, André (1749–1813) 206, 247
Jemappes 197, 198, 202, 206
Jersey 256, 309
Jesuits 35, 37, 48, 49, 54, 56, 218
Jews 9, 24, 137, 141, 367, 411
Joly de Fleury, Jean François (1718–1802) 67
Joseph II (1741–99) 60, 137, 159, 161, 162, 163, 164, 211, 298, 350, 357
Joubert, Barthélemy (1769–99) 346, 371, 372, 374
Jourdan, Jean-Baptiste (1762–1833) 204, 340, 349, 367, 371, 373, 374, 385
Jouy 20
Joyous Entry 162, 163
Jullien, Marc Antoine (1775–1848) 255, 257, 264
Jura 240, 262, 413
juries 125

Kant, Immanuel (1724–1804) 160
Kellermann, François Christophe (1735–1820) 192
Kellgren, Johan Henrik (1751–95) 160
Killala 342
Klopstock, Friedrich (1724–1803) 160
Koblenz 147, 171, 302, 303, 304, 305
Kosciuszko, Tadeusz (1746–1817) 198, 207, 208, 211

La Barre, Jean François, Chevalier de (1747–66) 55, 58
Lacombe, Claire (b. 1765) 420

Lafayette, Marie-Josèphe Paul Yves Roche Gilbert du Motier, Marquis de (1757–1834) 64, 72, 74, 90, 99, 112, 113, 121, 122, 127, 129, 148, 154, 176, 177, 178, 185, 186, 187, 188, 189, 190, 202
La Harpe, Frédéric César (1754–1838) 354, 355
Lajaunye 289
Lally-Tollendal, Trophime-Gérard de (1751–1830) 119, 310
La Mabilais 289, 312, 314
Lamballe, Marie-Thérèse Louise, Princess de (1749–92) 192
Lameth brothers (Alexandre de (1760–1829); Charles de (1757–1832)) 120, 129, 149, 154, 155, 310
Lamoignon, Chrétien François de (1735–89) 73, 78, 82, 83, 84, 85, 89, 93
Lancashire 404
*Landes* 6
*Landsturm* 416
*Landwehr* 416
Langhe 367
Languedoc 2, 4, 7, 9, 54, 55, 61, 71, 86, 88, 145, 229, 292
Lanjuinais, Jean-Denis (1753–1827) 240, 290
La Réole 248
La Revellière-Lépeaux, Louis-Marie (1753–1824) 321, 330, 335, 370–1, 372
La Rochefoucauld-Liancourt, François, Duke de (1747–1827) 111
La Rochelle 145
La Rouërie, Armand Taffin, Marquis de (1751–93) 305
Latin 49
Laval 256
Law, John (1671–1729) 133, 402
*lazzaroni* 364
Leblanc de Castillon, Jean François André (b. 1719) 72
Le Chapelier, Isaac René Guy (1754–94) 105, 149; Law 149, 276, 405
Leclerc, Jean Théophile Victoire (b. 1771) 250
Le Creusot 8
Legendre, Louis (1752–97) 278, 284
Leghorn 358
Legion of Honour 390, 410
Legislative Assembly 124, 150, 155, 174–80, 183, 184–93, 198, 220, 221, 230, 238, 304, 399, 412
Legislative Body 377, 388, 389, 410
Le Havre 13, 21, 286, 391
Leipzig 207
Le Mans 256, 309, 374

Le Mercier de la Rivière, Pierre Paul (1720–92) 57
Lenin, Vladimir Ilich (1870–1924) 422
Leo X (Pope 1513–21) 34
Leoben 214, 215, 217, 315, 329, 332, 360
Leopold II (1747–92) 156, 163–4, 165, 171, 177, 178, 179, 180, 199, 211, 301, 302, 357
Le Peletier de Saint-Fargeau, Louis Michel (1760–93) 222, 245, 367
Letourneur, Louis François (1715–1817) 321, 329
*lettres de cachet* 80, 83
*levée en masse* 204, 207, 250, 270, 371
liberty 63, 81, 104, 118, 135, 162, 165, 167, 172, 173, 193, 199, 200, 210, 222, 236, 238, 242, 245, 251, 254, 261, 263, 269, 272, 274, 275, 279, 325, 327, 343, 349, 354, 357, 360, 366, 378, 392, 406, 409, 418–19, 422
liberty trees 130, 186, 277, 287, 346, 350, 353, 359, 373, 418
*liberum veto* 165
Libourne 77, 80
Libraries 23, 47, 48
Liège 161, 162, 164, 197
Ligurian Republic 217, 362, 379 see also Genoa
Lille 147, 217
Limousin 19
Lindet, Robert (1746–1825) 248, 265, 323, 324, 325, 371
linen 13
Linguet, Simon Nicolas Henri (1736–94) 45
Lisbon 52
literacy 5, 22, 47, 49, 399
literary societies 47, 67
*lits de justice* 37, 76, 77, 79, 80, 82, 106
*livret* 20
loans 34, 37, 67, 68, 69, 70, 75, 78, 79, 80, 81, 106, 131, 132; forced 242, 290, 323, 352, 363; 1793 265; 1799 371, 384
Locke, John (1632–1704) 50
Lodi 382
Loire 5, 226, 232, 240, 243, 256, 257, 264, 289, 309, 314
Lombardy 213, 214, 357, 358, 359, 360, 364, 379
Loménie de Brienne, Étienne Charles, Cardinal (1727–94) 35, 71, 74, 75, 77, 78, 79, 81, 82, 83, 84, 85, 88, 89, 90, 93
London 169, 170, 200, 202, 216, 256, 298, 313, 380
Longwy 190, 191
Lorient 5
Lorraine 2, 8, 9, 10, 58

Louis XIV (1638–1715) 2, 23, 30, 31, 35, 37, 42, 43, 44, 50, 388, 393
Louis XV (1710–74) 2, 13, 38, 39, 42, 43, 55, 58, 59, 60, 63, 177
Louis XVI (1754–93) 1, 7, 11, 12, 13, 15, 18, 20, 23, 25, 28, 29, 31, 32, 34, 38, 39, 42, 43, 44, 47, 48, 55, 58, 59, 62, 66, 67, 68, 69, 70, 72, 73, 74, 75, 76, 77, 79, 80, 81, 82, 83, 84, 86, 88, 89, 92, 93, 97, 98, 101, 103, 105, 106, 107, 108, 110, 111, 112, 114, 117, 120, 121, 122, 123, 129, 132, 140, 141, 144, 146, 147, 148, 149, 150, 151, 152, 153, 154, 155, 156, 157, 164, 167, 171, 172, 175, 176, 177, 178, 179, 180, 184, 185, 186, 188, 189, 190, 194–6, 197, 200, 201, 202, 203, 221, 222, 223, 224, 231, 236, 237, 293, 296, 297, 298, 300, 301, 302, 306, 307, 310, 326, 381, 390, 420
Louis XVII (1785–95) 202, 227, 249, 255, 290, 295–6, 307, 310, 314
Louis XVIII see Provence
Louisiana 380
Loustalot, Élisée (1762–90) 127
Louvet, Jean Baptiste (1760–97) 221, 241, 290
Lozère 235
Lucerne 10
Lunéville 379, 391, 414
Lutherans 9
Luxembourg 151, 350, 353, 367, 414; palace 322
Lyons 8, 12, 18, 19, 20, 23, 24, 46, 87, 96, 109, 127, 147, 231–2, 234, 235, 238, 239, 242, 245, 247, 249, 253–4, 257, 258, 259, 260, 264, 267, 268, 286, 292, 300, 308–9, 315, 402, 404–5

Macdonald, Alexandre (1765–1840) 364
Machecoul 243
Madrid 164, 210, 218, 299, 413
Maine 5, 11, 406
Mainz 171, 177, 178, 197, 199, 202, 203, 218, 247, 256, 298, 304
Maistre, Joseph de (1753–1821) 422
maize 6, 10
Malesherbes, Chrétien-Guillaume Lamoignon de (1721–94) 51
Mallet du Pan, Jacques (1749–1800) 310, 311, 317, 327
Malouet, Pierre Victor (1740–1814) 119, 155, 310, 394
Malta 338, 339, 380, 381
Mamelukes 338
Manchester 5
mandates 106, 117, 118, 297

Manège Club 371, 372
Mantua 214, 215, 360
Marat, Jean Paul (1743–93) 26, 120, 134, 154, 191, 194, 221, 223, 228–9, 233, 236, 245, 246, 249, 250, 261, 269, 283, 284, 287, 367
*Maréchaussée* 36
Marengo 379, 382, 388
Maria Carolina (1753–1814) 219, 365
Maria Theresia (1717—80) 44, 416
Marie Antoinette (1755–93) 42, 58, 60, 77, 102, 105, 108, 112, 122, 146, 147, 151, 155, 156, 167, 175, 177, 179, 191, 219, 252, 253, 297, 298
Marseilles 7, 13, 18, 98, 113, 127, 143, 182, 187, 229–30, 231, 234, 238, 239, 240, 242, 243, 245, 247, 249, 255, 292, 403, 404
Martinique 13
Martinovics, Ignàcz Joseph (1755–95) 211
Mas d'Eu 203
Massif Central 6, 7, 11, 130, 174, 183
Master of Requests 40
Martial Law 127, 154
Marx, Karl (1818–88) 422
Maupeou, René Nicolas de (1714–92) 38, 39, 40, 56, 59, 60, 78, 84
Maurepas, Jean Frédéric Phélypeaux, Count de (1701–81) 42–3, 63, 67
Mauritius 13
Maury, Jean-Siffrein (1746–1817) 301
maximum 223, 229, 231, 232, 236, 237, 252, 258, 264, 265, 269, 270, 275–6, 281, 285–6
Mayo 342 ·
Mays 130
Mazarin, Jules, Cardinal de (1602–61) 43
Mediterranean 4, 6, 202, 203, 217, 229, 249, 338–9, 341, 380
Ménétra, Jacques-Louis (b. 1738) 19
merchants 23–4, 26, 40, 48, 125, 230, 357
Mercier, Louis-Sébastien (1740–1814) 20, 23
Méricourt, Théroigne de 420
Merlin de Douai, Philippe Auguste (1754–1838) 331, 351, 370–1, 372
Mesmerism 64
metallurgy 8, 88, 404
*métayage* 9, 405
*métiers libres* 20
metric system 393
Metz 83, 147, 411
Middle Ages 2, 6
Midi 6, 7, 143, 183, 230, 300, 305
migration 6, 8, 15, 16, 18
Milan 214, 357, 358, 359, 360, 361, 362, 363, 379, 386, 417

Miles, William Augustus (1753–1817) 150
militia 27, 31, 32, 109, 224, 406, 416
Mirabeau, Honoré Gabriel Riquetti, Count de (1749–91) 64, 72, 90, 97, 101, 103, 104, 106, 108, 119, 123–4, 129, 132, 133, 134, 136, 146, 149, 150, 156, 180, 222, 283, 299, 300, 301
Mirabeau, Vicomte de ('Mirabeau-Tonneau') (1754–92) 301, 302
Mirabeau, Victor Riquetti, Marquis de (1715–89) 57
Miranda, Francisco (1659–1816) 414
Miromesnil, Armand Thomas Hue de (1723–96) 73
Modena 215, 359
Moira, Francis Rawdon Hastings, Earl of (1754–1826) 309
Mombello 360
Momoro 270
Monarchical Club 149
*monarchiens* 119–20,. 123, 124, 149, 155, 298, 301, 306, 310, 319
monasteries 11, 15, 34, 35, 54, 96, 98, 109, 114, 115, 137, 140, 141, 149, 349, 363, 387, 391, 397, 399, 400, 402, 424
Monck, George (1608–70) 382
Montagnards 194, 208, 221, 222, 223, 227, 228, 229, 230, 231, 232, 233, 234, 235, 236–8, 239, 240, 241, 242, 243, 244, 245, 246, 247, 248, 249, 250, 279, 285, 291, 292, 294, 295, 411, 418
Montauban 7, 75, 139, 142
Montélimar 230
Montesquieu, Charles Louis de Secondat, Baron de (1689–1755) 50–1, 59, 123
Montesquiou, Anne-Pierre de (1739–98) 197
Montlosier, François Dominique (1755–1838) 310
Montmédy 151, 152
Montmorin, Armand Marc, Count de (1745–92) 78, 192
Montpellier 7, 239
Moreau, Jean Victor (1763–1813) 374, 379
Morocco 59
Mortmain 15
Moulin, Jean François (1752–1810) 371, 375
Mounier, Jean-Joseph (1758–1806) 64, 89, 95, 101, 119, 123, 129, 146, 300, 310
Mulhouse 2, 354
Munich 379
Muscadins 232, 248, 284, 287, 290, 291, 295 *see also* Gilded Youth

Nancy 2, 113, 147, 185

Nantes 5, 6, 13, 18, 21, 23, 47, 54, 92, 95, 143, 243, 247, 255, 257–8, 264, 283, 285, 374, 404
Naples 44, 202, 214, 218, 219, 339, 357, 361, 363, 364, 365, 380
Narbonne, Louis, Count de (1755–1815) 177–8, 180
national agents 264
National Assembly 103, 104, 107, 109, 110, 111, 113, 114, 115, 116–17, 118, 120, 122, 123, 124, 125, 127, 129, 130, 131, 132, 133, 135, 136, 137, 139, 140, 142, 143, 144, 146, 147, 149, 150, 151, 152, 156, 161, 162, 164, 167, 171, 299, 300, 301, 303, 385, 387, 388, 393, 394, 396, 400, 402, 411, 412
National Guard 112, 113, 115, 120, 121, 122, 125, 127–8, 130, 138, 139, 143, 147, 148, 151, 153, 154, 161, 174, 182, 184, 186, 187, 188, 189, 205, 220, 223, 224, 227, 231, 232, 233, 234, 235, 247, 261, 280, 291, 292, 293–4, 300, 305, 320, 322, 325, 330, 345, 373, 384, 420
nationalism 417
natural frontiers 199–200, 338, 348, 351, 414
Navarre 1, 96
navy 32, 42, 66, 210, 216, 240, 249, 255, 311, 341
Necker, Jacques (1732–1804) 28, 29, 55, 61, 62–3, 66–8, 71, 72, 73–4, 79, 85, 86, 87, 88, 89, 90, 91, 92, 93, 97, 98, 101, 102, 105, 106, 107, 108, 109, 112, 113, 120, 121, 131–2, 133, 134, 297, 298, 420
Neerwinden 202, 227
Nelson, Horatio, Viscount (1758–1805) 338, 339, 364, 380
Netherlands 45, 152, 159, 161, 197, 202, 211, 291, 298, 311, 330, 352, 414 *see also* Belgium, Holland
Neuchâtel 46, 48
Neufchâteau, François de (1750–1828) 331, 337
Nevers 259–60
Newton, Isaac (1642–1727) 49, 50
Nice 197, 201, 213, 298, 338
Nièvre 259
Nîmes 7, 12, 87, 138, 142, 143, 147, 230, 231, 292, 300; *bagarre* of 138, 143, 300
Nine Sisters Lodge 65
Noailles, Louis, Vicomte de (1756–1804) 116
nobility 22, 26–30, 32, 33, 34, 39–40, 41, 48, 50, 51, 64, 70, 71, 83, 88, 90, 91, 92, 94, 95, 96, 97, 99, 100, 101, 102,

103, 104, 105, 106, 113, 114, 116, 119, 120, 123, 127, 129, 135, 148, 157, 163, 165, 169, 174, 183, 197, 198, 199, 207, 226, 251, 275, 297, 298, 299, 301, 303, 305, 308, 309, 334, 361, 372, 390, 394–6, 398, 401, 409
Noble Revolt (1788) 83–4
Nootka Sound 164–5
Nore 216
Normandy 2, 5, 22, 109, 115, 229, 240, 242, 243, 245, 247, 322, 332, 406
North Sea 381
Notables 407, 420
Notables, Assembly of 70–5, 76, 79, 82, 83, 89, 90, 91, 92, 93, 95
Notaries 25, 101, 167
Notre-Dame 260, 261, 335, 388, 390
Novi 372
*noyades* 257

Oath of the Clergy 144, 145, 146, 147, 152, 153, 174, 177, 304, 396, 397, 399, 400, 420
Oberkampf, Christoff Philippe (1738–1815) 20
Ochs, Peter (1752–1821) 354–5
October Days 121–3, 127, 146, 166, 167, 169, 298
offices 23, 25, 26, 28, 30, 36, 37, 39, 40, 41, 82, 101, 116, 125, 133, 135 *see also* venality
Ogé, Vincent (1750–90) 412
Oléron 335
olives 86, 286
Orange 284, 292, 347
Orléans 277; Louis Philippe Joseph, Duke d' (1747–93) 80, 91, 99, 104, 112, 193, 221, 253, 327; Louis Phillippe, Duke d' (1773–1850) 327
owner–occupiers 9

Pache, Jean Nicolas (1746–1823) 233
Pacific 164
Padua 156; Circular 156, 302
Paine, Thomas (1737–1809) 63, 169–70, 194, 212
Palais Royal 104, 107, 108, 109, 120, 284, 392
Pantheon 222, 282, 287; Club 324, 325
Papal States 215, 338, 359, 361, 362
Paris 1, 2, 5, 6, 8, 9, 10, 11, 13, 15, 16, 18, 19, 20, 21, 22, 23, 29, 36, 37, 38, 39, 40, 41, 43, 44, 46, 50, 52, 53, 54, 55, 58, 59, 61, 62, 63, 64, 65, 68, 73,

74, 76, 77, 78, 80, 81, 82, 83, 85, 86,
87, 88, 89, 90, 91, 92, 96, 97, 98, 99,
100, 102, 103, 104, 105, 107, 108, 109,
110, 111, 112, 113, 114, 115, 120, 121,
122, 123, 127, 132, 135, 142, 144, 145,
146, 148, 151, 152, 153, 154, 155, 156,
157, 160, 161, 162, 168, 170, 172, 175,
176, 177, 178, 179, 181, 182, 184, 185,
186, 187, 189, 190–1, 192, 193, 194,
195, 199, 200, 202, 203, 204, 207, 215,
219, 220, 221, 222, 223, 226, 227, 228,
229, 230, 231, 232, 233, 236, 237, 238,
239, 240, 241, 242, 243, 244, 245, 246,
248, 249, 250, 253, 254, 255, 256, 257,
258, 260, 261, 262, 266, 267, 268, 269,
270, 271, 275, 276, 277, 280, 282, 283,
284, 285, 286, 288, 290, 291, 293, 294,
299, 301, 306, 308, 315, 316, 317, 320,
321, 322, 324, 326, 328, 330, 331, 335,
336, 342, 343, 346, 347, 348, 350, 354,
355, 358, 359, 360, 362, 363, 368, 369,
372, 373, 374, 381, 383, 385, 387, 389,
390, 391, 392, 397, 399, 401, 402, 403,
407, 412, 420; Peace of (1763) 13
parlements 2, 25, 27, 37–40, 46, 51, 53,
56, 57, 59, 60, 61, 62, 67, 70, 71, 75,
76–7, 78, 80–1, 82, 84, 87, 89, 125,
131, 135, 299–300, 402; of Aix 7, 305;
of Besançon 8, 36, 38, 61, 83; of
Bordeaux 38, 50, 58, 61, 63, 76, 77, 80,
81, 83; of Dijon 83; of Douai 2; of
Grenoble 61, 83; of Metz 83; of Nancy
2; of Paris 2, 8, 37, 38, 39, 40, 50, 60,
67, 68, 71, 73, 76–7, 78, 79, 80, 87, 88,
89–90, 91, 92, 222, 298; of Pau 2, 38;
of Rouen 2, 83; of Toulouse 7, 38, 55,
83
Parliament 161, 166, 167, 170, 200, 201,
212, 213, 380, 424
Parma 214, 357, 380
Parthenopean Republic 339, 364, 380
Pascalis, Jean Joseph Pierre (1732–90) 305
*patente* 131
Patriotic Contribution 132, 133–4
Pau 83
Paul I (1754–1801) 339, 379, 380
Pavia 358
*pays d'états* 27, 61, 70, 81, 96, 395
peasants 9–13, 16–18, 21, 29, 31, 32, 57,
84, 97, 114, 117, 130, 138, 145, 163,
164, 183, 207, 224–7, 242, 244, 261,
271, 307, 309, 317, 349–50, 355, 359,
365, 366, 367, 369, 373, 401, 402, 406,
407
Pembrokeshire 341
pensions 116, 177
Périgord 130

Perpignan 147
Pétion, Jerôme (1756–94) 154, 156, 170,
176, 180, 186, 187, 188, 189, 193, 195,
228, 232, 241, 253
*petite culture* 6
Philanthropic Institute 328, 376
philanthropic societies 15
Physiocrats 57–8, 60, 61, 131, 402 *see also*
Economists
Picardy 14, 109, 131, 391
Pichegru, Charles (1761–1804) 291, 315,
316, 329, 330, 331
Picornell, Juan (1757–1825) 210
Piedmont 253, 356, 357, 361, 365–6, 367,
381, 414
Pillnitz, Declaration of 156–7, 171, 175,
179, 302, 304
Pitt, William (1759–1805) 166, 169, 200,
201, 204, 211, 212, 213, 215, 217, 236,
246, 267, 311, 313, 341, 380
Pius VI (1717–99) 139, 141, 146, 215,
338, 362, 385, 386, 398
Pius VII (1740–1823) 386, 387, 388
plague 7
Plain 221, 279
Plenary Court 82
pluralism 116
Poitou 104
Poland 46, 91, 165–6, 171, 198, 201, 204,
206, 207–9, 214, 218, 316, 339, 343,
414, 422
police 36, 88, 107, 229, 242, 272, 284,
285, 290, 319, 389, 392, 416; Bureau of
General 277; Legion 325–6
Polignac, Yolande, Duchess de (1749–93)
42
Pompadour, Jeanne Poisson, Marquise de
(1721–64) 42
Pont Neuf 89, 127
Pont Saint-Esprit 7, 182, 183
Pope 2, 48, 136, 140, 141, 143, 146, 147,
150, 215, 277, 304, 338, 357, 360, 361,
368, 385–90, 398, 424 *see also* Pius VI,
Pius VII
popular societies 185, 232, 276, 287
population 2, 6, 7, 14, 16, 23, 96, 125,
198, 341, 343, 346, 365, 401
*portion congrue* 35–6, 137, 145
Portsmouth 313
Portugal 202, 211
potatoes 9, 10, 405
poverty 14–16, 18, 23, 61, 87, 161, 347,
363, 399–400, 401
Praga 208
Prairial, Law of 22 275, 277–8, 284;
uprising of 293–5, 315, 317, 320, 321,
324, 330, 383, 420

prefects 384, 388
press 23, 45–7, 89, 95, 103, 104, 120, 124, 132, 142, 148, 155, 156, 161, 172, 194, 227, 250, 297, 310, 320, 321, 323, 324, 326, 327, 328, 332, 335, 336, 361, 371, 372, 373, 389
Price, Richard (1723–91) 167
prices 98, 109, 112, 121, 149, 181, 182, 185, 223, 229, 231, 232, 236, 245, 250, 252, 264, 270, 286, 303, 319, 333, 367, 401, 403, 408
Priestley, Joseph (1733–1804) 170, 194
Prieur de la Côte d'Or (1763–1827) 248
privilege 27, 28, 33, 46, 51, 57, 73, 90, 91, 92, 94, 95, 96, 99, 100, 106, 114, 116, 117, 119, 136, 149, 162, 199, 259, 297, 303, 358, 394, 395, 401, 406, 408, 419
professions 24, 25, 41, 48, 408
property 81, 99, 106, 109, 113, 117, 118, 119, 132, 152, 167, 168, 174, 194, 200, 240, 242, 289, 302, 303, 311, 318, 319, 322, 323, 324, 336, 372, 378, 383, 388, 395, 407, 409, 418, 419, 420, 421, 422, 423
prostitution 15–16, 19, 210
Protestants 7, 9, 24, 26, 36, 54–5, 62, 64, 79, 80, 95, 99, 133, 136, 137, 138, 142, 143, 144, 145, 147, 206, 212, 300, 317, 342, 343, 387, 406, 410–11
Provence 7, 86, 93, 98, 145, 177, 183, 262, 292, 305
Provence, Count de (Louis XVIII) (1755–1824) 91, 152, 171, 296, 299, 302, 306, 307, 309, 310, 314, 315, 316, 327, 329, 347, 376, 382, 383
provinces 2, 60, 61, 134, 168, 242–3
Prussia 30, 31, 45, 76, 77, 156, 159, 161, 164, 165, 170, 171, 179, 180, 184, 188, 190, 192, 193, 201–2, 204, 208, 209, 210, 211, 293, 299, 302, 305, 306, 311, 343, 351, 381, 414–15, 416, 424
public opinion 37, 38, 56, 62, 75, 93, 103, 331, 392
Puisaye, Joseph, Count de (1755–1827) 289, 290, 308, 309, 311, 312, 313, 314, 315
pyramids 338
Pyrenees 2, 4, 6, 145, 200, 247, 313

Quercy 14, 130
Quesnay, François (1694–1774) 57
Quiberon 212, 312–13, 314, 396
Quimper 240–1, 288
Quincey 115

Rabaut de Saint-Étienne, Jean Paul (1743–93) 95, 117, 137, 138

Raclawice 207
Radischev, Alexander (1749–1802) 172
railways 11, 405
Ramel 323, 332–3, 384
Rastadt 217, 337–8, 339, 351
Raynal, Guillaume Thomas (1713–96) 63
Ré 334
Reeves, John 200
Reformation 392
regency 50, 56, 152
Reggio 359
regicide 55
Reichenbach, Convention of 164, 166, 302
remonstrances 37, 38, 59, 63, 70, 80, 81, 82
Rennes 5, 18, 83, 92, 94, 95, 113, 143, 240, 248, 257
Representatives on Mission 227, 228, 230, 237, 240, 241, 242, 248, 254, 258, 259, 263–4, 267, 292
republicanism 63, 150, 152, 153, 154, 169, 170, 194, 196, 204, 218, 231, 241, 301, 321, 328, 335, 337, 356, 357, 361, 363, 381, 398
*ressorts* 2, 3, 38
Reubell, Jean François (1747–1807) 321, 329, 330, 351, 354, 370, 411
Réunion 13
Reveillon Riots 20, 98, 107, 321
Revolutionary Armies 244, 250, 251, 252, 254, 258, 260, 261, 263, 264, 265, 267, 272, 282
Revolutionary Government 252, 262–4, 284
Revolutionary Tribunal 227, 228, 230, 237, 241, 251, 255, 263, 269–70, 274, 275, 281, 283, 285, 293
Revolution Society 167, 170
Rheims 1, 21, 34, 260
Rhine 9, 171, 199, 200, 201, 202, 209, 214, 215, 217, 218, 286, 304, 305, 306, 315, 348, 351–3, 357, 373, 378, 379, 381, 384, 387, 414
Rhône 4, 6, 7, 8, 146, 182, 239, 249, 286, 292, 315, 328
Richer, Edmond (1559–1631) 141
Richerism 141
Rivoli 214
roads 5, 7, 11, 87, 391
Robespierre, Augustin (1764–94) 280
Robespierre, Maximilien (1758–94) 25, 26, 95, 101, 120, 150, 151, 153, 155, 156, 176, 178, 179, 180, 183, 188, 191, 192, 193, 194, 202, 210, 221, 222, 228, 234, 240, 246, 251, 252, 253, 255, 257, 262, 263, 264, 266, 267, 268, 269, 272, 273, 274, 276, 277–8, 282, 283, 284, 285,

288, 289, 311, 319, 324, 325, 371, 412, 419, 420
Rochefort 32
Rohan, Édouard, Cardinal de (1734–1803) 60
Roland, Jean-Marie (1734–93) 14, 27, 180, 185, 221, 222, 231, 235, 236, 253; Mme Manon Phlipon (1754–93) 185, 221, 253, 420
Roman Law 3
Romans 89, 93
Rome 49, 136, 139, 140, 141, 144, 147, 160, 215, 267, 301, 338, 339, 362, 367, 385, 387, 397, 398
Roman Republic 338, 362, 363, 418, 419
Ronsin, Henri (1752–94) 252, 267, 268, 269, 270
Rossignol 247, 256
Rouen 2, 5, 12, 83, 87, 96, 113, 145, 186, 391, 404
Rouget de L'Isle, Jean Claude (1760–1836) 183, 187
Rousseau, Jean-Jacques (1712–78) 48, 52–3, 56, 57, 63, 235, 276, 278, 283, 376
Rousillon 20, 203, 210
Roux, Jacques (d. 1794) 185, 223, 237, 245, 250, 252, 261, 290
Rowan, Archibald Hamilton (1751–1834) 280–1
royalism 217, 230, 241, 242, 247, 253, 267, 274, 288–90, 290, 291–2, 293, 295–6, 308–9, 311, 315, 317, 318, 320, 321, 327, 328, 329, 330–1, 334, 335, 336, 369, 372, 373, 376, 377, 382, 383, 384, 388
Royal Session, 19 November 1787 79–80, 81, 107; 23 June 1789 105, 106, 107, 297, 298, 310
Ruffo, Fabrizio, Cardinal (1724–1827) 364–5
Ruhl, Philippe Jacques (d. 1795) 260
Russia 46, 160, 165, 171, 172, 198, 201, 204, 207–8, 215, 218, 304, 307, 316, 339, 346, 355, 356, 364, 366, 367, 368, 372, 373, 379, 380, 415, 417

Sainfoin 10
Saint-Antoine 20, 98, 229, 294, 295
Saint-Cloud 148, 374–5
Saint-Denis 261
Saint-Domingue 13, 151, 181, 210, 212, 403, 412–13
Sainte-Marguérite 98
Sainte Menehould 151
Saint-Germain 402

Saint-Germain l'Auxerrois 144
Saint-Huruge, Marquis de (d. 1810) 120
Saint-Just, Louis de (1767–94) 194, 252, 266, 269, 270, 274, 277, 279–80, 419
Saint-Lazare 109
Saint-Marcel 294
Saint-Médard 54
Saintonge 6
Saint Peter's 385
Saint Petersburg 44, 160, 198, 208, 307, 380
Saint-Séverin 144
Saint Vincent 216
Saltpetre 98
Sambre-et-Meuse 351
Sanfedists 364–5
sansculottes 186, 187, 190, 191, 196, 204, 220, 229, 233, 235, 236, 237, 242, 244, 245, 247, 251, 254, 255, 261, 264, 269, 270, 271, 272, 282, 287, 290, 291, 293, 294, 317, 321, 322, 324, 325, 372, 401, 407, 409, 418, 419, 420, 424
Santerre, Antoine Joseph (1752–1809) 220, 223, 232, 234
Saône 4, 8
Saône-et-Loire 264
Sardinia 147, 202, 211, 213, 366, 414
Sarthe 308
Saumur 232, 247, 256
Savary, Jacques (1622–90) 24
Savenay 257, 288, 309, 317
Savoy 197, 199, 201, 213, 231, 298, 414
Scaevola, Quintus Mucius 418
Scandinavia 46
Scheldt 200, 210, 348
Schérer, Barthélemy (1747–1804) 372
Schiller, Friedrich (1759–1805) 160
Schönbrunn 44
scientific revolution 49
Scotland 169, 170, 212, 314, 416
scrofula 1, 295
sections 127, 185, 186, 187–8, 189, 190, 191, 193, 204, 220, 222, 223, 226–7, 228, 230, 231, 233, 234, 238, 240, 242, 244, 245, 249, 250, 251, 252, 267, 270, 271, 276, 281, 283, 290, 293, 294, 295, 320, 321, 322, 325; Gravilliers 185, 261, 290; Le Peletier 320; Marat 269, 270; Théâtre-Française 127, 187
Sedan 6, 12
Ségur, Louis Philippe, Count de (1753–1830) 29
Ségur Ordinance 27, 29, 30, 31
Seine 5, 243, 245
Seine-et-Oise 369
Senate 355, 360, 362, 377, 388, 389
Senez 143

September Massacres 191–2, 207, 220, 221, 226, 236, 306, 397, 418
serfdom 8, 106, 116, 172, 199
Servan, Joseph (1741–1808) 184, 185, 186
servants 18–19, 22, 148, 193
Seychelles 383
Sèze, Romain de (1748–1828) 195
share-cropping *see* métayage
Sheffield 170
Sicily 160, 339, 364, 367
Sieyès, Emmanuel Joseph (1748–1836) 90, 94, 101, 103, 104, 120, 321, 370, 371, 372, 373–4, 375–6, 377, 388
Silesia 201
silk 8, 12, 19, 23, 87, 231, 402, 405
silver mark 124, 155, 174
Sirven 55
slavery 5, 13, 59, 151, 161, 172, 181, 353, 403, 411–13
smallpox 43, 61
Smollett, Tobias (1721–71) 29
smuggling 15
Social Circle 153, 154
socialism 422
Soissons 143
Sonthonax, Léger Félicité (1763–1813) 412
Sorbonne 46
sovereignty 105, 118, 297, 417, 418, 421
Spain 8, 44, 164, 165, 171, 172, 202, 203, 210, 211, 212, 215, 216, 217, 218, 222, 240, 254, 293, 299, 304, 309, 313, 380, 381, 385, 412, 413, 415, 417
spinning-jennies 87, 113
Spithead 216
Staël, Germaine Necker, Mme de (1766–1817) 420
Stamp Tax 69, 76, 78
Stanislas (Poniatowski), king of Poland (1732–98) 198
statists 163–4
Stockholm 160, 197
Stofflet, Jean-Nicolas (1761–96) 255, 289, 314
Stokach 368
Strasbourg 113, 183
strikes 19, 20, 149
Stroganov, Paul Alexandrovich, Count (1772–1817) 161
Stuarts 161
Suez 332
sugar 13, 23, 180, 223
suicide 286
Suleau, François Louis (1758–92) 303
Supreme Being 262, 276–7, 278, 288
Suspects, Law of 251, 258, 263, 270, 275, 372

Suvorov, Alexander (1729–1800) 208, 368, 378, 379
Sweden 44, 160, 165, 171, 172, 197, 316
Swiss Guards 31, 36, 189, 192
Switzerland 50, 55, 129, 134, 240, 300, 302, 315, 327, 338, 354–6, 361, 364, 367, 368, 373, 378, 381, 392, 414

*taille* 4, 27, 28, 131
Talleyrand, Charles-Maurice de (1754–1838) 34, 71, 90, 129, 132, 144, 145, 332, 374, 375, 387
Tallien, Jean Lambert (1767–1820) 249, 264, 278, 279, 280, 281, 282, 283; Mme *see* Cabarrus
Tarascon 143, 292
Target, Guy Jean Baptiste (1733–1807) 90, 101, 105
Targowica 198, 207
taxation 3, 4, 7, 11, 17, 27, 28, 33, 36, 37, 38, 41, 57, 58, 59, 60, 61, 62, 67, 69, 71, 72, 74, 75, 76, 78, 84, 92, 98, 105, 106, 113, 114, 115, 118, 124, 130–1, 135, 155, 162, 215, 232, 263, 286, 296, 297, 308, 311, 319, 323, 333–4, 346, 348, 349, 350, 355, 357, 363, 365, 366, 384, 395, 400, 402, 405, 408, 416
tax-farming 28 *see also* Farmers-General
Temple 189, 195, 290, 326
Tennis Court Oath 105, 106, 179, 186
Terray, Joseph-Marie, Abbé (1715–78) 35, 59, 79, 85
territorial mandates 323–4, 358
territorial subvention 69, 74, 78
Terror 250–71, 272–81, 282, 283, 284, 287, 290, 291, 312, 318, 321, 324, 325, 326, 334, 335, 340, 343, 367, 372, 393, 394, 396, 397, 406, 407, 410, 411, 424; White 291–3, 315, 327, 410
textiles 5, 6, 12, 87, 138
theatres 23, 26, 49, 109, 325, 400
Theophilanthropy 335, 410
third estate 61, 88, 89, 90, 91, 92, 93, 94, 95, 96, 99, 100–1, 102, 103, 104, 105, 106, 108, 112, 120, 162, 163, 197, 198, 401
Thirty, Society of 90–1, 95, 99, 394
Thouars 232
Thugut, Franz Maria, Baron von (1736–1818) 204, 209, 218, 373, 378, 379
Thuriot, Jacques Alexis (1753–1829) 277, 278
tithe 11, 17, 33, 34, 35, 36, 98, 114, 115, 116, 117, 132, 136, 137, 140, 145, 169,

199, 308, 353, 356, 369, 396, 399, 401, 407
tobacco 131, 276, 334
tocsin 121, 189, 227, 234, 293
Tolentino 215, 360, 362
toleration 50, 54–5, 99, 423
Tone, Theobald Wolfe (1763–98) 169, 213, 216, 322, 325, 342, 343, 345, 422
Torfou 256
torture 55, 342, 384
Toulon 7, 32, 203, 206, 211, 213, 239–40, 242, 247, 249, 250, 254–5, 280, 283, 292, 309, 310, 314, 332, 355
Toulouse 7, 11, 18, 22, 35, 55, 71, 83, 127, 239, 300, 373
Tourcoing 206
Tours 390
Toussaint L'Ouverture (1748–1803) 413
towns 14–15, 17–18
Treilhard, Jean Baptiste (1742–1810) 337, 370
Trent, Council of 54
Tribunate 362, 377, 388, 389
tricolour 113, 207, 359, 360, 364, 391, 414, 422
Trier 147, 171, 177, 178, 298, 352
Trinidad 381
Trotsky, Leon (1879–1940) 422
Troyes 77, 78
Tsarskoje Selo 44
Tuileries 109, 122, 123, 148, 151, 175, 186–7, 188, 189, 190, 192, 194, 220, 222, 277, 306, 355, 371, 392, 418, 420
Tulle 142
Turgot, Anne Robert Jacques, Baron de L'Aulne (1727–81) 21, 22, 60, 61, 62, 66, 67, 68, 69, 79, 85, 143, 146, 171, 298, 299, 300, 303, 365–6, 368
Turkey 164, 165, 166, 339
Turreau, Louis-Marie (1756–1816) 288
Tuscany 163, 211, 357, 358, 366, 379
*tutoiement* 252
Two Thirds Law 219, 320, 321, 376
Tyrol 356

Ulster 169, 341, 342
unemployment 148
*Unigenitus* 53, 54
United Irishmen 213, 216, 341–3, 422
universities 399, 408
Utrecht 343

Vadier, Marc Guillaume Alexis (1736–1828) 273, 279, 282, 287, 290, 291
Valais 356

Valence 338
Valenciennes 203
Valmy 192, 193, 197, 198, 202, 206, 306, 415
Vancouver 164
Van Der Noot, Heintje (1731–1827) 162, 163, 164
Varennes, Flight to 151–2, 153, 155, 156, 157, 170, 171, 172, 173, 175, 176, 196, 200, 301, 302, 303, 304, 326
Varlet, Jean François (1764–1832) 223–4, 227, 233, 234, 237, 245, 252
Vaud 354
venality 23, 25, 26, 28, 32, 37, 38, 39, 40, 41, 116, 117, 125, 135, 405, 408, 423
*see also* offices
Vendée 5, 175, 202, 204, 215, 224–6, 227, 232, 235, 240, 242, 243, 247, 249, 255–7, 262, 266, 275, 288–90, 307–8, 309, 311, 312, 313, 314, 315, 316, 317, 327, 340, 343, 349, 350, 353, 366, 406
Vendémiaire, uprising of 320–1, 322, 325, 327, 334
Vendôme 326, 327, 328, 330, 335; place 323
*Vengeur* 278
Venice 214, 217, 310, 315, 316, 360–1, 379, 414
Ventôse, Laws of 266, 270, 279, 326
Verdun 191
Vergennes, Charles Gravier, Count de (1717–87) 63, 66, 67, 68, 69, 70, 71, 75, 78, 159
Vergniaud, Pierre Victurnien (1753–93) 178, 188, 189, 221, 238, 253
Verona 296, 297, 299, 310, 314, 315, 317, 329, 360
Versailles 1, 22, 41–2, 44, 58, 68, 76, 77, 82, 83, 97, 98, 100, 101, 103, 104, 107, 108, 110, 112, 113, 114, 115, 118, 120, 121, 122, 123, 127, 133, 142, 159, 162, 192, 229, 298, 392, 402, 420
Vesoul 115
veto 120, 123, 155, 176, 185, 187
Victor-Amadeus III (king 1773–95) 213, 298, 300, 356
Vienna 44, 177, 179, 206, 211, 214, 315, 357, 366, 368, 379
Villèle, Joseph, Count de (1773–1854) 396
Vilno 207, 218
Vincennes 148, 149
Vincent 267, 268, 269, 270
Vinegar Hill 342
vines 86
*vingtièmes* 27, 33, 38, 68, 69, 71, 75, 78, 80, 131

Vizille 89, 92
Volney, Constantin Frédéric de Chassebœuf, Count de (1757–1820) 95
Voltaire, François Marie Arouet (1694–1778) 7, 49, 50, 53, 55, 56, 59, 65, 387, 411
Vonck, Jan-Frans (1743–92) 162, 163, 164
Vosges 9

wages 86–7, 251, 264, 276, 281, 185, 403
Walpole, Horace (1717–97) 54
wars, Seven Years' 30, 38, 57, 58, 62, 66, 180; American Independence 32, 62–3, 64, 67, 68, 69, 70, 159, 198, 204; of the French Revolution 156, 176, 177, 179, 180, 183, 185, 197–219, 228, 236, 237, 242, 246, 247–8, 308, 310, 329, 338–40, 341, 378–81, 390, 403, 416, 424
Warsaw 165, 208, 209, 218, 259, 343
Washington, George (1732–97) 72
Waterloo 409
Wattignies 204, 206
Weimar, Duke of 193
Wellington, Arthur Wellesly, Duke of (1769–1852) 415
Westermann, François-Joseph (1751–94) 256
West Indies 5, 13, 23, 181, 212, 223, 230,

311 *see also* Guadeloupe, Martinique, Saint-Domingue
Westphalia, Peace of 9, 171, 200
Wexford 342
wheat 10
Whigs 161, 166, 167, 201, 212
Wickham, William (1761–1840) 327
Wieland, Christoff-Martin (1733–1813) 160
William III 167
William V (1748–1806) 75, 159, 162, 200, 209, 343, 346, 347, 381
Wimpffen, Louis-Félix de (1744–1814) 241, 308
wine 6, 8, 12
women 16, 21, 33, 65, 121–2, 138, 148, 181, 205, 223, 231, 245, 256, 284, 290, 293, 309, 361, 397, 400, 420–1
woollens 13, 404

Yeu 313, 314
York, Frederick Augustus, Duke of (1763–1827) 204, 209, 211
Young, Arthur (1741–1820) 5, 9, 10, 11, 14, 23, 27, 32, 41, 78, 104, 107, 108, 113, 391, 392
Ysabeau, Claude Alexandre (1754–1831) 255

Zurich 354